Research Anthology on Machine Learning Techniques, Methods, and Applications

Information Resources Management Association
USA

Volume I

IGI Global
PUBLISHER of TIMELY KNOWLEDGE

Published in the United States of America by
    IGI Global
    Engineering Science Reference (an imprint of IGI Global)
    701 E. Chocolate Avenue
    Hershey PA, USA 17033
    Tel: 717-533-8845
    Fax: 717-533-8661
    E-mail: cust@igi-global.com
    Web site: http://www.igi-global.com

Library of Congress Cataloging-in-Publication Data

Names: Information Resources Management Association, editor.
Title: Research anthology on machine learning techniques, methods, and
  applications / Information Resources Management Association, editor.
Description: Hershey, PA : Engineering Science Reference, an imprint of IGI
  Global, [2022] | Includes bibliographical references and index. |
  Summary: "This reference set provides a thorough consideration of the
  innovative and emerging research within the area of machine learning,
  discussing how the technology has been used in the past as well as
  potential ways it can be used in the future to ensure industries
  continue to develop and grow while covering a range of topics such as
  artificial intelligence, deep learning, cybersecurity, and robotics"--
  Provided by publisher.
Identifiers: LCCN 2022015780 (print) | LCCN 2022015781 (ebook) | ISBN
  9781668462911 (h/c) | ISBN 9781668462928 (ebook)
Subjects: LCSH: Machine learning--Industrial applications. | Computer
  security--Data processing. | Medical care--Data processing. | Data
  mining. | Artificial intelligence.
Classification: LCC Q325.5 .R46 2022 (print) | LCC Q325.5 (ebook) | DDC
  006.3/1--dc23/eng20220628
LC record available at https://lccn.loc.gov/2022015780
LC ebook record available at https://lccn.loc.gov/2022015781

British Cataloguing in Publication Data
A Cataloguing in Publication record for this book is available from the British Library.

The views expressed in this book are those of the authors, but not necessarily of the publisher.

For electronic access to this publication, please contact: eresources@igi-global.com.

List of Contributors

Table of Contents

Section 5
Organizational and Social Implications

Section 6
Emerging Trends

Preface

Machine learning, due to its many uses across fields and disciplines, is becoming a prevalent technology in today's modern world. From medicine to business, machine learning is changing the way things are done by providing effective new techniques for problem solving and strategies for leaders to implement. Machine learning is driving major improvements in society including the promotion of societal health, sustainable business, and learning analytics. The possibilities for this technology are endless, and it is critical to further investigate its myriad of opportunities and benefits to successfully combat any challenges and assist in its evolution.

Staying informed of the most up-to-date research trends and findings is of the utmost importance. That is why IGI Global is pleased to offer this three-volume reference collection of reprinted IGI Global book chapters and journal articles that have been handpicked by senior editorial staff. This collection will shed light on critical issues related to the trends, techniques, and uses of various applications by providing both broad and detailed perspectives on cutting-edge theories and developments. This collection is designed to act as a single reference source on conceptual, methodological, technical, and managerial issues, as well as to provide insight into emerging trends and future opportunities within the field.

The *Research Anthology on Machine Learning Techniques, Methods, and Applications* is organized into six distinct sections that provide comprehensive coverage of important topics. The sections are:

1. Fundamental Concepts and Theories;
2. Development and Design Methodologies;
3. Tools and Technologies;
4. Utilization and Applications;
5. Organizational and Social Implications; and
6. Emerging Trends.

The following paragraphs provide a summary of what to expect from this invaluable reference tool.

Section 1, "Fundamental Concepts and Theories," serves as a foundation for this extensive reference tool by addressing crucial theories essential to understanding the concepts and uses of machine learning in multidisciplinary settings. Opening this reference book is the chapter "Introduction to Machine Learning and Its Implementation Techniques" by Profs. Sathiyamoorthi V. and Arul Murugan R. from Sona College of Technology, India, which aims in giving a solid introduction to various widely adopted machine learning techniques and serves as a simplified guide for the aspiring data and machine learning enthusiasts. This first section ends with the chapter "Machine Learning Applications in Nanomedicine and Nanotoxicology: An Overview" by Prof. Gerardo M. Casañola-Martin from North Dakota State

University, USA and Prof. Hai Pham-The of Hanoi University of Pharmacy, Vietnam, which discusses the recent advances in the conjunction of machine learning with nanomedicine.

Section 2, "Development and Design Methodologies," presents in-depth coverage of the design and development of machine learning techniques for their use in different applications. This section starts with the chapter "Classification and Machine Learning" by Prof. Damian Alberto from the Indian Institute of Technology Bombay, India, which addresses the classification concept in detail and discusses how to solve different classification problems using different machine learning techniques. This section ends with "A Process for Increasing the Samples of Coffee Rust Through Machine Learning Methods" by Prof. David Camilo Corrales from the University of Cauca, Colombia & Carlos III University of Madrid, Spain and Profs. Juan Carlos Corrales and Jhonn Pablo Rodríguez from the University of Cauca, Colombia, which describes how coffee rust has become a serious concern for many coffee farmers and manufacturers and provides a process about coffee rust to select appropriate machine learning methods to increase rust samples.

Section 3, "Tools and Technologies," explores the various tools and technologies utilized in the implementation of machine learning for various uses. This section begins with "Artificial Intelligence and Machine Learning Algorithms" by Prof. Amit Kumar Tyagi from Vellore Institute of Technology, India and Prof. Poonam Chahal of MRIIRS, India, which considers how machine learning and deep learning techniques and algorithms are utilized in today's world. This section closes with the chapter "Identifying Patterns in Fresh Produce Purchases: The Application of Machine Learning Techniques" by Profs. Malgorzata W. Korolkiewicz, Timofei Bogomolov, and Svetlana Bogomolova from the University of South Australia, Australia, which applies machine learning techniques to examine consumer food choices, specifically purchasing patterns in relation to fresh fruit and vegetables.

Section 4, "Utilization and Applications," describes how machine learning is used and applied in diverse industries for various technologies and applications. The opening chapter in this section, "Machine Learning Algorithms," by Profs. Namrata Dhanda and Stuti Shukla Datta from Amity University, India and Prof. Mudrika Dhanda from Royal Holloway University, UK, introduces the concept of machine learning and the commonly employed learning algorithm for developing efficient and intelligent systems. The closing chapter in this section, "Classification of Traffic Events in Mexico City Using Machine Learning and Volunteered Geographic Information," by Profs. Magdalena Saldana-Perez, Miguel Torres-Ruiz, and Marco Moreno-Ibarra from Instituto Politecnico Nacional, Mexico, implements a traffic event classification methodology to analyze volunteered geographic information and internet information related to traffic events with a view to identify the main traffic problems in a city and to visualize the congested roads.

Section 5, "Organizational and Social Implications," includes chapters discussing the impact of machine learning on society and business. The opening chapter, "Challenges and Applications for Implementing Machine Learning in Computer Vision: Machine Learning Applications and Approaches," by Prof. Hiral R. Patel from Ganpat University, India; Prof. Ajay M. Patel of AMPICS, India; and Prof. Satyen M. Parikh from FCA, India, discusses the fundamentals of machine learning and considers why it is important. The closing chapter, "Machine Learning Based Program to Prevent Hospitalizations and Reduce Costs in the Colombian Statutory Health Care System," by Prof. Alvaro J. Riascos from the University of los Andes and Quantil, Colombia and Prof. Natalia Serna of the University of Wisconsin-Madison, USA, suggests a hospitalization prevention program in which the decision of whether to intervene on a patient depends on a simple decision model and the prediction of the patient risk of an annual length-of-stay using machine learning techniques.

Section 6, "Emerging Trends," highlights areas for future research within the machine learning field. Opening this final section is the chapter "Current Trends: Machine Learning and AI in IoT" by Profs. Jayanthi Jagannathan and Anitha Elavarasi S. from Sona College of Technology, India, which addresses the key role of machine learning and artificial intelligence for various applications of the internet of things. The final chapter in this section, "The Role and Applications of Machine Learning in Future Self-Organizing Cellular Networks," by Profs. Muhammad Ali Imran, Paulo Valente Klaine, and Oluwakayode Onireti from the University of Glasgow, UK and Prof. Richard Demo Souza of Federal University of Santa Catarina (UFSC), Brazil, provides a brief overview of the role and applications of machine learning algorithms in future wireless cellular networks, specifically in the context of self-organizing networks.

Although the primary organization of the contents in this multi-volume work is based on its six sections, offering a progression of coverage of the important concepts, methodologies, technologies, applications, social issues, and emerging trends, the reader can also identify specific contents by utilizing the extensive indexing system listed at the end of each volume. As a comprehensive collection of research on the latest findings related to machine learning, the *Research Anthology on Machine Learning Techniques, Methods, and Applications* provides computer scientists, managers, researchers, scholars, practitioners, academicians, instructors, and students with a complete understanding of the applications and impacts of machine learning techniques. Given the vast number of issues concerning usage, failure, success, strategies, and applications of machine learning, the *Research Anthology on Machine Learning Techniques, Methods, and Applications* encompasses the most pertinent research on the applications, impacts, uses, and development of machine learning.

Section 1
Fundamental Concepts and Theories

Chapter 1

Introduction to Machine Learning and Its Implementation Techniques

Arul Murugan R.
Sona College of Technology, India

Sathiyamoorthi V.
Sona College of Technology, India

ABSTRACT

Machine learning (ML) is one of the exciting sub-fields of artificial intelligence (AI). The term machine learning is generally stated as the ability to learn without being explicitly programmed. In recent years, machine learning has become one of the thrust areas of research across various business verticals. The technical advancements in the field of big data have provided the ability to gain access over large volumes of diversified data at ease. This massive amount of data can be processed at high speeds in a reasonable amount of time with the help of emerging hardware capabilities. Hence the machine learning algorithms have been the most effective at leveraging all of big data to provide near real-time solutions even for the complex business problems. This chapter aims in giving a solid introduction to various widely adopted machine learning techniques and its applications categorized into supervised, unsupervised, and reinforcement and will serve a simplified guide for the aspiring data and machine learning enthusiasts.

INTRODUCTION

In the past decade there has been a rapid paradigm shift in the field of computer science due to apex achievements in artificial intelligence .Machine learning which is a sub field of artificial intelligence has taken the capabilities of imparting the intelligence across various disciplines beyond the horizon. In 1959, Arthur Samuel defined machine learning as a "Field of study that gives computers the ability to learn without being explicitly programmed" (Samuel 1959).The machine learning algorithms works on the fact that the learning happens persistently from the training data or with the past experience and

DOI: 10.4018/978-1-6684-6291-1.ch001

can enhance their performance by synthesizing the underlying relationships among data and the given problem without any human intervention. In contrast with the optimization problems, the machine learning algorithms generally encompasses a well-defined function that can be optimized through learning. This optimization of the decision-making processes based on learning has led to rapid rise in employing automation in innumerable areas like Healthcare, Finance, Retail, E-governance etc. However, machine learning has been considered as the giant step forward in the AI revolution the development in neural networks has taken the AI to a completely new level. Deep learning which a subset of machine learning is incorporates neural networks as their building blocks have remarkable advances in natural language and image processing.

With big data landscape being able to store massive amount of data that is generated every day by various businesses and users the machine learning algorithms can harvest the exponentially growing data in deriving accurate predictions. The complexity raised in maintaining a large computational on primes infrastructure to ensure successful learning has been efficiently addressed through cloud computing by eliminating the need to maintain expensive computing hardware, software and dedicated space. The businesses have started adopting Machine Learning as a service (MLaaS) into their technology stacks since they offer machine learning as a part of their service, as the name suggests. The major attraction is that these services offer data modeling APIs, machine learning algorithms, data transformations and predictive analytics without having to install software or provision their own servers, just like any other cloud service. Moreover MLaas can help manage big data better by collecting huge amounts of data to get insights by correlating the data, crunching numbers and understanding patterns of the data to helps business take quick decisions. As data sources proliferate along with the computing power to process them, going straight to the data is one of the most straightforward ways to quickly gain insights and make predictions. The combination of these two mainstream technologies yields beneficial outcome for the organizations. Machine learning is heavily recommended for the problems that involve complex learning. However, it is essential to remember that Machine learning is not always an optimal solution to every type of problem. There are certain problems where robust solutions can be developed without using Machine-learning techniques.

This chapter will explore the end-to-end process of investigating data through a machine-learning lens from how to extract and identify useful features from the data; some of the most commonly used machine-learning algorithms, to identifying and evaluating the performance of the machine learning algorithms. Section 2 introduces steps for developing suitable machine learning model and various paradigms of machine learning techniques such as supervised, unsupervised and reinforcement learning. Section 3 discusses about various applications of machine learning in various fields and then concludes whole chapter with research insights.

DEVELOPING A MACHINE LEARNING MODEL

As discussed, machine Learning is the field where an agent is said to learn from the experience with respect to some class of tasks and the performance measure P. The task could be answering exams in a particular subject or it could be of diagnosing patients of a specific illness. As shown in the figure 1 given below, it is the subset of Artificial intelligence (AI) where it contains artificial neurons and reacts to the given stimuli whereas machine learning uses statistical techniques for knowledge discovery. Deep learning is the subset of machine learning where it uses artificial neural networks for learning process.

Figure 1. Taxonomy of Knowledge Discovery

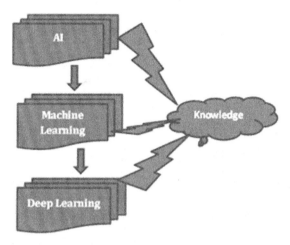

Further, machine learning can be categorized into supervised, unsupervised and reinforcement learning. In any kind of tasks, the machine learning involves three components. The first component is, defining the set of tasks on which learning will take place and second is setting up a performance measure P. Whether learning is happening or not, defining some kind of performance criteria P is mandatory in machine learning tasks. Consider an example of answering questions in an exam then the performance criterion would be the number of marks that you get. Similarly, consider an example of diagnosing patient with specific illness then the performance measure would be the number of patients who did not have adverse reaction to the given drugs. So, there exists different ways for defining various performance metrics depending on what you are looking for within a given domain. The last important component machine learning is experience. For an example, experience in the case of writing exams could be writing more exams which means the better you write, the better you get or it could be the number of patient's in the case of diagnosing illnesses i.e. the more patients that you look at the better you become an expert in diagnosing illness. Hence, these are three components involved in learning; class of tasks, performance measure and well-defined experience. This kind of learning where you are learning to improve your performance based on experience is known as inductive learning. There are various machine-learning paradigms as shown in the figure 2.

The first one is supervised learning where one learns from an input to output map. For an example, it could be a description of the patient who comes to the clinic and the output would be whether the patient has a certain disease or not in the case of diagnosing patients. Similarly, take an example of writing the exam where the input could be some kind of equation then output would be the answer to the question or it could be a true or false question i.e. it will give you a description of the question then you have to state whether it is true or false as the output. So, the essential part of supervised learning is mapping from the given input to the required output. If the output that you are looking for happens to be a categorical output such as whether he has a disease or does not have a disease or whether the answer is true or false then the learning is called supervised learning. If the output happens to be a continuous value like how long will this product last before it fails right or what is the expected rainfall tomorrow then those kinds of problems would be called as regression problems. Thus, classification and regression are called classes of supervised learning process.

Figure 2. Categorization of Various Machine Learning Algorithms

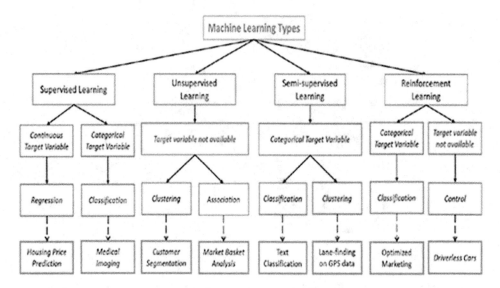

The second paradigm is known as unsupervised learning problems where input to output is not required. The main goal is not to produce an output in response to the given input indeed it tries to discover some patterns out of it. Therefore, in unsupervised learning there is no real desired output that we are looking for instead it looks for finding closely related patterns in the data. Clustering is one such task where it tries to find cohesive groups among the given input pattern. For an example, one might be looking at customers who comes to the shop and want to figure out if they are into different categories of customers like college students or IT professionals so on so forth. The other popular unsupervised learning paradigm is known as association rule mining or frequent pattern mining where one is interested in finding a frequent co-occurrence of items in the data that is given to them i.e. whenever A comes to the shop B also comes to the shop. Therefore, one can learn these kinds of relationship via associations between data.

The third form of learning which is called as reinforcement learning. It is neither supervised nor unsupervised in nature. In reinforcement learning you have an agent who is acting in an environment, you want to figure out what actions the agent must take at every step, and the action that the agent takes is based on the rewards or penalties that the agent gets in different states.

Apart from these three types of learning, one more learning is also possible which is called as semi-supervised learning. It is the combination of supervised and unsupervised learning i.e. you have some labeled training data and you also have a larger amount of unlabeled training data and you can try to come up with some learning out of them that can work even when the training data is limited features.

Irrespective of domain and the type of leaning, every task needs to have some kind of a performance measure. In classification, the performance measure would be classification error i.e. how many instances are misclassified to the total number of instances. Similarly, the prediction error is supposed to be a performance measure in regression i.e. if I said, it's going to rain like 23 millimeters and then it would ends up raining like 49 centimeters then this huge difference in actual and predicted value is called prediction error. In case of clustering, it is little hard to define performance measures as we do not know what is a good clustering algorithm and do not know how to measure the quality of clusters. Therefore, there exists different kinds of clustering measures and so one of the measures is a scatter or spread of the cluster that essentially tells you how to spread out the points that belong to a single group. Thus, good clustering algorithms should minimize intra-cluster distance and maximize inter-cluster distance. Association rule mining use variety of measures called support and confidence whereas reinforcement learning tries to minimize the cost to accrue while controlling the system. There are several challenges exists when trying to build a machine learning solution to the given problem and few of these are given below.

First issue is about how good is a model and type of performance measures used. Most of the measures discussed above were finds to be insufficient and there are other practical considerations that come into play such as user skills, experience etc. while selecting a model and measures. The second issue is of course presence of noisy and missing data. Presence of these kinds of data leads to an error in the predicted value. Suppose medical data is recorded as 225. so what does that mean it could be 225 days in which case it is a reasonable number it could be twenty two point five years again is a reasonable number or twenty two point five months is reasonable but if it is 225 years it's not a reasonable number so there's something wrong in the data. Finally, the biggest challenge is size of the dataset since algorithms perform well when data is large but not all. The following are the basic steps to be followed while developing any kind of machine-learning applications. They are,

A. Formulating the Problem/ Define Your Machine Learning Problem
B. Collecting Labeled Data/ Gathering Data
C. Preparing that data/ Analyzing Your Data
D. Feature selection/ Feature Processing
E. Splitting the Data into Training and Evaluation Data
F. Choosing a model:
G. Training
H. Evaluation
I. Parameter Tuning
J. Prediction/ Generating and Interpreting Predictions

The following subsections will give a detailed scheme for developing a suitable machine-learning model for the given problem.

Describing the Problem

The first step in developing a model is to clearly define and describe about the problem that need to be addressed with machine learning. In other words formulating the core of the problem will help in deciding what the model has to predict. The formulation can be done in different ways such as understanding problem through sentence description, deriving problem from the solved similar problems from the past. Choosing how to define the problem varies depending upon the use case or business need. It is very important to avoid over-complicating the problem and to frame the simplest solution as per the requirement. The motivation for solving the problem is to be evaluated against how the solution would benefit the business. Some of the common ways of describing the problems are

Similar Problems

After detailed discussions with stakeholders, identifying the pain-points the common and most affordable strategy is to derive the problem with previous similar experiences. Other problems can inform details about the current problem by highlighting limitations in the problem such as time dimensions and conceptual drift and can point to algorithms, data transformations that could be adapted to spot check performance.

Informal Description

The other simplest way is to describe the problems informally by highlighting the basic spaces of the problem in a sentence for initial understanding about the possible solution. However, this step must be considered only for initial level problem formation substituted with any other approach for detailed problem formation.

Using Assumptions

Creating a list of assumptions about the problem such as domain specific information that will lead to a viable solution that can be tested against real data .It can also be useful to highlight areas of the problem specification that may need to be challenged, relaxed or tightened.

Formalism

The most structured approach is Tom Mitchell's machine learning formalism. A computer program is said to learn from experience E with respect to some class of tasks T and performance measure P, if its performance at tasks in T, as measured by P, improves with experience E.

Use this formalism to define the T, P, and E for your problem.

- **Task** (T):
- **Experience** (E):
- **Performance** (P):

Data Collection

This step is the most expensive and most time-consuming aspect of any machine learning project because the quality and quantity of data that you gather will directly determine the success of the project .The paper published by Yuji Roh et al. (2018) discuss in detail about high level research landscape of data collection for machine learning such as data acquisition, data labeling and improve the labeling of any existing data. The Machine learning problems require many data for better prediction. With the rapid adoption of standard IOT solution enormous volume of sensor data can be collected from the industries for the Machine learning problems, other sources like social media and third party data providers can provide enough data for better solution predictions. The labeled data is a group of samples that have been tagged with one or more labels. Labeling typically takes a set of unlabeled data and augments each piece of that unlabeled data with meaningful tags that are informative. In supervised Machine learning, the algorithm teaches itself to learn from the labeled examples. Labeled data typically takes a set of unlabeled data and augments each piece of that unlabeled data with some sort of meaningful "tag," "label," or "class" that is somehow informative or desirable to know. Often, data is not readily available in a labeled form. Collecting and preparing the variables and the target are often the most important steps in solving a problem. The example data should be representative of the data that is used by the model to make a prediction. Unsupervised learning is the opposite of supervised learning, where unlabeled data is used because a training set does not exist. Semi-supervised learning is aimed at integrating unlabeled and labeled data to build better and more accurate models.

Data Preparation

Data preparation is the process of combining, structuring and organizing data so it can be analyzed through machine learning applications. Good enough visualizations of the data will help in finding any relevant relationships between the different variables and to find any data imbalances present. The Collected data is spilt into two parts. The first part that is used in training the model will be the majority of the dataset and the second will be used for the evaluation of the trained model's performance.

The data might need a lot of cleaning and preprocessing before it is feed into the machine learning system. The process of cleaning involves various processes such as getting rid of errors & noise and removal of redundancies to avoid ambiguities that arise out of the data. The preprocessing involves renaming categorical values to numbers, rescaling (normalization), abstraction, and aggregation.

The appropriate usage of attributes can lead to unexpected improvements in model accuracy. Deriving new attributes from the training data in the modeling process can boost model performance. Similarly, removal of redundant or duplicate attributes can increase the performance. Transformations of training data can reduce the skewness of data as well as the prominence of outliers in the data. Outliers are extreme values that fall a long way outside of the other observations. The outliers in input data can skew and mislead the training process of machine learning algorithms resulting in longer training times, less accurate models and ultimately poorer results. Outliers can skew the summary distribution of attribute values in descriptive statistics like mean and standard deviation and in plots such as histograms and scatterplots, compressing the body of the data. Charu C. Aggarwal in his book "Outlier Analysis "suggests following methods such as,

- **Extreme Value Analysis**: Determine the statistical tails of the underlying distribution of the data. For example, statistical methods like the z-scores on univariate data.
- **Probabilistic and Statistical Models**: Determine unlikely instances from a probabilistic model of the data.
- **Linear Models**: Projection methods that model the data into lower dimensions using linear correlations.
- **Proximity-based Models**: Data instances that are isolated from the mass of the data as determined by cluster, density or nearest neighbor analysis.
- **Information Theoretic Models**: Outliers are detected as data instances that increase the complexity (minimum code length) of the dataset.
- **High-Dimensional Outlier Detection**: Methods that search subspaces for outliers give the breakdown of distance-based measures in higher dimensions (curse of dimensionality).

Feature Engineering and Feature Selection

Feature engineering is about creating new input features from your existing ones. Feature engineering is the process of transforming raw data into features that had better represent the underlying problem to the predictive models, resulting in improved model accuracy on unseen data. An iterative process interplays with data selection and model evaluation, repeatedly, until better prediction is achieved. The process of involves the following steps

- **Brainstorm features**: Examining the problem and data closely and by study feature engineering on other problems to extract similar patterns
- **Devise features**: Decide on using use automatic feature extraction or manual feature construction and mixtures of the two.
- **Select features**: Using different feature importance scorings and feature selection methods to prepare different view of the model.
- **Evaluate models**: Estimate model accuracy on unseen data using the chosen features.

Feature selection is the process of selecting a subset of relevant features (variables, predictors) for use in machine learning model construction. Feature selection is also called variable selection or attributes selection. The data features are used to train the machine learning models have a huge influence on the performance. Hence choosing irrelevant or partially relevant features can negatively influence the model performance. A feature selection algorithm can be seen as the combination of a search technique for proposing new feature subsets, along with an evaluation measure, which scores the different feature subsets. In real world, applications the models usually choke due to very high dimensionality of the data presented along with exponential increase in training time and risk of over fitting with increasing number of features. Identifying better features can provide the flexibility in even choosing a slightly wrong algorithm but ending up in getting good results. The three general classes of feature selection algorithms are filter methods, wrapper methods and embedded methods.

Filter Methods

Filter feature selection methods apply a statistical measure to assign a scoring to each feature. The features are ranked by the score and either selected to be kept or removed from the dataset. Some examples of filter methods include Pearson's Correlation, Linear discriminant analysis, ANOVA, Chi-Square.

Wrapper Methods

The Wrapper Methods generate considers the selection of a set of features as a search problem, where different combinations are prepared, evaluated and compared to other combinations. Some examples of wrapper methods include recursive feature elimination, forward feature selection, backward feature elimination.

Embedded Methods

Embedded methods combine the qualities' of filter and wrapper methods. Algorithms that have their own built-in feature selection methods implement it. Some examples of embedded methods include regularization algorithms (LASSO, Elastic Net and Ridge Regression), Memetic algorithm, and Random multinomial logit.

Splitting up the Data

The crux of any machine-learning model is to generalize beyond the instances used to train the model. In other words, a model should be judged on its ability to predict new, unseen data. Hence evaluating (testing) the model with the same data used for training will generally result in over fitting. It should be noted that the data should not either over fit or underfit. The common strategy is to take into consideration of all the available labeled data and split it into training and evaluation (testing) subsets. The Training set used to fit and tune the model while the test sets are put aside as unseen data to evaluate the model. The split is usually done with a ratio of 70-80 percent for training and 20-30 percent for evaluation based upon the nature of the problem and the model that is been adapted. One of the best practices that is adopted is to make this split before starting the training process in order to get reliable outcomes of the models performance. In addition, the test data should be kept aside until the model is trained good enough to handle unseen data. The performance comparison against the entire test dataset and training dataset will give a clear picture about the data over fits the model. Some of the common ways of splitting up the labeled data are

Sequentially Split

Sequential split is the simplest way to guarantee distinct training and evaluation data split. This method is extremely convenient if the data holds date or time range since it retains the order of the data records.

Random Split

Random split is the most commonly adopted approach since it is easy to implement. However, for models that are more complex the random selection will result high variance.

Cross-validation

Cross-validation is a method for getting a reliable estimate of model performance using only the training data. There are several ways to cross-validate the commonly used method is k-fold cross-validation. In k-fold cross-validation the data is split into k-equally sized folds, k models are trained and each fold is used as the holdout set where the model is trained on all remaining folds.

Choosing an Appropriate Model

Choosing a suitable Machine-learning model can be very confusing because it depends on a number of following factors

Nature of Problem

The nature of the problem can be a significant factor in deciding which Machine-learning model works best among the possible models.

Volume of the Training Set

The training set volume can be helpful in selecting the Machine-learning models based on bias and variance factors

Accuracy

Deciding on the level of accuracy can sometimes guide in determine the suitable model. If the project does not require most accurate results then approximate methods can be adopted. The approximation can provide better results due to reduces processing time and usually avoid overfitting.

Training Time

The training time heavily depends on the accuracy and the volume of the dataset. If the training time is limited then it can be a considerable factor in picking a model particularly when the data set is large.

Number of Parameters

The number of parameters can tamper the model behavior in various ways like error tolerance or number of iterations. Moreover, algorithms with large numbers parameters require the most trial and error to find a good combination.

Number of Features

The amount of features incorporated in the datasets can be very large compared to the number of data points. The huge amount of features can pull down the efficiency some learning models, making training time very long.

The following two-step process can guide in choosing the model

Step 1: Categorize the problem

The categorization of the problem can be by the input feed into the machine-learning model or the output expected out of the machine-learning model. If the input data is labeled then, supervised learning model can be a good choice in contrast if input data is unlabeled data then unsupervised learning model can be adopted. The reinforcement learning models can be used for optimizing the objective function interacting with the environment. Similarly, if the output of the model is a number then regression models suits best whereas the classification models can an ideal solution if the output of the model is a class. The clustering models will be most appropriate for models that output a set of input groups.

Step 2: Find the available algorithms

Once the categorization of the problem is completed, the apposite model can be pinpointed with ease. Some of the commonly used algorithms discussed below for better understanding. Classification of Machine Learning Algorithms as follow;

- Supervised learning
- Unsupervised learning
- Semi-supervised learning
- Reinforcement learning

Training the Model

The process of training works by finding a relationship between a label and its features. The training dataset is used to prepare a model, to train it. Each sample in the selected training data will define how each feature affects the label. This data is used to incrementally improve the model's ability to predict. This process then repeated and updated to fit the data as best as possible. A single iteration of this process is called one training step. In general, a trained model is not exposed to the test dataset during training and any predictions made on that dataset are designed to be indicative of the performance of the model. Model training is the crux of machine learning that is done by fitting a model to the data. In other words, training a model with existing data to fit the model parameters. Parameters are the key to machine learning models since they are the part of the model that is learned from historical training data. There are two types of parameters that are used in machine learning models.

Model Parameters

A model parameter is a configuration variable that is internal to the model and whose value can be estimated from data. These parameters are learnt during training by the classifier or other machine-learning model. The Model parameters provide the estimate of learning during the training. Example: The support vectors in a support vector machine.

Hyper Parameters

A model hyper parameter is a configuration that is external to the model and whose value cannot be estimated from data. Hyperactive parameters are usually fixed before the actual training process begins. Example: number of clusters in a k-means clustering. In essence, a hyperactive parameter is a parameter whose value is set before the learning process begins. While the values of other parameters are derived via training. Model hyper parameters, on the other hand, are common for similar models and cannot be learnt during training but are set beforehand. The key distinction is that model parameters can be learned directly from the training data while hyperactive parameters cannot. Other training parameters are

Learning Rate

The amount of change to the model during each step of this search process, or the step size, is called the "*learning rate*" and provides perhaps the most important hyperparameter to tune for your neural network in order to achieve good performance on your problem. The learning rate is an important parameter in Gradient descent.

Model Size

Model size depends on the product being used and what is included in the model. This can vary from implementation to implementation, type of problem (classification, regression), algorithm (SVM, neural net etc.), data type (image, text etc.), feature size etc. Large models have practical implications, such as requiring more RAM to hold the model while training and when generating predictions. We can reduce the model size by using regularization or by specifically restricting the model size by specifying the maximum size.

Regularization

Generalization refers to how well the concepts learned by a machine-learning model apply to specific examples not seen by the model when it was learning. Overfitting refers to a model that models the training data too well and performs poorly with unseen data. Regularization helps prevent models from overfitting training data examples by penalizing extreme weight values. Some of the common types of regularization techniques are L2 and L1 regularization, Dropout, Data augmentation and early stopping.

Figure 3 gives the most popular and widely used algorithms in machine learning based applications. The following subsections discusses in detail about these techniques.

Figure 3. Popular Machine Learning Algorithms

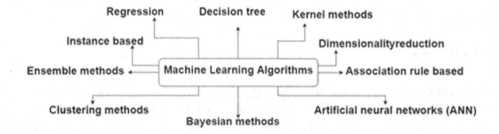

Supervised Learning

As shown in the figure 4, it is categorized into two types.

- Classification
- Regression

It is one of the machine learning techniques used for data analysis and used to construct the classification model. It is used to predict future trends analysis. It is also known as supervised learning.

Classification

The classification models used to predict categorical class labels whereas and prediction models predict continuous valued.

For example, classification model for bank is used to classify bank loan applications as either safe or risky one. A prediction model is used to predict the potential customers who will buy computer equipment given their income and occupation.

Some other examples of data analysis task of classification are given below.

- A bank loan officer wants to analyze the data in order to predict which loan applicant is risky or which are safe.
- A marketing manager at a company needs to analyze a customer with a given profile, who will buy a new computer as shown in figure 3.

In both the cases, a model is constructed to predict the categorical labels. These labels are risky or safe for loan application and yes or no for marketing data.

Figure 4. Supervised Learning Algorithms

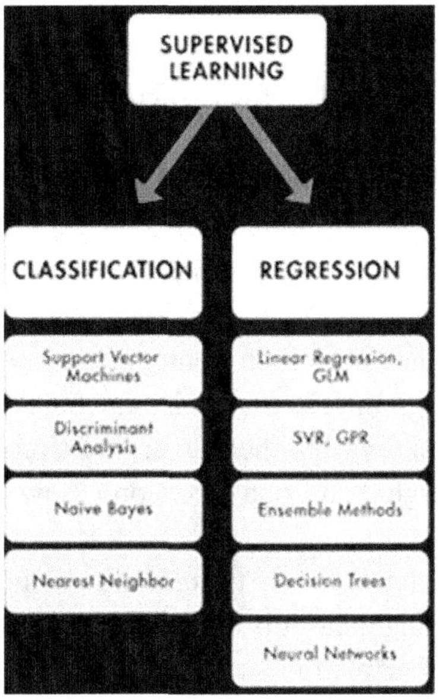

It is the task of building a model that describe and distinguish data class of an object. This is used to predict class label for an object where class label information is not available (Jiwei et al. 2006). It is an example of learning from samples. The first phase called model construction is also referred to as training phase, where a model is built based on the features present in the training data. This model is then used to predict class labels for the testing data, where class label information is not available. A test set is used to determine the accuracy of the model. Usually, the given data set is divided into training and test sets, with training set used to construct the model and test set used to validate it.

Decision trees are commonly used to represent classification models. A decision tree is similar to a flowchart like structure where every node represents a test on an attribute value and branches denote a test outcome and tree leaves represent actual classes. Other standard representation techniques include K-nearest neighbor, Bayesians classification algorithm, if-then rules and neural networks (Han et al. 2006). It is also known as supervised learning process. Effectiveness of prediction depends on training dataset used to train the model.

The classification is two steps process. They are,

Phase I: Building the Classifier(Training Phase)
Phase II: Using Classifier (Testing Phase)

Phase I: Training Phase

This is the first step in classification and in this step a classification algorithm is used to construct the classifier model shown in figure 6. The model is built from the training dataset which contain tuples called records with the associated class labels. Each tuple presents in the training dataset is called as category or class.

Consider that training dataset of a bank_loan schema contains value for the following attributes.

```
<Name, Age, Income, Loan_decision>
```

Once the decision tree was built, then it uses the IF-THEN rules on nodes present in the node to find the class label of a tuple in the testing dataset.

May be following six rules are derived from the above tree.

1. If Age=young and Income=low then Loan_decision= risky
2. If Age=Senior and Income=low then Loan_decision= risky
3. If Age=Middle_Aged and Income=low then Loan_decision= risky
4. If Age=young and Income=High then Loan_decision= Safe
5. If Age=Middle_Aged and Income=High then Loan_decision=Safe
6. If Age=Senior and Income=High then Loan_decision= Low_risky

Once the model is built then next step is testing the classifier using some sample testing dataset which is shown above figure. Here, the testing dataset is used to measure the accuracy of classification model shown in figure 7. There are two different metrics such as precision and recall used for measuring accuracy of a classification model. Figure 8 gives the sample decision tree construction based on ID3 algorithm.

Figure 5. Decision Tree

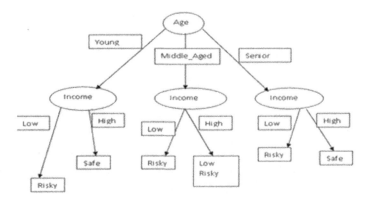

Figure 6. Training Process of Classification

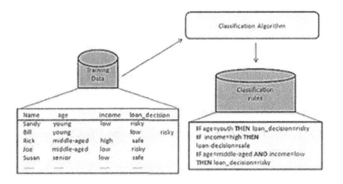

Phase II: Testing Phase

Figure 7. Testing Process of Classification

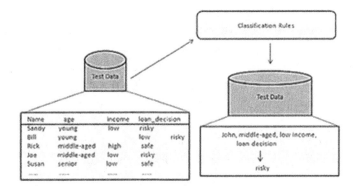

Figure 8. Sample Decision tree using ID3 Algorithm

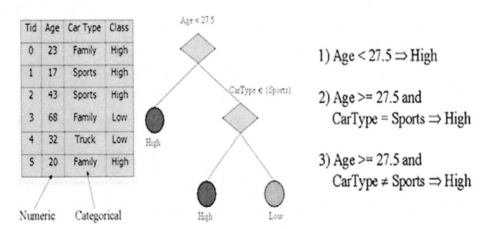

1) Age < 27.5 ⇒ High

2) Age >= 27.5 and
   CarType = Sports ⇒ High

3) Age >= 27.5 and
   CarType ≠ Sports ⇒ High

Regression

Prediction is an analytic process designed to explore data for consistent patterns or systematic relationships among variables and then to validate the findings by applying the detected patterns to new subsets of data. (Jiawei et al. 2006) uncover that the predictive data mining is the most common type of data mining and it has the most direct business applications.

The process of predictive data mining task consists of three stages:

- Data exploration
- Model building
- Deployment

Data Exploration usually starts with data preparation which may involve data cleaning, data transformations, selecting subsets of records and feature selection. Feature selection is one of the important operations in the exploration process. It is defined as reducing the numbers of variables to a manageable range if the datasets are with large number of variables performing some preliminary feature selection operations. Then, a simple choice of straightforward predictors for a regression model is used to elaborate exploratory analyses. The most widely used graphical and statistical method is exploratory data analysis. Model building and validation steps involve considering various models and choosing the best one based on their predictive performance. Deployment is the final step which involves selecting the best model in the previous step and applying it to a new data in order to generate predictions or estimates of the expected outcome.

Both classification and prediction are used for data analysis but there exists some issues dealing with preparing the data for data analysis. It involves the following activities,

- **Data Cleaning:** Data cleaning involves removing the noisy, incomplete and inconsistent data and methods for handling missing values of an attribute. The noisy data is removed by applying smoothing techniques such as binning and then problem of missing values is handled by replacing a missing value with most commonly occurring value for that attribute or replacing missing value by mean value of that attribute or replacing the missing value by global constant and so on.

- **Relevance Analysis:** Datasets may also have some irrelevant attributes and hence correlation analysis is performed to know whether any two given attributes are related or not. All irrelevant attributes are removed.

- **Normalization:** Normalization involves scaling all values for given attribute in order to make them fall within a small-specified range. Ex. Min_Max normalization.

- **Generalization:** it is data generalization method where data at low levels are mapped to some higher level there by reducing the number of values of an attributes. For this purpose, we can use the concept hierarchies. Example is shown in figure 8.

Unsupervised Learning

Figure 9. Unsupervised Learning Categorization

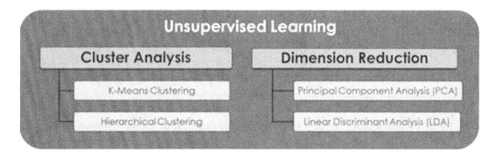

Unsupervised learning is the process of grouping the objects based on the similarity present in it. It can be classified into three types as shown in the figure 9.

- Clustering
- Association Rule
- Dimensionality Reduction

Clustering

Clustering is the process of grouping of objects into classes of similar objects based on some similarity measures between them (Sathiyamoorthi & Murali Baskaran 2011b). It is unsupervised leaning method. Each cluster can be represented as one group and while performing cluster analysis, first partition objects into groups based on the similarity between them and then assign the class labels to those groups. The main difference between clustering and classification is that, clustering is adaptable to changes and helps select useful features that distinguish objects into different groups. Some of the popular algorithms are shown in the figure 10.

Figure 10. Popular Algorithms in Unsupervised Learning

All these algorithms will belong to any one of the following methods as shown in the figure 11.

- Partitioning Method
- Hierarchical Method
- Density-based Method
- Grid-Based Method
- Model-Based Method
- Constraint-based Method

Figure 11. Types of Clustering

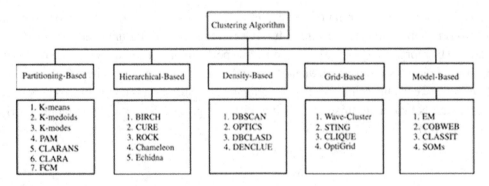

Partitioning Method

Given a database of 'n' objects and then the partitioning algorithm groups the objects into 'k' partition where k ≤ n. Each group should have at least one object. Also, objects in the same group should satisfy the following criteria.

- Each group contains at least one object.
- Each object must belong to exactly one group.
- Objects within clusters are highly similar and objects present in the different clusters are highly dissimilar.
- Kmeans algorithm is the most popular algorithm in this category. It works as follows.
- For a given number of partitions (say K), the Kmeans partitioning will create an initial partitioning representing K clusters using some distance measure.
- Then it uses the iterative technique to improve the partitioning by moving objects from one group to other. The problem with Kmeans algorithm is that K (number of partition) value is fixed before executing cluster and it does not change.
- Another algorithm is Kmedoid which is an improvement of Kmeans algorithm and provides better performance.

Hierarchical Clustering

In this method, it tries to create a hierarchical decomposition of given objects into various groups. There are two approaches used here for decomposition.

- Agglomerative Approach
- Divisive Approach

In agglomerative approach, clustering starts with each object forming a different group. Then, it keeps on merging the objects that are close to one another into groups. It repeats it until all of the groups are merged into one or until the termination condition holds. It is also known as bottom-up approach.

In divisive approach, clustering starts with all the objects representing a single cluster as a root. In each iteration, it tries to split the cluster into smaller clusters having similar i.e. objects that are close to one another. It proceeds towards down and split the cluster until each object in one cluster or the termination condition holds. This method is inflexible means that once a merging or splitting is done then it cannot be undone. It is also known as top-down approach.

Density-Based Clustering

It is based on the concept of density i.e. each clusters should have minimum number of data objects within the cluster radius. Here a cluster is continuing growing as long as the density in the neighborhood exceeds some threshold.

Grid-Based Clustering

In this clustering, the objects together form a grid. The object space is quantized into finite number of cells that form a grid structure. The main advantage of this approach is that it produces the cluster faster and takes less processing time.

Model-Based Clustering

In this approach, a model is used to build each cluster and find the best fit of data object for a given clusters. This method locates the clusters by using the density function. It reflects spatial distribution of the data objects among the clusters. It determines the number of clusters based on statistics, taking outlier or noise into account. Also, it yields robust clustering algorithm.

Constraint-Based Clustering

In this approach, the clustering is performed by incorporating the user and application constraints or requirements. Here, a constraint is the user expectation or the properties of desired clustering results. It is so interactive since constraints provide an interactive way of communication with the clustering process. Constraints can be specified by the user or by the application.

Association Rule Mining

As defined by (Han et al. 2006), an association rule identifies the collection of data attributes that are statistically related to one another. The association rule mining problem can be defined as follows: Given a database of related transactions, a minimal support and confidence value, find all association rules whose confidence and support are above the given threshold. In general, it produces a dependency rule that predicts an object based on the occurrences of other objects.

An association rule is of the form X->Y where X is called antecedent and Y is called consequent. There are two measures that assist in identification of frequent items and generate rules from it. One such measure is confidence which is the conditional probability of Y given X, Pr(Y|X), and the other is support which is the prior probability of X and Y, Pr(X and Y) (Jiawei et al 2006). It can be classified into either single dimensional association rule or multidimensional association rule based on number of predicates it contains (Jiawei et al. 2006). It can be extended to better fit in the application domains like genetic analysis and electronic commerce and so on. Aprior algorithm, FP growth algorithm and vertical data format are some of the standard algorithm used to identify the frequent items present in the large data set (Jiawei et al. 2006). Association rule mining metrics is shown in the figure 12.

Algorithms used for association rule mining are given below.

- Aprior algorithm
- FP-Growth
- Vertical Data format algorithm

Figure 12. Evaluating Association Rules

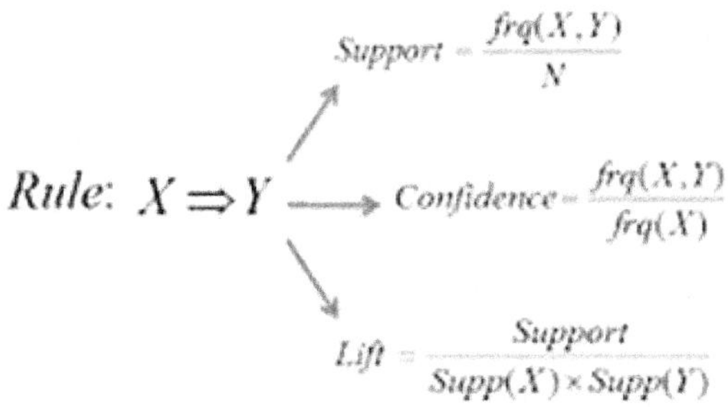

$$Support = \frac{frq(X,Y)}{N}$$

$$Rule: \quad X \Rightarrow Y \longrightarrow Confidence = \frac{frq(X,Y)}{frq(X)}$$

$$Lift = \frac{Support}{Supp(X) \times Supp(Y)}$$

Issues Related to Clustering

- **Scalability**: Clustering algorithms should be scalable and can handle large databases.
- **Ability to deal with different kinds of attributes: clustering a**lgorithms should be in such a way that it should be capable of handling different kinds of data such as numerical data, categorical, and binary data and so on.
- **Discovery of clusters with attribute shape**: Clustering algorithms should be capable of producing clusters of arbitrary shape using different measures.
- **High dimensionality:** Clustering algorithm should be designed in such way that it should be capable of handling both low as well as high dimensional data.
- **Ability to deal with noisy data**: Data sources may contain noisy, missing or erroneous data. So presence of these data may leads too poor quality clusters. Hence clustering algorithm should be designed in such way that it should handle noisy, missing and error data and produce high quality clusters.
- **Interpretability**: The results of clustering should be readable, interpretable, comprehensible into different form and useful to the end users

Dimensionality Reduction

In statistics, machine learning, and information theory, dimensionality reduction or dimension reduction is the process of reducing the number of random variables under consideration by obtaining a set of principal variables. It can be divided into feature selection and feature extraction.

Principal Component Analysis(PCA) is one of the most popular linear dimension reduction. Sometimes, it is used alone and sometimes as a starting solution for other dimension reduction methods. PCA is a projection based method which transforms the data by projecting it onto a set of orthogonal axes.

Evaluating the Model

Choosing the right evaluation metrics for the machine learning models will help the model to learn patterns that generalize well for unseen data instead of just memorizing the data. This will help in evaluating the model performs and to select better parameters. However using all the different metrics available will create chaos due to different outputs generated from these metrics. The different machine learning tasks have different performance metrics so the choice of metric completely depends on the type of model and the implementation plan of the model. There are different metrics for the tasks of classification, regression, ranking, clustering, topic modeling, etc.

Underfitting vs. Overfitting

Figure 13. Model Evaluation based on Overfitting and Underfitting

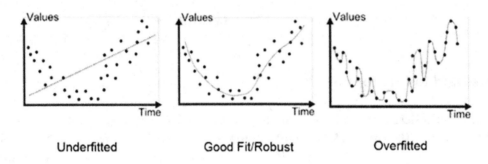

| Underfitted | Good Fit/Robust | Overfitted |

Underfitting

A statistical model or a machine-learning algorithm is said to have underfitting when it cannot capture the underlying trend of the data in other words model does not fit the data well enough. Overfitting occurs if the model or algorithm shows low bias but high variance.

Overfitting

A statistical model is said to have overfitted, when trained with large data but the model cannot capture the underlying trend of the data. Underfitting occurs if the model or algorithm shows low variance but high bias. Both overfitting and underfitting lead to poor predictions on new data sets. Some of the commonly used metrics are Hold-Out Validation, Bootstrapping, Hyperparameter, Tuning, Classification Accuracy, Logarithmic Loss, Confusion Matrix, Area under Curve, F1 Score, Mean Absolute Error, and Mean Squared Error.

Tuning the Parameter

The machine models applied to vary according to the Machine learning models are parameterized so that their behavior can be tuned for a given problem. These models can have many parameters and finding the best combination of parameters can be treated as a search problem. However, this very term called parameter may appear unfamiliar to you if you are new to applied machine learning. Some of the parameters to tune when optimizing neural nets (NNs) include:

- learning rate
- momentum

- regularization
- dropout probability
- batch normalization

Once the evaluation is over, any further improvement in your training can be possible by tuning the parameters. A few parameters were implicitly assumed when the training was done. Another parameter included is the learning rate that defines how far the line is shifted during each step, based on the information from the previous training step. These values all play a role in the accuracy of the training model, and how long the training will take.

For models that are more complex, initial conditions play a significant role in the determination of the outcome of training. Differences can be seen depending on whether a model starts training with values initialized to zeroes versus some distribution of values, which then leads to the question of which distribution is to be used. Since there are many considerations at this phase of training, it is important that you define what makes a model good. These parameters are referred to as Hyper parameters. The adjustment or tuning of these parameters depends on the dataset, model, and the training process. Once you are done with these parameters and are satisfied, you can move on to the last step.

Once you have done evaluation, it is possible that you want to see if you can further improve your training in any way. We can do this by tuning our parameters. We implicitly assumed a few parameters when we did our training, and now is a good time to go back, test those assumptions, and try other values. One example is how many times we run through the training dataset during training. What I mean by that is we can "show" the model our full dataset multiple times, rather than just once. This can sometimes lead to higher accuracies. Another parameter is *"learning rate"*. This defines how far we shift the line during each step, based on the information from the previous training step. These values all play a role in how accurate our model can become, and how long the training takes.

For more complex models, initial conditions can play a significant role in determining the outcome of training. Differences can be seen depending on whether a model starts off training with values initialized to zeroes versus some distribution of values, which leads to the question of which distribution to use. As you can see there are many considerations at this phase of training, and it's important that you define what makes a model "good enough", otherwise you might find yourself tweaking parameters for a very long time. These parameters are typically referred to as *"hyper parameters"*. The adjustment, or tuning, of these hyperactive parameters, remains a bit of an art, and is more of an experimental process that heavily depends on the specifics of your dataset, model, and training process. Once you're happy with your training and hyper parameters, guided by the evaluation step, it's time to finally use your model to do something useful!

Generating Predictions

Machine learning is using data to answer questions. The final step is where the model can predict the outcome and establish a learning path. The predictions can be generated in two ways real-time predictions and batch predictions.

Real-Time Predictions

The real-time predictions, when you want to obtain predictions at low latency. The real-time prediction API accepts a single input observation serialized as a JSON string, and synchronously returns the prediction and associated metadata as part of the API response. You can simultaneously invoke the API more than once to obtain synchronous predictions in parallel.

Batch Predictions

Use asynchronous predictions, or *batch predictions*, when you have a number of observations and would like to obtain predictions for the observations all at once. The process uses a data source as input, and outputs predictions into a .csv file stored in an S3 bucket of your choice. You need to wait until the batch prediction process completes before you can access the prediction results.

APPLICATIONS OF DATA MINING

Data mining applications include (Sathiyamoorthi, 2016),

- Market Basket Analysis and Management
  - Helps in determining customer purchase pattern i.e. what kind of consumer going to buy what kind of products.
  - Helps in finding the best products for different consumers. Here prediction is a data mining technique used to find the users interests based on available data.
  - Performs correlations analysis between product and sales.
  - Helps in finding clusters of consumers who share the same purchase characteristics such as user interests, regular habits, and monthly income and so on.
  - Is used in analyzing and determining customer purchasing pattern.
  - Provides multidimensional analysis on user data and support various summary reports.
- Corporate Analysis and Risk Management in Industries
  - It performs cash flow analysis and prediction, contingent claim analysis to evaluate assets.
  - Where it summarizes and compares the resource utilization i.e. how much resources are allocated and how much are currently available. it, helps in production planning and control system
  - Current trend analysis where it monitors competitors and predict future market directions.
- Fraud Detection or Outlier Detection
  - It is also known as outlier analysis which is used in the fields of credit card analysis and approval and telecommunication industry to detect fraudulent users.
  - In communication department, it helps in finding the destination of the fraud call, time duration of the fraud call, at what time the user made a call and the day or week of the calls and so on.
  - It helps in analyzing the patterns that are deviating from the normal behavior called outlier.

- Spatial and Time Series Data Analysis
  - ◦ For predicting stock market trends and bond analysis
  - ◦ Identifying areas that shares similar characteristics
- Image Retrieval and analysis
  - ◦ Image segmentation and classification
  - ◦ Face recognition and detection
- Web Mining
  - ◦ Web content mining
  - ◦ Web structure mining
  - ◦ Web log mining

REFERENCES

Aggarwal, C. C. (2016). *Outlier analysis*. New York: Springer.

Han, J., Kamber, M., & Pei, J. (2012). Data Preprocessing. *Data Mining*, 83-124. doi:10.1016/b978-0-12-381479-1.00003-4

Roh, Y., Heo, G., & Whang, S. E. (2018). *A survey on data collection for machine learning: a big data – AI integration perspective*. Retrieved from: https://arxiv.org/pdf/1811.03402.pdf

Samuel, A. L. (1959). Some Studies in Machine Learning Using the Game of Checkers. *IBM Journal of Research and Development*, *44*(1), 210–229.

Sathiyamoorthi & Baskaran. (2011). Data pre-processing techniques for pre-fetching and caching of web data through proxy server. *International Journal of Computer Science and Network Security*, *11*(1), 92–98.

Chapter 2
Review and Applications of Machine Learning and Artificial Intelligence in Engineering:
Overview for Machine Learning and AI

Melda Yucel
ⓘ https://orcid.org/0000-0002-2583-8630
Istanbul University-Cerrahpaşa, Turkey

Gebrail Bekdaş
Istanbul University-Cerrahpaşa, Turkey

Sinan Melih Nigdeli
Istanbul University-Cerrahpaşa, Turkey

ABSTRACT

This chapter presents a summary review of the development of artificial intelligence (AI). The chapter provides definitions of AI, together with its basic features, and illustrates the development process of AI and machine learning. Further, the authors outline the developments of applications from the past to today and the use of AI in different categories. Finally, they describe prediction applications using artificial neural networks for engineering applications. The outcomes of this review show that the usage of AI methods to predict optimum results is the current trend and will be more important in the future.

ARTIFICIAL INTELLIGENCE AND MACHINE LEARNING

Alongside generally related to computer sciences and engineering disciplines, artificial intelligence (AI) pertains to science and technology, and benefits many fields, such as biology and genetics, psychology, language learning and comprehension, and mathematics.

DOI: 10.4018/978-1-6684-6291-1.ch002

As AI is accepted as a branch of a science, being considered as a field of research and technology at the same time, its various definitions are from many different sources. Some of these are as follows:

1. This approach, which is human-oriented, should be an experimental science that includes hypothesis and experiences within (Russell & Norvig, 1995).
2. AI can be defined as an effort for developing computer operations, which will ensure to find out the similarities of this structure, via an understanding of the human thinking structure (Uygunoğlu & Yurtçu, 2006).
3. McCarthy (2007) remarked that of AI is a science and engineering discipline, which is generated by intelligent machines, especially computer programming, too.
4. Luger (2009) defined AI as a computer science branch that is related to automation of intelligent behaviors.
5. AI is an expert system to understand intelligent beings, and establish and make the process of decision-making productive, rapid, and simple (Patil et al., 2017).

Based on these different definitions, AI is a technology, which is made of computers, which function similarly to humans' intelligent structure and thinking behaviors, intelligently thinking software or computer-controlled robots.

However, although this technology is a case, which is related to using computers in order to understand human intelligence, it should not be limited to methods that are measurable only according to biological factors (McCarthy, 2007). On the other hand, in recent times, the main reason of importantly advancing of AI technology consists in developments in computer functions, which are integrated with human intelligence, such as reasoning, nominated ability of discernment, learning, and solving probles.

Machine learning, which is seen as a subfield of AI, is a technology related to designing and developing algorithms and techniques, which ensure devices to learn, such as computers (Olivas, Guerrero, Sober, Benedito, & López, 2009). In this respect, the concept of machine learning expresses the generated changes in systems by tasks, which include the actions which are realized with AI, such as recognition, robot-controlling, detection/identification, and prediction. Also, with occurring changes, previously generated systems are developed or new systems are synthesized. Figure 1 shows the structure of a typical AI tool, which illustrates this case more clearly.

This tool senses information coming from its surrounding and realizes a suitable modelling. Actions are calculated based on the possible effects from the models being predicted. Conversely, changes, which can occur in any of AI components Figure 1 shows, may be regarded as learning. Also, different learning mechanisms may be run, based on the change of subsystems.

The definition of learning in the dictionary is gain of knowledge and success through study, understanding or experience, become skillful and changes that occurred via experience in behavioral tendencies (Nilsson, 1998). Consequently, learning happens in a long and iterative process, and generates alterations, which ensure certain attainments and experiences as a result of this process, too. The development of many technological devices (e.g., computer) and becoming like humans are unavoidable when various activities are carried out. In this case, machine learning is considered as gain of experience or information of machines, such as computers, as a result of a variety of events (e.g., developing various decision-making mechanisms and foreknowing similar states) which may be lived in the future.

Figure 1. Artificial intelligence system
(Nilsson, 1998)

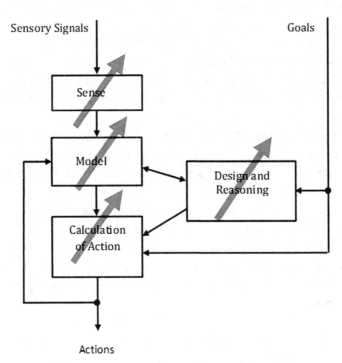

As the authors remarked above, in order to have a successful learning process in devices, firstly actualized learning actions of biologic beings, namely people and animals, and the features of processes should be understood properly. However, this information is insufficient alone and in terms of engineering, too; some vital information and calculations are needed (Nilsson, 1998). Some of these are as follows:

1. The use of metalevel knowledge makes the control of solving-problem strategies more advanced. Although this is a very hard problem, investigation of some current systems can be relatively considerable as an area of research (Luger, 2009).
2. A program can only learn behaviors and factors, and which formation (mathematical or logical definition) of itself may be represented. However, unfortunately, almost all of learned systems depend on very limited abilities about representing the knowledge (McCarthy, 2007).
3. Some tasks are not described well without a sample. Therefore, it is possible to determine input-output couples for tasks. Yet, a clear relation may not occur between inputs and desired outputs.
4. The current amount of information of specific duties can be too much, because open coding can be performed by people.

DEVELOPMENT PROCESS OF ARTIFICIAL INTELLIGENCE AND MACHINE LEARNING

Machine learning technology is a branch of AI that focuses on independent computers and machines, and realizes the conversion of these to smart entities. Various features which belong to humans (e.g., physical, genetic, and intelligence) benefit from this conversion.

Since the discovery and usage of computers and various technological calculators, hand in hand with the continuous development of technology, the development of more innovative and differentiated machines has occurred. Nevertheless, only in the 20th century these machines were able to think, experience, and learn lessons from mistakes, by making various comparisons like humans.

In this respect, one of the first studies in the literature is cybernetics, meaning communication science and automatic control systems between livings and machines, which Arturo Rosenblueth, Norbert Wiener, and Julian Bigelow developed in 1943. In 1948, Weiner's famous book was published with this name, too. Between 1948 and 1949, Grey Walter performed an experiment in Bristol, based on the opinion that little count brain cells can cause complex behaviors with autonomous robots, which are turtles called Elsie and Elmer. Also, in 1949, Donald Hebb proved a simple and current rule for altering connection weights between neurons which ensure to realize the learning (Buchanan, 2006).

The real important developments about AI in terms of machine learning occurred in 1950 and after. For example, in 1950, Alan Turing published the Turing test, which is required for measuring intelligent behaviors and which he included in the book called *Computing Machinery and Intelligence*. In this book, the author discussed the required conditions to be able to think that a machine is intelligent. According to Turing, it must be thought that the machine is certainly smart in case a machine shams a human successfully, compared to a smart observer (McCarthy, 2007).

The application in Figure 2 is a method which Turing generated and named as a simulation game. In this test, a machine and a human are brought to face opposite, and in a separate section another person, called querier, is present. The querier cannot see directly any entities within the test and talk with them. However, the querier actually does not know which entity is a machine or a human, and can communicate with them using a device, such as a terminal, which can write only text. From the querier's perspective, the distinction of a human from a computer is based on given answers by entities existed in test, to ask questions, which are asked with just the device. When the machine or the human cannot be distinguished, it may be assumed the machine is intelligent, according to Turing.

Nevertheless, the querier is free to ask any question, regardless how deceptive or indirect, to reveal the identity of the computer. For example, the querier can want arithmetic calculation from both, by assuming a high probability that the computer gives more accurate results than the human. Contrary to this strategy, the computer may need to know when it may be unsuccessful about finding correct answers to a set of problems as these, to resemble the human. The querier can want to ask both entities to discuss a poem or artwork, to find out their identity based upon human sensitive structure. Also, a strategy is required to allow the computer for information related to the sensual formation of mankind (Luger, 2009).

In this respect, the Turing test is a significant application to measure similarity between a machine and a human. The results showed that machines have similarities with humans at high rate, but these results cannot be considered as right exactly. The clearest reason stands in some features, which come from human creation; machines do not have such sensual and humanized features. Therefore, machines cannot carry out everything as humanoid and, consequently, the fact that machines are more successful than or superior to humans may not be deduced through all kinds of applications.

Figure 2. Application of Turing test
(Luger, 2009)

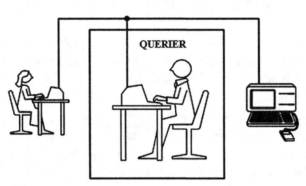

On the other hand, in the 1950s, the use of the k-means algorithm started. It is one of the commonly attracted clustering methods in machine learning and works to estimate the values of a complex and multidimensional dataset with the help of its several average points (Olivas et al., 2009).

In the same period, another study consisted in chess programs, which Claude Shannon (1950) and Alan Turing (1953) wrote for von-Neumann-style traditional computers. Then, in 1951, Marvin Minsky and Dean Edmonds, who were graduate students at the Mathematics Department of Princeton University, set up the first neural network computer. Between the years 1952 and 1962, Arthur Samuel wrote the first program which can play games, with the aim of having the upper hand in a world champion by gaining adequate skill in checkers. In this period, which started in 1952, the idea that computers can carry out only determined actions by themselves was refuted, because this written program learned rapidly playing a game better than its designer did. Logic Theorist, which was written by Allen Newell, J. C. Shaw, and Herbert Simon, was a demonstration of the first functioning AI program (Russell & Norvig, 1995).

In addition, in 1958, Rosenblatt proposed a simple neural network called "perceptron," which was seen as a milestone in machine learning history (Han & Kamber, 2006). Again, in 1958, McCarthy, who became an important name in the field of AI, discovered the LISP programming language, which is the second oldest programming language still used today. At the beginning of 1960s, Margaret Masterman and friends designed semantic networks for machine translation. In 1964, the thesis of Danny Bobrow at the MIT sustained that computers were good at understanding natural language as well as solving algebraic problems, too. Joel Moses demonstrated the power of symbolic reasoning for integral problems through the Macsyma program (a computer-aided algebra system) in his doctoral thesis, which the MIT published in 1967. This program is the first successful knowledge-based program in the field of math. Another event in this year was the design of a chess program named MacHack, which is based on knowledge, and as good as being able of getting a degree of C-class in a tournament. Its author was Richard Greenblatt, from the MIT (Buchanan, 2006).

In conjunction with an increased adoption of the approach of knowledge-based systems, the intelligibility problem of a molecular structure was solved through the information which was acquired with the mass spectrometer Ed Feigenbaum, Bruce Buchanan, and Joshua Lederberg had developed in 1969. The program input was formed from the base (beginning) formula of the molecule, and, when the created molecule was bombarded by cathode (electron) rays, the mass spectrometer put forth masses of various parts of the molecule. For instance, the mass spectrometer can include a density at m=15 corresponding to the mass of a methyl part. By producing all possible structures, which were interconnected with the formula, with a simple version of the program, the effect on each part of the mass spectrometer was compared with an original spectrometer by being predicted (Russell & Norvig, 1995).

In 1970 and after, with the rising of machine learning capabilities, more developments were experienced in the fields of industry and neural networks. Moreover, with machines and robots designed for space studies, the aim to use them to simulate the human became widespread gradually.

Coming to 1980, the first expert systems and commercial applications became more and more developed. For example, Lee Erman, Rick Hayes-Roth, Victor Lesser, and Raj Reddy developed the Hearsay-II speech-understanding system, which has a blackboard model as a skeleton structure. With respect to the middle of the 1980s, Werbos defined how to work neural networks by using the back-propagation algorithm, for the first time in 1974. Pattern recognition, which is another technology, is an issue closely related to machine learning; Bishop (1995) and Ripley (1996) explained the usage of neural networks for it. On the other hand, Mitchell (1997) wrote a book covering many machine learning techniques, also including genetic algorithms and reinforcement learning. Again, in 1997, the program called The Deep Blue defeated Garry Kasparov, who was then world chess champion. At the end of the 20th century, Rod Brooks improved the Cog Project at the MIT, which allowed a major progress on building a humanoid robot. With these advances, it is sighted that any machines and systems have abilities on human level and even come to a grade that will rival the human. For example, Cynthia Breazeal's thesis *Social Machines* described Kismet, which is a robot whose face can express its feelings. Also, in 2005, Robot Nomad explored Antarctica's far areas, to search for meteorite samples (Buchanan, 2006; Witten, Hall, & Frank, 2011).

ARTIFICIAL INTELLIGENCE AND MACHINE LEARNING

Machine learning improved with AI technology can be used for many different applications in various areas. Performed applications and developments in these areas are explained as follows:

1. **Expert Systems:** These systems generate solutions to existing problems in a similar way to solve-style of any problem by an expert. When viewed from this aspect, expert systems were created through conversion to a format that computers can apply for solving similar problems by gaining information from a human expert.

Dendral, which is one of the oldest expert systems and is benefiting from domain knowledge about solving problems, was developed at the end of the 1960s, at Stanford. Generally, the structure of organic molecules is too big; this increases the possibility of the probable number of structures for molecules is higher. Therefore, this system was developed to determine the structure of organic molecules, with mass spectrometer information related to chemical bonds in molecules, and chemical formulas. Another system that has a feature to be first is Mycin, which was developed in 1974. Mycin was improved by using expert medical information, in a way to present cure advices by diagnosing spinal meningitis and bacterial infections in the blood (Luger, 2009).

As another example, in 1991 Bell Atlantic developed a system which allows to assign a company's suitable technician based on the problem the customer reports on the phone. The system, which Bell Atlantic developed with machine learning methods, has features for becoming an expert system, which provides savings for more than ten billion dollars per year through carrying out this decision of improvement in 1999 (Witten et al., 2011). The following systems were also developed as machine learning methods: *Internist*, to diagnose internal diseases; *Prospector*, to determine the kind of mineral deposits and possible locations, according to geological information about a site; *Dipmeter Advisor*, to comment the results of oil well drilling (Luger, 2009).

2. **Robotics:** Besides, AI is generated in order to perform the tasks and actions, which are carried out by people, with a better and quick performance; numbers and usage areas of robots, which are one of the practices developing with AI technology for fulfilling these tasks, increase day by day.

Indeed, AI technology and machine learning, which is a branch of it, are closely related to robotics technology. The reason is that, generally, artificial neural networks (ANNs) or other classification systems are used for various tasks, which are required to control robots (Onwubolu & Babu, 2004). However, nowadays, structures with a simple form (e.g., algorithms, all sort software, Internet robots, and apps), which are AI tools, together with structures with an advanced form (e.g., robots, driverless vehicles, smart watches, and the other mechanical devices) exist. On the other hand, Floridi (2017) predicted that generated digital technologies and automations would take place of employees in fields such as agricultural and production sectors, while in service industry robots would come instead of humans. Even so, the human performs as an interface between a vehicle and a GPS, documents in different languages, a finished meal and its ingredients, or in cases such as diagnosing a disease which matched with symptoms. Thus, robots replacing humans are posing a danger.

3. **Gaming:** Gaming is one of the oldest fields of work of AI. In 1950, as soon as computers became programmable, Claude Shannon and Alan Turing wrote the first chess program. Since that time, a resolute progression has been at stake in game standards, reaching up to the point that today's systems can challenge across to a world champion (Russell & Norvig, 1995).

The largest part of the first researches in this field was performed by using common board games, such as checkers, chess, and fifteen crosswords. As board games have specific features, they represent an ideal topic for AI research. Many games are played by using a well-described set of rules. This condition facilitates the definition of the field of research and saves the researcher from most of the complexities and uncertainness, which is inherent to less structured problems (Luger, 2009). Less abstract games, such as football or cricket, did not attract AI researchers' attention much. As increasing number of competitors in games makes more complex and affects the operating of the installed functions.

Together with the progress in technology, researchers have included other kinds of games (e.g., football, tennis, and volleyball), which require human talent, physical capacity or humanoid responses such as reflex, alongside intelligent games (e.g., chess and checkers), which are preferred as a beginning-phase study field. Researchers obtained real-like values, besides observing the usage AI technology in these kinds of game.

4. **Speech Recognition with Natural Language Process**: Natural language processing is a research and development field, which deals with written and talked (digitized and recorded) language and its data. Natural language processing is known as the science and technology of features and usage of human language, and is mentioned as NLP technology. NLP comes from the first letters of the

words "Natural Language Process," and emphasizes the origins of the languages people talk and their role in information processing. The substantial execution areas of theory, tool, and techniques developed in the NLP contain the topics of machine translation, text summarization, text mining, and information extraction.

Further, Olivas et al. (2009) sustained that NLP methods are able to process a manageable amount of data, like people do, and analyze big amounts of data easily. For example, NPL's combination of speech parts automatically is close to faultless performance, which belongs to an adequate human.

One of the first designs is the Lunar system, which William Woods developed in 1973. This system was the first natural language program, which allowed geologists for asking English questions about rock/stone samples from the Apollo Moon Mission, and was used by other people practically (Russell & Norvig, 1995). Besides, examples of modern-day developments of this technology are especially virtual assistants as smart phones applications that transcribe speech, and systems which automatically correct errors in messages and e-mails (Biswas, 2018).

5. **Finance, Banking, and Insurance Applications**: Expenditures, banking actions, and various financial activities reflect the various features of people, and finance, bank, and insurance institutions benefit from new technologies for increasing the number of customers who earn and for meeting these customers' expectations (i.e., customer satisfaction).

An example of application of these technologies can be determining which persons a loan corporation will give how much credit. In this case, loan companies apply a decision procedure by calculating a numeric parameter according to the information they obtain from surveys to applicants. If this parameter is above the defined threshold, the application is accepted, while it is refused if the parameter is below the threshold (Witten et al., 2011). Another example of application of NPL technologies is that, in various sectors, it is possible to plan sale timing by predicting the next purchasing time of a product/service, buying operations for a travel, flight, car or house, the customer's profile, when the operation may be realized, and its rate of possibility of occurrence (Maimon & Rokach, 2010).

6. **Medicine and Health**: Medicine and health science is the primary areas area in which AI and, especially, machine learning applications are used most. They are used for diagnosing and treating of many diseases; moreover, machine learning practices are adopted for recognizing genetic and biological features and improving new technologies.

For instance, determining the most proper medicine dose for a person in treatment of chronic diseases generally occurs by trial and error. Machine learning methods are used in order to speed this process, and identify the suitable medicine treatment for each person (Olivas et al., 2009). Also, these methods help deduce phenotype information from the data of the gene expression, determine how the sequencing of protein and DNA will occur, examine pattern regulations on biological gene sequences and with regard to the generation of different gene patterns, and find out recurrence frequency (Han & Gao, 2008; Maimon & Rokach, 2010; Olivas et al. 2009).

7. **Vision Systems and Image Recognition Technology**: Systems, which are created by benefitting from sight sense and characters of beings within nature, are vision systems. These systems can

perform position determination, image selection and combination, pattern and photo analogy, debugging, and many similar processes with image detection actions, mainly by using properties and advantages of the sight sense.

The vision system based on optical flow is an example, and is used for controlling of responses of airplanes during landing. In addition, these systems are intended for aims, such as performing the movement of mobile robots in an environment by detecting location of existing barriers and free spaces, monitoring many astronomical bodies in space, determining varying land cover because of abrupt changes in green zones by identifying damages, which are natural or man-made within ecosystems (Han & Gao, 2008; Russell & Norvig, 1995).

Except from these applications, vision systems are frequently preferred in various areas with many purposes, especially geographical positioning, face recognition, determining vehicle route, detecting faulty products, which can occur during production activities, and diagnosing diseased/healthy cells.

8. **Publication, Web, and Social Media Applications**: Increase of the spending time on the Web and social media, and varying of carried out actions cause to create of a big data stack. Also, the improvement of the new technologies is becoming possible via using the data from people's use of social media accounts and various Internet sites in many scopes.

Particularly, one of these is the sequencing of Web pages by search engines. This problem can be solved via machine learning, depending on a training set creating the data, which is obtained in line with the decisions persons make previously. By analyzing training data, a learning algorithm can predict the relation level of query, thanks to its features, such as URL address content for a new query or whether it takes place at a header label. On the other hand, machine learning applications uses the search terms to select adverts (e.g., choices of other users about advices to similar products on shopping a book or a film/music CD) (Witten et al., 2011).

PREDICTION APPLICATIONS VIA ARTIFICIAL NEURAL NETWORKS

In various study fields, ANNs benefit many topics, such as feature extraction, clustering, classification, notably prediction and forecasting. In engineering science, which is the primary of these fields, ANNs can represent quite successful results, especially about predicting the values of design parameters in handled problems.

Also, in civil engineering, some studies were performed to rapidly predict parameter values belong to a problem, for designing a model. One of these is a study that developed of a model which can predict salinity rate of Murray River in South Australia from 14 days ago, by used ANN and GA methods by Bowden, Maier, and Dandy (2002).

Atici (2011) used ANNs, besides multiple regression analyses, to predict the compressive strength in different curing periods of concrete mixtures consisting of various amounts of blast furnace slag and fly ash. These amounts depend on values and features of additives which are obtained with ultrasonic pulse velocity and nondistructive testing. Momeni, Armaghani, and Hajihassani (2015) used ANNs combined with the particle swarm optimization method, with the aim of increasing network performance, to predict the unconfined compressive strength of granite and limestone rock samples from an area in Malaysia.

In 2015, Aichouri et al. (2015) developed an ANN with the aim of modeling the rain-runoff relation in a basin, which has a semiarid Mediterranean climate in Algeria. Veintimilla-Reyes, Cisneros, and Vanegas (2016) created a model based on ANN, which allowed to predict the water flow in Tomebamba River in real time and for a specific day of the year. In addition, model inputs were precipitation and flow information, which occurred in determined stations. The reseaarchers used real data from a system which was placed in the stations.

On the other hand, Chatterjee et al. (2017) determined the structural damages of multi-storey reinforced buildings via ANN, which they used to train the particle swarm optimization algorithm. Also, Cascardi, Micelli, and Aiello (2017) devised a model based on ANN for predicting the compression strength of reinforced circular columns, which are covered unremittingly by a wrap with fiber reinforced polymer. Shebani and Iwnicki (2018) used ANNs to predict the wearing rate of wheel and ray according to different wheel-rail contact cases, such as under dry, wet, and oiled conditions and after sanding.

At the same time, ANNs together with metaheuristic algorithms work well, and become hybrid, too. Besides, they are quite suitable in prediction issues, and enable various applications that determined by predicting optimum parameters for design problems under investigation.

For example, Ormsbee and Reddy (1995) realized optimum control of pumping systems to supply water. Their study aimed at handling the working times of a pump as decision variable, and at minimizing its operating costs. The researchers trained with a neural network the prediction data they had obtained from the simulation model they used for the purpose, and then provided the optimization of the system control by using the trained data in a genetic algorithm. Further, they compared the performance with genetic algorithm and ANN methods, by developing a multi-stages prediction model that included the firefly algorithm that is used to determine optimum values of the parameters in model, which is used in prediction duration, with the support of a vector machine for predetermining the daily lake level according to three different horizon lines, in Kişi et al.'s (2015) study. Sebaaly, Varma, and Maina (2018) developed a model which combined ANNs with a genetic algorithm, by using a data set including information belonging to numerous asphalt mixtures.

The above-mentioned examples show that the use of AI methods, mainly ANNs, are the increasing trend in science and engineering when the problem solving is too complex, impossible or the process needs too much time.

REFERENCES

Aichouri, I., Hani, A., Bougherira, N., Djabri, L., Chaffai, H., & Lallahem, S. (2015). River flow model using artificial neural networks. *Energy Procedia, 74*, 1007–1014. doi:10.1016/j.egypro.2015.07.832

Atici, U. (2011). Prediction of the strength of mineral admixture concrete using multivariable regression analysis and an artificial neural network. *Expert Systems with Applications, 38*(8), 9609–9618. doi:10.1016/j.eswa.2011.01.156

Biswas, J. (2018). *9 Complex machine learning applications that even a beginner can build today* Retrieved from https://analyticsindiamag.com/machine-learning-applications-beginners/

Bowden, G. J., Maier, H. R., & Dandy, G. C. (2002). Optimal division of data for neural network models in water resources applications. *Water Resources Research, 38*(2), 2–1. doi:10.1029/2001WR000266

Buchanan, B. G. (2006). *Brief history.* Retrieved from https://aitopics.org/misc/brief-history

Cascardi, A., Micelli, F., & Aiello, M. A. (2017). An Artificial Neural Networks model for the prediction of the compressive strength of FRP-confined concrete circular columns. *Engineering Structures, 140,* 199–208. doi:10.1016/j.engstruct.2017.02.047

Chatterjee, S., Sarkar, S., Hore, S., Dey, N., Ashour, A. S., & Balas, V. E. (2017). Particle swarm optimization trained neural network for structural failure prediction of multistoried RC buildings. *Neural Computing & Applications, 28*(8), 2005–2016. doi:10.100700521-016-2190-2

Floridi, L. (2017). *If AI is the future, what does it mean for you?* Retrieved from https://www.weforum.org/agenda/2017/01/the-future-ofai-and-the-implications-for-you

Han, J., & Gao, J. (2008). Data mining in e-science and engineering. In H. Kargupta, J. Han, S. Y. Philip, R. Motwani, & V. Kumar (Eds.), *Next generation of data mining* (pp. 1–114). Boca Raton, FL: CRC Press. doi:10.1201/9781420085877.pt1

Han, J. & Kamber, M. (2006). Data mining: concepts and techniques (2nd ed.). CL: Morgan Kaufmann.

Kisi, O., Shiri, J., Karimi, S., Shamshirband, S., Motamedi, S., Petković, D., & Hashim, R. (2015). A survey of water level fluctuation predicting in Urmia Lake using support vector machine with firefly algorithm. *Applied Mathematics and Computation, 270,* 731–743. doi:10.1016/j.amc.2015.08.085

Luger, G. F. (2009). *Artificial intelligence: structures and strategies for complex problem solving* (6th ed.). Boston, MA: Pearson Education.

Maimon, O., & Rokach, L. (2010). *Data mining and knowledge discovery handbook* (2nd ed.). New York, NY: Springer. doi:10.1007/978-0-387-09823-4

McCarthy, J. (2007). *What is artificial intelligence?* Retrieved from http://www.formal.stanford.edu/jmc/whatisai.html

Momeni, E., Armaghani, D. J., & Hajihassani, M. (2015). Prediction of uniaxial compressive strength of rock samples using hybrid particle swarm optimization-based artificial neural networks. *Measurement, 60,* 50–63. doi:10.1016/j.measurement.2014.09.075

Nilsson, N. J. (1998). *Introduction to machine learning an early draft of a proposed textbook.* Retrieved from http://ai.stanford.edu/~nilsson/MLBOOK.pdf

Olivas, E. S., Guerrero, J. D. M., Sober, M. M., Benedito, J. R. M., & López, A. J. S. (Eds.). (2009). *Handbook of research on machine learning applications and trends: algorithms, methods, and techniques.* Hershey, PA: IGI Global.

Onwubolu, G. C., & Babu, B. V. (2004). *New optimization techniques in engineering* (Vol. 141). Heidelberg, Germany: Springer-Verlag. doi:10.1007/978-3-540-39930-8

Ormsbee, L. E. & Reddy, S. L. (1995). Pumping system control using genetic optimization and neural networks. *IFAC Proceedings Volumes, 28*(10), 685-690.

Patil, A., Patted, L., Tenagi, M., Jahagirdar, V., Patil, M., & Gautam, R. (2017). Artificial intelligence as a tool in civil engineering – a review. In *Proceedings of National conference on advances in computational biology, communication, and data analytics (ACBCDA 2017)*. India: IOSR Journal of Computer Engineering.

Russell, S. J., & Norvig, P. (1995). *Artificial intelligence: a modern approach*. Englewood Cliffs, NJ: Prentice Hall.

Sebaaly, H., Varma, S., & Maina, J. W. (2018). Optimizing asphalt mix design process using artificial neural network and genetic algorithm. *Construction & Building Materials*, *168*, 660–670. doi:10.1016/j.conbuildmat.2018.02.118

Shebani, A., & Iwnicki, S. (2018). Prediction of wheel and rail wear under different contact conditions using artificial neural networks. *Wear*, *406*, 173–184. doi:10.1016/j.wear.2018.01.007

Uygunoğlu, T., & Yurtçu, Ş. (2006). Yapay zekâ tekniklerinin inşaat mühendisliği problemlerinde kullanımı. *Yapı Teknolojileri Elektronik Dergisi*, *1*, 61–70.

Veintimilla-Reyes, J., Cisneros, F., & Vanegas, P. (2016). Artificial neural networks applied to flow prediction: A use case for the Tomebamba river. *Procedia Engineering*, *162*, 153–161. doi:10.1016/j.proeng.2016.11.031

Witten, I. H., Hall, M. A., & Frank, E. (2011). *Data mining: practical machine learning tools and techniques*. USA: Morgan Kaufmann Series.

This research was previously published in Artificial Intelligence and Machine Learning Applications in Civil, Mechanical, and Industrial Engineering; pages 1-12, copyright year 2020 by Engineering Science Reference (an imprint of IGI Global).

Chapter 3
Machine Learning Applications in Nanomedicine and Nanotoxicology: An Overview

Gerardo M. Casañola-Martin
North Dakota State University, Fargo, USA

Hai Pham-The
ⓘ https://orcid.org/0000-0003-4531-7223
Hanoi University of Pharmacy, Hanoi, Vietnam

ABSTRACT

The development of machine learning algorithms together with the availability of computational tools nowadays have given an increase in the application of artificial intelligence methodologies in different fields. However, the use of these machine learning approaches in nanomedicine remains still under-explored in certain areas, despite the development in hardware and software tools. In this review, the recent advances in the conjunction of machine learning with nanomedicine are shown. Examples dealing with biomedical properties of nanoparticles, characterization of nanomaterials, text mining, and image analysis are also presented. Finally, some future perspectives in the integration of nanomedicine with cloud computing, deep learning and other techniques are discussed.

INTRODUCTION

Nanomaterials have arisen as one of the promising fields in material sciences and technologies in the current century. The most prominent that should be mentioned include among others the development of new fuel cells (Liu, Ling, Su, & Lee, 2004), electronic devices (Novoselov et al., 2012), coatings (Ragesh, Anand Ganesh, Nair, & Nair, 2014), diagnostic imaging (Wu et al., 2002), and drug delivery (Muller & Keck, 2004). The field of nanomedicine has gained a great importance in the last years. In the case of nanomedicine successful applications of computational approaches, most of them related with QSAR (quantitative-structure activity relationships) studies.

DOI: 10.4018/978-1-6684-6291-1.ch003

In this sense in this review we cover the main applications of machine learning methods in medicine, where the most relevant publications are discussed for this field. This has led to the development of different approaches, based in the predictions of the effects of nanoparticles, the enzyme inhibition of carbon nanotubes and others in the use of artificial intelligence for the study of nanoimages to predict the response to certain effects, or the improvement of personalized cancer treatment based in nanometer-scale drug delivery systems.

The State of the Art of Machine Learning and Nanomedicine

In the era of data, machine learning (ML) algorithms have played a crucial role by helping to improve the predictions of biological, physical, chemical and toxicological effects. As the size of the information increase these artificial intelligence methods are of valuable important to analyze this huge amount of data.

One of the main practical use is for virtual throughput screening of new chemical entities, based on the information gathered from previous one. A common procedure to perform this kind of study is by the Quantitative Structure-Activity Relationships (QSAR) methods, a statistical method, in a general way which try to correlate the biological effect with the features describing the compounds, molecular descriptors gathered directly from the chemical structure through mathematical equations of the connectivity graph. In the case of nanomaterials other descriptors can also be obtained like shape, size, composition, surface modifications, and propensity to agglomerate, interaction with different molecules, and aqueous solubility that could influence the properties of the nanomaterials affecting the biological responses.

The impact of this field was analyzed by retrieving in the Scopus database a search using the search criteria "Machine Learning" AND "Nanomedicine". As can be observed in Figure 1 the time period for Machine Learning-Nanomedicine search comprises the time period from 1999-present, with 921 documents this is compressible because this is novel multidisciplinary field. As can be noted a constant increased in this field is observed. From this could be said that this thematic constitutes a hot topic nowadays due to the increased interest in drug discovery and design.

Figure 1. Yearly publications based on 'Machine Learning'-'Nanomedicine' keywords

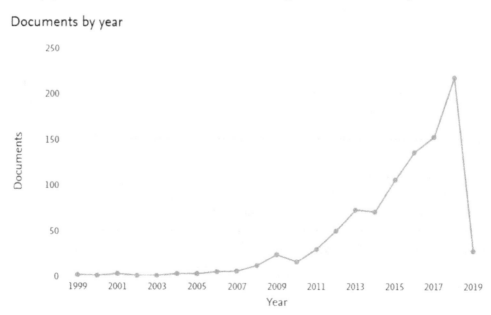

Innovative Applications and Methods

One of the big challenges for nanomedicine is the management of high volumes of data generated through all the years of experimental research. The improvement of the tools for information retrieval is a crucial step in order to organize the big datasets and compile the necessary and relevant information to be processed for its use in studies. In this sense, a work developed by de la Iglesia et al. make use of a machine learning method combined with Natural Language Processing (NLP) methods (de la Iglesia et al., 2014). In the mentioned report is done the classification of clinical trials (CT) in the ClinicalTrials. gov database that test nanotechnology products (nanodrugs and nanodevices) from those one that make testing of conventional drugs.

In the proposed method, the authors developed a workflow (see Figure 2) that comprises the extraction and manual annotation of the CT into two categories: nano and non-nano, with 500 CTs selected as positives (nano) and 500 CTs as negatives (non-nano). In a second step is performed the preprocessing of the data eliminating the irrelevant information, the standardization and filtering, by using Natural Language Toolkits to convert the information into textual features using a vector-based representation. In the following state several machine learning algorithms implemented in the Weka workbench are used and the best predictions model showed an F-measure value equal to 0.955. In summary this study helps to retrieve and organize the big data in CTs database, making useful for researchers.

Figure 2. Graphical workflow of the work developed by de la Iglesia et al. (2014)

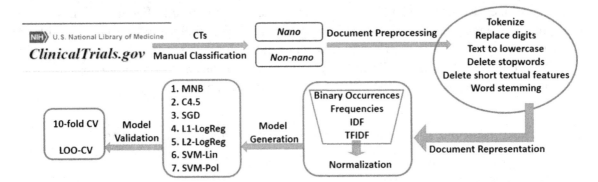

In a recent review from Jones et al. are described the applications of machine learning in nanomedicine focused mainly in the prediction of biomedical responses (Jones, Ghandehari, & Facelli, 2016). In the first section, the authors show the QSAR studies related with nanoparticles and its responses related with nanoparticle adherence, nanoparticle size, cellular uptake, molecular release and so on (Epa et al., 2012; Fourches et al., 2010; Puzyn, Leszczynska, & Leszczynski, 2009; Toropova & Toropov, 2017; Winkler et al., 2014). The authors noted that the Artificial Neural Networks (ANN) are the main algorithms used through most of the works. From their point of view this choice is due to the complexity of the data given by the great heterogeneity in the nanomaterials (Tantra et al., 2015). This led to a large number of different features that also the difficulty to develop prediction studies.

In the same way, Winkler et al. (Papa, Doucet, Sangion, & Doucet-Panaye, 2016), modelled the bioactivity of gold nanoparticles in cell association studies. In this study, several machine learning algorithms are proved, and all showed accuracy values (Ac) > 0.88 for the training set, and Ac > 0.73 for the prediction set. The same researcher published a review of computational modeling of nanomaterials, where are described most of the research related with the use of machine learning models in the prediction of biological effects (Winkler, 2016). The reports included here are based mainly in the strongest research teams and researchers working in the field. This review article helps to complement the previous ones already commented, to give a picture of the state of the art of the thematic.

However, some interesting approaches in modeling of nanomaterial properties are not included, like the case of the works of Michael et al. that predicting the energy gap of graphene nanoflakes by ML methods (Fernandez, Abreu, Shi, & Barnard, 2016). In this work the topological information gathered from the structure was used as features. The E_G values (response variable) were well predicted in the ML regression models with $R^2 > 0.80$. In a previous work these authors use the ML algorithms to establish a structure-property approach for some nanomaterial properties such as: ionization potential, electronic band gap, energy of Fermi level, and electron affinity Fernandez, Shi, & Barnard, 2016). The remarkable aspect in these studies is the encoding of the molecular structures to obtain the features (molecular descriptors) to perform the QSAR studies. These two studies and those commented below are summarized in Table 1.

Table 1. Summary of recent studies on QSPR-ML nanomedicine

Property Under Study[a]	ML Algorithm[b]	Accuracy	Reference
Graphene nanoflakes- E_G	SVM	$R^2_{train} = 0.862$ $R^2_{ext} = 0.812$	Fernandez 2016
Graphenes nanoflakes- E_A	SVM	$Q^2_{train} = 0.77$ $R^2_{ext} = 0.90$	(Fernandez, Shi, et al., 2016)
Graphenes nanoflakes- E_F	kNN	$Q^2_{train} = 0.99$ $R^2_{ext} = 0.89$	(Fernandez, Shi, et al., 2016)
Graphenes nanoflakes- E_G	SVM	$Q^2_{train} = 0.66$ $R^2_{ext} = 0.89$	(Fernandez, Shi, et al., 2016)
Graphenes nanoflakes- E_I	ANN	$Q^2_{train} = 0.78$ $R^2_{ext} = 0.90$	(Fernandez, Shi, et al., 2016)
Carbon Nanotube -ATPase Inhibitors	ANN	Sp = 99.6 Sn = 99.3	(González-Durruthy et al., 2019)
Carbon Nanotubes- Mitochondrial Oxygen Flux Dynamics	RF	$R^2_{train} = 0.855$ $R^2_{ext} = 0.856$	(González-Durruthy et al., 2017)
Computer Tomography images	kNN	97%	(Rani & Jawhar, 2019)

[a]Properties: E_G (Energy band gap), E_A (Electron affinity), E_F (Energy of the Fermi level), E_I (Ionization potential)
[b]Machine Learning Algorithms: ANN (Artificial Neural Networks), kNN (K-Nearest Neighbor), SVM (Support Vector Machine), RF (Random Forest)

Recently, some novel approaches have been developed in the efforts to apply the QSAR methodologies to challenging problems. As an example, a study performed by González-Durruty et al. (González-Durruthy et al., 2019) is shown. The authors studied the mitochondrial F0F1-ATP ATPase a target that offer a higher selectivity for selecting positive response (inhibitors) from inactive ones(non-inhibitors). In this sense, fractal SEM (scanning electron microscopy) nanodescriptors were calculated by using the original SEM-image in a box counting algorithm linked to the calculation of the fractal dimension of the object by a linear fit of the data (Odziomek et al., 2017). Besides, subset of descriptors based in the different conditions (moving averages) an approach widely used in QSAR studies (González-Durruthy et al., 2017). These features were then fed into Artificial Neural Networks (ANN) for development of the classification models and adequate statistical parameters (Specificity >98.9% and Sensitivity >99.0%). The general theoretical workflow for this study is showed in Figure 3.

The nanoscale imaging technique has emerged as another interesting and very useful approach as is showed in the study performed by Rani et al. (Rani & Jawhar, 2019). IN this case, the Computer To-mography (CT) images were used to develop a measuring tool to detect lung tumor areas. The Support Vector Machine and K-Nearest Neighbor were the selected ML algorithms for the image classification and feature engineering. The performance of this classifier (Ac = 97%) provide an efficient method for the segmentation of lung lesion and the diagnosis and shows an interesting application for the field of medical informatics.

Figure 3. Theoretical workflow on mitochondrial F0-ATPase mitotoxic inhibition. Reprinted (adapted) with permission from (González-Durruthy et al., 2012).

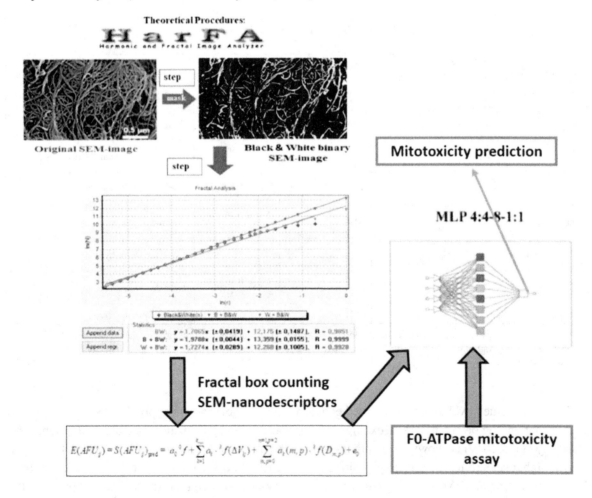

CONCLUSION

Nanomedicine represents a challenge for nanoinformatics because of the widely spread data generated by the scientists for decades. This big amount of data is very heterogeneous and requires the use of powerful computational resources. These requirements could be satisfied with the integration of the machine learning algorithms in high performance computing (HPC) or Cloud computing platforms. Besides, the use of consensus models could benefit the predictions for this kind of studies, avoiding the bias that a single classifier/regressor could have on a collected data.

The combination of these approaches, with those showed in this review, such as text mining, image acquisition, multi-scale modeling could improve the effectiveness for the management of the data and information on nanomedical research and hence the discovery of new knowledge about the biomedical properties of nanomaterials.

ACKNOWLEDGMENT

GMCM is grateful for computer access, financial and administrative support provided by North Dakota State University, Department of Coatings and Polymer Materials.

REFERENCES

De La Iglesia, D., García-Remesal, M., Anguita, A., Munoz-Marmol, M., Kulikowski, C., & Maojo, V. (2014). A machine learning approach to identify clinical trials involving nanodrugs and nanodevices from ClinicalTrials.gov. *PLoS One, 9*(10), e110331. doi:10.1371/journal.pone.0110331 PMID:25347075

Epa, V. C., Burden, F. R., Tassa, C., Weissleder, R., Shaw, S., & Winkler, D. A. (2012). Modeling Biological Activities of Nanoparticles. *Nano Letters, 12*(11), 5808–5812. doi:10.1021/nl303144k PMID:23039907

Fernandez, M., Abreu, J. I., Shi, H., & Barnard, A. S. (2016). Machine Learning Prediction of the Energy Gap of Graphene Nanoflakes Using Topological Autocorrelation Vectors. *ACS Combinatorial Science, 18*(11), 661–664. doi:10.1021/acscombsci.6b00094 PMID:27598830

Fernandez, M., Shi, H., & Barnard, A. S. (2016). Geometrical features can predict electronic properties of graphene nanoflakes. *Carbon, 103*, 142–150. doi:10.1016/j.carbon.2016.03.005

Fourches, D., Pu, D., Tassa, C., Weissleder, R., Shaw, S. Y., Mumper, R. J., & Tropsha, A. (2010). Quantitative Nanostructure– Activity Relationship Modeling. *ACS Nano, 4*(10), 5703–5712. doi:10.1021/nn1013484 PMID:20857979

González-Durruthy, M., Manske Nunes, S., Ventura-Lima, J., Gelesky, M. A., González-Díaz, H., Monserrat, J. M., ... Cordeiro, M. N. D. S. (2019). MitoTarget Modeling Using ANN-Classification Models Based on Fractal SEM Nano-Descriptors: Carbon Nanotubes as Mitochondrial F0F1-ATPase Inhibitors. *Journal of Chemical Information and Modeling, 59*(1), 86–97. doi:10.1021/acs.jcim.8b00631 PMID:30408958

González-Durruthy, M., Monserrat, M. J., Rasulev, B., Casañola-Martín, M. G., Barreiro Sorrivas, M. J., Paraíso-Medina, S., ... Munteanu, R. C. (2017). Carbon Nanotubes' Effect on Mitochondrial Oxygen Flux Dynamics: Polarography Experimental Study and Machine Learning Models using Star Graph Trace Invariants of Raman Spectra. *Nanomaterials (Basel, Switzerland)*, 7(11), 386. doi:10.3390/nano7110386 PMID:29137126

Jones, D. E., Ghandehari, H., & Facelli, J. C. (2016). A review of the applications of data mining and machine learning for the prediction of biomedical properties of nanoparticles. *Computer Methods and Programs in Biomedicine*, 132, 93–103. doi:10.1016/j.cmpb.2016.04.025 PMID:27282231

Liu, Z., Ling, X. Y., Su, X., & Lee, J. Y. (2004). Carbon-Supported Pt and PtRu Nanoparticles as Catalysts for a Direct Methanol Fuel Cell. *The Journal of Physical Chemistry B*, 108(24), 8234–8240. doi:10.1021/jp049422b

Muller, R. H., & Keck, C. M. (2004). Challenges and solutions for the delivery of biotech drugs – a review of drug nanocrystal technology and lipid nanoparticles. *Journal of Biotechnology*, 113(1), 151–170. doi:10.1016/j.jbiotec.2004.06.007 PMID:15380654

Novoselov, K. S., Fal'ko, V. I., Colombo, L., Gellert, P. R., Schwab, M. G., & Kim, K. (2012). A roadmap for graphene. *Nature*, 490, 192. doi:10.1038/nature11458 PMID:23060189

Odziomek, K., Ushizima, D., Oberbek, P., Kurzydłowski, K. J., Puzyn, T., & Haranczyk, M. (2017). Scanning electron microscopy image representativeness: Morphological data on nanoparticles. *Journal of Microscopy*, 265(1), 34–50. doi:10.1111/jmi.12461 PMID:27571322

Papa, E., Doucet, J. P., Sangion, A., & Doucet-Panaye, A. (2016). Investigation of the influence of protein corona composition on gold nanoparticle bioactivity using machine learning approaches. *SAR and QSAR in Environmental Research*, 27(7), 521–538. doi:10.1080/1062936X.2016.1197310 PMID:27329717

Puzyn, T., Leszczynska, D., & Leszczynski, J. (2009). Toward the Development of "Nano-QSARs": Advances and Challenges. *Small*, 5(22), 2494–2509. doi:10.1002mll.200900179 PMID:19787675

Ragesh, P., Anand Ganesh, V., Nair, S. V., & Nair, A. S. (2014). A review on 'self-cleaning and multifunctional materials'. *Journal of Materials Chemistry. A, Materials for Energy and Sustainability*, 2(36), 14773–14797. doi:10.1039/C4TA02542C

Rani, K. V., & Jawhar, S. J. (2019). Novel Technology for Lung Tumor Detection Using Nanoimage. *Journal of the Institution of Electronics and Telecommunication Engineers*, 1–15. doi:10.1080/03772063.2019.1565955

Tantra, R., Oksel, C., Puzyn, T., Wang, J., Robinson, K. N., Wang, X. Z., ... Wilkins, T. (2015). Nano(Q)SAR: Challenges, pitfalls and perspectives. *Nanotoxicology*, 9(5), 636–642. doi:10.3109/17435390.2014.952698 PMID:25211549

Toropova, A. P., & Toropov, A. A. (2017). Nano-QSAR in cell biology: Model of cell viability as a mathematical function of available eclectic data. *Journal of Theoretical Biology*, 416, 113–118. doi:10.1016/j.jtbi.2017.01.012 PMID:28087422

Winkler, D. A. (2016). Recent advances, and unresolved issues, in the application of computational modelling to the prediction of the biological effects of nanomaterials. *Toxicology and Applied Pharmacology, 299*, 96–100. doi:10.1016/j.taap.2015.12.016 PMID:26723909

Winkler, D. A., Burden, F. R., Yan, B., Weissleder, R., Tassa, C., Shaw, S., & Epa, V. C. (2014). Modelling and predicting the biological effects of nanomaterials. *SAR and QSAR in Environmental Research, 25*(2), 161–172. doi:10.1080/1062936X.2013.874367 PMID:24625316

Wu, X., Liu, H., Liu, J., Haley, K. N., Treadway, J. A., Larson, J. P., ... Bruchez, M. P. (2002). Immunofluorescent labeling of cancer marker Her2 and other cellular targets with semiconductor quantum dots. *Nature Biotechnology, 21*(1), 41–46. doi:10.1038/nbt764 PMID:12459735

This research was previously published in the International Journal of Applied Nanotechnology Research (IJANR), 4(1); pages 1-7, copyright year 2019 by IGI Publishing (an imprint of IGI Global).

Section 2
Development and Design Methodologies

Chapter 4
Classification and Machine Learning

Damian Alberto
Indian Institute of Technology Bombay, India

ABSTRACT

The manual classification of a large amount of textual materials are very costly in time and personnel. For this reason, a lot of research has been devoted to the problem of automatic classification and work on the subject dates from 1960. A lot of text classification software has appeared. For some tasks, automatic classifiers perform almost as well as humans, but for others, the gap is still large. These systems are directly related to machine learning. It aims to achieve tasks normally affordable only by humans. There are generally two types of learning: learning "by heart," which consists of storing information as is, and learning generalization, where we learn from examples. In this chapter, the authors address the classification concept in detail and how to solve different classification problems using different machine learning techniques.

INTRODUCTION

The manual classification of a large amount of textual materials are very costly in time and personnel for this reason a lot of research has been devoted to the problem of automatic classification and work on the subject dates from 1960.

These days a lot of text classification software have appeared For some tasks, automatic classifiers perform almost as well as humans, but for others, the gap is still large, these systems are directly related to machine learning (machine learning) it aims to achieve tasks normally affordable only by human there are generally two types of learning: learning "by heart" which consists of storing information as is, and learning generalization where we learn from examples a model we will recognize new examples (Ko, 2012).

In this chapter we will address the classification concept in detail how to solve different classification problems were appealed to different machine learning kind. The text classification is a generic task of assigning one or more categories from a predefined list or not a document by finding a functional link

DOI: 10.4018/978-1-6684-6291-1.ch004

between a set of texts and a set of categories (tags, classes) according to criteria. They apply to many human activities and particularly suited to the problems of automated decision-making.

For example: we are faced with a set of target text and the goal is to make a computer application capable of autonomously determine in which category classified each text, based on statistical data. Habitually the categories refer to the text subjects, but for particular applications, they can take other forms (Nigam, 2000).

Figure 1. Classification of texts (Sriram, 2010)

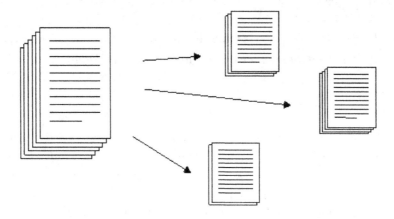

Classification can be found in several application domains as the language identification, recognition of writing, Categorization of multimedia document, spam detection, speech recognition, aid to medical diagnosis.

CLASSIFICATION DUAL CLASS AND MULTI CLASS

The Bi-Classes Classification

The bi-classes classification is a kind of problem examples for which the classification system answers the question: Does the text belongs to the category "C" or to its complementary class (Wu, 2004). some tasks Typical of binary classification are: determining whether a document is it plagiarize or not, Medical tests to determine if a patient has certain disease or not, quality control in the factories decide whether a new product is good enough to be sold, or whether it should be eliminated.

III 3-2-The Multi-Class Classification

The multi-class classification is the problem of the classification of examples in more than two classes or given example can be associated with one or more classes or no class is the most general case of the classification, which can be used in multiple domain: such as handwriting recognition which is part of the marking speech, speech recognition. The classification methods Binary can be generalized in many ways to manage multiple classes there are two approaches to perform this generalization. (Wu, 2004).

- **Approach One-Against-All (OAA):** Allows the direct use of standard binary classifiers to encode and form the output label and assume that for each class, there is only one (single) separation between this class and all other classes that is to say each class is opposed to all other classes. The mth classifier separates the data from the M class all data remains latter takes one sign and another class -1.
- **One Against One (OAO):** Is a more expressive alternative that assumes the existence of a separator between each two classes this method is called a one against this is to say that each class is discriminated from another or one must calculate M (M-1) / 2 classifier (Polat, 2009).

WHY AUTOMATIC DOCUMENT CLASSIFICATION?

The major consequences that pose a manual processing (by a human) classification of textual documents are:

- The classification of textual material is difficult to be manually performed by a human being because it takes a long time for:
  - Read and reread each document line by line and memorize it.
  - Much time is used in reflection to the final decision (associate a text category).
  - The number of class play a very important role in the classification of costs.
- The playback speed changes from one person to another so it is on decision making also not going to be the same for each person.
- Check other texts that are in the same category as the text filed to validate the decision.
- The difference between the class of such classified document into two category "Medicine" and "right" is easier than classified document any of the following categories "Natural Language Processing" and "Artificial Intelligence"
- The classification shall be made in a way that the groups obtained are made of similar observations and that the groups are as different as possible between them.
- The generalization of a manual classification to other areas is almost impossible. (Lodhi, 2002)

The classification of texts is a problem that can be directly related to machine learning (artificial).

Machine Learning (Machine Learning)

Machine learning is at the crossroads of many other areas: artificial intelligence, statistics, cognitive science, probability theory, which refers to computer algorithms that allow a machine to evolve through a learning process, it is based on a kind of observation or data as examples or experiences to fulfill the tasks that it is difficult to fill by algorithmic means more classics such as make precise prediction or retrieve and operate automatically information presented in a dataset. (Liu, 2002)

In general: machine learning is to learn to do better in the future on the basis of what was known in the past or we can consider it as programming example.

"Learning denotes changes in a system that allows it to do the same task more efficiently the next time," Herbert Simon. Machine learning is surrounded by several disciplines as shown in the following figure (Kubat, 1998).

Figure 2. Discipline around machine learning

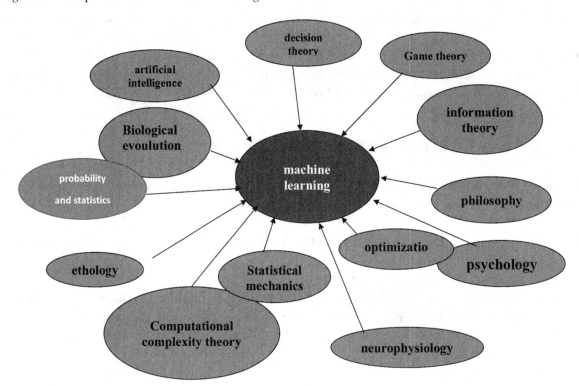

5-1-FROM LEARNING NATURAL TO THE ARTIFICIAL

Natural learning is done differs from the artificial it is achieved not by a machine but by a human For example:

We ask a human review to classify by theme how it will make no particular or prior knowledge?

If he is alone he reads the magazine and try to observe points of similarity or difference between them so he can find a way to combine the review theme.

If it is accompanied by an expert can help the problem but it No there's not much time for him so he just some example classified by the expert for the rest classified examples that did not had time them classified. all his shows the machine learning process. The machine can be faced with situation where she must learn only (not supervise learning) or on the contrary with the help of an expert (learning supervision). (Liu, 2002)

Learning Algorithm

Learning algorithm is an algorithm taking into entering a given set of "D" (set of training or learning) and returns a function F (model) model obtained was train on all "D".

Set "D" contains the form of vector information needed to solve a problem (e.g. classification) Learning .Algorithme enables automatic adaptation to the production of a stain or each algorithm is known to work on some type of spot and unsure else.

Choosing a learning algorithm usually depends on the type of text to be classified (form, article, quiz, etc.), purpose and scope of application. For example, applications designed for the medical field requires the most accurate algorithms learning possible that different learning algorithms used to design a search engine in a bookstore website and DEPOND also the task to solve (classification, estimation values, ect) and for each task there are a variety of algorithms (Nasrabadi, 2007).

Learning Models

The model will allow the learner to learn effectively as a means for achieving the desired task. The choice of model to use is therefore essential for success optimal learning. This bias is different in nature depending on the model chosen:

- **Functional:** He is then based on a decision function on the input attributes for establishing a separation. The most famous and easiest is probably the linear function (eg SVM Support Vector Machine).
- **Probabilistic:** It is then based on a probability distribution on the attributes of entries. Bayesian networks are probably typical of this kind of model.
- **Connexionnis:** The is then based on a neural network. This type of model is based on the basis of how the human brain We quote perceptrons and multilayer neural networks (MLP) as typical examples connectionist.
- **Time:** It will be based on a temporal coupling between the inputs. This type of model describes different temporal states in which one is likely to be the typical example is the Hidden Markov Model.

Why Machine Learning

- Certain tasks are well defined as via a set an example to clearly specify the relationship between the output entries.
- The amount of data can contain important relationships that the methods of machine learning allow to find out.
- The machine learning may better exploit the knowledge or the human brain can not explicit.
- The machine learning, machine to adapt to environmental changes without systematically redesign after changing the environment.

TYPES OF LEARNING

Supervised Learning

A supervisor (expert or oracle) is available to correctly labeled learning or training data in this case, D is a set of "n" pairs of inputs "xt" and associated label "yl" and the "F" going to be defined in an explicit way by the learning algorithm such learning consists of two Phase

- **Learning Phase (Training):** In this phase the learning algorithm receives input labeled learning example "D" and produced a most powerful predictive model possible, that is to say the model that produces the lowest prediction errors as presented in Figure 3.
- **Prediction:** This task is to predict one or more unknown characteristics from a set of characteristic known .For example: predicting the quality of a customer based on his back and his many children. (Liu, 2002)

Figure 3. Learning Phase

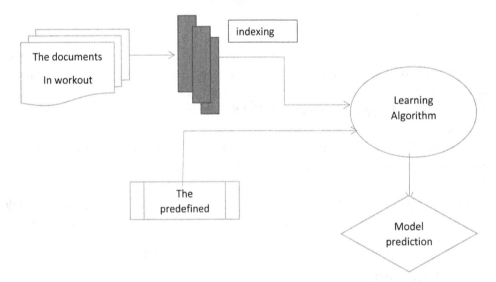

- **The Test Phase**: This is the phase of prediction of the new instance depending on the model obtained during the learning phase that going associating each enter "X" any outlet (label) "Y" which typically will have been given by the supervisor (test the accuracy of the model).

These two phases can be Executed consecutively ways supervised learning offline or iterative supervised learning online.

Figure 4. Test phase

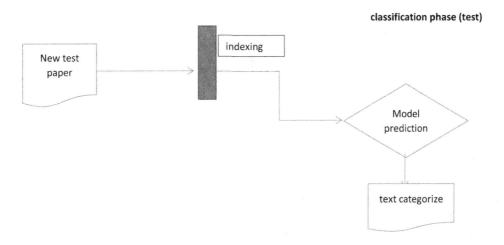

PROBLEM SOLVED BY LEARNING OVERSEE

the application of learning oversee concerns medicine: given a patient's test results and the knowledge of the other patients state where the same analyzes were carried out it is possible to assess the risk sick of this new patient based on the similarity of its analyzes with those of another patient. in general, two major types of problems that the supervised learning is applied: the supervised classification (categorization), the regression.

Text Categorization (Supervised Classification): She predicts whether a text is a member of a group or a predefined class .It classification of each text $x \in X$ from a class together existing (known in advance).

The general principle is to seek a prediction model estimated by supervised learning.This classification can be used to type in a number field, for example.

Spam Filtering: Identify emails as spam or non-spam.
Medical Diagnosis: Diagnose a patient as a sick or not sick from a disease.
Forecast Weather: Predicting, for example, whether it will rain tomorrow.

Unsupervised Machine Learning

No supervisor is available and D training data contains entries "X" label and not the prediction model produced by the learning algorithm will be implied. The algorithm must discover for himself the similarities and differences between data and aims to characterize the distribution of data, and relationships between variables, without discriminating between the observed variables and variables to predict. for this type of learning rather it is the user who has to specify the problem to solve .the figure **5** presents a learner who receives three input X1, X2, X3 and X1 and X2 are label output by Y1 and Y2 with X3.

Figure 5. Unsupervised learning operation

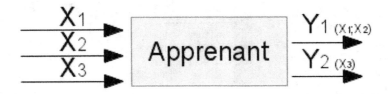

Problem Solved by Learning Unsupervised

Learning not monitor can be adapted as a problem: feature extraction, dimensionality reduction, clustering.

Unsupervised classification (clustering): the clustering problem is a problem Logical partitioning of the set of D data sub set (cluster) or each cluster has a certaindegree of internal coherence as shown in Figure 6 (Pedregosa, 2011).

The classification is not oversee the search for main classes of distribution through the process of learning not supervise because the class are not known in advance (data cache).

Similarly one can also consider that each instance can belong has one group (hard clustering) Consider that each example has a given probability of belonging to each of the groups (clustering software). [C03] [C01]

The problem here is more difficult because the available observations are not initially identified as belonging to a particular population: it will deduct this information at our classification (Arai, 2007).

Figure 6. Clustering (Arai, 2007)

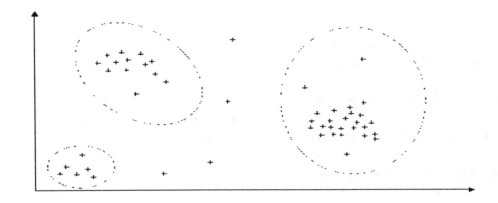

Application Example

Marketing: Market Segmentation by finding groups of separate customers from purchasing databases. city planning: identification of groups of dwellings according to the type of dwelling, value, geographical location ect ......

Insurance: identification of distinct groups of insured associated with a large number of claims.

NO-SUPERVISED LEARNING ALGORITHM

The Hierarchical Classification

Allows you to build a cluster tree, called dendrogram which shows how clusters are organized .or the number of cluster "K" is not required as data By cutting the dendrogram at the desired level, a classification of data into disjoint groups is obtained with the use of a distance matrix as clustering criterion. (de Hoon, 2004)

The hierarchical classification methods are divided into two types of approaches: ascending and descending that are presented in the following figure:

Figure 7. Upward and downward classification (Arai, 2007)

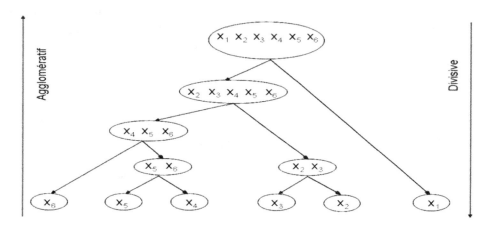

The Data-Partitioning Algorithm (Non-Hierarchical)

The algorithm shares data into several together and seeks to directly decompose the database in a cluster together disjointed More specifically, they try to determine a number of scores that optimize certain criteria (objective function). [C04] The objective function can enhance the local or global data structure and its optimization is an iterative process Among the non-hierarchical algorithms most used:

Kmeans (k-Average)

K-means with the intention of n objects into k classes where each object belongs to the cluster with the nearest average. This method produces exactly k different groups distinguish the greatest. The best number of clusters k leading to greater separation (distance) is not known as a priori and must be calculated from the data. The objective of K-means is to minimize total intra-cluster variance, or function of the squared error (Jain, 2010).

Algorithm

Input: x1 data sample, ..., xm

1.   Select k random points as the classes.c1 centers ..., ck
2.   Assign each of the m data in group i whose center is nearest. using the Euclidean distance function
3.   If no element group changes then stop and get out groups
4.   Calculate the new centers: for all i, is the average of the i group elements.
5.   Go 2 and repeating steps until the same points are assigned to each group

Advantages

*   Relatively extensible in the overall processing of large
*   The results are relatively effective
*   Generally produces a local optimum and global optimum can be obtained by using another technique: genetic algorithms ... .ECT
*   The downside: Applicable only if the average of the objects is defined to specify the number of cluster K a priori unable to process noisy data, the point isolate poorly managed.

Method Based on the Density

the use of similarity measures (distance) is less efficient than using central idea neighborhood density is to group related items of all data in classes according to a density function for minimizing the distance inter -clusters is not always a good criterion to recognize the "form".

The Semi-Supervised Machine Learning Algorithm (Hybrid)

It's a mix between the basic principle of learning and not supervise supervise use when labeling example is expensive this type of learning that has been very important in recent years improves outcome.

A supervisor is partly available and some label data. The algorithm will then learn the classification task based on the supervisor put labels and discovering for himself the missing information (the unlabeled example).

Semi-supervised algorithms operate on the same two phases but accept more untagged data during the training phase as the figure or the training set (not labeled x1 and x2 labeled). [C05]

Ex: In medicine, it can be an aid to diagnosis.

Reinforcement Learning

The main objective is to lead an agent to act intelligently in a given environment. An agent interacts with the environment by choosing, at any given time to perform an action from a set of allowable actions. The intelligent behavior must learn this agent is given implicitly via enhanced signal after each officer's decision, says it has right or wrong and the officer enter as an indicator or set of characteristic describing the environment as shown in the following figure:

Figure 8. Semi supervised learning operation

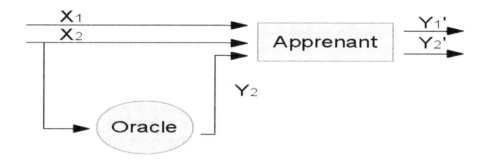

Figure 9. Learning operation by strengthening (Lin, 1992)

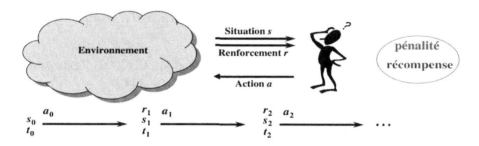

Ex: The algorithm Q-learning(The concept of time does not exist) or Td-Learning (dynamic: the concept of time exists). This type of learning is applied in many fields such as games (ladies), robotics .... ect.

CONCLUSION

This chapter includes the text classification problem and how to solve this problem at Eid a machine learning as we view the type of learning defeated their limits and areas of application of each of them in detail some popular learning algorithm.

REFERENCES

Arai, K., & Barakbah, A. R. (2007). Hierarchical K-means: An algorithm for centroids initialization for K-means. *Reports of the Faculty of Science and Engineering, 36*(1), 25–31.

de Hoon, M. J., Imoto, S., Nolan, J., & Miyano, S. (2004). Open source clustering software. *Bioinformatics (Oxford, England), 20*(9), 1453–1454. doi:10.1093/bioinformatics/bth078 PMID:14871861

Guo, G., Wang, H., Bell, D., Bi, Y., & Greer, K. (2003, November). KNN model-based approach in classification. In *OTM Confederated International Conferences On the Move to Meaningful Internet Systems* (pp. 986-996). Springer. 10.1007/978-3-540-39964-3_62

Jain, A. K. (2010). Data clustering: 50 years beyond K-means. *Pattern Recognition Letters, 31*(8), 651–666. doi:10.1016/j.patrec.2009.09.011

Jambu, M., & Lebeaux, M. O. (1978). *Classification automatique pour l'analyse des données* (Vol. 1). Paris: Dunod.

Ko, Y. (2012, August). A study of term weighting schemes using class information for text classification. In *Proceedings of the 35th international ACM SIGIR conference on Research and development in information retrieval* (pp. 1029-1030). ACM. 10.1145/2348283.2348453

Kubat, M., Holte, R. C., & Matwin, S. (1998). Machine learning for the detection of oil spills in satellite radar images. *Machine Learning, 30*(2-3), 195–215. doi:10.1023/A:1007452223027

Lin, L. J. (1992). Self-improving reactive agents based on reinforcement learning, planning and teaching. *Machine Learning, 8*(3-4), 293–321. doi:10.1007/BF00992699

Liu, B., Lee, W. S., Yu, P. S., & Li, X. (2002, July). *Partially supervised classification of text documents* (Vol. 2). ICML.

Lodhi, H., Saunders, C., Shawe-Taylor, J., Cristianini, N., & Watkins, C. (2002). Text classification using string kernels. *Journal of Machine Learning Research, 2*(Feb), 419–444.

Nasrabadi, N. M. (2007). Pattern recognition and machine learning. *Journal of Electronic Imaging, 16*(4), 049901. doi:10.1117/1.2819119

Nigam, K., McCallum, A. K., Thrun, S., & Mitchell, T. (2000). Text classification from labeled and unlabeled documents using EM. *Machine Learning, 39*(2-3), 103–134. doi:10.1023/A:1007692713085

Pedregosa, F., Varoquaux, G., Gramfort, A., Michel, V., Thirion, B., Grisel, O., ... Vanderplas, J. (2011). Scikit-learn: Machine learning in Python. *Journal of Machine Learning Research, 12*(Oct), 2825–2830.

Polat, K., & Güneş, S. (2009). A novel hybrid intelligent method based on C4. 5 decision tree classifier and one-against-all approach for multi-class classification problems. *Expert Systems with Applications, 36*(2), 1587–1592. doi:10.1016/j.eswa.2007.11.051

Sriram, B., Fuhry, D., Demir, E., Ferhatosmanoglu, H., & Demirbas, M. (2010, July). Short text classification in twitter to improve information filtering. In *Proceedings of the 33rd international ACM SIGIR conference on Research and development in information retrieval* (pp. 841-842). ACM. 10.1145/1835449.1835643

Wu, T. F., Lin, C. J., & Weng, R. C. (2004). Probability estimates for multi-class classification by pairwise coupling. *Journal of Machine Learning Research, 5*(Aug), 975–1005.

This research was previously published in Advanced Metaheuristic Methods in Big Data Retrieval and Analytics; pages 180-193, copyright year 2019 by Engineering Science Reference (an imprint of IGI Global).

Chapter 5
A Novel Resource Management Framework for Fog Computing by Using Machine Learning Algorithm

Shanthi Thangam Manukumar

https://orcid.org/0000-0001-5026-4889

Anna University, India

Vijayalakshmi Muthuswamy

Amity University, India

ABSTRACT

With the development of edge devices and mobile devices, the authenticated fast access for the networks is necessary and important. To make the edge and mobile devices smart, fast, and for the better quality of service (QoS), fog computing is an efficient way. Fog computing is providing the way for resource provisioning, service providers, high response time, and the best solution for mobile network traffic. In this chapter, the proposed method is for handling the fog resource management using efficient offloading mechanism. Offloading is done based on machine learning prediction technology and also by using the KNN algorithm to identify the nearest fog nodes to offload. The proposed method minimizes the energy consumption, latency and improves the QoS for edge devices, IoT devices, and mobile devices.

INTRODUCTION

In this era, the most upcoming technique is the edge devices IoT and mobile device users are increasing in drastic manner. By this same speed, the high complexity real time applications and data intensive applications gadgets such as Virtual Reality, Augmented Reality, Drones are developed. The resources limitations, energy consumption, mobile network traffic, high computation and storage are the main difficulties facing by the user. It is very difficult to solve these limitations with cloud computing model

DOI: 10.4018/978-1-6684-6291-1.ch005

to support the cloud, a new concept to deploy task and storage, edge computing, fog computing, mobile edge computing are introduced.

To overcome the challenges and to support the cloud fog computing is proposed by Cisco, virtual platform provides storage, computation, network services and plays its role between the end devices and cloud (Bonomi et al., 2012). A decentralized networks which performs actions as cloud server but it relays on the cloud computing for high computation (Mahmud & Buyya, 2017). It performs wonders for edge devices, IoT devices and mobile devices due its low latency for real time applications and low mobile network traffic. In fog computing, main challenge is resource allocation and heterogeneous devices.

Offloading (Hyytia, Spyropoulos & Ott, 2015) is the way of transferring the task from the edge device to the fog nodes or to the cloud. Due to large complex applications and lack of resource its task or the part of the task offloaded is to the cloud or to the fog node to overcome the above mentioned challenges. Offloading decision is made based on the prediction technology and KNN algorithms to provide the best resource management for fog nodes. The important of fog computing and its characteristics are represented the energy minimization IoT devices resource management is discussed (Dastjerdi & Buyya, 2017).

Machine learning is way to increase the intelligence of the system and it is important to analyze. It is the way of learning the system for high computational real time applications (Angra & Ahuja, 2017). Detailed learning process about the data to understand and to classify accordingly will lead to improve the knowledge about the data (Mitchell, 1997). Machine learning algorithms applied to large data set to learn the data. Machine learning algorithm is used to improve problem solving with the prior knowledge about the data. It leads the dataset to train according to the learned information and it will find the way to reduce the problem and improves its performance. There some challenges in the machine learning while using in the data like how much data need to learn?, what algorithm is fit for this data? etc.,

The proposed method of this system used the machine learning algorithm KNN for resource allocation in fog nodes. It will show the nearest fog node to the user by using the machine learning KNN algorithm for efficient offloading and resource management. K- Nearest Neighbors (KNN) (Parsian, 1015) is the machine learning classification algorithm, here K is a numerical value always greater than 0.

KNN algorithm is used to find out the nearest data points in the dataset using the standard Euclidean distance. The (KNN) is a non-parametric method used for classification, to calculate the accuracy and for the validation of the KNN classification confusion matrix and the statistical method likelihood-ration is also used (Huang et al., 2013).

This chapter covers the introduction about this proposed work with brief discussion. It also includes about the new techniques, machine learning algorithms how it supports to this proposed system and also about the issues and challenges with the technique. In related works it shows analyse and survey about how the fog computing works and its issues, how the machine learning technique and KNN is useful for making decision and its challenges. In this related work, the discussion about offloading and its challenges are in wide manner. In the proposed work part it shows how to find the execution location and how KNN is works with this proposed system.

In the experimental result part, shows how the implementation takes part, how the task identify its execution location and it also gives how to evaluate and performance accuracy in classification is done, how R programming is used for statistical learning and how this proposed system implemented using R. In the last section, discussed about what this proposed system achieves, how the resource managed in the complex application and it shows the latency and high resource utilization, future work is also discussed related to this proposed system.

RELATED WORKS

Redowan Mahmud and R. Buyya (2017) provide a detailed fog taxonomy, survey and challenges facing in cloud computing and the how the fog computing techniques is supported. In addition to that, discussed about how the fog computing is acts an intermediate between the cloud and IoT devices, high computation mobile applications. They also tell how the fog computing technique works and its current research challenges. Luis M. Vaquero and Luis Rodero-Merino (2014) proposed the fog with a comprehensive definition. They discussed about the device ubiquity as the main and addressed how the fog connects with mobile devices and other IoT/sensor devices and challenges on services and network management in fog applications. Ben Zhang et al. (2015) discussed about why moving from the cloud to fog and tell us about how the cloud is not enough and how to change from cloud computing to fog computing. They argued that the level of abstraction to a data-centric design and showed the information how IoT is protected and much better computation performance in the fog than cloud. Ashkan Yousefpour et al. (2018) showed a complete survey about fog computing and its research topics and tutorial on fog computing and its paradigms. Chenn-Jung Huang et al. (2013) proposed machine learning prediction mechanism realized by using Support Vector Regressions (SVRs) to find the low latency time and the resources allocation. A. Singh et al. (2016) reviewed about the machine learning supervised algorithm to predict the future instances, to classify, and for clustering and discussed about the speed of the learning, complexity of the applications. Mario Bkassiny et al. (2013) reviewed the learning problem in cognitive radios and feature classification and decision making are done using the learning algorithms. Deng et al. (2016) proposed the investigation between power consumption and transmission delay in the fog to cloud computing system. They suggested the workload allocation problem between the fog and cloud to achieve the minimum delay and power consumption. Muhammad Aamir Nadeem et al. (2016) provide the survey about the fog computing emerging paradigm and issues and the challenges of the fog architecture is mentioned. Pengfei Hu et al. (2017) presented the hierarchical architecture of fog computing its characteristics and comparison with cloud computing and edge computing. They analyzed the key technologies like computing, communication and storage technologies, naming, resource management, security, privacy protection and also considers the bandwidth, latency to improve the performance of fog and cloud computing. Katrina Wakefield (n.d.) discussed about predicting models and machine learning algorithm, it also gives the information about the how to use the prediction technology and how machine learning algorithms are powerful for the prediction. Eren Balevi and Richard D. Gitlin (2018) determine the optimum number of normal nodes is changes to fog nodes with more computational capabilities to increase the data rate and to minimize the transmission delay. Changsheng You et al. (2018) studied the energy efficient resource management policies for asynchronous mobile edge computation offloading and determines by using the deadlines and also by considering arrival time of heterogeneous input data. By considering the arrival and deadlines and minimum mobile energy consumption in achieved. Yueyue Dai et al. (2018) proposed joint computation offloading and user association to provide the better offloading decision and for minimizing the overall energy consumption.

The motivation for this method is to improve the resource allocation in the fog nodes and to achieve the Quality of Service (QoS) by providing the services from the nearest fog nodes to the user. Tom M. Mitchell (1997) described the instance-based learning methods the KNN algorithm a machine learning techniques which are defined using the Euclidean distance. Learning in this algorithm simply provides the training dataset in the sorted manner, K is numerical value which is always greater than 0. The KNN algorithm is efficient memory indexing algorithm, and the distance- weighted KNN is effective inductive inference method for many practical problems. It is good and effective to noisy training data and also for large dataset of training data.

PROPOSED METHOD

The proposed method is to improve the resource allocation in the fog nodes and to achieve the Quality of Service (QoS) by providing the services from the nearest fog nodes to the user also by reducing the delay and improving resource. To improve the offloading mechanism, machine learning algorithm is used for predicting the fog nodes. KNN algorithm is used to find and to analyze the fog nodes which are available and provides accurate resource provider for the task so that it will improve the quality and minimizes the delay and latency (Saed Sayad, n.d.). KNN algorithm is simple that stores all the cases and classifies new cases based on the learned class and distance measured based on the similarity of the dataset and it is used in the statistical evaluation.

In this proposed system the task are offloaded either in the cloud side or in the fog side from the edge devices, IoT/sensor devices and mobile devices to avoid the resource constraints. In this system there is a resource provider pool which is having number resources provider such as resource provider 1; resource provider 2 up to resource provider N depends upon resource available. When the needed resource is not available in the resource pool and in the smart devices then the system will dynamically decide to offload the task and the decision making is need to decide which part of the task is offloaded to the cloud or to the fog. Here in the system the pools of resource are provided based on the availability and need. The prediction of the fog nodes and available resources is achieved by using the machine learning engines.

The offloading decision is made based on the machine learning KNN algorithm classification prediction technique. The KNN algorithm (Wikipedia, n.d.; Singh, Thakur & Sharma, 2016; Bkassiny, Li & Jayaweera, 2013) is used to learn about the fog node dataset which contains the details about fog node depends upon the price, CPU utilization, RAM, instance, queue length and it describes the detail about whether the fog node service is available or not. If the fog service is not available then tasks are offloaded to the cloud side for execution. The decision making using the machine learning algorithm reduces the power consumption and the task execution time is reduced. Here the Figure 1 shows system architecture for resource allocation in fog computing.

Figure 1. System architecture for resource allocation in fog computing

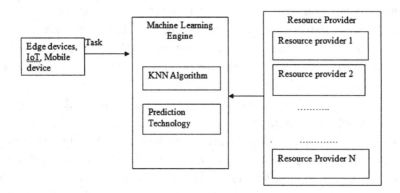

Algorithm

```
Input: Tasks T currently need to execute with their decision
Output: Updation of the execution location
Identify the resource need r, resource availability r
                           i                          a
for all methods do
        if r ==availability then execute local
           i
        else search(r ) then
                    i
        make decision d and check to execute in remote
                        if d==cloud then execute
                        else execute in fog then
                        update ri
        end
        end
end
```

The algorithm shows that if the task is currently needed to execute with the decision as input and update of the execution location whether in local, or either in the cloud side or in the fog side. While executing the task, it should identify the resource which is needed to execute the task. In all the methods it needs to check whether the resource available or not, if not need to take decision for the offloading location.

EXPERIMENTAL RESULTS

The implementation of the offloading decision making system is done using RStudio. Paul Teetor (2011) explained about the R programming getting started, data structures, probability and how to initialize the variables, and to load the dataset and export the dataset implementation. It also shows how the R programming is used in statistical computing. R studio (Teetor, 2011; James et al., 2013) is one of the best tools for statistics; it is free, open source using R programming. Gareth James et al. (2013) discussed about statistical learning which refers to the tools for understanding the complex dataset and it supports for the machine learning algorithms. This system uses KNN algorithm to make decision based on the availability of the fog service among the nearest fog. In the fog node data 50 patterns are classified two classes, each node has 6 numerical properties. This algorithm implemented using the RStudio; the decision to implement a particular task either in the cloud side or in the fog node is based on the availability of fog services, this decision is purely based on the accuracy and the prediction of the fog nodes.

In this system, the execution of task in smart devices are maintained and monitored, when there is high computation task is performed. If there is lack of the resource in smart device side then it will look out for the resource provider and check whether the resource is available in the resource pool. If the required resource is not available then the machine learning engine will pays it attention to make decision and to find the fog nodes to execute.

Figure 2. Service availability prediction by using KNN algorithm

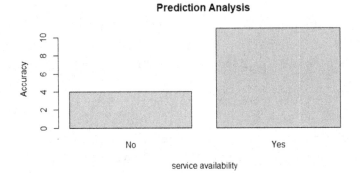

Prediction Analysis

Figure 3. Confusion matrix and statistics

```
Confusion Matrix and Statistics

              Reference
Prediction No Yes
       No    4   0
       Yes   3   8

              Accuracy : 0.8
                95% CI : (0.5191, 0.9567)
   No Information Rate : 0.5333
   P-Value [Acc > NIR] : 0.03209

                 Kappa : 0.5872
 Mcnemar's Test P-Value : 0.24821

           Sensitivity : 0.5714
           Specificity : 1.0000
        Pos Pred Value : 1.0000
        Neg Pred Value : 0.7273
            Prevalence : 0.4667
        Detection Rate : 0.2667
  Detection Prevalence : 0.2667
     Balanced Accuracy : 0.7857

      'Positive' Class : No
```

Resource management is done by using accuracy, prediction given by KNN algorithm which reduces the delay and response time. Figure 2 describes about the service availability prediction by using KNN algorithm it classified as yes or no. Based on the accuracy the selection of fog service is done to implement the task in the fog. Figure 3 describes the confusion matrix and the statistics about the data set. Figure 4 shows the response time of the task due to the decision prediction and implementing the task as per its requirements.

The validation and the estimation for performance accuracy of the classification machine learning KNN algorithm is validated using confusion matrix. For estimating performance for classification (Kuhn, 2013) a confusion matrix is a cross-tabulation of the observed and the predicted classes. R functions for confusion matrix are in the caret package. The performance accuracy of this proposed system is 80% and this system provides better performance by using the fog computing nodes and the high end resource provider cloud.

Figure 4. Response time of the task due to the decision prediction

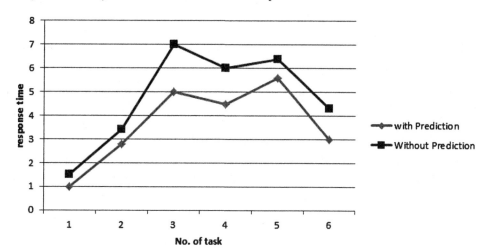

CONCLUSION

This system achieves the efficient resource allocation by using the machine learning techniques. It improves the QoS, response time and reduced the delay by using the nearest fog nodes for task allocation. In this system machine learning plays a vital role in classification and decision making which provides efficient offloading decision to achieve the execution of task with low latency, high resource utilization.

In future, very large dataset is learned using deep learning techniques and planned to include, achieving the improved resource allocation in the fog side as well as in the smart device side, or in the IoT/ sensor nodes. Energy consumption and battery power consumption also measure and minimized to achieve green computing based smart device. Location based smart devices and fog nodes or the cloud are analyzed to provide resource in the efficient resource management.

ACKNOWLEDGMENT

This work is funded by the Ministry of Electronics and Information Technology has initiated "Visvesvaraya PhD Scheme for Electronics and Information Technology (IT)", India.

REFERENCES

Angra, S., & Ahuja, S. (2017). Machine learning and its applications: A review. *2017 International Conference on Big Data Analytics and Computational Intelligence (ICBDAC)*, 57-60. 10.1109/ICB-DACI.2017.8070809

Balevi & Gitlin. (2018). Optimizing the Number of Fog Nodes for Cloud-Fog-Thing Networks. *IEEE Access, 6*, 11173-11183.

Ben Zhang, Kolb, Chan, Lutz, Allman, Wawrzynek, … Kubiatowicz. (2015). The cloud is not enough: Saving iot from the cloud. HotStorage.

Bkassiny, M., Li, Y., & Jayaweera, S. K. (2013). A Survey on Machine-Learning Techniques in Cognitive Radios. *IEEE Communications Surveys and Tutorials, 15*(3), 1136–1158. doi:10.1109/SURV.2012.100412.00017

Bonomi, F., Milito, R., Zhu, J., & Addepalli, S. (2012). Fog computing and its role in the internet of things. *Proceedings of the first edition of the MCC workshop on Mobile cloud computing*, 13–16. 10.1145/2342509.2342513

Dai, Y., Du Xu, S. M., & Zhang, Y. (2018). Joint Computation Offloading and User Association in Multi-Task Mobile Edge Computing. *IEEE Transactions on Vehicular Technology, 67*(12), 12313–12325. doi:10.1109/TVT.2018.2876804

Dastjerdi, A. V., & Buyya, R. (2017). Fog computing: Helping the internet of things realize its potential. *Computer, 49*(8), 112–116. doi:10.1109/MC.2016.245

Deng, R., Lu, R., Lai, C., & Luan, H. (2016). *Optimal Workload Allocation in Fog-Cloud Computing Towards Balanced Delay and Power Consumption. IEEE Internet of Things Journal.*

Hu, Dhelim, Ning, & Qiu. (2017). Survey on fog computing: architecture, key technologies, applications and open issues. *Journal of Network and Computer Applications.*

Huang, Wang, & Guan, Chen, & Jian. (2013). Applications of Machine Learning to Resource Management in Cloud Computing. *International Journal of Modeling and Optimization, 3*(2).

Hyytia, Spyropoulos, & Ott. (2015). Offload (only) the right jobs: Robust offloading using the Markov decision processes. *World of Wireless, Mobile and Multimedia Networks (WoWMoM), 2015 IEEE 16th International Symposium*, 1–9.

James, G. (2013). *An Introduction to Statistical Learning with Applications in R. In Springer Texts in Statistics.* Springer.

Kuhn, M. (2013). *Predictive Modeling with R and the caret Package useR!* Retrieved from https://www.r-project.org/nosvn/conferences/useR- 2013/Tutorials/kuhn/user_caret_2up.pdf

Mahmud, R., & Buyya, R. (2017). Fog computing: A taxonomy, survey and future directions. In *Internet of Everything.* Springer.

Mahmud, R., Kotagiri, R., & Buyya, R. (2018). Fog Computing: A Taxonomy, Survey and Future Directions. In B. Di Martino, K. C. Li, L. Yang, & A. Esposito (Eds.), *Internet of Everything. Internet of Things (Technology, Communications and Computing)* (pp. 103–130). Singapore: Springer. doi:10.1007/978-981-10-5861-5_5

Mitchell. (1997). *Machine Learning*. McGraw-Hill Science/Engineering/Math.

Nadeem. (2016). *Fog Computing: An Emerging Paradigm*. IEEE Xplorer.

Parsian. (2015). *Data Algorithms*. O'Reilly Media, Inc.

Sayed, S. (n.d.). K nearest neighbors – classification. *Saed Sayed*. Retrieved from: https://www.saedsayad.com/k_nearest_neighbors.htm

Singh, A., Thakur, N., & Sharma, A. (2016). A review of supervised machine learning algorithms. *2016 3rd International Conference on Computing for Sustainable Global Development (INDIACom)*, 1310-1315.

Teetor, P. (2011). R Cookbook. O'Reilly Media, Inc.

Vaquero, L. M., & Rodero-Merino, L. (2014). Finding your way in the fog: Towards a comprehensive definition of fog computing. *Computer Communication Review*, *44*(5), 27–32. doi:10.1145/2677046.2677052

Wakefield, K. (n.d.). Predictive analytics and machine learning. *Sas*. Retrieved from: https://www.sas.com/en_gb/insights/articles/analytics/a-guide-to-predictive-analytics-and-machine-learning.html

Wikipedia. (n.d.). K nearest neighbors algorithm. *Wikipedia*. Retrieved from: https://en.wikipedia.org/wiki/K-nearest_neighbors_algorithm

You, C., Zeng, Y., Zhang, R., & Huang, K. (2018). Asynchronous Mobile-Edge Computation Offloading: Energy-Efficient Resource Management. *IEEE Transactions on Wireless Communications*, *17*(11), 7590–7605. doi:10.1109/TWC.2018.2868710

Yousefpour, Fung, Nguyen, Kadiyala, Jalali, Niakanlahiji, … Jue. (2018). *All one needs to know about fog computing and related edge computing paradigms: A complete survey*. CoRR, abs/1808.05283

This research was previously published in Architecture and Security Issues in Fog Computing Applications; pages 42-52, copyright year 2020 by Engineering Science Reference (an imprint of IGI Global).

Chapter 6

High Performance Concrete (HPC) Compressive Strength Prediction With Advanced Machine Learning Methods:
Combinations of Machine Learning Algorithms With Bagging, Rotation Forest, and Additive Regression

Melda Yucel

 https://orcid.org/0000-0002-2583-8630
Istanbul University-Cerrahpaşa, Turkey

Ersin Namlı

 https://orcid.org/0000-0001-5980-9152
Istanbul University-Cerrahpasa, Turkey

ABSTRACT

In this chapter, the authors realized prediction applications of concrete compressive strength values via generation of various hybrid models, which are based on decision trees as main a prediction method. This was completed by using different artificial intelligence and machine learning techniques. In respect to this aim, the authors presented a literature review. The authors explained the machine learning methods that they used as well as with their developments and structural features. Next, the authors performed various applications to predict concrete compressive strength. Then, the feature selection was applied to a prediction model in order to determine parameters that were primarily important for the compressive strength prediction model. The authors evaluated the success of both models with respect to correctness and precision prediction of values with different error metrics and calculations.

DOI: 10.4018/978-1-6684-6291-1.ch006

INTRODUCTION AND LITERATURE REVIEW

Concrete, which is a structural material frequently used in civil engineering, is composed from water, cement, and various mineral or chemical materials. Engineers use this material to connect structural components to each other. For instance, in a beam and a column, and each component in place during the construction of structures. In this regard, strength and quality of concrete is important for ensuring resistance and sustainability of structures to various factors.

This case causes a considerable problem related to determining concrete strength with precision based on the features of the materials themselves, together with their mixture rates, acting to quality of concrete (Küçük, 2000). However, the process of calculating the compressive strength of concrete is a time-intensive and expensive operation. Altogether, calculating and observing concrete strength takes 28 days (Turkish Standards Institute, 2000). On the other hand, various environmental effects, such as air and gas rates, temperature, humidity, and the properties of the sample tools or techniques used for measurement contribute to the strength of concrete. For this reason, the strength values could deviate from the real results and so, show change.

Nowadays, various advanced methods, which can be useful alternatives to traditional laboratory analyses and test methods, may be utilized in to effectively and rapidly calculate and determine numerical values for structural materials. Considering that these methods are frequently machine learning and artificial intelligence prediction techniques, serve the benefit of preventing loss of time and effort, with cost residuals.

In the first periods when researchers operated machine learning and statistical applications, nondestructive tests were greatly preferred by many researchers, and numerous studies were realized with these techniques. One example of this technique is the ultrasonic pulse velocity method, which may be beneficial to researchers because it uses its own values to predict compressive strength. With this aim, the authors carried out various studies in the literature review that follows:

Hoła and Schabowicz (2005) performed artificial neural networks (ANNs) implementation using the features obtained by means of the nondestructive testing as input variables for prediction of concrete compressive strengths. Next, Kewalramani and Gupta (2006) used multiple regression analysis and ANNs to predict the concrete compression strength of samples belonging to concrete mixtures that have two different sizes and forms in longtime, by used ultrasonic pulse velocities and weight values. In another study, the authors applied multilayer neural network, which is one kind of ANNs technique, to estimate compressive strength of concrete by values of ultrasonic pulse velocity besides concrete mixtures properties (Trtnik, Kavčič & Turk, 2009).

On the other hand, Bilgehan and Turgut (2010) presented an application regard to performing predictions for the compressive strength of concrete based on the ultrasonic pulse velocity method. In this study, the authors generated a great deal of data through the usage of different concrete parts of a variety of ages and concrete rates. The authors did this by taking samples from concrete structures with the aim of training of ANNs. Nevertheless, Atici (2011) performed a study that assessed compressive strength in different curing times of concrete mixtures containing several amounts blast furnace cinder and fly ash by depend on qualities and values. The authors obtained this information via rebound number from a non-destructive test, ultrasonic pulse velocity of additive agents forecasted via ANNs, and multiple regression analysis methods.

In addition to these studies, intelligent systems working with various algorithms have started to come into prominence and use thanks to advancing technology and computational methods. One of these is fuzzy logic methods, and some studies are as follows:

Topcu and Sarıdemir (2008) used fuzzy logic methods and ANNs in forecasting the daily period compressive strength of three different types of concrete with fly ashes inside and high and low-level lime. Next, Cheng, Chou, Roy and Wu (2012) developed a prediction tool by combining three different methods, including fuzzy logic, support vector machine, and a genetic algorithm under the name of "Evolutionary Fuzzy Support Vector Machine Inference Model for Time Series Data" to foresee of the value of compressive strength for high performance concretes (HPC). by depend on an opinion that determining of these concretes' behavior is more difficult opposite to traditional concretes.

Nevertheless, from other respects, methods like artificial neural networks, various kinds of regression analysis, and decision tree models are some of the principal techniques that have the most usage and preferability with regards to artificial intelligence applications, such as prediction, forecasting, recognition, classification by researchers and performers of machine learning. In this direction, Naderpour, Kheyroddin and Amiri (2010) carried out a study that dealt with ANNs. In this study, the authors determined the compressive strengths of concretes covered with fiber-reinforced polymer (FRP) by using the properties of FRPs and concrete sample. Also, the authors composed five separate models to determine HPC compression strength with usage of k-nearest neighbor machine learning method. This was optimized using a type of differential evolution, together with generalized regression neural networks and stepwise regressions (Ahmadi-Nedushan, 2012). An application in which recycled aggregates were used, was actualized by Duan, Kou, and Poon in 2013. In this study, an ANN model operating via back propagation algorithm was established with 14 inputs for estimation of the compressive strength for concrete varieties with recycled aggregate, which were obtained from 168 different mixture data taking place in literature.

Authors executed a prediction application made in 2013 for high performance concrete, and they applied many advanced machine learning techniques and algorithms to determine compressive strength. These techniques are ensemble-structured ANNs, which consisted of using methods such as bagging and gradient boosting. Moreover, authors implemented a wavelet transform operation combined with prediction models for the purpose of increasing of precision of these models (Erdal, Karakurt & Namli, 2013). Furthermore, Akande, Owolabi, Twaha and Olatunji (2014) investigated the support vector machines by comparing them with ANNs from respects that observing of estimation success for concrete compressive strength. Chou, Tsai, Pham and Lu (2014) presented an extent study regarding the compressive strength prediction issue of high-performance concrete. from the authors used several enhanced machine learning algorithms, such as multilayer perceptron (a kind of artificial neural network), support vector machines, classification and regression tree method (CART), and linear regression. In addition to these applications, the authors applied ensemble models for prediction of this mechanic property.

Additionally, another study in which Deshpande, Londhe, and Kulkarni (2014) applied three various methods is the prediction of compression strength 28-day values of concrete consisting of recycled aggregates which was used as additives material. With this aim, specific input parameters, such as different aggregate types, water and cement amounts, and the other material rates were determined to realize the prediction process using two different methods besides ANNs; model tree and non-linear regression.

Nikoo, Zarfam, and Sayahpour (2015) used a different type of ANNs. The authors ran these neural networks, consisting of self-organizing feature maps, to estimate the compressive strength of 173 concrete mixtures. Additionally, the authors turned ANNs models with self-organizing maps to optimized-case design through use of genetic algorithm. Furthermore, in 2016, Chopra, Sharma and Kumar performed a study via ANNs and genetic programming methods by using the data obtained in different curing times consisting from 28, 56, and 91 days. This study served the purpose of developing models for determining concrete compressive strength values.

Furthermore, Chithra, Kumar, Chinnaraju, and Ashmita (2016) used multiple regression analysis with ANNs to predict the compression strength of numerous high-strength concrete samples, including particular rates of different additions materials, such as nano silica and copper slag. In addition, these predictions were directed to curing times consisting of six different days, like 1, 3, 7, and so. Additionally, Behnood, V. Behnood, Gharehveran, and Alyamac (2017) utilized an algorithm that is called M5P model tree to estimate compressive strength for normal and high strength concretes (HPC).

In another study conducted by Akpinar and Khashman in 2017, the authors used ANNs to carry out classification, which is a type of machine learning applications. In this direction, separating the mixture of concretes according to different strength level became possible through an improved model.

ANN models, which possesses a feed-forward structure working via a back propagation algorithm were developed to estimate the compressive strength and concrete tensile strength that have steel-slag aggregate. For modeling of ANN prediction structure in this study, the authors determined various input parameters, including different curing times, water/cement rate, and value that replacement of a type of blast furnace slag with certain amounts of granite (Awoyera, 2018).

Behnood and Golafshani (2018) applied a two-stage work that grey wolf optimization method was benefited for construction of the most proper ANNs model to predict the compressive strength of concrete mixtures that a part of Portland cement was constituted by alter with silica fume material, which comes in use for nature from many respects. However, Bui, Nguyen, Chou, Nguyen-Xuan and Ngo (2018) developed an expert system consisting of combinations of ANNs and metaheuristic firefly algorithm (FA) to estimate tensile and compression strengths of high-performance concretes. Yu, W. Li, J. Li and Nguyen (2018) also developed a prediction model with support vector machines for high performance concretes. In addition to this, the authors optimized the operated technique parameters, which is important on increasing of model performance and success, via cat swarm optimization, which is one of the metaheuristic algorithms.

Also, Yaseen et al. (2018) used extreme learning machine technique besides multivariate adaptive regression spline, M5 tree model, and support vector regression, for determination of compressive strength of concrete adding foamed. Similarly, Al-Shamiri, Kim, Yuan and Yoon (2019) realized the prediction of concrete compressive strength for concrete with high-strength quality by using a newer method compared to other methods, called extreme learning machine. For this purpose, mentioned method is benefited respect to training of a model, which was developed with the usage of many experiment data, by artificial neural networks.

In this study, the authors improved hybrid prediction models with one of the decision tree models, which consisted of Random Forest and ANNs as base learners. These were combined with different advanced machine learning techniques, namely Additive Regression, Rotation Forest, and Bagging, which are ensemble learning algorithms, with the aim of determining the HPC compressive strength for concretes. In addition, following this process, the authors performed feature selection application to determine mainly effective parameters on a model developed for prediction of values of concrete compressive strength.

Also, the authors calculated various error metrics, composing mean absolute error (MAE), root mean squared error (RMSE), relative absolute error (RAE) and root relative squared error (RRSE), and coefficient of correlation (R) to evaluate prediction success belonging to first main models and next models, which are performed for the optimization of features.

MATERIAL AND METHODS

Base Algorithms

Rotation Forest

Rotation Forest (RotF) is a method that applies a principle that is based on generating ensemble classifiers through decision trees, which are trained separately (Kuncheva & Rodríguez, 2007).

The Rotation Forest algorithm operates in a similar way to random forest in that the classification (or regression) process is realized by using more one tree. In this direction, Bootstrap algorithm, which is one of ensemble-based classification methods, is used as a base classifier method with the aim of training each of the data groups. On the other hand, in this method, analysis of principal component (PCA) determines attributes belonging to Bootstrap data groups, which is generated in order to train each decision tree. In the end of the process, the user determines the main/principal components belonging to K attribute parts, and the user generates a new attribute set by combining each of these components obtained in each attribute group for the data groups (Kılınç, Borandağ, Yücalar, Özçift & Bozyiğit, 2015; Kuncheva & Rodríguez, 2007). Ensuring difference is made possible by performing the process separately for all decision trees.

In this paper, this new attribute set is constructed with nonlinearly, arranged from the relationships between attributes of PCA technique, which was proposed by Karl Pearson in 1901 (Rokach & Maimon, 2015).

Figure 1 shows the pseudo code of rotation forest algorithm, which is explained by the operating logic of this method. In Figure 1, as expressed that in previous, initially, attributes are split for base classifiers, namely decision trees of sub data groups ($S_{i,j}$) for training. This division is made randomly with M number, which is the same in each attribute subset ($F_{i,j}$). Also, sample quantity within each data groups is composed from three-quarters of $S_{i,j}$, and this portion of samples is called as *'Bootstrap sample'* ($S_{i,j}'$). Following this step, PCA analysis is applied to all $S_{i,j}'$ samples, and the main classifier is built after in various steps.

Bagging

Bagging (bootstrap aggregating) is one of the best-known ensemble-based machine learning algorithms. In order to form an aggregated predictor, bagging method produces multiple predictor variants (Breiman, 1996). The bagging algorithm improves the prediction accuracy of model by operating a training data set before base learner's prediction process (Dietterich, 2000).

Bagging algorithm makes the selection of subsamples without any replacement for training data. After that, the subsample is used instead of original data set for fitting base classifier or predictor, which finally builds the model for next iteration. Nevertheless, bagging ensemble method, which is proposed for regression models, was clarified via several equations that follow (Aydogmus et al., (2015); Bühlmann, & Yu, 2002).

Figure 1. Rotation forest pseudo code
(Rokach & Maimon, 2015)

Rotation Forest

Require: I (a base inducer), S (the original training set), T (number of iterations), K (number of subsets),

1: **for** $i = 1$ to T **do**
2:   Split the feature set into K subsets: $F_{i,j}$ (for $j=1..K$)
3:   **for** $j = 1$ to K **do**
4:     Let $S_{i,j}$ be the dataset S for the features in $F_{i,j}$
5:     Eliminate from $S_{i,j}$ a random subset of classes
6:     Select a bootstrap sample from $S_{i,j}$ of size 75% of the number of objects in $S_{i,j}$. Denote the new set by $S'_{i,j}$
7:     Apply PCA on $S'_{i,j}$ to obtain the coefficients in a matrix $C_{i,j}$
8:   **end for**
9:   Arrange the $C_{i,j}$, for $j = 1$ to K in a rotation matrix R_i as in the equation:

$$R_i = \begin{bmatrix} a_{i,1}^{(1)}, a_{i,1}^{(2)}, \ldots, a_{i,1}^{(M_1)} & [0] & \cdots & [0] \\ [0] & a_{i,2}^{(1)}, a_{i,2}^{(2)}, \ldots, a_{i,2}^{(M_2)} & \cdots & [0] \\ \cdots & \cdots & \cdots & \cdots \\ [0] & [0] & \cdots & a_{i,k}^{(1)}, a_{i,k}^{(2)}, \ldots, a_{i,k}^{(Mk)} \end{bmatrix}$$

10:   Construct R_i^a by rearranging the columns of R_i so as to match the order of features in F
11: **end for**
12: Build classifier M_i using (SR_i^a, X) as the training set

Figure 2. Bagging algorithm structure
(Erdal et al., 2013)

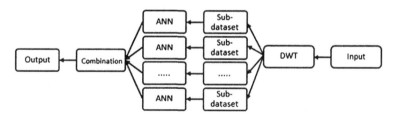

In these equations, D is a training set that includes data couples composed from $(X_i Y_i)$ as $i=1,2,\ldots,n$. X_i components express the multi-dimensional predictor variables, and Y_i is a realization of a variable with a real value. A predictor variable is given in Equation (1) and denoted by Equation (2).

$$E(Y|X=x) = f(x). \tag{1}$$

$$C_n(x) = h_n(D_1,\ldots,D_n)(x) \tag{2}$$

Theoretically, bagging is described in this way: bagging starts with the bootstrapped sample construction process that follows:

$$D_i^* = \left(Y_i^*, X_i^*\right)$$ (3)

In accordance with the experimental distribution of the pairs $D_i = (X_i, Y_i)$, where ($i = 1, 2, \ldots, n$). After that, prediction of the bootstrapped predictors, defined via Equation (4), is carried out by using the principle of plug-in:

$$C_n^*\left(x\right) = h_n\left(D_i^*, \ldots, D_n^*\right)\left(x\right)$$ (4)

Finally, the bagged predictor can be obtained with Equation (5).

$$C_{n;B}\left(x\right) = E^*\left[, D_n^*\left(x\right)\right]$$ (5)

Additive Regression

On one hand, regression is a method that is used to observe the effect of one or more independent variables on a dependent variable and determine the statistical relationship between these variables. On the other hand, Additive Regression (*AddReg*)is an amplified version of regression method via any algorithm. In this regard, besides that basically regression analysis is performed, this analysis is carried out by applying a learning algorithm to each data set.

Generally, this method expresses that the way of producing any prediction is by collocating the contributions obtained through all off the other separate models. While most of learning algorithms cannot generate the base models on their own, they try to generate a main model group, which optimizes predicted performance according to specific standard by completing each other together with a regression model (Witten, Hall, & Frank, 2011).

Learner Algorithms

Artificial Neural Networks

The method of ANN is an algorithm inspired by the human nervous system. ANNs are black box operations that are based on nonlinear basis functions (Malinov, Sha, & McKeown, 2001). ANN algorithms have wide application areas due to the ability of solving highly non-linear complex problems (Seyhan, Tayfur, Karakurt, & Tanoglu, 2005). ANNs models have ability, which is made possible that be able to learn the connection of input parameters with the output or target parameter because they benefit from mathematical training processes (Dahou, Sbartaï, Castel, & Ghomari, 2009).

Back-propagation is explained as a technique that calculates an error between actual values and predicted values and propagates the error information back through the network to each node in each layer. Error back-propagation method includes two significant parameters for learning the target variable or variables. These are composed of learning rate and momentum. Learning rate expresses the quantity of comprehension by network – in other words changing or updating of weight values according to observed errors. Also, momentum value means that weights wish to perform gradient in a direction, where weight values are changed.

Conventional backpropagation is formulated in the equation that follows (Erdal et al., 2013). Output value, which belongs to any l th neuron exists in the n th layer and can be calculated with Equation (6).

$$y_l^n\left(t\right) = \phi\left[\sum_{j=1}^{p} w_{lj}^n\left(t\right) y_j^{n-1}\left(t\right) + \Psi_l^n\right] \tag{6}$$

In Equation (6), ϕ.is the activation function used for the ultimate summation obtained with weight values for inputs. Also, w_{lj}^n indicates the weight values for connections between neurons in layers, y_j^{n-1} is the input value for any j neuron within the previous layer, t is value of iteration or time indicator, and $\Psi_l^n = w_{l_0}^n\left(t\right)$ defines the bias value for related l neuron. Furthermore, value of synaptic connection weight ($w_{ji}^n\left(t\right)$ can be calculated via Equation (7), where $\Delta w_{ji}^n\left(t\right)$ expresses the differentiation of weight value compared to the previous time.

$$w_{ji}^n\left(t+1\right) = w_{ji}^n\left(t\right) + \Delta w_{ji}^n\left(t\right) \tag{7}$$

Figure 3. Structure of artificial neural networks (ANNs)

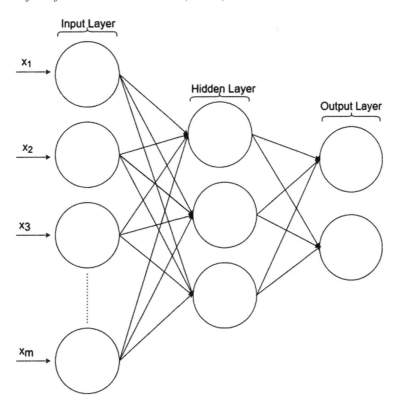

In Figure 3, an ANN structure generates from three layers, which correspond to the input layer, the hidden layer, and the output layer respectively, is shown representatively. Hidden layers can become as more from indicating in this presentation. In this Figure, x_m is expressed the data given to each ith input nodes by i=1, 2, ..., m.

Random Forest

On one hand, each node within a forest structure is parted according to the best split among all model parameters. On the other hand, each node existing in a random forest is split using the best predictor among a subset of predictor variables randomly chosen at that node. At the same time, RF also is expressed as a different model of Bagging ensemble algorithm. The intercorrelation of each independent tree classifiers in the forest ensures that researchers find out the error rate of the random forest base learner. Thus, accuracy for performance belonging to the RF model arises by based on each tree learner (Khoshgoftaar, Golawala, & Van Hulse, 2007; Ozturk, Namli, & Erdal, 2016).

In regression problems, RF is defined as non-parametric regression approximation. This process forms of a set of M trees (Adusumilli, Bhatt, Wang, Bhattacharya, & Devabhaktuni, 2013).

The following expression as p-dimension input vector, which builds a forest, is $\{T_1(X), T_2(X), ..., T_M(X)\}$ where, $(X_1, X_2, ..., X_p)$.

The authors present M outputs related to each tree produced by ensemble algorithm via Equation (8).

$$\hat{Y}_1 = T_1\left(X\right), ..., \hat{Y}_M = T_M\left(X\right) \tag{8}$$

where, $\hat{Y}_m, m = 1, .., M$ is the mth tree output. Also, the average value of predictions determines the output value.

Feature Selection

Researchers apply feature, or attribute or variable selection application, with the purpose of observing and determining the essential and significant components that are effective over any data model, and owing to this, reducing the load of input space (Rokach & Maimon, 2015). Actually, the aim of this technique is improving prediction success and decreasing of error that occurs according to the real values of data samples for any machine-learning model. However, this cannot be possible every time.

Moreover, researchers regard the principal subject in terms of machine learning technology as selection of features. The reason for this is to ensure usage of less quantity during learned of data, to improve learning possibility of more intense things, and to complete the operation process in less time by the feature selection technique (Hall, 1999). In addition, for the selection of features, numerous different technique and algorithms can be used in machine learning applications, such as prediction, classification, pattern recognition, etc.

Backward elimination by Marill and Green, best-first search by Winston, and genetic algorithms by Goldberg, nearest-neighbor learning by Kibler with Aha, and Cardie, and correlation-based feature selection method by Hall (which the authors utilized in this study for feature selection), are among some of these techniques (Witten & Frank, 2005).

Correlation-based feature selection method (CFS; seen as '*Cfs subset evaluator*' in Weka software) is a technique used in statistical relationships between attributes. For this reason, the technique determines the effective features by some select features according to relations between each, other besides relations according to the output or target features (Cichosz, 2015). This case can be considered as correlation, and so, this technique may become a correlation-based selector or evaluator.

On the other hand, the CFS evaluator has many advantages for selecting principal features, such as operating easily and rapidly, ability of clear the not effective features, and so prediction can be improved many times. In this regard, the technique uses a heuristic function related with correlation and realizes of rank the subsets of features. The evaluation function for CFS is given in Equation (9) (Hall, 1999).

$$M_s = \frac{k\overline{r_{cf}}}{\sqrt{k + k(k-1)\overline{r_{ff}}}} \tag{9}$$

In this equation, M_S indicates the heuristic value belonging to any S subset of features, including k features. Also, $\overline{r_{cf}}$ is the average value of correlations existing among each feature with output class, and $\overline{r_{ff}}$ is the average of features' correlations according to each other.

CALCULATIONS AND EMPIRICAL RESULTS

Dataset Description

In this study, the authors obtained a dataset containing various parameters acting to measure concrete compressive strength. This dataset includes defined information obtained from performed experiments at the University of California (Yeh, 1998a, 1998b). In addition, these samples amount to 1030, and the samples consisted of normal Portland cement, which has various additives and was cured via normal conditions. Also, these numerical observations for model samples were gained from research laboratories taking place in a different university.

Table 1 represents the dataset and its various properties, and Figures 4-12 show the number of each feature label for samples within dataset.

Cross Validation

Cross validation is a technique applied for observation by collecting the data samples inside independent groups (namely, fold) for developing prediction performance of any machine learning algorithm to design a model.

In this respect, this method applies an approach that is related to dividing samples into two separate groups consisting of training, in other words learning, and testing part, which is preferred for validating of model. Thus, these groups should be sequenced consecutively. On the other hand, k folds exist in classic form of this method (Refaeilzadeh, Tang, & Liu, 2009).

Table 1. Properties of inputs and output in data set

Features	Unit	Ultimate Values	
		Min	Max
Cement	kg/m³	102.0	540.0
Blast-furnace slag	kg/m³	11.0	359.4
Fly ash	kg/m³	24.5	200.1
Water	kg/m³	121.8	247.0
Superplasticizer	kg/m³	1.7	32.2
Coarse aggregate	kg/m³	801.0	1145.0
Fine aggregate	kg/m³	594.0	992.6
Age of testing	Day	1.0	365.0
Concrete compressive strength	MPa	2.3	82.6

Figure 4. Frequency of age input feature for data samples

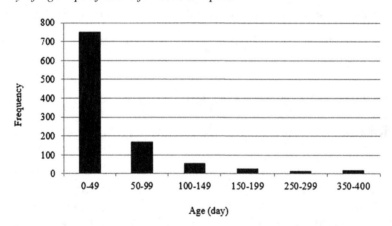

Figure 5. Frequency of blast furnace input feature for data samples

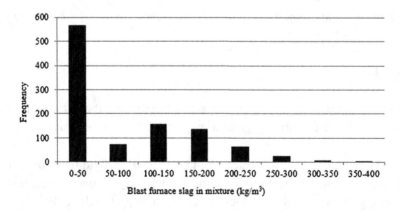

Figure 6. Frequency of fly ash input feature for data samples

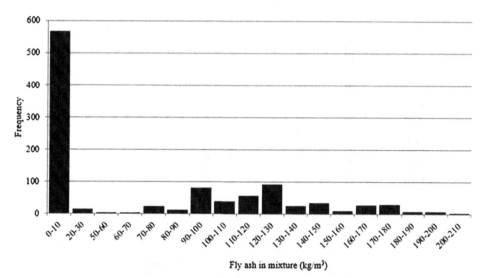

Figure 7. Frequency of superplasticizer input feature for data samples

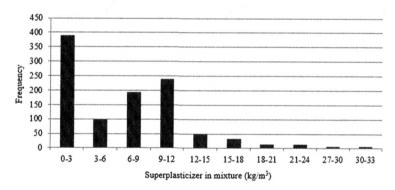

Figure 13 represents the operation logic of k-fold cross validation method. As mentioned before, this data model is first split as training and testing data, and then each testing fold is evaluated by means of learning and modelling of all training folds (as (k-1) fold). As a result of realizing all cross-validation operations, obtained performance results are collected in the final prediction value for operated algorithm.

However, in this study, the authors preferred cross-validation, as k is equal to 10-fold to detect of prediction success and performances of proposed machine and ensemble machine learning models. In this study, the dataset, which was randomized initially, is composed of 10 separate folds, and their single fold is a test and the remaining 9 folds are training folds. The authors carry out calculation of error values belonging to each cross-validation set, and the following total error value can be obtained after this sequential process.

Figure 8. Frequency of cement input feature for data sample

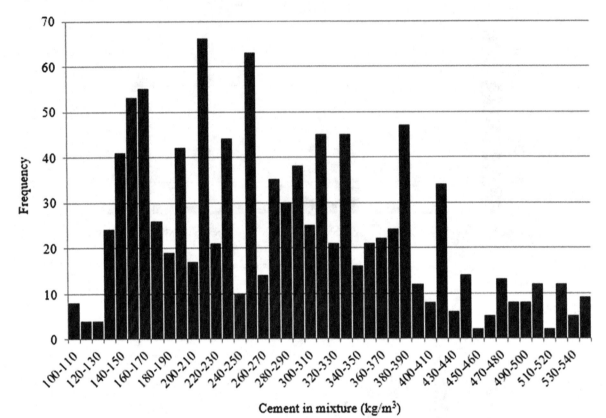

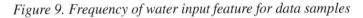

Figure 9. Frequency of water input feature for data samples

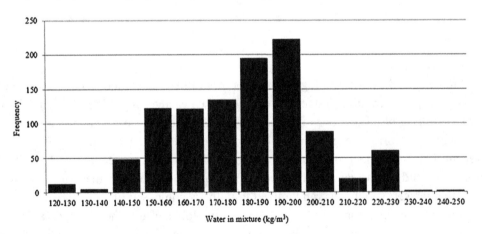

Figure 10. Frequency of coarse aggregate input feature for data samples

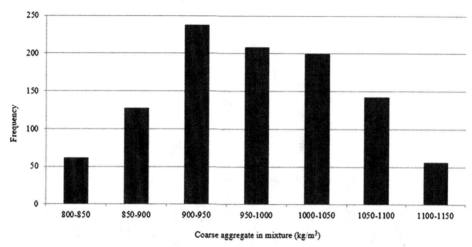

Figure 11. Frequency of fine aggregate input feature for data samples

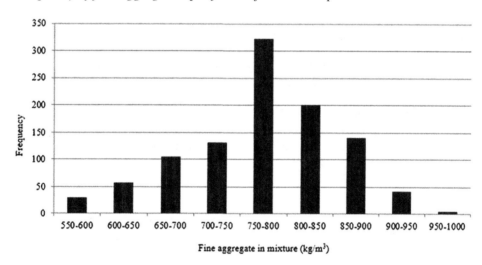

Table 2. Error evaluation metrics

Abbreviations	Definitions
R	Correlation Coefficient
MAE	Mean Absolute Error
RAE	Relative Absolute Error
RMSE	Root Mean Squared Error
RRSE	Root Relative Squared Error

Figure 12. Frequency of concrete compressive strength output feature for data samples

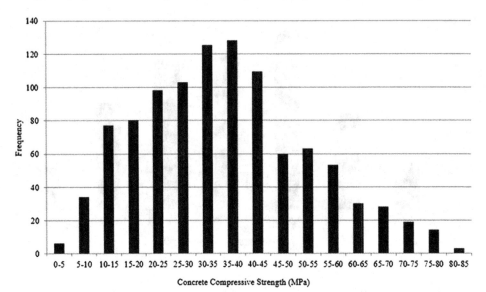

Figure 13. k-fold cross validation method
(Chou, Lin, Pham, & Shao,2015)

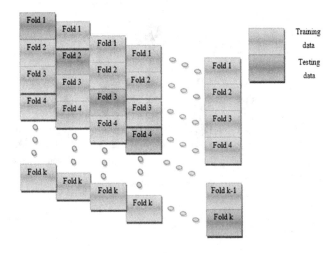

Performance Evaluation Metrics

In Table 2, various error evaluation metrics are composed from mean absolute error, relative absolute error, root mean squared error, and root relative squared error, which are considered generally as basic observations and are frequently used. These are given and intended for evaluating of success of machine-learning prediction models.

Table 3 represents formulations of metrics used in this study.

Table 3. Formulation of evaluation metrics

Evaluation Metrics	Equations
Correlation Coefficient (R)	$$\frac{n\sum y \cdot y' - \left(\sum y\right)\left(\sum y'\right)}{\sqrt{n\left(\sum y^2\right)-\left(\sum y\right)^2}-\sqrt{n\left(\sum y'^2\right)-\left(\sum y'\right)^2}}\cdot$$
Mean Absolute Error (MAE)	$$\frac{1}{n}\sum_{i=1}^{n}\left|y - y'\right|.$$
Root Absolute Error (RAE)	$$\frac{\sum_{i=1}^{n}\left|y'-y\right|}{\sum_{i=1}^{n}\left|\hat{y}-y\right|}$$
Root Mean Squared Error (RMSE)	$$\sqrt{\frac{1}{n}\sum_{i=1}^{n}\left(y_i - y_i'\right)^2}$$
Root Relative Squared Error (RRSE)	$$\sqrt{\frac{\sum_{i=1}^{n}\left(y'-y\right)^2}{\sum_{i=1}^{n}\left(\hat{y}-y\right)^2}}$$

On the other hand, a different measurement was realized for evaluating error as commonly. This method is called Synthesis Index (SI) calculation. In this respect, the authors used ΣSI as a comprehensive performance measure, and its equation is expressed via Equation (10).

$$\Sigma SI = (1\text{-ErrorSI}) + \text{PerformanceSI} \tag{10}$$

Where ErrorSI (E-SI) and PerformanceSI (P-SI) are calculated by the following formula as in Equation (11) (Huang et al., 2016):

$$s1 = \frac{1}{m}\sum_{i=1}^{m}\left(\frac{P_i - P_{min,i}}{P_{max,i} - P_{min,i}}\right) \tag{11}$$

Discussion and Results

According to these results, the authors found AddReg-RF hybrid model to be superior to other methods. One of the causes was that the correlation coefficient (R) belonging to mentioned hybrid model is the best value with the point of prediction performance, according to other ones. In addition to this performance, the authors observed the least values in terms of all of the error evaluation metrics towards this hybrid model.

Table 4. Performance results of machine and ensemble machine learning models

	RF	ANN	Bagging-RF	Bagging-ANN	AddReg-RF	AddReg-ANN	RotF-RF	RotF-ANN
R	0.9630	0.9023	0.9598	0.9149	0.9713	0.9187	0.9464	0.9165
MAE	3.1963	5.5957	3.5096	5.2329	2.4945	5.1139	4.0526	5.1697
RMSE	4.6031	7.2950	4.8649	6.7596	4.0025	6.6883	5.6928	6.8207
RAE	23.7152	41.5172	26.0397	38.8257	18.5076	37.9422	30.0726	37.3617
RRSE	27.5379	43.6426	29.104	40.439	23.9449	40.013	34.0613	40.8102

After the feature selection process, which was used to determine the fundamental effective parameters for the concrete compressive strength prediction model, the authors observed that the results were close to the results obtained with eight features existing in the initial model. However, observed values for prediction performance were a decreased to a lesser degree compared to the initial model. On the other hand, the selected features are cement, water, superplasticizer, and age.

Table 5. Performance results of machine and ensemble machine learning models applied selection of features

	RF	ANN	Bagging-RF	Bagging-ANN	AddReg-RF	AddReg-ANN	RotF-RF	RotF-ANN
R	0.9259	0.8501	0.9229	0.8633	0.9444	0.8573	0.9111	0.8662
MAE	4.5607	6.9468	4.7796	6.5228	3.6391	6.7875	5.2162	6.4578
RMSE	6.3130	9.0045	6.4429	8.4303	5.4946	8.7302	6.9190	8.4017
RAE	33.8425	51.5491	35.4670	48.4025	27.0039	50.3671	38.7069	47.9203
RRSE	37.7721	53.8767	38.5499	50.4410	32.8754	52.2352	41.3982	50.2696

Table 6 shows the percentage change of performance results (error metrics) between the first model and after feature selection process. The percentage change in R values are in an acceptable range.

Table 6. Percentage change of performance results (error metrics) between first model and after feature selection process

	RF	ANN	Bagging-RF	Bagging-ANN	AddReg-RF	AddReg-ANN	RotF-RF	RotF-ANN
R	-3.85	-5.79	-3.84	-5.64	-2.77	-6.68	-3.73	-5.49
MAE	42.69	24.15	36.19	24.65	45.88	32.73	28.71	24.92
RMSE	37.15	23.43	32.44	24.72	37.28	30.53	21.54	23.18
RAE	42.70	24.16	36.20	24.67	45.91	32.75	28.71	28.26
RRSE	37.16	23.45	32.46	24.73	37.30	30.55	21.54	23.18

In Table 7 and Table 8, the authors combined all performance metrics with error SI method, and the authors ranked the results for readers to easily interpret them.

Table 7. SI results of machine and ensemble machine learning models

	1-R	MAE	RMSE	RAE	RRSE	SI Average Value	Rank
RF	0.12	0.23	0.18	0.23	0.18	0.19	2
ANN	1.00	1.00	1.00	1.00	1.00	1.00	8
Bagging-RF	0.17	0.33	0.26	0.33	0.26	0.27	3
Bagging-ANN	0.82	0.88	0.84	0.88	0.84	0.85	7
AddReg-RF	0.00	0.00	0.00	0.00	0.00	0.00	1
AddReg-ANN	0.76	0.84	0.82	0.84	0.82	0.82	5
RotF-RF	0.36	0.50	0.51	0.50	0.51	0.48	4
RotF-ANN	0.79	0.86	0.86	0.82	0.86	0.84	6

Table 8. SI results of machine and ensemble machine learning models after feature selection process

	1-R	MAE	RMSE	RAE	RRSE	SI Average Value	Rank
RF	0.20	0.28	0.23	0.28	0.23	0.24	2
ANN	1.00	1.00	1.00	1.00	1.00	1.00	8
Bagging-RF	0.23	0.34	0.27	0.34	0.27	0.29	3
Bagging-ANN	0.86	0.87	0.84	0.87	0.84	0.86	6
AddReg-RF	0.00	0.00	0.00	0.00	0.00	0.00	1
AddReg-ANN	0.92	0.95	0.92	0.95	0.92	0.93	7
RotF-RF	0.35	0.48	0.41	0.48	0.41	0.42	4
RotF-ANN	0.83	0.85	0.83	0.85	0.83	0.84	5

CONCLUSION

As the authors mentioned before, researchers presented various methods and models for prediction of HPC compressive strength. Machine learning-based studies showed that ML is one of most influential methods in this area. The construction sector is an industry where international competition is very intense. To survive in this intense and ruthless competitive environment, managing time efficiently will be a great advantage. In this case, waiting for the results of concrete compressive strength for days will cause unnecessary time loss, increase construction completion time, and increase costs.

The authors have proposed an advanced ML based prediction model of HPC in this study. The prediction model could be used as a decision support system that could eliminate the time to wait for laboratory test results. According to sudden solutions of ML model execution, the process of construction never stops.

In this study, the authors explained eight different ML and EML techniques, composed from RF and ANN algorithms, which were used as base learners for prediction performance comparison of Rotation Forest, Additive Regression, and Bagging EML methods, besides only themselves. In addition, the authors applied a feature selection process to the model to decrease calculation time and to make accurate predictions with less information. The results obtained showed that there are acceptable declines in R values. Finally, the results also demonstrate that the Additive Regression method with Random Forest base learner is the most accurate model in predicting HPC compressive strength, according to evaluation metrics.

REFERENCES

Adusumilli, S., Bhatt, D., Wang, H., Bhattacharya, P., & Devabhaktuni, V. (2013). A low-cost INS/GPS integration methodology based on random forest regression. *Expert Systems with Applications, 40*(11), 4653–4659. doi:10.1016/j.eswa.2013.02.002

Ahmadi-Nedushan, B. (2012). An optimized instance-based learning algorithm for estimation of compressive strength of concrete. *Engineering Applications of Artificial Intelligence, 25*(5), 1073–1081. doi:10.1016/j.engappai.2012.01.012

Akande, K. O., Owolabi, T. O., Twaha, S., & Olatunji, S. O. (2014). Performance comparison of SVM and ANN in predicting compressive strength of concrete. *IOSR Journal of Computer Engineering, 16*(5), 88–94. doi:10.9790/0661-16518894

Akpinar, P., & Khashman, A. (2017). Intelligent classification system for concrete compressive strength. *Procedia Computer Science, 120*, 712–718. doi:10.1016/j.procs.2017.11.300

Al-Shamiri, A. K., Kim, J. H., Yuan, T. F., & Yoon, Y. S. (2019). Modeling the compressive strength of high-strength concrete: An extreme learning approach. *Construction & Building Materials, 208*, 204–219. doi:10.1016/j.conbuildmat.2019.02.165

Atici, U. (2011). Prediction of the strength of mineral admixture concrete using multivariable regression analysis and an artificial neural network. *Expert Systems with Applications, 38*(8), 9609–9618. doi:10.1016/j.eswa.2011.01.156

Awoyera, P. O. (2018). Predictive models for determination of compressive and split-tensile strengths of steel slag aggregate concrete. *Materials Research Innovations, 22*(5), 287–293. doi:10.1080/14328 917.2017.1317394

Aydogmus, H. Y., Erdal, H. İ., Karakurt, O., Namli, E., Turkan, Y. S., & Erdal, H. (2015). A comparative assessment of bagging ensemble models for modeling concrete slump flow. *Computers and Concrete, 16*(5), 741–757. doi:10.12989/cac.2015.16.5.741

Behnood, A., Behnood, V., Gharehveran, M. M., & Alyamac, K. E. (2017). Prediction of the compressive strength of normal and high-performance concretes using M5P model tree algorithm. *Construction & Building Materials, 142*, 199–207. doi:10.1016/j.conbuildmat.2017.03.061

Behnood, A., & Golafshani, E. M. (2018). Predicting the compressive strength of silica fume concrete using hybrid artificial neural network with multi-objective grey wolves. *Journal of Cleaner Production, 202*, 54–64.

Bilgehan, M., & Turgut, P. (2010). Artificial neural network approach to predict compressive strength of concrete through ultrasonic pulse velocity. *Research in Nondestructive Evaluation*, *21*(1), 1–17. doi:10.1080/09349840903122042

Breiman, L. (1996). Bagging predictors. *Machine Learning*, *24*(2), 123–140. doi:10.1007/BF00058655

Bühlmann, P., & Yu, B. (2002). Analyzing bagging. *Annals of Statistics*, *30*(4), 927–961. doi:10.1214/aos/1031689014

Bui, D. K., Nguyen, T., Chou, J. S., Nguyen-Xuan, H., & Ngo, T. D. (2018). A modified firefly algorithm-artificial neural network expert system for predicting compressive and tensile strength of high-performance concrete. *Construction & Building Materials*, *180*, 320–333. doi:10.1016/j.conbuildmat.2018.05.201

Cheng, M. Y., Chou, J. S., Roy, A. F., & Wu, Y. W. (2012). High-performance concrete compressive strength prediction using time-weighted evolutionary fuzzy support vector machines inference model. *Automation in Construction*, *28*, 106–115. doi:10.1016/j.autcon.2012.07.004

Chithra, S., Kumar, S. S., Chinnaraju, K., & Ashmita, F. A. (2016). A comparative study on the compressive strength prediction models for high performance concrete containing nano silica and copper slag using regression analysis and artificial neural networks. *Construction & Building Materials*, *114*, 528–535. doi:10.1016/j.conbuildmat.2016.03.214

Chopra, P., Sharma, R. K., & Kumar, M. (2016). Prediction of compressive strength of concrete using artificial neural network and genetic programmings. *Advances in Materials Science and Engineering*, *2016*, 1–10. doi:10.1155/2016/7648467

Chou, J. S., Lin, C. W., Pham, A. D., & Shao, J. Y. (2015). Optimized artificial intelligence models for predicting project award price. *Automation in Construction*, *54*, 106–115. doi:10.1016/j.autcon.2015.02.006

Chou, J. S., Tsai, C. F., Pham, A. D., & Lu, Y. H. (2014). Machine learning in concrete strength simulations: Multi-nation data analytics. *Construction & Building Materials*, *73*, 771–780. doi:10.1016/j.conbuildmat.2014.09.054

Cichosz, P. (2015). *Data mining algorithms: explained using R*. Chichester, UK: John Wiley & Sons. doi:10.1002/9781118950951

Dahou, Z., Sbartaï, Z. M., Castel, A., & Ghomari, F. (2009). Artificial neural network model for steel–concrete bond prediction. *Engineering Structures*, *31*(8), 1724–1733. doi:10.1016/j.engstruct.2009.02.010

Deshpande, N., Londhe, S., & Kulkarni, S. (2014). Modeling compressive strength of recycled aggregate concrete by artificial neural network, model tree and non-linear regression. *International Journal of Sustainable Built Environment*, *3*(2), 187–198.

Dietterich, T. G. (2000). An experimental comparison of three methods for constructing ensembles of decision trees: Bagging, boosting, and randomization. *Machine Learning*, *40*(2), 139–157. doi:10.1023/A:1007607513941

Duan, Z. H., Kou, S. C., & Poon, C. S. (2013). Prediction of compressive strength of recycled aggregate concrete using artificial neural networks. *Construction & Building Materials*, *40*, 1200–1206. doi:10.1016/j.conbuildmat.2012.04.063

Erdal, H. I., Karakurt, O., & Namli, E. (2013). High performance concrete compressive strength forecasting using ensemble models based on discrete wavelet transform. *Engineering Applications of Artificial Intelligence, 26*(4), 1246–1254. doi:10.1016/j.engappai.2012.10.014

Hall, M. A. (1999). *Correlation-based feature selection for machine learning* (Doctoral dissertation). Retrieved from https://www.cs.waikato.ac.nz/~mhall/thesis.pdf

Hoła, J., & Schabowicz, K. (2005). Application of artificial neural networks to determine concrete compressive strength based on non-destructive tests. *Journal of Civil Engineering and Management, 11*(1), 23–32. doi:10.3846/13923730.2005.9636329

Huang, S., Wang, B., Qiu, J., Yao, J., Wang, G., & Yu, G. (2016). Parallel ensemble of online sequential extreme learning machine based on MapReduce. *Neurocomputing, 174*, 352–367.

Kewalramani, M. A., & Gupta, R. (2006). Concrete compressive strength prediction using ultrasonic pulse velocity through artificial neural networks. *Automation in Construction, 15*(3), 374–379. doi:10.1016/j. autcon.2005.07.003

Khoshgoftaar, T. M., Golawala, M., & Van Hulse, J. (2007). An empirical study of learning from imbalanced data using random forest. In *Proceedings of 19th IEEE International Conference on Tools with Artificial Intelligence (ICTAI 2007)*. Patras, Greece: IEEE. 10.1109/ICTAI.2007.46

Kılınç, D., Borandağ, E., Yücalar, F., Özçift, A., & Bozyiğit, F. (2015). Yazılım hata kestiriminde kolektif sınıflandırma modellerinin etkisi. In *Proceedings of IX. Ulusal Yazılım Mühendisliği Sempozyumu*. Bornava-İzmir.

Küçük, B. (2000). Factors providing the strength and durability of concrete. *Pamukkale Üniversitesi Mühendislik Bilimleri Dergisi, 6*(1), 79–85.

Kuncheva, L. I., & Rodríguez, J. J. (2007). An experimental study on rotation forest ensembles. In M. Haindl, J. Kittler, & F. Roli (Eds.), *Multiple classifier systems* (pp. 459–468). Heidelberg, Germany: Springer-Verlag. doi:10.1007/978-3-540-72523-7_46

Malinov, S., Sha, W., & McKeown, J. J. (2001). Modelling the correlation between processing parameters and properties in titanium alloys using artificial neural network. *Computational Materials Science, 21*(3), 375–394. doi:10.1016/S0927-0256(01)00160-4

Naderpour, H., Kheyroddin, A., & Amiri, G. G. (2010). Prediction of FRP-confined compressive strength of concrete using artificial neural networks. *Composite Structures, 92*(12), 2817–2829.

Nikoo, M., Zarfam, P., & Sayahpour, H. (2015). Determination of compressive strength of concrete using self organization feature map (SOFM). *Engineering with Computers, 31*(1), 113–121.

Ozturk, H., Namli, E., & Erdal, H. I. (2016). Modelling sovereign credit ratings: The accuracy of models in a heterogeneous sample. *Economic Modelling, 54*, 469–478.

Refaeilzadeh, P., Tang, L., & Liu, H. (2009). Cross-validation. In L. Liu & M. T. Özsu (Eds.), *Encyclopedia of database systems* (pp. 24–154). Boston, MA: Springer.

Rokach, L., & Maimon, O. (2015). *Data mining with decision trees theory and applications* (2nd ed., Vol. 81). Singapore: World Scientific.

Seyhan, A. T., Tayfur, G., Karakurt, M., & Tanoglu, M. (2005). Artificial neural network (ANN) prediction of compressive strength of VARTM processed polymer composites. *Computational Materials Science*, *34*(1), 99–105. doi:10.1016/j.commatsci.2004.11.001

Topcu, I. B., & Sarıdemir, M. (2008). Prediction of compressive strength of concrete containing fly ash using artificial neural networks and fuzzy logic. *Computational Materials Science*, *41*(3), 305–311.

Trtnik, G., Kavčič, F., & Turk, G. (2009). Prediction of concrete strength using ultrasonic pulse velocity and artificial neural networks. *Ultrasonics*, *49*(1), 53–60. doi:10.1016/j.ultras.2008.05.001 PMID:18589471

Turkish Standards Institute (TSE). (2000). *Requirements for design and construction of reinforced concrete structures (ICS 91.080.40)*. Ankara, Turkey: Turkish Republic Ministry of Public Works and Settlement.

Wang, Q. (2007). Artificial neural networks as cost engineering methods in a collaborative manufacturing environment. *International Journal of Production Economics*, *109*(1-2), 53–64. doi:10.1016/j.ijpe.2006.11.006

Witten, I. H., & Frank, E. (2005). *Data Mining: Practical machine learning tools and techniques* (2nd ed.). San Francisco, CA: Morgan Kaufmann.

Witten, I. H., Hall, M. A., & Frank, E. (2011). *Data mining: practical machine learning tools and techniques*. Burlington, MA: Morgan Kaufmann Series.

Yaseen, Z. M., Deo, R. C., Hilal, A., Abd, A. M., Bueno, L. C., Salcedo-Sanz, S., & Nehdi, M. L. (2018). Predicting compressive strength of lightweight foamed concrete using extreme learning machine model. *Advances in Engineering Software*, *115*, 112–125. doi:10.1016/j.advengsoft.2017.09.004

Yeh, I. C. (1998a). Modeling of strength of high-performance concrete using artificial neural networks. *Cement and Concrete Research*, *28*(12), 1797–1808. doi:10.1016/S0008-8846(98)00165-3

Yeh, I. C. (1998b). Modeling concrete strength with augment-neuron networks. *Journal of Materials in Civil Engineering*, *10*(4), 263–268. doi:10.1061/(ASCE)0899-1561(1998)10:4(263)

Yu, Y., Li, W., Li, J., & Nguyen, T. N. (2018). A novel optimised self-learning method for compressive strength prediction of high-performance concrete. *Construction & Building Materials*, *184*, 229–247.

This research was previously published in Artificial Intelligence and Machine Learning Applications in Civil, Mechanical, and Industrial Engineering; pages 118-140, copyright year 2020 by Engineering Science Reference (an imprint of IGI Global).

Chapter 7

Modern Statistical Modeling in Machine Learning and Big Data Analytics:
Statistical Models for Continuous and Categorical Variables

Niloofar Ramezani
George Mason University, USA

ABSTRACT

Machine learning, big data, and high dimensional data are the topics we hear about frequently these days, and some even call them the wave of the future. Therefore, it is important to use appropriate statistical models, which have been established for many years, and their efficiency has already been evaluated to contribute into advancing machine learning, which is a relatively newer field of study. Different algorithms that can be used within machine learning, depending on the nature of the variables, are discussed, and appropriate statistical techniques for modeling them are presented in this chapter.

INTRODUCTION

Machine learning is an important topic these days as it involves a set of many different methods and algorithms that are suited to answer diverse questions about a business or problem. Therefore, choosing an algorithm is a critical step in the machine learning process to ensure it truly fits the solution proposed in answering a problem at hand (Segal, 2004). To better understand machine learning algorithms and when each algorithm needs to be used, it is helpful to understand them within the framework of statistics and separate them into two main groups based on the data and the format of their outcomes. These two types of machine learning methods are classification and regression for categorical and continuous response variables, respectively. Within this book chapter, we will differentiate these two types and mention related algorithms and statistical techniques that can be used to answer real world problems.

DOI: 10.4018/978-1-6684-6291-1.ch007

Then the concept of high-dimensional data and some of the methods that are appropriate for handling such data will be discussed.

An outline of the sections and subsections within this chapter are discussed below. First, the continuous approaches are discussed and regression algorithm and regression algorithm, as the most commonly used approach for such scenarios, is explained. Such methods help modeling the continuous response variables. On the other hand, generalized linear models and classification techniques assist researchers to model discrete, binary, and categorical responses. While discussing the statistical models, which are appropriate in predicting the categorical response variables, binary logistic regression as well as multinomial and ordinal logistic regression models are introduced and discussed here. These models can assist researchers and applied practitioners in modeling binary and categorical response variables. Within the section that discusses ordinal logistic models, different logit models are briefly discussed. These logit functions are cumulative logit, adjacent-categories logit, and continuation-ratio logit.

The next section of this chapter is dedicated to introducing and discussing dimension reduction methods. Dimension reduction techniques applied within the two classification and regression algorithms, paired with the analytically powerful computers, will assist researchers in handling data sets with higher dimensions of variables and observations efficiently within a reasonable timeline. Different models to address each set of techniques are introduced in this chapter to provide different statistical and research tools that can be used by researchers and practitioners in machine learning and data analysis. Selected dimension reduction methods are discussed in this chapter. These subsections are principal components analysis, decision trees and their use in building random forest, regression decision trees and random forest for continuous responses, classification decision trees and random forest for categorical responses, LASSO and ridge regression, and finally cluster analysis.

This chapter adopts an introductory and educational approach, rather than rushing into the programming or data analysis details, to familiarize the readers with different data scenarios and the proper statistical and machine learning algorithms to appropriately model the data. The author believes the first step in ensuring the quality, correctness, and reliability of any quantitative analysis is to learn about the characteristics of the data, by exploring them, and then choosing the proper statistical and machine learning approach to model the data. Years of teaching statistics, data analytics, and quantitative methodology, as well as providing statistical consultation, have taught the author the importance of strengthening the foundations of statistical knowledge of students, clients, or data analysts before diving into running codes and printing output to ensure the accuracy of the results. This chapter is meant to educate the readers about the correct modeling options to minimize the chances of choosing the wrong methods of data analysis while exploring and modeling real-world data.

CONTINUOUS DATA

When dealing with continuous data and predicting such outcome measures, regression approaches and algorithms can be used. Linear regression is by far the simplest and most popular example of a regression algorithm used in many fields. Though it is often underrated due to its simplicity, it is a flexible prediction tool. Regression trees and support vector regressions are more advanced algorithms within the framework of regression that can be used for high dimensions of data.

Regression

Every machine learning problem is an optimization problem. This means we want to find either a maximum or a minimum of a specific function of predictors and responses. This function is usually called the loss function, which is defined for each machine learning algorithm we use. A regression function can be optimized using the same procedure. Linear regression is widely used in different supervised machine learning problems and focuses on regression problem. Linear regression uses the optimization technique in linear programming. This means linear regression is generally considered as an optimization problem. Concepts such as regression help with investigating and establishing a relationship between the vast amounts of data required for learning through the relationships that exist among different variables in a model. If we have an explanatory or predictor variable and a response variable, we would like to make predictions of the expected values of the response variable based on the observed values of the explanatory variable. If we fit a line to the data, which is called regression line if it is the best and most optimal fit, then we can use this line's equation in predicting the response variable by estimating the coefficients of the regression model. This is achievable by executing an iterative process that updates the coefficients, which are now considered the parameters of the model, at every step by reducing the loss function as much as possible. Once we reach the minimum point of the loss function, we can say that we have completed the iterative process and estimated the parameters.

For the simple linear regression model, we use only one predictor variable to predict the response. In this case, we will end up with two coefficients; the intercept and the slope. Within multiple linear regression, we can have multiple predictors that together they can explain a higher amount of the variation of the response. The multiple regression model can be written as below,

$$Y = \beta_0 + \beta_1 X_1 + \beta_2 X_2 + \beta_3 X_3 + \ldots + \beta_k X_k + \epsilon,$$

Where Y is the response, $X_1, X_2, \ldots, X_k$ are k predictors, β_0 is the intercept of the regression line, $\beta_1, \beta_2, \ldots, \beta_k$ are the slopes, and ϵ is the random error term.

In order to solve the linear regression problem, we will use the same iterative algorithm and minimize the loss function. The main difference will be that we will end up with multiple β coefficients instead of only two, which was the case for a simple linear regression. Least square estimation is the most common algorithm, and one of the most efficient techniques, used to minimize the loss function and estimate the best coefficients for the regression model (Montgomery, Peck & Vining, 2012). Many assumptions need to be checked before fitting the regression model to the data which is not the main focus of this chapter. For more details on the regression assumptions and how to fit a regression model, see Montgomery et al. (2012). We also recommend reading chapters 2 and 3 of "The elements of statistical learning" book by Friedman, Hastie, and Tibshirani (2001) to learn more about structured regression models within supervised learning and linear methods for regression, respectively. Chapter 3 of "An introduction to statistical learning with application in R" by James, Witten, Hastie, and Tibshirani (2013) provides examples and applications of regression. Applications of this method can be found in almost any field.

CATEGORICAL DATA

When dealing with categorical outcomes, the assumption of normality is not met and therefore, the linear regression approaches cannot be fitted to such data anymore. Additionally, the relationship between the response variable and predictors is no longer linear, hence more advanced models than linear approaches need to be adopted to appropriately model this nonlinear relationship. Binary, multinomial, and ordinal logistic regression approaches are some examples of the robust predictive methods to use for modeling the relationship between non-normal discrete response and the predictors. Readers can consult Ramezani and Ramezani (2016) that discusses multiple methods and algorithms to fit predictive models to non-continuous non-normal responses. Agresti (2007) is another resource that is recommended if readers are interested in learning more details regarding such techniques. These methods are briefly discussed below.

Binary classification in machine learning will model binary responses while multi-label classification captures everything else, and is useful for customer segmentation, audio and image categorization, and text analysis for mining customer sentiment (James, Witten, Hastie & Tibshirani, 2013). Algorithms like naive Bayes, decision trees, logistic regression, kernel approximation, and K-nearest neighbors are among the methods that can be used within this framework. Within this chapter, these models will be expanded and tools for fitting such models will be provided. We briefly discuss two of the most important models within logistic regression in this chapter.

Binary Logistic Regression

Logistic regression allows one to form a multiple regression relation between a dependent variable and several independent variables. Logistic regression is useful for predicting the presence or absence of a characteristic or outcome based on values of a set of predictor variables. The advantage of logistic regression is that, through the addition of an appropriate link function to the usual linear regression model, the variables may be either continuous or discrete, or any combination of both types and they do not necessarily have normal distributions. Where the dependent variable is binary, the logit link function is applicable (Atkinson & Massari, 1998). Logistic regression coefficients can be used to estimate ratios for each of the independent variables in the model (Lee, 2005).

Quantitatively, the relationship between the occurrence and its dependency on several variables can be expressed as:

$$p = \frac{1}{1 + e^{-z}},$$

where p is the probability of an event occurring. The probability varies from 0 to 1 on an S-shaped curve and z is the linear combination. It follows that logistic regression involves fitting an equation of the following form to the data:

$$z = \beta_0 + \beta_1 X_1 + \ldots + \beta_k X_k,$$

where β_0 is the intercept of the model, the $\beta_i (i=0,1,2,\ldots,k)$ are the slope coefficients of the logistic regression model, and the $X_i (i=0,1,2,\ldots,k)$ are the independent variables.

In logistic regression, probability of the outcome is measured by the odds of occurrence of an event. Change in probability is not constant (linear) with constant changes in X. This means that the probability of a success (Y = 1) given the predictor variable (X) is a non-linear function, specifically a logistic function.

The most common form of logistic regression uses the logit link function so it is easily understandable to show the logistic regression equation as

$$logit\left(p\right) = \beta_0 + \beta_1 X_1 + \ldots + \beta_k X_k.$$

Different methods are then applied to do the analysis of the logistic regression model, which are explained in detail in different books like Hosmer and Lemeshow (2013) and Agresti (2007). Application of this method can be found in different fields such as education and biology (Peffer & Ramezani, 2019), psychology and education (Cokluk, 2010), and geographical information system (Lee, 2005).

Ordinal Logistic Regression

Ordinal logistic regression models have been applied in recent years in analyzing data with ranked multiple response outcomes. Ordered information has been increasingly used in health indicators but their use in the public health is still rare (Abreu et al., 2009). This may be attributed to these models' complexity, assumptions validation, and limitations of modeling options offered by statistical packages (Lall, 2002).

The multinomial logistic regression model is an extension of the binomial logistic regression model. This type of model is used when the dependent variable has more than two nominal (unordered) categories. When the response categories are ordered, a multinomial regression model still can be used. According to Agresti (2007), the disadvantage is that some information about the ordering is thrown away. An ordinal logistic regression model preserves that information, but it is slightly more involved (Ramezani, 2015).

There are different logit functions such as Cumulative Logit, Adjacent–Categories Logit, and Continuation Ratio Logit which are used within regression models to provide useful extensions of the multinomial logistic model to ordinal response data. Each of these models are briefly explained below, based on the description of Ramezani (2015), and notations used in Agresti (2007).

Cumulative Logit Models

The cumulative logit function used in ordinal multinomial logistic models is as below which basically models categories $\leq j$ versus categories $>j$, where j is the cut-off point category decided by the data analyst or researcher based on the research question. This division dichotomizes the multiple categories that exists within each categorical response by aggregating the before and after categories at a certain point.

$$logit\left(P\left(Y \leq j\right)\right) = \log\left(\frac{P\left(Y \leq j\right)}{P\left(Y > j\right)}\right) = \log\left(\frac{P\left(Y \leq j\right)}{1 - P\left(Y \leq j\right)}\right)$$

$$= \log\left(\frac{\pi_1 + \cdots + \pi_j}{\pi_{j+1} + \cdots + \pi_J}\right), for\ j = 1, \cdots, J-1$$

Using this logit function, the cumulative logit based ordinal logistic regression model can be written as below

$$\log it\left(P\left(Y \le j\right)\right) = \alpha_j + \sum_{k=1}^{K}\beta_k X_k.$$

Adjacent–Categories Logit Models

The adjacent-categories logit function used in ordinal multinomial logistic models is as below modeling two adjacent categories

$$\log\left(\frac{P\left(Y = j\right)}{P\left(Y = j+1\right)}\right) = \log\left(\frac{\pi_j}{\pi_{j+1}}\right).$$

Using this logit function, the adjacent-categories logit model is as below

$$\log\left(\frac{\pi_j}{\pi_{j+1}}\right) = \alpha_j + \sum_{k=1}^{K}\beta_k X_k.$$

Within this model, only adjacent categories will be used in odds resulting in using local odds ratios for interpretations, whereas within the cumulative logit models, the entire response scale is used for the model and cumulative odds ratio is used for their interpretation.

Continuation–Ratio Logit

The continuation-ratio logit function used in ordinal multinomial logistic models is as below

$$logit\left(\omega_j\left(X\right)\right) = \log\left(\frac{P\left(Y = j\right)}{P\left(Y \ge j+1\right)}\right)$$

$$= \log\left(\frac{\pi_j}{\pi_{j+1} + \cdots + \pi_J}\right), for\ j = 1, \cdots, J-1$$

where

$$\omega_j\left(X\right) = \frac{\pi_j\left(X\right)}{\pi_j\left(X\right) + \cdots + \pi_J\left(X\right)}.$$

Using this logit function, the continuation-ratio logit model is as below

$$logit\left(\omega_j\left(X\right)\right) = \alpha_j + \sum_{k=1}^{K}\beta_k X_k.$$

As described in Agresti (2007), this model is useful when a sequential mechanism determines the response outcome. Mechanisms like survival through various age periods would be suitable for such models. For more details and examples about the application of these models to real data see Ramezani (2016).

DIMENSION REDUCTION

When dealing with high dimensional data, methods such as principal component analysis, cluster analysis, discriminant analysis, and random forest are highly recommended (Wickham & Grolemund, 2016). Radom forest can be used for both categorical and continuous variables in two forms of classification random forest and regression random forest, respectively. Breiman (2001) proposed random forests, which uses decision trees. In addition to constructing each tree using a different bootstrap sample of the data, random forests change how the classification or regression trees are constructed to build the most optimal group of trees. This strategy turns out to perform very well compared to many other classifiers, including discriminant analysis, support vector machines and neural networks, and is robust against overfitting of the data (Liaw & Wiener, 2002).

Principal Component Analysis

Pearson (1901) and Hotelling (1933) introduced principal component analysis (PCA) to describe the variation in a set of multivariate data in terms of a set of uncorrelated variables. PCA is a variable dimension-reduction tool that can be used to reduce a large set of variables to a small set of new variables that still contains most of the information in the large set while reducing the dimension of the data. PCA is a mathematical procedure that transforms a number of correlated variables into a smaller number of uncorrelated variables called principal components. This will assist researchers with the multicollinearity issue that can negatively affect regular multiple linear regression models through creating a new set of uncorrelated variables. Multicollinearity happens when predictors are correlated with each other (Montgomery et al., 2012).

Among the newly created components of PCA, the first principal component accounts for as much of the variability in the data as possible, and each succeeding component accounts for as much of the remaining variability as possible.

Figure 1 shows a sample of a Scree plot, which is a widely used plot within PCA. Scree plots can list eigenvalues or percentage of variances as criteria of component selection. As seen on the following scree plot, the percentage of variance of the data explained by each component is listed on the Y-axis. The first principal component explains 42 percent of the variance, which is a significant amount of explained variation. This guarantees that this is the most important component, hence the first principal component, which should be kept in the model. The second principal component explains 18 percent of the variance, which in addition to the first one, these two principal components explain 60 percent of the model variation. Therefore, if someone wishes to ensure that 80 percent of variation is being captured, four components should be chosen and possibly used in future models. Of course, if the researchers are wishing to capture higher variation of the data, they would need to choose to keep higher number of components in their model.

The shape of scree plot and number of principal components, and how much variance each explains, vary in each data set but following the same steps can help researchers choose the appropriate number of principal components to use.

Figure 1. Scree plot using percentage of variances as component selection criterion

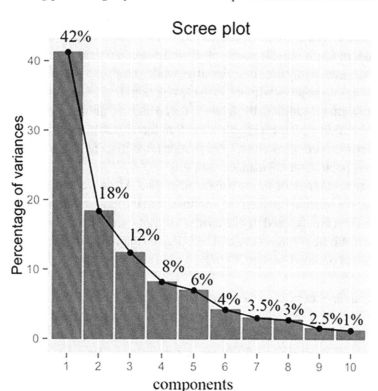

Within PCA, we typically have a data matrix of n observations on p correlated variables x_1, x_2,..., x_p. PCA looks for a transformation of the x_i into p new variables that are uncorrelated (Jolliffe, 2011). Principal component analysis is useful for finding new, more informative, uncorrelated features while reducing dimensionality by rejecting low variance features. One important point that should be considered by researchers is to make sure PCA is applied on data that have approximately the same scale in each variable.

For more details on this topic see Jolliffe (2011) and Wold, Esbensen, and Geladi (1987). "A user's guide to principal components" is another informative book by Jackson (2005) regarding PCA and its application, which we recommend reading. Chapter 8 of "Applied Multivariate Statistical Analysis" by Johnson and Wichern (2002) is another reference that provides more technical information about principal component analysis. Dunteman's book "Principal components analysis" shows interesting applications of PCA in social sciences (1989). Articles such as Raychaudhuri, Stuart, and Altman (1999) and Wiegleb (1980) provide examples of applications of PCA in microarray experiments within sporulation time series and ecological research, respectively.

Decision Trees and Random Forest

Random forest is an ensemble classifier that consists of many decision trees and outputs the class that is the mode of the class's output by individual trees. The term came from random decision forests, that was first proposed by Tin Kam Ho in 1995. The method combines Breiman's "bagging" idea and the random selection of features.

Decision trees, used in building random forests, are individual learners that are combined. They are one of the most popular learning methods commonly used for data exploration. We discuss some of the advantages of random forest here. It is one of the most accurate learning algorithms available. For many data sets, it produces a highly accurate classifier while running efficiently on large databases and handling thousands of input variables without variable deletion. It gives estimates of what variables are important in the classification. Additionally, it generates an internal unbiased estimate of the generalization error as the forest building progresses. Also, random forest has an effective method for estimating missing data and maintains accuracy when a large proportion of the data are missing. It has methods for balancing error in class population unbalanced data sets.

Generated forests can be saved for future use on other data. Moreover, prototypes are computed that give information about the relation between the variables and the classification. It computes proximities between pairs of cases that can be used in clustering, locating outliers, or give interesting views of the data by scaling. The capabilities of the above can be extended to unlabeled data, leading to unsupervised clustering, data views and outlier detection. Finally, it offers an experimental method for detecting variable interactions.

Some of the disadvantages of random forests are that they have been observed to overfit for some data sets with noisy classification or regression tasks. For data including categorical variables with different number of levels, random forests are biased in favor of those attributes with more levels. Therefore, the variable importance scores from random forest are not reliable for this type of data (Segal, 2004).

A tree is called a classification tree when the dependent variable is categorical and it is called a regression tree when the dependent variable is continuous. When classification decision trees are used while building the random forest for modeling categorical response variables, the respective random forest is referred to as classification random forest. On the other hand, when regression decision trees are used while building the random forest for modeling continuous response variables, the respective random forest is referred to as regression random forest.

For more details on each of the aforementioned random forest models, see Breiman (2001) and Liaw and Wiener (2002). We also recommend reading chapters 9 and 15 of "The elements of statistical learning" book by Friedman, Hastie, and Tibshirani (2001) to learn more about regression trees and random forests, respectively. Additionally "Decision trees and random forests: a visual introduction for beginners" by Smith (2017) has an easy-to-understand introduction to decision trees, random forests, and their applications. "Machine Learning With Random Forests And Decision Trees: A Visual Guide For Beginners" book by Hartshorn (2016) discusses these methods from a machine learning perspective, which we recommend to the readers.

Regression Shrinkage Methods

Two extensions of linear regression are ridge regression and LASSO, which are used for regularization. When applying multiple linear regression models, more features could be added to the model compared to the simple linear regression. Having more features may seem like a perfect way for improving the accuracy of the trained model by reducing the loss within the loss function. This is because the model that will be trained will be more flexible and will take into account more parameters that can potentially explain more variation of the response variable. On the other hand, we need to be extremely careful while adding more features to the model as this may increase the likelihood of overfitting the data. As we know, every research study, and the related data set, can have noisy samples as the samples are taken at random. Such noisy samples may lead to inaccuracies within each fitted model and hence it can lead to a low-quality model if not trained carefully. The model might end up memorizing the noise that exists within the noisy data set instead of learning the trend of the data. Overfitting can happen in linear models as well when dealing with multiple features. If not filtered and explored up front, some features can be more destructive to the accuracy of the model than helpful, repeat information that are already expressed by other features, and add high noise to the data set.

Therefore, statisticians have always tried assisting the applied researchers in avoiding overfitting. One of the most common mechanisms for avoiding overfitting is called regularization. A regularized machine learning model is a model that its loss function contains another element that should be minimized as well. The loss function includes two elements. The first one is what is used within regular linear regression models; it is the sum of the distances between each prediction and its ground truth or the observed value. The second element added to the loss function which is used in Ridge regression and LASSO models is the regularization term. It sums over squared β values and multiplies it by another parameter λ. The reason for doing that is to "punish" the loss function for high values of the coefficients β and prevent the overfitting of the regression models while using many variables in building it.

In general, simple models are better than complex models and usually do not face overfitting issues. Therefore, we should try to simplify the model as much as possible. The goal of the iterative process is to minimize the loss function. By punishing the β values, we add a constraint to minimize them as much as possible. Chapters 3 and 10 of "The elements of statistical learning" book by Friedman, Hastie, and Tibshirani (2001), as well as chapter 6 of "An introduction to statistical learning with application in R" by James, Witten, Hastie, and Tibshirani (2013), discuss shrinkage, related methods and examples using R, which is a statistical programing language.

Ridge Regression

There is a gentle trade-off between fitting the model and at the same time making sure that we are not overfitting it. This approach is called Ridge regression.

Ridge regression is an extension for linear regression. It is basically a regularized linear regression model, which was explained above. The λ parameter, also called tuning parameter, is a scalar that should be learned as well, using a method called cross validation, which is beyond the topic of this chapter.

An important fact we need to notice about ridge regression is that it enforces the β coefficients to be lower, but it does not enforce them to be zero. So, it shrinks them to zero but does not set them equal to zero. That is, it will not get rid of irrelevant features and variables but rather minimize their impact on the trained model to reduce the likelihood of the overfitting.

Another way to look at it, beyond the overfitting issue, is that having many variables at play in a multiple linear regression sometimes poses a problem of choosing the inappropriate variables for the linear model, which gives undesirable and unreliable output as a result. Ridge regression can help overcoming this issue. This method is a regularization technique in which an extra variable (tuning parameter) is added and optimized to offset the effect of multiple variables in linear regression, which can reduce the noise.

As described above, ridge regression essentially is an instance of linear regression with regularization. Mathematically, the model with ridge regression is given by

$$Y = X\beta + \epsilon$$

where Y is the dependent variable, X is the independent variable or a matrix of all predictors if there are multiple independent variables (features), β represents all the regression coefficients and ϵ represents the residuals or errors. Based on this, the variables are now standardized by subtracting the respective means and dividing by their standard deviations.

The tuning parameter (λ) is now included in the ridge regression model as part of regularization. The higher the value of λ is, the residual sum of squares tend to be closer to zero. The lower the λ is, the solutions conform to least square method. In simpler words, this parameter helps the model in deciding the effect of coefficients. λ is estimated using a technique called cross-validation.

For more details regarding ridge regression, LASSO, and their application in machine learning see Hastie, Tibshirani, and Wainwright (2015). Earlier applications of this method can be found in Marquardt and Snee (1975), Mahajan, Jain, and Bergier (1977), and Price (1977).

Lasso Method

Least absolute shrinkage and selection operator, abbreviated as LASSO, is a linear regression technique which also performs regularization on variables in consideration. LASSO is another extension built on regularized linear regression, but with a small difference. The only difference from ridge regression is that the regularization term is in absolute value. Setting the coefficient equal to zero, when the tuning parameter allows the model to do so, has a huge impact on the results. LASSO method overcomes the disadvantage of ridge regression by not only punishing high values of the coefficients β, but actually setting them to zero if they are not relevant. Therefore, one might end up with fewer features included in the model than originally entered into the model, which is a huge advantage. This also qualifies the LASSO to be considered a variable selection technique.

In fact, it almost shares a similar statistical analysis evident in ridge regression, except it differs in the regularization values. This means, it considers the absolute values of the sum of the regression coefficients (hence the 'shrinkage' feature). It even sets the coefficients to zero which reduces the errors and noise completely. In the ridge equation mentioned earlier, the error component has absolute values instead of squared values.

This method was proposed by Professor Robert Tibshirani. Tibshirani said, *Lasso minimizes the residual sum of squares to the sum of the absolute value of the coefficients being less than a constant. Because of the nature of this constraint, it tends to produce some coefficients that are exactly 0 and hence gives interpretable models.*

In his journal article titled *Regression Shrinkage and Selection via the Lasso,* Tibshirani gives an account of this technique with respect to various other statistical models such as all subset selection and ridge regression. He goes on to say that LASSO can even be extended to generalized linear regression models and tree-based models. In fact, this technique provides possibilities of even conducting statistical estimations. This method is widely applied in different fields. For more details about LASSO, its applications and extensions, we recommend "Statistical learning with sparsity: the lasso and generalizations" by Tibshirani and Wainwright (2015). Grouped LASSO, an extension of the LASSO technique, is frequently used in biomedical studies such as Lin, Wang, Liu, and Holtkamp (2013) and Rao, Nowak, and Rogers (2013).

Cluster Analysis

Clustering is a case reduction technique and can be viewed as a way of grouping together data samples that are similar in some way according to some criteria that researchers pick. Both similarities and dissimilarities can be used while defining different clusters and grouping cases together. It also is a form of unsupervised learning meaning that we generally do not have examples demonstrating how the data should be grouped together and instead the data guide us through this grouping based on the characteristics of them.

Therefore, one can say that clustering is a method of data exploration and a way of looking for patterns or structure in the data that are of interest. The goal is to group together "similar" data and the important question is how to find the similarities and dissimilarities and use them to group the data.

There exists no single answer in how to define the similarities. It depends on what we want to find or emphasize in the data; this is one reason why clustering can be a flexible tool based on what researchers need. The similarity measure is often more important than the clustering algorithm used in the data exploration as if the similarity is not measured properly, the clustering algorithm cannot do anything to fix that issue. Measures such as Pearson correlation coefficient and Euclidean distance are some examples of measures that quantifies the similarities among the data points.

Instead of talking about similarity measures and using them to define the clusters within the cluster analysis, we often equivalently refer to dissimilarity measures. Jagota (2013) defines a dissimilarity measure as a function $f(x,y)$ such that $f(x,y) > f(w,z)$ if and only if x is less similar to y than w is to z. This is always a pair-wise measure:

$$d_{euc}(x,y) = \sqrt{\sum_{i=1}^{n}(x_i - y_i)^2}$$

where n is the number of dimensions in the data vector.

Sometimes researchers care more about the overall shape of variables rather than the actual magnitudes of dissimilarities. In that case, we might want to consider cases similar when they are "up" and "down" together based on the measured variable of interest. In that case, Pearson linear relationship can be used as a measure of the overall shape.

$$\rho(x,y) = \frac{\sum\limits_{i=1}^{n}(x_i - \bar{x})(y_i - \bar{y})}{\sqrt{\sum\limits_{i=1}^{n}(x_i - \bar{x})^2}\sqrt{\sum\limits_{i=1}^{n}(y_i - \bar{y})^2}}$$

$$\bar{x} = \frac{1}{n}\sum_{i}^{n}x_i$$

$$\bar{y} = \frac{1}{n}\sum_{i}^{n}y_i$$

Within this calculation, the variables are shifted down by subtracting the means and then scaling them by dividing them by the standard deviations. This will standardize our data and make them have the mean of zero and standard deviation of one regardless of the unit of measurement. Pearson linear correlation is a measure that is invariant to vertically scaling and shifting of the expression values. The values are always between −1 and +1, where -1 shows a perfect negative linear correlation between two variables and +1 shows a perfect positive linear correlation between two variables. This is a similarity measure, but we can easily make it into a dissimilarity measure as below by defining d,

$$d = \frac{1 - \rho(x,y)}{2}$$

Pearson linear correlation only measures the degree of a linear relationship between two variables. If one wants to measure other relationships, there are many other possible measures.

Different clustering algorithms include, but are not limited to, hierarchical agglomerative clustering, K-means clustering and quality measures, and self-organizing maps.

To read more about this model and its applications in different fields, we recommend the following books and articles to the readers of this chapter. Books such as "Cluster Analysis for Researchers" by Charles Romesburg (2004) provides detailed information about this method and includes multiple examples. "Cluster analysis for applications: probability and mathematical statistics: a series of monographs and textbooks" by Michael R. Anderberg (2014) is another book discussing the applications of this method in detail. Chapter 12 of "Applied Multivariate Statistical Analysis" by Johnson and Wichern (2002) is another reference that provides more technical information about clustering methods. Additionally, we recommend reading chapters 13 and 14 of "The elements of statistical learning" book by Friedman, Hastie, and Tibshirani (2001) to learn more about unsupervised learning and clustering algorithms.

Articles such as Punj and Stewart (1983), Ketchen and Shook (1996), and Sturn, Quackenbush, and Trajanoski (2002) provide interesting examples of application of culuster analysis in marketing research, strategic management research, and microarray data and bioinformatics, respectively.

CONCLUSION

To summarize, in this chapter, we tried to assist reader in the understanding of different statistical methods and using their algorithms within machine learning and data analytics. We organized and explained various statistical strategies and algorithms based on the type of response variables used in each model. We first explained models used for modeling of continuous and categorical response variables and then moved on to explaining different approaches used for dimension reduction while working with various types of response and predictors when dealing with high dimensional data. These techniques can assist researchers in modeling of the big data, describing them and making inferences about them, and predicting the behavior of the data. Different approaches, based on the type of the variables involved in a study, were presented to help working with data sets in different dimensions and formats, reduce the dimensions of a big data set, and get efficient results. Once these methods are understood and the differences become clear, the data analysis stage is much easier to perform and many resources are available for programming and modeling in different software packages.

FUTURE RESEARCH DIRECTIONS

Different statistical algorithms and machine learning approaches were introduced, and discussed, in this chapter. Categorical statistical methods, especially ordinal logistic models, and classification approaches, such as classification random forest, are among the models not used by researchers as often as they should duo to their complexities and longer run time using different software packages. The computational burden and time-consuming nature of the existing algorithms for such approaches, based on the current computational capabilities, make such methods less popular among applied researchers and practitioners and therefore results in the use of less appropriate models by researchers when dealing with categorical and discrete response variables. This happens in both low and high dimensional data analysis.

Author suggests, and are currently working on, developing more powerful algorithms, which are computationally more advanced in terms of programming, that can handle applying such methods more efficiently, computationally. Developing such algorithms can encourage researchers to use these more appropriate models, which can guarantee reliable results, rather than using faster algorithms that ignore the categorical nature of variables to optimize the speed of the computation procedure.

We propose the development of such computationally efficient algorithms, in addition to using them within random forest, in neural network, deep learning, and artificial intelligence areas of research. Such methods and their application in neural network and deep learning can greatly benefit researchers in handling high dimensional data with varying types of variables.

ACKNOWLEDGMENT

This research received no specific grant from any funding agency in the public, commercial, or not-for-profit sectors. The author would like to thank Dr. Ali Ramezani and Dr. Iman Raeesi Vanani for their assistance with research and the compilation of this chapter.

REFERENCES

Agresti, A. (2007An Introduction To Categorical Data Analysis (2nd ed.). Wiley.

Anderberg, M. R. (2014). *Cluster analysis for applications: probability and mathematical statistics: a series of monographs and textbooks* (Vol. 19). Academic Press.

Breiman,L.(2001).Breiman.Randomforests.*MachineLearning*,*45*(1),5–32.doi:10.1023/A:1010933404324

Cokluk, O. (2010). Logistic Regression: Concept and Application. *Educational Sciences: Theory and Practice*, *10*(3), 1397–1407.

Dunteman, G. H. (1989). *Principal components analysis (No. 69)*. Sage. doi:10.4135/9781412985475

Friedman, J., Hastie, T., & Tibshirani, R. (2001). *The elements of statistical learning* (Vol. 1). New York: Springer Series in Statistics.

Hartshorn, S. (2016). *Machine Learning With Random Forests And Decision Trees: A Visual Guide For Beginners*. Kindle Edition.

Hastie, T., Tibshirani, R., & Wainwright, M. (2015). *Statistical learning with sparsity: the lasso and generalizations*. CRC Press. doi:10.1201/b18401

Hosmer, D., & Lemeshow, S. (2013). *Applied Logistic Regression* (3rd ed.). Willey Series in Probability and Statistics. doi:10.1002/9781118548387

Hosmer, D., Lemeshow, S., & May, S. (2008). Regression Modeling of Time-to-Event Data. Willey Series in Probability and Statistics, second edition. doi:10.1002/9780470258019

Jackson, J. E. (2005). *A user's guide to principal components* (Vol. 587). John Wiley & Sons.

Jagota, A. (2013). *Machine Learning Basics Kindle Edition* [Kindle Fire version]. Retrieved from Amazon.com.

James, G., Witten, D., Hastie, T., & Tibshirani, R. (2013). *An introduction to statistical learning* (Vol. 112). New York: Springer.

Johnson, R. A., & Wichern, D. W. (2002). Applied multivariate statistical analysis: Vol. 5. *No. 8*. Upper Saddle River, NJ: Prentice Hall.

Jolliffe, I. (2011). Principal component analysis. In *International encyclopedia of statistical science* (pp. 1094–1096). Berlin: Springer. doi:10.1007/978-3-642-04898-2_455

Ketchen, D. J. Jr, & Shook, C. L. (1996). The application of cluster analysis in strategic management research: An analysis and critique. *Strategic Management Journal*, *17*(6), 441–458. doi:10.1002/(SICI)1097-0266(199606)17:6<441::AID-SMJ819>3.0.CO;2-G

Lee, S. (2005). Application of logistic regression model and its validation for landslide susceptibility mapping using GIS and remote sensing data. *International Journal of Remote Sensing*, *26*(7), 1477–1491. doi:10.1080/01431160412331331012

Liaw, A., & Wiener, M. (2002). Classification and regression by randomForest. *R News*, *2*(3), 18–22.

Lin, H., Wang, C., Liu, P., & Holtkamp, D. J. (2013). Construction of disease risk scoring systems using logistic group lasso: Application to porcine reproductive and respiratory syndrome survey data. *Journal of Applied Statistics, 40*(4), 736–746. doi:10.1080/02664763.2012.752449

Mahajan, V., Jain, A. K., & Bergier, M. (1977). Parameter estimation in marketing models in the presence of multicollinearity: An application of ridge regression. *JMR, Journal of Marketing Research, 14*(4), 586–591. doi:10.1177/002224377701400419

Marquardt, D. W., & Snee, R. D. (1975). Ridge regression in practice. *The American Statistician, 29*(1), 3–20.

Montgomery, D. C., Peck, E. A., & Vining, G. G. (2012). *Introduction to linear regression analysis* (Vol. 821). John Wiley & Sons.

Peffer, M. E., & Ramezani, N. (2019). Assessing epistemological beliefs of experts and novices via practices in authentic science inquiry. *International Journal of STEM Education, 6*(1), 3. doi:10.118640594-018-0157-9

Price, B. (1977). Ridge regression: Application to nonexperimental data. *Psychological Bulletin, 84*(4), 759–766. doi:10.1037/0033-2909.84.4.759

Punj, G., & Stewart, D. W. (1983). Cluster analysis in marketing research: Review and suggestions for application. *JMR, Journal of Marketing Research, 20*(2), 134–148. doi:10.1177/002224378302000204

Ramezani, N. (2015). Approaches for missing data in ordinal multinomial models. In *JSM Proceedings, Biometrics section, New Methods for Studies with Missing Data Session*. Alexandria, VA: American Statistical Association Journal.

Ramezani, N. (2016). Analyzing non-normal binomial and categorical response variables under varying data conditions. In *Proceedings of the SAS Global Forum Conference*. Cary, NC: SAS Institute Inc.

Ramezani, N., & Ramezani, A. (2016). *Analyzing non-normal data with categorical response variables. In proceedings of the Southeast SAS Users Group Conference*. Cary, NC: SAS Institute Inc.

Rao, N., Cox, C., Nowak, R., & Rogers, T. T. (2013). Sparse overlapping sets lasso for multitask learning and its application to fmri analysis. In Advances in neural information processing systems (pp. 2202-2210). Academic Press.

Raychaudhuri, S., Stuart, J. M., & Altman, R. B. (1999). Principal components analysis to summarize microarray experiments: application to sporulation time series. In Biocomputing 2000 (pp. 455-466). Academic Press. doi:10.1142/9789814447331_0043

Romesburg, C. (2004). *Cluster analysis for researchers*. Lulu.com.

Segal, M. R. (2004). *Machine learning benchmarks and random forest regression*. Academic Press.

Smith, C. (2017). *Decision trees and random forests: a visual introduction for beginners*. Blue Windmill Media.

Sturn, A., Quackenbush, J., & Trajanoski, Z. (2002). Genesis: Cluster analysis of microarray data. *Bioinformatics (Oxford, England), 18*(1), 207–208. doi:10.1093/bioinformatics/18.1.207 PMID:11836235

Wickham, H., & Grolemund, G. (2016). *R for data science: import, tidy, transform, visualize, and model data*. O'Reilly Media, Inc.

Wiegleb, G. (1980). Some applications of principal components analysis in vegetation: ecological research of aquatic communities. In *Classification and Ordination* (pp. 67–73). Dordrecht: Springer. doi:10.1007/978-94-009-9197-2_9

Wold, S., Esbensen, K., & Geladi, P. (1987). Principal component Analysis. *Chemometrics and Intelligent Laboratory Systems*, 2(1-3), 37–52. doi:10.1016/0169-7439(87)80084-9

This research was previously published in the Handbook of Research on Big Data Clustering and Machine Learning; pages 135-151, copyright year 2020 by Engineering Science Reference (an imprint of IGI Global).

Chapter 8
Machine Learning Applications for Anomaly Detection

Teguh Wahyono
Satya Wacana Christian University, Indonesia

Yaya Heryadi
Bina Nusantara University, Indonesia

ABSTRACT

The aim of this chapter is to describe and analyze the application of machine learning for anomaly detection. The study regarding the anomaly detection is a very important thing. The various phenomena often occur related to the anomaly study, such as the occurrence of an extreme climate change, the intrusion detection for the network security, the fraud detection for e-banking, the diagnosis for engines fault, the spacecraft anomaly detection, the vessel track, and the airline safety. This chapter is an attempt to provide a structured and a broad overview of extensive research on anomaly detection techniques spanning multiple research areas and application domains. Quantitative analysis meta-approach is used to see the development of the research concerned with those matters. The learning is done on the method side, the techniques utilized, the application development, the technology utilized, and the research trend, which is developed.

INTRODUCTION

The aim of this chapter is to describe several applications of machine learning for anomaly detection. Although has received considerable attention from many researchers since 90's, the anomaly detection problem remained an interesting problem in computer vision field. Its wide potential applications ranging from climate change, computer network intrusion detection, financial transaction fraud detection, engines fault detection, spacecraft anomaly detection to vessel track and the airline safety detection. The emerging applications of machine learning methods in the past ten years has received great interests from many researchers to adopt machine lerning to address anomaly detection.

DOI: 10.4018/978-1-6684-6291-1.ch008

This paper started with literature review using quantitative analysis meta approach to analyze the main research progress, opportunities and trends, and research applications in the anomaly detection field. This systematic literature review will identify the most significant journals in the anomaly detection field, the opportunities and trends for anomaly detection method, identify research applications and trends in anomaly detection system and give the proposed method improvements for anomaly detection in the future.

This chapter is an attempt to provide a structured and a broad overview of extensive research on anomaly detection techniques spanning multiple research areas and application domains. quantitative analysis meta approach to see the development of the research concerned with those matters. The learning is done both on the method side, the techniques utilized, the application development, the technology utilized and the research trend which is developed.

BACKGROUND

Anomaly, also known as outliers, is a term refers to irregularity or deviation from the normal pattern (Chandola, et al., 2007). Yang (2007) refered the term anomaly to observation data that strongly inconsistent with the previous compiled data. Recently, Bloomquist (2015) defined anomaly as "*patterns or data points that do not conform to a well defined notion of normal behaviour.*"

Anomaly detection problem refers to the task of finding patterns in data that do not conform to expected behavior (Chandola, 2007). The problem is an interesting computer vision problem with many potential applications ranging from climate change detection, anomaly detection of fault tolerant robotic system (Jakimovski, 2011) to fraud transaction detection. In the past decade, anomaly detection problem has raised wide attention from various research domains due to its potential applications for recognizing indication that the underlying process that induces the data does not happen as expected. Depending on the context of the data, the detected anomalous data can be interpreted as either extreme climate change (Kawale, 2011), network security intrusion (Tsai, et al., 2010), medical diagnosis (Park, et al., 2015), engines fault (Djurdjanovic, et al., 2007), spacecraft anomaly detection (Fujimaki, et al., 2007), Mobility-Based Anomaly Detection in Cellular Mobile (Sun, et al., 2006) or vessel track and the airline safety diagnosis (Budalakoti et al., 2009).

Despite many studies have been reported, anomaly detection remained a challenging problem. A prominent study reported by (Chandola, et al., 2007) summarized several challenges in detecting anomaly as follows.

1. Defining a normal region which encompasses every possible normal behavior is very difficult. In addition, the boundary between normal and anomalous behavior is often not precise. Thus an anomalous observation which lies close to the boundary can actually be normal, and vice-versa.
2. When anomalies are the result of malicious actions, the malicious adversaries often adapt themselves to make the anomalous observations appear like normal, thereby making the task of defining normal behavior more difficult.
3. In many domains normal behavior keeps evolving and a current notion of normal behavior might not be sufficiently representative in the future. In medical research domain, concluded that the general pattern to be used as the expected behavior or reference is often unavailable.

4. The exact notion of an anomaly is different for different application domains. For example, in the medical domain a small deviation from normal (e.g., fluctuations in body temperature) might be an anomaly, while similar deviation in the stock market domain (e.g., fluctuations in the value of a stock) might be considered as normal. Thus applying a technique developed in one domain to another is not straightforward.

5. Availability of labeled data for training/validation of models used by anomaly detection techniques is usually a major issue.

6. Often the data contains noise which tends to be similar to the actual anomalies and hence is difficult to distinguish and remove.

There are two prominent applications of anomaly detection. *First*, detecting climate change. Climate anomaly refers to the irregularity of climate patterns that occurred in a region over a particular period (Kawale, 2011). The oddity or deviation of the climate from the previous patterns strongly affected variation and inconsistency of some other weather variables. Due to its important effect to various aspect of human life, climate anomaly has raised research attention from various research communities. In Indonesia, for example, one of the anomalies phenomenons is the occurrence of an extreme climate change called El Nino and La Nina. This phenomenon strung out the season irregularity. For example: rainfall declines between 40-80% of the normal circumstances, the air temperature increases sharply accompanied by various extreme phenomenons, such as whirlwind, dryness and declining in the food production (Prasetyo, et al., 2011).

Second, detecting computer network security violation. Many reports showed some evidences that the advent of computer network has to be followed by the technical development of the data securing (Yang, et al., 2015). The security of a network is often interrupted by the presence of a threat from inside or from outside of the network. That offensive can be hacker attacks which purposely to damage the network, or an intruder who is going to steal the important information which is available on the network. The anomaly detection method is very instrumental to analyze the beginning conditions of the emergence of an attack; capturing the suspicious packets of data in order that the system can anticipate the occurrence of an intrusion.

This chapter starts with a detailed analysis of various methods for anomaly detection using quantitative analysis meta-approach to analyze the development of the research on anomaly detection. The analysis will emphasize on several aspects mainly: theoretical, applications, and the research trend. Next, some machine learning methods for addressing one-class classification will be discussed.

LITERATURE REVIEW

Anomaly

Chandola, Banerjee & Kumar (2011) classified anomalies into four wide categories as follows.

Point Anomalies

A point anomaly is a single point that is classified to have a different value from the common data group. The example of the point anomaly can be seen in Figure 1, in which the single point A and the single point B have deviant values from the rest.

Figure 1. Point anomalies represented by A and B

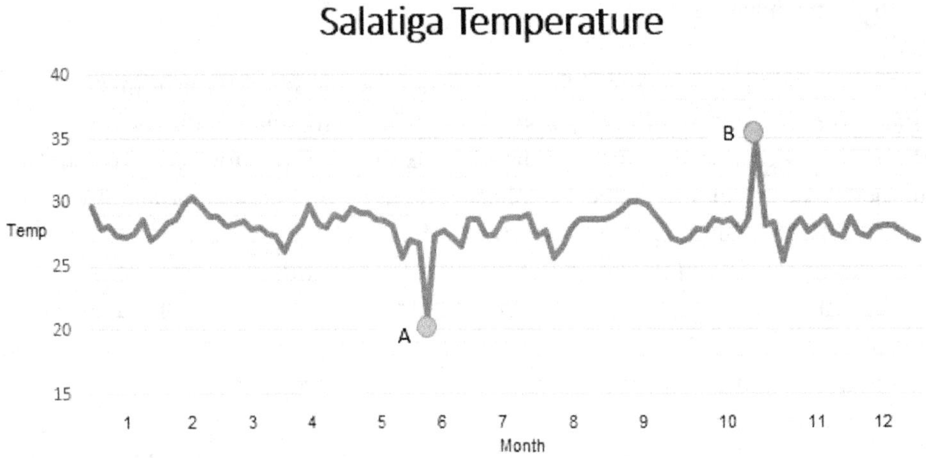

Salatiga Temperature

Contextual Anomalies

A contextual anomaly happens if the data is called as anomaly based on a context, whereas on another context, it is considered normal. A simple illustration on the contextual anomaly is the number of access on a server when the university students register their lessons in the beginning of the semester. The number of access will increase significantly in the registration period. In the context of the registration periode, this occurrence cannot be said as an anomaly, but when it is an anomaly when it happens outside the registration periode (Figure 2).

Collective Anomalies

A collective anomaly happens when it seen individually, the data is considered as normal, but it becomes anomaly when it happens simultaneously for a long period of time, longer from the same range of the other data surrounds it. The example of the point anomaly can be seen in Figure 3.

On the other hand, Xie et.al. said that anomaly can be classified into four types (Xie, et al., 2015):

1. **Constant**: The anomaly happens when sequential observations show constant values.
2. **Burst**: The anomaly happens when the observation data shows significant bursts in some points.
3. **Small Noise**: The anomaly happens when the observation data shows small noise that can influence the variance.
4. **Large Noise**: The anomaly happens when a large noise appears and increase the variance value.

Figure 2. Contextual anomalies

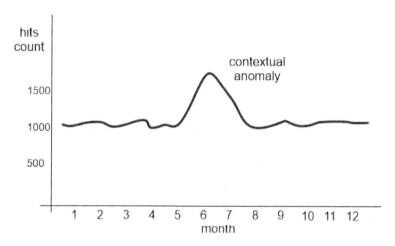

Figure 3. Collective anomalies from stackexchange.com
(Stack Exchange, 2017)

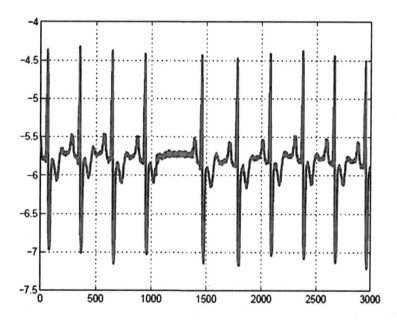

Further, detection is seen as a process to check something by using a specific way or technique. This detection can be done for various problems, such as a disease detection system, where the system identifies the problems connected to a disease, which is common to be called as symptoms. In this context, detection is used to find the anomaly in a group of data.

Figure 4. Four types of anomaly
(Xie, et al., 2015)

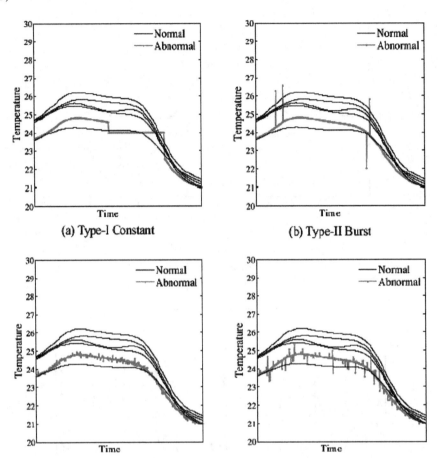

(a) Type-1 Constant   (b) Type-II Burst

(c) Type-III Small Noise   (d) Type-IV Large Noise

Methods, Applications, and Technological Issues

We have done a survey paper to know the method used, application and technological issues in anomaly detection. Following Kitchenham (2007) and Adisasmito (2007), literature mapping is implemented using systematic literature review (SLR) method. Several finding from literature review are as follows.

Research Question

Research Question is a beginning part and a running basic of SLR. Research Question is used to guide the seeking process and the literature extraction. The analysis and the synthesis of data, as a result of SLR, is the answer from Research Question which we decide on the front. The Research Question formulation should be based on the five elements which come to be called PICOC criteria consisted of: Population, Intervention, Comparison, Outcomes, and Context. Table 1 shows PICOC criteria in this research.

There are five research question in this study as shown in Table 2.

Table 1. PICOC criteria

Population	software, anomaly detection system
Intervention	anomaly detection technique, prediction methods, application area, technological issues
Comparison	n/a
Outcomes	Performance
Context	studies in academia, small and large datasets

Table 2. Research questions

ID	Research Question	Motivation
RQ1	Which journal is the most significant with anomaly detection field?	Identify the most significant journals in the anomaly detection field.
RQ2	What kind of methods are used for anomaly detection system?	Identify opportunities and trends for anomaly detection method
RQ3	What kind of research applications are selected by researchers in anomaly detection field?	Identify research applications and trends in anomaly detection system
RQ4	Which method performs best when used for anomaly detection?	Identify the best method for anomaly detection
RQ5	What kind of method improvements are proposed for anomaly detection?	Identify the proposed method improvements for anomaly detection

Search Strategy

The searching strategy is started from the source determination of the literature headed for. In this research, it is determined six sources as follow: (1) IEEE Explore Digital Library (ieeexplore.ieee.org), (2) ACM Digital Library (dl.acm.org), (3) Semantic Scholar (www.semanticscholar.org), (4) Science Direct (sciencedirect.com), (5) Springer Link (springerlink.com), and (6) EBSCO (www.ebscohost.com).

The next stage is the determination stage of keyword (search string) from the literature searched accordance with the PICOC which had been designed before. The selection of the right keyword will determine the level of the literature accuracy discovered.

The following search string in this research was eventually used:

(anomaly OR outlier* OR intrusion OR security) AND (detect* OR predict* OR prone* OR probability OR assess* OR estimat* OR classificat*) AND (system OR software OR application OR methods)

Significant Journal Publications

This research discovers 28 articles related to the Research Question that has been defined previously. Those articles come from a variety of digital library website which has been predetermined with the compositions such as in Figure 5 below.

Figure 6 shows the paper's distribution by the year of publication. From those data can be seen that every year, there are always be the research related to the anomaly detection of data. That matter shows that this research was conducted continuously and growing from year to year.

Figure 5. The composition of the article based on a data source

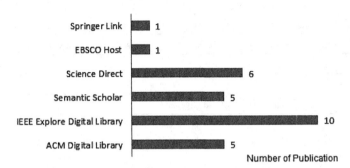

Figure 6. Distribution of selected paper over the year

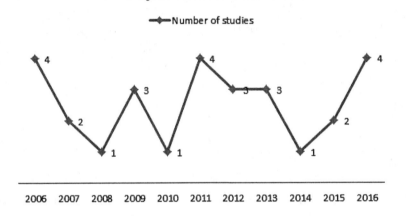

Methods Used in Anomaly Detection System

Anomaly Detection Systems are generally designed using four methods to execute the predictions, those are; statistical, data mining, machine learning, and graphical modeling as shown in Figure 7. The most popular method and used a lots are data mining (45% utilization), followed by machine learning (29% utilization).

The statistical method is the most basic method for used in the forecasting study. This study discovers two statistical methods used, those are; regression modeling and exponentially weighted moving average. A multinomial logistic regression modeling approach is used for detecting the attacks on the computer networks (Wang, 2005). Whereas the exponentially weighted moving average approach is used for enhancing security using mobility-based anomaly detection system (Sun, et al., 2006).

The data mining method is most widely used in the study of this anomaly detection. The various methods used are seen in Figure 8. There are seven data mining methods used in these studies, namely Clustering and outlier detection, DBScan, Fuzzy Logic, Genetic Algorithm (GA), Hidden Markov Models (HMM), Selection Criteria and Support Vector Machines (SVM). Fuzzy Logic and SVM are the most widely used methods, that is each at 25% of the researches by the method of data mining.

Figure 7. Methods used in anomaly detection system

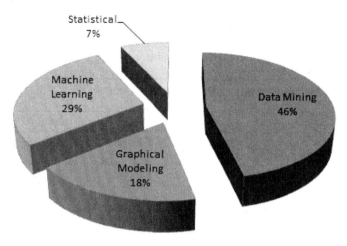

Figure 8. The various methods of data mining are used

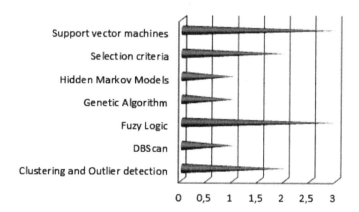

Data mining is a method that concerned with uncovering patterns, associations, changes, anomalies, and statistically significant structures and events in data (Grossman, 1997). Data mining can help improve the process of intrusion detection by adding a level of focus to anomaly detection (Patcha, 2007). Table 3 shows list of the papers that using data mining in their research, with the highlighting features and specific methodology.

The machine learning methods used in this research can be seen in Figure 9. There are five methods which are used, namely semi-supervised learning, Discrete Wavelet Transform (DWT), decision tree, Principal Component Analysis (PCA) and Bayesian approach. Bayesian approach is the most widely used methods, that is 40% of the existing research.

Basically, machine learning is a computer process to learn from the data. It is a type of Artificial Intelligence (AI). With machine learning, systems have the ability to change their execution strategy on the basis of newly acquired information (2007). Machine learning system can automatically build the model based on the training dataset, which contains data instances that can be described using a set of attributes and associated labels (2013). Table 4 shows list of the papers that using machine learning in their research, with the highlighting features and specific methodology.

Table 3. A summary of data mining based anomaly detection

Reference	Highlighting Features	Specific Methodology
Abadeh, et.al (2007)	This research is design and analysis of genetic fuzzy systems, implemented for intrusion detection in computer networks	Genetic Fuzzy
Ensafi et.al (2008)	It is optimizing Fuzzy K-means for network anomaly detection using PSO	Fuzzy Swarm Intelligent
Kawale et.al (2011)	Anomaly Construction in Climate Data	Selection Criteria
Das and Parthasarathy (2009)	It detects anomaly Detection and Spatio-Temporal Analysis of Global Climate System	Spatial-Temporal
Kao et.al (2009)	It is motivating Complex Dependence Structures in Data Mining: A Case Study with Anomaly Detection in Climate	dependence structure and the use of copulas
Budalakoti (2009)	Anomaly Detection and Diagnosis Algorithms for Discrete Symbol Sequences with Applications to Airline Safety	Sequence Miner vs Hidden Markov Models
Tsai et.al (2010)	A triangle area based nearest neighbors approach to intrusion detection	Triangle area based nearest neighbors (TANN)
Horng et.al (2011)	A novel intrusion detection system based on hierarchical clustering and support vector machines	Support Vector Machines
Yi et.al (2011)	Incremental SVM based on reserved set for network intrusion detection	Support Vector Machines
Celik et.al (2011)	Anomaly Detection in Temperature Data Using DBSCAN Algorithm	DBScan
Kavitha et.al (2012)	An ensemble design of intrusion detection system for handling uncertainty using Neutrosophic Logic Classifier	Fuzzy (Neutrosophic Logic Based Classifier)
Fu et.al (2012)	A Hybrid Anomaly Detection Framework in Cloud Computing Using One-Class and Two-Class Support Vector Machines	One Class and two Class SVM
Karami et.al (2016)	A fuzzy anomaly detection system based on hybrid PSO-Kmeans algorithm in content-centric networks	Fuzzy- Kmeans algorithm

Figure 9. The various methods of machine learning are used

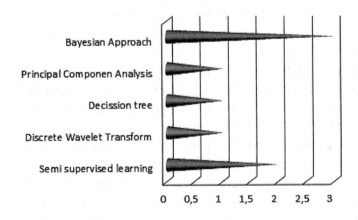

Table 4. Summary of machine learning based anomaly detection

Reference	Highlighting Features	Specific Methodology
Fujimaki et.al (2006)	An Approach to Spacecraft Anomaly Detection Problem Using Kernel Feature Space	Principal Component Analysis
Yairi et.al (2006)	Telemetry-mining: A Machine Learning Approach to Anomaly Detection and Fault Diagnosis for Space Systems	Dynamics Bayesian Networks
Djurdjanovic et.al (2007)	Immune Systems Inspired Approach to Anomaly Detection and Fault Diagnosis for Engines	Exponentially Weighted Moving Average (EWMA)
Farid et.al (2010)	Combining Naive Bayes and Decision Tree for Adaptive Intrusion Detection	Naïve Bayes and Decision tree
Chitrakar et.al (2012)	Anomaly-based Intrusion Detection using Hybrid Learning Approach of combining k-Medoids Clustering and Naïve Bayes Classification	k-Medoids Clustering and Naive Bayes Classification
Gornitz et.al (2013)	Toward Supervised Anomaly Detection	semi-supervised anomaly detection
Mascaro et.al (2014)	Anomaly detection in vessel tracks using Bayesian networks	Bayesian Networks
Casas et.al (2016)	Machine-Learning Based Approaches for Anomaly Detection and Classification in Cellular Networks	Discrete Wavelet Transform

The researches which are using a graphical modeling and spatio-temporal approach are the latest researches in the imaging field, satellite imagery and several papers with a spatio-temporal thematic. Rembold (2013) using low-resolution satellite imagery for yield prediction and yield of anomaly detection. Another papers are imaging of neuronal activity (Park, 2015), visual anomaly detection in spatio-temporal (Alcaide, et al., 2016), and spatio-temporal graphical modeling approach to anomaly detection in distributed cyber-physical systems (Liu, 2016).

Research Application in Anomaly Detection System

Anomaly detection system so far has been applied in a variety of applications. Figure 6 showing that there are seven applications which are implementing this model. This research is applied in various fields such as Network Intrusion Detection, Spatial Detection, Medical, Diagnosis for Engine, Tracking and Safety, Climate Data and Cellular Mobile.

Figure 10. Research application in anomaly detection system

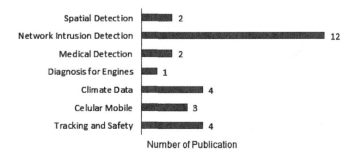

The Most field which is using anomaly detection system is a field of the Network Intrusion Detection that is as many as 12 papers or 43% of all the exciting papers. Next came after by the research topics in the field of Tracking and Safety along with Climate Data that each at 15% of the existing research.

Performance Methods Used in Anomaly Detection

At this section will be selected the papers which are discussing up to the performance of each of the methods applied for the anomaly detection. After a further selection, there were elected 10 papers that have a discussion up to the performance testing, shown with the value of the Detection Rate. The exciting data shows in Table 5 that the anomaly detection by using Data Mining-Genetic Fuzzy approach has the highest level of the detection rate that is at 99,53.

Table 5. Performance methods by detection rate

Author	Method	Detection Rate
Gornitz et.al (2013)	Machine learning-semi supervised anomaly detection	70,00
Casas et.al (2016)	Machine learning-Discrete Wavelet Transform	80,00
Kavitha et.al 2012)	Data Mining-Fuzzy Neutrosophic Logic Based	99,02
Abadeh, et.al (2007)	Data Mining-Genetic Fuzzy	99,53
Tsai et.al (2010)	Data Mining-Triangle area based nearest neighbors	99,27
Ensafi et.al (2008)	Data Mining-Fuzzy Swarm Intelligent	95,88
Horng et.al (2011)	Data Mining-support vector machines	95,70
Yi et.al (2011)	Data Mining-support vector machines	81,38
Chitrakar (2012)	Machine learning - k-Medoids Clustering and Naive Bayes	99,43
Farid et.al (2010)	Machine learning-Naïve Bayes and Decision tree	99,00

Strategy to Improve Accuracy for Anomaly Detection

According to the selected papers in this study, anomaly detection systems are generally designed using four methods to execute the predictions, those are; statistical, data mining, machine learning, and graphical modeling. To improve the accuracy for anomaly detection, the researchers proposed some strategy.

The first, if anomaly detection system using a machine learning method, note that there are two techniques in the application of machine learning. Both of these techniques are supervised and unsupervised learning. The results of several studies indicate that the supervised learning methods significantly outperform the unsupervised ones if the test data contains no unknown attacks (Omar, 2013). Among the supervised methods, the best performance is achieved by the non-linear methods, such as Support Vector Machines methods (Horng, et al., 2011; Yi, et al., 2011).

Secondly, data mining has been used in anomaly detection system by many researchers in recent years (Agrawal, 2015). In this area, hybrid approaches provide better results and overcome the drawback of one approach over the other (Fu, et al., 2012; Agrawal, 2015; Karami, et al., 2016). In hybrid approaches, researchers can combine the modified version of already existing algorithms. For example, there are one-class and two-class Support Vector Machines for a hybrid anomaly detection framework (Fu, et al., 2012) and a novel fuzzy anomaly detection based on Hybrid PSO-Kmeans (Karami, 2016). Chitrakar (2012) using a hybrid approach to combine Support Vector Machine classification and K-Medoids clustering for the network intrusion detection system. The experimental results demonstrate that hybrid approach performs high performance, higher accuracy, increase in detection rate and reduction in mean time of false alarm rate.

MACHINE LEARNING CONCEPT

Definition of Machine Learning

Machine learning is an emerging research field which has raised wide attention in the past ten years due to many successfull reports to address many problems, such as classification, using big data. As a branch of Artificial Intelligence [42. 43], machine learning focuses on the development of algorithm that automatically improves its performance with experiences. Specifically, Mitchell (1997) defined machine learning as algorithms that "*learn from experience E with respect to some class of tasks T and performance measure P, if its performance at tasks in T, as measured by P, improves with experience E.*" In the machine learning context, the process in which an algorithm improving its performance with experiences commonly refers to learning process.

Following Mitchell (1997), the learning process of a machine learning algorithm can be characterized by the following factors.

1. Training experience which depends on the following factors. *First*, the type of training experience from which a machine learning algorithm will learn. *Second*, the degree to which the learning algorithm controls the sequence of training examples. *Third*, how well the training dataset represents the distribution of examples over which the final system performance P must be measured.
2. Target function.
3. Representation of the learned function.
4. Learning algorithm.

Issues in Machine Learning

According to Mitchell (1997) the main issues in using machine learning approach can be summarized into Table 6.

Types of Learning

Learning types in machine learning can be categorized as shown in Figure 11.

Table 6. Main issues in machine learning

Categories	Issues
Learning algorithm	• What algorithms exist for learning general target functions from specific training examples? • In what settings will particular algorithms converge to the desired function, given sufficient training data? • Which algorithms perform best for which types of problems and representations?
The size of training dataset	• How much training data is sufficient? • What general bounds can be found to relate the confidence in learned hypotheses to the amount of training experience and the character of the learner's hypothesis space?
Prior knowledge	• When and how can prior knowledge held by the learner guide the process of generalizing from examples? • Can prior knowledge be helpful even when it is only approximately correct?
Model testing	• What is the best strategy for choosing a useful next training experience, and how does the choice of this strategy alter the complexity of the learning problem?
Target function representation	• What is the best way to reduce the learning task to one or more function approximation problems? • What specific functions should the system attempt to learn? • Can this process itself be automated?
Optimization algorithm	• How can the learner automatically alter its representation to improve its ability to represent and learn the target function?

Figure 11. Types of machine learning

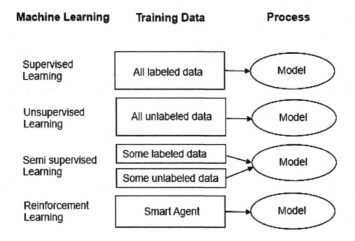

Supervised Learning

Supervised learning uses the training data in performing prediction or classification. The data in the supervised learning is labeled data. The final purpose of this method is to identify the new input label by using the existing feature in the new data.

Some algorithms include in the supervised learning are:

- Multiple Regressions
- Decision Tree.

- Random Forest
- Naive Bayes Classifier
- Nearest Neighbor Classifier
- Support Vector Machine
- Artificial Neural Network

Unsupervised Learning

Unsupervised learning does not use training data in prediction or clarification. In the unsupervised learning, the system learns unlabeled data based on the features of the data. This algorithm does not have target variable and aims to classify almost similar objects in a specific area. For an example, if we want to classify the customers of a company based on similar traits like age, education, and hobby, we do not need any training data.

Some algorithms include in the unsupervised learning are:

- Hierarchical Clustering
- K-Means
- DBSCAN
- Fuzzy C-Means
- Self-Organizing Map

Semi-Supervised Learning

Semi-supervised Learning combines supervised and unsupervised learning. In this process, the system learns the labeled data and unlabeled data simultaneously to be made as training data.

Reinforcement Learning

Reinforcement learning is a method that teaches us how to act to face a problem, in which the action has impacts. This method is applied in a smart agent so that it can adapt with the condition in its environment.

MACHINE LEARNING APPROACH TO ANOMALY DETECTION

A plethora of machine learning methods to address anomaly detection tasks can be categorized broadly into supervised and unsupervised method categories (Park, 2015; Rembold, 2016). The supervised methods view anomaly detection as classification problem in which converting the problem into one or binary classification problem. The unsupervised methods, on the other hand, convert the problem into clustering task followed by apply thresholds to decide whether or not the data conform the "normal" data.

The term one-class classification was coined by Moya et.al (1996) refers to a task of "*learning to characterize the target class by examining only target data without requiring training samples of non-target data.*" This task can be viewed as a special type of classification problem. However, in contrast to binary or multi-class classification, one-class classification typically uses only samples from the as-signed class called target class. In anomaly detection problem, as an example of one-class classification problem, the target class is typically called "normal" classes. Any sample which does not conform the "normal" class is categorized as "anomaly" data.

Wide potential application of one-class classification have gained research interest resulted in a plethora of proposed methods. Among the prominent methods based on support vector machine were proposed by Schölkopf *et al.* (2000) and Tax *et al.* (2004).

K-Nearest Neighbor

k-Nearest Neighbor (kNN) is a prominent machine learning method categorized as a supervised learning algorithm. Given *n*-samples

$$S = \left\{ \left(x_1, y_1\right), \left(x_2, y_2\right), \ldots, \left(x_n, y_n\right) \right\} \subseteq \mathcal{R}^m \times Y$$

as input data such that each $x_i \in \mathcal{R}^m$ represented by *m*-atributes (feature) a_j as follows:

$$x_i = a_1\left(x_i\right), a_2\left(x_i\right), \ldots, a_m\left(x_i\right)$$

where: $y_i \in Y = \left\{v_1, v_2, \ldots, v_p\right\}$ are x_i labels. The objective of k-NN method is to approximate a target function $f : \mathcal{R}^m \rightarrow Y$ with an approximation function $h : \mathcal{R}^m \rightarrow Y$ such that for a new data x, $h\left(x\right) = \hat{f}\left(x\right)$.

Many studies have adopted k-NN as a classifier to categorize samples into either normal or anomaly class. Following Yang & Liu (1999) the decision rule in k-NN can be written as:

$$y\left(x, c_j\right) = \sum_{d_i \in kNN} sim\left(x, d_i\right) y\left(d_i, c_j\right) - b_j$$

where: $y(x,c_j) \in \{0,1\}$ the classification for sample d_i with respect to category c_j; $sim(x,d_i)$ be similarity between the test sample x and the training data d_i which can be measured using various distance functions such as: Euclidean distance between x and d_i points, cosine value between x and d_i vectors; and b_j is the optimal threshold for binary decisions which can be learned from training dataset. From learning process, the value of b_j is selected from all possible values that give the best performance of k-NN. From eq (1), the thresholding parameter (b_j) is very instrumental to categorize data as normal data or anomaly data in anomaly detection (Liao, et al., 2002).

The advantages of k-NN for anomaly detection are mainly: (1) no prior probabilities required, and (2) the algorithm is computationally efficient compared to other methods such as Bayesian classifier. The main computation is finding the k-nearest neighbors for the test data that involves sorting training data.

One-Class SVM

One-class Support Vector Machine (OCSVM) model proposed by Schölkopf (2000) is a kernel-based techniques for supervised learning. In general, the objective of this model is to estimate functions that describes the underlying distributions of the input data which have been mapped into a feature space using a kernel. Next, the knowledge about the data distribution can be used to address problem on the basis of the raw data. In the context of anomaly detection, the estimated function describe distribution of the target (normal) dataset. So that, any data does not conform the estimated distribution of the dataset is categorized as anomaly data.

In general, the OCSVM algorithm works by firstly mapping the target data into the feature space $\mathcal{F}$ corresponding to the kernel k followed by separating the data in feature space $\mathcal{F}$ using a hyperplane from the origin with maximum margin. Finally, the algorithm returns a function f that takes the value +1 in a region capturing most of the data points, and -1 elsewhere. For a new point x, the value $f(x)$ is determined by evaluating which side of the hyperplane it falls on in the feature space $\mathcal{F}$.

The OCSVM model can be viewed as an adaptation of SVM (Vapnik, 1998) for one-class classification problem. In contrast to binary/multi-class SVM model, which is trained using dataset with two (or more) classes, the OCSVM model is trained using only one class dataset called "normal" or target samples to learn pattern of the given samples. Having been trained using the normal cases, the model is then used to predict new samples.

The term "planar OCSVM" often used in literature to differentiate the model (Schölkopf, 2000) from similar model proposed (Tax, 2004). The former model estimates a hyperplane to separate data in feature space that maximized the margin between the target data and the origin point; whilst, the later model estimates the smallest hypersphere that encloses the target data points. The later model will be described in 3.

The theoretical foundation of OCSVM can be described as follows. Consider some samples $x_1, x_2, \ldots,$ $x_l \in \mathcal{X} \subseteq \mathcal{R}^{\mathbb{N}}$ where l is the number of samples are samples drawn from an unknown underlying probability distribution P. Mathematically, the aims of OCSVM algorithm is to estimate a set S so that a new, previously unseen, pattern x_{l+1} lies in S with an apriori-specified probability. The OCSVM model training comprises of several steps. *First*, mapping the data into the feature space $\mathcal{F}$ using kernel k. Consider ϕ be a feature map, $\phi : \mathcal{X} \rightarrow \mathcal{F}$ such that the image of ϕ (the dot product in $\mathcal{F}$) can be computed using kernel:

$$k\left(x, y\right) = \left(\phi\left(x\right) \cdot \phi\left(y\right)\right) \tag{1}$$

For example: Gaussian kernel which can be formulated as:

$$k\left(x, y\right) = e^{\frac{-x-y^2}{c}} \tag{2}$$

where c is a kernel parameter.

Second, minimizing the objective function which can be represented as follows.

$$\min_{w \in \mathcal{F}, \xi \in \mathcal{R}^n, \rho \in \mathcal{R}} \frac{1}{2} w^2 + \frac{1}{vl} \sum_i \xi_i - \rho \tag{3}$$

subject to:

$$\left(w \cdot \phi\left(x_i \right) \right) \geq \rho - \xi_i \text{ for all } i=1,2,3,\ldots,l \tag{4}$$

$$\xi_i \geq 0 \text{ for all } i=1,2,3,\ldots,l \tag{5}$$

where: w be the weight vector parameters, $\upsilon \in \{0,1\}$ is a parameter, ρ be the offset parameterizing a hyperplane in the feature space $\mathcal{F}$ associated with the kernel k, and ξ_i or slack variable are penalized in the objective function. The minimization problem can be solved by setting out Lagrangian multipiers $\alpha_i, \beta_i \geq 0$.

$$\mathcal{L}\left(w, \xi, \rho, \alpha, \beta \right) = \frac{1}{2} w^2 + \frac{1}{\upsilon l} \sum_i \left(\xi_i - \rho \right) - \sum_i \alpha_i \left(\left(w \cdot \phi\left(x_i \right) \right) - \rho + \xi_i \right) - \sum_i \beta_i \xi_i \tag{6}$$

where: ξ_i or slack variable are penalized in the objective function. The coefficient α_i can be computed as the solution of the dual problem:

$$\sum_i \alpha_i = 1 \tag{7}$$

$$\min_\alpha \frac{1}{2} \sum_{i,j} \alpha_i \alpha_j \phi\left(x_i, x_j \right) \text{ subject to } 0 \leq \alpha_i \leq \frac{1}{\upsilon l} \tag{8}$$

If w and ρ solve this problem then the decision function is:

$$f\left(x \right) = \text{sgn}\left(\sum w.\phi\left(x \right) - \rho \right) \tag{9}$$

By using substitution,

$$f\left(x \right) = \text{sgn}\left(\sum_i \alpha_i \phi\left(x_i, x \right) - \rho \right) \tag{10}$$

where:

$$\rho = \sum_j \alpha_j \phi\left(x_j, x_i \right) \tag{11}$$

The function f will be positive (+1) for most examples x_i contained in the training dataset and negative (-1) elsewhere.

The immediate advantages of OCSVM models are: (1) the model required less number of samples in compared to binary/multi-class SVM; and (2) highly applicable for detecting anomaly data when there was only a small proportion of labeled data from the whole dataset (Chen, et al., 2001); and (3) the model can handle imbalanced data.

Support Vector Data Description

Support Vector Data Description (SVDD) is a model proposed Tax and Duin (2004) to address one-class classification problem. The proposed model estimates a hypersphere, characterized by center a and radius $R>0$, that gives a closed boundary around the normal data points in feature space $\mathcal{F}$ with minimum diameter.

Consider l-samples $x_1, x_2, \ldots, x_l \in \mathcal{X} \subseteq \mathcal{R}^{\mathbb{N}}$ as target data for which we want to obtain a description. Consider the error function:

$$F(R, a) = R^2 + C\sum_i \xi_i \text{ for } 1=1,2,\ldots,l \tag{12}$$

subject to:

$$x_i - a^2 \leq R^2 + \xi_i \text{ for } 1=1,2,\ldots,l. \tag{13}$$

where: $\xi_i \geq 0$ be slack parameter, and C be penalty parameter to control the trade-off between the volume and the errors. This problem can be transformed into minimization problem using Lagrangian multiplier $\alpha_i \geq 0$ and $\gamma_i \geq 0$ as follows.

$$\mathcal{L}(R, a, \alpha_i, \gamma_i, \xi_i) = R^2 + C\sum_i \xi_i - \sum_i \alpha_i \left\{ R^2 + \xi_i - \left(x_i^2 - 2a \cdot x_i + a^2 \right) \right\} - \sum_i \gamma_i \xi_i \tag{14}$$

By minimizing $\mathcal{L}$ with respect to R, a and ξ_i; and maximizing $\mathcal{L}$ with respect to α_i and γ_i followed by setting partial derivatives to zero gives the constraints:

$$\sum_i \alpha_i = 1 \tag{15}$$

$$a = \sum_i \alpha_i x_i \tag{16}$$

$$C - \alpha_i - \gamma_i = 0 \text{ or } \alpha_i = C - \gamma_i \tag{17}$$

Since $\alpha_i \geq 0$ and $\gamma_i \geq 0$, by substitution, $0 \leq \alpha_i \leq \gamma_i$. Further substitution resulted:

$$\mathcal{L}\left(R, a, \alpha_i, \gamma_i, \xi_i\right) = \sum_i \alpha_i \left(x_i \cdot x_i\right) - \sum_{i,j} \alpha_i \alpha_j \left(x_i \cdot x_j\right) \qquad (18)$$

Equation (16) shows that the center of the sphere is a linear combination of the data points. However, for data description, only data points x_i with $\alpha_i > 0$ are needed. These data points are called the support vectors of the description (SV's). By definition, R2 is the distance from the center of the sphere a to (any of the support vectors on) the boundary.

Testing a new data point z is implemented in two steps as follows. First, the distance of the data point to the center of the sphere (a), $d(z,a)$, has to be calculated using the following formula.

$$d\left(z, a\right) = \left(z.z\right) - 2\sum_i \alpha_i \left(z.x_i\right) + \sum_{i,j} \alpha_i \alpha_j \left(x_i.x_j\right) \qquad (19)$$

Finally, a test data point z is accepted when this distance is smaller or equal than the radius. Hence, $d(z,a) \leq R^2$

$$R^2 = \left(x_k.x_k\right) - 2\sum_i \alpha_i \left(x_i.x_k\right) + 2\sum_{i,j} \alpha_i \alpha_j \left(x_i.x_j\right) \qquad (20)$$

where: x_k is any support vector whose $\alpha_k < C$.

Zero-Boundary Long Short-Term Memory Model

Anomaly detection task from discrete sequence (time-series) of data has gained considerable attention from many researchers due to its wide applications in various fields such as cybersecurity and weather analysis. The study from Chandola (2012), for example, reviewed some prominent anomaly detections from time-series data. The main objective of anomaly detection from discrete sequence is locating a segment of data sequences that does not follow the pattern in a normal dataset.

Zero-boundary Long Short-term Memory Model was proposed by Roberts & Nair (2018). Architecture of the proposed model comprises of two parts. The first part (encoder) is based on Long Short-term Memory model and the second part (decoder) is based on one-class SVM model. Having this architecture, the model can be viewed as a mixed of LSTM model proposed by Hochreiter & Schmidhuber (1997) and one-class SVM model (2000).

The proposed model comprises of a modified LSTM autoencoder and an array of One-Class SVMs. The LSTM takes in elements from a sequence and creates context vectors that are used to predict the probability distribution of the following element. These context vectors are then used to train an array of One-Class SVMs. These SVMs are used to determine an outlier boundary in context space.

The mathematical foundation for this model can be described as follows. Let $D = \{x_1, x_2, \ldots, x_n\}$ is n-samples where $x_i = x_{i1}, x_{i2}, \ldots, x_{2m} \in \mathcal{R}^m$ for $i = 1, 2, \ldots, n$ be a discrete sequence with length m. Let's define a language as a finite subset $L \subseteq \mathcal{R}^m$. A discrete sequence x_i is categorizd as normal if $x_i \in L$; otherwise it is categorized as anomaly. If x_i as an anomaly data then there exists $x_{ij}, 1 \leq j \leq m$ such that

Figure 12. Architecture of Zero-Boundary LSTM
(Roberts & Nair, 2018)

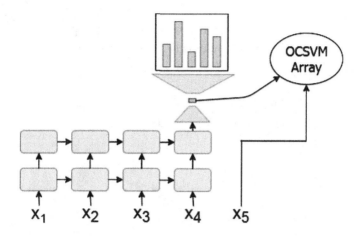

$P\left(x_{ij} \mid x_{i1},\ldots,x_{i,j-1}; L\right) = 0$. Following this definition, machine learning algorithm aims to appriximate the target function $f(x,L)$ where:

$$f\left(x,L\right) = \begin{cases} 1, & \textit{if there is } x_{ij} \textit{ such that } P\left(x_{ij} \mid x_{i1},\ldots,x_{i,j-1}; L\right) = 0 \\ 0, & \textit{otherwise} \end{cases} \tag{21}$$

Since $P\left(x_{ij} \mid x_{i1},\ldots,x_{i,j-1}; L\right) = 0$ then $P\left(x_{i1},\ldots,x_{i,j-1} \mid x_{ij} ; L\right) = 0$. Consequently:

$$f\left(x,L\right) = \begin{cases} 1, & \textit{if there is } x_{ij} \textit{ such that } P_{x_{ij}}\left(x_{i1},\ldots,x_{i,j-1}; L\right) = 0 \\ 0, & \textit{otherwise} \end{cases} \tag{22}$$

where: $P_{x_{ij}}$ be the probability under a specified x_{ij}.

The objective function of the model can be represented as follows.

$$\mathcal{L} = \sum_{i=1}^{n-1} - \log\left(P\left(x_{i+1} \mid D\left(E\left(x;\theta_{E}\right)_{i} ;\theta_{D}\right)\right)\right) \tag{23}$$

where:

$$E\left(x;\theta_{E}\right) : \Sigma^{n} \rightarrow \mathcal{R}^{n \times e} \text{ is LSTM encoder} \tag{24}$$

$$D\left(y;\theta_{D}\right) : \mathcal{R}^{e} \rightarrow \mathcal{R}^{|\Sigma|} \text{ is MLP decoder} \tag{25}$$

$$O_{\sigma}\left(cv\right): \mathcal{R}^{\varepsilon} \to \mathcal{R} \text{ is OCSVM for element } \sigma \in \Sigma \tag{26}$$

The LSTM autoencoders are trained by reconstructing their own input. Output of the encoder is the expected probability distribution for the $i+1$ element given the first i elements. The model is trained using stochastic gradient descent learning algorithm to learn θ_E and θ_D with the cross entropy as the objective function.

We can then train each OCSVM O$\sigma \in$ O with the context vector set from the corresponding Y$\sigma \in$ Y using the method from Schölkopf (2000). We now describe how to approximate the function f(x). Given, $\theta 0$ E and O, we define g $\approx$ f as

$$g\left(x\right) = \begin{cases} 1, & \text{if there is } x_i \in x \text{ such that } O_{x_i}\left(E\left(x;\theta_E'\right)_{i-1}\right) < t_{\alpha} \\ 0, & \text{otherwise} \end{cases} \tag{27}$$

where: t_{α} be a threshold hyperparamater.

CONCLUSION

The study regarding on the anomaly detection is a very important thing in the life of human being. The various phenomenon often occurs related to the anomaly study. The network intrusion detection is the most widely fields using the technique of the anomaly detection. Followed by the tracking and safety field, climate prediction, cellular technology, medical, spatial detection and diagnosis for the engine.

The Anomaly Detection System are generally designed using four methods to execute the predictions, namely statistical, data mining, machine learning and graphical modeling. The most popular method and widely used are data mining (45%), followed by machine learning (29% utilization). Whereas the approach of graphical modeling used in the latest researches at the field of imaging, satellite imagery and several researches with a spatiotemporal thematic.

Machine learning is basically the process by which a computer learns from the data. Anomaly detection is an interesting problem in machine learning with any applications. Two most effective machine learning techniques used to detect anomaly are supervised and unsupervised learning. For supervised learning anomaly detection case, the detection is done by training the data points so that the can be classified into two groups of anomaly and non-anomaly, while in the unsupervised learning, we can apply a threshold to decide whether or not the data is anomaly.

Furthermore, to improve the accuracy for anomaly detection, this study suggest to using a hybrid approach in data mining to combine the modified version of already existing algorithms. Hybrid approaches provide better results, higher accuracy, increase in detection rate and reduction in mean time of false alarm rate.

REFERENCES

Abadeh, M. S., Habibi, J., & Lucas, C. (2007). Intrusion detection using a fuzzy genetics-based learning algorithm. *Journal of Network and Computer Applications, 30*(1), 414–428. doi:10.1016/j.jnca.2005.05.002

Adisasmito, W. (2007). Systematic Review Penelitian Akademik Bidang Kesehatan Masyarakat. Jurnal Makara Kesehatan, 11.

Agrawal, S., & Agrawal, J. (2015). Survey on Anomaly Detection using Data Mining Techniques. International Conference on Knowledge Based and Intelligent Information and Engineering Systems. *Procedia Computer Science, 60*, 708–713. doi:10.1016/j.procs.2015.08.220

Alcaide. (2016). Visual Anomaly Detection in Spatio-Temporal Data using Element-Specific References. *2016 IEEE VIS.*

Blomquist, H., & Moller, J. (2015). *Anomaly detection with Machine learning.* Uppsala Universitet.

Budalakoti, S., Srivastava, A. N., & Otey, M. E. (2009). Anomaly Detection and Diagnosis Algorithms for Discrete Symbol Sequences with Applications to Airline Safety. *IEEE Transactions on Systems, Man, and Cybernetics Part C, 39*(1), 101–113.

Casas, P. (2016). *Machine-Learning Based Approaches for Anomaly Detection and Classification in Cellular Networks. 2016 The Traffic Monitoring and Analysis workshop.* TMA.

Celik, M., Dadaser-Celik, W., & Dokuz, A. S. (2011). Anomaly detection in temperature data using DBSCAN algorithm. *11 International Symposium on Innovations in Intelligent Systems and Applications.* 10.1109/INISTA.2011.5946052

Chandola, V., Banerjee, A., & Kumar, V. (2007). *Anomaly detection – a survey.* Technical Report 07-017. Computer Science Department, University of Minnesota.

Chandola, V., Banerjee, A., & Kumar, V. (2012). Anomaly detection for discrete sequences: A survey. *IEEE Transactions on Knowledge and Data Engineering, 24*(5), 823–839. doi:10.1109/TKDE.2010.235

Chen, Y., Zhou, X. S., & Huang, T. S. (2001). One-class SVM for learning in image retrieval. In *Image Processing, 2001. Proceedings 2001 International Conference on* (Vol. 1, pp. 34-37). IEEE.

Chitrakar, R., & Chuanhe, H. (2012). Anomaly detection using Support Vector Machine classification with k-Medoids clustering. *Proceedings of IEEE Third Asian Himalayas International Conference on Internet (AH-ICI).* 10.1109/AHICI.2012.6408446

Das, M., & Parthasarathy, S. (2009). Anomaly detection and spatio-temporal analysis of global climate system. In *Proceedings of the Third International Workshop on Knowledge Discovery from Sensor Data.* ACM. 10.1145/1601966.1601989

Djurdjanovic, D., Liu, J., Marko, K. A., & Ni, J. (2007). Immune Systems Inspired Approach to Anomaly Detection and Fault Diagnosis for Engines. *2007 International Joint Conference on Neural Networks.* 10.1109/IJCNN.2007.4371159

Ensafi, R., Dehghanzadeh, S., Mohammad, R., & Akbarzadeh, T. (2008). Optimizing Fuzzy K-means for network anomaly detection using PSO. *Computer Systems and Applications, IEEE/ACS International Conference.*

Farid, D. M., Harbi, N., & Rahman, M. Z. (2010). Combining naive bayes and decision tree for adaptive intrusion detection. *International Journal of Network Security & Its Applications, 2*(2).

Fu, S., Liu, J., & Pannu, H. (2012). A Hybrid Anomaly Detection Framework in Cloud Computing Using One-Class and Two-Class Support Vector Machines. In *Advanced Data Mining and Applications.* Springer Berlin Heidelberg. doi:10.1007/978-3-642-35527-1_60

Fujimaki, R., Yairi, T., & Machida, K. (2005). An approach to spacecraft anomaly detection problem using kernel feature space. In *Proceedings of the eleventh ACM SIGKDD international conference on Knowledge discovery in data mining (KDD '05).* ACM. 10.1145/1081870.1081917

Gornitz, N., Kloft, M., Rieck, K., & Brefeld, U. (2013). Toward supervised anomaly detection. Journal Artificial Intelligence. *Intestinal Research, 46,* 235–262.

Grossman, R. (1977). *Data Mining: Challenges and Opportunities for Data Mining During the Next Decade.* Academic Press.

Hochreiter, S., & Schmidhuber, J. (1997). Long short-term memory. *Neural Computation, 9*(8), 1735–1780. doi:10.1162/neco.1997.9.8.1735 PMID:9377276

Horng, S.-J., Su, M.-Y., Chen, Y.-H., Kao, T.-W., Chen, R.-J., Lai, J.-L., & Perkasa, C. D. (2011). A novel intrusion detection system based on hierarchical clustering and support vector machines. *Expert Systems with Applications, 38*(1), 306–313. doi:10.1016/j.eswa.2010.06.066

Jakimovski, B. (2011). Biologically Inspired Approaches for Anomaly Detection within a Robotic System. In Biologically Inspired Approaches for Locomotion. Anomaly Detection and Reconfiguration for Walking Robots (pp. 127-150). Springer. doi:10.1007/978-3-642-22505-5_7

Kao, A. R., Ganguly, S. C., & Steinhaeuser, K. (2009). Motivating Complex Dependence Structures in Data Mining: A Case Study with Anomaly Detection in Climate. *2009 IEEE International Conference on Data Mining Workshops,* 223-230. 10.1109/ICDMW.2009.37

Karami, A. (2016). *A Novel Fuzzy Anomaly Detection Algorithm Based on Hybrid PSO-Kmeans in Content-Centric Networking. In Handbook of Research on Advanced Hybrid Intelligent Techniques and Applications.* IGI Global.

Kavitha, B., Karthikeyan, D. S., & Maybell, P. S. (2012). An ensemble design of intrusion detection system for handling uncertainty using Neutrosophic Logic Classifier. *Knowledge-Based Systems, 28*(0), 88–96. doi:10.1016/j.knosys.2011.12.004

Kawale, J. (2011). *Anomaly Construction in Climate Data: Issues and Challenges. Technical Report.* Department of Computer Science, University of Minnesota.

Kitchenham, B., & Charters, S. (2007). *Guidelines for performing Systematic Literature Reviews in Software Engineering.* EBSE Technical Report Version 2.3.

Liao, Y., & Vemuri, V. R. (2002). Use of k-nearest neighbor classifier for intrusion detection. *Computers & Security, 21*(5), 439–448. doi:10.1016/S0167-4048(02)00514-X

Liu, C., Ghosal, S., Jiang, Z., & Sarkar, S. (2016). An unsupervised spatiotemporal graphical modeling approach to anomaly detection in distributed CPS. In *Proceedings of the 7th International Conference on Cyber-Physical Systems (ICCPS 2016)*. IEEE Press. 10.1109/ICCPS.2016.7479069

Mascaroa, S., Nicholson, A., & Korb, K. (2014). Anomaly detection in vessel tracks using Bayesian Networks. *International Journal of Approximate Reasoning*, 55.

Michell, T. (1997). *Machine Learning*. Mc Graw Hill.

Moya, M., & Hush, D. (1996). Network constraints and multi- objective optimization for one-class classification. *Neural Networks, 9*(3), 463–474. doi:10.1016/0893-6080(95)00120-4

Omar, S. (2013). Machine Learning Techniques for Anomaly Detection: An Overview. *International Journal of Computer Applications, 79*(2).

Park, Y., Wang, H., Nobauer, T., Vaziri, A., & Priebe, C. E. (2015). Anomaly Detection on Whole-Brain Functional Imaging of Neuronal Activity using Graph Scan Statistics. *Computer Networks, 51*, 3448–3470.

Prasetyo, S.Y.J.P., Subanar, W. E., & Daryono, B.S. (n.d.). ESSA: Exponential Smoothing and Spatial Autocorrelation, Methods for Prediction of Outbreaks Pest In Indonesia. *International Review Computer and Software*.

Rembold. (2013). Using Low Resolution Satellite Imagery for Yield Prediction and Yield Anomaly Detection. *Yaogan Xuebao, 5*, 1704–1733.

Roberts, C., & Nair, M. (2018). *Arbitrary Discrete Sequence Anomaly Detection with Zero Boundary LSTM*. arXiv preprint arXiv:1803.02395

Schölkopf, B., Williamson, R. C., Smola, A. J., Shawe-Taylor, J., & Platt, J. C. (2000). Support vector method for novelty detection. *Advances in Neural Information Processing Systems*, 582–588.

Stack Exchange. (2017). *Difference between contextual anomaly and collective anomaly*. Retrieved from https://stats.stackexchange.com/questions/323553

Sun, B., Yu, F., Wu, K., Xiao, Y., & Leung, V. C. M. (2006). Enhancing Security Using Mobility-Based Anomaly Detection in Cellular Mobile Networks. *IEEE Transactions on Vehicular Technology, 55*(4), 1385–1396. doi:10.1109/TVT.2006.874579

Tax, D. M., & Duin, R. P. (2004). Support vector data description. *Machine Learning, 54*(1), 45–66. doi:10.1023/B:MACH.0000008084.60811.49

Tsai, C.-F., & Lin, C.-Y. (2010). A triangle area based nearest neighbors approach to intrusion detection. *Pattern Recognition, 43*(1), 222–229. doi:10.1016/j.patcog.2009.05.017

Vapnik, V. (1998). *Statistical learning theory*. Chichester, UK: Wiley.

Wahyono, T. (2017). Anomaly detection to evaluate in-class learning process using distance and density approach of machine learning. *International Conference on Innovative and Creative Information Technology (ICITech)*. 10.1109/INNOCIT.2017.8319138

Wang, Y. (2005). A multinomial logistic regression modeling approach for anomaly intrusion detection. *Computers & Security, 24*(8), 662–674. doi:10.1016/j.cose.2005.05.003

Xie, M., Hu, J., & Guo, S. (2015). Segment-based anomaly detection with approximated sample covariance matrix in wireless sensor networks. Parallel and Distributed Systems. *IEEE Transactions on, 26*(2), 574–583.

Yairi, T., & Kawahara. (2006). Telemetry-mining: a machine learning approach to anomaly detection and fault diagnosis for space systems. *2nd IEEE International Conference on Space Mission Challenges for Information Technology (SMC-IT'06)*. 10.1109/SMC-IT.2006.79

Yang, Y., & Liu, X. (1999). A re-examination of text categorization methods. In *Proceedings of the 22nd annual international ACM SIGIR conference on Research and development in information retrieval* (pp. 42-49). ACM.

Yang, Z., Meratnia, N., & Havinga, P. (2007). *Outlier Detection Techniques For Wireless Sensor Networks: A Survey*. Department of Computer Science, University of Twente.

Yi, Y., Wu, J., & Xu, W. (2011). Incremental SVM based on reserved set for network intrusion detection. *Expert Systems with Applications, 38*(6), 7698–7707. doi:10.1016/j.eswa.2010.12.141

This research was previously published in Computational Intelligence in the Internet of Things; pages 49-83, copyright year 2019 by Engineering Science Reference (an imprint of IGI Global).

APPENDIX

Case Study: Detecting Anomaly Data Using Distance kNN Method

Wahyono et.al (2017) did a simple research to see the data anomaly of the students' grades, especially for Religion and Civics lessons of 140 students is a school in Salatiga. The research was implemented in an application by using an R Programming.

The program codes for the data initiation are shown in Box 1.

Box 1.

```
1  #Call Data Set Nilai.csv
2  set.seed(1000)
3  x1=rnorm(50)
4  y1=rnorm(50)
5  nilai <- "nilai.csv"
6  mydata1 <- read.csv(nilai)
7  plot(mydata1,pch=16)
```

Those codes produced outputs sowed in the diagram below, which illustrate the plots of the students' grades' data (Figure 13).

Figure 13. Data plot

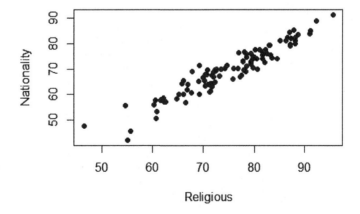

The anomaly detection was done by using distance based approach, using *distance to k-Nearest Neighbor* (k-NN) as the outlier score. The algorithms from the anomaly detection by using distance based with k-NN as the outlier score were:

1. Determine the number of the closest neighbors ((k) parameter).
2. Determine the distance of every pair of data and sort them.

3. Determine the closest neighbor based on the minimum distance to –k.
4. Determine the category of the closest neighbors.
5. The conclusion was, a data can be called as anomaly if the point had the longest distance from the k of the clossest neighbors or if the point had largest distance average from the closest neighbors.

The program codes for determine distance matrix and distance to nearest neighbor are shown in Box 2.

Box 2.

```
 9   #Determine Distance Matrix and Distance to kth nearest neighbor (k=5)|
10   DMatrix=as.matrix(dist(mydata1))
11   kdist=1:140
12 ▾ for(i in 1:140){
13     kdist[i]=(sort(DMatrix[i,]))[6]
14   }
15
16   #Plotting data
17   library(ggplot2)
18   library(gridExtra)
19
20   #ordinary plot
21   ggplot(data=mydata1,aes(x=Religious,y=Nationality,size=3))+geom_point()
```

Ordinary plot could be shown as in Figure 14.

Figure 14. Ordinary plot

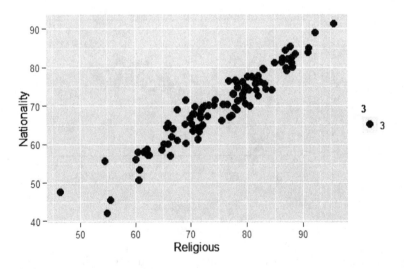

The program codes for ploting with color determined by kdist are shown in Box 3.

Box 3.

```
26  #Plot with Color Determined by kdist
27  #and with Gradient Plot (Heatmap)
28  ggplot(data=mydata1,aes(x=Religious,y=Nationality,col=kdist,size=3))+geom_point()+
29    scale_colour_gradientn(colours=c("black", "red"))
30
```

Gradient plot could be shown as in Figure 15.

Figure 15. Gradient plot

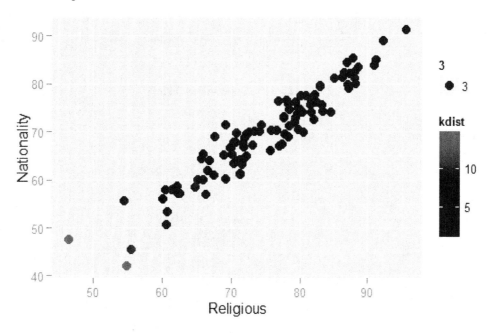

By applying distance to k-Nearest Neighbor as the score, the Density Curve for the Outlier Score could be shown as in Figure 16.

Based on the above graphic, the lines perceives as outliers could further be found. Next, an analysis based on k-dist could provide Ggplot graphic shown in Figure 17.

Finding rows with outliers is shown in Box 4.

Box 4.

```
> #Finding Rows with Outliers
> (1:140)[kdist>=6]
[1]    7   30   35   98 107 110 134 138 139
```

After finding rows with outliers were performed, it could also be concluded that the distance based model could identify 9 students whose grades could be seen as anomaly, which were students number 7, 30, 35, 98, 107, 110, 134, 138 dan 139.

Figure 16. Density curved

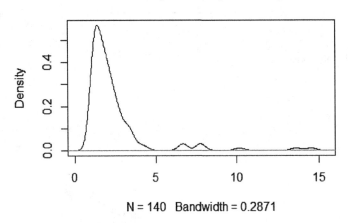

Figure 17. Ggplot analysis based on k-dist

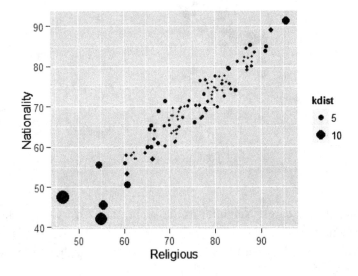

Chapter 9
Machine Learning With Avatar-Based Management of Sleptsov Net-Processor Platform to Improve Cyber Security

Vardan Mkrttchian
 https://orcid.org/0000-0003-4871-5956
HHH University, Australia

Leyla Ayvarovna Gamidullaeva
 https://orcid.org/0000-0003-3042-7550
Penza State University, Russia

Sergey Kanarev
Penza State University, Russia

ABSTRACT

The literature review of known sources forming the theoretical basis of calculations on Sleptsova networks and on the basis of authors' developments in machine learning with avatar-based management established the basis for the future solutions to hyper-computations to support cyber security applications. The chapter established that the petri net performed exponentially slower and is a special case of the Sleptsov network. The universal network of Sleptsov is a prototype of the Sleptsov network processor. The authors conclude that machine learning with avatar-based management at the platform of the Sleptsov net-processor is the future solution for cyber security applications in Russia.

DOI: 10.4018/978-1-6684-6291-1.ch009

INTRODUCTION

Information and Communication Technology is acknowledged as crucial part of our current society, accessing within every level of our social environment. Along with the implementation of Information and Communication Technology, comes an important part of securing it. Their evolution and development has brought many benefits and have also given rise to cybercrime actors, serious cyber-attacks that had been demonstrated over the past few years. Cyber security has become an important subject of national, international, economic, and societal importance that affects multiple nations (Walker, 2012). Many countries have come to understand that this is an issue and has developed policies to handle this in an effort to mitigate the threats (Dawson, Omar, & Abramson, 2015). To address the issue of cyber security, various frameworks and models have been developed. Traditional approaches to managing security breaches is proving to be less effective as the growth of security breaches are growing in volume, variation and velocity (Bhatti & Sami, 2015). The purpose of this chapter is to show what future cyber security as engineering science and technology expects. In addition, the authors propose future solutions for the use of computer with a Sleptsov net processor when it will be actually created and practically implemented. The authors of the chapter did not consider the credibility issues of Sleptsov nets computing but completely trusted the creator of Sleptsov net as a processor, based on open sources, in particular on publications and webinars of IGI Global (Zaitsev, 2016; Zaitsev, et al., 2016; Zaitsev, 2018). Based solely on these publications in recent years in IGI Global and own experience, the authors research the emerging trends and perspectives of digital transformation of the economy using machine learning with avatar-based management at the platform of Sleptsov net processor and propose further prospects for development of hyper-computation.

BACKGROUND

Many researchers compare machine learning solutions for cyber security by considering one specific application (e.g., Buczak and Guven, 2016; Blanzieri and Bryl, 2008; Gardiner and Nagaraja, 2016) and are typically oriented to Artificial Intelligence experts.

The term "cyber security" refers to three things:

1. A set of activities and other measures, technical and non-technical, intended to protect computers, computer networks, related hardware devices and software, and the information they contain and communicate, including software and data, as well as other elements of cyberspace, from all threats, including threats to national security;
2. The degree of protection resulting from the application of these activities and measures;
3. The associated field of professional endeavor, including research and analysis, aimed at implementing those activities and improving their quality (Jenab, et al., 2018).

At the same time, our previous research of the problem of cyber security showed that cyber security is a section of information security, within the framework of which the processes of formation, functioning and evolution of cyber objects are studied. It is necessary to identify sources of cyber-danger formed while determining their characteristics, as well as their classification and formation of regulatory documents, implementation of security systems in future. However, working on the application of the machine learning for Cyber Security applications with the use of developed by the authors Avatars-Based Management techniques, we came to the conclusion that this is not so, and the built-in cyber security systems can be destroyed by the same artificial intelligence.

The search for a solution to this discrepancy leads to a thought about advantages of natural intelligence displayed by humans where everything is interconnected, logical and protected (Mkrttchian, et al., 2015).

This paper is specifically aims to research the emerging trends and perspectives of digital transformation of the economy using machine learning with avatar-based management at the platform of Sleptsov net processor, and to identify their main limitations.

Sleptsov net concept mends the flaw of Petri nets, consisting in incremental character of computations, which makes Sleptsov net computing a prospective approach for ultra-performance concurrent computing (Zaitsev, 2018).

A Sleptsov net (SN) is a bipartite directed multi-graph supplied with a dynamic process (Zaitsev, 2016). An SN is denoted as $N=(P,T,W,\mu0)$, where P and T are disjoint sets of vertices called places and transitions respectively, the mapping F specifies arcs between vertices, and $\mu0$ represents the initial state (marking). The mapping $W: (P \times T) \rightarrow N \cup \{-1\}$, $(T \times P) \rightarrow N$ defines arcs, their types and multiplicities, where a zero value corresponds to the arc absence, a positive value – to the regular arc with indicated multiplicity, and a minus unit – to the inhibitor arc which checks a place on zero marking. N denotes the set of natural numbers. To avoid nested indices we denote w,i j j− = w(p, t) and+ =) . The mapping $\mu: P \rightarrow N$ specifies the place marking (Zaitsev, 2018).

Based on the previous research, performed by D. Zaitsev (2018; 2019), the main conclusion was drawn that Sleptsov networks are executed exponentially faster than Petri nets that makes it possible to recommend them as a parallel computing model for subsequent practical implementation.

Calculations on the networks of Sleptsov acquire all new applications presented in the works. First of all, computations on Sleptsov networks may be used for those applications in which parallel programming style can bring significant acceleration of computations.

Effective practical implementation of computations on Sleptsov networks requires the development of appropriate specialized automation systems for programming and hardware implementation of processors of Sleptsov networks. In addition, further development of theoretical methods of proving the correctness of programs in the language of Sleptsov networks and the development of universal networks that use mass parallelism are needed.

The advantages of computing on the Sleptsov networks are visual graphic language, the preservation of the natural domain parallelism, fine granulation of parallel computing, formal verification methods for parallel programs, fast mass-parallel architectures that implement the computation model (Zaitsev, 2018).

MAIN FOCUS OF THE CHAPTER

Issues, Controversies, Problems, Solutions and Recommendations

Machine learning (ML) was introduced in the late 1950's as a technique for artificial intelligence (AI) (Ambika, 2018). Over time, its focus evolved and shifted more to algorithms that are computationally viable and robust. One of the classical definitions of Machine Learning is the development of computer models for learning processes that provide solutions to the problem of knowledge acquisition and enhance the performance of developed systems (Duffy, 1995).

Machine learning is the use of artificial intelligence (AI) that provides systems with the capability to learn and automatically improve from experience (data) without being explicitly programmed. Machine learning focuses on developing computer programs that can access data and use them to learn by themselves.

Ideology of Machine Learning based on the principles of multiple use (reusability) and free distribution (share ability) copyright courses. Therefore, developers of training courses must adhere to generally accepted standards. To date, the most widely used models of the following courses:

1. Model IEEE LOM (Learning Object Model), developed by the LTSC (Learning Technology Standard Committee) in 2002. The entire set of learning objects is divided into 9 composite hierarchies (categories): General (General), life cycle (Life Cycle), metadata (Metadata), technical (Technical), education (Education), legal (Rights), communication (Relation), annotation and classification (Annotation and Classification).

2. System specifications consortium IMS (such as egg Content Packaging Specification, Metadata Specification, Digital Repositories Interoperability, Digital Repositories).

3. Specifications Committee AICC (Aviation Industry Computer-Based Training Committee) originally intended for the development of computer-based training systems and technologies in the aviation industry.

4. Specification SCORM (Shareable Course Object Reference Model), developed in the framework of the ADL (Advanced Distributed Learning), carried out by the Ministry of Defense. This is the industry standard for exchange of training materials based on tailored specifications ADL, IEEE, IMS. AICC. SCORM is the basis of the model modular design of educational material by separating the individual autonomous educational units (SCO - Shareable Content Objects) and their representation in the Web- specific repositories. SCO modules can be assembled together in various combinations and compiled into electronic textbooks using LMS- system. Thus, if in the first E-Learning systems, a teacher was expected to collect their own training courses to keep in his personal computer, and then manually organize a nationwide educational content, with the advent of such specifications as SCORM, this work is automated with the possibility of using Web 2.0 technologies and service-oriented approach.

Another pressing problem of modern machine learning systems is the problem of creating a student model based on the tracking of personal information related to learning trajectories passing on various training modules or web-services, the courses tendered tests. For these purposes, there is also a range of specifications, the most famous of which are:

- IEEE PAPI (Personal and Private Information);
- IMS LIP (Learner Information Package).

It uses the language XML (eXtension Markup Language) to write to the user's profile his curriculum vitae, teaching history, language skills, preferences to use computer platforms, passwords, access to training, etc. These data are then used to account for the individual characteristics of the student in determining the best means and methods of teaching.

Competency assessments for learning (learning competency assessment) are also used standardized specifications.

Figure 1. Screen-stop of the modeling supercomputer with Sleptsov net processor to visualize of a report on the work of Cyber Security system

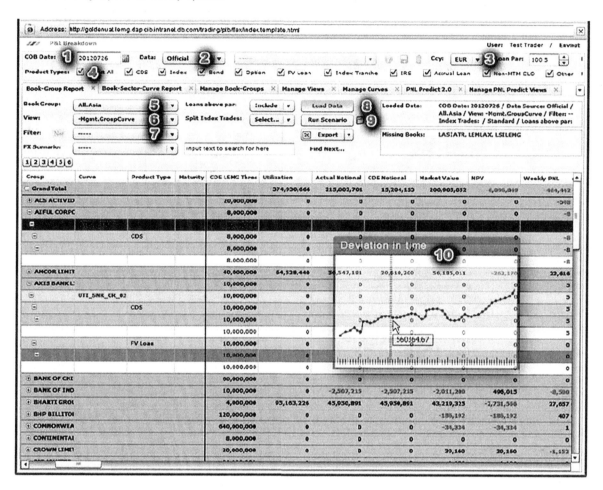

Having considerable experience in Intellectual Control and Communication, Avatar–Based Learning, Teaching and Training, and Avatar-Based Management, there is a need in modelling a joint system of Machine Learning with Avatar-Based Management with the use of Sleptsov net processor.

We define as an Avatar-Based Management (A-BM) model variability hypergraph VMG, consisting of two sets and predicate:

$$VMG = (V, U, P), \tag{1}$$

Set *V* describes the structure of a hypergraph on the vertex level:

$$V = \{v_{i,(weight)}\}, \, i = 1, 2, \ldots, N, \tag{2}$$

where N – is the total number of peaks is corresponding to the total number of characteristics of the A-BM model variability; *weight* - vertex weight in form n.1.1.1 (Figure 3) corresponding to the index of the corresponding characteristics in the hierarchical structure of the A-BM model variability.

Figure 2. Block diagram of the model of platform for supercomputer with Sleptsov net processor in support cyber security applications

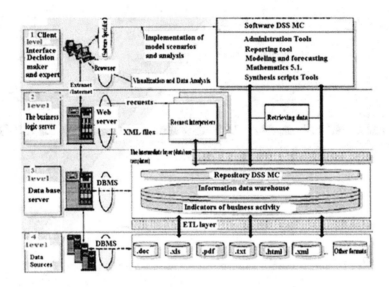

Set U has a capacity corresponding to the number of possible configurations of the A-BM:

$$U = \{u_j\} \; ; j = 1, 2, ..., K, \tag{3}$$

where K - the numbers of hyperedges.

Obviously, depending on the size and structure of each elements of Block diagram the Model of Platform of the supercomputer with Sleptsov net processor in the Support Cyber Security Applications (fig.2), from the technical and communications capabilities available to the user at some point and some other features of the cardinality of the set U can vary significantly.

Predicates P - determines incidence of vertices and hyperedges of each layer. P is defined on the set of all pairs ($v \in V, u \in U$). Truth domain predicate P is the set R of variable cardinality $Bt \neq const$:

$$F(P) = \{(v, u) \mid P(v, u)_r\}, \tag{4}$$

Where $v \in V, u \in U, r \in R = \{1, 2... B_t\}$

Variability of the cardinality of R is due to the same causes as the variability of U in Equation 3.

Considered a set-theoretic representation of the A-BM model to determine the variability of the matrix representation of this A-BM model is useful for creating software for Machine learning application with Avatar-Based Management technique use. Matrix representation (incidence matrix size NxK) hypergraph will have the form (Mkrttchian, et al., 2014) (5):

Figure 3. Hypergaph, in which weights of vertices correspond to indices characteristics in the A-BM model supercomputer with Sleptsov net processor model and the hyper-cores correspond possible A-BM model configurations

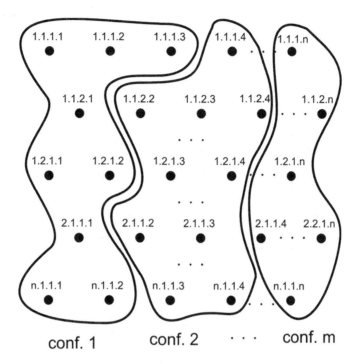

$$M_f = \| m_{ij} \|_{N \times K},$$ (5)

where:

1, if $(v_i, u_j) \in F(P)$, $v \in V$, $u \in U$

$m_{ij} = 0$, if $(v_i, u_j) \notin F(P)$, $v \in V$, $u \in U$

In some cases it is more convenient to use the matrix of connected vertices of the hypergraph (Equation 6), which has a size *NxN* and reflects pairwise connectivity relations through vertices incident hyperedges.) .

$$M_c = \| m_{ij} \|_{N \times N},$$ (6)

where:

1, if (v_i, v_j) $\exists u_k$, $(v_i, u_k) \in F(P)$, $(v_i, u_k) \in F(P)$, $v \in V$, $u \in U$

$m_{ij} = 0$, if (v_i, v_j) $\neg(\exists u_k)$, $(v_i, u_k) \in F(P)$, $(v_i, u_k) \in F(P)$, $v \in V$, $u \in U$

Figure 4 shows the interaction model variability and configurations A-BM model depending on the success of the Machine learning applications, available technical and telecommunications capacity psychophysical characteristics of the people work in Cyber Security Systems. Based on the analysis of the current profile of this people, selects the optimal configuration of the A-BM (hyperedge in graph *VMG*), defined technical, interface and content component (vertices that is incident to this hyperedges).

Figure 4. Block diagram of the model of platform for supercomputer with Sleptsov Net processor

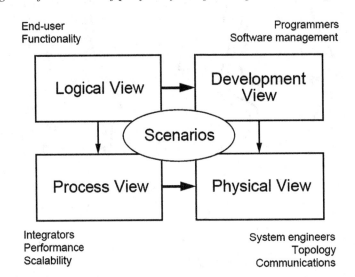

CONCLUSION

In this chapter, the authors studied machine-learning application with the use of Avatar-Based Management technique for cyber security issues. Our previous research devoted to the cyber security problem showed that cyber security is a section of information security, within the framework of which the processes of formation, functioning and evolution of cyber objects are studied. It is necessary to identify sources of cyber-danger formed while determining their characteristics, as well as their classification and formation of regulatory documents, implementation of security systems in future. However, working on the application of the machine learning for Cyber Security applications with the use of developed by the authors Avatars-Based Management techniques, we came to the conclusion that this is not so, and the built-in cyber security systems can be destroyed by the same artificial intelligence.

We proposed some prospects on Machine Learning with Avatar-Based Management at the Platform of the Sleptsov net processor, which are the Future Solutions to hyper-computations in the Support Cyber Security Applications.

ACKNOWLEDGMENT

The reported study was funded by RFBR according to the research project No. 18-010-00204_a.

REFERENCES

Ambika, P. (2018). Machine Learning. In P. Raj & A. Raman (Eds.), *Handbook of Research on Cloud and Fog Computing Infrastructures for Data Science* (pp. 209–230). Hershey, PA: IGI Global. doi:10.4018/978-1-5225-5972-6.ch011

Bhatti, B. M., & Sami, N. (2015). Building adaptive defense against cybercrimes using real-time data mining. *2015 First International Conference on Anti-Cybercrime (ICACC)*. 10.1109/Anti-Cybercrime.2015.7351949

Blanzieri, E., & Bryl, A. (2008). A survey of learning-based techniques of email spam filtering. *Artificial Intelligence Review*, *29*(1), 63–92. doi:10.100710462-009-9109-6

Buczak, A. L., & Guven, E. (2016). A Survey of Data Mining and Machine Learning Methods for Cyber Security Intrusion Detection. *IEEE Communications Surveys and Tutorials*, *18*(2), 1153–1176. doi:10.1109/COMST.2015.2494502

Dawson, M., Omar, M., & Abramson, J. (n.d.). Understanding the Methods behind Cyber Terrorism. *Encyclopedia of Information Science and Technology, 3*, 1539–1549. doi:10.4018/978-1-4666-5888-2.ch147

Duffy, J. (1975). IFToMM symposium—Dublin, September 1974. *Mechanism and Machine Theory*, *10*(2-3), 269. doi:10.1016/0094-114X(75)90030-0

Gardiner, J., & Nagaraja, S. (2016). On the Security of Machine Learning in Malware C8C Detection. *ACM Computing Surveys*, *49*(3), 1–39. doi:10.1145/3003816

Jenab, K., Khoury, S., & LaFevor, K. (2016). Flow-Graph and Markovian Methods for Cyber Security Analysis. *International Journal of Enterprise Information Systems*, *12*(1), 59–84. doi:10.4018/IJEIS.2016010104

Jenab, K., Khoury, S., & LaFevor, K. (2018). Flow-Graph and Markovian Methods for Cyber Security Analysis. In I. Management Association (Ed.), Cyber Security and Threats: Concepts, Methodologies, Tools, and Applications (pp. 674-702). Hershey, PA: IGI Global. doi:10.4018/978-1-5225-5634-3.ch036

Mkrttchian, V. (2015). Use Online Multi-Cloud Platform Lab with Intellectual Agents: Avatars for Study of Knowledge Visualization & Probability Theory in Bioinformatics. International Journal of Knowledge Discovery in Bioinformatics, 5(1), 11-23. Doi:10.4018/IJKDB.2015010102

Mkrttchian, V., & Aleshina, E. (2017). *Sliding Mode in Intellectual Control and Communication: Emerging Research and Opportunities*. Hershey, PA: IGI Global. doi:10.4018/978-1-5225-2292-8

Mkrttchian, V., & Belyanina, L. (Eds.). (2018). *Handbook of Research on Students' Research Competence in Modern Educational Contexts*. Hershey, PA: IGI Global. doi:10.4018/978-1-5225-3485-3

Mkrttchian, V., Bershadsky, A., Bozhday, A., & Fionova, L. (2015). Model in SM of DEE Based on Service-Oriented Interactions at Dynamic Software Product Lines. In G. Kurubacak & T. Yuzer (Eds.), *Identification, Evaluation, and Perceptions of Distance Education Experts* (pp. 231–248). Hershey, PA: IGI Global. doi:10.4018/978-1-4666-8119-4.ch014

Mkrttchian, V., Bershadsky, A., Bozhday, A., Kataev, M., & Kataev, S. (Eds.). (2016). *Handbook of Research on Estimation and Control Techniques in E-Learning systems*. Hershey, PA: IGI Global. doi:10.4018/978-1-4666-9489-7

Mkrttchian, V., Kataev, M., Shih, T., Kumar, M., & Fedotova, A. (2014). Avatars "HHH" Technology Education Cloud Platform on Sliding Mode Based Plug- Ontology as a Gateway to Improvement of Feedback Control Online Society. International Journal of Information Communication Technologies and Human Development, 6(3), 13-31. Doi:10.4018/ijicthd.2014070102

Mkrttchian, V., Veretekhina, S., Gavrilova, O., Ioffe, A., Markosyan, S., & Chernyshenko, S. V. (2019). The Cross-Cultural Analysis of Australia and Russia: Cultures, Small Businesses, and Crossing the Barriers. In U. Benna (Ed.), *Industrial and Urban Growth Policies at the Sub-National, National, and Global Levels* (pp. 229–249). Hershey, PA: IGI Global. doi:10.4018/978-1-5225-7625-9.ch012

Walker, S. (2012). Economics and the cyber challenge. *Information Security Technical Report*, *17*(1-2), 9–18. doi:10.1016/j.istr.2011.12.003

Zaitsev, D. A. (2018). Sleptsov Net Computing. In M. Khosrow-Pour (Ed.), Encyclopedia of Information Science and Technology (4th ed.; pp. 7731-7743). Hershey, PA: IGI Global. doi:10.4018/978-1-5225-2255-3.ch672

Zaitsev, D. A. (2019). Sleptsov Net Computing. In M. Khosrow-Pour (Ed.), Advanced Methodologies and Technologies in Network Architecture, Mobile Computing, and Data Analytics (pp. 1660-1674). Hershey, PA: IGI Global. doi:10.4018/978-1-5225-7598-6.ch122

ADDITIONAL READING

Bershadsky, A., Bozhday, A., Evseeva, J., Gudkov, A., & Mkrtchian, V. (2017). Techniques for Adaptive Graphics Applications Synthesis Based on Variability Modeling Technology and Graph Theory, In A. Kravets, M. Shcherbakov, M. Kultsova, & O. Shabalina, (Eds.), *Proceedings of CIT&DS 2017*, (pp. 169–179). Switzerland: Springer International Publishing AG. DOI: 10.1007/978-3-319-65551-2_33

Bershadsky, A., Evseeva, J., Bozhday, A., Gudkov, A., & Mkrtchian, V. (2015), Variability modeling in the automated system for authoring intelligent adaptive applications on the basis of three-dimensional graphics, In A. Kravets, M. Shcherbakov, M. Kultsova, & O. Shabalina, (Eds.), *Proceedings of CIT&DS 2015*, (pp. 149–159). Switzerland: Springer International Publishing AG. DOI: 10.1007/978-3-319-23766-4

Glotova, T., Deev, M., Krevskiy, I., Matukin, S., Mkrttchian, V., & Sheremeteva, E. (2015). Individualized learning trajectories using distance education technologies, In A. Kravets, M. Shcherbakov, M. Kultsova, & O. Shabalina, (Eds.), *Proceedings of CIT&DS 2015*, (pp. 778–793). Switzerland: Springer International Publishing AG. DOI: 10.1007/978-3-319-23766-4

Mkrttchian, V. (2011). Use 'hhh' technology in transformative models of online education. In G. Kurubacak & T. Vokan Yuzer (Eds.), *Handbook of research on transformative online education and liberation: Models for social equality* (pp. 340–351). Hershey, PA, USA: IGI Global; doi:10.4018/978-1-60960-046-4.ch018

Mkrttchian, V. (2012). Avatar manager and student reflective conversations as the base for describing meta-communication model. In G. Kurubacak, T. Vokan Yuzer, & U. Demiray (Eds.), *Meta-communication for reflective online conversations: Models for distance education* (pp. 340–351). Hershey, PA, USA: IGI Global; doi:10.4018/978-1-61350-071-2.ch005

Mkrttchian, V. (2015). Modeling using of Triple H-Avatar Technology in online Multi-Cloud Platform Lab. In M. Khosrow-Pour (Ed.), Encyclopedia of Information Science and Technology (3rd Ed.). (pp. 4162-4170). IRMA, Hershey: PA, USA: IGI Global. Doi:10.4018/978-1-4666-5888-2.ch409

Mkrttchian, V. (2016). The Control of Didactics of Online Training of Teachers in HHH University and Cooperation with the Ministry of Diaspora of Armenia. In V. Mkrttchian, A. Bershadsky, A. Bozhday, M. Kataev, & S. Kataev (Eds.), *Handbook of Research on Estimation and Control Techniques in E-learning systems* (pp. 311–322). Hershey, PA, USA: IGI Global; doi:10.4018/978-1-4666-9489-7.ch021

Mkrttchian, V., & Aleshina, E. (2017). The Sliding Mode Technique and Technology (SM T&T) According to Vardan Mkrttchian in Intellectual Control(IC). In *Sliding Mode in Intellectual Control and Communication: Emerging Research and Opportunities* (pp. 1–9). Hershey, PA: IGI Global; doi:10.4018/978-1-5225-2292-8.ch001

Mkrttchian, V., Amirov, D., & Belyanina, L. (2017). Optimizing an Online Learning Course Using Automatic Curating in Sliding Mode. In N. Ostashewski, J. Howell, & M. Cleveland-Innes (Eds.), *Optimizing K-12 Education through Online and Blended Learning* (pp. 213–224). Hershey, PA, USA: IGI Global; doi:10.4018/978-1-5225-0507-5.ch011

Mkrttchian, V., Aysmontas, B., Uddin, M., Andreev, A., & Vorovchenko, N. (2015). The Academic views from Moscow Universities of the Cyber U-Learning on the Future of Distance Education at Russia and Ukraine. In G. Eby & T. Vokan Yuzer (Eds.), *Identification, Evaluation, and Perceptions of Distance Education Experts* (pp. 32–45). Hershey, PA, USA: IGI Global; doi:10.4018/978-1-4666-8119-4.ch003

Mkrttchian, V., & Belyanina, L. (2016). The Pedagogical and Engineering Features of E- and Blended Learning of Adults Using Triple H-Avatar in Russian Federation. In V. Mkrttchian, A. Bershadsky, A. Bozhday, M. Kataev, & S. Kataev (Eds.), *Handbook of Research on Estimation and Control Techniques in E-Learning Systems* (pp. 61–77). Hershey, PA, USA: IGI Global; doi:10.4018/978-1-4666-9489-7.ch006

Mkrttchian, V., Bershadsky, A., Bozhday, A., Noskova, T., & Miminova, S. (2016). Development of a Global Policy of All-Pervading E-Learning, Based on Transparency, Strategy, and Model of Cyber Triple H-Avatar. In G. Eby, T. V. Yuser, & S. Atay (Eds.), *Developing Successful Strategies for Global Policies and Cyber Transparency in E-Learning* (pp. 207–221). Hershey, PA, USA: IGI Global; doi:10.4018/978-1-4666-8844-5.ch013

Mkrttchian, V., Kataev, M., Hwang, W., Bedi, S., & Fedotova, A. (2014). Using Plug-Avatars "hhh" Technology Education as Service-Oriented Virtual Learning Environment in Sliding Mode. In G. Eby & T. Vokan Yuzer (Eds.), *Emerging Priorities and Trends in Distance Education: Communication, Pedagogy, and Technology*. Hershey, PA, USA: IGI Global; doi:10.4018/978-1-4666-5162-3.ch004

Mkrttchian, V., Kataev, M., Hwang, W., Bedi, S., & Fedotova, A. (2016), Using Plug-Avatars "hhh" Technology Education as Service-Oriented Virtual Learning Environment in Sliding Mode. Leadership and Personnel Management: Concepts, Methodologies, Tools, and Applications (4 Volumes), (pp.890-902), IRMA, Hershey: PA, USA: IGI Global. Doi:10.4018/978-1-4666-9624-2.ch039

Mkrttchian, V., & Potapova, I. (2018). Professors of Innovative Implementations in Sliding Mode Digital Technology for Enhancing Students Competence. In Mkrttchian, V., & Belyanina, L., (Eds.) Handbook of Research on Students' Research Competence in Modern Educational Contexts, (189-204), Hershey, PA, USA: IGI Global. Doi:10.4018/978-1-5225-3485-3.ch010

Mkrttchian, V., & Stephanova, G. (2013). Training of Avatar Moderator in Sliding Mode Control. In G. Eby & T. Vokan Yuzer (Eds.), *Project Management Approaches for Online Learning Design* (pp. 175–203). Hershey, PA, USA: IGI Global; doi:10.4018/978-1-4666-2830-4.ch009

Mkrttchian, V., Vasin, S., Surovitskaya, G., & Gamidullaeva, L. (2018). Improving the mechanisms of formation of MS students' research competencies in Russian core universities. In Mkrttchian, V., & Belyanina, L., (Eds.), Handbook of Research on Students' Research Competence in Modern Educational Contexts, (90-105), Hershey, PA, USA: IGI Global. Doi:10.4018/978-1-5225-3485-3.ch005

Tolstykh, T., Vasin, S., Gamidullaeva, L., & Mkrttchian, V. (2017). The Control of Continuing Education Based on the Digital Economy. In P. Isaias & L. Carvalho (Eds.), *User Innovation and the Entrepreneurship Phenomenon in the Digital Economy* (pp. 153–171). Hershey, PA, USA: IGI Global; doi:10.4018/978-1-5225-2826-5.ch008

Tolstykh, T., Vertakova, J., & Shkarupeta, E. (2018). Professional Training for Structural Economic Transformations Based on Competence approach in the Digital Age. In Mkrttchian, V., & Belyanina, L., (Eds.) Handbook of Research on Students' Research Competence in Modern Educational Contexts, (209-229), Hershey, PA, USA: IGI Global. Doi:10.4018/978-1-5225-3485-3.ch011

KEY TERMS AND DEFINITIONS

Hypercomputation or Super-Turing Computation: Is a multi-disciplinary research area with relevance across a wide variety of fields, including computer science, philosophy, physics, electronics, biology, and artificial intelligence; models of computation that can provide outputs that are not Turing computable.

Machine Learning: Is the use of artificial intelligence (AI) that provides systems with the capability to learn and automatically improve from experience (data) without being explicitly programmed.

Machine Learning Application With Avatar-Based Management Technique Use: Is a class of methods of natural intelligence, the characteristic feature of which is not a direct solution of the problem, but training in the process of applying solutions to a set of similar problems.

Shareable Content Object Reference Model (SCORM): Is a collection of standards and specifications for web-based electronic educational technology (also called e-learning).

Sleptsov Net (SN): Is a bipartite directed multi-graph supplied with a dynamic process.

This research was previously published in Machine Learning and Cognitive Science Applications in Cyber Security; pages 139-153, copyright year 2019 by Information Science Reference (an imprint of IGI Global).

Chapter 10
Malware and Anomaly Detection Using Machine Learning and Deep Learning Methods

Valliammal Narayan

Avinashilingam Institute for Home Science and Higher Education for Women, India

Barani Shaju

Avinashilingam Institute for Home Science and Higher Education for Women, India

ABSTRACT

This chapter aims to discuss applications of machine learning in cyber security and explore how machine learning algorithms help to fight cyber-attacks. Cyber-attacks are wide and varied in multiple forms. The key benefit of machine learning algorithms is that it can deep dive and analyze system behavior and identify anomalies which do not correlate with expected behavior. Algorithms can be trained to observe multiple data sets and strategize payload beforehand in detection of malware analysis.

INTRODUCTION

Today, technology has become most essential part of our life. Internet usage has grown rapidly for the past years. Internet has brought about a new revolution in the fields of computing and communicating technology as it connects billions of infinitesimal devices. Potential intelligent support is provided by internet and the limitations of workplace is exempted using the wireless network providing excess mobility and flexibility over the conventional networks (Altaher. A, 2016). The sensitive information can be exposed by the transactions which were performed using the internet. Apart from the benefits of internet there are some drawbacks too like all our records, personal as well as professional, banking, medical, passwords, communication etc. can be made easily available to the antagonists using various illegal techniques and can finally receive our complete information, misuse our records imprecating the transactions which are online.

DOI: 10.4018/978-1-6684-6291-1.ch010

Figure 1. Tabulation and graph on malware statistics

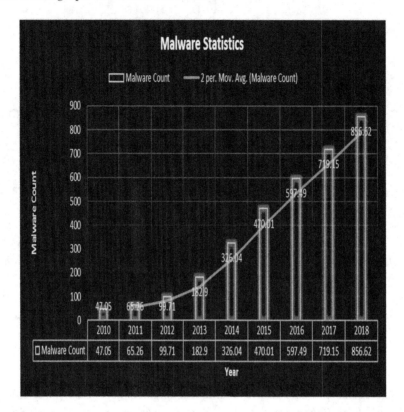

In the year 2018, the number of internet users has significantly increased. There are about 55.1% internet users as compared to the world population in table as Figure 1.

Definition

Malware: It is a term used to describe malicious software, including spyware, ransomware, viruses, and worms. Malware breaches a network through vulnerability, typically when a user clicks a dangerous link or email attachment that then installs risky software (Bhattacharya A, 2017). Inside the system, malware can do the following access:

Box 1.

- Blocks access to key components of the network (ransomware)

- Installs malware or additional harmful software

- Covertly obtains information by transmitting data from the hard drive (spyware)

- Disrupts certain components and renders the system inoperable

Malvertising: This is the usage of web-based exposing to stretch malware. It ordinarily includes infusing malware-loaded commercials into genuine web-based publicizing systems and website links.

Figure 2. Distribution of attacks in cyber security

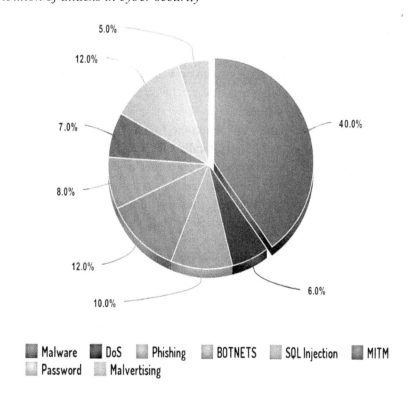

The number of cyber attacks has grown gradually during the last few years. In Figure 2, upshots shown that the malware attack have the highest percentage rate compared to other attacks. The increase of malware has presented a long-lasting and serious threat to the security of computer systems and internet. For example, the well-known WannaCry ransomware attack has affected millions of devices and caused billions of dollars damage. The number of malware has increased greatly every year, and it is reported that every 4.6 seconds a new malware specimen emerged in 2018.

Major Consequence

- More attacks are launched from the web - and not from executable files (PE-files)
- Overall numbers are decreasing, as attacks are more targeted
- Illegal hidden crypto mining (Crypto jacking) is on the rise
- Attackers make use of novel standards such as Web assembly for better efficiency

KNOW-HOW: UNDERSTANDING ABOUT MALWARE IN ITS DEPTH AND BREADTH

Malware is deployed by cyber attackers to concession computer systems by developing their security vulnerabilities. This software is utilized to change the PC settings, delete software, cause errors, watch browsing habits, or open computer to attacks without user knowledge. It uses deceptive and unethical tactics to install itself on your computer without user consent. For instance, they may visit a website and receive an unrequested download, and mistakenly run this software on their computer (F. Alotaibi,2016). It may also use vulnerabilities in the operating system or web browser to install itself without requiring the user to manually run the software. Malware access can be disastrous consequences include data theft, extortion or the crippling of network systems.

The journey of malware started around 1982 when the first virus with replicating features and malicious intent was written by a high-school student called Rich Skrenta for the Apple II systems. The virus was named "The Elk Cloner". It used to infect a computer when the machine was booted from an infected floppy disk, copying itself to the new machine. When an uninfected floppy disk was inserted in an infected machine, it copied itself to the floppy, thus spreading itself. Even though its behavior was relatively harmless but it displayed a small poem on every 50th boot, however, it also had the unintended effect of overwriting code on particular systems.

A system can be affected by malware by clicking an infected website, downloading/ installing infected software. Antivirus and anti-spyware software are used to prevent, detect and remove the malware from the computer. Most antivirus software can clean malware but at the same time, it's a smart thought to run an anti-malware. An example of malware infecting a PC is shown in Figure 3,

Figure 3. Ways of spread on PC

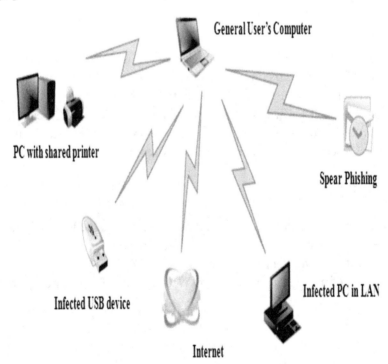

To create countermeasures to malware contagions, investigate has been dynamic in innovation for recognizing infections and deciding their basis and innovation for dissecting malware.

Makers of Malware

Malware customers go by a collection of names. Presumably the most outstanding names are dark caps, programmers, and saltines. The real individuals or affiliations that go up against the previously mentioned names could be an outer/interior risk, an outside government, or a mechanical covert operative.

There are basically two stages in the lifecycle of programming amid which malware are embedded. These phases are alluded to as the pre-discharge stage and the post-discharge stage. An inward threat is commonly the main kind of programmer equipped for embeddings malware into programming before its discharge to the end-clients. An insider is a confided in the developer, regularly inside an association, of some product to be conveyed to its end clients. Every single other individual or associations that go up against the programmer job embed malware amid the post-discharge stage, which is the point at which the product is accessible for its target group.

In making new malware, black hats, by and large, utilize either of the accompanying systems: muddling and conduct expansion/adjustment so as to go around malware identifiers. Muddling endeavors to conceal the genuine goals of pernicious code without expanding the practices displayed by the malware. Conduct expansion/adjustment viably makes new malware, in spite of the fact that the substance of the malware probably won't have changed.

Types of Malware

Malware is classified into multiple points of view. Sometimes they are classified on the basis of behavior, on the basis of their target platform or on the basis of their attack directive. In this section classifies the malware randomly by mixing all the categories (Kai Huang, 2009).

The different classes and terms related to malware are shown in Figure 4.

Each of the above-mentioned classes causes a massive amount of damage to the system or software (Boukhtouta A, 2016). The details of the given malware classes are as follows:

- **Virus:** Virus is a category of malware that, when executed, tries to replicate itself into other executable code, when it succeeds, the code is said to be infected. At the point when the tainted code is executed, the infection likewise executes. A computer virus is a kind of bad software code (malware) that, when runs, multiplies by reproducing itself (copying its own program code) or tainting other computer programs by editing them. Corrupting the computer programs also includes data files or the "boot" sector of the hard disk.
  - **Boot Infectors**
    - A virus can contaminate a framework as an occupant infection by introducing itself as a component of the working framework with the goal that it stays in the RAM from the time a PC is booted up to when shutdown. These kinds of infections are exceptionally uncommon nowadays, what with the approach of the Internet, and security methods incorporated with current working frameworks like Windows 10.

Figure 4. Types of malware

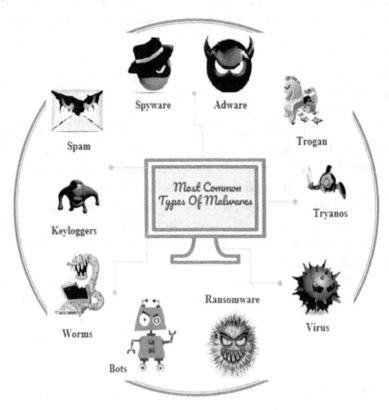

- ○ **File Infectors**
  - ▪ Numerous viruses creep up into common executable records like.EXE and.COM so as to up their odds of being controlled by a client. Any program that documents type that Windows can call for execution is vulnerable, including clump and content records like. BAT, .JS. .VB and considerably screensaver records with the.SCR extension.
- ○ **Macro Viruses**
  - ▪ These sorts of infections are the ones that kept running inside explicit applications that enable full-scale programs so as to broaden the capacities of given programming. Infections that focused Microsoft Office were across the board a couple of years back, however, the risk of large scale infections has additionally declined as of late as unsigned macros are consequently incapacitated in Office and are not permitted to run.
- • **Worm:** A worm is a computer program that can run without any support that means it runs independently and can propagate a complete working version of itself onto other hosts on a network. A computer worm may also be thought of as an independent vindictive computer program that creates copies of itself in order to spread to other machines. Most of the times, it uses a distributed environment to spread itself, depending on vulnerabilities or weaknesses on the target computer to access it. Unlike a computer virus, it does not require to attach itself to an existing program.
- • **Logic Bomb:** It is a program inserted into System or Software by an intruder. It remains in the dormant state until a predefined condition is met. On meeting the condition an unauthorized action is performed. Software that is intrinsically vindictive, such as viruses and worms, mostly

consist of logic bombs that run a certain consignment at a pre-decided time or when some other criteria are fulfilled. This method can be used by a virus or worm to attain impulse and spread before being caught. Some viruses attack their host systems on particular dates only, such as Friday the 13th or April Fools' Day. Trojans that attack particular dates are frequently called time bombs.

- **Trojan Horse:** It is a computer program which appears harmless but is actually a harmful program. It has a hidden and potentially malicious function which evades the security process, sometimes by exploiting legitimate authorizations of a system entity that invokes the Trojan horse program. Trojans are most of the times propagated by some form of social engineering, for example where a user is lured into running an e-mail attachment disguised to be harmless. Although their consignment can be anything, many new forms act as a backdoor, communicating with a controller which can then have illegitimate access to the smitten computer system. This corruption allows an attacker to access system owner's personal details such as banking credentials, passwords, or personal identification details.

- **Backdoor:** A backdoor virus is a software program that makes entry into a computer system without being notices and caught and executes in the background to open ports. It allows third parties to control the computer surreptitiously. These harmful backdoor programs can pass themselves off as legitimate ones. It is a type of program that bypasses a normal security check; it may allow the unauthorized access to the crucial information.

- **Mobile Code:** It is software which may be a script, macro or any other type of portable instruction that can be moved unaltered to different types of platforms and get executed with similar semantics. Mobile code is any software program, application, or data content that is able to perform movement while existing in an email, document or website. Mobile code uses distributed environment or storage media, such as a Universal Serial Bus (USB) thumb drive, to execute local program execution from another machine.

- **Exploits:** These are the kind of codes which are specific to a particular type of vulnerability or a set of vulnerabilities. Exploits attack on the system on finding certain type of weakness. An exploit is a part of software program, a piece of data, or a serial arrangement of commands that takes benefit of an error or weakness in order to cause unintentional or unanticipated demeanor to exist in computer software, hardware, or anything electronic. Such behavior mostly includes acts like gaining control of a computer system, allowing privilege rise, or a denial-of-service (DoS or related DDoS) attack.

- **Downloader's:** It is a kind of program which if gets executed on a machine installs other program or items on a machine. Normally downloader's are sent through emails. On opening the email, the user is lured to download a program which in turn downloads other malicious items. Downloader's are harmful programs with the intention to seditious download and install malware on a victim's machine. Once executed, a downloader communicates with its command-and-control (C&C) server(s) through C&C channels. After receiving download guidelines, it then directs at least one download channel to load malware through the network.

- **Auto Rooter:** Auto rooters are the harmful program or software's that act as tools that are used to break into new machines lying at different locations through network. The phrase "auto rooter" is based on security jargon for successfully breaking and obtaining privileged access to a Computer system. Auto rooters can be designed to scan a network for weak machines in terms of security or attack everything they encounter. Once a computer system is successfully captured or compromised, or rooted, some type of harmful code can be installed and configured: data might be caught using a software component known as sniffer, Web pages defaced, servers installed. Some autorooters are destroyed after sending the results back to the cracker, others may install bots that wait for further directions from the attacker.

- **Kit (Virus Generator):** These are the set of programs or software's which act as tools and have capability to generate new viruses on their own. These work through an automated system. It is a program that creates a virus or worm on its own with any role of the user. They make it possible for those people who have very small knowledge of viruses or even computers to develop viruses. As early viruses were almost entirely coded in Assembly language, it was nearly impossible for anyone to create a virus or worm without having good experience with computers.

- **Spammer:** These are the software programs used to send large volumes of unwanted emails which fill the mailbox of person under attack. These mails are sometimes called junk mails or spam mails. These are sometimes a list of individuals and organizations noteworthy for engaging in bulk electronic spamming using the spamming software program, either on their own behalf or on behalf of others.

- **Flooders:** These are the types of malware form or software programs that are used to attack the networked computers with a massive amount of data traffic to carry out a DOS (Denial of Service) attack.

- **Keyloggers:** These are the programs which capture keystrokes and log them. These are the types of information stealers which record keypresses and store them locally for later retrieval or pass them to a server lying at remote location that the attacker has access to. Keystroke logging, mostly referred to as keylogging or keyboard capturing, is the process of recording the keys pressed on a keyboard, usually secretly, so that the person typing on the keyboard is ignorant of the fact that their events are being recorded. Keylogging may also be used for studying human–computer communication. Large number of keylogging techniques exist, they range from hardware and software-based methodology to auditory investigation.

- **Zombie or Bot:** Zombie is a program stored or activated on a compromised machine used to launch different types of attacks on other machines. "Robot" is otherwise called as "Bot", which is another type of malware as well as is a sort of machine-driven undertaking that connects with other disseminated administrations. An exemplary use of bots is to collect information (such as web crawlers), or communicate on its own with instant messaging (IM), Internet Relay Chat (IRC), or other web based interactive tools. A typical bot software allows an operator to remotely control each machine and group them together to form what is commonly referred to as a bot army or botnet.

- **Spyware:** Spyware is a software program that collects information without the victim's knowledge and transmits it to another system. It is software that aims to collect information about an individual or a company without their awareness and that may send such information to another entity without the owner's permission, or that claim control over a computer without the consumer's consent. Whenever spyware is used for harmful reasons, its presence is normally hidden from the user and can be intricate to detect. Some spyware, such as keyloggers, may be sent by the owner of a shared, commercial, or public computer deliberately in order to monitor users.

- **Adware:** It is a kind of badware that displays pop up commercial ads or it redirects the browsers to other business websites. The term adware is frequently used to describe a form of malevolent software which presents unwanted ads to the user of a computer. The advertisements produced by adware are sometimes in the form of pop-ups or sometimes in a Window that cannot be closed.

Adware, or advertising-supported software, is any software packages that automatically deliver commercials in order to produce monetary gain for its developer. The advertisements may be in the user interface of the software program or on a screen shown to the user during the installation procedure.

- **Ransomware:** It is a kind of malicious software program that takes control of data files and keep them as hostage and asks for the ransom amount from the owner in lieu of making such files are held by the ransomware, the user or owner of such files is unable to access them. Ransomware is a computer malware that installs secretly on a one's computer, executes an attack by encrypting all the document files that badly affects it, and demands a ransom payment to decrypt it or not publish it. Simple ransomware programs may freeze the system in such a way which is not difficult for an experienced person to overturn, and display a message asking for a payment to unlock the system. Highly developed and superior malware encrypts the victim's computer's useful files, making them unapproachable, and insists a ransom amount to decrypt them or unlock them. The ransomware may also encode the computer's Master File Table (MFT) or the entire contents hard drive. Thus, ransomware is a kind of denial-of-access attack that avoids computer users from accessing files since it is difficult to decrypt the files without the decryption key. Ransomware attacks are normally carried out using a Trojan that has a consignment concealed as a genuine file.

- **Grayware**: It is a recently coined term that came into use around 2004. It is utilized to depict undesirable applications and records that however are not named malware, can exacerbate the execution of PCs and lead to security threats. At the base, these projects carry on in an irritating or unwanted way, and even from a pessimistic standpoint, they screen a framework and telephone home with data. Grayware suggests both adware and spyware. Practically all financially accessible antivirus programming can identify these possibly undesirable projects, and offer separate modules to distinguish, isolate and expel malware that shows commercials.

- **Adware**

Albeit advertisement bolstered programming is currently substantially more typical and known as adware in a few circles, the word has been connected to malware for a long while. While adware can refer to any program that is supported by advertising, malicious adware usually shows ads in the form of pop-ups and windows that cannot be closed.

It is the maybe the most rewarding and least unsafe malware, planned with the particular reason for showing promotions on your PC. Adware usage is on the rise on mobile, in particular, with some Chinese firms bundling in adware by default in certain low-cost Android smart phones.

- **Spyware**

Spyware is programming that continually keeps a spies on you its principle intention is to monitor your Internet exercises so as to send adware. Spyware is likewise used to accumulate data around an association without their insight, and send that data to another substance, without the assent of the person in question.

- **Rootkits:** It is a collection of software specifically designed to permit malware that gathers information, into your system. These work out of sight with the goal that a client may not see anything suspicious. Be that as it may, out of sight, a rootkit will allow a few kinds of malware to get into the framework. These product work like a secondary passage for malware to enter and unleash devastation, and are presently being utilized broadly by programmers to contaminate frameworks. A rootkit establishment can either be programmed, or an assailant can introduce it once they have gotten overseer benefits.

Malwares at Recent Years

- **Kovter:** It is a Trojan, which has been observed acting as click fraud malware or an ansomware downloader. It is spread through malspam email connections containing noxious office macros. Kovter is lifeless malware that sidesteps discovery by covering up in vault keys. A few reports demonstrate that Kovter diseases have gotten refreshed directions from order and control framework to fill in as a remote access indirect access.

- **Emotet:** It is a modular Trojan that downloads or drops banking Trojans. Introductory contamination happens by means of malspam messages that contain malevolent download joins, a PDF with installed connections, or a large scale empowered Word connection. Emotet joins spreader modules so as to engender all through a system. Emotet is known to download/drop the Pinkslipbot and Dridex managing an account Trojans. Presently, there are 4 known spreader elements: Outlook scraper, WebBrowserPassView, Mail PassView, and a credential enumerator.

  - **Outlook Scraper:** This is a device that rub names and email addresses from the injured individual's Outlook records and uses that data to convey phishing messages from the traded off record.

  - **WebBrowserPassView:** This is a password recovery tool that captures passwords stored by Internet Explorer, Mozilla Firefox, Google Chrome, Safari, and Opera and passes them to the credential enumerator module.

  - **Mail PassView:** It is a password recovery tool that reveals passwords and account details for various email clients such as Microsoft Outlook, Windows Mail, Mozilla Thunderbird, Hotmail and so on;

  - **Credential Enumerator:** It is a self-extracting RAR file containing a bypass and a service component. The detour part is utilized for specification of system assets and either fined writable offer drives or attempts to animal power client accounts, including the director account. When an accessible framework is found, Emotet then composes the administration segment on the framework, which composes Emotet onto the plate.

- **WannaCry:** It is a ransomware worm that utilizes the EternalBlue endeavor to spread. Adaptation 1.0 is known to have a "killswitch" space, which stops the encryption procedure. Later forms are not known to have a "killswitch" space. WannaCry is dispersed by means of malspam.

- **ZeuS/Zbot:** A Trojan malware that has affected thousands of devices for a long time, Zbot has been labeled as one of the ruthless malicious attacks in the recent era. It is a modular banking Trojan which uses keystroke logging to compromise victim credentials when the user visits a banking website.

- **CoinMiner:** It is a cryptocurrency miner that was initially disseminated via malvertising. When a machine is tainted, CoinMiner utilizes Windows Management Instrument (WMI) and EternalBlue to misuse SMB and spread over a system. CoinMiner utilizes the WMI Standard Event Consumer scripting to execute contents for diligence.

- **Gh0st:** It is a RAT used to control infected endpoints. Gh0st is dropped by other malware to make a secondary passage into a gadget, enabling an assailant to completely control the tainted gadget.
- **NanoCore:** It is a Remote Access Trojan (RAT) spread via malspam as a malicious Excel XLS spreadsheet. As a RAT, NanoCore can acknowledge directions to download and execute records, visit sites, and include library keys for steadiness.
- **Ursnif:** Ursnif and its variant Dreambot, are banking trojans known for weaponizing documents. Ursnif as of late overhauled its web infusion assaults to incorporate TLS callbacks so as to muddle against hostile to malware programming. Ursnif gathers unfortunate casualty data from login pages and web shapes.
- **Mirai:** It is a malware botnet known to compromise Internet of Things (IoT) devices in order to conduct large-scale distributed denial of service (DDoS) attacks.
- **Redyms:** It is a click-fraud Trojan that is primarily downloaded via exploit kit.
- **Loyphish:** This is fundamentally a phishing page which camouflages as a real saving money site. These site pages are very advanced in structure, which influences you to trust that you're interfacing with the first site of your bank. These pages are astutely worked with all the first pictures, logos, and content. These assaults are focused against essentially everybody. In this way, on the off chance that you ever enter your managing an account data into any of these pages, you may lose generous measures of cash. More often than not, malware phishing pages can be maintained a strategic distance from by twofold checking the URL of the page in your program's location bar. Likewise, utilizing an Internet Security apparatus can help you significantly in keeping away from such dangers.
- **Sirefef:** This is a standout amongst the most progressive malware dangers out there. Numerous gadgets have been influenced by this in the ongoing occasions. Otherwise called ZeroAccess, this malevolent danger works in total stealth mode, leaving practically no hint of its reality in your gadget. Besides, it additionally has the capacity of crippling the security resistances of your PC. This document normally gets into your gadget when you're downloading pilfered records, programming, and comparative others. In this way, in case you're downloading split programming or keygens, you could be making your PC powerless. Sirefef likewise transmits your private data to remote servers. Moreover, it can likewise cripple your Windows Firewall and Windows Defender too.
- **Suspicious.Emit:** It is a Trojan malware that can complete a genuine mischief to your PC. Typically, Trojan steeds are truly malignant documents that camouflage themselves as valuable applications, for example, utility apparatuses. Suspicious. Radiate is among such Trojan dangers, which could display unfortunate harm to your gadget. It works through code infusion procedure, where it picks up invulnerability from location. Alongside that, it additionally makes an autorun. inf document and places it in the root catalog of the injured individual's gadget. This kind of risk is normally conveyed through removable gadgets, for example, USB drives. Suspicious. Emit additionally can take your data and transmits to different gadgets and servers.
- **FBI Virus:** An exceedingly perilous malware, FBI infection which is on the other hand known as FBI Money pack Scam, is an astutely planned pernicious record. At the point when assaulted by this risk, your PC will show a ready which expresses that your PC has been secured because of infringement of copyrights. This alarm attempts to swindle you that you've been hindered because of an illicit access or downloads of documents, for example, music, programming, motion pictures, and numerous others. So as to get your PC unblocked, you would need to pay two hundred

dollars. Numerous ordinary citizens have succumbed to this trick, making it one of the dangerous assaults in the ongoing past.

MALWARE ANALYSIS AND DETECTION TECHNIQUES

Malware Analysis

Malware examination considering malicious records with the point of having improved comprehension around a few parts of malware like malware conduct, development after some time, and their chose targets. The result of malware investigation ought to permit security firms to fortify their resistance procedures against malware assaults. It is important to create successful malware recognition system. Procedures utilized for malware investigation for the most part classified into three sections: Static, Dynamic, and Hybrid examination. Figure 5 demonstrates malware analysis methods as well as their general features,

Figure 5. Types of malware analysis with features

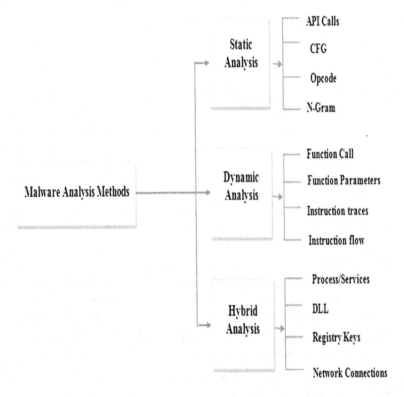

Static Analysis

It is additionally called as code examination. It is the way toward dissecting the code by analyzing it for example programming code of malware is seen to pick up the learning of how malware's capacities function. In this strategy figuring out is performed by utilizing dismantle apparatus, decompile device, debugger, source code analyzer devices, for example, IDA Pro and Ollydbg so as to comprehend structure of malware. Before program is executed, static data is found in the executable including header information and the grouping of bytes is utilized to decide if it is vindictive. Dismantling system is one of the strategies of static examination. With static examination executable record is dismantled utilizing dismantling instruments like XXD, Hexdump, NetWide direction, to get the low level computing construct program document. From this record the opcode is separated as a component to statically dissect the application conduct to recognize the malware (Nikolopoulos SD, 2016).

This procedure alludes to examining the PE records without executing code. Malware ordinarily utilizes binary packer, for example, UPX and ASP Pack Shell, to abstain from being examined. A PE records should be unloaded and decompressed before being examined. To decompile windows executable document a dismantle apparatus can be utilized, for example, IDA Pro and OlleyDbg that show get together directions, give data about the malware, and concentrate example to distinguish the assailant. The recognition example can be separated in static investigation like Windows API calls, string mark, control stream diagram, opcode recurrence and byte grouping n-grams (Siddiqui M, 2008).

Application Programming Interface (API)

Practically all projects use Windows API calls to converse with the working framework. For instance, the "OpenFileW" is a Windows API in "Kernel32.dll" that makes another record or opens a current one. Thusly, API calls uncover the conduct of projects and could be considered as a fundamental stamp in malware discovery. For example, the Windows API calls "WriteProcessMemory", "LoadLibrary" and "CreateRemoteThread" are a presumed conduct utilized by malware for DLL infusion into a procedure, while infrequently met up in an authentic set. DLL infusion is examined in the memory investigation area. Strings are a decent pointer of malignant presence.

Control Flow Graph (CFG)

A CFG is a coordinated diagram that shows the control flow of a code, where squares of code are exhibited by hubs and control flow sends through edges. In malware identification, CFG can be utilized to catch the conduct of a PE record as well as concentrate the program formation.

Opcodes(Operation Codes)

It is the initial segment of a machine language guidance that distinguishes what task to be executed by the CPU. Full machine dialect guidance made out of opcode and, alternatively, at least one operands. Opcode can be utilized as a component in malware recognition by testing opcode frequency or computing the similitude between opcode arrangements.

N-grams

N-grams are the majority of the coterminous subsequences of a grouping of a length N. For instance, "MALWARE" is a grouping of letters of length 7, it very well may be divided into 3-grams as: "MAL", "ALW", "LWA", "WAR" and "ARE". N-Grams have been connected with different discovery highlights like API calls as well as opcodes. Adjacent to the past features, there are different highlights that have been utilized in static assessment like size and capacity length of the file. Networking elements such as TCP/ UDP ports, destination IP as well as HTTP request are also features in static analysis.

Dynamic Analysis

It is additionally called a behavioral investigation. Assessment of tainted code amid its execution is known as unique investigation. After that malware scientists use SysAnalyzer, Process Explorer, ProcMon, Reg-Shot, and different apparatuses to recognize the general conduct of record. In the dynamic investigation, the record is recognized in the wake of executing it in a genuine domain, amid the execution of document its framework association, its conduct and impact on the machine are checked. The upside of dynamic investigation is that it precisely dissects the referred to just as obscure, new malware.

Hybrid Analysis

Hybrid method accumulates data about malware from static and dynamic method. By utilizing half and half examination, security scientists gain the advantages of the two investigations, static and dynamic. In this manner, expanding the capacity to identify vindictive projects accurately. The two examinations have their very own points of interest and constraints. Static examination is shabby, quick and more secure contrasted with dynamic investigation. Be that as it may, malware dodges it by utilizing confusion strategies. Then again, dynamic examination is dependable and can beat jumbling methods. Besides, it can perceive malware variations and obscure malware families. In any case, it is time escalated and assets expending.

Malware Detection Framework

Malware identification methods are utilized to distinguish the malware and keep the PC framework from being tainted, shielding it from potential data misfortune and framework trade off. Malware identification has to do with the speedy recognition and approval of any occurrence of malware so as to avert further harm to the framework. The last piece of the activity is control of the malware, which includes exertion at halting the heightening and forestalling further harms to the framework (Wuechner T, 2017). Malware recognition strategies are in a general sense gathered in various classes from various perspectives. The following figure Figure 6 illustrates the general framework of malware detection system:

The general framework for malware detection using machine learning exhibits three distinct stages: Feature extraction, feature selection sometimes followed by dimensionality reduction techniques, and then classification using machine learning algorithm. This flow of malware detection process is as shown in Figure 6. Each stage demonstrates diverse measure and strategies utilized in already existing techniques. Initially the dataset is readied which comprises of malware and generous executables. These files are preprocessed depending on the FE method and next feature selection is done to quantify the correlation of feature for improving performance and reducing number of computations to attain the learning speed. Further after generalizing the feature capability, classifier is trained on the basis of the filtered results of feature selection. Researchers have adopted supervised machine learning approach which uses classifiers Decision trees, Support vector machine, Nave bayes, Bayesian network, KNN algorithm, etc. The best classifier is chosen which gives the clear margin, and reduces interference and misclassification between maliciousness and benignancy of executables. The dataset is tested corresponding to the trained classifier and results are generated as malicious or benign software. The obtained outcomes are evaluated with consequent performance metrics (Wu S, 2016).

Figure 6. General framework of malware detection system

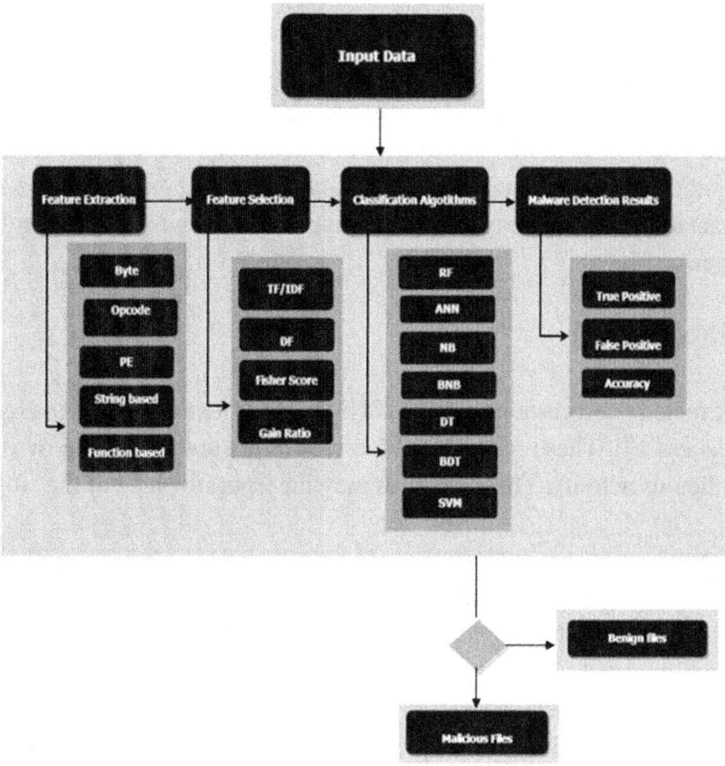

Feature Extraction

Feature extraction is a dimension reduction method that reduces the number of random variables being considered. This extraction process is performed through either static or dynamic analysis, or a combination of both, while examination and correlation are carried out by using machine learning techniques. Approaches based on static analysis look at the content of samples without requiring their execution, while dynamic analysis works by running samples to examine their behavior.

Debuggers are used for instruction level analysis. Simulators model and show a behavior similar to the environment expected by the malware, while emulators replicate the behavior of a system with higher accuracy but require more resources. Sandboxes are virtualized operating systems providing an isolated and reliable environment where to detonate malware.

Byte n-Gram Features

Byte n-gram highlights are successions of n bytes removed from malware utilized as the mark for perceiving malware. Despite the fact that this kind of highlight does not give important data, it yields high exactness in identifying new malware.

Opcode n-Gram Features

Previous studies represented that opcodes feature extraction was more efficient and successful for classification. They reveal statistical diversities between malicious and legitimate software. Some rare opcodes are better predictor's of malicious behavior. First all dataset executable files are disassembled and opcodes are extracted. Opcodes are capable to statistically derive the variability between malicious and legitimate software.

Portable Executables (PE)

These features are extracted from certain parts of EXE files. PE features are extracted by static analysis by using structural data of PE. These meaningful features indicate that the file was manipulated or infected to perform malicious activity. These features may incorporate piece of the snippets of data given as pursues:

- **File Pointer:** Pointer denotes the position within the file as it is stored on disk, CPU type.
- **Import Section:** Functions from which DLLs were used and Object files, list of DLLs of the executable can be imported.
- **Exports Section:** Describes which functions were exported.
- **Resource Directory:** Indexed by a multiple-level binary-sorted tree structure, resources like dialogs and cursors used by a given file.

String Features

These features are based on plain text which is encoded in executables like windows, get version, get start up info, get module filename, message box, library, etc.

Function Based Features

Function based features are extracted over the runtime behavior of the program file. Function based features functions that reside in a file for execution and utilize them to produce various attributes representing the file. Dynamically analyzed function calls including system calls, windows application programming interface (API) calls, their parameter passing, information flow tracking, instruction sets, etc. These functions increase the code reusability and maintenance. It is semantically richer representation. In this system, addressed automatic behavior analysis using Windows API calls, instruction set, control flow graph, function parameter analysis and system calls are used as features.

Hybrid Analysis Features

These features are obtained by combining both techniques static analysis as well as dynamic analysis. It decreases the impact of countermeasures of every static and dynamic procedure for breaking down malware and enhances the execution and identification rates.

Feature Selection

Feature selection is an important step for this process. The main objective is to select the smallest number of features that keep the detection rate as high as possible to allow using the minimum quantity of resources for the malware detection task. Besides, include determination and decrease is now realize that can diminish the clamor, enhance the exactness, and obviously enhance speed for preparing the arrangement calculations as given that time increased in $O(n^2)$ with respect to the number of features as state by Kolter and Maloof. The stages of feature selection methods are listed as follows,

- TF/IDF (term frequency/ inverse document frequency)
- DF (document frequency)
- Fisher Schore
- Gain Ration

Many researchers are developing malware detection, analysis, classification and antidote technologies in a four-phase manner to solve the malware attacks. These phases are described below.

- In the primary stage, identification method is being produced to gather information about attacks, which is a mystery framework for pulling in assaults and gathering malware. It also collects access destinations and communication patterns at time of malware infection.
- In the second stage, analysis method is being created to break down the gathered malware. The fact of the matter is to understand the malware's abilities and choose the hazard that it presents, and all around, to acquire distinct information about the attack
- After that, the classification of malware is carried out. It is a difficult process. Software that allows unauthorized control of a system is obviously malicious. Malware comes in various forms and categories. These are usually classified according to their propagation method and their actions that are performed on the infected machine using the designed malicious program.
- The characterization of malware is completed. It is a troublesome procedure. Programming that permits unapproved control of a framework is clearly pernicious. Malware comes in different structures and classes. These are generally grouped by their proliferation strategy and their activities that are performed on the contaminated machine utilizing the structured malevolent program.
- At last, in the third stage, cure innovation is being created to utilize the data acquired by the above identification and investigation advancements to produce boycotts in an arrangement that can be utilized by administrations. Addresses of access goals showing up at the season of a malware contamination extricated by discovery innovation can be utilized to create boycotts comprising of URL records, IP address records, and so forth.

Malware Classification Methodology

Methodologies towards characterization of malware can be gotten from Machine Learning, information mining, and content order. The most common way is to use the n-grams approaches which are extracted from executables to form training examples. Then after extracting these ngrams we can apply several learning methods such as

- Instance Based Learner
- Naïve Bayes (NB)
- Support Vector Machines (SVM)
- Decision Tree (DT)
- RF(Rain)
- J48
- ANN
- BN
- Boosted Classifiers

Malware Detection Approach

This chapter strategizes Malware Detection approaches are classified into signature-based and behavior-based. Malware Family Attribution technique of binding a malicious element as a "family" associated to its "Ancestors". Machine learning algorithm provides defensive support with varied guards and provisions as provided by Swiss Army Knife to disseminate and decode the resources found in binaries (Sheen S, 2015). Three types of malware detection methods are illustrated in Figure 7.

Figure 7. Types of malware detection techniques

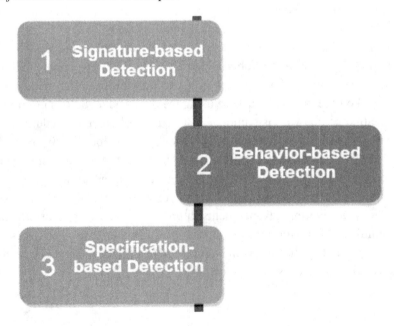

Signature-Based Detection

This method is used to checking the substance of PC files and cross-referencing their substance with the "code marks" having a place with known infections. A library of known code marks is refreshed and revived continually by the counter infection programming merchant. On the off chance that a viral mark is distinguished, the product demonstrations to shield the client's framework from harm. Suspected files are typically quarantined or encrypted in order to render them inoperable and useless. Unmistakably, there will dependably be new and rising infections with their very own special code marks. So by and by, the counter infection programming merchant works continually to survey and absorb new mark based identification information as it ends up accessible, frequently progressively so updates can be pushed out to clients quickly and zero-day vulnerabilities can be evaded. However, this technique has certain disadvantages:

Susceptible to Evasion: Since the check byte plans are gotten from known malware, these byte structures are in like manner normally known. From now on they can be viably avoided by software engineers using fundamental confusing frameworks, for example, embeddings no-operations and code re-requesting. Thus malware code can be altered and signature-based recognition can be equivocated.

Zero-Day Attacks: While the check-based adversary of malware structures are created dependent on known malware, they can't recognize darken malware or even varieties of known malware. Hence, without exact marks, they can't successfully distinguish polymorphic malware. Subsequently, signature-based location does not give zero-day security. What's more, since a stamp-based pointer uses an alternate check for each malware variety, the database of imprints creates at an exponential rate (Norouzi M, 2016).

Behavioral-Based Detection

This malware detection method is made out of a few applications, which together give the assets and components expected to recognize malware on the Android stage. Each program has its own particular usefulness and reason in the framework and the blend of every one of them makes the Behavior-Based malware discovery framework. The Android information mining contents and applications referenced in are the in charge of gathering information from Android applications, and the content running on the server will be the in charge of parsing and putting away all gathered information. Besides, the content will be in charge of making the framework call vectors for the k-implies grouping calculation (Ming J, 2016).

Specification-Based Malware Detection

Specification based discovery makes utilization of a specific principle set of what is considered as would be expected so as to choose the malevolence of the program disregarding the predefined rule set. Therefore programs damaging the standard set are considered as a vindictive program. In detail-based malware identification, where a discovery calculation that tends to the inadequacy of example coordinating was produced. This calculation consolidates guidance semantics to recognize malware occurrences. The methodology is high strength to basic jumbling systems. It utilized format T to depict the noxious practices of malware, which are the arrangement of directions spoken to by factors and representative constants. The impediment of this methodology is that the property of a program can't be precisely indicated. Particular based recognition is the derivate of oddity-based discovery (Mohaisen A, 2015).

Flexibility: It monitoring decouples strategy production from enforcement. For instance, one can think about having a plan in a specification-based monitoring system that is derived using anomaly detection.

Lower False-Positives: While methodologies in an overall structured, specific based watching system can be viably tuned, it can effect in low false positives.

Table 1. Comparison of the reviewed malware classification algorithms

S.NO	Author (Year)	Classification approach	Data analysis method	Usage	Total dataset	Accuracy %
1	Bhattacharya et al., (2017)	Random forest	Dynamic	Android malware detection	170	86
2	Mohaisen A et al.,(2015)	Decision trees	Dynamic	Automated malware analysis	2086	98
3	Altaher A (2016)	Neuro fuzzy inference system	Dynamic	Android malware detection	500	90
4	BoukhtoutaA et al.,(2016)	Naïve Bayesian	Dynamic	Deep Packet Inspection for Malware	4560	99
5	Sheen S et al.,(2015)	SVM	Static	Android based malware	2000	98.91
6	Norouzi M et al., (2016)	J48	Dynamic	Behavioral Malware	7000	98.3
7	Siddiqui M et al.,(2008)	Boosted Classifiers	Static	Malware Feature extraction method in cloud	15,000	99.69
8	Wu S et al., (2016)	BN	Static	Data flow android malware detection	2200	97.66
9	Wuechner T et al., (2017)	Compression based malware detection	Dynamic	ANN	7507	99.3
10	Dali Z et al., (2017)	Deep-learning malware detection	Hybrid	Hybrid (Naive Bayes, PART, Logistic Regression, SVM and MLP)	11,000	95.05
11	Yuan Z, et al.,(2016)	Deep belief networks	Hybrid	Android malware characterization and detection	1860	96.76
12	Nikolopoulos et al., (2016)	SaMe-NP	Dynamic	System-call malware	2667	95.9
14	Y. Ye et al., (2010)	Adapting Post processing Techniques	Dynamic	API calls and function calls of malware	15,000	88
15	Kai Huang et al., (2009)	ISMCS	Dynamic	Automated malware (e.g., viruses, backdoors, spyware, Trojans and worms) categorization	2029	79

A COMPARISON OF THE REVIEWED MALWARE CLASSIFICATION ALGORITHMS

In this part, a measurable investigation of surveyed methodologies of malware elucidation utilizing different systems is displayed. Beneath figure demonstrates the measurable graph for the majority of the order strategies in the chose malware discovery approaches.

According to the various author's researches, the comparison of the existing classification methods has illustrated in Table 1. Additionally, Table 1 demonstrates a specialized correlation of the order factors in each article.

From Figure 8, the SVM strategy has the most rates for malware classification approach with 29%, j48 has 17%, NB has 10%, RF has 5%, ANN has 3% and alternate techniques have fewer than 2% utilization in existing research results. In this way, this investigation finds that the SVM strategy simply has the best precision in the malware order approaches among different procedures.

Figure 8. An analysis of classification algorithms

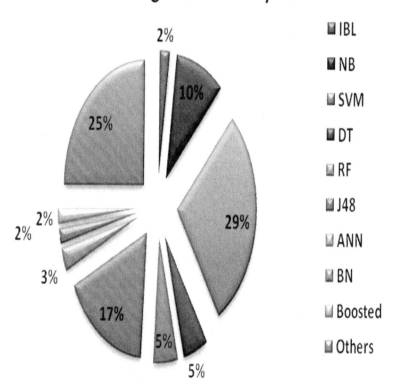

Machine Learning (Ml)

ML has developed from the investigation of computational learning hypothesis and example acknowledgment. It is the most effective method used in the field of classification in order to predict something by developing algorithms (N. Srivastava, 2014). These algorithms allow researchers to produce reliable and valid results and decisions. It also helps to discover some hidden features through historical learning's and trends in data. Feature selection is the mainly imperative mission of ML. Algorithm is created based on the results gathered from the training data that is why machine-learning algorithms are non-interactive. It thinks about the past perceptions to make exact expectations. It is an exceptionally troublesome undertaking to make a precise expectation rule dependent on which calculation can be produced. Fundamentally machine learning can be assembled into three classifications:

Box 2.

- *Supervised learning:* The majority of practical machine learning uses supervised learning. All data is labeled and the algorithms learn to predict the output from the input data.

- *Unsupervised learning:* All data is unlabeled and the algorithms learn to inherent structure from the input data.

- *Semi-supervised:* Some data is labeled but most of it is unlabeled and a mixture of supervised and unsupervised techniques can be used.

- *Reinforcement learning:* Reinforcement learning is an area of Machine Learning. It is all about making decisions sequentially. In simple words, it can define that the out depends on the state of the current input and the next input depends on the output of the previous input. In Reinforcement learning decision is dependent, so user gives labels to sequences of dependent decisions.

The figure Figure 9 shows the categories.

Machine Learning in Cyber Security

ML systems have been connected in numerous territories of science because of their one of kind properties like versatility, adaptability, and potential to quickly change in accordance with new and obscure difficulties. Digital security is a quickly developing field requesting a lot of consideration on account of astounding advances in informal communities, cloud and web innovations, and web-based saving money, versatile condition, brilliant matrix, malware grouping and so forth (Y. Ye, 2010). Diverse machine learning methods have been successfully deployed to address such wide-ranging problems in cyber security.

A variety of approaches have been attempted to tackle the problem of Malware detection and classification. According to the fundamental principles, machine learning approaches can be broadly used into malware classification system. These approaches try to analyze the information of a malware and by extracting good feature representations of malware, and training a prediction model on training data of both malicious and benign. The three phases such as data collection, feature extraction and machine learning classification are outlined in Figure 10.

Figure 9. Categorization of machine learning algorithms

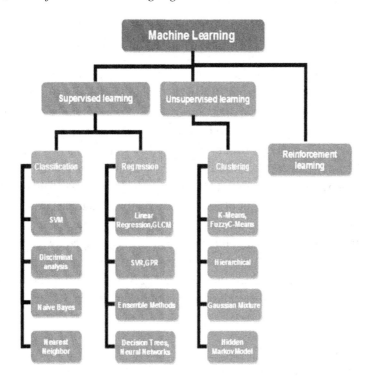

Figure 10. Malware classification approach by using machine learning system

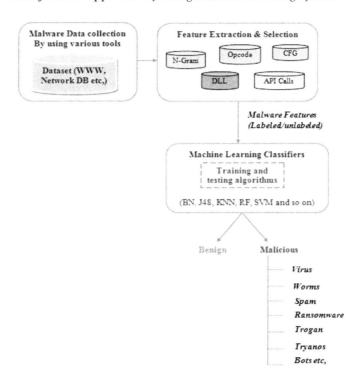

DEEP LEARNING (DL)

It is an almost human personification of knowledge given to computer systems. The whole system is relied on the way that the mind can absorb learning at a fast rate, and this information can be effectively changed over for various employments. Individuals regularly underestimate a great deal of things, and the capacity of the cerebrum is downplayed. When the human cerebrum absorbs data, it nearly turns out to be second nature for it to spread this data. For instance, if the human cerebrum recognizes a type of a puppy, it has normally engraved on the brain. On the off chance that the human is, demonstrated a very pixilated type of a canine, the cerebrum is as yet ready to recognize this shape as a pooch. This is somewhat how Deep Learning functions for digital security and malware recognition. It is compared to a cerebrum that is always learning and developing. It is along these lines ready to distinguish these illnesses and malware absent much exertion in light of its capacity to absorb data at a fast rate (Dali Z, 2017).

DL is a propelled model of conventional machine learning. This has the capacity to extricate ideal component portrayal from crude info tests. This method is been employed by researchers in recent days. This has been connected to different use cases in digital security, for example, interruption recognition, malware order, android malware identification, spam and phishing location and binary investigation as shown in Figure 11 There are many other classification algorithms like MLP and J48 that can be used for different problem statements.

Figure 11. Perception of deep learning

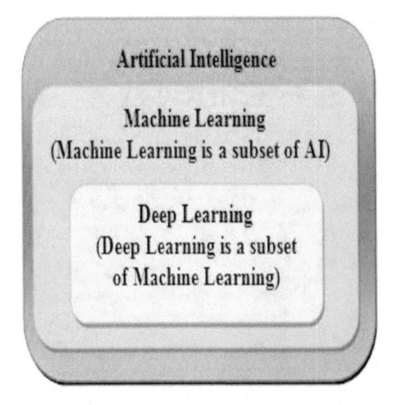

- A class of machine learning techniques that exploit many layers of non-linear information processing for supervised or unsupervised feature extraction and transformation, and for pattern analysis and classification.
- Deep learning is a set of algorithms in machine learning that attempt to learn in multiple levels, corresponding to different levels of abstraction. It typically uses artificial neural networks.
- The levels in these learned statistical models correspond to distinct levels of concepts, where higher-level concepts are defined from lower-level ones, and the same lower-level concepts can help to define many higher-level concepts.

The key concept within deep learning is the notion of layers, where each layer recognizes progressively more complex features and learns from the previous layer (Yuan Z, 2016). The following graphic illustrates the types of deep learning techniques

Box 3.

- *Deep convolutional network* is a special category the feed-forward multilayer neural network. It involves convolutional multiple layers followed by a few fully-connected layers.

- *Deep neural network* represents a multilayer perceptron with several hidden layers. The weights are entirely linked and are initialized using supervised/unsupervised pre-training method.

- *Boltzmann machine* represents a symmetrically linked network, where the stochastic decisions are determined based on the neuron.

- *Deep belief network* represents a probabilistic generative scheme consists of multiple stochastic layers of hidden variables. The first (top) two layers have symmetric/undirected connections.

Deep Learning in Cyber Security

The DL is sub-field of AI that is gaining an ever increasing extent of concentration. It holds the promise of attaining many of the long-standing goals for AI. Over the coming years, advances in unsupervised deep learning (interpreting unlabeled data) will propel AI's success in cyber security. While the promise of DL is amazing, the current state of the art is still complex.

MACHINE LEARNING(ML) VS DEEP LEARNING(DL)

In the course of the most recent couple of years' ML in has moved from the research center to the cutting edge of operational frameworks. Google, Amazon, and Facebook use ML each day to show signs of improvement customer encounters, recommended buys/associate individuals socially with new applications and encourage individual associations. ML's amazing capacity is likewise there for cyber security. Cyber security is situated to use machine learning out how to enhance malware identification, triage occasions, and perceive breaks and ready associations to security issues. ML can be used to perceive advanced concentrating on and risks, for instance, affiliation profiling, establishment vulnerabilities, and potential dependent vulnerabilities and attempts. Machine learning can fundamentally change the digital security scene. Malware independent from anyone else can speak to upwards of three million new examples sixty minutes.

Conventional malware identification and malware examination can't pace with new assaults and variations. New assaults and modern malware have possessed the capacity to sidestep system and end-direct identification toward convey digital assaults at disturbing rates. New procedures like profound learning must be utilized to address the developing malware issue. As opposed to progressively ordinary machine learning and highlight designing calculations, Deep Learning has favorable position of possibly giving an answer for location the information investigation and learning issues found in gigantic volumes of info information. All the more explicitly, it helps in naturally separating complex information portrayals from expansive volumes of unsupervised information. This makes it a profitable apparatus for digital security. The profound learning answer for learning highlight chains of importance is to illuminate an arrangement of basic shallow issues. In each progression, profound strategies become familiar with another dimension highlights increasing new bits of knowledge into the info information circulation in transit.

Table 2 represents the features of two learning paradigms.

Table 2. Features of learning paradigms

Features	Machine Learning	Deep Learning
Accuracy	Moderate, with a false positive rate at up to 5%	Extremely high with a false positive rate at nearly zero
Domain Expert	Required for feature engineering & extraction	Not required
Analysis of Data Set	Only 2.5-5% of available data	Processes 100% of available raw data
Correlations	Only simple, linear correlations	Non-linear correlations, i.e. correlations that exist in complex patterns, rather than simple 1-1 correlations.

The recent development in learning deep representations has demonstrated its wide applications in traditional vision tasks like classification and detection. Deep learning is a prominent algorithm employed in several malware classifications. Considering several traditional methods and machine learning methods deep learning algorithms considered as a robust way to solve problems. It is clear that most of the deep learning algorithms come up with better accuracy rate, which will be helpful in building a real time application for analyzing malware activities.

CONCLUSION

The growth and assortment of malware tests intensifies the requirement for development in programmed discovery and characterization of the malware variations. Machine learning is a characteristic decision to adapt to this expansion, since it tends to the need of finding hidden examples in vast scale datasets. These days, neural system procedure has been developed to the express that can outperform impediments of past machine learning strategies, for example, Hidden Markov Models and Support Vector

Machines. As an outcome, neural systems would now be able to offer unrivaled arrangement precision in numerous areas, for example, PC vision or natural language processing. This enhancement originates from the likelihood of building neural systems with a higher number of conceivably various layers and is known as Deep Learning.

During the past few years, deep learning has achieved a 20-30% improvement in most of application in computer vision. The domain of deep learning has a multitude of powerful algorithms that may be applied to almost any problem in cyber security. In view of the rising demand for responses and solutions to malware classification, applying other deep learning techniques onto cyber security problems holds an extremely large prospect for future work.

REFERENCES

Alotaibi, F., Furelli, S., Stengeli, I., & Papadakii, M. (2016). A Survey of Cyber-Security Awareness in Saudi Arabia. *11th International Conference for Internet Technology and Secured Transactions (IC-ITST-2016)*. 10.1109/ICITST.2016.7856687

Altaher, A. (2016). An improved Android malware detection scheme based on an evolving hybrid neuro-fuzzy classifier (EHNFC) and permission-based features. *Neural Computing & Applications*, 28(12), 4147–4157. doi:10.100700521-016-2708-7

Bhattacharya, A., & Goswami, R. T. (2017). DMDAM: data mining based detection of android malware. *Proceedings of the first international conference on intelligent computing and communication*, 187–194. 10.1007/978-981-10-2035-3_20

Boukhtouta, A., Mokhov, S. A., Lakhdari, N.-E., Debbabi, M., & Paquet, J. (2016). Network malware classifcation comparison using DPI and fow packet headers. *J Computer Virol Hacking Tech*, 12(2), 69–100. doi:10.100711416-015-0247-x

Dali, Z., Hao, J., Ying, Y., Wu, D., & Weiyi, C. (2017). Deep Flow: deep learning-based malware detection by mining Android application for abnormal usage of sensitive data. In 2017 IEEE symposium on computers and communications (ISCC), (pp. 438–443). IEEE.

Huang, K., Ye, Y., & Jiang, Q. (2009). Ismcs: an intelligent instruction sequence based malware categorization system. In *ASID'09: Proceedings of the 3rd international conference on Anti-Counterfeiting, security, and identification in communication*, (pp. 509–512). Piscataway, NJ: IEEE Press. 10.1109/ICASID.2009.5276989

Ming, J., Xin, Z., Lan, P., Wu, D., Liu, P., & Mao, B. (2016). Impeding behavior-based malware analysis via replacement attacks to malware specifications. *J Computer Virol Hacking Tech*, 13(3), 193–207. doi:10.100711416-016-0281-3

Mohaisen A., Alrawi O., & Mohaisen M. (2015). *AMAL: high-fidelity, behavior-based automated malware analysis and classification*. Academic Press.

Nikolopoulos, S.D., & Polenakis, I. (2016) A graph-based model for malware detection and classification using system-call groups. *J Comput Virol Hacking Tech, 13*, 29–46.

Norouzi, M., Souri, A., & Samad Zamini, M. (2016). A data mining classification approach for behavioral malware detection. *J Comput Netw Commun, 2016*, 9.

Sheen, S., Anitha, R., & Natarajan, V. (2015). Android based malware detection using a multi feature collaborative decision fusion approach. *Neurocomputing, 151*(2), 905–912. doi:10.1016/j.neucom.2014.10.004

Siddiqui, M., Wang, M. C., & Lee, J. (2008). A survey of data mining techniques for malware detection using fle features. In *Proceedings of the 46th annual southeast regional conference on xx.* ACM. 10.1145/1593105.1593239

Srivastava, N., Hinton, G., Krizhevsky, A., Sutskever, I., & Salakhutdinov, R. (2014). Dropout: A Simple Way to Prevent Neural Networks From Over fitting. *Journal of Machine Learning Research, 15*(1), 1929-1958.

World Internet, . (2010, May). *World internet users and 2016 population stats*. World Internet.

Wu, S., Wang, P., Li, X., & Zhang, Y. (2016). Effective detection of android malware based on the usage of data fow APIs and machine learning. *Information and Software Technology, 75*, 17–25. doi:10.1016/j.infsof.2016.03.004

Wuechner, T., Cislak, A., Ochoa, M., & Pretschner, A. (2017). Leveraging compression-based graph mining for behavior-based malware detection. *IEEE Trans Dependable Secur Comput.*

Ye, Y., Li, T., Jiang, Q., & Wang, Y. (2010). CIMDS: Adapting postprocessing techniques of associative classification for malware detection. *IEEE Transactions on Systems, Man, and Cybernetics, Part C (Applications and Reviews), 40*(3), 298–307.

Yuan, Z., Lu, Y., & Xue, Y. (2016). Droid detector: Android malware characterization and detection using deep learning. *Tsinghua Science and Technology, 21*(1), 114–123. doi:10.1109/TST.2016.7399288

This research was previously published in the Handbook of Research on Machine and Deep Learning Applications for Cyber Security; pages 104-131, copyright year 2020 by Information Science Reference (an imprint of IGI Global).

Chapter 11

Machine Learning–Based Subjective Quality Estimation for Video Streaming Over Wireless Networks

Monalisa Ghosh

Indian Institute of Technology Kharagpur, India

Chetna Singhal

Indian Institute of Technology Kharagpur, India

ABSTRACT

Video streaming services top the internet traffic surging forward a competitive environment to impart best quality of experience (QoE) to the users. The standard codecs utilized in video transmission systems eliminate the spatiotemporal redundancies in order to decrease the bandwidth requirement. This may adversely affect the perceptual quality of videos. To rate a video quality both subjective and objective parameters can be used. So, it is essential to construct frameworks which will measure integrity of video just like humans. This chapter focuses on application of machine learning to evaluate the QoE without requiring human efforts with higher accuracy of 86% and 91% employing the linear and support vector regression respectively. Machine learning model is developed to forecast the subjective quality of H.264 videos obtained after streaming through wireless networks from the subjective scores.

INTRODUCTION

This chapter provides insight into the emerging applications of machine learning for catering the needs of the next generation wireless networks. It is expected that the next generation wireless networks must reinforce ultra-reliable, low-latency communication in addition to bestowing high video quality to users playing real time streaming or ongoing download applications. Several deployment of LTE femto cells, WiFi hotspots not only makes accessing faster, but also increases the number of users enormously.

DOI: 10.4018/978-1-6684-6291-1.ch011

In next generation wireless networks, substantial volumes of data has to be gathered periodically and in real time across several sensing devices. The wireless uplink will confront growth of traffic due to large number of short-packet transmissions, opposed to general view of uplink being less congested compared to downlink. Tomorrow's wireless network must support cloud-based gaming, real-time HD streaming and several multimedia services. Infact, this will lead to varying networking environment whose applications and their heterogeneous quality-of-service (QoS) along with need for efficient network resource utilization, while maintaining reasonable cost endorse a fundamental change in the way in which next generation wireless networks are modeled, designed and optimized. Upcoming trends also aim at solutions that optimize the Quality of Experience (QoE) of the end users. This necessity for meeting the QoE can be realized by implementing the fundamental notions of machine learning across network infrastructure and the end-user equipments. This chapter presents basic architecture, training procedure, as well as the associated challenges and opportunities for communication problems that can be addressed using machine learning.

Recent studies are coming up that address the current state-of the-art applications of machine learning for QoE evaluation. The work by Grazia et al., (2018) devised a machine learning approach to carry out QoE-deployed video admission control and resource management algorithms. They developed a multi-stage learning system that combines the unsupervised learning of video features from the size of H.264-encoded video frames with a supervised classifier trained to automatically extract the quality-rate characteristics of unknown video sequences. They have developed a multi-stage machine learning system that blends the unsupervised learning of features obtained from video from the size of H.264-encoded video frames with a supervised classifier trained to spontaneously withdraw the quality-rate characteristics of unknown video sequences. This characterization of QoE is then used to govern parallel video transmissions via a shared channel in order to assure a minimum quality level conveyed to the destined users. The discussions by Casa & Wassermann (2017) presented a new proposal to multi-dimensional Quality of Experience (QoE) prediction incase of mobile video by use of machine learning models. A high dimensional input space is used by them inorder to model influence of buffering and beginning delay on QoE. The proposed models are trained and tested on publicly available mobile video dataset. The work by Bampis, Li, Katsavounidis, & Bovik (2018), deploy diverse recurrent dynamic neural networks that carry out continuous time subjective QoE prediction. They trained a variety of recurrent neural networks and non-linear autoregressive models to estimate the QoE using different available subjective QoE database. Another work by Gao, Kwong, & Jia (2017) devise a joint framework consisting of machine learning and game theory (MLGT) for inter frame coding tree unit (CTU) level bit allocation and rate control (RC) optimization in high efficiency video coding (HEVC). At first, the authors have devised a support vector machine-based multi classification scheme inorder to improve the prediction accuracy of CTU-level rate-distortion (R-D) model. Second, they have proposed a mixed R-D model-based cooperative bargaining game theory for bit allocation optimization. The minimum utility is adjusted by the reference coding distortion and frame-level quantization parameter (QP) change.

With extensive utilization of internet in today's world, it can be foreseen that several multimedia applications like video teleconferencing, video on demand, video streaming over the wireless, online streaming sites like YouTube, Hotstar etc. will occupy a huge proportion in the next generation wireless networks. Videos undergo ample distortions during any of these processes i.e. processing, compression or transmission which results in degradation of visual quality before reaching the destined users. Fluctuating bandwidth is a distinctive feature of the wireless channels that corrupts the transmitting bitstream. The recent advances in video coding and compression techniques make it feasible to deliver high quality video services to the end users. Majority of the video coding and compression standards deploy block-based coding schemes and motion compensation techniques. Due to application of these techniques, the decoded videos are subjected to one or multiple compression artifacts i.e. blurriness, false edges, color bleeding, jagged motion, chrominance mismatch, ringing and flickering. Study of video quality metrics provides insight into the video distortions. Hence, proper error correction and concealment techniques can be applied to ameliorate the quality of the video.

MEETING THE QOE AND QOS PARAMETERS

The issue of video quality evaluation is essential for video service providers from the perspective of better service delivery and maintaining acceptable performance levels across common network impairments. Human beings visual perception of the video gives assessment of video quality. Since network-related video impairments negatively influence quality of experience (QoE), so its evaluation is utmost important. Various video quality evaluation methods help in quality monitoring; thus maintaining quality of service (QoS) requirements and improving overall system performance.

NEED FOR REDUCING HUMAN EFFORTS IN SUBJECTIVE VIDEO QUALITY ASSESSMENT

As per the Recommendation of ITU-R BT.500-11 (2000), obtaining subjective scores from several groups of non-expert assessors for each and every video is a tedious and expensive process. Assessors need to be made familiar with assessment methods, type of impairment, grading scale etc. Discussions by Seshadrinathan, Soundararajan, Bovik, & Cormack (2010) show the presence of correlation between several objective quality metrics and human mean opinion scores. The dependence of several objective metrics on subjective scores can be made use for applying machine learning algorithms for forecasting the subjective scores. So, in this chapter a machine learning model is proposed which predicts the subjective scores

Many robust error detection mechanisms for H.264 and H.263++ encoding schemes are discussed by Farrugia & Debono (2008, 2009). Their methodology employs check sum of transport protocols and subjective scores for dividing the corrupted and uncorrupted Macro blocks (MBs) in a frame. Numerous error concealment techniques are used to mask the corrupted MBs. Only few corrupted MBs result in quality loss of the video. Some corrupted MBs incorporate extremely little distortions; thus removing them will adversely affect the video quality. The process involves classification of MBs in the scale of 1 to 5, followed by highly corrupted MBs detection. Subsequently, the content in these extremely corrupted MBs is used for training the Support Vector Machine (SVM).

The rest of the chapter is organized as follows. The next section discusses the significance of video quality and different assessment methods associated with it. These include subjective quality as well as objective quality methodologies. A brief description of the objective metrics i.e. PSNR, SSIM, MS-SSIM, SVD and MOVIE is also presented. Another section includes discussion on main motive behind proposing the machine learning model with a view to forecast the subjective scores of videos obtained through wireless transmission from the objective metrics. A short description of different wireless transmission methods used to obtain the distorted video sets is provided. The complete process involved in DMOS scores calculation is outlined. The further section provide details of the process involved in implementing the machine learning model. The process starts with correlation computation between the objective and subjective scores, followed by predictive model training and performance analysis of different regression models. A discussion on some of the open challenges is provided. The final section presents scope for future works and conclusion.

IMPORTANCE OF VIDEO QUALITY AND ITS ASSESSMENT METHODS

Quality of a video is assessed after passing the video through video transmission system. Several assessment techniques give an estimate of perceived degraded video compared to reference video. This methodology can be subjective as well as objective. Subjective quality assessment methods gather opinion scores of the quality from the users. On the contrary, Objective quality assessment methods make use of spatial as well as temporal information of the video.

Subjective Quality Methodology

Subjective video quality methods involve conducting the subjective tests, directly asking the human subjects for their point of view regarding the perceived quality. Choice of subjects should be such that they are not skilled in this field. An atmosphere that is isolated from the common environment is provided for viewing the videos aiming for better results. Subjective quality assessment is carried out as per Recommendation of ITU-R BT.500-11 (2000). The assessor has to give an unbiased score of his choice to video sequences. The options range from excellent to bad. Different scores and their corresponding opinions is given in Table-1. Approximately, 20-40 subjects are required to give their opinion scores. This methodology is much time and resource consuming.

Table 1. Quality and corresponding opinion scores of a video

Video Quality	Opinion Score
Excellent	5
Good	4
Fair	3
Poor	2
Bad	1

Objective Quality Methodology

1. **Peak Signal to Noise Ratio (PSNR):** PSNR is most easily interpreted through Mean Squared Error (MSE) between the original video and distorted videos. Generally, PSNR is a basic standard for objective video quality assessment metric. The MSE is given as

$$MSE = \frac{\sum_{l=1}^{L} \sum_{m=1}^{M} \left[S\left(l,m\right) - s\left(l,m\right) \right]^2}{L \times M}$$

$L \times M$ is the pixel resolution of the video. $S(l,m)$ is the original image. $s(l,m)$ is the distorted image. The expression for PSNR is given as,

$$PSNR = 20 \log_{10} \frac{255}{MSE} \tag{1}$$

2. **Structural Similarity Index (SSIM):** SSIM is one of the approaches for quality evaluation of still images. Structural information comprises of those attributes in an image which depicts the construction of objects in the scene, independent of mean luminance and contrast (Wang, Bovik, Sheikh, & Simoncelli, 2004). A good perception of image distortion is given by the computation of structural information change, considering that human visual system is adjusted to obtain structural information from viewing field. The SSIM is calculated on luminance component of the video frame-by-frame basis. Then, the mean of all the frame level gives the overall SSIM index for complete video sequence. SSIM index is expressed as

$$SSIM = \frac{\left(2\mu_y \mu_z + d_1\right)\left(2\sigma_{yz} + d_2\right)}{\left(\mu_y^2 + \mu_z^2 + d_1\right)\left(\sigma_y^2 + \sigma_z^2 + d_2\right)} \tag{2}$$

where Y,Z are reference and distorted frames. d_1, d_2 assume some constant values. σ_y, σ_z are the standard deviations of luminance intensities for reference and test videos.

3. **Multi-Scale Similarity Index (MS-SSIM):** The details of the image at various resolutions can be incorporated conveniently using the multi-scale method. Prolongation of single scale approach in SSIM leads to MS-SSIM (Wang, Lu, & Bovik, 2004). In MS-SSIM, original and test image are taken as inputs. Low pass filtering is performed by the system. The filtered image is then down sampled by a factor of two. MS-SSIM is represented as,

$$MS - SSIM\left(y,z\right) = \left[l_m\left(y,z\right)\right]^\alpha \prod_{m=1}^{M} c_m\left(y,z\right)^\beta \left[S_m\left(y,z\right)^\gamma\right] \tag{3}$$

where

$$l_m\left(y,z\right) = \frac{2\mu_y \mu_z + d_1}{\left(\mu_y^2 + \mu_z^2 + d_1\right)}, \quad c_m\left(y,z\right) = \frac{2\sigma_y \sigma_z}{\sigma_y^2 + \sigma_z^2 + d_2}, \quad S_m\left(y,z\right) = \frac{\sigma_{yz} + d_3}{\sigma_y \sigma_z + d_3}$$

4. **M-Singular Value Decomposition Metric (SVD):** M-SVD is one of the parameters used for image quality assessment that is established on SVD concept (Shnayderman, Gusev, & Eskicioglu, 2006). M-SVD is expressed as a function of distance between singular values of the reference and distorted image block. SVD is expressed as,

$$SVD = \sqrt{\sum_{j=1}^{n} \left(F_j - F_j' \right)^2}$$

(4)

where F_j, F_j' are the singular values of original and distorted blocks, n is the number of blocks.

5. **Motion-Tuned Video Integrity Evaluation (MOVIE):** MOVIE records perceptually significant distortions all along the motion trajectories; thus combining motion information into the video quality assessment process. In this way, MOVIE enhances spatial artifacts measurement in videos (Seshadrinathan, & Bovik, 2010). MOVIE uses Gabor filter family to decompose the original and distorted videos into the spatio-temporal bandpass channels. MOVIE model is distinct in the sense that it utilizes neuroscience based models as to how brain involves in visual information processing. In a video, spatial and temporal distortions are captured using the "Spatial MOVIE Index" and "Temporal MOVIE Index" model respectively. Spatial MOVIE and Temporal MOVIE indices are integrated to give overall MOVIE index.

6. **Spatial Motion-Tuned Video Integrity Evaluation Index:** Different spatial distortions include blurring, false contouring, ringing, mosaic patterns, noise and so on. Apart from primarily processing the spatial distortions, Spatial MOVIE index captures temporal distortions to a very little extent.

7. **Temporal Motion-Tuned Video Integrity Evaluation Index:** Various distortions like mosquito noise, ghosting, smearing, motion compensation mismatch etc. constitute the temporal distortions. For temporal video quality assessment, motion statistics is calculated from original video in the pattern of optical flow fields. The optical flow fields obtained is then combined with the spatio-temporal Gabor decomposition of original and test videos to evaluate temporal quality. Temporal MOVIE index primarily captures temporal distortions.

8. **Spatial Perceptual Information (SI):** Spatial perceptual information determines the quantity of spatial characteristics of a picture. The scenes with are more spatially complex usually contain higher spatial information. SI does not convey entropy measurement (Recommendation ITU-T P.910, 2008). SI calculation depends on Sobel filter. At given time n, every video frame (Fr_n) is initially filtered using Sobel filter [$Sobel(Fr_n)$]. In every Sobel filtered frame, the computation of standard deviation is performed over the pixels (Std_{space}). This process is continued for every frame contained in the video sequence. This in turn leads to creation of a time series of SI of the scene. Out of this time series, the maximum value is selected to depict the SI content of the scene (max m_{time}). This complete procedure can be represented in equation as

$$SI = \max m_{time} \left\{ Std_{space} \left[Sobel \left(Fr_n \right) \right] \right\}$$

(5)

9. **Temporal Perceptual Information (TI):** Temporal perceptual information gives a measure of temporal changes taking place in a video sequence. Sequences with high motion usually contain higher temporal information. Like SI, TI also does not convey entropy measurement (Recommendation ITU-T P.910, 2008). TI computation depends on motion difference feature [$Motion_n(j,k)$]. This motion difference evaluates the difference between pixel values (of luminance plane) that are at identical locations in space, but at consecutive times or frames. $Motion_n(j,k)$ can be expressed as function of time n as

$$Motion_n\left(j,k\right) = Fr_n\left(j,k\right) - Fr_{n-1}\left(j,k\right) \tag{6}$$

where $F_{rn}(j,k)$ denotes pixel location at j^{th} row and k^{th} column of nth time frame.

$Fr_{n-1}\left(j,k\right)$ denotes pixel location at j^{th} row and k^{th} column of $(n–1)^{th}$ time frame. TI is expressed as-

$$TI = \max m_{time}\left\{Std_{space}\left[Motion_n\left(j,k\right)\right]\right\} \tag{7}$$

where max m_{time} gives maximum value of time, Std_{space} gives standard deviation over space. The SI and TI values for the sample videos are given in Table 2.

OBJECTIVE OF PROPOSING THE MACHINE LEARNING MODEL

This chapter introduces a machine learning model that is developed to forecast the subjective scores of videos obtained through wireless transmission from the objective metrics. This particular model reduces tremendous human efforts needed in accessing the video. Obtaining a prediction of the subjective scores provides an estimate of QoE. Flow diagram depicting the model is given in Figure 1. The process of training this model involves providing objective and subjective scores that can predict subjective scores of new test sequence.

Ten different sets of video sequences consisting of natural sceneries, pedestrian area etc. have been used in this study. These video sequences are obtained after transmission through wireless networks collected from LIVE video quality database (2003). Each set consists of one reference video sequence and eleven distorted video sequences. The distortions are obtained in the following ways-

1. **H.264 Compression:** There are four test videos per reference which are H.264 compressed. The compression rate ranges from 200 kbps to 5 Mbps. The H.264 compressed videos were created using the JM reference software (Version 12.3) which was made accessible by Joint Video Team (JVT) (available online- H.264/AVC Software Coordination) (2007).
2. **Transmission Over IP Networks:** Different applications like video conferencing, Video on Demand require transmission of videos over IP networks. The database consists of three "IP" test videos per reference which were obtained by simulating IP losses on H.264 compressed videos. The JM reference software from H.264/AVC Software Coordination [available online] was used to create H.264 compressed videos with compression range varying between 0.5 and 7 Mbps. S. Wenger

in "H.264/AVC over IP" gives a detailed study of transmitting H.264 videos over IP networks. Generally, the packet losses occur in IP network because of buffer overflow at intervening nodes in congested network. The test videos obtained after transmission of compressed H.264 videos over error prone IP networks contain between 1 and 4 slices per frame and 1 slice per packet. Use of one slice per frame leads overhead reduction caused by IP headers with compromise in terms of robustness. Use of 4 slices per frame enhances robustness to error, but in turn decreases the compression efficiency.

Figure 1. Flow diagram of proposed machine learning model

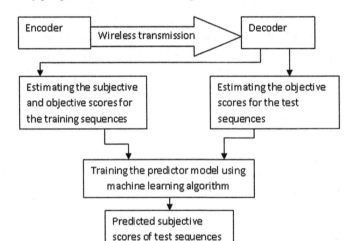

The IP error patterns with four different loss rate of 3%, 5%, 10% and 20% is used which is provided by VCEG (Video Coding Experts Group). After obtaining the H.264 compressed packetized video; the test videos were created by dropping the packets defined in error pattern. Two packets were not dropped inorder to allow decoding- (i) the first packet carrying Instantaneous Data Refresh (IDR) and (ii) the last packet (as decoder fails to detect this last packet). The H.264 bit stream obtained was further decoded employing H.264 Software coordination. Further, losses were suppressed deploying built-in error concealment mechanism (mode 2-motion copy) given in H.264/MPEG-4 AVC Reference software manual (2007).

Several observed artifacts in transmission over IP networks rely on different factors such as (i) whether the Intracoded frame (I frame) or Predicted frame (P frame) is lost (ii) the ordering of Flexible Macroblock (iii) whether each frame transmission takes place in 1 packet or 4 packets. Loss of I frame results in more distortions of the video sequence compared to P frame. Transmission of complete frame as one slice leads to remarkable distortions than transmission using four slices. Regular as well as dispersed modes of Flexible Macroblock ordering was used in the simulations. More distortions was observed in regular mode. In dispersed mode, the frames were subsampled by 2 along both rows as well as columns. Four packet groups were composed using these subsampled frames.

3. **Transmission Over Wireless Networks:** The following assumptions are made while simulating transmission of H.264 compressed videos over wireless networks. While simulating transmission of

H.264 compressed videos over wireless networks; it is assumed that packet loss occurs although it contains single bit error. As a consequence of this assumption, probability of loss of longer packet is more compared to shorter sized packets. So, sending shorter sized packets is advantageous. Video stream is encoded employing multiple slices for each frame. Each packet comprises roughly 200 bytes per packet providing equal liability to bit errors. The errors in wireless networks are produced using bit error patterns and software made available by VCEG. The packet error rate varies between 0.5-10%. Decoding as well as error concealment mechanism is similar to IP simulations. Observed artifacts in wireless transmission also rely on whether it results in loss of I or P frames. Also Flexible Macroblock Ordering contributes to observed artifacts.

In total, hundred and ten distorted video sequences (11 distorted sequences for each video sample) are H.264 compressed, produced by simulating losses carried by H.264 compressed video stream in a wireless environment. Spatial resolution of each video is 768×432. Detailed description of the video sets is provided in Table 2 and snapshot of video samples is shown in Figure 2.

Table 2. Description of the video sets

Video	Description	Camera Movement	Video Duration	Frame Rate	SI	TI
Blue sky (bs)	Blue sky and some trees	Circular camera motion	8.68	25	125.6266	26.0787
Mobile and Calendar (mc)	Toy train moving horizontally and a calendar moving vertically in the background	Recorded by camera pan	10	50	109.2197	0.0063
Pedestrian area (pa)	Few people walking about in a street intersection	Recorded by still camera	10	25	51.5969	7.4527
Park run (pr)	A person running across a park and comes to stand still.	Recorded by camera pan	10	50	146.5951	0
River bed (rb)	A river bed containing some pebbles and water	Recorded by still camera	10	25	104.4118	17.2233
Rush hour (rh)	Rush hour traffic on a street	Recorded by still camera	10	25	85.7463	7.9567
Sunflower (sf)	A bee moving over a sunflower in close-up	Recorded by still camera	10	25	49.1202	4.4439
Shields (sh)	A person walking across a display pointing at shields	Camera pans, then becomes still and zooms in	10	50	111.1766	0.0063
Station (st)	A railway track, a train and some people walking across the track	Recorded by still camera	10	25	107.9593	0.4670
Tractor (tr)	A tractor moving across some fields	Recorded by camera pan	10	25	53.6444	0.8260

Figure 2a. Video samples: bs

Figure 2b. Video samples: mc

Figure 2c. Video samples: pa

Figure 2d. Video samples: pr

Figure 2e. Video samples: rb

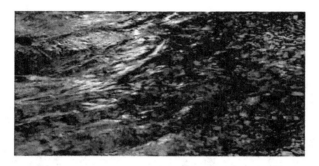

Figure 2f. Video samples: rh

Figure 2g. Video samples: sf

Figure 2h. Video samples: sh

Figure 2i. Video samples: st

Figure 2j. Video samples: tr

Subjective Quality Metric

Subjective quality tests were carried out with the help of 38 human subjects. The opinion scores were computed according to ITU- R Absolute category rating (ACR) scale. There were different sessions when the tests were conducted. Over all sessions, the mean opinion score was calculated for a video. These opinion scores obtained from assessors were transformed to difference opinion scores with a view to remove assessor preferences for any particular reference videos. The difference opinion score is computed as

$$D_{pqs} = r_{pq_{ref}s} - r_{pqs} \qquad (8)$$

where r_{pqs} represent the rate (score) allocated by assessor p to video q in session $s=\{1,2\}$.

This is termed as hidden reference removal. The difference scores obtained per session was subsequently converted to Z-scores.

$$z_{pqs} = \frac{D_{pqs} - \mu_{ps}}{\sigma_{ps}} \tag{9}$$

where

$$\mu_{ps} = \frac{1}{T_{ps}} \sum_{q=1}^{T_{ps}} D_{pqs} \text{ and } \sigma_{ps} = \left(\frac{1}{T_{ps}-1} \sum_{q=1}^{T_{ps}} \left(D_{pqs} - \mu_{ps} \right)^2 \right)^{1/2}.$$

T_{ps} denotes the number of test videos watched by assessor p in session s.

In the process of test conduction, the assessor sees each video contained in database only once- either in first or second session. The matrix $\{z_{pq}\}$. results after combining the Z-scores of both the sessions. $\{z_{pq}\}$ corresponds to Z-scores given by assessor p to video q where q varies from 1 to T_{ps}. T_{ps}=110 distorted videos collected from LIVE Video Quality Database (LIVE VQD) (2003).

A procedure is laid down in ITU-R BT 500.11 to reject scores from unreliable assessors. The recommendation of ITU-R BT 500.11 at first governs if the scores given by an assessor are normally distributed by evaluating kurtosis of the scores. When the kurtosis lies between the values of 2 and 4, the scores are deemed to be normally distributed. Incase of normally distributed scores, an assessor gets rejected when greater than 5% of scores allocated by him falls beyond the range of two standard deviations from mean scores. Generally, those subjects that are constantly pessimistic or optimistic in judging the quality are retained.

Linear rescaling was done to make the Z-scores remain in the range of [0,100]. Under the assumption that Z-scores given by an assessor follow standard Gaussian distribution, 99% of the scores fell in the range of [-3,3]. The authors in ("Study of subjective and objective quality assessment of video") performed rescaling following linear mapping from [-3,3] to [0,100] using

$$z'_{pq} = \frac{100\left(z_{pq} + 3\right)}{6} \tag{10}$$

For each video, the DMOS was calculated as mean of rescaled Z-scores from rest subjects left after rejection. Only 29 subjects were left after subject rejection (R=29).

$$DMOS_q = \frac{1}{R} \sum_{p=1}^{R} z'_{pq} \tag{11}$$

In In this study, the DMOS scores were collected from LIVE VQD. LIVE VQD aimed to sample the extent of visual quality in almost uniform manner. The histogram of DMOS scores acquired from LIVE VQD is shown in Table-3. Table-3 shows out of total videos, the number of videos with good and poor quality are almost equal. Table-3 depicts that the DMOS scores obtained from LIVE VQD lies in the range of [30,90]. This range seems apparently small to subjects dealing with evaluating subjective scores employing Double Stimulus Continuous Quality Scale (DSCQS) method. The authors- Seshadrinathan,

Soundararajan, Bovik, & Cormack (2010) applied the DSCQS method in VQEG phase 1 study, where a rating in the scale of [0,100] was given by the subjects to original and test videos. The difference between the rating of original and test videos was calculated as DMOS. On the contrary, LIVE VQD applies a sole stimulus paradigm with hidden reference removal and DMOS is calculated taking the average of Z-scores over all sessions; not as difference between ratings of original and test videos. Transforming difference scores to Z-scores is essential to justify for differences in applying ratings by the subjects. Under the assumption that Z-scores given by an assessor follow standard Gaussian distribution, 99% of the scores fell in the range of [-3,3] which is analogous to DMOS score in range of [0,100]. DMOS range of [30,90] in LIVE VQD is equivalent to range of [-1.2,1.92] on average Z-scores, which is roughly 86% of area of standard normal distribution.

Table 3. Distribution of DMOS scores over the video sequences

DMOS Scores	Number of Videos
30-40	10
40-50	27
50-60	35
60-70	25
70-80	10
80-90	3

Objective Quality Metric

PSNR, SSIM, MS-SSIM, SVD, Spatial MOVIE, Temporal MOVIE and MOVIE index constitute the objective quality metrics. Out of them, PSNR, SSIM, MS-SSIM and SVD are computed on luminance component at each frame with respect to reference video in similar set. Concatenations of frames result in formation of sequence files. Calculating the mean of corresponding metric across all frames gives the metrics of that video sequence. Spatial MOVIE, Temporal MOVIE and MOVIE index were estimated for all test (distorted) video sequence with reference to original video sequence. For implementing the machine learning model, dataset was composed of all the hundred and ten distorted video sequences. The subjective and objective scores of distorted videos were incorporated in the data set. The objective quality metrics was computed for distorted videos of blue sky, park run, shields, tractor and so on. Distribution of PSNR for complete dataset of videos is shown in Figure 3.

IMPLEMENTING THE MACHINE LEARNING MODEL

The dataset for study of proposed machine learning model contains subjective and objective scores of 110 test videos. Keeping in mind the fact that the model intends to predict the subjective score i.e. DMOS, it is at first necessary to make out the dependence of each and every objective score on the subjective score. Distribution of objective metrics incase of river bed is shown in Figure 4.

Figure 3a. PSNR distribution for complete dataset of videos: PSNR boxplot

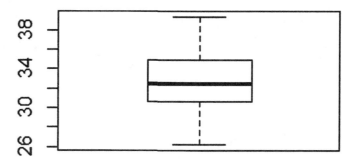

Figure 3b. PSNR distribution for complete dataset of videos: Scatter plot of PSNR~DMOS

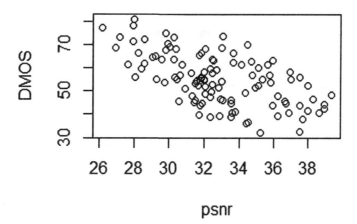

Figure 4a. Objective metrics for test videos in river bed (rb): SSIM and MS-SSIM

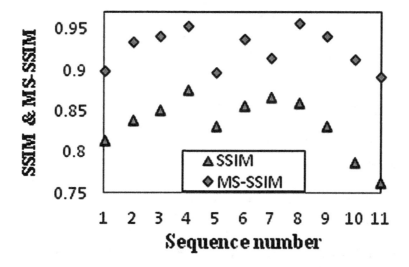

Figure 4b. Objective metrics for test videos in river bed (rb): PSNR and SVD

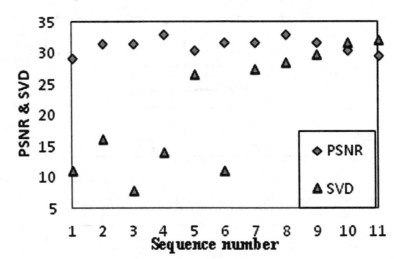

Figure 4c. Objective metrics for test videos in river bed (rb): Spatial, Temporal and MOVIE index

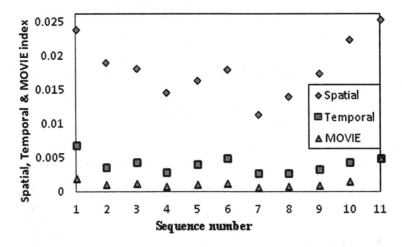

So, the following steps need to be followed to execute the model-

1. Finding out the association (correlation) between every objective score and subjective score.
2. Training the predictive model.
3. Applying the Linear regression model to predict the response variable i.e. DMOS.
4. Applying the Support Vector regression model to predict the response variable i.e. DMOS.
5. Performance comparison of Linear and Support Vector Regression models.

Computing Correlation Between Objective Scores and Subjective Score

Correlation test is carried out to assess the association between objective scores and the subjective score. The correlation coefficient shows the dependency of DMOS on a specific objective score. Correlation coefficient gives the statistical relationship between PSNR and DMOS, SSIM and DMOS, MS-SSIM and DMOS, Spatial MOVIE and DMOS etc. The computed correlation coefficient values are depicted in Table 4.

Table 4. Correlation between Objective scores and DMOS

Objective Score~DMOS	Correlation Coefficient
PSNR	-0.5847
SSIM	-0.4583
MS-SSIM	-0.6674
SVD	-0.3906
Spatial MOVIE	0.7607
Temporal MOVIE	0.5660
MOVIE index	0.3355

Training the Predictive Model

The complete dataset is separated into training and test datasets. The predictive model is trained using 90% of the dataset, while rest 10% of the dataset is used for evaluating the performance of trained model.

This predictive model comprises of two variables- predictor and response variable. The predictor variables include the objective metrics- PSNR, SSIM, MS-SSIM, SVD, Spatial MOVIE, Temporal MOVIE and MOVIE index. The response variable contains the subjective score- DMOS. Linear regression and support vector regressions are used for predicting the response variable considering its quantitative nature.

Performance Analysis of Linear Regression Model

Linear regression is one of the simplest approach for predicting the quantitative response. A linear regression model helps in determining the values of the coefficients used in the representation with the aid of available data (Tibshirani, James, Witten, & Hastie, 2013). Linear regression considers that there exists a linear relationship between the response variable 'y' and the predictor variables 'x_1' and 'x_2' of the sort $y=K+Lx_1+Mx_2$, where K, L and M are the coefficients of the given equation. After the training set is fed, linear regression builds a linear equation for prediction on the test set.

The response variable–DMOS is predicted from objective metrics using a simple linear regression model constructed in R studio. The contents in training dataset are used to train the model and its performance on the test dataset is obtained as shown in Table 5. Mean absolute error and variance of linear regression model is 5.6904 and 15.6630 respectively. The adjusted R –squared value obtained for this model in R-studio is 0.5716.

Performance Analysis of Support Vector Regression (SVR) Model

The support vector machine (SVM) is an augmentation of the support vector classifier which is the outcome of expanding the feature space in a distinct way by applying kernels. Support vector machine

(SVM) provides an approach for classification whereas the support vector regression finds application in regression problem (Tibshirani et al., 2013). SVR provides a quantitative approach than a qualitative approach. In case of non-linear SVR, the kernel functions modify the data into higher dimensional feature space for attaining the linear separation.

The response variable is predicted using a support vector regression model constructed in R studio. SVR is trained using training instances and tested on the test dataset. In this study, a polynomial kernel is used to construct the SVR model because of its better performance compared to others. Mean absolute error obtained here is 5.0842 and variance of 9.3213.

Table 5. Performance comparison of Linear Regression and Support Vector Regression

Parameters	Linear Regression	Linear Regression With Bagging	Support Vector Regression (SVR)	SVR With Bagging
Mean absolute Error	5.6904	5.8544	5.0842	6.2757
Standard deviation of error	3.9576	3.8252	3.0530	3.7334
Root mean square error	6.9314	6.9933	5.9304	7.3022
Variance of error	15.6630	14.6325	9.3213	13.9388
Mean absolute percentage error(%)	10.9747	11.3196	10.0237	11.7442

Performance Comparison of Linear Regression and SVR

In every simulation, the mean absolute error value varies due to the random sampling of the train and test sequences. With a view to analyse the actual performance of these models, Bagging (Bootstrap Aggregation) is performed on these models. The bootstrap is used to quantify the doubt related to a particular estimator. Bootstrap estimates the actual performance of Linear regression and SVR. Linear regression and SVR performance comparison and their corresponding bagged models is depicted in Table 5. It can be noted that SVR has a better performance compared to linear regression.

K-Fold Cross Validation

Sometimes it leads to over fitting while trying to fit the model with training instances. This degrades the performance of the model while testing. This problem can be overcome using the K-fold Cross validation, a resampling technique that helps to avoid over fitting (Rodriguez, Perez, & Lozano, 2010). In this process, observation set is randomly divided into k folds of almost equal size. The starting fold is the validation set and method is fit on the rest $k-1$ folds.

In this study, 10 fold cross validation is applied. Figure 5 shows the corresponding fold number and mean absolute error value of linear regression (LR) and support vector regression (SVR). Mean absolute error of 7.414 and 6.275 is obtained using LR and SVR respectively on all folds.

Figure 5. Variation of error in LR and SVR in 10-fold cross validation

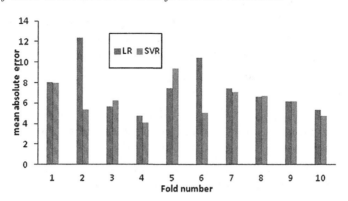

Performance of SVR on an Unseen Sequence

In order to test the unbiased performance of SVR on any particular video sequence, some tests were carried out. SVR was trained on starting 9 tractor (tr) videos and its performance on 10th tr video was evaluated. This gives mean absolute error of 5.6388 and variance of 9.905. It is seen that the performance is almost similar to SVR in section 4.5. Thus, unbiased performance of SVR is proved.

OPEN CHALLENGES

The study presented in this chapter was intended to reduce the efforts involved in video quality evaluation by the use of machine learning model. Although few objective metrics have been considered in this chapter, still other major QoE metrics are not taken into account that could have affected sharp quality changes. The identification of a function that quantifies the quality degradation due to change in SSIM, PSNR, SVD etc can be a research challenge. Any small change in any of the objective metrics will affect the QoE immensely. The amount of trade off that can be obtained by reducing the SSIM characteristics, thus providing space for more numbers of end users to be served can be looked into. The process of allowing new users to be served at the cost of minimal degradation of the objective metrics is still an open area of challenge. A model can be devised that must be optimized in terms of maximum users served at the cost of minimum quality degradation in the overall system. Steps can be taken forth inorder to further improve the accuracy of the machine learning models. Feature set can be extended to include the initial delay, jitter and rebuffering events to predict the QoE. Brief analysis of complexity involved in the end user side for implementing the machine learning model can be considered.

CONCLUSION AND FUTURE DIRECTIONS

This chapter has presented a novel machine learning model that is applied to evaluate the Quality of Experience of a video sequence from its objective quality metrics. Infact, this provides an insight of how machine learning finds applications in next generation wireless networks. Averaging of quality assessment techniques at frame level for a video gives the objective score for that video. Certain observations were deduced from this study. Spatial MOVIE was found to have highest correlation with subjective scores. Training objective scores with machine learning algorithms provides better evaluation of subjective quality. To check the accurate performance of Linear and Support vector regression model, bootstrap aggregation was performed. The performance of support vector regression was better compared to linear regression. Further, it was noticed that this model operates well on unseen sequences which tells that the model is unbiased by a particular set of sequences.

In future, several objective features that have good correlation with subjective scores can be simulated to increase the predictive capacity of our model. Exploiting the spatial and temporal information of video sequences and deploying them for enhancing video quality can be carried out. Many no- reference quality assessments metric like video intrinsic integrity and distortion evaluation oracle (VIIDEO) can be included as features. Apart from this, numerous full reference quality assessment metrics can also be incorporated. Using the principal component analysis to remove those features (from multiple available features) that may adversely affect the response variable.

REFERENCES

Bampis, C. G., Li, Z., Katsavounidis, I., & Bovik, A. C. (2018). Recurrent and Dynamic Models for Predicting Streaming Video Quality of Experience. *IEEE Transactions on Image Processing*, *27*(7), 3316–3331. doi:10.1109/TIP.2018.2815842 PMID:29641409

Casa, P., & Wassermann, S. (2017). Improving QoE prediction in mobile video through machine learning. *8th International Conference on the Network of the Future (NOF)*, 1-7. 10.1109/NOF.2017.8251212

Farrugia, R. A., & Debono, C. J. (2008). A Robust Error Detection Mechanism for H.264/AVC Coded Video Sequences Based on Support Vector Machines. *IEEE Transactions on Circuits and Systems for Video Technology*, *18*(12), 1766–1770. doi:10.1109/TCSVT.2008.2004919

Farrugia, R. A., & Debono, C. J. (2009). A Support Vector Machine Approach for Detection and Localization of Transmission Errors Within Standard H.263++ Decoders. *IEEE Transactions on Multimedia*, *11*(7), 1323–1330. doi:10.1109/TMM.2009.2030651

Gao, W., Kwong, S., & Jia, Y. (2017). Joint Machine Learning and Game Theory for Rate Control in High Efficiency Video Coding. *IEEE Transactions on Image Processing*, *26*(12), 6074–6089. doi:10.1109/TIP.2017.2745099 PMID:28858792

Grazia, M. D. F. D., Zucchetto, D., Testolin, A., Zanella, A., Zorzi, M., & Zorzi, M. (2018). QoE Multi-Stage Machine Learning for Dynamic Video Streaming. *IEEE Transactions on Cognitive Communications and Networking*, *4*(1), 146–161. doi:10.1109/TCCN.2017.2784449

H.264/AVC Software Coordination. (2007). Retrieved from http://iphome.hhi.de/suehring/tml/

H.264/MPEG-4AVC Reference Software Manual. (2007). Retrieved from http://iphome.hhi.de/suehring/tml/JM(JVT-X072).pdf

Int. Telecommun. Union. (2000). *Methodology for the Subjective Assessment of the Quality of Television Pictures*. ITU-R Recommendation BT.500-11, Tech. Rep.

LIVE -Labaratory for Image and Video Quality Engineering, an Image Quality Assessment Database. (2003). Retrieved from http://live.ece.utexas.edu/research/quality/subjective.htm

Rodriguez, J. D., Perez, A., & Lozano, J. A. (2010). Sensitivity Analysis of k-Fold Cross Validation in Prediction Error Estimation. *IEEE Transactions on Pattern Analysis and Machine Intelligence*, *32*(3), 569–575. doi:10.1109/TPAMI.2009.187 PMID:20075479

Seshadrinathan, K., & Bovik, A. C. (2010). Motion tuned spatio-temporal quality assessment of natural videos. *IEEE Transactions on Image Processing*, *19*(2), 335–350. doi:10.1109/TIP.2009.2034992 PMID:19846374

Seshadrinathan, K., Soundararajan, R., Bovik, A. C., & Cormack, L. K. (2010). Study of Subjective and Objective Quality Assessment of Video. *IEEE Transactions on Image Processing*, *19*(6), 1427–1441. doi:10.1109/TIP.2010.2042111 PMID:20129861

Shnayderman, A., Gusev, A., & Eskicioglu, A. M. (2006). An SVD-based grayscale image quality measure for local and global assessment. *IEEE Transactions on Image Processing*, *15*(2), 422–429. doi:10.1109/TIP.2005.860605 PMID:16479812

Telecommunication Standardization Sector of, ITU. (2008). Subjective video quality assessment methods for multimedia applications. [Tech. Rep.]. *ITU-T P*, *910*, 4–5.

Tibshirani, R., James, G., Witten, D., & Hastie, T. (2013). Linear Regression, Support Vector Machines, Tree-Based Methods. In An Introduction to Statistical Learning with Applications in R (pp. 59-102, 344-354, 316-321). New York, NY: Springer.

Wang, Z., Bovik, A. C., Sheikh, H. R., & Simoncelli, E. P. (2004). Image quality assessment: From error visibility to structural similarity. *IEEE Transactions on Image Processing*, *13*(4), 600–612. doi:10.1109/TIP.2003.819861 PMID:15376593

Wang, Z., Lu, L., & Bovik, A. C. (2004). Video quality assessment using structural distortion measurement. *Signal Processing Image Communication*, *19*(2), 121–132. doi:10.1016/S0923-5965(03)00076-6

This research was previously published in Next-Generation Wireless Networks Meet Advanced Machine Learning Applications; pages 235-254, copyright year 2019 by Information Science Reference (an imprint of IGI Global).

Chapter 12
Architecting IoT based Healthcare Systems Using Machine Learning Algorithms:
Cloud–Oriented Healthcare Model, Streaming Data Analytics Architecture, and Case Study

G. S. Karthick
https://orcid.org/0000-0002-9340-6928
Bharathiar University, India

P. B. Pankajavalli
https://orcid.org/0000-0003-1992-7386
Bharathiar University, India

ABSTRACT

The rapid innovations in technologies endorsed the emergence of sensory equipment's connection to the Internet for acquiring data from the environment. The increased number of devices generates the enormous amount of sensor data from diversified applications of Internet of things (IoT). The generation of data may be a fast or real-time data stream which depends on the nature of applications. Applying analytics and intelligent processing over the data streams discovers the useful information and predicts the insights. Decision-making is a prominent process which makes the IoT paradigm qualified. This chapter provides an overview of architecting IoT-based healthcare systems with different machine learning algorithms. This chapter elaborates the smart data characteristics and design considerations for efficient adoption of machine learning algorithms into IoT applications. In addition, various existing and hybrid classification algorithms are applied to sensory data for identifying falls from other daily activities.

DOI: 10.4018/978-1-6684-6291-1.ch012

INTERNET OF THINGS AND HEALTHCARE INTERNET OF THINGS: AN INTRODUCTION

The IoT is an outcome of the technological revolution which interrelates the unified computing devices, mechanical instruments, hi-tech electronic machines and humans that are equipped with the capacity to exchange data over a network. The IoT was first formulated with the back support of Radio Frequency Identification (RFID) that can be applied to track the location of objects. For example, products in the shopping malls are interconnected to their own network, which enables tracking the location of products and increases the billing process flexible at the point of sales depots. Every individual product is exclusively identified and categorized based on its RFID. This uses machine-to-machine networks and these resemble the IoT through network connected systems and data/information. The likelihood of connecting objects to the network allows tagging, tracking and reading of data from objects with greater technical efforts, the technology of this era established called as IoT.

The essentials that emerged the IoT in current and future applications have been elaborated comprehensively and have been characterized by many authors. Gubbi et al., and Li et al., have discussed the major components and architectural elements in IoT (Gubbi, 2013) (Li, 2015). The millions of sensing elements, actuators, and other devices exist at the lowest level of the IoT. Each of which requires a unique identification and addressing schemes because of their deployment are at large scale and also have a high degree of constraints such as energy and computational resources. Communication is another important element which interconnects 'n' number of heterogeneous devices for providing smart services. Some of the short and long-range technologies used for communications in IoT applications which may include Wireless Sensor Networks (WSNs), Radio Frequency Identification (RFID), IETF Low power Wireless Personal Area Networks (6LoWPAN) and protocols like IEEE 802.11 (Wi-Fi), IEEE 802.15 (Bluetooth). As IoT devices generate a vast amount of raw data, thus increases the need for data storage and analytics. The data analytics, processing and machine learning in most of the IoT applications are deployed via cloud services. The IoT services are classified as identity-related, information aggregation, collaboration-aware and ubiquitous services (Montenegro, 2007). Identity-related services provide unique identification for every deployed thing. Information aggregation services are responsible for collecting and storing the data received from sensors. Collaborative aware services make use of the data provided by information aggregation services to take decisions and to provide smartness to the system. Ubiquitous services enable users to access services without geographical restrictions (Montenegro, 2007). Li et al., 2015 categorized the generic service-oriented architecture as sensing layer, network layer, service layer and interface layer (Al-Fuqaha, 2015).

The healthcare domain is in a state of a highly miserable situation, where its services are becoming more costly than ever before due to an increase in global population and a huge rise of chronic diseases. Even the basic healthcare services are out of reach to the people and this would be prone to chronic diseases. The technological revolution could never eradicate the population from aging and chronic diseases completely. But the accessibility to the healthcare services can be made easier with incomparable innovation and applicability of the Internet of things (IoT) in the healthcare domain. The application of IoT technology in healthcare allows doctors to communicate with their patients via smart wearable gadgets and devices without human interventions. On the other hand, major two crucial purposes of Healthcare Internet of things (HIoT) are: (i) Enhanced disease management that satisfies the patients and offers a better experience. (ii) Offers a higher level of interaction which allows patients to gain more information and medical intervention at every situation.

HIoT consists of medical devices, remote patient monitoring tools, wearables and various sensors which transmit the data to other end devices via the Internet. One of the interesting examples of IoT in healthcare is the automated insulin delivery system that entirely differs from continuous glucose monitoring system which can able to measure the amount of glucose in a patient's blood and intimate the end-users via mobile applications. But automated insulin delivery system automatically adjusts the quantity of insulin delivered to the patient's and thus prevents them from hyperglycemia and hypoglycemia. Such kind of applications generates a vast amount of data that has to be stored, incorporated and analyzed for spawning the useful insights for managing the patients with chronic diseases.

The high-level information extraction requires the application of machine learning techniques which processes the data automatically and intelligently. The efficiency of machine learning techniques tends to evaluate the data recorded by devices continuously in order to identify the stability or condition of patients. This streamlined data processing also helps the medical practitioners to predict the secondary illness in accordance with the patient primary illness. IoT improves the lives of patients through seamless connectivity, intelligent data processing, and remote monitoring. IoT technology tends to reshape the healthcare domain in such a way to reduce the hurdles in accessing healthcare services. Few key areas acknowledged where healthcare is reshaped by IoT are: (i) define the regulations for the industries which manufacture the pharmaceutical and medical devices that comply with patient safety, reliability and flexibility,(ii) aging of population simultaneously increase the demand of medical devices, (iii)the relevant data captured from patient's IoT devices to be communicated autonomously and accurately without data tampering.

HEALTHCARE BENEFITS FROM IoT

The number of healthcare service providers opt the IoT solutions is constantly increasing due to the adherence of the following benefits as shown in Figure 1:

Reporting and Monitoring

Remote health monitoring, diagnosing and patient's deterioration condition alerting. Medical gadgets send useful information on patient's conditions to practitioners or healthcare service providers without any human intervention. For example, HIoT device gathers health data like blood pressure, heartbeat, glucose level and oxygen in blood and temperature and stores the data in the cloud. Then stored data can be made available to the authorized person.

End-to-End Connectivity

Innumerable medical equipment is connected together to the centralized hub that eases monitoring and management. Thus avoid human participation, reduces error and time consumption.

Figure 1. Healthcare benefits from IoT

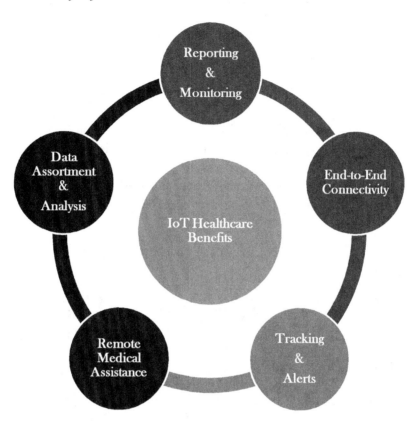

Data Assortment and Analysis

IoT devices generate a huge amount of data in seamlessly and manual analysis of such data is impossible. Therefore, streaming data analytics enables healthcare providers to receive structured data by avoiding data processing distractions.

Remote Medical Assistance

Remote medical device configuration allows the healthcare service providers to change the home-based health monitoring devices which avoid the patient's frequent visits to the hospital.

Tracking and Alerts

IoT-based medical devices drop notifications via mobile applications during life-threatening situations rather than gathering health data. Thus, provides better accuracy, appropriate intervention by healthcare providers and improves the healthcare service delivery.

A CLOUD-ORIENTED MODEL FOR INTERNET OF THINGS HEALTHCARE SYSTEM

IoT healthcare systems are developed to offer various medical services to the people, which incorporate reliability, integrity, and security. Furthermore, healthcare applications notify the patient's status by observing the activities of patients and vital signs. A well-formed healthcare system must offer accurate and reliable services in a timely manner for patients, doctors, and caregivers. Existing healthcare model does not guarantee the integrity and confidentiality of data stored in the cloud. Also, there is no reliable communication and latency time is too high. In order to meet all the drawbacks, a new cloud-oriented model is developed for IoT-based healthcare system, which includes fog computing for offering processing and storage services to the users. Figure 2 shows the Cloud-Oriented Model for Internet of things Healthcare System and the functionalities of each layer are explained as follows:

Figure 2. Cloud-oriented model for Internet of things healthcare system

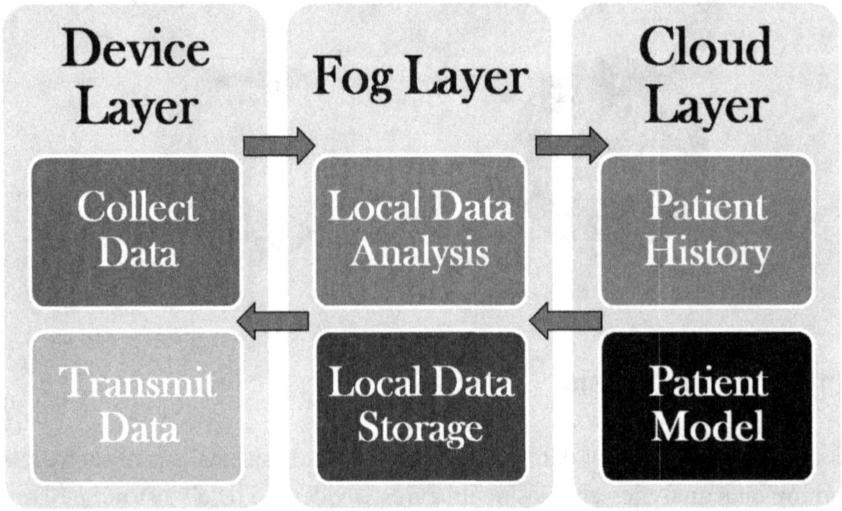

Device Layer

This layer encompassing the 'n' number of physical objects such as medical sensors which are incorporated with the wireless module to gather physiological information of a patient. Every sensory device is enabled with patient identification data tends to capture the physiological patterns from the body. The captured physiological patterns are analyzed and used for predicting patient conditions. These captured patterns are transmitted over wired or wireless communications.

Fog Layer

This layer resembles the fog computing platform which offers storage, computational facility, and network infrastructure between the end devices and cloud. In addition, the main characteristic of fog computing is providing services to the edge of the network. Since IoT generates an enormous amount of data cloud platform is not affordable to maintain these data. To overcome this issue, the edge of the network performs various tasks which include data fusion, data compression, encrypting and local processing and then forwards the data to cloud storage.

Cloud Layer

The cloud layer provides many functions that include data storage, data sharing, and data analysis, where data synchronized periodically to ensure the integrity of the data. In this layer, the patient's information is stored into two groups: public data unit and private data unit. The information stored in the public data unit can be accessible to everyone whereas the private data unit holds the confidential information that cannot be available for public access.

ARCHITECTING IoT SYSTEM WITH MACHINE LEARNING TECHNIQUES

Connected IoT devices generate a huge amount of data which has to be monitored and analyzed continuously without any human intervention. Such kind of analyzes makes the system smarter by the adoption of machine learning techniques. Several machine learning techniques and algorithms are available to analyze the flooding data within a minimum span of time. Techniques like decision trees, classification, clustering, neural network, and fuzzy logic assist the IoT devices to find the patterns in diversified data and make an appropriate decision depends on the analysis. In the case of embedded devices, there is no support for implementing the machine learning algorithms. Without machine learning techniques, it would be a major drawback and the device becomes meaningless.

IoT is still in the state of infancy; it has to flourish in the near future and will play a primary role in walks of our lives. Machine learning can be considered as an important area of computer science domain which has the ability to make any system to act smarter and allows such systems to learn to act autonomously based on the historical inference. In recent times, many factors joined together to make machine learning into reality- heterogeneous data sources, increased processing power required for solving complex computational problems within limited time and the requirement of reliable inference. The primary purpose of embracing machine learning into IoT system is to automate the generation of data analytics models allows the algorithms to learn seamlessly with the help of streaming data. Machine learning can be implemented in any domain other than IoT, which depends on 3W's.

- When expected inference is known in advance - Supervised Learning
- When expected inference is not known in advance - Unsupervised Learning
- When inference depends on the relationship between any specific model and the concerned environment – Reinforcement Learning

IoT without Machine Learning

Even though IoT uses the Internet remarkably, there are some challenges exists in implementing IoT application without machine learning. Traditional procedures cannot handle the huge amount of data generated by multiple devices. Hence some of the challenges that are faced by IoT without machine learning will be discussed in this section.

Diversified Devices and Interoperability

A single domain products and services are developed by diversified manufacturers in the field of IoT. In the case of smart healthcare systems, a wide variety of sensors available from several organizations that measure the body temperature and each of which operates differs in their standards. The integration of such kind of sensors together for accomplishing a particular task becomes a major challenge, which has to be resolved by machine learning techniques.

Device Management

IoT applications are comprised of countless small devices which are connected via the Internet in order to communicate with each other and also deployed over diversified locations. In some cases, the possibility of connecting a few devices together is less due to different communication link issues that require efficient management. For instance, the deterioration condition of patients has to be intimated to the healthcare service providers immediately through the wireless communication links. This requires all possible communication links among the various body sensors and networking devices to be managed for smooth operation.

Multi-Source Data Integration

On deploying the IoT systems, it is anticipated to acquire an abundant variety of data from multiple sources which includes sensors, actuators, mobile devices and so on. To develop an analytics model for data integration and processing of such diversified data might be a major challenge.

Performance and Scalability

IoT systems must be scalable for managing the huge volume of real-time streaming data, as well as the performance of the system, should be equally balanced. Hence, handling and analyzing the real-time streaming data in IoT system is another challenging factor that has to deal with machine learning.

Application Flexibility

Various IoT devices and sensors will tend to evolve with new potentials and enhanced functionalities. This may require more effort to develop new test cases and business models. To develop a flexible IoT system with minimal effort to cope up with the changing requirements, machine learning support is needed for enabling the system to learn varied applications.

How Machine Learning Improves the Efficiency of IoT?

- Traditional data analytics models work on static data and have certain limitations so that they cannot be implemented over dynamic and unstructured data. In the case of IoT, the correlations between enormous sensor data and their external factors must be identified. Traditional data analytics model performs operations on historical data and also requires an expert opinion for identifying the relationship among the variables. But machine learning can able to directly focus on predicting the resultant variable through automatic identification of predictor variables and their relationships. Hence, machine learning really helps in identifying important variables during the decision-making process and thus machine learning becomes a valuable phenomenon.

- Since traditional data analytics models are well suited for static data but various machine learning algorithms are quite simple which accurately predicts the future events. Moreover, machine learning algorithms can be improved constantly due to increased scaling of data. This denotes the algorithms can make better predictions when compared to their historical predictions.

- The predictive abilities of machine learning algorithms are tremendously useful in the healthcare domain. The physiological data gathered from patients from multiple sensors allows the machine learning algorithms to point out the distinctive data and also predicts the abnormality in patients before the condition worsening.

Design Considerations

Some of the IoT system designing factors may affect the decisions made by machine learning algorithms. In order to assure the accuracy of decisions, the following design factors must be considered while developing the system.

Battery Lifetime of IoT Device

The battery power is consumed during the duty cycle (may depend on power modes like active, standby, off) and minimal power is consumed by the sensors, processors and communication interfaces. The power consumption at the communication interface will increase during the raw data transmission from the sensor node to cloud and processors power consumption rate will also increase during local data processing.

On-Time Needs

Most of the IoT systems cannot tolerate the delayed transmission of sensor data to cloud and response from the cloud. So, the systems must afford on-time transmission and response.

Communication Channel Load

The transmission of a huge volume of data to cloud via communication channel may block the entire channel due to traffic. This may sometimes affect the decision-making process.

Sensitivity to the Communication Link Disturbance

Few machine learning algorithms cannot tolerate the communication link disturbance. For example, in a healthcare monitoring system, an emergency alarm must be raised even under the absence of disturbance of the communication link when a patient's condition starts worsening. When the system fails to raise alarm, then the prediction of the patient's condition using machine learning algorithms will be insignificant.

Needy of Algorithms and Multiple Platforms

In many cases, algorithms are needy because the analyst cannot handle the massive amount of IoT data arrival. The algorithm is playing a significant role in processing the IoT data at backend and do a meaningful job (i.e. decision making). Thus, the selection of an appropriate algorithm and attaining accurate results will be a challenging task. Another important challenge is to make algorithms to work on multiple environments without affecting the usual performance of the algorithms.

Agility and Flexibility

Prior to the deployment of IoT devices, the processor capacity and memory size must be fixed. Since they are fixed by default, scaling or replacing the IoT device in terms of computational resources will highly expensive and the degree of complexity will also increase. Meanwhile, using cloud resources and edge resources are more agile in nature. Because it can be scaled up and down depends upon the needs.

Privacy and Security

IoT applications like smart healthcare and smart home are stick on to deal with privacy or sensitive data. For example, transferring entire sensor data to the cloud may expose the IoT device towards the security risks. Instead, incorporating the sensitive wall on the edges will help to filter the sensitive data and transfers the data to the cloud.

SMART DATA CHARACTERISTICS

IoT represents a new paradigm "smart data", which is a challenging domain in the area of computing for researchers. The main challenges are with preparing and processing IoT data. S. Bin et al. proposed four data mining model for IoT data processing (Bin, 2010, April). The first model is a multi-layer model, which concentrates on data collection, data management, event processing, and mining services. The next model is a distributed data mining model which has been proposed for data deposition at various sites. The third model is a grid-oriented model that concentrates on heterogeneous, scalable and high-performance IoT applications. Finally, the fourth model provides the integration functions for the frameworks of the future Internet technologies.

In (Gonzalez, 2006, April), the author has focused on radio frequency identification (RFID) data warehousing with respect to the management and analysis of RFID stream data. F. Chen et al. reviewed many data mining techniques like classification, clustering, association rule mining, time series analysis and outlier detection (Chen, 2015). This work has revealed that the data originated from e-commerce, industries, healthcare, and social media are much similar to that of IoT data. Therefore, it has been identified that traditional data mining algorithms are highly fit for various IoT applications driven data.

C.W.Tsai et al. surveyed many challenges in preparation and processing IoT data using data mining algorithms (Tsai, 2013). They presented their study into three various divisions, which includes the explanation of IoT, data and its challenges existing in building the data mining model for IoT.

In (Zanella, 2014), the authors examined the infrastructure of a smart city in IoT and conversed the advanced communication technologies that support the services provided to the city and citizens. They offered an overview of various enabling technologies, protocols and architectures for smart city and in which the authors studied the data of Padova Smart City.

The IoT devices deployed in the cities generate the data in the streaming manner, signifying that data collected from health, energy management, and traffic applications would provide a huge volume of data. Therefore, the generation of data from various devices, processing of such data with differed generation rates is a major challenge (Qin, 2016) (Costa, 2015) (Jara, 2014, May). As the data generated from heterogeneous devices, the quality of the gathered data is mandatory. The characteristics of IoT data is depicted in Figure 3.

Figure 3. Characteristics of IoT data

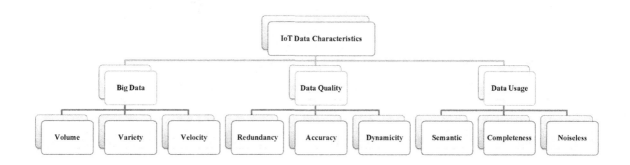

From the study [(Barnaghi, (2015))], it has been identified that the information quality depends on three major factors (i) measurement errors, (ii) device noise and (iii) discrete observation and measurements. The characteristics of smart data collected from smart cities are tabulated in Table 1.

Table 1. Smart city data characteristics

Smart City Use Cases	Type of Data	Data Processing Area	References
Smart Traffic	Stream/Massive	Data Edge	(Kafi, 2013) (Qin, 2016)
Smart Health	Stream/Massive	Data Edge/Cloud	(Toshniwal, 2013, February)
Smart Environment	Stream/Massive	Data Cloud	(Jakkula, 2010, July)
Smart Weather	Prediction Stream	Data Edge	(Ni, 2014, August)
Smart Home	Massive/Historical	Data Cloud	(Souza, 2015)
Smart Air Controlling	Massive/Historical	Data Cloud	(Costa, 2015)

MACHINE LEARNING ALGORITHMS FOR IoT

Machine learning is a major sub-field of computer science, provides the ability to machines, to learn without explicit programming. It has been developed from pattern recognition and computational theory. Frequently used machine learning algorithms for smart data analysis are discussed below. Generally, learning can be of three categories: supervised learning, unsupervised learning and reinforcement learning (Bishop, 2006) (Murphy, 2012)are shown in the Figure 4. A learning algorithm works upon the set of input samples which is termed as a training set.

Figure 4. Categories of machine learning algorithms

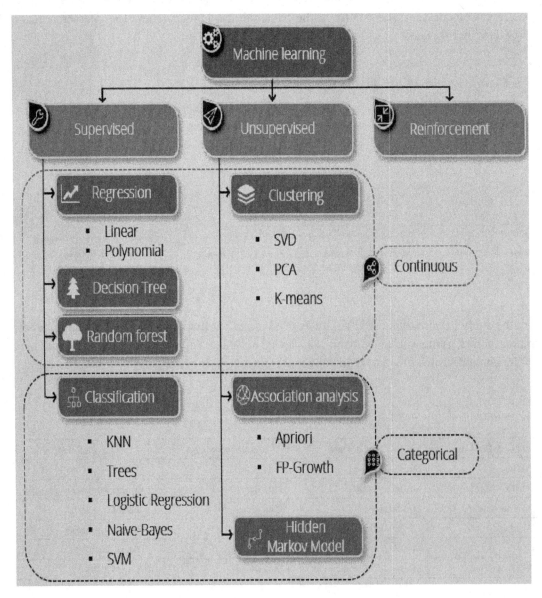

Supervised learning contains a set of input samples in which each of their samples belongs to a particular target group, known as labels whereas in unsupervised learning labels are not required. Reinforcement learning tends to learn from the appropriate action for a given situation. This review article depicts the supervised and unsupervised learning techniques since it is being commonly applied to IoT smart data analytics. The aim of supervised learning is to learn how to forecast the accurate target group (finite number of distinct categories) for a given input sample and it's called as classification tasks. When the target group is a collection of one or more continuous variables is termed as regression (Goodfellow, 2016). The major aim of unsupervised learning is to predict the clusters of related samples from the set of input data is called clustering. The most frequently used machine learning algorithms for smart data analysis are presented in Table 2 and the various machine learning algorithms that can be applied IoT applications are tabulated in Table 3.

Table 2. Machine learning algorithms for smart data analysis – an outline

Machine Learning Algorithm	Data Processing Tasks	References
K-Nearest Neighbors	Classification	(Cover, 1967), (H.V. Jagadish, 2005)
Naive Bayes	Classification	(McCallum, 1998, July), (Zhang, 2004)
Support Vector Machine	Classification	(C. Cortes, 1995), (Guyon, 1993), (Cristianini, 2000), (Scholkopf, 2001)
Linear Regression	Regression	(Neter, 1996), (Seber, 2012), (Montgomery, 2012)
Support Vector Regression	Regression	(Drucker, 1997), (Smola, 2004)
Classification and Regression Trees	Classification/Regression	(Breiman, 2017), (Prasad, 2006), (Loh, 2011)
Random Forests	Classification/Regression	(Breiman, 2001)
Bagging	Classification/Regression	(Breiman, 1996)
K-Means	Clustering	(Likas, 2003), (Coates, 2012), (Jumutc, 2015)
Density-Based Spatial Clustering of Applications with Noise	Clustering	(Ester, 1996), (Kriegel, 2011), (Campello, 2013)
Principal Component Analysis	Feature extraction	(Pearson, 1901), (Hotelling, 1933), (Jolliffe, 2011), (Abdi, 2010), (Bro, 2014)
Canonical Correlation Analysis	Feature extraction	(Hotelling, 1992), (Bach, 2002)
Feed Forward Neural Network	Regression/Classification/Clustering/Feature extraction	(LeCun Y. B., 1998), (Glorot, 2010), (Eberhart, 2014), (He, 2016),
One-class Support Vector Machines	Anomaly detection	(Schölkopf, 2001), (Rätsch, 2002)

A PROPOSED MACHINE LEARNING ARCHITECTURE FOR STREAMING IoT HEALTHCARE DATA

The increasing ratio of IoT devices analogously generates a huge amount of data; machine learning will provide a wide opportunity to make IoT applications highly effective and intelligent. Applying machine learning on healthcare data helps healthcare providers to improve the quality of patient's life. Additionally, it allows healthcare providers to take more optimal decisions. Machine learning is broadly classified into two types such as supervised and unsupervised machine learning. Supervised learning uses training

Table 3. Machine learning algorithms applied IoT applications

Machine learning Algorithm	IoT Use Cases	Metric to Optimize	References
Classification	Smart Traffic	Traffic Prediction, Increase Data Abbreviation	(M.A. Kafi, 2013)
Clustering	Smart Traffic, Smart Health	Traffic Prediction, Increase Data Abbreviation	(M.A. Kafi, 2013), (D. Toshniwal, 2013)
Anomaly Detection	Smart Traffic, Smart Environment	Traffic Prediction, Increase Data Abbreviation, Finding Anomalies in Power Dataset	(M.A. Kafi, 2013), (V. Jakkula, 2010)
Support Vector Regression	Smart Weather Prediction	Forecasting	(P. Ni, 2014)
Linear Regression	Economics, Market analysis, Energy usage	Real Time Prediction, Reducing Amount of Data	(W. Derguech, 2014)
Classification and Regression Trees	Smart Citizens	Real Time Prediction, Passengers Travel Pattern	(X. Ma, 2013), (W. Derguech, 2014)
Support Vector Machine	All Use Cases	Classify Data, Real Time Prediction	(W. Derguech, 2014)
K-Nearest Neighbors	Smart Citizen	Passengers' Travel Pattern, Efficiency of the Learned Metric	(X. Ma, 2013)
Naive Bayes	Smart Agriculture, Smart Citizen	Food Safety, Passengers Travel Pattern, Estimate the Numbers of Nodes	(X. Ma, 2013), (W. Han, 2014)
K-Means	Smart City, Smart Home, Smart Citizen, Controlling Air and Traffic	Outlier Detection, fraud detection, Analyze Small Data set, Forecasting Energy Consumption, Passengers Travel Pattern, Stream Data Analyze	(X. Ma, 2013)
Density-Based Clustering	Smart Citizen	Labeling Data, Fraud Detection, Passengers Travel Pattern	(X. Ma, 2013)
Feed Forward Neural Network	Smart Health	Reducing Energy Consumption, Forecast the States of Elements, Overcome the Redundant Data and Information	(I. Kotenko, 2015)
Principal Component Analysis	Monitoring Public Places	Fault Detection	(D.N. Monekosso, 2013)
Canonical Correlation Analysis	Monitoring Public Places	Fault Detection	(D.N. Monekosso, 2013)
One-class Support Vector Machines	Smart Human Activity Control	Fraud Detection, Emerging Anomalies in the data	(M. Shukla, 2015), (A. Shilton, 2015)

data for predicting the rules whereas unsupervised learning uses unknown data for predicting the rules. The HIoT systems can be made intelligent combining streaming medical data with machine learning. The application of machine learning into healthcare system allows the doctor to provide smart treatment to the patient's with improved quality at a lower cost. Figure 5 depicts the procedure of applying the streaming data into machine learning, which comprised of four components such as stream data source, data collection, data processing, and dashboard. The stream data source represents the medical devices which observe the patient's vital signs and stores the observed data in assembling unit called streaming data collection. The streaming data is being analyzed to make a prediction about health conditions and it has been done using two functions: batch processing and stream processing. The batch processing creates an offline model using historical medical data that exhibits the normal condition of the patient.

The offline model is validated against the streaming data to recognize the variations. The observed behavior pattern is compared with the normal behavior pattern to identify abnormal patterns. On finding the abnormal pattern, an alert is generated at the dashboard through which healthcare providers can take a necessary intervention.

Figure 5. Application of machine learning algorithm on streaming data

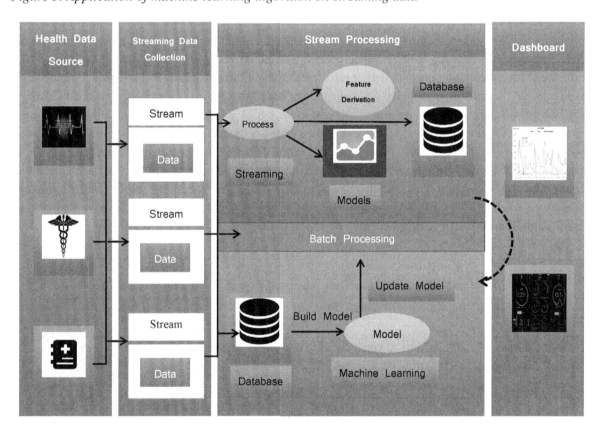

Chiuchisan and Geman proposed the decision support and home monitoring system composed of diagnosis, treatment, prescriptions, rehabilitation for Parkinson's disease (IulianaChiuchisan&Geman, 2014). Thomas Bruschwiler stated that machine learning algorithms can assist doctors and patients to diagnose diseases before worsening. Fizar Ahmed presented an IoT-based architecture for monitoring and it uses the kNN classification algorithm for predicting the number of patients suspected to have a heart attack in the future (Ahmed, 2017) . IBM researchers focused on developing an IoT-based system for monitoring chronic obstructive pulmonary disease (COPD) with machine learning technologies. This work encourages the patient-physician communication and slightly reduces the cost involved in healthcare systems. J. Jin Kang et al. presented a new way of predicting the health status by making an inference on the cloud itself (J. Jin Kang, 2015). Thus, it reduces the data overloading issues at sensor nodes. A hybrid density-based clustering for data stream algorithm is proposed in (AmineshAmini, 2014), which use the merits of density-grid based method and density based micro-clustering method for searching and selecting data point only in the potential list. If it is not found, then it is mapped to the grid as an outlier. The growth of IoT is driven by many supporting technologies, in that machine learning plays a predominant role because it makes IoT systems more intelligent. Three fuelling ways are identified through which machine learning shapes the IoT, includes increasing the usability of real-time data, enhancing security features and expanding the scope of IoT.

CASE STUDY: FALL DETECTION USING MACHINE LEARNING ALGORITHMS

Falls are an indisputable medical issue and possibly dangerous for individuals and this case study responds to the challenge of arranging diverse developments as a piece of a framework intended to satisfy the requirement for a wearable device to gather information about fall and nearly fall analysis. Four diverse fall directions (forward, in reverse, left and right); three ordinary activities (standing, walking and lying) and close fall circumstances are distinguished and identified. Fall recognition frameworks are ordered into the accompanying three groups: ambient device, camera-based frameworks, and wearable devices whose pros and cons are depicted in Table 4. Ambiance devices are connected around an area which can recognize falls utilizing the add-on sensors: PIR, pressure, Doppler, amplifier and accelerometer sensors. Computer vision utilizes cameras to follow user developments. A fall might be distinguished when the user is latent for quite a while. Wearable devices which are connected on the user incorporate the following sensors: an accelerometer and a gyrator.

Table 4. Pros and cons of fall recognition systems

Type of Devices	Pros	Cons
Ambience devices	Cheap and Non-intrusive	Range and environmental factors which can result in low accuracy
Camera-based systems	Detect multiple events simultaneously, less intrusive	Limited to a specific area and does not guarantee privacy, expensive
Wearable devices	Portable, cheap and easy to use	Intrusive, false alarms

The performance of the framework relies upon the sensors utilized and classification methods. The speed and accuracy of the fall identification classifier are taken into the major considerations of fall detection systems. Components that impact the identification and classification of fall activities and ADLs incorporate difference in movements, environmental conditions and the relocation of the sensor. Classification algorithms can be categorized into two models as supervised and unsupervised models. In a supervised model, the output can be controlled and can be effectively modeled when contrasted with the unsupervised model. Unsupervised models have been utilized in fall detection frameworks, for example, one-class support vector machine. Supervised models contain a support vector machine (SVM), k-Nearest Neighbor (k-NN), Naive Bayes, least squares method (LSM), artificial neural networks (ANNs) and hybrid k-NN. Supervised models are used in this case study for fall detection and categorization of various activities. Fall detection frameworks can be characterized using five phases: data collection, pre-processing, feature extraction, feature selection, model training and classification as shown in Figure 6.

Figure 6. Machine learning architecture for fall detection

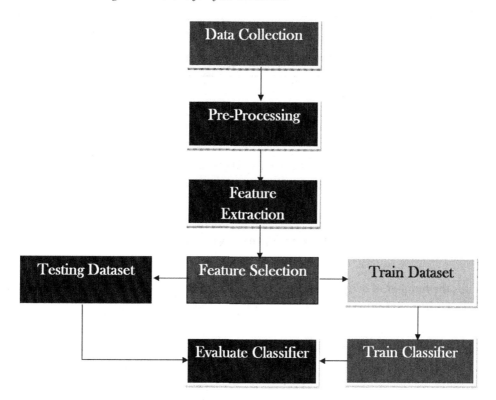

Data Collection

The major intention of this case study is to implement various classification algorithms on fall detection dataset which has been downloaded from Kaggle dataset repository (Özdemir, 2014). Fourteen volunteers play out an institutionalized arrangement of activities including 20 deliberate falls and 16 Activities of Daily Living (ADLs), bringing about a substantial dataset with 2520 preliminaries. Several machine learning classification algorithms including SVM, ANN, k-NN, LSM, Naïve Bayes and Hybrid High Probability Nearest Neighbor SVM classifier were implemented and evaluated to determine the best classification model. The primary objective is to classify the various daily activities like standing, walking, sitting, falling, cramps and running. In this study, the rank-based method is used to select the features and activities are classified. Table 5 shows that the columns were used in the dataset and its associated description.

Pre-Processing

Pre-Processing involves obtaining pure data from the dataset, and then it will be used for training and testing. This application tends to gather data from multiple sensors which are not acquired at a regular sampling rate. Hence the stored timestamp will be used for calculating the regular sampling rate. The following formula was used to validate the sampling rate,

Table 5. Dataset and its description

Attributes	Description
ACTIVITY	Activity Classification
TIME	Monitoring Time
SL	Sugar Level
EEG	EEG Monitoring Rate
BP	Blood Pressure
HR	Heart Beat Rate
CIRCULATION	Blood Circulation

$$\text{Sampling Rate} = \frac{1}{\text{Timestamp}(x+1) - \text{Timestamp}(x)} \tag{1}$$

where x denotes the number of sensor data. Using Equation 1, the sampling rate has been calculated to be 100 Hz. The median filter function was used to remove the sensors attenuated noises.

Feature Extraction and Feature Selection

Feature extraction is an important stage in the classification process since it decides the accuracy of any classification schemes. Features are extracted based on the data acquired from a window intervals, the time index of the maximum signal magnitude vector (SMV) peak has been identified in each activity record and the features were normalized between 0-1. On the other hand, various features have been extracted using the statistical methods which include mean, median, maximum, minimum, standard deviation and so on.

The performance of any classification scheme depends on the size of the features extracted. In order to improve the performance, the features must be minimized and also it can extensively differentiate the fall activities from normal activities. An aggregate of 6 features was extracted and a filter rank based system was utilized to eliminate features with no data.

Classifiers Evaluation

The best six features were utilized in the classification model which gives better than average outcomes. The classification model can deliver the accompanying four feasible results:

1. True Positive (TP) when a system accurately detects a fall when a fall takes place
2. False Positive (FP) when a system detects a fall when no fall take place
3. True Negative (TN) when a system detects no fall when no fall takes place.
4. False Negative (FN) when a system detects no fall when a fall takes place.

Table 7. Classifiers applied on fall detection dataset

Classification Algorithms	Pros & Cons	Algorithm Description
k-Nearest Neighbor	i. Classes need not be linearly separable ii. Zero cost of the learning process iii. Sometimes it is robust with regard to noisy training data iv. Well suited for multimodal v. Time to find the nearest neighbors in a large training dataset can be excessive vi. It is sensitive to noisy or irrelevant attributes vii. Performance of the algorithm depends on the number of dimensions used	k-NN classifier has been highly applied on fall detection applications which use distance function for identifying the similarity between two activity records.
Naïve Bayes	i. Simple to implement ii. Great computational efficiency and classification rate iii. It predicts accurate results for most of the classification and prediction problems iv. The precision of the algorithm decreases if the amount of data is less v. For obtaining good results, it requires a very large number of records	Generally, this algorithm follows the principle of Bayes theorem and the probabilities are used for classifying the features.
Artificial Neural Networks	i. It is easy to use with few parameters to adjust ii. A neural network learns and reprogramming is not needed. - Easy to implement iii. Applicable to a wide range of problems in real life. iv. Requires high processing time if a neural network is large v. Difficult to know how many neurons and layers are necessary - Learning can be slow	This algorithm consists of a two-layer feedforward network that includes hidden layers and neurons. The gradient backpropagation has been for training.
Support Vector Machine	i. High accuracy ii. Work well even if the data is not linearly separable in the base feature space iii. Speed and size requirement both in training and testing is more iv. High complexity and extensive memory requirements for classification in many cases	"svmtrain" and "svmpredict" functions are used for training and testing. The radial basis kernel has been used to classify the activities and fall occurrence.
Hybrid Nearest Neighbor integrated SVM Classifier	i. Very minimal computational complexities ii. Very high accuracy	k-NN has been used for creating the feature space as it requires less computational complexities and then, SVM is used for classifying the various activities.

Various performance measures used to evaluate the classification algorithms used for detecting the falls are accuracy, specificity, and sensitivity, which are given by,

$$\text{Accuracy} = \frac{(TP + TN)}{(TP + TN + FN + FP)} \tag{2}$$

$$\text{Sensitivity} = \frac{(TP)}{(TP + FN)} \tag{3}$$

$$Specificity = \frac{(TN)}{(TN + FP)} \tag{4}$$

Generally k-NN, SVM, ANN offers the best precision than Naive Bayes. Elements that impact the accuracy are the position of sensors on the body. The two existing algorithms k-NN and SVM outperforms well when compared to other algorithms. Therefore, k-NN and SVM algorithms are hybridized for classifying the various activities and to detect the fall. This hybrid algorithm can be used successfully for detecting fall and other activities with reduced computational complexities in both training and testing phases. k-NN has been used for creating the feature space as it requires less computational complexities and then, SVM is used for classifying the various activities. The pseudo code of the hybrid algorithm is shown below:

Algorithm: Hybrid Nearest Neighbor integrated SVM Classifier

```
Inputs:  Set of sample x to classify, Training Set T
         Number of nearest neighbors K= {k₁, k₂....kₙ}
         Adjustment parameter for balancing errors
Output:  Classified Dataset
Steps:
1.       Order the training samples in ascending order
2.       Minimum Error=1000; Value= 0;
3.       if initial k values are from same class label c then
4.       print c
5.       end if
6.       for all k do
7.       Train SVM model on training samples
8.       Classify x using built SVM model
9.       Classify the same training sample using built SVM model
10.       Evaluate the Error Positive and Error Negative
11.       Update Minimum Error
12.       Calculate Value
13.       End for
14.       Return Value
```

RESULTS AND DISCUSSION

Table 8 illustrates the summary classifiers performance. The best classifier is the Hybrid Nearest Neighbor integrated SVM Classifier with 89.01% of accuracy, the sensitivity of 90.27%, and specificity of 85.63%. Figure 7, Figure 8 and Figure 9 depicts the compares the performance of various classifiers in terms of accuracy, sensitivity and specificity .

Table 8. Classification summary

Classifiers	Accuracy (%)	Sensitivity (%)	Specificity (%)
NB	80.00	85.11	72.73
ANN	85.87	89.23	81.43
k-NN	87.5	90.70	83.78
SVM	86.75	89.74	82.93
Hybrid Classifier	89.01	91.27	85.63

Figure 7. Comparison of accuracy

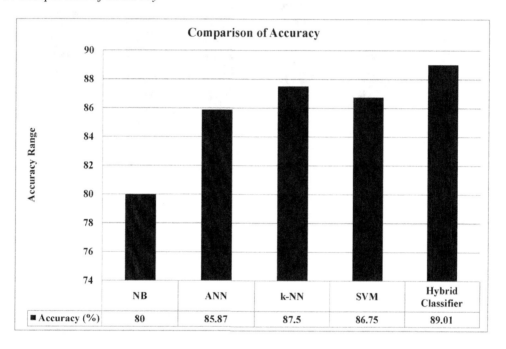

CONCLUSION

IoT is a developing broad domain consists of enormous different devices that are connected together and generates a vast amount of smart data. In which, the healthcare is a major application of IoT that offers various services like remote health monitoring, disease prediction and assisted the living. The services provided by the smart applications have to be optimized and improved by analyzing the smart data gathered. Many machine learning algorithms have been applied on gathered to extract high-level information. Selecting an appropriate algorithm for certain IoT applications is an important issue. This chapter addresses the design considerations for building efficient healthcare IoT systems and also focuses on major factors must be considered while applying machine learning algorithms to smart data. An exclusive machine learning architecture has been proposed for applying streaming healthcare data which radically improves the decision-making capability of healthcare systems. This chapter anticipates the application of existing classification algorithms and a hybrid algorithm on sensory IoT data for detecting the fall from other regular activities. The hybrid algorithm outperforms when compared with other existing techniques.

Figure 8. Comparison of sensitivity

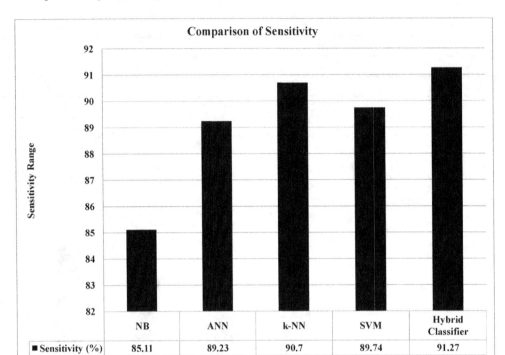

Figure 9. Comparison of specificity

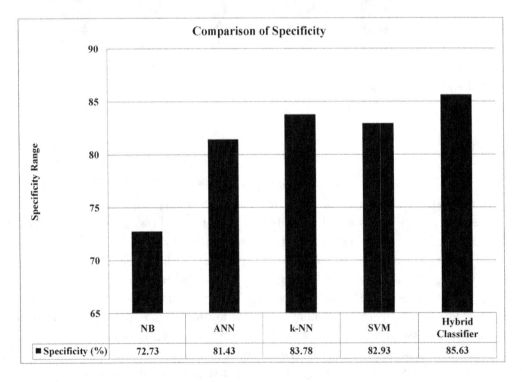

REFERENCES

Abdi, H., & Williams, L. J. (2010). Principal component analysis. *Wiley Interdisciplinary Reviews: Computational Statistics*, *2*(4), 433–459. doi:10.1002/wics.101

Ahmed, F. (2017). An internet of things (IoT) Application for Predicting the Quantity of Future Heart Attack Patients. *International Journal of Computers and Applications*, *164*(6), 36–40. doi:10.5120/ijca2017913773

Al-Fuqaha, A., Guizani, M., Mohammadi, M., Aledhari, M., & Ayyash, M. (2015). Internet of things: A survey on enabling technologies, protocols, and applications. *IEEE Communications Surveys and Tutorials*, *17*(4), 2347–2376. doi:10.1109/COMST.2015.2444095

Amini, A., Saboohi, H., Ying Wah, T., & Herawan, T. (2014). A fast density-based clustering algorithm for real-time Internet of things stream. *The Scientific World Journal*. doi:10.1155/2014/926020

Bach, F. R., & Jordan, M. I. (2002). Kernel independent component analysis. *Journal of Machine Learning Research*, *3*(Jul), 1–48.

Barnaghi, P. M., Bermudez-Edo, M., & Tönjes, R. (2015). Challenges for Quality of Data in Smart Cities. *J. Data and Information Quality*, *6*(2-3), 6–1.

Bin, S., Yuan, L., & Xiaoyi, W. (2010, April). Research on data mining models for the internet of things. In 2010 *International Conference on Image Analysis and Signal Processing* (pp. 127-132). Piscataway, NJ: IEEE.

Bishop, C. M. (2006). Pattern recognition and machine learning. Berlin, Germany: Springer.

Breiman, L. (1996). Bagging predictors. *Machine Learning*, *24*(2), 123–140. doi:10.1007/BF00058655

Breiman, L. (2001). Random forests. *Machine Learning*, *45*(1), 5–32. doi:10.1023/A:1010933404324

Breiman, L. (2017). Classification and regression trees. Abingdon-on-Thames, UK: Routledge. doi:10.1201/9781315139470

Bro, R., & Smilde, A. K. (2014). Principal component analysis. *Analytical Methods*, *6*(9), 2812–2831. doi:10.1039/C3AY41907J

Campello, R. J., Moulavi, D., & Sander, J. (2013, April). Density-based clustering based on hierarchical density estimates. In *Pacific-Asia conference on knowledge discovery and data mining* (pp. 160–172). Berlin, Germany: Springer. doi:10.1007/978-3-642-37456-2_14

Chen, F., Deng, P., Wan, J., Zhang, D., Vasilakos, A. V., & Rong, X. (2015). Data mining for the internet of things: Literature review and challenges. *International Journal of Distributed Sensor Networks*, *11*(8). doi:10.1155/2015/431047

Coates, A., & Ng, A. Y. (2012). Learning feature representations with k-means. In *Neural networks: Tricks of the trade* (pp. 561–580). Berlin, Germany: Springer. doi:10.1007/978-3-642-35289-8_30

Cortes, C., & Vapnik, V. (1995). Support-vector networks. *Machine Learning*, *20*(3), 273–297. doi:10.1007/BF00994018

Costa, C., & Santos, M. Y. (2015). Improving cities sustainability through the use of data mining in the context of big city data. *Lecture Notes in Engineering and Computer Science, 1*, 320–325.

Cover, T. M., & Hart, P. E. (1967). Nearest neighbor pattern classification. *IEEE Transactions on Information Theory, 13*(1), 21–27. doi:10.1109/TIT.1967.1053964

Cristianini, N., & Shawe-Taylor, J. (2000). *An introduction to support vector machines and other kernel-based learning methods.* Cambridge University Press. doi:10.1017/CBO9780511801389

Derguech, W., Bruke, E., & Curry, E. (2014). An autonomic approach to real-time predictive analytics using open data and internet of things. In *IEEE 11th Intl Conf on Ubiquitous Intelligence and Computing, and IEEE 11th Intl Conf on Autonomic and Trusted Computing, and IEEE 14th Intl Conf on Scalable Computing and Communications and its Associated Workshops (UTC-ATC-ScalCom)* (pp. 204–211). Piscataway, NJ: IEEE. 10.1109/UIC-ATC-ScalCom.2014.137

Drucker, H., Burges, C. J., Kaufman, L., Smola, A. J., & Vapnik, V. (1997). Support vector regression machines. In Advances in neural information processing systems (pp. 155-161).

Eberhart, R. C. (Ed.). (2014). *Neural network PC tools: a practical guide.* Academic Press.

Ester, M., Kriegel, H. P., Sander, J., & Xu, X. (1996, August). A density-based algorithm for discovering clusters in large spatial databases with noise. *In Proceedings of International Conference on Knowledge Discovery & Data Mining, 96*(34), 226–231.

Glorot, X., & Bengio, Y. (2010, March). Understanding the difficulty of training deep feedforward neural networks. In *Proceedings of the thirteenth international conference on artificial intelligence and statistics* (pp. 249-256).

Gonzalez, H., Han, J., Li, X., & Klabjan, D. (2006, April). Warehousing and Analyzing Massive RFID Data Sets (Vol. 6, p. 83). Oslo, Norway: ICDE. doi:10.1109/ICDE.2006.171

Goodfellow, I., Bengio, Y., & Courville, A. (2016). *Deep learning.* Cambridge, MA: MIT Press.

Gubbi, J., Buyya, R., Marusic, S., & Palaniswami, M. (2013). Internet of things (IoT): A vision, architectural elements, and future directions. *Future Generation Computer Systems, 29*(7), 1645–1660. doi:10.1016/j.future.2013.01.010

Guyon, I., Boser, B., & Vapnik, V. (1993). Automatic capacity tuning of very large VC-dimension classifiers. In Advances in neural information processing systems (pp. 147-155).

Han, W., Gu, Y., Zhang, Y., & Zheng, L. (2014). Data driven quantitative trust model for the Internet of agricultural things. In *International Conference on the internet of things (IoT)* (pp. 31–36). Piscataway, NJ: IEEE. 10.1109/IOT.2014.7030111

He, K., Zhang, X., Ren, S., & Sun, J. (2016). Deep residual learning for image recognition. In *Proceedings of the IEEE conference on computer vision and pattern recognition* (pp. 770-778).

Hotelling, H. (1933). Analysis of a complex of statistical variables into principal components. *Journal of Educational Psychology, 24*(6), 417–441. doi:10.1037/h0071325

Hotelling, H. (1992). Relations between two sets of variates. In *Breakthroughs in statistics* (pp. 162–190). New York, NY: Springer. doi:10.1007/978-1-4612-4380-9_14

Jagadish, H. V., Ooi, B. C., Tan, K.-L., Yu, C., & Zhang, R. (2005). Idistance: An adaptive bþ-treebased indexing method for nearest neighbor search [TODS]. *ACM Transactions on Database Systems, 30*(2), 364–397. doi:10.1145/1071610.1071612

Jakkula, V., & Cook, D. (2010, July). Outlier detection in a smart environment structured power datasets. In *Sixth International Conference on Intelligent Environments* (pp. 29-33). Piscataway, NJ: IEEE. 10.1109/IE.2010.13

Jakkula, V. & Cook, D. (2010). Outlier detection in smart environment structured power datasets. In *Sixth International Conference on Intelligent Environments (IE)* (pp. 29–33). Piscataway, NJ: IEEE. 10.1109/IE.2010.13

Jara, A. J., Genoud, D., & Bocchi, Y. (2014, May). Big data in smart cities: from poison to human dynamics. In *28th International Conference on Advanced Information Networking and Applications Workshops* (pp. 785-790). Piscataway, NJ: IEEE. 10.1109/WAINA.2014.165

Jin Kang, J., Sdibi, S., Larkin, H., & Luan, T. (2015). Predictive data mining for Converged Internet of things: A Mobile Health perspective. *International Telecommunication Networks and Application Conference (ITNAC)*, Sydney, Australia, pp. 5-10. 10.1109/ATNAC.2015.7366781

Jolliffe, I. (2011). Principal component analysis (pp. 1094–1096). Berlin, Germany: Springer.

Jumutc, V., Langone, R., & Suykens, J. A. (2015, October). Regularized and sparse stochastic k-means for distributed large-scale clustering. In *2015 IEEE International Conference on Big Data (Big Data)* (pp. 2535-2540). Piscataway, NJ: IEEE. 10.1109/BigData.2015.7364050

Kafi, M. A., Challal, Y., Djenouri, D., Doudou, M., Bouabdallah, A., & Badache, N. (2013). A study of wireless sensor networks for urban traffic monitoring: Applications and architectures. *Procedia Computer Science, 19*, 617–626. doi:10.1016/j.procs.2013.06.082

Kriegel, H. P., Kröger, P., Sander, J., & Zimek, A. (2011). Density-based clustering. *Wiley Interdisciplinary Reviews. Data Mining and Knowledge Discovery, 1*(3), 231–240. doi:10.1002/widm.30

LeCun, Y., Bottou, L., Bengio, Y., & Haffner, P. (1998). Gradient-based learning applied to document recognition. *Proceedings of the IEEE, 86*(11), 2278–2324. doi:10.1109/5.726791

Li, S., Da Xu, L., & Zhao, S. (2015). The internet of things: A survey. *Information Systems Frontiers, 17*(2), 243–259. doi:10.100710796-014-9492-7

Likas, A., Vlassis, N., & Verbeek, J. J. (2003). The global k-means clustering algorithm. *Pattern Recognition, 36*(2), 451–461. doi:10.1016/S0031-3203(02)00060-2

Loh, W. Y. (2011). Classification and regression trees. *Wiley Interdisciplinary Reviews. Data Mining and Knowledge Discovery, 1*(1), 14–23. doi:10.1002/widm.8

Ma, X., Wu, Y.-J., Wang, Y., Chen, F., & Liu, J. (2013). Mining smart card data for transit riders 'travel patterns. *Transportation Research Part C, Emerging Technologies, 36*, 1–12. doi:10.1016/j.trc.2013.07.010

McCallum, A. & Nigam, K. (1998, July). A comparison of event models for naive bayes text classification. In AAAI-98 workshop on learning for text categorization, 752(1), (pp. 41-48).

Monekosso, D. N., & Remagnino, P. (2013). Data reconciliation in a smart home sensor network. *Expert Systems with Applications, 40*(8), 3248–3255. doi:10.1016/j.eswa.2012.12.037

Montenegro, G., Kushalnagar, N., Hui, J., & Culler, D. (2007). Transmission of IPv6 packets over IEEE 802.15. 4 networks (No. RFC 4944).

Montgomery, D. C., Peck, E. A., & Vining, G. G. (2012). *Introduction to linear regression analysis* (Vol. 821). Hoboken, NJ: John Wiley & Sons.

Murphy, K. P. (2012). *Machine learning: a probabilistic perspective.* Cambridge, MA: MIT Press.

Neter, J., Kutner, M. H., Nachtsheim, C. J., & Wasserman, W. (1996). *Applied linear statistical models* (Vol. 4). Chicago, IL: Irwin.

Ni, P., Zhang, C., & Ji, Y. (2014, August). A hybrid method for short-term sensor data forecasting in Internet of things. In *11th International Conference on Fuzzy Systems and Knowledge Discovery (FSKD)* (pp. 369-373). Piscataway, NJ: IEEE. 10.1109/FSKD.2014.6980862

Ni, P., Zhang, C., & Ji, Y. (2014). A hybrid method for short-term sensor data forecasting in Internet of Things. In *11th International Conference on Fuzzy Systems and Knowledge Discovery (FSKD)*. 10.1109/FSKD.2014.6980862

Chiuchisan, I. U. L. I. A. N. A. & Geman, O. A. N. A. (2014). An Approach of a Decision Support and Home Monitoring System for Patients with Neurological Disorders Using Internet of things Concepts. *WSEAS Transaction on Systems, 13,* 460–469.

Özdemir, A. T., & Barshan, B. (2014). Detecting Falls with Wearable Sensors Using Machine Learning Techniques. *Sensors (Basel), 14*(6), 10691–10708. doi:10.3390140610691 PMID:24945676

Pearson, K. (1901). LIII. On lines and planes of closest fit to systems of points in space. *The London, Edinburgh and Dublin Philosophical Magazine and Journal of Science, 2*(11), 559–572. doi:10.1080/14786440109462720

Prasad, A. M., Iverson, L. R., & Liaw, A. (2006). Newer classification and regression tree techniques: Bagging and random forests for ecological prediction. *Ecosystems (New York, N.Y.), 9*(2), 181–199. doi:10.100710021-005-0054-1

Qin, Y., Sheng, Q. Z., Falkner, N. J., Dustdar, S., Wang, H., & Vasilakos, A. V. (2016). When things matter: A survey on data-centric internet of things. *Journal of Network and Computer Applications, 64,* 137–153. doi:10.1016/j.jnca.2015.12.016

Rätsch, G., Mika, S., Schölkopf, B., & Müller, K. R. (2002). Constructing boosting algorithms from SVMs: An application to one-class classification. *IEEE Transactions on Pattern Analysis and Machine Intelligence, 24*(9), 1184–1199. doi:10.1109/TPAMI.2002.1033211

Schölkopf, B., Platt, J. C., Shawe-Taylor, J., Smola, A. J., & Williamson, R. C. (2001). Estimating the support of a high-dimensional distribution. *Neural Computation*, *13*(7), 1443–1471. doi:10.1162/089976601750264965 PMID:11440593

Scholkopf, B., & Smola, A. J. (2001). *Learning with kernels: support vector machines, regularization, optimization, and beyond*. Cambridge, MA: MIT Press.

Seber, G. A., & Lee, A. J. (2012). *Linear regression analysis* (Vol. 329). Hoboken, NJ: John Wiley & Sons.

Shilton, A., Rajasegarar, S., Leckie, C., & Palaniswami, M. (2015). A dynamic planar one-class support vector machine for internet of things environment. In *International Conference on Recent Advances in Internet of things (RIoT)*. Piscataway, NJ: IEEE. pp. 1–6. 10.1109/RIOT.2015.7104904

Shukla, M., Kosta, Y., & Chauhan, P. (2015). Analysis and evaluation of outlier detection algorithms in data streams. In *International Conference on Computer, Communication and Control (IC4) (pp. 1–8)*. Piscataway, NJ: IEEE.

Smola, A. J., & Schölkopf, B. (2004). A tutorial on support vector regression. *Statistics and Computing*, *14*(3), 199–222. doi:10.1023/B:STCO.0000035301.49549.88

Souza, A. M., & Amazonas, J. R. (2015). An outlier detect algorithm using big data processing and internet of things architecture. *Procedia Computer Science*, *52*, 1010–1015. doi:10.1016/j.procs.2015.05.095

Toshniwal, D. (2013, February). Clustering techniques for streaming data-a survey. In *3rd IEEE International Advance Computing Conference (IACC)* (pp. 951-956). Piscataway, NJ: IEEE.

Tsai, C. W., Lai, C. F., Chiang, M. C., & Yang, L. T. (2013). Data mining for the internet of things: A survey. *IEEE Communications Surveys and Tutorials*, *16*(1), 77–97. doi:10.1109/SURV.2013.103013.00206

Zanella, A., Bui, N., Castellani, A., Vangelista, L., & Zorzi, M. (2014). Internet of things for smart cities. IEEE Internet of things journal, 1(1), 22-32.

Zhang, H. (2004). The optimality of naive Bayes. AA, 1(2), 3.

This research was previously published in Incorporating the Internet of Things in Healthcare Applications and Wearable Devices; pages 40-66, copyright year 2020 by Medical Information Science Reference (an imprint of IGI Global).

Chapter 13
Machine Learning Techniques for Analysis of Human Genome Data

Neelambika Basavaraj Hiremath

Department of Computer Science and Engineering, J.S.S. Academy of Technical Education Bengaluru, India

Dayananda P.

Department of Information Science and Engineering. J.S.S. Academy of Technical Education, Bengaluru, India

ABSTRACT

Human genome data analysis is one of the molecular level information in health informatics, which enables genetic epidemiological analysis of complex data sets. The recent studies of the genomic sequence, a part of genome-wide association studies (GWAS) have led to understand the genetic architecture to identify the area of focus i.e. interactions with single-nucleotide polymorphism (SNP) is linked to causing complex diseases. The study and identification of these interactions and splicing of nucleic acids involves complexity in processing and computation. This article reviews current methods and trends in various machine learning and data mining approaches which are very complex and challenging to model and evaluate the performances.

INTRODUCTION

The field of health care domain comprises lots of information and data where it helps to relies goal of diagnosing, treating, helping and healing all patients in need. This domain needs quality of care and research and development (R &D) for new discoveries. The basic goal of Health Informatics is to analyse at all levels of human existence, helping to advance our understanding of medicine and medical practice. The computational models and study real-world medical data with use of biological systems, and to understand the technology for optimizing treatment strategy (Ji, Yan, Li, Hu, & Zhu, 2017) for discovering new drug. According to (Herland et al., 2014) health informatics, is a broader subject where

DOI: 10.4018/978-1-6684-6291-1.ch013

the following studies are covered. Micro level data which deals with molecular level information such as gene expression data which helps clinical predication of diseases of patient. The assessment of gene expression is used to identify histological types of lung cancer disease (Podolsky et al., 2016). The health informatics also covers tissue level, Patient level and Population data for various informational insights.

Bioinformatics research is an important source of health information which revolves around micro

Figure 1. Interactions of disciplines contributed to bioinformatics

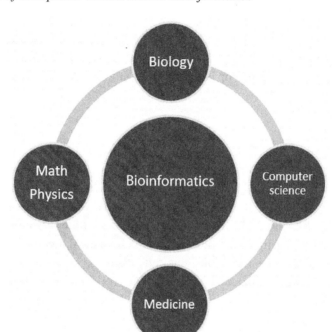

level data and focuses on analytical research using molecular data to learn the process of how the human body works. Figure 1 displays the knowledge contribution between another subject domain. Predictive models can be built by measuring gene expression, splicing, and proteins binding to nucleic acids, which is inclusive of cell variables through the principles of modern biology (Leung et al., 2016). With the growing availability of large-scale data sets, (Olson et al., 2017) mentioned that there are about 165 publicly available datasets were used with machine learning algorithms to fine tune the performance of algorithms, open source packages were used. Advanced computational technique called deep learning architecture which comprises of deep neural networks, recurrent neural networks, convolutional neural networks and emergent architectures were discussed by authors (Min, Lee, & Yoon, 2016). The research community can help users in the advanced age of genomic medicine. Deep learning is used as a computational technique. The study of inheritance and variation of individuals based on DNA (deoxyribonucleic acid) is called genetics. The study of the structure and function of the genome is called genomics. To determine the nucleic acid structure, both bioinformatics and computational techniques are used by the data generated from methods of namely DNA and RNA (ribonucleic acid) sequencing, microarrays, proteomics, and electron microscopy, or optical methods. A genome is an instruction book for building an organism (Leung et al., 2016). The introns and exons are called as alternating regions in a typical gene and they are the most significant valuable information structures. The patterns in the nucleotide sequence (SNP) determines the boundaries between these regions. Disease-causing mutations act by disrupting these patterns. The genomic events which are associated with complex and dynamic aspects of the disease. There are computational models (Sun et al., 2017) built to identify insights on cancer progression.

TYPES OF DATASETS AND TOOLS

The literature survey is being carried out using genome wide association studies (GWAS), which facilitates the genetic variants of individuals associated with disease risk. Various related research papers and literature found in National Centre for Biotechnology Information (NCBI) instituted by National library of Medicine.

Datasets

National Centre for Biotechnology Information (NCBI) is a research organization established in the year 1988 as a branch of National library of medicine (NLM). The research organization is built to discover modern molecular biology at National institutes of Health (NIH). It facilitates data by way of various databases, software and tools to the medical community, it is responsible to conduct research and training in molecular biology problems using computational and mathematical methods, develops and promotes database standards and structures to store molecular data. It's made available to different medical institutes, industry and government organizations all around the world for future research.

Database availability is made through well-organized web site (NCBI, n.d.) under the following broad categories as displayed in Figure 2.

Figure 2. Displays categories of available (significant) database related to molecular bioinformatics

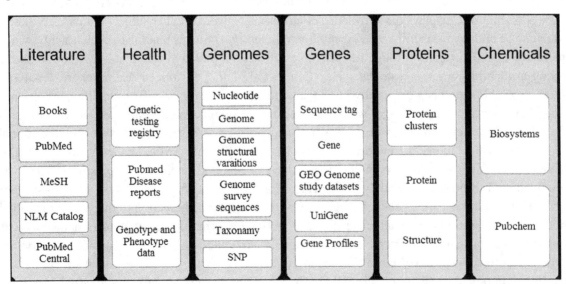

A huge available data in the form of database, for example, PubMed comprises about 22 million abstracts and citations of literature pertaining to biomedical, it is related to the category of literature. Avatar (A value added transcriptome database) which identifies 174k alternative splicing events with covering of Homo sapiens (Hsu, Shia, & Lo, 2007). There are experimental data available to download Genome data in various international standards, GenBank is a collection of such publicly available nucleotide sequences which are annotated. This database is produced by NCBI in collaboration with other national research laboratories like data library from the European Bioinformatics Institute (EBI), DNA Data Bank of Japan (DDBJ) and the European Molecular Biology Laboratory (EMBL), GenBank receives sequences from all over the world about distinct organisms, to name, it has over 167 million sequences as on year 2013. These sequences have been uploaded by various sequence centres and with standard structure and annotation. Related to human genome, the sequence variations within genome, expresses phenotypic characteristics to various complex diseases, so variations will be used for gene mapping. Single Nucleotide Polymorphism database (SNP) has a typical data which is related to human genome, called as "human_9606" and it is compressed to contain data for 23 typical chromosomes. In which each chromosome data file size varies from 100 MB (megabyte) to 2.6 GB (gigabyte) file, available in formats of flat, xml and binary (Kitts et al., 2013). The data will be uploaded in releases with a plan and build management with all standard documentation. This will be uploaded quarterly and yearly dumps, then the data will be made available to the public through FTP address (file transfer protocol). Figure 3 flow chart displays the NCBI process of releasing dataset.

Figure 3. Typical build cycle for data dump of SNP to the FTP site

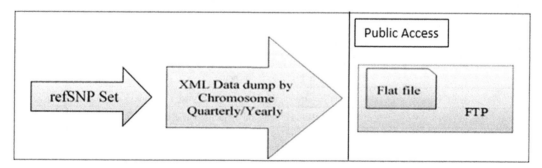

Dataset for SNP Interactions for Genomic Data

A review of machine learning and systems of genomics along with multi-omics data are analysed (Lin & Lane, 2017). Few researchers have processed 27k datasets and simulated, the authors have evaluated the real data set for analysing the effectiveness of interaction models. Genome wide association studies (GWAS) suggests that data obtained by Welcome Trust Case Control Consortium (WTCCC) and disease related dataset obtained from the cancer genome atlas (TCGA), which has about 33 types of cancer disease related data, available from genomic data commons (GDC) (National Cancer Institute, n.d.). Dataset for training gene patterns can be obtained from leukaemia and it has about 38 bone marrow samples (NCBI, n.d.).

Dataset for Splice Site Prediction for Human Genome (HS3D)

Gene prediction is a problem of challenge in identifying gene, splice site prediction is one of the significant processes, splice site prediction (Pashaei, Ozen, & Aydin, 2016; Pashaei, Yilmaz, & Aydin, 2016) have proposed AdaBoost classifier to nucleotide which is modified and encoded, called as tenfold cross validation. The experimental results show an accuracy of 92.78 percent on acceptor splice site over the early method of support vector machine with Markova (SVM-MM) model.

Omics Informatics Data (Integration)

Informatics data is a subject under bioinformatics deals with multi omics data (Boekel et al., 2015) analysis, a subfield of bioinformatics. The scope of this analysis represents involving of proteomics, genomics, metabolomics and transcriptomics data, which has complete set of sequencing including RNA and DNA. there are methods that integrate omics data to bridge the gap between phenotype and genotype to understand role of genetics and genomics (Ritchie et al., 2015). As the data is of high volume, an ecosystem of big data is proposed to manage to reduce computational complexity, so NCBI has stored omics data in EBI ftp servers. Ma and Zhang, (2017) have proposed integrated framework to manage and to make novel findings and new discoveries. i.e. integrating multi omics data and clinical data makes sense to further determining insights in an efficient way, the following are the key drivers which should be robust to frame solution, a. The search methodology: b. Efficient data storage; c. Analysis of data; d. Management of data Authors (Ma & Zhang, 2017) have proposed few toolkits as listed in Table 1.

Table 1. Toolkits for specific tasks

Name of Toolkit	Usage Details
Crossbow	Complete genome resequencing
GATK	Analyse sequencing data and genotyping
Picard	Manipulation of high throughput sequencing data
SAMtools	Interaction of sequencing data
Churchill	Scalable, efficient variant discovery tool
SNPtools	Analysis of SNP and genotype variant discovery

There are few integrated workflow management systems built with best practices available as user friendly platforms in Python, Java and multiple languages. They are available in cloud infrastructure with Amazon web services (AWS). A list of Integrated workflow systems for analysis through Multi-Omics data (Giardine et al., 2005) is shown in Table 2.

GEO (Gene expression Omnibus dataset) dataset is a genomics data, the type is array and sequence-based data, the repository exists in NCBI. Chlis, Bei, and Zervakis, (2016) have used datasets of GSE9574, GSE18672 and found evaluation in the support vector machines (SVM) methodology. This methodology has achieved significant accuracy over relevance vector machine (RVM) which is a probabilistic equivalent and a Bayesian approach method.

Table 2. Integrated workflow systems for analysis through Multi-Omics data

Name of System Framework	Usage Details
Galaxy	GUI and web-based platform for multi-omics work analysis
GenePattern	For Genomic analysis with various analytical tools
GenomeSpace	Multi-omics work analysis with web interface
Taverna	Desktop and cloud based with web interface
Omics Pipe	Automation and cloud based with no GUI

DIFFERENT METHODOLOGY FOR MACHINE LEARNING TECHNIQUES

Big Data Analytics in Microlevel Data

Authors (Herland et al., 2014) elaborates about big data technology to be adapted as a computational method, because the genome data has large data set which is one of the five dimensions of big data viz., volume, velocity, variety, veracity and value. The latest methods are discussed with focus to all problem definitions of health informatics like bioinformatics, neuro informatics, public informatics, clinical informatics and translational bioinformatics. The main solution framework using big data revolves on data retrieval, storage, analytics and subject them to data mining techniques. The framework explains a subfield which is in a developing area called as translational bioinformatics, it's a field which links the biomedical, genome data and clinical data as well, which improves the performance of the findings from research. Butte and Shah (2011) discusses in detail about translational bioinformatics published in Journal of American medical informatics association. The big data capability has increased recently to handle complexities in algorithms, so it's critical to use these tools in bioinformatics. It concludes more efficient methods and will be developed to frame solutions in health informatics at all levels.

Machine Learning and Statistical Approaches

Machine learning is the logical field, managing the routes in which machines gain as a matter of fact. For some researchers, the term "machine learning" is indistinguishable to the expression "computerized reasoning", given that the likelihood of learning is the fundamental principle for an element. The motivation behind machine learning is the development of personal computer frameworks that can adjust and gain from their experience. Machine learning (Kavakiotis et al., 2017) are classified into three categories.

Supervised Learning

Here system infers labelled data from training processes. An expression of a model comprises data, this has input and output variables, the input variables represent a set of features of a domain. The expression must learn for a target, the output variables is called as training data. Mainly there are two types of tasks, they are, regression and classification, regression predicts the numerical values whereas the classification predicts the distinct values. The commonly used techniques are Genetic Algorithms (GA), k-Nearest Neighbours (k-NN), Decision Trees (DT), Artificial Neural Networks (ANN) and support vector machines (SVM).

Unsupervised Learning

The system learns using an unlabeled data, this method discovers hidden structures of data, without any labelled data, the association rule mining algorithm is Apriori, commonly, the gene expression in bio-informatics will be carried out by sequence analysis as exploratory data analysis by unsupervised task.

Reinforcement Learning

The whole learning processes takes the dynamic interaction. The technique is through direct environment interaction, and behaviour of the environment will be understood by trial and error method. Its relation is independent to the environment.

Clustering

The whole dataset is grouped by way of different clusters, the patterns, information will be derived out of these patterns. It is an unsupervised learning, where the exact number of clusters is unknown. There are various algorithms used by researchers. Gupta, Singh, & Kumar (2016) has proposed hybridized methods of clustering techniques, there are two types of clustering. Hierarchical Clustering - All the objects are grouped together and then vector will be determined by Principle component analysis and Non-Hierarchical clustering - The datasets are grouped in predefined numbers, as self-organizing maps (SOM) which gives orientation of clusters and K-means which partitions datasets into groups, the methods gave optimal solutions in giving partitions for gene expression data analysis, the process of cluster analysis is displayed in Figure 4.

Figure 4. Process flow clustering method

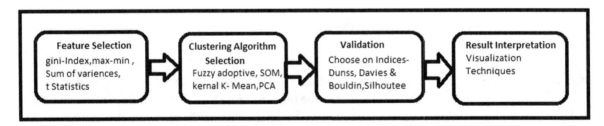

SINGLE-NUCLEOTIDE POLYMORPHISM (SNP)

The SNP (Wang, Elston, & Zhu, 2011) is one of the significant interactions in human genome that reasons for genetic epidemiology of human diseases. The Webster meaning of interaction means transitional activity and activity on each other. SNP interactions have become strong identifying biomarkers for susceptibility of cancer disease in prostate (Vaidyanathan et al., 2017). To build a model and identify the features, as it is a multidimensional problem requires statistical and data mining techniques with machine learning capability. As there are various researches are carried out using different models in the history. Uppu, Krishna, and Gopalan (2018) have laid out detailed comparative study on few approaches by using real data sets. The interactions are two types: 1. Gene interaction with environment (G*E) which has modification by the effects of genes by exposure to environment. 2. Gene interaction with other gene (G*G) called as 'epistasis' (Van Steen, 2012), (Wei, & Hemani, 2014) it has its definition by statisticians, biologists, geneticists and epidemiologists. To detect SNP interactions, methods are reviewed by identification of interactions (G*G) in high-dimensional genomic data, they are highly complex as it's a multidimensionality problem by mathematics and are addressed in the following methods, the authors have explained the performance and achievements of these methods in the proposed approaches. The key issues (Qi, 2012) considered for identifying interactions are selection of variables, models and interpreting the models. The gene architecture comprises large dimensional datasets, in a set of 3-billion-base pairs of human genome, about 12 million SNPs are present all along and maybe they are useful because of their associations with complex disease strains. The challenge in computing these many dimensions are addressed by dimensionality reduction (Sheet and Uppu, Krishna, & Gopalan, 2015) method by way of feature extraction with the help of algorithms. The model building challenge is overcome by cross validation of nonlinear approaches. The biological interpretation of the built SNP interaction model is challenging, few of the following software packages are useful. Software packages like Gene pattern, Pathway studio from Ariadne and ingenuity pathway. Analysis from Ingenuity systems which aids the biologists to interpret the model. The following methods have been discussed in detail with their strengths and limitations. Sheet (n.d.) suggests that future work prevails with SNP interaction identification and existing methods require improvement in minimizing limitations by consolidating knowledge of statistics, biology, genetics epidemiology. Analysis is done by both interactions (G*E) and (G*G) are important to discover insights from the genetic architecture. Few of the methods are discussed and listed in the Table 3.

Table 3. Data mining methods and their strengths/limitations

Methods	Strengths	Limitations
Random forest (Breiman, 2001), Neural Networks (Qi, 2012) Support vector machine (Koo, Liew, Mohamad, & Salleh, 2013) Regression models Bayesian models	No overfit Handle large dataset Robust method to noisy data Performs well on dynamic phenotypes The limitations of p- values are reduced	Under estimates scores of SNP's More complex Do not cope with missing data Substantial number of phenotypes require small p-values Computationally intensive

Biological Filters and Multifactor Dimensionality Reduction (MDR)

Uppu et al., (2018) identified the chances of missing SNP interactions as they may get filtered in the process of statistics, so it's worthwhile to use novel alternative filters such as using filters with biological knowledge, these filters can be derived by bio chemical pathways. Computational optimization is necessary as the dataset is large, the current parallel computing, cloud computing by sharing infra resources and grid computing helps to overcome the complexity to handle limitations. Evaluation of models are being done by data simulation as it is difficult to evaluate with real dataset i.e. with unknown SNP. The simulators recommended are forward-time, resampling and coalescent (Carvajal-Rodríguez, 2008). It is concluded that further developments should be carried out on SNP interaction studies to highlight advances in optimizing algorithms and computing power, the study and advancement of interaction effects on factors of genetic and environment will discover insights of genetic architecture that contribute to diseases.

In an era of genomic wide association studies, the advances in genotyping, generation sequencing and technologies have enabled identification of number of SNPs which are directly related to the cause of complex diseases responsiveness, but these studies prompt to identify SNP interactions which are complex and challenging computationally. So, choosing a method depends on the performance and the efficiency of giving the result as expected, will be entirely based on doing more tests with real data, different methods and compares them, if need new process with minor changes in validation and testing can be considered in every experiment. In identifying the SNP interactions, formation of full genetic architecture places a key role in, Genome wide association studies. It is important to identify multi loci SNP interactions which enables a complete genetic architecture which are to be finalized by researchers. Lin et al., (2013) have tried by conducting experiments in the available efficient techniques, these techniques have procedures of latest data mining and machine learning methods.

According to (Lin et al., 2013) MDR is a method which reduces high dimension data into single dimension, the input data would be genotypic combination data. In Figure 5, p-value is a smallest level of significance to prove null hypothesis. A common consideration for p-value is 0.05 means, convincing evidence against null hypothesis. The flow chart diagram displays, the process of classifier and prediction. There are few limitations like, this may not be scalable for a substantial number of SNP's. To speed up the computational time, there are a two-way ANOVA tests are performed.

Figure 5. Process of MDR method

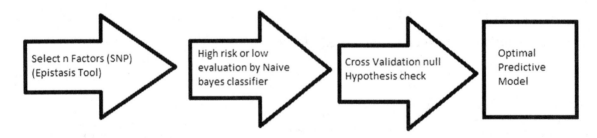

Random Forest (RF) and Neural Networks (NN)

A node is represented by binary split and terminates in leaf, implemented in R program, Weka tool packages, it's an ensemble classification and regression trees (CART), each split has subset of child nodes, so the child node is purer than parent node. This method is suitable for large p- value problems, these errors can overcome by using advanced RF methods like Epiforest, Random Jungle and other hybrid models i.e. combined with multivariate adaptive regression splines (MARS), integrated methods like combining random forest and multivariate adaptive regression splines of machine learning methods can be used effectively to identify patterns of interactions in SNP (Lin et al., 2013), tests with real genetic data is preferable. Random Forest Algorithm (Qi, 2012) is used mainly to reduce the over fitting in classification problem and regression task, it identifies the important feature from training dataset. Method provides accurate predictions on various applications and improve the model performance for computational biology problems having nonlinear problems, is applied successfully for wide range of data types, viz., statistical genetics, mass spectrum protein expression analysis, sequence annotation, gene expression classification. This method used by (Nguyen et al., 2015) for detecting SNP interactions is more accurate to generate trees with a low error rate for prediction to reduce dimensionality of Genome - wide association data.

Neural networks (NN) is a machine learning model where each neuron node is a processing unit, they are trained as an input layer with known SNPs and disease strains as output, there are weight attributes to reduce prediction errors. Two methods to detect SNPs associated with disease strains, first one is linkage between locus of disease and marker, second is linkage disequilibrium of locus of disease and marker. Authors (Keedwell and Narayanan, 2005) have proposed algorithms and combined to achieve opted solution. A combination of genetic algorithm with NN is used to identify temporal gene expression datasets and Back propagation algorithm is to detect interactions between non-functional SNPs, there are two locus models implemented on real genetic data. Genetic programming (GPNN) will identify association in human diseases; it is an optimized neural network process. This has limitation, that it will not cope for complex dataset because of limited number of layers, to overcome a grammatical evolution, a method is used to identify strong pair-wise interactions.

Support Vector Machines (SVM) and Regression Models

Supervised learning methods, two feature vectors are used to train data i.e. Positive - Presence of SNP interactions and negative - lack of SNP interactions, but the SVM method fails to cope with larger and missing SNP data. Chen et al., (2008) have implemented few techniques which optimizes SVM method, they are Genetic Algorithm (SVM-GA) and Recursive feature addition (SVM-RFA). Regression models are statistically based approaches and they follow linear regression equation $(Y = mX+C)$ the function is a predictor variable, whereas logistic regression follows $(p/1-p)$, p is a probability of a risk for a disease. The limitation of these methods is computationally complex, as they require to $2*N$ equations for N interactions. An effective tool called PLINK is used for whole Genome analysis. The other models merging with monte carlo (MCLR), Full Bayesian logic regression (FBLR) are also proposed by other researchers.

Bayesian Method and Ant Colony Optimization Method (ACO)

Genotype distribution are different for a disease related SNP, it is a stepwise method by adopting regression and Bayesian-based. WINBUGS is a software which is implemented for single locus models. The other method Markov chain Monte Carlo (MCMC) used to identify multiclass SNP interactions. The process of prediction happens in three groups:

Group 0: Do not relate to disease.
Group 1: Contribute to disease.
Group 2: Disease risks due to interaction effects.

WTCCC uses Bayesian epistasis association mapping (BEAM). There are limitations in this method, as it cannot be implemented to detect SNP in the absence of main effects. Ant Colony Optimization Method is a probabilistic feedback approach is used by modelling behaviour of ants in detecting optimal path, they do feedback communication with more levels of pheromone. It searches parallelly for SNP interactions for large association studies, the procedure is called AntEpiSeeker and it has two stages of process, highly suspected SNP determination by x2 and reduced SNP sets and for SNPs with large marginal effects. Ant colony optimization with logistic regression is proposed for better results, ACO along with novel encoding is being used by WTCCC for type II Diabetes disease risks. But these methods pose difficulty in increasing number of hypothesis for three loci interactions.

Detection of SNP Interactions With Deep Learning Approaches

The current data mining methods has limitations in identifying SNP interactions, as the problem is a multidimensional, the recent publication of research article (Uppu, Krishna, & Gopalan, 2016b) carried out works on recent deep learning methods to find reduction techniques for multidimensional features (MDR). The method is most suitable for large sized datasets with unique variants (Gola et al., 2016). This method uses labelled training data, for inferring a function also called as machine learning task of supervised learning. Method searches multi-locus SNP Interactions with a non-parametric technique. Researchers have discussed that marginal effect on at least one pair of SNP is required, that will reduce performance of the technical reference model (TRM) (Vansteen, 2012), sampling random forest (Sheet, n.d.) and SNPInterForest (Goodfellow et al., 2011). After reviewing the current methods, it is proposed to use deep feed forward neural networks with an analysis five-stages is done:

- **Stage One:** A simulation of data sets is generated with the use of GAMETES tool (Uppu, Krishna, & Gopalan, 2016c).
- **Stage Two:** A combination of SNP's of various locations are used to improve the prediction accuracy.
- **Stage Three:** A new process of cross validation is used with ten folds.
- **Stage Four and Five:** It uses deep learning algorithms which classifies and discovers multi locus SNP interactions.

A deep feed forward neural network, authors (LeCun, 2015 and Goodfellow et al., 2011) have proposed three hidden layers with a width of each hidden layer of 50. The model is trained with samples of 320k which takes a duration of 17.658 seconds. Current studies identify twenty highly ranked two-locus SNP interactions. Feed forward network comprises one input and an output with three hidden layers, the output of each neuron is weighted by sum of $\sum W_{jj}X_i \leq$ at threshold level, W is the weight associated with input x of each neuron. The deep feed forward network method is used for the following set of samples displayed in Table 4 which are samples from published breast cancer data.

Table 4. Details about samples tested in feed forward method

Training Samples	Time Taken to Train in Seconds	Training Speed Samples / Seconds	The Validation Error
320,000	17.658 Seconds	8122.098	0.294

It is suggested that researchers can analyse with higher order interactions in high dimensional data. Authors have highlighted the importance of pre-processing of data sets. In Figure 6, the accuracy of deep learning method in percentage is displayed, compared to other conventional methods.

HISEEKER METHODOLOGY WITH OPTIMIZATION FOR HIGH ORDER SNP INTERACTIONS

It is concluded that detecting SNP interactions is the best approach to explain missing heritability of complex diseases, so far, the researchers focus on pair wise interactions and the existing methods has limitations in analysing high order interactions of genome-wide data, hence Liu, Yu, Jiang, & Wang, (2017) suggested an adaptable two-stage methodology (called HiSeeker). The first stage of screening utilizes the chi-squared test and logistic regression model should proficiently acquire hopeful pairwise combinations, in the next stage, two search methods by candidate combinations are used to detect high-order interactions from different strategies (exhaustive search and ant colony optimization-based search), such as dynamic clustering of high order genome, epistatic interactions detecting (DCHE) and CINOEDV, used for top-k most significant two-locus interactions. HiSeeker detected various significant high-order interactions on two-real WTCCC datasets (Dubois et al., 2010) (breast cancer and Celiac disease). HiSeeker limits performance in few tests and time consuming for high-order interaction detection. It is proposed in the future work to use with graphics processing units (GPUs) to speedup HiSeeker for GWAS studies (Sapin, Keedwell, & Frayling, 2015). Nguyen et al., (2015) proposes new methodology of machine learning, which is used for identification of genetic variants. Authors (Nguyen et al., 2015) recommend utilizing another two-stage quality-based testing technique for random forests, named ts-RF, for SNP subspace choice for GWAS. The process uses a new SNP sampling method to generate splits at the nodes of CART trees (Deng, 2013). The splits represent week informative and highly informative SNPs. An experiment is conducted on real time datasets of complex disease with 10 gene sets and found reduction in prediction error.

COMPUTATIONAL EVALUATION SYSTEMS (CES) AND COMPARATIVE STUDY

The problem is of multiclass, a binary classification algorithm (Crabtree et al., 2017) is introduced to carry out bio marker discovery in bioinformatics domain. It's a knowledge discovery engine to identify synergetic relationships for large data sets. This technique is compared with classical algorithms like random forest and support vector machine. The performance of CES advantageous in deep learning algorithm compared to random forest, logistic regression, naive based and gradient boosting method is shown in Figure 6.

The Table 5 lists a view of various researches and their findings, the research papers selected are relevant to gene sequencing data analysis for SNP and splicing problems, a data integration framework is also discussed in a research finding.

Figure 6. Accuracy of predictions with deep learning, random forest, logistic regression, naive based and gradient boosting method

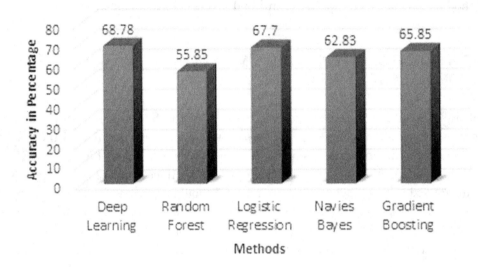

Table 5. Comparison details about research findings on techniques

Future work	Limitation	Authors	Dataset	Processes	Methods	Algorithm	Achievement
To explore more biological features like pre mRNA secondary structures	Motifs may not accurate	2017 Jing Xia et.al	For Alternate splicing -exons of C.elegans(3 & 5)- 487 alt exons, 2531	Feature selection-Basic sequence feature, splice site strength	simple linear SVM classifier	SVM algorithm +j48 decision tree algorithm	SVM classifier is better than using sophisticated kernel methods
Can focus prediction drug efficiency techniques	1) Challenging to avoid overfitting 2) Transforming into intermediate form	2017 Eugene Lin and Lane	Multi omics data		1) Model based integration 2) Transformation based integration		1) Various data type can be obtained by same phenotype 2) Unique variables are used economically and clinically
Efficient and less expensive methods	Growing number of genetic variants causes high dimensional data which limits efficiency	2016 Suneetha Uppu, et.al	GWAS and real dataset from wellcome	Using Data simulators with real data set - Performance Assessments	MDR, RF, NN, SVM, RM, Bayesian models	Ant colony optimization along with regression	Analysing Interaction in SNP
To do three loci, high dimensional data in unsupervised learning	Two locus data used	2016 Suneetha Uppu, et.al	SNP variation data in GAMETES tool	Ten fold cross validation	Deep learning algorithm	Trained multilayer NN	Predication accuracy efficient over other methods (68%)
Interpretability methods to be standardised, Promising direction in Genome editing	Complexity in computation	2016 Michael K.K Leung et.al (Review)	Reference is made to "omics" data set,GTEx, NCI-60, ENCODE, ICGC,	Cell variable related to genomic regulatory	Machine learning methods RNN(Recurrent Neural network)	Splicing patterns also to be identified	gene expression, splicing, protein binding- all are training targets for predictive models
Mode based approaches to be experimented		2016 Shelly et.al	Gene micro array data	Hybridized methods	Clustering	1) Cluster centre initialization 2) Quadtree structure 3) Expectation maximization	Promising result
Stress on analytical Strategy using integrated data rather than data in silo	Few approaches are theoretical distribuitions - Simulation and permutation testing is needed, Inference and interpretations are not strong	2015 Marylyn D. Ritchie et.al	genome sequencing date (genomics), genome wide RNA-sequencing data (transcriptomics), methylation and histone modification data (epigenomics), mass spectrometry protein data (proteomics)	Data integration: Multistage analysis Meta dimensional analysis	a) Trans eQTL(expression quantitative trait loci), b) Cis-eQTL, Allele specific, c) Overlap with functional unit 1) Concatenation, 2) Transformation, 3) Model based integration		

CONCLUSION

Detail study is made and summarized on various computational methods, algorithm and techniques to identify disease traits by the way of gene splicing and SNP interactions. To identify SNP interactions, a deep learning approach is experimented as preferable computational method. The researchers have proposed few pre-processing steps called a tenfold cross validation. In future, multi loci analysis are to be carried out to obtain higher order accuracy, because the multi loci parameters poses high dimensional dataset. The review also suggests that, use of hybrid approaches is important, as advancement in computational technology helps in building ecosystem to effectively manage genome datasets. There are potential challenges like imbalanced data and interpretation of results, but selection of appropriate architecture or techniques makes effective discovery.

REFERENCES

Boekel, J., Chilton, J. M., Cooke, I. R., Horvatovich, P. L., Jagtap, P. D., Käll, L., ... Griffin, T. J. (2015). Multi-omic data analysis using Galaxy. *Nature Biotechnology*, *33*(2), 137–139. doi:10.1038/nbt.3134 PMID:25658277

Breiman, L. (2001). Random forests. *Machine Learning*, *45*(1), 5–32. doi:10.1023/A:1010933404324

Butte, A. J., & Shah, N. H. (2011). Computationally translating molecular discoveries into tools for medicine: Translational bioinformatics articles now featured in *JAMIA*. *Journal of the American Medical Informatics Association*, *18*(4), 352–353. doi:10.1136/amiajnl-2011-000343 PMID:21672904

Carvajal-Rodriguez, A. (2008). Simulation of Genomes: A Review. Current Genomics.

Chen, S. H., Sun, J., Dimitrov, L., Turner, A. R., Adams, T. S., Meyers, D. A., ... Hsu, F.-C. (2008). A support vector machine approach for detecting gene-gene interaction. *Genetic Epidemiology*, *32*(2), 152–167. doi:10.1002/gepi.20272 PMID:17968988

Chlis, N. K., Bei, E. S., & Zervakis, M. (2018). Introducing a stable bootstrap validation framework for reliable genomic signature extraction. *IEEE/ACM Transactions on Computational Biology and Bioinformatics*, *15*(1), 181–190. doi:10.1109/TCBB.2016.2633267 PMID:27913357

Crabtree, N. M., Moore, J. H., Bowyer, J. F., & George, N. I. (2017). Multi-class computational evolution: Development, benchmark evaluation and application to RNA-Seq biomarker discovery. *BioData Mining*, *10*(1), 13. doi:10.118613040-017-0134-8 PMID:28450890

Deng, H. (2013). Guided Random Forest in the RRF Package. Retrieved from http://arxiv.org/abs/1306.0237

Dubois, P. C. A., Trynka, G., Franke, L., Hunt, K. A., Romanos, J., Curtotti, A., ... van Heel, D. A. (2010). Multiple common variants for celiac disease influencing immune gene expression. *Nature Genetics*, *42*(4), 295–302. doi:10.1038/ng.543 PMID:20190752

Giardine, B., Riemer, C., Hardison, R. C., Burhans, R., Elnitski, L., Shah, P., ... Miller, W. (2005). Galaxy: A platform for interactive large-scale genome analysis. *Genome Research*, *15*(10), 1451–1455. PMID:16169926

Gola, D., Mahachie John, J. M., Van Steen, K., & König, I. R. (2016). A roadmap to multifactor dimensionality reduction methods. *Briefings in Bioinformatics*, *17*(2), 293–308. doi:10.1093/bib/bbv038 PMID:26108231

Goodfellow, I., Bengio, Y., & Courville, A. (2011). Deep Learning. In *ICML2013 Tutorial* (pp. 1–800). doi:10.1038/nmeth.3707

Gupta, S., Singh, S. N., & Kumar, D. (2016). Clustering methods applied for gene expression data: A study. In *2016 Second International Conference on Computational Intelligence & Communication Technology (CICT)* (pp. 724–728). 10.1109/CICT.2016.149

Herland, M., Khoshgoftaar, T. M., & Wald, R. (2014). A review of data mining using big data in health informatics. *Journal of Big Data*, *1*(1), 2. doi:10.1186/2196-1115-1-2

Hsu, F. R., Lin, H. C., & Chang, H.-Y. (2007). Discovery the relationship between single nucleotide polymorphisms and alternative splicing events. In IFMBE Proceedings (Vol. 15). doi:10.1007/978-3-540-68017-8_132

Human Genome Project. (n.d.). US Department of Energy genome Program's biological and environmental research information system (BERIS). Retrieved from http://www.ornl.gov/sci/techresources/Human_Genome/

Ji, Z., Yan, K., Li, W., Hu, H., & Zhu, X. (2017). Mathematical and computational modeling in complex biological systems. *BioMed Research International*, 1–16. doi:10.1155/2017/5958321 PMID:28386558

Kavakiotis, I., Tsave, O., Salifoglou, A., Maglaveras, N., Vlahavas, I., & Chouvarda, I. (2017). Machine learning and data mining methods in diabetes research. *Computational and Structural Biotechnology Journal*, *15*, 104–116. doi:10.1016/j.csbj.2016.12.005 PMID:28138367

Keedwell, E., & Narayanan, A. (2005). Discovering gene networks with a neural-genetic hybrid. *IEEE/ACM Transactions on Computational Biology and Bioinformatics*, *2*(3), 231–242. doi:10.1109/TCBB.2005.40 PMID:17044186

Kitts, A., Phan, L., Minghong, W., & Holmes, J. B. (2013). The database of short genetic variation (dbSNP). *The NCBI Handbook* (2nd ed.). Retrieved from http://www.ncbi.nlm.nih.gov/books/NBK174586/

Koo, C. L. C., Liew, M. M. J., Mohamad, M. S., & Salleh, A. H. M. (2013). A review for detecting gene-gene interactions using machine learning methods in genetic epidemiology. *BioMed Research International*, *13*. doi:10.1155/2013/432375 PMID:24228248

LeCun, Y., Bengio, Y., & Hinton, G. (2015). Deep learning. *Nature*, *521*(7553), 436–444. doi:10.1038/nature14539 PMID:26017442

Leung, M. K. K., Delong, A., Alipanahi, B., & Frey, B. J. (2016). Machine Learning in Genomic Medicine: A Review of Computational Problems and Data Sets. *Proceedings of the IEEE*, *104*(1), 176–197. doi:10.1109/JPROC.2015.2494198

Lin, E., & Lane, H.-Y. (2017). Machine learning and systems genomics approaches for multi-omics data. *Biomarker Research*, *5*(1), 2. doi:10.118640364-017-0082-y PMID:28127429

Lin, H., Chen, Y. A., Tsai, Y., Qu, X., Tseng, T., & Jong, Y. (2013). TRM: A Powerful Two-Stage Machine Learning Approach for Identifying SNP-SNP Interactions. *NIH Public Access*, *76*(1), 53–62. doi:10.1111/j.1469-1809.2011.00692.x.TRM

Liu, J., Yu, G., Jiang, Y., & Wang, J. (2017). HiSeeker: Detecting high-order SNP interactions based on pairwise SNP combinations. *Genes*, *8*(6), 2–19. doi:10.3390/genes8060153 PMID:28561745

Ma, T., & Zhang, A. (2017). Omics informatics: From scattered individual software tools to integrated workflow management systems. *IEEE/ACM Transactions on Computational Biology and Bioinformatics*, *14*(4), 926–946. doi:10.1109/TCBB.2016.2535251 PMID:26930689

Min, S., Lee, B., & Yoon, S. (2017). Deep learning in bioinformatics. *Briefings in Bioinformatics*, *18*(5), 851–869. doi:10.1093/bib/bbw068 PMID:27473064

National Cancer Institute. (n.d.). Retrieved October 30, 2017, from https://gdc-portal.nic.nih.gov/

NCBI Sitemap. (n.d.). Retrieved from http://www.ncbi.nlm.nih.gov/Sitemap/index.html

Nguyen, T.-T., Huang, J., Wu, Q., Nguyen, T., & Li, M. (2015). Genome-wide association data classification and SNPs selection using two-stage quality-based Random Forests. *BMC Genomics*, *16*(Suppl. 2), S5. doi:10.1186/1471-2164-16-S2-S5 PMID:25708662

Olson, R. S., La Cava, W., Mustahsan, Z., Varik, A., & Moore, J. H. (2017). Data-driven Advice for Applying Machine Learning to Bioinformatics Problems. doi:10.1142/9789813235533_0018

Pashaei, E., Ozen, M., & Aydin, N. (2016). Splice sites prediction of human genome using AdaBoost. In *2016 IEEE-EMBS International Conference on Biomedical and Health Informatics (BHI)* (pp. 300–303). 10.1109/BHI.2016.7455894

Pashaei, E., Yilmaz, A., & Aydin, N. (2016). A combined SVM and Markov model approach for splice site identification. In *2016 6th International Conference on Computer and Knowledge Engineering (ICCKE)* (pp. 200–204). doi:10.1109/ICCKE.2016.7802140

Podolsky, M. D., Barchuk, A. A., Kuznetcov, V. I., Gusarova, N. F., Gaidukov, V. S., & Tarakanov, S. A. (2016). Evaluation of machine learning algorithm utilization for lung cancer classification based on gene expression levels. *Asian Pacific Journal of Cancer Prevention*, *17*(2), 835–838. doi:10.7314/APJCP.2016.17.2.835 PMID:26925688

Qi, Y. (2012). Random Forest for Bioinformatics. In C. Zhang & Y. Ma (Eds.), *Ensemble machine learning*. Boston, MA: Springer. doi:10.1007/978-1-4419-9326-7_11

Ritchie, M. D., Holzinger, E. R., Li, R., Pendergrass, S. A., & Kim, D. (2015). Methods of integrating data to uncover genotype–phenotype interactions. *Nature Reviews. Genetics*, *16*(2), 85–97. doi:10.1038/nrg3868 PMID:25582081

Sapin, E., Keedwell, E., & Frayling, T. (2015). An ant colony optimization and tabu list approach to the detection of gene-gene interactions in genome-wide association studies. *IEEE Computational Intelligence Magazine*, *10*(4), 1–21. doi:10.1109/MCI.2015.2471236

Sun, Y., Yao, J., Le, Y., Chen, R., Nowak, N. J., & Goodison, S. (2017). Computational approach for deriving cancer progression roadmaps from static sample data. *Nucleic Acids Research*, *45*(9), 1–16. doi:10.1093/nar/gkx003 PMID:28108658

Uppu, S., Krishna, A., & Gopalan, R. P. (2015). A multifactor dimensionality reduction based associative classification for detecting SNP interactions. In Neural Information Processing (pp. 328-336).

Uppu, S., Krishna, A., & Gopalan, R. P. (2016b). A deep learning approach to detect SNP interactions. *Journal of Software*, *11*(10), 960–975. doi:10.17706/jsw.11.10.965-975

Uppu, S., Krishna, A., & Gopalan, R. P. (2016c). Towards deep learning in genome-wide wssociation interaction studies. In Pacis (p. 20).

Uppu, S., Krishna, A., & Gopalan, R. P. (2018). A review on methods for detecting SNP interactions in high-dimensional genomic data. *IEEE/ACM Transactions on Computational Biology and Bioinformatics*, *15*(2), 599–612. doi:10.1109/TCBB.2016.2635125 PMID:28060710

Vaidyanathan, V., Naidu, V., Karunasinghe, N., Jabed, A., Pallati, R., Marlow, G., & Ferguson, L. R. (2017). SNP-SNP interactions as risk factors for aggressive prostate cancer. *F1000 Research*, *6*(May), 621. doi:10.12688/f1000research.11027.1 PMID:28580135

Van Steen, K. (2012). Travelling the world of gene-gene interactions. *Briefings in Bioinformatics*, *13*(1), 1–19. doi:10.1093/bib/bbr012 PMID:21441561

Wang, X., Elston, R. C., & Zhu, X. (2011). The meaning of interaction. *Human Heredity*, *70*(4), 269–277. doi:10.1159/000321967 PMID:21150212

Wei, W.-H., Hemani, G., & Haley, C. S. (2014). Detecting epistasis in human complex traits. *Nature Reviews. Genetics*, *15*(11), 722–733. doi:10.1038/nrg3747 PMID:25200660

This research was previously published in the International Journal of Smart Education and Urban Society (IJSEUS), 10(1); pages 49-63, copyright year 2019 by IGI Publishing (an imprint of IGI Global).

Chapter 14
A Fast Feature Selection Method Based on Coefficient of Variation for Diabetics Prediction Using Machine Learning

Tengyue Li
University of Macau, Macau

Simon Fong
University of Macau, Macau SAR

ABSTRACT

Diabetes has become a prevalent metabolic disease nowadays, affecting patients of all age groups and large populations around the world. Early detection would facilitate early treatment that helps the prognosis. In the literature of computational intelligence and medical care communities, different techniques have been proposed in predicting diabetes based on the historical records of related symptoms. The researchers share a common goal of improving the accuracy of a diabetes prediction model. In addition to the model induction algorithms, feature selection is a significant approach in retaining only the relevant attributes for the sake of building a quality prediction model later. In this article, a novel and simple feature selection criterion called Coefficient of Variation (CV) is proposed as a filter-based feature selection scheme. By following the CV method, attributes that have a data dispersion too low are disqualified from the model construction process. Thereby the attributes which are factors leading to poor model accuracy are discarded. The computation of CV is simple, hence enabling an efficient feature selection process. Computer simulation experiments by using the Prima Indian diabetes dataset is used to compare the performance of CV with other traditional feature selection methods. Superior results by CV are observed.

DOI: 10.4018/978-1-6684-6291-1.ch014

INTRODUCTION

Diabetes is a global health concern in both developed and developing countries, and its prevalence is rising. In just UK alone, 2.9 million people are suffering from diabetes mellitus in 2011 that constitutes to 4.45% of the population (Holman et al., 2011). By 2025, it is projected to have 5 million people in UK inflicted with diabetes. This incurable metabolic disorder is chronic and characterized by deficiency of insulin secretion or insensitivity of the body tissues to insulin. The former is known as Type-I insulin-dependent diabetes mellitus (IDDM) where the body defects to produce sufficient insulin due to autoimmune destruction of pancreatic β-cells. As a result, the patients' body cells may wither because they cannot absorb the needful amount of glucose in the bloodstream without this important hormone. The second type is called Type-II non-insulin-dependent diabetes mellitus which is usually associated with obesity and lack of bodily exercises. It will inevitably lead to insulin treatment, probably for lifelong. Early detection of diabetes has become vital and the detection techniques are maturing over the years. However, it is reported that about half of the patients with Type II diabetes are undiagnosed and the latency from disease onset to diagnosis may exceed over a decade (American diabetes association) (International Diabetes Federation). Therefore, the importance of early prediction and detection of diabetes that enables timely treatment of hyperglycaemia and related metabolic abnormalities is escalating.

In the light of this motivation, diabetes prediction models are being formulated and developed in machine-learning research community that claimed to be able to do blood glucose prediction based on the historical records of diabetes patients and their relevant attributes. One of the most significant works is by Jan Maciejovski (Maciejowski, 2002) who formulated predictive diabetic control by using a group of linear and non-linear programming functions that take into consideration of variables and constraints. The other direction related to blood glucose prediction is time-series forecasting (Ståhl & Johansson, 2009), which take into account of the measurements of the past blood glucose cycles, in order to do some short-term blood glucose forecasts. Another popular choice of algorithm in implementing a blood glucose predictor is artificial neural network (Otto et al., 2000; Gogou et al., 2001; Akmal et al., 2011) which non-linearly maps daily regimens of food, insulin and exercise expenditure as inputs to a predicted output. Although neural network predictors usually can achieve a relatively high accuracy (88.8% as in (Akmal et al., 2011)), the model itself is a black-box where the logics in the process of decision making are mathematical inference. For example, numeric weights associated in each neuron and the non-linear activation function. Recently some researchers advocated applicability of decision trees in predicting diabetic prognosis such as batch-training model (Han et al., 2009) and real-time incremental training model (Zhang et al., 2012). The resultant decision tree is in a form of predicate logics IF-THEN-ELSE rules which are descriptive enough for decision support when the rules are embedded in some predictor system, as well as for reference and studies by clinicians. However, one major drawback on decision tree is the selection of the appropriate data attributes or features that should be general enough to model the historical cases, while providing sufficiently high prediction accuracy in the event of unseen case.

Potentially there exist many factors (so-called features) for analysis and diagnosis of the diabetes of patients; these factors may be direct physiological symptoms or lifestyle habits that contribute to the disease. However, there is no standard rule-of-thumb in deciding which of these factors into the inclusion of the model induction (Janecek et al., 2008), given different physicians might have their own opinions. At convenience when all the available features are included in the process of model construction, quite often some of these features may found to be insignificant or irrelevant. Consequently, the accuracy of the prediction model reduces because these the inappropriate feature might have added randomness to the data or the values of these features lead to biased results. Although the topic of feature selection has been widely studied, to the best of the authors' knowledge, a comprehensive evaluation of feature selection methods pertaining to the neural network and decision tree classification has not been done so far. The existing research works either focus on a classification model, especially support-vector-machine (SVM) or on a few feature selection techniques. For instance, research teams of the works (Alakrishnan & Narayanaswamy, 2009; Praharsi et al., 2013; Giveki et al., 2012) dedicated research efforts on solving the feature selection by using SVM classifier and its variants. Huang et al, (Huang et al., 2004) researched the diabetes prediction problem with a variety of classifiers such as CART decision tree and so forth, a singular feature selection called ReliefF was used. In this paper, we propose a novel feature selection method called Coefficient of Variation (CV) which is characterized by its simple and efficient computation. In comparison to other popular feature selection methods which are based on calculating the information gain or correlation among attributes and to the target classes, CV only calculates the ratio of the standard deviation and the mean of each column of attribute data. The underlying principle is that a good attribute should have its data that vary considerably in value, and the data should adequately spread over a certain range, in order to characterize a quality prediction model. Otherwise having an attribute whose data values diverge insufficiently implies certain bias may exist in the data. At least such attribute contributes little to the generality of the induction model, by a relatively narrow data range that it covers. In the context of stochastic optimization, a model induced by such data would likely lead the result falls into a local optimum.

The reminder of this article is structured as follow. Section 2 describes the diabetes dataset and the related data mining techniques to be applied in the experiment. It is known as the data mining framework as a whole. Section 3 reports the results of the experiment, followed by some discussion. Section 4 concludes the paper.

PROPOSED PREDICTIVE MODEL DESIGN

This section describes the data to be used in the experiment, the feature selection algorithms and the model induction algorithms. Though sometimes this is commonly known as KDD, the details especially the attributes are clearly presented so to appreciate the efficacy of the CV feature selection method which follows.

Diabetes Dataset

One of the most popularly used datasets in testing machine learning algorithms for diabetes prediction is Pima Indian diabetes dataset. Generally, the dataset is challenging to building a highly accurate model because all the attributes do not have a profound relation to the predictable class, though these attributes are believed to be subtly related to the diabetes diseases somehow. The dataset has eight potentially useful attributes or features, that describe 768 sample cases of whether the case is of diabetes or not. The binary class is of normal with 500 cases and abnormal (diagnosed with Pima Indian diabetes) with 268 cases. The ratio is considered quite balanced, with a ratio of diabetes-free and confirmed diabetes 65.10%: 39.89%. The diabetes cases are those that are diagnosed with diabetes onset within five years. The data are owned by Peter Turney, National Institute of Diabetes and Digestive and Kidney Diseases. And the database is donated by Vincent Sigillito, Research Center, RMI Group Leader, Applied Physics Laboratory, The Johns Hopkins University, Johns Hopkins Road, Laurel, United States. The eight features are briefly described as follow together with their acronyms:

Feature 1 *preg*: Number of times pregnant
Feature 2 *plas*: Plasma glucose concentration 2 hours in an oral glucose tolerance test
Feature 3 *pres*: Diastolic blood pressure (mm Hg)
Feature 4 *skin*: Triceps skin fold thickness (mm)
Feature 5 *insu*: 2-Hour serum insulin (mu U/ml)
Feature 6 *mass*: Body mass index (weight in kg/(height in m)^2)
Feature 7 *pedi*: Diabetes pedigree function
Feature 8 *age*: Age (in years)
Class *class*: variable (0 or 1)

Feature Selection

The dataset has not been pre-processed, cleansed, nor filtered in our experiment. All the 768 instances are used as they originally are in the model induction. Nevertheless, feature selection is applied prior to model induction; the standard feature selection algorithms are those made available by Weka (Weka 3) which is a popular software platform of machine learning algorithms for solving data mining problems implemented in Java and open sourced under the GPL license by the University of Waikato, New Zealand. Most of these algorithms are documented, and their implementations are provided by Weka as built-in functions as follow. Readers who want further information about these algorithms can refer to the user's manual of Weka or the survey (Molina et al., 2002):

- *cfsubseteval*: Evaluates the worth of a subset of attributes by considering the individual predictive ability of each feature along with the degree of redundancy between them;
- *ChiSquaredAttributeEval*: Evaluates the worth of an attribute by computing the value of the chi-squared statistic with respect to the class;
- *InfoGainAttributeEval*: Evaluates the worth of an attribute by measuring the information gain with respect to the class;
- *PrincipalComponents*: Performs a principal components analysis and transformation of the data;
- *SignificanceAttributeEval*: Evaluates the worth of an attribute by computing the Probabilistic Significance as a two-way function;
- *CorrelationAttributeEval*: Evaluates the worth of an attribute by measuring the correlation (Pearson's) between it and the class;
- *SVMAttributeEval*: Evaluates the worth of an attribute by using an SVM classifier;
- *ReliefFAttributeEval*: Evaluates the worth of an attribute by repeatedly sampling an instance and considering the value of the given attribute for the nearest instance of the same and different class;
- *SymmetricalUncertAttributeEval*: Evaluates the worth of an attribute by measuring the symmetrical uncertainty with respect to the class.

A new feature selection method is proposed in this paper, based on Coefficient of Variation, called *CVAttribeEval*. The method is programmed as a Weka extension plug-in in Java language. It is founded on the belief that a good attribute in a training dataset should have its data vary sufficiently wide across a range of values, so that it is significant to characterize a useful prediction model. To illustrate this concept, visually, the eight attributes of the Pima Indian diabetes dataset are plotted by using the Projection Plot in Weka. Since the original attribute values take in various unit scales, e.g. Age or Body mass index usually is a double-digit number, and Diabetes pedigree function has at least a 3-digit number, the attributes are first subject to normalization into fixed range of [0, 1]. In the visualization program, the attribute values are displayed in seven different scales of color tones, indicating the ranges of values that the data fall into. The farthest ends of values are in solid red and blue, the central values are in pale, and those in between are in mild color. The color chart is shown in Figure 1. The outputs of the eight attributes are shown in Figures 2 (a-h).

Figure 1. Color chart for displaying the values of attribute data in different hues

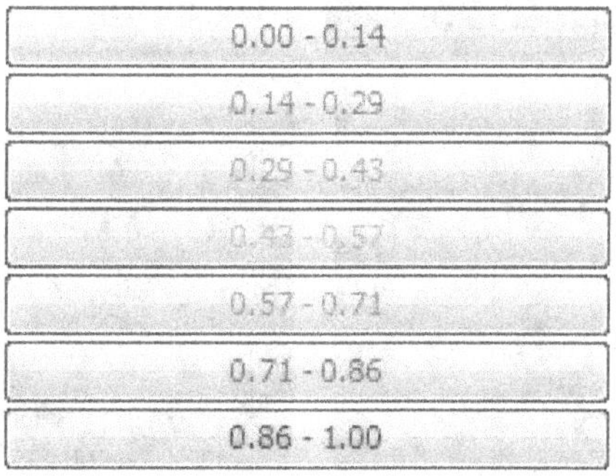

As it can be observed from the collection of visualizations, the attributes do have a good distribution over the data space except *plas*, *pres*, *mass* and *age*, which are shown in Figures 2 (b) (c) (f) and (h) respectively. These attributes which do not have a far spread in the data space often too are carrying mediocre data ranges, as represented by white to grey colors in the data points. That is, the data of these attributes do not vary much in the data scale; hence these attributes may not contribute significantly to an accurate prediction model. These visual patterns can be quantified by using CV computation.

Let X is a training dataset with n instances of vector whose values are characterized by a total of m attributes or features. An instance is a m-dimensional tuple, in the form of $(x_1, x_2, \ldots x_m)$. For each x_a where $a \in [1...m]$, can be partitioned into subgroups of different classes where $c \in C$ is the total number of prediction target classes. So that $x_a \subseteq \{x_a^1, x_a^2, \ldots, x_a^C\}$. Setting a threshold $\tau=1$, if a coefficient of variation of a feature $a \in [1...m]$, $v_a < 1$, then the ath feature can be removed according to the CV feature selection. The coefficient of variation is defined as:

$$v_a = \sum_{c=1}^{C} \frac{\sqrt{\frac{1}{n}\left[\left(x_1^c - \bar{x}_a^c\right)^2 + \left(x_2^c - \bar{x}_a^c\right)^2 + .. + \left(x_n^c - \bar{x}_a^c\right)^2\right]}}{\bar{x}_a^c} \tag{1}$$

where $\bar{x}_a^c$ is the mean of all the ath feature values that belong to class c. v_a is the sum of all coefficients of variation for each class c where $c \in [1...C]$, for that particular a^{th} feature. The coefficient of variation is expressed as a real number from $-\infty$ to $+\infty$ and it describes the standard deviation relative to the mean.

Figure 2. (a) Visualization of data values of attribute preg; (b) Visualization of data values of attribute plas; (c) Visualization of data values of attribute pres; (d) Visualization of data values of attribute skin; (e) Visualization of data values of attribute insu; (f) Visualization of data values of attribute mass; (g) Visualization of data values of attribute pedi; (h) Visualization of data values of attribute age Colo

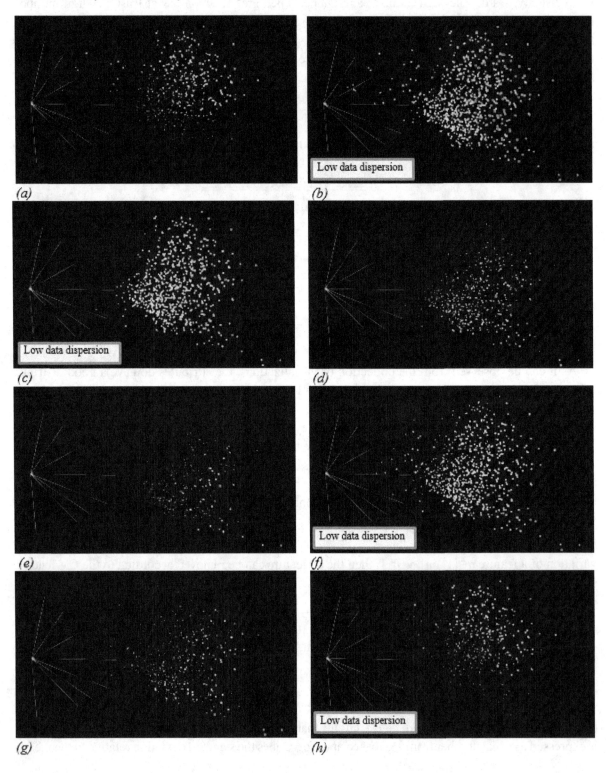

It can be used to compare variability even when the units are different (the units will divide out, providing just a pure number).

In general CV informs us about the size of variation relative to the size of the observation, and it has the advantage that the coefficient of variation is independent of the units of observation. The coefficient of variation, however, will be the same over all the features as it does not depend on the unit of measurement. So you can obtain information about the data variation throughout all the features, by using the coefficient of variation to look at all the ratios of standard deviations to mean in each feature.

It is therefore effectively a normalized or relative measure of the variation in a data set, (e.g. a time series) in that it is a proportion (and therefore can be expressed as a single numeric indicator). Intuitively, if the mean is the expected value, then the coefficient of variation is the expected variability of a measurement, relative to the mean. This is useful when comparing measurements across multiple heterogenous data sets or across multiple measurements taken on the same data set - the coefficient of variation between two data sets or calculated for two attributes of measurements in the case of feature selection, can be directly compared, even if the data in each are measured on very different scales, sampling rates or resolutions. In contrast, standard deviation is specific to the measurement/sample it is obtained from, i.e. it is an absolute rather than a relative measure of variation. In statistics, it is sometimes known as measure of dispersion, which helps compare variation across variables with different units. A variable with higher coefficient of variation is more dispersed than one with lower CV. In our programmed *CVAttribeEval* function, a feature with a composite CV of all the target classes, lower than one is deemed to be removed.

Data Mining Experiment

The goal of the data mining experiment to be conducted is to evaluate the efficacy of the above-mentioned feature selection algorithms including the newly proposed *CVAttribeEval*. The whole Pima Indian diabetes, without any pre-processing are applied with the 10 feature selection algorithms. The filtered dataset, with the redundant features trimmed off, is then used to train a classification model with 10-folds cross-validation assessment method. Two Weka classification algorithms are used, Decision Tree which is implemented as *J48* pruned decision tree function, and Neural Network which is implemented as *MultilayerPerceptron* function.

By using the *CVAttribeEval* approach, the coefficients of variation are calculated for each feature with respective each of the two classes, and they are shown in Table 1. It can be seen that some features of which the CV are higher than one would be retained for subsequent model training. They are highlighted in Table 1. On the other hand, the other features that should be removed (in sorted order) are: *mass*, *plas*, *pres*, and *age*.

After eliminating the low CV features, four features remain. These four features, however, can form different combination of feature subset; up to $p!/[(p-q)!q!]$ combinations can be formed given p is the maximum cardinality of the feature subset ($p=4$) and q is the choice length of the feature subset ($q=1,2,3$ or 4). A snapshot of classification results by using the possible combinations of feature subsets is shown in Table 2. Note that the accuracy is averaged over each group of feature subsets for each cardinality q. The classification results are generated by using J48, where both accuracy in terms of correctly classified instances over the total instances, and the size of the induced decision tree which is the sum of nodes and leaves, are shown.

Table 1. Results of CVAttribeEval feature selection method applied on the diabetes dataset

Feature	class 1			class 2			Total
	mean	stddev	sd/m	mean	stddev	sd/m	
preg	3.4234	3.0166	0.881171	4.9795	3.6827	0.739572	1.620743
plas	109.9541	26.1114	0.237475	141.2581	31.8728	0.225635	0.463111
pres	68.1397	17.9834	0.26392	70.718	21.4094	0.302743	0.566663
skin	19.8356	14.8974	0.751044	22.2824	17.6992	0.794313	1.545357
insu	68.8507	98.828	1.435396	100.2812	138.4883	1.381	2.816395
mass	30.3009	7.6833	0.253567	35.1475	7.2537	0.206379	0.459946
pedi	0.4297	0.2986	0.694903	0.5504	0.3715	0.674964	1.369867
age	31.2494	11.6059	0.371396	37.0808	10.9146	0.294346	0.665742

Table 2. Classification results for possible feature subsets by CVAttribeEval feature selection method and J48 algorithm

cardinality=4						Average accuracy	Average size
{insu, preg, skin, pedi}							
75.7813						75.7813	21
21							
cardinality=3							
{insu, preg, skin}	{insu, preg, pedi}	{insu, skin, pedi}	{preg, skin, pedi}				
75.9115	75.5208	75.9115	74.7396			75.52085	24
31	21	23	21				
cardinality=2							
{insu, preg}	{insu, skin}	{insu, pedi}	{preg, skin}	{preg, pedi}	{skin, pedi}		
75.2604	75.1302	75.651	73.9583	74.4792	74.349	74.80468	28.33333333
33	39	23	31	21	23		
cardinality=1							
{insu}	{preg}	{skin}	{pedi}				
74.8698	73.6979	73.9583	73.9583			74.12108	33.5
39	33	39	23				
					Overall average:	75.05698	26.70833333

The classification experiment repeats for each of the ten feature selection algorithms. The corresponding performance in terms of averaged accuracies and averaged tree sizes are recorded. After it is done with *J48*, the whole data mining experiment is reiterated with exactly the same steps with *MultilayerPerceptron*.

EXPERIMENT RESULT

Performance results are tabulated in Table 3 and Table 4 for decision tree model and neural network model respectively. For each type of feature selection, the overall accuracy which is averaged over all the possible combinations of feature subset that are formed by the features selected by the feature selection algorithm, and the maximum accuracy are reported. Both sets of results point to the fact that CV feature selection can achieve the highest averaged accuracy and the best possible accuracy in different feature subsets.

By plotting the average accuracy versus the average decision tree size for the J48 model, a comparison diagram is shown in Figure 3. It shows essentially CV has attained the highest average accuracy over all the other feature selection algorithms. However, in terms of tree size, *PrincipalComponents* yields the smaller tree but its accuracy is the worst, even lower than the accuracy of a model built without using any feature selection. This may be due to the phenomenon that an individual feature which may not be significant by itself, but when joined with others they map an important relation to the class. CV however can accomplish a good accuracy together with a relatively compact decision tree size.

Table 3. Performance results for all the feature selection algorithms applied for building a decision tree model

J48				
FS algorithm	Average accuracy	Best accuracy	Average size	Best size
None	73.8281	73.8281 (39)	39	39 (73.8281)
FeatureSelection_CV	75.05698	75.9115 (23)	26.70833	21 (75.7813)
cfsubseteval	74.8698	74.8698 (29)	29	29 (74.8698)
ChiSquaredAttributeEval	74.25403	74.8698 (39)	27.58333	19 (74.349)
InfoGainAttributeEval	74.25403	74.8698 (39)	27.58333	19 (74.349)
PrincipalComponents	73.01702	75.651 (23)	18.25	9 (73.0469)
SignificanceAttributeEval	74.67449	75.9115 (23)	28	15 (75.1302)
CorrelationAttributeEval	74.67449	75.9115 (23)	28	15 (75.1302)
SVMAttributeEval	74.60396	75.1302 (39)	31.29167	21 (75)
ReliefFAttributeEval	74.35168	75.651 (23)	27.70833	15 (75.1302)
SymmetricalUncertAttributeEval	74.17265	74.7396 (21)	27.83333	19 (73.6979)

Table 4. Performance results for all the feature selection algorithms applied for building a neural network model

MultilayerPerceptron		
FS algorithm	Average accuracy	Best accuracy
None	75.3906	73.8281 (39)
FeatureSelection_CV	76.14746	77.0833
cfsubseteval	74.8698	74.8698
ChiSquaredAttributeEval	75.52896	76.6927
InfoGainAttributeEval	75.74054	76.6927
PrincipalComponents	74.26758	75.1302
SignificanceAttributeEval	75.46386	76.3021
CorrelationAttributeEval	75.49641	76.3021
SVMAttributeEval	75.32552	75.61848
ReliefFAttributeEval	75.01627	75.55338
SymmetricalUncertAttributeEval	75.74054	76.6927

Figure 3. Comparison chart that shows average accuracies and decision tree sizes produced by J48 model built with different feature selection algorithms

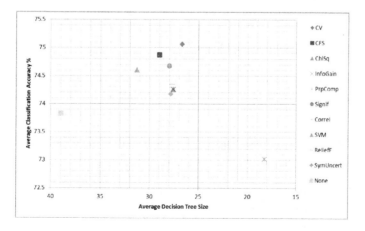

CONCLUSION

Diabetes prediction has drawn much attention recently as the instances of the disease increase worldwide. In machine learning research communities, researchers have been trying to improve the accuracy of such prediction model. In this paper, a novel feature selection method called Coefficient of Variation is proposed. Experiment results show that the new method outperformed nine other conventional feature selection methods. The proposed CV method has potential to be applied with other modern classification algorithms for unprecedented performance improvement.

ACKNOWLEDGMENT

The authors are thankful for the financial support from the Research Grant Temporal Data Stream Mining by Using Incrementally Optimized Very Fast Decision Forest (iOVFDF), Grant no. MYRG2015-00128-FST, offered by the University of Macau, FST, and RDAO. Research Grant entitled "A scalable data stream mining methodology: stream-based holistic analytics and reasoning in parallel", Grant no. 126/2014/A3, offered by the FDCT Macao government.

REFERENCES

Akmal, S. M., Ismail, K., & Zainudin, S. (2011). Prediction of Diabetes by using Artificial Neural Network. In *Proc 2011 International Conference on Circuits, System and Simulation* (Vol. 7, pp. 299-303).

American diabetes association, Retrieved from http://www.diabetes.org/diabetes-basics

Balakrishnan, S., Narayanaswamy, R. (2009). Feature Selection Using FCBF in Type II Diabetes Databases. *International Journal of the Computer, the Internet and Management, 17*(SP1), 50.2-50.8.

Giveki, D., Salimi, H., Bahmanyar, G. R., & Khademian, Y. (2012). Automatic detection of diabetes diagnosis using feature weighted support vector machines based on mutual information and modified cuckoo search. *International Journal of Computational Engineering Research, 2*(5), 1384–1387.

Gogou, G., Maglaveras, N., Ambrosiadou, B. V., Goulis, D., & Pappas, C. (2001). A neural network approach in diabetes management by insulin administration. *Journal of Medical Systems, 25*(2), 119–131. doi:10.1023/A:1005672631019 PMID:11417199

Han, J. C., Rodriguez, J. C., & Beheshti, M. (2009). Discovering Decision Tree Based Diabetes Prediction Model. In *Conf Proc ASEA* (pp. 99–109). 10.1007/978-3-642-10242-4_9

Holman, N., Forouhi, N. G., Goyder, E., & Wild, S. H. (2011). The Association of Public Health Observatories (APHO) Diabetes Prevalence Model: Estimates of total diabetes prevalence for England, 2010-2030. *Diabetic Medicine, 28*(5), 575–582. doi:10.1111/j.1464-5491.2010.03216.x PMID:21480968

Huang, Y., McCullagh, P., Black, N., & Harper, R. (2004). Feature Selection and Classification Model Construction on Type 2 Diabetic Patient's Data. In *ICDM 2004, LNAI* (Vol. 3275). Springer-Verlag. Retrieved from http://www.idf.org

Janecek, A. G. K., Gansterer, W. N., Demel, M. A., & Ecker, G. F. (2008). On the Relationship Between Feature Selection and Classification Accuracy. *JMLR Workshop and Conference Proceedings*, *4*, 90–115.

Maciejowski, J. M. (2002). *Predictive control with constraints, Prentice-Hall, Pearson Education Limited*. Harlow, UK: PPR.

Molina, L. C., Belanche, L., & Nebot, A. (2002). Feature selection algorithms: a survey and experimental evaluation. In *Proceedings. IEEE International Conference on Data Mining* (pp. 306-313. 10.1109/ICDM.2002.1183917

Otto, E., Semotok, C., Andrysek, J., & Basir, O. (2000). An intelligent diabetes software prototype: Predicting blood glucose levels and recommending regimen changes. *Diabetes Technology & Therapeutics*, *2*(4), 569–576. doi:10.1089/15209150050501989 PMID:11469620

Pima Indians Diabetes Data Set. (n.d.). UCI Machine Learning Repository, Center for Machine Learning and Intelligent Systems. Retrieved from http://archive.ics.uci.edu/ml/datasets/Pima+Indians+Diabetes

Praharsi, Y., Miaou, S. G., & Wee, H. M. (2013). Supervised learning approaches and feature selection - a case study in diabetes. *Int. J. of Data Analysis Techniques and Strategies*, *5*(3), 323–337.

Ståhl, F., & Johansson, R. (2009). Diabetes mellitus modeling and short-term prediction based on blood glucose measurements. *Mathematical Biosciences*, *217*(2), 101–117. doi:10.1016/j.mbs.2008.10.008 PMID:19022264

Weka 3. (n.d.). Data Mining Software in Java, Retrieved from http://www.cs.waikato.ac.nz/ml/weka/

Zhang, Y., Fong. S., Fiaidhi, J., & Mohammed, S. (2012). Real-Time Clinical Decision Support System with Data Stream Mining, *Journal of Biomedicine and Biotechnology*.

This research was previously published in the International Journal of Extreme Automation and Connectivity in Healthcare (IJEACH), 1(1); pages 55-65, copyright year 2019 by IGI Publishing (an imprint of IGI Global).

Chapter 15
Development of a Classification Model for CD4 Count of HIV Patients Using Supervised Machine Learning Algorithms:
A Comparative Analysis

Peter Adebayo Idowu

https://orcid.org/0000-0002-3883-3310

Obafemi Awolowo University, Nigeria

Jeremiah Ademola Balogun

https://orcid.org/0000-0002-6510-6127

Obafemi Awolowo University, Nigeria

ABSTRACT

This chapter was developed with a view to present a predictive model for the classification of the level of CD4 count of HIV patients receiving ART/HAART treatment in Nigeria. Following the review of literature, the pre-determining factors for determining CD4 count were identified and validated by experts while historical data explaining the relationship between the factors and CD4 count level was collected. The predictive model for CD4 count level was formulated using C4.5 decision trees (DT), support vector machines (SVM), and the multi-layer perceptron (MLP) classifiers based on the identified factors which were formulated using WEKA software and validated. The results showed that decision trees algorithm revealed five (5) important variables, namely age group, white blood cell count, viral load, time of diagnosing HIV, and age of the patient. The MLP had the best performance with a value of 100% followed by the SVM with an accuracy of 91.1%, and both were observed to outperform the DT algorithm used.

DOI: 10.4018/978-1-6684-6291-1.ch015

INTRODUCTION

HIV is a human immunodeficiency virus. It is the virus that can lead to acquired immunodeficiency syndrome or AIDS if not treated (Lakshmi and Isakki, 2017). HIV is spread primarily by unprotected sex, contaminated blood transmission, hypodermic, and from mother during pregnancy, delivery, or breastfeeding. HIV attacks the body's immune system, specifically the CD4 cells (T cells), a type of white blood cell, which help the immune system fight off infections. Untreated, HIV reduces the number of CD4 cells (T cells) in the body, making the person more likely to get other infections or infection-related cancers. Anti-retro viral treatment is one of the best treatment for HIV patients. Anti-retroviral treatment can slow the course of the disease, and may lead to a near-normal life expectancy (Kama and Prem, 2013).

There is no cure for HIV but it is being managed with antiretroviral drugs (ARV) and Highly Active Antiretroviral drugs (HAART) which is the optimal combination of ARV (Rosma et al., 2012). ARV does not kill the virus but slow down the growth of the virus (Ojunga *et al.*, 2014). Antiretroviral therapy (ART) and highly antiretroviral therapy (HAART) are the mechanisms for treating retroviral infections with drugs. (Brain *et al.*, 2006). Monitoring of the progression of the disease is made even more important due to the emergence of HIV drug resistance, especially in developing countries with limited resource. HIV drug resistance refers to the inability of the ARV drug to reduce the viral reproduction rate sufficiently. Poor management of HIV drug resistance will lead to opportunistic infections that make treatment of HIV more difficult and even may lead to fatalities.

Common clinical markers of disease progression are weight loss, mucocutaneous manifestations, bacterial infections, chronic fever, chronic diarrhea, herpes zoster, oral candidiasis, and pulmonary tuberculosis (Morgan et al., 2002). One of the best available surrogate markers for HIV progression is the use of CD4 cell count information (Post *et al.*, 1996). Although this is also standard of care in developing countries, the measurement of CD4 cell count requires many complex and expensive flow cytometric procedures which burden the minimal resources available. There have been previous attempts to predict CD4 cell count information using cheaper chemical assays and even correlating a patient's total lymphocyte count (TLC) with CD4 cell counts using logistic and linear regression (Schechter *et al.,* 1994; Mwamburi *et al.*, 2005).

The CD4 cell count remains the strongest predictor of HIV related complications, even after the initiation of therapy. The baseline pretreatment value is informative: lower CD4 counts are associated with smaller and slower improvements in counts. However, precise thresholds that define treatment failure in patients starting at various CD4 levels are not yet established. As a general rule, new and progressive severe immunodeficiency is demonstrated by declining longitudinal CD4 cell counts which should trigger a switch in therapy. Another problem associated with CD4 count is, frequent failure happening on the CD4 counting machine which creates a great challenge in taking CD4 counts regularly in the scheduled time.

Machine learning algorithms provide a means of obtaining objective unseen patterns from evidence-based information especially in the public health care sector. These techniques have allowed for not only substantial improvements to existing clinical decision support systems, but also a platform for improved patient-centered outcomes through the development of personalized prediction models tailored to a patient's medical history and current condition (Moudani *et al.*, 2011a). Predictive research aims at predicting future events or an outcome based on patterns within a set of variables and has become increasingly popular in medical research (Olayemi *et al.*, 2016). Accurate predictive models can inform patients and physicians about the future course of an illness or the risk of developing illness and thereby help guide decisions on screening and/or treatment (Waijee *et al.*, 2013).

The aim of this study is to apply machine learning to the identification of the relevant variables that are important for developing a predictive model for the classification of the level of CD4 count. The model will provide decision support to healthcare providers regarding alternate therapy to patients thereby improving HIV survival. There is a need for the development of a predictive model for the classification of the CD4 count of HIV patients receiving ART treatment using machine learning techniques needed for providing clinical decision support and improving the survival of HIV patients receiving ART treatment.

RELATED WORKS

Singh *et al.* (2013) applied machine learning algorithms to the prediction of patient-specific current CD4 cell count in order to determine the progression of human immunodeficiency virus (HIV) infections. This work shows the application of machine learning to predict current CD4 cell count of an HIV-positive patient using genome sequences, viral load and time. A regression model predicting actual CD4 cell counts and a classification model predicting if a patient's CD4 cell count is less than 200 was built using a support vector machine and neural network. The most accurate regression and classification model took as input the viral load, time, and genome and produced a correlation of co-efficient of 0.9 and an accuracy of 95%, respectively, proving that a CD4 cell count measure may be accurately predicted using machine learning on genotype, viral load and time.

Ojunga *et al.* (2014) applied logistic regression in modeling of survival chances of HIV -positive patients on highly active antiretroviral therapy (HAART) in Nyakach District, Kenya. The aim of this study was to outline the various social and economic factors affecting survival of HIV patients on highly active antiretroviral therapy (HAART). The study was expected to provide suitable model for predicting the chances of survival among the HIV positive patients attending ART clinic in Nyakachi District and also provide information for policy makers on the factors affecting survival of HIV positive individual on ARV drugs. The strength shows that the survival of infected patient under study can be improved if their access to socio-economic factors is considered. The outcome may only be obtained in services that have smaller numbers of patients. Socioeconomic factors are not enough to predict survival as CD4, viral load; opportunistic infections and nutritional status were added to the existing study in this thesis as predictive factors.

Idowu *et al.* (2016) developed a predictive model for the survival of HIV/AIDS in pediatric patients in Nigeria. The study identified survival variables for HIV/AIDS Peadiatric patients, developed predictive model for determining the survival of the patients who were receiving antiretroviral drug in the South-western Nigeria based on identified variables, compared and validate the developed model. Interviews were conducted with the virologists and Pediatricians at two health institutions from the study area in order to identify survival variables for HIV/AIDS Peadiatric patients. 216 Peadiatric HIV/AIDS patients' data were also collected, preprocessed and the 10-fold cross validation technique was used to partition the datasets into training and testing data. Predictive model was developed using supervised learning technique and WEKA was used to simulate the models in which CD4 count, Viral Load, Opportunistic infections and Nutritional status were used as the independent variables for the prediction. The result showed that The Multi-layer Perception (MLP) was suitable for carrying out the task of forecasting the survival of Peadiatric HIV/AIDS patients with an accuracy of 99.07%. Additional study involved the use of naïve Bayes' classifier (Idowu *et al.*, 2017a) and C4.5 decision trees classifier (Idowu *et al.*, 2017b) for the development of a predictive model for the survival of HIV/AIDS among pediatrics. However, the study by Idowu *et al.* (2017b) revealed that the variables viral load and CD4 count were redundant and recommended instead of using both variables only one of them should be used for classifying survival of HIV/AIDS among pediatrics.

Tarekegn and Sreenivasaro (2016) applied data mining techniques on Pre ART data. The dataset for the study contains pre ART records of the year 2005 and 2006 produced by the ART office of patients Felege Hiwot Referral Hospital. The dataset has been utilized for the purpose of predicting clients' eligibility for ART. Before these data has been used for the purpose of classification a number of pre-processing steps such as data cleaning, data reduction and data transformation have been effectively used which helped in achieving the objective finally or to increase the speed and efficiency of mining process. The final goal of this paper is to build ART eligibility predictive model that helps to deciding whether HIV positive individual should start Anti-retroviral treatment or not. For building ART eligibility predictive model, Naive Bayesian Classifier and J48 Decision Tree Classifier are used. After experimenting J48 decision tree and Naive Bayesian classifier using both 10-fold cross validation and percentage split (66%) test modes, J48 classifier using 10-fold cross validation (95.83%) that performs well and can be used as a best predicting model algorithm than Naive Bayesian classifier (93.64%%) in predicting clients' eligibility for ART was created.

Lakshmi and Isakki (2017) performed a comparative study of data mining classification techniques using HIV/AIDS and STD data. The performance of classifiers is actively dependent on the data set used for learning. It leads to better performance of the classification models in terms of their predictive or descriptive accuracy and computing time needed to build models as they learn faster and better understanding of the models. The paper performed a comparative analysis of data mining, classification techniques, Decision Tree, Support Vector Machine (SVM), and Naïve Bayes' Classification algorithms. The total of 800 medical data set having many attributes with Boolean value in addition to age and sex. The proposed algorithm uses four data sets called – Symptoms, Virus type, Cd4 count type of white blood cell and STD cell for Chlamydia count. There are numerical values allocated to each cell count and severe. The aim is to classify the diseases and predict the presence of HIV infection. The decision trees algorithm outperformed SVM and naïve Bayes classification with an accuracy of 90.07% compared to 77.5% and 85.05% for naïve Bayes and SVM respectively.

METHODS

The methodological approach of this study composes of a number of methods, namely: the identification of the required variables for CD4 count classification, the collection of historical datasets about CD4 count measures, formulation of the predictive models using the supervised machine learning algorithms proposed, the simulation of the predictive models using the WEKA simulation environment and the performance evaluation metrics applied during model validation for the evaluation of the performance of the predictive models. The model for the classification of CD4 count was formulated using decision trees, support vector machines and multi-layer perceptron algorithms with their performance compared.

Data Identification and Collection

For the purpose of this study, data was collected following the identification of the factors for determining CD4 count level from 45 patients located in the south-western part of Nigeria using structured questionnaires that consisted of two (2) main sections, namely: demographic section which included: gender, age, ethnicity, religion, educational qualification, occupation, weight, height and body mass index (BMI) while the clinical factors for determining CD4, namely: date of HIV diagnosis, baseline CD4 count measure, time since baseline CD4 count, opportunistic infection, total lymphocyte count, patient on ART, patient HAART, white blood cell count, level of hematocrit, platelets level, viral load, last recorded CD4 count level and the time since the last CD4 count level. The information collected consisted of the variables used to identify the CD4 count level risk factors associated with the osteoporosis for each patient as proposed by the medical expert. The variables that were identified following the review of related works regarding the CD4 count level are stated in Table 1.

Table 1. Identified variables for the classification of CD4 count level

Categories	Risk Factors	Labels
Demographic Factors	Gender	Male, Female
	Age (years)	Numeric
	Age Group	Youth, Adult, Aged, Teenager
	Ethnicity	Yoruba, Hausa, Ibo, Idoma
	Religion	Christian, Islam, Traditional
	Education	Primary, Secondary, Polytechnic, University
	Occupation	Nil, Trader, Teacher, Artisan, Student, Clerical
	Weight (Kg)	Numeric
	Height (m)	Numeric
	Body Mass Index (Kg/m)	Numeric
	BMI Class	Normal, Underweight, Overweight, Obese
Clinical Factors	Time of HIV Diagnosis	Numeric
	Baseline CD4 count	Numeric
	Time of Baseline count	Numeric
	Opportunistic Infection	Protozoa, Typhoid, Nil, Virus, Malaria, Bacteria, Gonorrhea, Ulcer, Asthma, Fungi
	Total Lymphocyte count	Numeric
	On ART Treatment	Yes, No
	On HAART	Yes, No
	White Blood Cell Count	Numeric
	Hematocrit Level	Numeric
	Platelets Level	Numeric
	Viral Load	Numeric
	Last recorded CD4 count	Numeric
	Time since last CD$ count	Numeric
Target	CD4 Count Level	Low, Moderate, High

Data-Preprocessing

Following the collection of data from the 45 patients alongside the attributes (22 factors in all) alongside the CD4 count level, the data collected was checked for the presence of error in data entry including misspellings and missing data. Following this process, there was no error in misspellings nor missing data in the cells describing the records for the identified factors. The data was stored in an .arff file format, the most acceptable file format for the simulation environment chosen for this study. The arff file is composed of three parts, namely:

1. The relation name section which contains the tag @relation CD4CountTrainingData, used to identify the name of the relation (or file) that contains the data needed for simulation. This section is located at the first line of the file and the tag 'name' following @relation must always be the same as the file name else the file loader of the simulation environment will cease to open the file. This section is followed in the next line by the attribute names section;

2. The attribute names section which contains the tag @attribute attribute_name label was used to identify the attributes that describe the dataset stored in the .arff file needed for simulation. Each attribute name alongside its labels is stated following the @relation tag on each line. The label can be a set of values inserted between brackets or a descriptor (e.g. date, numeric etc.). The last attribute is identified as the target class (CD4 count class) while the previous attributes are the input variables. This section is followed in the next line by the data section; and

3. The data section which contains the tag @data followed in the next line by the values of the attributes for each record of the HIV patients collected separated by a comma. Each value was listed on a row for each record in the same order as the attributes were listed in the attribute names section. The values inserted into each record must be the same values defined in each respective attribute; if there is an error in spelling or a label not defined is inserted then the file loader of the simulation environment will fail to load the file.

The dataset collected for the purpose of the development of the predictive model for the quality of service was stored in .arff in the name CD4CountTrainingData.arff while the number of attributes listed in the attribute section were 23 including the target attribute. Following this, the values of the input variables for the record of the 45 records recorded form the sites for this study was provided.

Model Formulation

Following the identification and validation of variables relevant to the CD4 count level in HIV patients and the collection of historical explaining the relationship between the identified risk factors and their respective class for each record of individuals, the predictive model for the CD4 count level in HIV patients was formulated using the decision trees algorithm, support vector machines and artificial neural networks. Supervised machine learning algorithms make it possible to assign a set of records (CD4 count indicators) to a target class – the CD4 count level. Equation 1 shows the mapping function that describes the relationship between the risk factors and the target class – CD4 count level.

$$\varphi: X \to Y \qquad\qquad (1)$$

defined as: $\varphi(X)=Y$

The equation shows the relationship between the set of identified factors represented by a vector, X consisting of the values of i factors and the label Y which defines the CD4 count level – low, moderate and high level as expressed in equation 3.2. Assuming the values of the set of risk factors for an individual is represented as $X= \{X_1, X_2, X_3, ..., X_i\}$ where X_i is the value of each risk factor, i = 1 to i; then the mapping φ used to represent the predictive model for osteoporosis risk maps the identified factors of each individual to their respective CD4 count level according to equation 2.

$$\varphi\left(X\right) = \begin{cases} Low\ Level \\ Moderate\ Level \\ High\ Level \end{cases} \tag{2}$$

Decision Trees Algorithm

The theory of a decision tree has the following parts: a root node is the starting point of the tree; branches connect nodes showing the flow from question to answer. Nodes that have child nodes are called interior nodes. Leaf or terminal nodes are nodes that do not have child nodes and represent a possible value of target variable given the variables represented by the path from the root. The rules are inducted by definition from each respective node to branch to leaf. Given a set X_{ij} of j number of cases, the decision trees algorithm grows an initial tree using the divide-and-conquer algorithm as follows:

- If all the cases in X_{ij} belong to the same class or X_{ij} is small, the tree is a leaf labeled with the most frequent class in X_{ij}.
- Otherwise, choose a test based on a single attribute X_i with two or more outcomes. Make this test the root of the tree with one branch for each outcome of the test, partition X_{ij} into corresponding subsets according to the outcome for each case, and apply the same procedure recursively to each subset.

The C4.5 decision trees algorithm builds decision trees from a set of training dataset, X_{ij} the same way as ID3, using the information entropy. For this study, the C4.5 decision trees algorithm was used for the formulation of the predictive model for the diagnosis of hypertension due to its advantages over the ID3 decision trees algorithm due to its ability to: handle continuous and discrete attributes, handle missing values, handle attributes with differing costs and prune trees after creation. The two criteria used by the C4.5 decision trees in developing its decision trees are presented in equations (3) and (4) defined as the information gain and the split criteria respectively. Equation (3) is used in determining which attribute is used to split the dataset at every iteration while equation (4) is used to determine which of the selected attribute split is most effective in splitting the dataset after attribute selection by equation (3).

$$IG\left(X_i\right) = H\left(X_i\right) - \sum_{t \in T} \frac{|t|}{|X_{ij}|} \cdot H\left(X_i\right) \tag{3}$$

where:

$$H\left(X_i\right) = -\sum_{t \in T} \frac{|t, X_i|}{|X_{ij}|} \cdot \log_2 \frac{|t, X_i|}{|X_{ij}|}$$

$$Split\left(T\right) = -\sum_{t \in T} \frac{|t|}{|X_{ij}|} \cdot \log_2 \frac{|t|}{|X_{ij}|} \tag{4}$$

T is the set of values for a given attribute X_i.

Perceptron-Based Networks

The support vector machines and the artificial neural networks both fall under the class of machine learning algorithms called the perceptron network systems since input values are fired into nodes using synaptic weights attached to the nodes – inputs are sum of products of weights w_i and input x_i, equation (5) shows the expression. The variables selected by the decision trees algorithm in tree construction will also be used in the formulation of the predictive model for CD4 count level of HIV patients using support vector machines and the artificial neural networks' multi-layer perceptron architecture.

$$\sum_{k=1}^{i} w_k x_k = w_1 x_1 + w_2 x_2 + \ldots + w_i x_i = \left\langle w.x \right\rangle \tag{5}$$

Support Vector Machines

An SVM model is a representation of the examples as points in space, mapped so that the examples of the separate categories are divided by a clear gap that is as wide as possible. New examples are then mapped into that same space and predicted to belong to a category based on which side of the gap they fall on. In formal terms, SVM constructs a hyper-plane or set of hyper-planes in a high-dimensional space, which can be applied for classification, regression or any other task. A good separation is achieved by the hyperplane that has the largest distance to the nearest training data points x called the support vectors since in general the larger the margin the lower the generalization error of the classifier. Therefore, the SVM during model formulation attempts to minimize the cost by maximizing the distance between hyper-planes. A good separation is achieved by the hyperplane $\left\langle w, x \right\rangle + b = 0$ that has the largest distance $\dfrac{2}{\|w\|}$ to the neighbouring data points of either classes at opposite ends, since in general the larger the margin the lower the generalization error of the SVM classifier. Figure 1 shows the separation of the different classes of CD4 count level in the dataset. Figure 1 (left) shows how two hyper-planes were used to separate the dataset into three classes, such that hyperplane 1 was used to extract the low CD4 level records after which hyperplane2 was used to separate the moderate CD4 level records and the high CD4 level records. Figure 1 (right) shows a clear description of the relationship between the parameters and the hyper-plane and separating margins from the support vectors *x*.

Figure 1. Separation of Support Vectors Using Hyper-planes

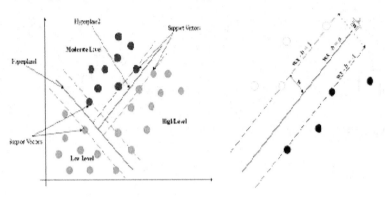

A hyperplane created is defined as $\langle w, x \rangle + b = 0$ where $w \in \mathbb{R}^p$ and $b \in \mathbb{R}$ while $\langle w, x \rangle + b = -1$ and $\langle w, x \rangle + b = 1$ are the margins required for the separation *w* of support vectors *x* within the *n* variables. Therefore, equation (6) was defined for a linearly separable function for which the decision function in equation (7) was used to propagate the output of equation (6) using a sigmoid function with interval {-1, 1}. The aim of the SVM is to maximize the separation of the hyper-planes in equation (8) subject to the decision function defined in equation (7).

$$CD4\_Count_i = f\left(x_i\right) = \left(\langle w, x_i \rangle + b\right) > 0, \forall i \in \left[1, n\right] \tag{6}$$

$$f_d\left(x_i\right) = sign\left(CD4\_count_i\right) = \left(\langle w, x_i \rangle + b\right) > 0, \forall i \in \left[1, n\right] \tag{7}$$

$$maximize \frac{1}{2}\left\|w\right\|^2 \tag{8}$$

Artificial Neural Network

An artificial neural network (ANN) is an interconnected group of nodes, akin to the vast network of neurons in a human brain. Multi-layer perceptron are ANNs which are generally presented as systems of interconnected neurons (containing activation functions) which send messages to each other such that each connection have numeric weights that can be tuned based on experience, making neural nets adaptive to inputs and capable of learning using the back-propagation algorithm. The word network refers to the inter-connections between the neurons in the different layers of each system. Figure 2 shows an MLP with 3 hidden layers having 2, 3 and 2 nodes located in each layer, in all there are *j=7* nodes.

Figure 2. Multi-Layer Perceptron Architecture

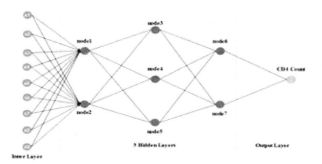

Therefore, the MLP propagates the sum of product of the weights and the inputs through nodes at multiple inner layers to the output layer. Using the back-propagation algorithm, the MLP compares the output calculated with the actual in order to compute an error-function. Gradient descent was then used to feed the error back to the system from output nodes through the nodes in the hidden layers to the nodes at the input layer while adjusting the weights as a function of the error determined at each node. The process was repeated for a number of training cycles for which the MLP network converged to a state where the error determined is small enough, then the MLP network was able to learn the target function.

The back-propagation learning algorithm can be divided into two phases: propagation and weight update.

1. **Phase 1 – Propagation:** Each propagation involves the following steps:
    a. Forward propagation of training pattern's input through each node *j* in the neural network in order to generate the propagation's output activations;

$$output\ O_j = \varphi\left(\sum_{k=1}^{i} w_{kj} x_k + b_k\right) = \varphi(z) = \frac{1}{1 + e^{-z}} \tag{9}$$

    b. Backward propagation of the propagation's output activations through the neural network using the training pattern target in order to generate deltas *δj* of all output and hidden neurons.

$$\delta_j = \frac{\partial E}{\partial O_j}\frac{\partial O_j}{\partial net_j} = \begin{cases} \left(O_j - p_j\right)\varphi\left(net_j\right)\left(1 - \varphi\left(net_j\right)\right) & j\ is\ output\ neuron, \\ \left(\sum_{l\ f\ L}\delta_j w_{jl}\right)\varphi\left(net_j\right)\left(1 - \varphi\left(net_j\right)\right) & j\ is\ inner\ neuron \end{cases} \tag{10}$$

2. **Phase 2 – Weight Update:** For each weight-synapse, hence the following:

a. Multiply its output delta and input activation to get the gradient of the weight

$$\frac{\partial E}{\partial w_{ij}} = \delta_j x_i \tag{11}$$

b. Subtract a ratio (percentage α) of the gradient from the weight.

$$\Delta w_{ij} = -\alpha \frac{\partial E}{\partial w_{ij}} \tag{12}$$

Performance Evaluation

In order to evaluate the performance of the supervised machine learning algorithms used for the classification of CD4 count level, there was the need to plot the results of the classification on a confusion matrix as shown in Figure 3. A confusion matrix is a square which shows the actual classification along the vertical and the predicted along the horizontal. Correct classifications were plotted along the diagonal from the north-west position for the low cases predicted as Low (A), Moderate (E) and High (I) on the south-east corner (also called true positives and negatives). The incorrect classifications were plotted in the remaining cells of the confusion matrix (also called false positives). These results are presented on confusion matrix – for this study the confusion matrix is a 3 x 3 matrix table owing to the three (3) labels of the output class.

Figure 3. Diagram of a Confusion Matrix

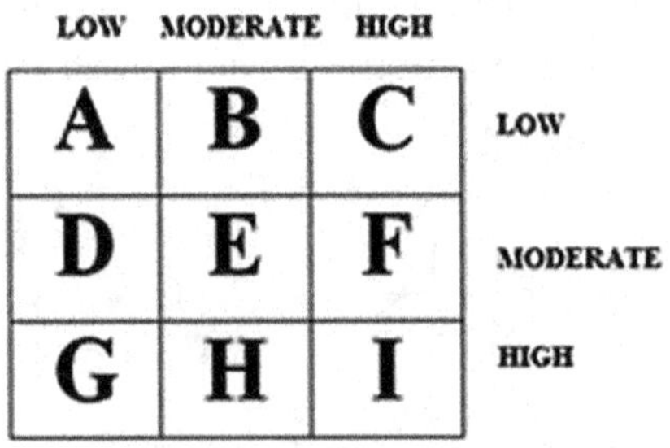

Also, the actual Low cases are A+B+C, actual Moderate cases are D+E+F and the actual High cases are G+H+I while the predicted Low are A+D+G, predicted Moderate are B+E+H and predicted High are C+F+I. The developed model was validated using a number of performance metrics based on the values of *A – I* in the confusion matrix for each predictive model. They are presented as follows.

1. **Accuracy:** The total number of correct classification

$$Accuracy = \frac{A + E + I}{total\_cases} \tag{13}$$

2. **True Positive Rate (Recall/Sensitivity):** The proportion of actual cases correctly classified

$$TP_{low} = \frac{A}{A + B + C} \tag{14}$$

$$TP_{moderate} = \frac{E}{D + E + F} \tag{15}$$

$$TP_{high} = \frac{I}{G + H + I} \tag{16}$$

3. **False Positive (False Alarm/1-Specificity):** The proportion of negative cases incorrectly classified as positive

$$FP_{low} = \frac{D + G}{actual_{high} + actual_{moderate}} \tag{17}$$

$$FP_{moderate} = \frac{B + H}{actual_{low} + actual_{high}} \tag{18}$$

$$FP_{high} = \frac{C + F}{actual_{moderate} + actual_{low}} \tag{19}$$

4. **Precision:** The proportion of predictions that are correct

$$Precision_{low} = \frac{A}{A + D + G} \tag{20}$$

$$Precision_{moderate} = \frac{F}{B + E + H} \tag{21}$$

$$Precision_{high} = \frac{K}{C + F + I} \tag{22}$$

RESULTS

This section presents the results of the methods that were applied for the development of the predictive model for the classification of CD4 count level. The results presented were that of the data collection, model formulation and simulation results using the WEKA software following the results of the model validation of the predictive model for osteoporosis.

Results of Data Description

For this study, data was collected from 45 patients using the questionnaires constructed for this study among which; the CD4 count of Nigerian HIV patients was identified for 45 patients. Table 2 gives a description of the number of patients with respect to their level of CD4 counts which shows that majority of the patients selected had moderate CD4 count levels with a proportion of 40% composing of 15.6% female and 24.4% male followed by the patients with low CD4 count levels with a proportion of 31.1% composing of 17.8% male and 13.3% female with minority of the patients with high CD4 count levels with a proportion of 28.9% composing of 13.3% male and 15.7% female.

Table 2. Distribution of Level of CD4 Count among Patients' Dataset

CD4 Count Class	Gender	Total	
		Frequency	**Percentage (%)**
High	Female	7	15.56
	Male	6	13.33
Sub-Total		13	28.89
Low	Female	6	13.33
	Male	8	17.78
Sub-Total		14	31.11
Moderate	Female	7	15.56
	Male	11	24.44
Sub-Total		18	40.00
TOTAL		45	100.00

Table results showed that among the adults, majority of the patients were male moderate CD4 count cases and female high CD4 count cases followed by female moderate CD4 count cases with the least patients selected from female low CD4 count and male high CD4 count levels while among the youths, an equal number of patients were selected from male moderate and female low CD4 count levels while none was selected for female moderate and high CD4 count levels. The results showed that among the Hausa, majority of the patients were selected from male low and moderate CD4 count levels followed by female low and moderate CD4 count levels and a minority selected from male high and female low CD4 count levels.

The results showed that among the Christian patients, none was selected among the male low CD4 count levels and none selected from female moderate and lowCD4 count levels while among the Islamic patients, an equal proportion of male and female high CD4 count levels were selected while majority were selected from male low CD4 count level cases and minority from female low and moderate CD4 count level cases. The results showed that majority of the patients were normal representing 42.2% followed by underweight representing 26.7% and obese representing 20% with minority been overweight representing 11.1% of patients selected while majority of the patients selected were male moderate CD4 count cases among normal, female low and female high CD4 count levels among obese, male high and low CD4 count levels among overweight patients and male low CD4 count levels among underweight patients. No patients were selected from male high CD4 count levels among normal patients, female low CD4 count levels among obese patients, female high, and low and moderate CD4 count levels among overweight patients.

Tables 3, 4 and 5 show the descriptive statistics of the numeric variables among the dataset selected from the patients receiving HIV treatment in Nigeria. The descriptive statistics used included the minimum which returns the lowest recorded value from the 45 records for each numeric variable; the maximum returns the greatest recorded value from the 45 records for each numeric variable; the mean returns the average recorded value from the 45 records for each numeric variable identified while the standard deviation gives the deviation with respect to the mean, minimum and maximum for a 95% confidence interval from the 45 records for each numeric variable identified for this study.

Table 3. Descriptive Statistics across High CD4 Count Patients

Variables	Descriptive Statistics			
	Minimum	Maximum	Mean	Deviation
Age (years)	19	69	43	12
Weight (Kg)	39	70	54	10
Height (m)	1.08	1.95	1.55	0.27
BMI (Kg/m2)	12.35	40.29	24.10	7.70
Time since HIV diagnosis (weeks)	8	18	13	4
Baseline CD4 count (cell/mm3)	340	1200	685	240
Time since baseline CD4 count (in weeks)	3	15	10	4
Total Lymphocyte Count (cell/mm3)	5	9	7	1
White Blood Cell	4000	8000	5546	1083
Level of Hematocrit (%)	27	51	39	7
Platelets	152000	600000	355154	120997
Viral Load	3	55	11	13
Time since last count CD4 (weeks)	10	19	13.85	2.764
Relative Time since Last CD4 count	.526	1.000	.729	.145
Last CD4 Count (cell/mm3)	13	24	18	3
Relative Last CD4 Count	10	18	13	3

Table 4. Descriptive Statistics across Moderate CD4 Count Patients

Variables	Descriptive Statistics			
	Minimum	Maximum	Mean	Deviation
Age (years)	25	61	38	9
Weight (Kg)	35	75	59	10
Height (m)	.96	1.80	1.55	.29
BMI (Kg/m2)	16.36	70.53	27.05	13.28
Time since HIV diagnosis (weeks)	4	19	13	5
Baseline CD4 count (cell/mm3)	350	1000	705	239
Time since baseline CD4 count (in weeks)	7	18	10	3
Total Lymphocyte Count (cell/mm3)	5	10	8	1
White Blood Cell	3000	7000	4679	1436
Level of Hematocrit (%)	20	60	37	12
Platelets	45000	500000	351722	162486
Viral Load	3	12	7	2
Time since last count CD4 (weeks)	6	15	9	2
Relative Time since Last CD4 count	.316	.789	.471	.119
Last CD4 Count (cell/mm3)	10	20	15	3
Relative Last CD4 Count	5	9	7	1

Table 5. Descriptive Statistics across Low CD4 Count Patients

Variables	Descriptive Statistics			
	Minimum	Maximum	Mean	Deviation
Age (years)	12	55	33	11
Weight (Kg)	20	70	54	14
Height (m)	1.20	1.80	1.60	0.21
BMI (Kg/m2)	10.21	38.54	21.72	7.46
Time since HIV diagnosis (weeks)	4	15	9	4
Baseline CD4 count (cell/mm3)	320	2800	808	604
Time since baseline CD4 count (in weeks)	5	15	9	2
Total Lymphocyte Count (cell/mm3)	5	10	8	1
White Blood Cell	4000	46200	8479	10901
Level of Hematocrit (%)	26	65	37	11
Platelets	5000	700000	357500	168874
Viral Load	3	19	9	5
Time since last count CD4 (weeks)	5	10	7	2
Relative Time since Last CD4 count	.263	.526	.383	.091
Last CD4 Count (cell/mm3)	6	18	10	3
Relative Last CD4 Count	2	5	4	1

Simulation Results

Two different supervised machine learning algorithms were used to formulate the predictive model for the classification CD4 count level, namely: decision trees, support vector machines and the multi-layer perceptron classifiers. They were used to train the development of the prediction model using the dataset containing 45 patients' records. The simulation of the prediction models was done using the Waikato Environment for Knowledge Analysis (WEKA). The models were trained using the 10-fold cross validation method which splits the dataset into 10 subsets of data – while 9 parts are used for training the remaining one is used for testing; this process is repeated until the remaining 9 parts take their turn for testing the model.

C4.5 Decision Trees Classifier

The J4.8 decision trees algorithm was used to implement the C4.5 decision trees algorithm for the formulation of the predictive model using the simulation environment. The results of the formulation of the predictive model for the CD4 count levels of HIV patients using the C4.5 decision trees algorithm showed that five (5) variables were the most important factors for determining the level of CD4 count and were used by the algorithm to develop the tree that was used in formulating the predictive model for level of CD4 count using the C4.5 decision trees algorithm. The variables identified in the order of their importance were: age group, white blood cell (WBC) count, age, time HIV was diagnosed and viral load of patient. Based on the five (5) variables identified by the C4.5 decision tees algorithm, the predictive model for the CD4 count levels of HIV patients was using the J48 decision trees algorithm on the WEKA simulation environment. Figure 4 shows the decision trees that was formulated based on the variables that were proposed by the algorithm.

Figure 4. Decision Tree formulated using C4.5 for CD4 Count in HIV Patients

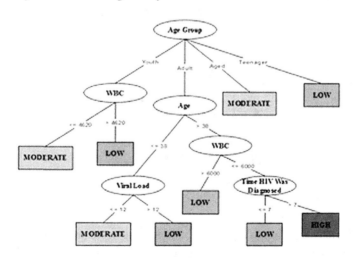

The tree was used to deduce the set of rules that are used for determining the CD4 count levels of HIV patients based on the values of the 5 variables identified by the algorithm. The rules extracted from the tree were 9 and are stated as follows:

1. If (Age Group = Youth) AND (White Blood Cell Count <= 4620 cell/mm3) Then (CD4 count level = Moderate);
2. If (Age Group = Youth) AND (White Blood Cell Count > 4620 cell/mm3) Then (CD4 count level = Low);
3. If (Age Group = Adult) AND (Age <= 38 years) AND (Viral Load <= 12 cell/mm3) Then (CD4 count level = Moderate);
4. If (Age Group = Adult) AND (Age <= 38 years) AND (Viral Load > 12 cell/mm3) Then (CD4 count level = Low);
5. If (Age Group = Adult) AND (Age > 38 years) AND (White Blood Cell Count <= 6000 cell/mm^3) AND (Time of HIV diagnosis <= 7 weeks) THEN (CD4 count level = Low);
6. If (Age Group = Adult) AND (Age > 38 years) AND (White Blood Cell Count <= 6000 cell/mm^3) AND (Time of HIV diagnosis > 7 weeks) THEN (CD4 count level = High);
7. If (Age Group = Adult) AND (Age > 38 years) AND (White Blood Cell Count > 6000 cell/mm^3) THEN (CD4 count level = Low);
8. If (Age Group = Aged) THEN (CD4 Count level = Moderate); and
9. If (Age Group = Teenager) THEN (CD4 Count Level = Low).

The results presented in Figure 4 was used to evaluate the performance of the C4.5 decision trees algorithm and thus, the confusion matrix determined. Figure 5 shows the confusion matrix that was used to interpret the results of the true positive and negative alongside the false positive and negatives of the validation results.

Figure 5. Confusion matrix of performance evaluation using C4.5

Low	Moderate	High	<-- Predicted as
13	1	0	Low
1	12	5	Moderate
3	1	9	High

From the confusion matrix shown in Figure 5, the following sections present the results of the model's performance. Out of the 14 actual low cases, 13 were correctly classified as low while 1 was misclassified as moderate, out of the 18 actual moderate cases, there were 12 correct classifications with 1 misclassified as low and 5 misclassified as high and out of the 13 high, there were 9 correct classifications with

3 misclassified as low and 1 misclassified as moderate. Therefore, there were 34 correct classifications out of the 45 records considered for the model development owing for an accuracy of 75.56%.

Results of the Support Vector Machines (SVM)

Following the simulation of the predictive model for CD4 count level using the SVM algorithm, the evaluation of the performance of the model following validation using the 10-fold cross validation method was recorded. The results were used to evaluate the performance of the SVM algorithm and thus, the confusion matrix determined. Figure 6 shows the confusion matrix that was used to interpret the results of the true positive and negative alongside the false positive and negatives of the validation results. The confusion matrix shown in Figure 6 was used to evaluate the performance of the predictive model for CD4 count level of HIV patients. From the confusion matrix shown in Figure 6, the results of the model's performance were presented. Out of the 14 actual low cases, 12 were correctly classified as low while 2 was misclassified as moderate, out of the 18 actual moderate cases, all were correctly classified with no misclassifications and out of the 13 high, there were 11 correct classifications with 2 misclassified as low. Therefore, there were 41 correct classifications out of the 45 records considered for the model development owing for an accuracy of 91.11%.

Figure 6. Confusion matrix of performance evaluation using SVM

Low	Moderate	High	<-- Predicted as
12	2	0	Low
0	18	0	Moderate
2	0	11	High

Results of the Multi-Layer Perceptron (MLP)

Following the simulation of the predictive model for CD4 count level using the MLP algorithm, the evaluation of the performance of the model following validation using the 10-fold cross validation method was recorded. The results presented were used to evaluate the performance of the MLP algorithm and thus, the confusion matrix determined. Figure 7 shows the confusion matrix that was used to interpret the results of the true positive and negative alongside the false positive and negatives of the validation results. The confusion matrix shown in Figure 7 was used to evaluate the performance of the predictive model for CD4 count level of HIV patients. From the confusion matrix shown in Figure 7, the results of the model's performance were presented. Out of the 14 actual low cases, all were correctly classified with no misclassifications, out of the 18 actual moderate cases, all were correctly classified with no misclassifications and out of the 13 high, all were correctly classified with no misclassifications. Therefore, all 45 records considered for the model development were correctly classified owing for an accuracy of 100%.

Figure 7. Confusion matrix of performance evaluation using MLP

Low	Moderate	High	<.. Predicted as
14	**0**	**0**	Low
0	**18**	**0**	Moderate
0	**0**	**13**	High

Discussion

The result of the performance evaluation of the machine learning algorithms are presented in Table 6 which presents the average values of each performance evaluation metrics considered for this study. For the C4.5 decision trees algorithm, the results showed that the TP rate which gave a description of the proportion of actual cases that was correctly predicted was 0.763 which implied that 76.3% of the actual cases were correctly predicted; the FP rate which gave a description of the proportion of actual cases misclassified was 0.120 which implied that 12% of actual cases were misclassified while the precision which gave a description of the proportion of predictions that were correctly classified was 0.755 which implied that 75.5% of the predictions made by the classifier were correct.

For the support vector machine (SVM) algorithm, the results showed that the TP rate which gave a description of the proportion of actual cases that was correctly predicted was 0.901 which implied that 90.1% of the actual cases were correctly predicted; the FP rate which gave a description of the proportion of actual cases misclassified was 0.046 which implied that 4.6% of actual cases were misclassified while the precision which gave a description of the proportion of predictions that were correctly classified was 0.919 which implied that 91.9% of the predictions made by the classifier were correct.

Table 6. Summary of Validation Results for C4.5, naïve Bayes' and MLP classifiers

Machine Learning Algorithm Used	Performance Evaluation Metrics				
	Correct Classification (Out of 45)	Accuracy (%)	TP Rate (Recall or Sensitivity)	FP Rate (False Positive)	Precision
C4.5 Decision Trees (DT) Algorithm	34	75.56	0.763	0.120	0.755
Support Vector Machines (SVM)	41	91.11	0.901	0.046	0.919
Multi-Layer Perceptron Algorithm (MLP)	45	100.00	1.000	0.000	1.000

For the multi-layer perceptron algorithm, the results showed that the TP rate which gave a description of the proportion of actual cases that was correctly predicted was 1 which implied that all of the actual cases were correctly predicted; the FP rate which gave a description of the proportion of actual cases misclassified was 0 which implied that none of actual cases were misclassified while the precision which gave a description of the proportion of predictions that were correctly classified was 1 which implied that all of the predictions made by the classifier were correct.

In general, the MLP and SVM algorithms were able to predict the CD4 count level better than the C4.5 decision trees algorithm. Although, the difference between the performance of the SVM and the MLP classifiers was 4 misclassification. Overall, the multi-layer perceptron was able to accurately classify all cases of CD4 count level with a value of 100% showing that it had the capacity to identify the complex patterns that existed within the dataset than the SVM and C4.5 DT algorithms. The variables identified by the C4.5 decision trees algorithm can also be given very close attention and observed in order to better understand the level of CD4 count in Nigerian HIV patients receiving treatment.

CONCLUSION

This study focused on the development of a prediction model for the classification of the level of CD4 count of patients receiving treatment in a Nigerian hospital. Historical dataset on the distribution of the classes of CD4 count among HIV patients was collected using questionnaires following the identification of associated factors needed for the classification of CD4 count level from physicians. The dataset containing information about the factors identified and collected from the respondents was used to formulate predictive models for the classification of the level of CD4 count using decision trees, support vector machine sand multi-layer perceptron algorithms. The predictive model development using the algorithms were formulated and simulated using the WEKA software.

Using the decision trees algorithm, the study was also able to identify 5 important variables among the initially identified 21 variables as most relevant for the classification of CD4 count level, namely: age group, white blood cell count, viral load, date of diagnosis of HIV and the age of the patient in addition to 9 rules that were formulated by using a combination of the 5 identified variables for the classification of the level of CD4 count of patients based on the values of the variables identified. The performance of the models developed using decision trees, support vector machines and multi-layer perceptron was done.

Following the comparison of the performance of the machine learning algorithms used in this study, it was observed that the multi-layer perceptron had the best capability to identify the unseen patterns existing within the variables used to classify CD4 count level while decision trees was able to identify the most relevant variables with an accuracy of 75.6%. Following the development of the prediction model for osteoporosis risk classification, a better understanding of the relationship between the attributes relevant to osteoporosis risk was proposed. The model can also be integrated into existing Health Information System (HIS) which captures and manages clinical information which can be fed to the CD4 count level classification prediction model thus improving the clinical decisions affecting the measurement of CD4 count levels and the real-time assessment of clinical information affecting CD4 count level from remote locations.

REFERENCES

Brain, L., Tshilidzi, M., Taryn, T., & Monica, L. (2006). Prediction of HIV Status from Demographic Data using Neural Networks. IEEE Conference on Systems Man and Cybernetics, Taipei, Taiwan.

Idowu, P. A., Aladekomo, T. A., & Agbelusi, O. (2016). Prediction of Pediatrics HIV/AIDS Patient's Survival in Nigeria: A Data Mining Approach. *Journal of Research in Science, Technology, Engineering and Management, 2*(2), 40–45.

Idowu, P. A., Aladekomo, T. A., Agbelusi, O., Alaba, O. B., & Balogun, J. A. (2017a). Prediction of Pediatric HIV/AIDS Survival in Nigeria using Naïve Bayes' Approach. *International Journal of Child Health and Human Development, 10*(2), 1–12.

Idowu, P. A., Aladekomo, T. A., Agbelusi, O., Alaba, O. B., & Balogun, J. A. (2017b). Prediction of Pediatric HIV/AIDS Survival in Nigeria using C4.5 Decision Trees Algorithm. *International Journal of Child Health and Human Development, 10*(2), 1–12.

Kama, K., & Prem, S. (2013). Utilization of Data Mining Techniques for Prediction and Diagnosis of Major Life Threatening Diseases Survivability-Review. *International Journal of Scientific & Engineering Research, 4*(6), 923–932.

Lakshmi, G. S., & Isakki, P. (2017). A Comparative Study of Data Mining Classification Technique Using HIV/AIDS and STD Data. *International Journal of Innovative Research in Computer and Communication Engineering, 5*(1), 134–139.

Morgan, D., Mahe, C., Mayanja, B., Whitworth, J. A. G., & Kilmarx, P. H. (2002). Progression to symptomatic disease in people infected with HIV-1 in rural Uganda: Prospective cohort study. *Biomedical Journal, 324*, 193–197. PMID:11809639

Mwamburi, D. M., Ghosh, M., Fauntleroy, J., Gorbach, S. L., & Wanke, C. A. (2005). Predicting CD4 count using total lymphocyte count: A sustainable tool for clinical decisions during HAART use. *The American Journal of Tropical Medicine and Hygiene, 73*(1), 58–62. doi:10.4269/ajtmh.2005.73.58 PMID:16014833

Ojunga, N., Peter, M., Otulo, W., Omollo, O., & Edgar, O. (2014). The Application of Logistic Regression in Modeling of Survival Chances of HIV-Positive Patients under Highly Active Antiretroviral Therapy (HAART): A Case of Nyakach District, Kenya. *Journal of Medicine and Clinical Sciences, 3*(3), 14–20.

Olayemi, O. C., Olasehinde, O. O., & Agbelusi, O. (2016). Predictive Model of Pediatric HIV/AIDS Survival in Nigeria using Support Vector Machines. *Communications on Applied Electronics, 5*(8), 29–36. doi:10.5120/cae2016652349

Post, F. A., Wood, R., & Maartens, G. (1996). CD4 and total lymphocyte counts as predictors of HIV disease progression. *The Quarterly Journal of Medicine, 89*(7), 505–508. doi:10.1093/qjmed/89.7.505 PMID:8759490

Rosma, M. D., Sameem, A. K., Basir, A., Adeeba, K., & Annapurni, K. (2012). The Prediction of AIDS Survival: A Data Mining Approach. *Proceedings of the 2nd WSEAS International Conference on Multivariate Analysis and Its Application in Science and Engineering*, 48 – 53.

Schechter, M., Zajdenverg, R., Machado, L. L., Pinto, M. E., Lima, L. A., & Perez, M. A. (1994). Predicting CD4 Counts in HIV-infected Brazilian Individuals: A Model Based on the World Health Organization Staging System. *Journal of Acquired Immune Deficiency Syndromes, 7*(2), 163–168. PMID:7905525

Singh, Y., Narsai, N., & Mars, M. (2013). Applying Machine Learning to predict Patient-Specific Current CD4 Cell Count in order to determine the Progression of Human Immunodeficiency Virus (HIV) Infection. *African Journal of Biotechnology*, *12*(23), 3724–3750.

Tarekegn, G. B., & Sreenivasarao, V. (2016). Application of Data Mining Techniques on Pre ART Data: The Case of Felege Hiwot Referral Hospital. *International Journal of Research Studies in Computer Science and Engineering*, *3*(2), 1–9.

This research was previously published in Computational Models for Biomedical Reasoning and Problem Solving; pages 149-176, copyright year 2019 by Medical Information Science Reference (an imprint of IGI Global).

Chapter 16
An Improved Retinal Blood Vessel Detection System Using an Extreme Learning Machine

Lucas S Sousa
Programa de Pós-Graduação em Ciências da Computação do IFCE, Fortaleza, Brazil

Pedro P Rebouças Filho
Programa de Pós-Graduação em Ciências da Computação do IFCE, Fortaleza, Brazil

Francisco Nivando Bezerra
Programa de Pós-Graduação em Ciências da Computação do IFCE, Fortaleza, Brazil

Ajalmar R Rocha Neto
Instituto Federal do Ceará, Fortaleza, Brazil

Saulo A. F. Oliveira
Programa de Pós-Graduação em Engenharia de Telecomunicações do IFCE, Fortaleza, Brazil

ABSTRACT

Retinal images are commonly used to diagnose various diseases, such as diabetic retinopathy, glaucoma, and hypertension. An important step in the analysis of such images is the detection of blood vessels, which is usually done manually and is time consuming. The main proposal in this work is a fast method for retinal blood vessel detection using Extreme Learning Machine (ELM). ELM requires only one iteration to complete its training and it is a robust and fast network in all aspects. The proposal is a compact and efficient representation of retinal images in which the authors achieved a reduction up to 39% of the initial data volume, while still keeping representativeness. To achieve such a reduction whilst maintaining the representativeness, three features (local tophat, local average, and local variance) were used. According to the simulations carried out, this proposal achieved an accuracy of about 95% for most results, outperforming most of the state-of-art methods. Furthermore, this proposal has greater sensitivity, meaning that more vessel pixels are detected correctly.

DOI: 10.4018/978-1-6684-6291-1.ch016

INTRODUCTION

Diseases, such as diabetic retinopathy, glaucoma, and hypertension can be diagnosed from retinal images. The detection of the blood vessels in these images plays an important role in the diagnosis. This detection task is usually done manually with specific tools and is very time consuming. In addition to using the detection of blood vessels in retinal images in the medical field, this technique can also be employed in personal identification systems. The main idea of this later use is for biometric devices where the retinal vascular network is used as input, as described in Köse et al. (2011). Therefore, the development of tools, methods, and techniques that automate vessel detection is very much in demand (Imani et al., 2015a).

Segmentation of blood vessels in retinal images have recently been carried out successfully with supervised and semi-supervised methods (Niemeijer et al., 2004b; You et al., 2011; Vega et al., 2015). Such methods follow the idea that each pixel is represented by a feature vector and then a supervised classifier classifies each pixel as vessel or non-vessel. Due to the size of retinal images, a large number of feature vectors are generated. Therefore, the choice of a classifier and the discriminant pixel descriptors becomes an important issue. Among the various existing neural networks, Extreme Learning Machine (ELM), is a neural network that belongs to the family of the single-hidden layer feedforward neural networks (SLFN). In SLFN the weights and the hidden layer biases can be randomly assigned, if the activation functions in the hidden layer are infinitely differentiable. Then the SLFNs can be simply considered as a linear system and the output weights of SLFNs can be analytically determined (Bala and Vijayachitra, 2015). Furthermore, ELM minimizes the empirical risk and only requires one iteration to complete its training.

In fact, using ELM for this particular task is not new in this field. Some methods using ELM employing different methodologies can be found in the literature (Sheeba and Vasanthi, 2011; Shanmugam and Wahida Banu, 2013; Bala and Vijayachitra, 2015). However, most of them lack a solid methodology. In one work for example, neither the setup parameters, nor the training methodology are clear (Sheeba and Vasanthi, 2011). Furthermore, some of them present results using only a few images from the dataset (Sheeba and Vasanthi, 2011; Shanmugam and Wahida Banu, 2013). Consequently, some questions concerning their methodology and achieved accuracies without any detailed explanations arise. Thus, it is difficult to make fair comparisons between models that employ a solid methodology and those that do not.

The objective of this work is to address the segmentation of blood vessels in retinal images using an ELM network. Considering that the performance of a classifier depends directly on the representativeness of the data used during the training stage, this work proposes a set of attributes extracted from the images. Such attributes represent information about the level of detail, mean and standard deviation of each pixel and its neighborhood. Thus, the main novelty of this work is the use of a compact and efficient representation of retina images, with a 36% reduction of the initial data in two of the three datasets used. Such compact and efficient representation decrease the computational cost because ELM requires the computation of inverse matrices and by reducing the matrix sizes, fewer computations are necessary to achieve the weight vectors and consequently less runtime. The proposed approach was evaluated using three common databases: the Digital Retinal Images for Vessel Extraction (DRIVE), the STructured Analysis of the Retina (STARE), and the High-Resolution Fundus (HRF). The first two have low-resolution images, while the last has high-resolution images.

BACKGROUND

In this section the ELM is described in detail and some of the more recent methods for retinal vessel segmentation, which were also used for performance comparison, are discussed in order to facilitate a full understanding of the proposed approach.

Extreme Learning Machine

ELM is a SLFN and was originally proposed by Huang et al. (2006). The main concept behind it lies in the random initialization of the weights and biases of the hidden neurons. Therefore, the input weights and biases do not need to be adjusted, and only the output weights have to be analytically determined as described in (Huang et al., 2006). The final network is obtained with very few steps and with a very low computational cost.

Consider a set of M distinct samples (x_i, y_i) with x_i R^{d1} and y_i R^{d2}; then, an SLFN with N hidden neurons is modeled as:

$$\sum_{i=1}^{N} \beta_i f_i\left(w_i x_j + b_i\right), s.t. 1 \leq j \leq M \tag{1}$$

where f is the activation function, w_i the input weights, b_i the biases, and β_i the output weights. When the SLFN closely represents the data, the errors between the estimated outputs $\hat{y}_i$ and the actual outputs y_i are zero and the relation is:

$$\sum_{i=1}^{N} \beta_i f_i\left(w_i x_j + b_i\right) = y, \qquad 1 \leq j \leq M \tag{2}$$

which rewrites compactly as $H\beta=Y$, where:

$$H = \begin{pmatrix} f\left(w_1 x_1 + b_1\right) & \cdots & f\left(w_N x_N + b_N\right) \\ \vdots & \ddots & \vdots \\ f\left(w_1 x_M + b_1\right) & \cdots & f\left(w_N x_M + b_N\right) \end{pmatrix} \tag{3}$$

$\beta = \left(\beta_1^T \ldots \beta_N^T\right)^T$ and $Y = \left(y_1^T \ldots y_N^T\right)^T$. The ELM training algorithm is presented in Algorithm 1.

Algorithm 1: ELM Training
Given a training set (x_i, y_i), $x_i \in \mathbb{R}^{d1}$, $y_i \in \mathbb{R}^{d2}$, an activation function $f : \mathbb{R} \to \mathbb{R}$, and the number of hidden nodes N: [1] Randomly assign input weight vectors w_i and biases b_i, $1 \leq i \leq n$; Calculate the hidden-layer output matrix H; Calculate output weights matrix $\beta = H^{\dagger}Y$.
The $H^{\dagger}$ stands for the generalized inverse of the matrix H, more details in Huang et al. (2006).

RELATED WORK

There are a significant number of methods in the literature that perform automatic or semiautomatic segmentation of blood vessels in retinal images. They can be separated into two main groups: the supervised and unsupervised methods.

The supervised methods tend to be more accurate. However, these methods often require "re-training" when performing on a new set of images in order to achieve optimal performance, i.e., they are highly dependent on the training dataset (Nguyen et al., 2013). Niemeijer et al. (2004b) proposed a method using the KNN classifier with a feature vector of 31 attributes, all extracted from the green channel that achieved an accuracy of 94.07% in DRIVE. Soares et al. (2005) used a Bayesian classifier to classify the pixels with features obtained by the Morlet wavelet transform and achieved an accuracy of 94.67% in DRIVE. Ricci and Perfetti (2007) used support vector machines (SVMs) with features based on analyses of the neighborhood and linear structures. These authors reported an accuracy of 95.63% and 95.84% in DRIVE and STARE, respectively. You et al. (2011) also employed SVMs for this task, but this time, the segmentation of the thinner and wider vessels was performed separately for better results, achieving an accuracy of 94% in DRIVE and STARE. Yu et al. (2012) presented an algorithm that uses information from a vessel probability map generated by computing the eigenvalues of the second derivatives of Gaussian filtered image at multiple scales. The authors reported an accuracy of 95.15% in HRF. Vega et al. (2015) used the neural network LNNDP for vessel detection, which does not require any segmentation parameters for the vessels in retinal images, yielding an accuracy of 94.83% and 94.12% in DRIVE and STARE, respectively.

On the other hand, the unsupervised methods do not require the ground truth images and demand less time because they do not have a training stage. Additionally, in cases where there is no overlap between classes, they work quite well. However, with overlapping data, the accuracy decreases significantly. Espona et al. (2007) developed a system based on the classical snake and incorporated blood vessels topological properties. The authors achieved 93.16% accuracy in DRIVE. Bankhead et al. (2012) addressed vessel segmentation using thresholding wavelet coefficients and localized vessel edges from image profiles; these authors achieved an accuracy of 93.71% in DRIVE. Li et al (2012) proposed a multiscale vessel extraction scheme for blood vessel detection by multiplying the responses of matched filters using different scales. Such a scheme produced an accuracy of 94.96% in DRIVE and 94.61% in STARE. The usage of line detectors with a combination of line lengths with different scales to produce the final segmentation was carried out by Nguyen et al. (2013) and Guyen et al. (2013). The authors reported accuracies of 94.07% and 93.24% in DRIVE and STARE, respectively. Odstrcilik et al. (2013) employed MF and the minimum error thresholding technique to extract the binary blood vessel tree with five different kernels. Each kernel was designed according to typical blood vessel cross-sectional profiles considering five width classes of retinal vessels to cover all blood vessel structures. The authors achieved 94.94% accuracy in HRF. Imani et al. (2015b) addressed the problem by employing morphological component analysis (MCA) and refining the results with Morlet Wavelet Transform, yielding an accuracy of 95.23% and 95.90% in DRIVE and STARE, respectively. Fraz et al. (2015) proposed an automated system for processing and analyzing retinal images. The system, called QUARTZ is divided into modules for specific tasks, such as vessel detection, optic disc localization, arteriole/venule classification and related tasks. The vessel detection task in QUARTZ is based on a multi-scale line detector with hysteresis morphological reconstruction. They reported an accuracy of 94.80% in DRIVE and 95.30% in STARE.

In this context, the blood vessel detection problem calls for approaches that provide higher accuracy at low cost. Also, this work meets both criteria by combining ELM, a robust and fast network, with simple feature vectors (2 R^3), which are described below in the Proposal section.

Proposal

The proposal of this work applies an ELM network to the detection of blood vessels, for which two processing stages are necessary. The first consists of extracting features from a random training image, from the database, and the second is the ELM training stage. Prior to the feature extraction stage a pre-processing is carried out on the original training image to obtain another one, from which the features are extracted. After removing the redundant patterns from this newly generated image, the classifier can then be trained. Once the training is completed, the classifier can be used to detect blood vessels in other images. It is important to highlight that, during generalization or the test phase, there is no need to remove redundant patterns in the feature extraction stage. Thereby, the ELM can classify each pixel/feature vector as a vessel or non-vessel. The feature extraction, training, and classification processes are described below in detail.

Feature Extraction

As stated, the performance of a classifier depends directly on the representativeness of the data. Thus, a set of features that can represent the ground truth image is highly desirable. This study has found a set of simple image processing techniques from the literature that can transform an input image to an intermediary one which is very close to its ground-truth. A few of these are employed later to extract features to build the proposed training dataset. All features are pixel based and they represent information about the level of detail, mean and standard deviation of each pixel and its neighborhood. Also, this study looks for simplicity and this compact representation is handy; on the other hand, in the literature, there are works that use patterns with a very large number of features.

The feature extraction is described next.

The first step in feature extraction is to use the green channel because it brings relevant information about the vessels, as reported in Niemeijer et al. (2004b) and Iemeijer et al. (2004b). The second step consists of applying a contrast adjustment on the image so that the vessels will be highlighted against the background. The top-hat operation on the complement image results in an image which shows the vessels with brighter pixels and the background with the darker pixels. The reason behind using the top-hat operation is because it decreases the variations in illumination in the image. Consequently, the resulting image also has low contrast, so, to overcome this, the contrast adjustment is applied once more. The final image is the input for the ELM network. The following steps show the pre-processing used in the proposed approach, see Figure 1:

1. Extract the green channel I_g from the input image I;
2. Compute the contrast adjusted image I_g^* from I_g;
3. Compute the complement image I_g^{*-} from I_g^*, so that $I_g^{*-} = 255 - I_g^*$;

4. Compute the top-hat image I_ς using the top-hat transform with a disk structuring element *se* of radius W, so that $I_\gamma = I_g^{*-} - \left(I_g^{*-} \circ se \right)$;

5. Finally, the resulting image I_γ^* is achieved by adjusting the contrast of the top-hat image I_γ.

Figure 1. Images from each step of the pre-processing phase. Original image I in (a) and its green channel with contrast adjusted I_g^* in (b). Top-Hat of green channel complement I_γ in (c) and the enhancement of the top-hat I_γ^* in (d). The images (b)-(c)-(d) are inverted (negative) for visualization purposes.

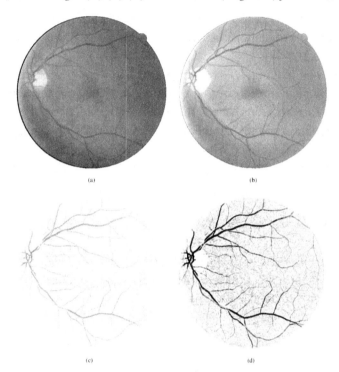

After obtaining the top-hat enhancement image I_γ^*, to extract from each pixel its value. For the sake of simplicity, consider the following description and notation to address the resulting images from the mean filter $I_\mu = \Psi_\mu \left(I_\gamma^* \right)$, and the local standard deviation filter $I_\sigma = \Psi_\sigma \left(I_\gamma^* \right)$ from I_γ^*, all using a window of size W. The mean filter μ and the local standard deviation filter $\circ$ compute, for each pixel in the input image, the average and standard deviation of its $W \times W$ neighborhood, respectively. Finally, for each pixel i is defined as feature vector as $x_i \in \mathbb{R}^3$ as follows:

$$x_i = \left[I_\gamma^*(i), I_\mu(i), I_\sigma(i) \right] \tag{4}$$

Note: Each feature is normalized to zero before training or classification.

ELM Training

Initially the ELM classifier has to be trained for blood vessel detection. To carry this out one image is randomly selected to build the training dataset $X = \{x_i\}_{i=1}^{N}$. Unsurprisingly, X has a large number of elements due to the size of the images. So, to reduce the number of elements X, the duplicate inputs are removed resulting in a training set X^* with only unique ones, i.e., $|X| \geq |X^*|$ where $|A|$ yields the cardinality of a set A. When the three features of two different inputs are the same, we have a duplicated input, i.e., given two inputs x_i and x_j with $i \neq j$, $I_\gamma^*(i) = I_\gamma^*(j)$, $I_\mu(i) = I_\mu(j)$, $I_\sigma(i) = I_\sigma(j)$. Reducing the number of the training set helps ELM in memory costs because the computational cost to compute weight vectors will be decreased. In this work, the reduction ratio of DRIVE and STARE was about 34% and 39%, respectively, and HRF was about 16%.

As ELM uses supervised training, a label (vessel and non-vessel) must be provided for each input in X^*. These labels are obtained directly from the ground truth image pixel values. After obtaining the training set X^* and their corresponding labels, the ELM parameters have to be tuned. This is done by choosing an activation function and the number of neurons from the hidden layer. To find the best parameter set, a grid search was performed with k-fold cross-validation using the training set and a fixed activation function for the whole process. Once the best parameter set is found, the ELM is trained as described in Algorithm 1.

ELM Classification

After training, each image of the dataset is transformed into feature vectors in the same way as in the training phase; however, in this case, the duplicated pixels are not removed. Finally, the classifier computes the output for each pixel, to form the output image.

Small Object Removal

After the classification, the output image is composed of detected vessels and some noise, small objects, obtained through miss-classification. So, to obtain a more appropriate output image, these unwanted objects based on their area are removed. If any object has an area smaller than the Rejection Area (RA) parameter, it is removed from the resulting image. A diagrammatic representation of this proposal is shown in Figure 2.

EXPERIMENTS AND RESULTS

Simulations using images from three well-known datasets, namely, DRIVE, STARE, and HRF were used to assess our proposal. The DRIVE (Niemeijer et al., 2004a) is a publicly available dataset, containing a total of 40 color fundus photographs divided into a test and a training set both containing 20 images with available ground truth images. The observers manually segmented all images. The STARE dataset (Hoover, 2000) contained 20 images for blood vessel segmentation. Two observers manually segmented all the images; the second observer provided more details concerning the small vessels. The final dataset, the HRF (Kohler et al., 2013), contains 45 images with three different classes of patients, namely, healthy, retinopathy, and glaucomatous, with their ground truth images.

Figure 2. Diagrammatic representation of the proposed approach

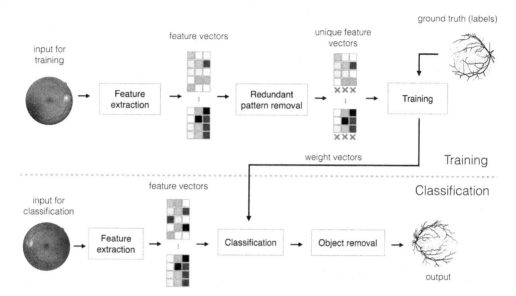

Experiment Setup

When it comes to supervised training, the methodologies used for training and test vary a lot from work to work. Part of this is because most of these datasets have a small number of images available and no clear definitions on how to separate them between training and test, except for the DRIVE dataset. Thus, different experimental methodologies for each dataset were carried out to make a fair comparison. The description of each experiment is as follows:

- **DRIVE:** This dataset contains 20 training images and the other 20 are test images. For this particular dataset, one image was chosen at random from the training set for the training and then, all the 20 test set images were used for the test;
- **STARE:** This dataset only contained 20 images. Here one image was chosen at random for training and then, the remaining 19 were used for the test;
- **HRF:** This dataset contains 45 images divided into three classes (Diabetic, Glaucoma and Healthy), forming three small sets. Then, for each small set, we choose one image at random for training and then, the remaining images were used for testing.

As the proposal has parameters to be tuned, namely, the number of neurons in the hidden layer (NHL), the window size (W) and the rejection area (RA), a cross-validation using the whole training dataset was carried out 10 times to find the best values to be used, see Table 1. In DRIVE and STARE, the same values for W and RA due to their image resolutions were obtained. However, higher values were required for HRF. Furthermore, each experiment was carried out ten times to analyze robustness.

Furthermore, all these experiments were performed on an AMD FX™-4300 1.4 GHz Quad-Core Processor with 8 GB of RAM without using parallel computing.

Table 1. Configuration adopted for each experiment concerning the dataset. The NHL values were obtained through cross-validation, 10 times, varying the number of neurons in [1,. .. 50] for STARE and DRIVE, while the variations for HRF were [1,. .. 20].

Dataset	NHL	W	RA
DRIVE	40	5	20
STARE	40	5	60
HRF	11	17	400

Validation

In order to improve the evaluation and the Discussion when comparing the proposed approach to the state-of-art methods, found in the literature, seven statistical measurements were considered. The following measures were used: sensitivity (SEN), specificity (SPC), precision (PRE), accuracy (ACC), F-Measure (F_β), the Matthews Correlation Coefficient (MCC) (Matthews, 1975) and the Jaccard Similarity Coefficient (J) (Jaccard, 1901). All of them were measured by true positive (TP), false positive (FP), true negative (TN), and false negative (FN) metrics. TP is defined as the number of vessel pixels correctly detected in the retinal images; FP is the number of non-vessel pixels detected as a vessel; TN is the number of non-vessel pixels correctly detected and FN is the number of vessel pixels detected as non-vessel pixels (Ammar Khatib and Shailaja, 2015):

$$SEN = \frac{TP}{TP + FN} \tag{5}$$

$$SPC = \frac{TN}{TN + FP} \tag{6}$$

$$PRE = \frac{TP}{TP + FP} \tag{7}$$

$$ACC = \frac{TP + TN}{TP + TN + FP + FN} \tag{8}$$

$$F_\beta = \left(1 + \beta^2\right) \frac{PRE \times SPC}{\beta^2 \times PRE \times SPC} \tag{9}$$

$$MCC = \frac{TP \times TN - FP \times FN}{\sqrt{\left(TP + FP\right)\left(TP + FN\right)\left(TN + FP\right)\left(TN + FN\right)}} \tag{10}$$

$$J = \frac{TP}{TP + FP + FN} \qquad (11)$$

Borji et al. (2012) reported that when F_β is used for evaluating, SPC is not as important as PRE because 100% of SPC can be easily achieved by classifying all pixels as non-vessel. Thus, weighting PRE more than SPC is necessary for comparative purposes. Therefore, we adopted two different values for β_2, 1 and 0.3, respectively. The MCC score is regarded as a balanced measure which can be employed to assess the classification quality of unbalanced class problems. It can assume any value in the interval between -1 and +1, in which a value of +1 indicates a perfect prediction, 0 no better than random prediction and -1 indicates a total disagreement between prediction and observation. Finally, the J score, a similarity metric, ranges from 0 (worst) to 1 (best) and characterizes the overall vessel detection performance.

In this work seven measures were used (see Table 4); however, there is a lack of evaluation metrics in the other studies discussed here. The methodology used to assess the results varies and some works only present part of these measures. ACC was the only common measure adopted among them. Thus, we used the same metrics for comparison. Furthermore, the vessel detection problem is an unbalanced one, i.e., there are more non-vessel pixels than vessel ones. The percentage of vessel pixels is reported to be somewhere around 10-15% in DRIVE and STARE, respectively. Thus, other statistical analyses must be included in the discussion concerning the actual vessel detection task.

Figure 3. The mean accuracy for the ten realizations for each image in the datasets DRIVE and STARE

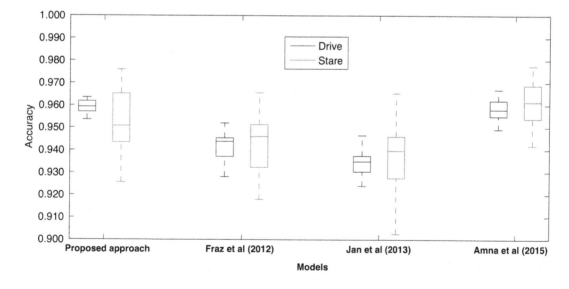

DISCUSSION

The main goal in detection applications is the correct detection of the class of interest, that is, missing a target in a scene is costly. Therefore, in these applications, metrics that are highly sensitive to incorrect classifications are perhaps the most appropriate to assess the performance. Moreover, as stated, the problem itself is an unbalanced one. Thus, analyzing how good the blood vessel detection was in terms of actual detection of vessels is highly desirable. Besides the sensitivity, the F_p, Mathews Correlation Coefficient and the Jaccard Similarity scoring metrics are the ones that most capture the essence of vessel detection.

Figure 3 and Table 2 show that the proposed approach achieved good accuracy with a lower standard deviation for the DRIVE dataset than in STARE. This is because there is a higher variation among the images in STARE. However, even the worst accuracy achieved by this work is better than the others found in the literature. For the DRIVE dataset, the proposal outperformed most of the results regarding accuracy, and sensitivity and the specificity stayed close to the state-of-art. The results comparing the proposed method using the HRF dataset are presented in Table 3. The proposed approach outperformed the one presented in Odstrc̆ilík et al. (2009) concerning accuracy. Also, the lower standard deviation in most metrics reinforces that this work has a low variation from image to image.

Table 2. The performance of different vessel segmentation models in terms of ACC, SEN and SPC using the DRIVE and STARE datasets. The results were extracted directly from Imani et al. (2015b). Only the works that had a similar methodology with respect to the usage of the entire training dataset were selected.

Method	SEN (%)	DRIVE SPC (%)	ACC (%)	SEN (%)	STARE SPC (%)	ACC (%)
Human observer	77.63	97.23	94.73	89.51	93.84	93.50
Proposed Method	97.46	78.16	95.85	96.20	77.47	95.25
(Ricci and Perfetti, 2007, Ricci and Perfetti, 2007)	-	-	95.63	-	-	95.84
(Imani et al., 2015b, Imani et al., 2015b)	75.24	97.53	95.23	75.02	97.45	95.90
(Fraz et al., 2015, Fraz et al., 2015)	74.00	98.00	94.80	75.54	97.60	95.30
(Lam et al., 2010, Lam et al., 2010)	-	-	94.72	-	-	95.67
(Soares et al., 2005, Soares et al., 2005)	-	-	94.67	-	-	94.74
(Li et al., 2012, Li et al., 2012)	78.43	96.76	94.96	80.69	95.78	94.61
(Akram and Khan, 2013, Akram and Khan, 2013)	-	-	94.62	-	-	-
(Miri and Mahloojifar, 2011, Miri and Mahloojifar, 2011)	-	-	94.58	-	-	-
(Marín et al., 2011, Marín et al., 2011)	70.67	98.01	94.52	70.67	98.01	94.52
(Staal et al., 2004, Staal et al., 2004)	-	-	94.42	-	-	95.16
(Fraz et al., 2012, Fraz et al., 2012)	71.52	97.69	94.30	73.11	96.80	94.42
(Niemeijer et al., 2004b, Niemeijer et al., 2004b)	-	-	94.16	-	-	-
(Nguyen et al., 2013, Nguyen et al., 2013)	-	-	94.07	-	-	93.24
(You et al., 2011, You et al., 2011)	74.00	97.00	94.00	72.00	97.00	94.00
(Bankhead et al., 2012, Bankhead et al., 2012)	70.27	97.17	93.71	-	-	-
(Espona et al., 2007, Espona et al., 2007)	66.34	96.82	93.16	-	-	-
(Delibasis et al., 2010, Delibasis et al., 2010)	72.88	95.05	93.11	-	-	86.76
(Jiang and Mojon, 2003, Jiang and Mojon, 2003)	-	-	92.00	-	-	-
(Vlachos and Dermatas, 2010, Vlachos and Dermatas, 2010)	74.00	95.00	92.00	-	-	-
(Kande et al., 2010, Kande et al., 2010)	-	-	89.11	-	-	89.76

Table 3. The performance of different vessel segmentation models in terms of SEN, SPC and ACC using the HRF dataset

Method	Class	SEN (%)	SPC (%)	ACC (%)
(Odstrc˘ilík et al., 2009, Odstrc˘ilík et al., 2009)	HEAL	78.61 ± 3.92	97.50 ± 0.65	95.39 ± 0.61
	DIAB	74.63 ± 5.66	96.19 ± 0.77	94.45 ± 0.84
	GLAU	79.00 ± 3.18	96.38 ± 0.69	94.97 ± 0.61
(Yu et al., 2012, Yu et al., 2012)	HEAL	79.38 ± 0.00	97.67 ± 0.00	95.66 ± 0.00
	DIAB	76.04 ± 0.00	96.25 ± 0.00	94.60 ± 0.00
	GLAU	78.90 ± 0.00	96.62 ± 0.00	95.18 ± 0.00
(Odstrcilik et al., 2013, Odstrcilik et al., 2013)	HEAL	78.61 ± 0.03	97.50 ± 0.00	95.39 ± 0.00
	DIAB	74.63 ± 0.05	96.19 ± 0.01	94.45 ± 0.01
	GLAU	79.00 ± 0.30	96.38 ± 0.00	94.97 ± 0.00
Proposed Method	HEAL	96.91 ± 0.40	83.77 ± 3.70	95.87 ± 0.10
	DIAB	96.92 ± 0.44	74.46 ± 3.99	95.68 ± 0.13
	GLAU	97.47 ± 0.20	77.85 ± 1.46	96.33 ± 0.13

In general, the proposed method has higher sensitivity scores and lower specificity scores. This is a strong indication that just a few vessel pixels are classified as non-vessel pixels, while some non-vessel pixels are erroneously classified as vessel ones (Table 4). This is exactly the opposite of what occurred in the other models, where the specificity scores are higher than the sensitivity ones, indicating that more non-vessel pixels are detect correctly than vessel pixels. Moreover, detecting the smaller blood vessels is a very challenging task as one can see in Figure 4, 5, and 6. As reported by Ramlugun et al. (2012), during the feature extraction stage, conventional smoothing techniques and other related techniques suppress these small blood vessels causing them to be similar to the background. In the proposed approach the input image contrast was adjusted so some of these smaller blood vessels were preserved. The authors believe that the proposal was very well trained using a very representative set of images especially for blood vessels. This behavior is confirmed by the higher sensitivity, F_1-Measure, Matthews Correlation Coefficient, and the Jaccard Similarity Coefficient values which are very close to those obtained by a specialist, as presented in Table 5.

Figure 4. Results for DRIVE

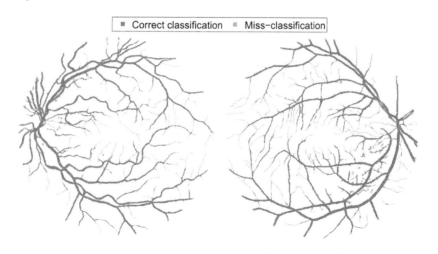

Table 4. Performance of the proposed method using the eight measures: Sensitivity (SEN), Specificity (SPC), Precision (PRE), F1- measure using two different values for β2· 0.3 and 1, the Matthews Correlation Coefficient (MCC), and the Jaccard Similarity Coefficient (J). Each score is the average μ and the standard deviation σ for each dataset.

Dataset		SEN	SPC	ACC	PRE	$F_\beta=0.3$	$F_\beta=1$	MCC	J
DRIVE	μ	0.9746	0.7816	0.9585	0.9802	0.9788	0.9773	0.7344	0.9557
	σ	0.0058	0.0532	0.0037	0.0055	0.0034	0.0021	0.0238	0.0011
STARE	μ	0.9620	0.7747	0.9525	0.9876	0.9815	0.9746	0.6184	0.9506
	σ	0.0131	0.1092	0.0144	0.0062	0.0060	0.0078	0.1059	0.0004
HRF D	μ	0.9692	0.7446	0.9568	0.9849	0.9812	0.9770	0.6341	0.9550
	σ	0.0077	0.0638	0.0058	0.0057	0.0036	0.0032	0.0401	0.0014
HRF G	μ	0.9747	0.7785	0.9633	0.9862	0.9835	0.9804	0.6949	0.9616
	σ	0.0038	0.0307	0.0037	0.0024	0.0019	0.0020	0.0216	0.0013
HRF H	μ	0.9691	0.8377	0.9587	0.9860	0.9820	0.9774	0.7400	0.9559
	σ	0.0065	0.0521	0.0046	0.0054	0.0034	0.0026	0.0261	0.0011

Figure 5. Results for STARE

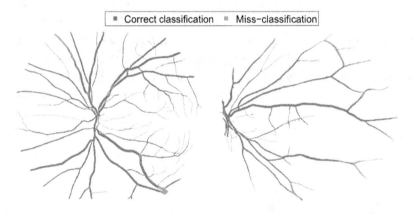

Figure 6. Results for HRF

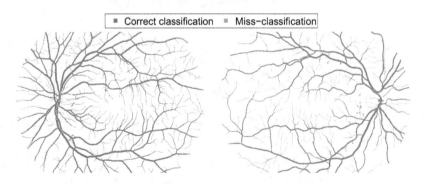

Table 5. Performance of the proposed method (PM) compared with the 2nd observer (SO) in each dataset using three measures: Precision (PRE), F_1-measure using two different values for β; 0.3 and 1, the Matthews Correlation Coefficient (MCC), and the Jaccard Similarity Coefficient (J). Each score is the average for each dataset.

Dataset		$F_\beta = 0.3$	$F_\beta = 1$	MCC	J
DRIVE	SO	0.9792	0.9801	0.7700	0.9611
	PM	0.9788	0.9773	0.7344	0.9557
STARE	SO	0.9832	0.9735	0.7316	0.9485
	PM	0.9815	0.9746	0.6184	0.9506

Table 6. The runtime performance of the proposed method for a single image from each dataset. All runtimes are approximate values.

	Drive	Stare	HRF
Runtime	(584×565)	(605×700)	(2336×3504)
Training	11.26 s	12.90 s	6 min
Classification	00.02 s	00.02 s	00.59 s

Concerning the dataset size and the duplicated pattern removal stage, each retinal image generates many training inputs since each pixel is treated as one. Therefore, the choice of a classifier that adapts to this situation well is essential. In this work, the choice of ELM was successful due to its fast training and its ability to work with a large amount of data. Moreover, the only information retained after the training stage is the weight vectors. Working with high-resolution datasets, such as HRF, in which a training set has a size of 6.8 million pixels (even after reduction), approximately, is very difficult for methods with high training complexity. This constraint makes SVMs, in their standard formulation, impractical even for a moderate problem as the number of training data reaches to the extent of hundreds of thousands of pixels (Shen et al., 2016).

As ELM is efficient for a large number of patterns, reducing the data set in a representative manner always brings performance benefits. Reducing the data set decreases the computational cost because ELM requires the computation of inverse matrices. Thus, reducing the size of the matrices decreases the number of computations necessary to determine the weight vectors, and consequently it decreases runtime. Moreover, as one can see in the results, these reductions did not affect the performance of the ELM negatively when compared to other supervised learning methodologies.

As aforementioned, the number of pixel vessels in DRIVE and STARE is about 10-15% and, in these datasets, even after the reduction, the proposed approach achieves a reduced training set with a size about 60-66% of the total number of pixels. That being said, we also believe that the proposed features are indeed very representative. Other models reported other features not used here. However, the proposal here has shown that simple techniques can achieve higher scoring values.

The results of the runtime are presented in Table 6. In fact, the training stage in supervised learning methodologies is known for requiring more runtime. However, it only takes place in the process once and the classification task is the one that is repeated over and over. As the proposal is sensitive to the input image size, datasets with small size images benefit and have a fast training while higher resolution datasets require more processing, and consequently more runtime. The proposed approach took, on average, less than 15 seconds to perform the training stage for low resolution datasets (DRIVE and STARE), while the classification task was complete in just a few seconds. However, for the higher resolution dataset it took about 6 min to train and almost half a second to classify.

CONCLUSION

In this work a novel method is proposed for retina blood vessel detection based on ELM. The proposal of this work is mainly based on computing descriptors for each pixel, based on a top-hat transform, mean and standard deviation values of its neighborhood. Indeed, the main advantage of this work lies in the compact and efficient representation of this type of image. Such compact and efficient representation decreases the computational cost because as ELM requires the computation of inverse matrices, with smaller matrices, fewer computations are necessary to achieve the weight vectors, and consequently less runtime. The reduction achieved was up to 36% of the original data.

The experimental results indicate that the proposed algorithm is competitive for retina vessel detection. The proposal outperformed most of the results regarding accuracy using three well-known datasets. Also, the lower standard deviation achieved in most results reinforces the robustness and stability of the proposed approach. The authors believe that the proposed feature extraction method produced a very representative training set, especially for the vessel class. This was confirmed by the higher sensitivities of the F1-Measure, Matthews Correlation Coefficient, and the Jaccard Similarity Coefficient results which were very close to those obtained by the specialist labeled data in DRIVE and STARE. The runtime for training and classification in this work took on average 13 seconds for the training stage using low-resolution datasets (DRIVE and STARE), while the classification task took less than one second per image. However, it took about 6 min for training and a half second per image for classification in the higher resolution dataset.

Presently, we are exploring other descriptors for ELM input. Furthermore, we are working on the choice of suitable current parameter values to be carried out automatically, without cross-validation. Also, there is a need to reduce the number of inputs even more to reduce the computational costs. Finally, once a set reduction strategy has been set up satisfactorily, we intend to employ Support Vector Machines, which is a model that minimizes the structural risk, as a means to improve the current approach even for high-resolution datasets.

ACKNOWLEDGMENT

This work was partially supported through Coordenação de Aperfeiçoamento de Pessoal de Nível Superior (CAPES), Fundação Cearense de Apoio ao Desenvolvimento Científico e Tecnológico (FUNCAP) and Federal Institute of Ceará (IFCE).

REFERENCES

Akram, M. U., & Khan, S. A. (2013). Multilayered thresholding-based blood vessel segmentation for screening of diabetic retinopathy. *Engineering with Computers*, *29*(2), 165–173. doi:10.100700366-011-0253-7

Bala, M. P., & Vijayachitra, S. (2015). Extraction of retinal blood vessels and diagnosis of proliferative diabetic retinopathy using extreme learning machine. *Journal of Medical Imaging and Health Informatics*, *5*(2), 248–256. doi:10.1166/jmihi.2015.1380

Bankhead, P., Scholfield, C. N., McGeown, J. G., & Curtis, T. M. (2012). Fast retinal vessel detection and measurement using wavelets and edge location refinement. *PLoS One*, *7*(3). doi:10.1371/journal.pone.0032435 PMID:22427837

Borji, A., Sihite, D. N., & Itti, L. (2012). Salient object detection: A benchmark. In *Computer Vision–ECCV 2012* (pp. 414–429). Springer. doi:10.1007/978-3-642-33709-3_30

Delibasis, K. K., Kechriniotis, A. I., Tsonos, C., & Assimakis, N. (2010). Automatic model-based tracing algorithm for vessel segmentation and diameter estimation. *Computer Methods and Programs in Biomedicine*, *100*(2), 108–122. doi:10.1016/j.cmpb.2010.03.004 PMID:20363522

Espona, L., Carreira, M. J., Ortega, M., & Penedo, M. G. (2007). A snake for retinal vessel segmentation. In *Pattern Recognition and Image Analysis* (pp. 178–185). Springer. doi:10.1007/978-3-540-72849-8_23

Fraz, M., Welikala, R., Rudnicka, A., Owen, C., Strachan, D., & Barman, S. (2015). Quartz: Quantitative analysis of retinal vessel topology and size–an automated system for quantification of retinal vessels morphology. *Expert Systems with Applications*, *42*(20), 7221–7234. doi:10.1016/j.eswa.2015.05.022

Fraz, M. M., Barman, S., Remagnino, P., Hoppe, A., Basit, A., Uyyanonvara, B., ... Owen, C. G. (2012). An approach to localize the retinal blood vessels using bit planes and centerline detection. *Computer Methods and Programs in Biomedicine*, *108*(2), 600–616. doi:10.1016/j.cmpb.2011.08.009 PMID:21963241

Hoover, A. (2000). Structured analysis of the retina.

Huang, G.-B., Zhu, Q.-Y., & Siew, C.-K. (2006). Extreme learning machine: Theory and applications. *Neurocomputing*, *70*(1), 489–501.

Imani, E., Javidi, M., & Pourreza, H.-R. (2015b). Improvement of retinal blood vessel detection using morphological component analysis. *Computer Methods and Programs in Biomedicine*, *118*(3), 263–279. doi:10.1016/j.cmpb.2015.01.004 PMID:25697986

Imani, E., Javidi, M., and Pourreza, H.-R. (2015a). Improvement of retinal blood vessel detection using morphological component analysis. *Computer Methods and Programs in Biomedicine*, *118*(3), 263–279.

Jaccard, P. (1901). *Etude comparative de la distribution florale dans une portion des Alpes et du Jura*. Impr. Corbaz.

Jiang, X., & Mojon, D. (2003). Adaptive local thresholding by verification-based multithreshold probing with application to vessel detection in retinal images. *Pattern Analysis and Machine Intelligence. IEEE Transactions on*, *25*(1), 131–137.

Kande, G. B., Subbaiah, P. V., & Savithri, T. S. (2010). Unsupervised fuzzy based vessel segmentation in pathological digital fundus images. *Journal of Medical Systems*, *34*(5), 849–858. doi:10.100710916-009-9299-0 PMID:20703624

Kohler, T., Budai, A., Kraus, M. F., Odstrcilik, J., Michelson, G., & Hornegger, J. (2013). Automatic no-reference quality assessment for retinal fundus images using vessel segmentation. In *2013 IEEE 26th International Symposium on Computer-Based Medical Systems (CBMS)* (pp. 95–100). IEEE.

Köse, C., & İki, C. (2011). A personal identification system using retinal vasculature in retinal fundus images. *Expert Systems with Applications*, *38*(11), 13670–13681.

Lam, B. S., Gao, Y., & Liew, A. W.-C. (2010). General retinal vessel segmentation using regularization-based multiconcavity modeling. *IEEE Transactions on* Medical Imaging, *29*(7), 1369–1381. PMID:20304729

Li, Q., You, J., & Zhang, D. (2012). Vessel segmentation and width estimation in retinal images using multiscale production of matched filter responses. *Expert Systems with Applications*, *39*(9), 7600–7610. doi:10.1016/j.eswa.2011.12.046

Marín, D., Aquino, A., Gegúndez-Arias, M. E., & Bravo, J. M. (2011). A new supervised method for blood vessel segmentation in retinal images by using gray-level and moment invariants-based features. *IEEE Transactions on* Medical Imaging, *30*(1), 146–158. PMID:20699207

Matthews, B. W. (1975). Comparison of the predicted and observed secondary structure of t4 phage lysozyme. *Biochimica et Biophysica Acta (BBA)- Protein Structure*, *405*(2), 442–451. doi:10.1016/0005-2795(75)90109-9 PMID:1180967

Miri, M. S., & Mahloojifar, A. (2011). Retinal image analysis using curvelet transform and multistructure elements morphology by reconstruction. *IEEE Transactions on* Biomedical Engineering, *58*(5), 1183–1192. PMID:21147592

Nguyen, U. T., Bhuiyan, A., Park, L. A., & Ramamohanarao, K. (2013). An effective retinal blood vessel segmentation method using multi-scale line detection. *Pattern Recognition*, *46*(3), 703–715. doi:10.1016/j.patcog.2012.08.009

Niemeijer, M., Staal, J., van Ginneken, B., Loog, M., & Abramo, M. D. (2004b). Comparative study of retinal vessel segmentation methods on a new publicly available database. In *Medical Imaging 2004* (pp. 648–656). International Society for Optics and Photonics. doi:10.1117/12.535349

Niemeijer, M., Staal, J. J., Ginneken, B., Loog, M., & Abramoff, M. D. (2004). DRIVE: digital retinal images for vessel extraction. In Methods for Evaluating Segmentation and Indexing Techniques Dedicated to Retinal Ophthalmology.

Odstrc˘ilík. J., Jan, J., Gazárek, J., and Kolá˘r, R. (2009). Improvement of vessel segmentation by matched filtering in colour retinal images. In *World Congress on Medical Physics and Biomedical Engineering*, Munich, Germany, September 7-12 (pp. 327-330). Springer.

Odstrcilik, J., Kolar, R., Budai, A., Hornegger, J., Jan, J., Gazarek, J., ... Angelopoulou, E. (2013). Retinal vessel segmentation by improved matched filtering: Evaluation on a new high-resolution fundus image database. *IET Image Processing*, *7*(4), 373–383.

Ramlugun, G. S., Nagarajan, V. K., & Chakraborty, C. (2012). Small retinal vessels extraction towards proliferative diabetic retinopathy screening. *Expert Systems with Applications, 39*(1), 1141–1146. doi:10.1016/j.eswa.2011.07.115

Ricci, E., & Perfetti, R. (2007). Retinal blood vessel segmentation using line operators and support vector classification. *Medical Imaging. IEEE Transactions on, 26*(10), 1357–1365. PMID:17948726

Shanmugam, V., & Wahida Banu, R. (2013). Retinal blood vessel segmentation using an extreme learning machine approach. In 2013 IEEE Point-of- Care Healthcare Technologies (PHT) (pp. 318–321. IEEE.

Sheeba, X. M., & Vasanthi, S. (2011). An efficient elm approach for blood vessel segmentation in retinal images. *Bonfring International Journal of Man Machine Interface, 1*, 15.

Shen, X.-J., Mu, L., Li, Z., Wu, H.-X., Gou, J.-P., & Chen, X. (2016). Large-scale support vector machine classification with redundant data reduction. *Neurocomputing, 172*, 189–197. doi:10.1016/j. neucom.2014.10.102

Soares, J. V., Leandro, J. J., Cesar-Jr, R. M., Jelinek, H. F., & Cree, M. J. (2005). Using the 2-d morlet wavelet with supervised classification for retinal vessel segmentation. In *18th Brazil. Symp. Comput. Graphics Image Process (SIBGRAPI).*

Staal, J., Abràmoff, M. D., Niemeijer, M., Viergever, M. A., & Van Ginneken, B. (2004). Ridge-based vessel segmentation in color images of the retina. *IEEE Transactions on Medical Imaging, 23*(4), 501–509.

Vega, R., Sanchez-Ante, G., Falcon-Morales, L. E., Sossa, H., & Guevara, E. (2015). Retinal vessel extraction using lattice neural networks with dendritic processing. *Computers in Biology and Medicine, 58*, 20–30. doi:10.1016/j.compbiomed.2014.12.016 PMID:25589415

Vlachos, M., & Dermatas, E. (2010). Multi-scale retinal vessel segmentation using line tracking. *Computerized Medical Imaging and Graphics, 34*(3), 213–227. doi:10.1016/j.compmedimag.2009.09.006 PMID:19892522

You, X., Peng, Q., Yuan, Y., Cheung, Y., & Lei, J. (2011). Segmentation of retinal blood vessels using the radial projection and semi-supervised approach. *Pattern Recognition, 44*(10), 2314–2324. doi:10.1016/j. patcog.2011.01.007

Yu, H., Barriga, S., Agurto, C., Zamora, G., Bauman, W., & Soliz, P. (2012). Fast vessel segmentation in retinal images using multiscale enhancement and second-order local entropy. In *SPIE medical imaging* (pp. 83151B–83151B). International Society for Optics and Photonics. doi:10.1117/12.911547

This research was previously published in the International Journal of E-Health and Medical Communications (IJEHMC), 10(3); pages 39-55, copyright year 2019 by IGI Publishing (an imprint of IGI Global).

Chapter 17
Classification of Staphylococcus Aureus FabI Inhibitors by Machine Learning Techniques

Vinicius Gonçalves Maltarollo

Faculty of Pharmacy, Federal University of Minas Gerais, Belo Horizonte, Brazil

ABSTRACT

Enoyl-acyl carrier protein reductase (FabI) is a key enzyme in the fatty acid metabolism of gram-positive bacteria and is considered a potential target for new antibacterial drugs development. Indeed, triclosan is a widely employed antibacterial and AFN-1252 is currently under phase-II clinical trials, both are known as FabI inhibitors. Nowadays, there is an urgent need for new drug discovery due to increasing antibacterial resistance. In the present study, classification models using machine learning techniques were generated to distinguish SaFabI inhibitors from non-inhibitors successfully (e.g., Mathews correlation coefficient values equal to 0.837 and 0.789 calculated with internal and external validations). The interpretation of a selected model indicates that larger compounds, number of N atoms and the distance between central amide and naphthyridinone ring are important to biological activity, corroborating previous studies. Therefore, these obtained information and generated models can be useful for design/ discovery of novel bioactive ligands as potential antibacterial agents.

1. INTRODUCTION

In the last decades, methicillin-resistant *Staphylococcus aureus* (MRSA) infections have been considered a threat to humanity due to their high mortality rate. The lower respiratory tract, skin (followed by necrosis) and bloodstream are the main tissues affected by MRSA infections (Lowy, 2003), and it is considered endemic in several hospitals worldwide (CDC, 2016; Klevens et al., 2006). Moreover, antibiotics resistance is a major public health issue and there is an urgent need for new antibacterial drugs. In this sense, the World Health Organization (WHO) recently released a priority list of microbial infections which needs discovery/design of new drugs treatment (Shrivastava, 2018; Wenzel, 2004).

DOI: 10.4018/978-1-6684-6291-1.ch017

In general, essential pathogen enzymes, which are not present in host cells, are considered good molecular targets for drug design. Furthermore, type II fatty acid biosynthesis (FAS-II) pathway is considered a good source of drug targets and its main difference from mammals (type I) fatty acid biosynthesis is that the last one occurs in a multidomain enzymatic complex (Chirala et al., 1997). The enoyl acyl-carrier-protein (ACP) reductase (FabI) is the key enzyme FAS-II pathway (Heath & Rock, 1995) and have known inhibitors, such as triclosan (McMurry et al., 1998) and AFN-1252 (an antibacterial designed specifically against *S. aureus* including MRSA which is tested in clinical phase-II) (Hafkin et al., 2015). In last decades, several new classes of *S. aureus* FabI (*Sa*FabI) inhibitors have been reported on literature: triclosan analogs (Gerusz et al., 2012), diazaborines (Baldock et al., 1996), 1,4-disubstituted imidazoles (Heerding et al., 2001), indole derivatives (Miller et al., 2002; Seefeld et al., 2001; Seefeld et al., 2003), thiopyridine (Ling et al., 2004), 4-pyridone derivatives (Kitagawa et al., 2007), spiro-naphthyridinones piperidines derivatives (Sampson et al., 2009), tetrahydropyridodiazepines (Ramnauth et al., 2009), azetidine ene-amides derivatives (Takhi et al., 2014), benzimidazole derivatives (Mistry et al., 2016), and N-carboxy pyrrolidine derivatives (Kwon et al., 2018). Most of these inhibitors were successfully tested mainly against wild-type *S. aureus* and MRSA, while a fraction was also tested against other strains and/or bacteria such as triclosan-resistant *S. aureus*, *Escherichia coli*, methicillin-resistant *Staphylococcus epidermidis*, and *Haemophilus influenzae*. Furthermore, selected molecules were tested against *in vivo* infection models indicating then their potential as therapeutic agents. Natural products also have been identified as FabI inhibitors such as luteolin, curcumin (Yao et al., 2010) and jaceosidin, a flavonoid isolated from *Artemisia californica* (Allison et al., 2017).

The diversity of FabI inhibitors in terms of chemical classes provides a large amount of structural information allowing the application of computer-aided drug design (CADD) techniques to study and design inhibitors as new antibacterial agents. Recently, a study combining molecular docking, molecular dynamics and binding free energy to describe the ligand-enzyme interactions was reported (Yang et al., 2017). Quantitative structure-activity relationship (QSAR) studies also were published highlighting the importance of molecular structures and its substituent to FabI inhibition (Lu et al., 2012; Kronenberger et al., 2017). In general, those computational works suggested three main findings: (i) interactions with Tyr-156 and NADPH are essential for inhibition; (ii) hydrophobic interactions at Tyr-146 pocket are important to biological activity and; (iii) H-bond with Ala-95 and π-stacking with NADPH ring A could be responsible for potency (Yang et al., 2017; Lu et al., 2012; Kronenberger et al., 2017).

QSAR models are generated with mathematical methods, which correlate molecular properties and structural features with biological activity, and thus providing direct or indirect insights of binding mode and/or other related molecular mechanisms. This approach has been widely used to predict the biological activities of unknown compounds in virtual screening and scaffold hopping campaigns (Braga et al., 2014; Passeri et al., 2018; Soufan et al., 2018). In the last decades, machine learning techniques (MLT) such as artificial neural networks (ANN), support vector machines (SVM) and random forest (RF) have been applied to generate regression and classification models to predict pharmacodynamics, pharmacokinetics and toxicological endpoints (Soufan et al., 2018; Lima et al., 2016; Gertrudes et al., 2012; Maltarollo et al., 2015). In this work, several MLT models were generated by using different techniques aiming to classify known compounds as *Sa*FabI inhibitors or non-inhibitors.

2. MATERIAL AND METHODS

2.1. Dataset Compounds

One hundred sixty-six different inhibitors of *Sa*FabI were retrieved from literature representing the diversity of scaffolds: 1,4-disubstituted imidazoles, indole derivatives, spiro-naphthyridinones piperidines derivatives, tetrahydropyridodiazepines, and azetidine ene-amides derivatives (Figure 1) . The dataset compounds were tested under the same experimental conditions by monitoring recombinant *Sa*FabI consumption of NADPH via changes in the absorption at 340 nm for 20 min (Heerding et al., 2001; Miller et al., 2002; Seefeld et al., 2001; Seefeld et al., 2003; Sampson et al., 2009; Ramnauth et al., 2009; Takhi et al., 2014). In this work, the compounds were classified as active and inactive according to IC_{50} cut-off equals to 1µM (Davis and Ward, 2014). Two classes of known non-inhibitors according our criteria (Kim et al.; 2015; Zheng et al., 2013) were also included in dataset. Table S1 at Supplementary Material displays all dataset structures and its respective biological activity class.

Two-dimensional molecular structures were generated with Marvin Sketch 15.8.31 (Chemaxon, 2015) followed by 3D most stable conformations which were generated by OMEGA 2.5.1.4 (Hawkins et al., 2010; Hawkins et al., 2016). Protonation states were also corrected for physiological pH (7.4) using fixpka software implemented in QUACPAC 1.6.3.1 (OpenEye Scientific Software, 2016).

2.2. Classification Models Generation Using MLT

Initially, compounds were separated in training and test sets (80% and 20% of total number, respectively) according a hierarchical cluster analysis (HCA) of three main spaces: physicochemical properties (molecular weight, calculated *n*-octanol/water partition coefficient, number of hydrogen bonds acceptor and donors, number of rotatable bonds, sp^3 carbon ratio, and topological polar surface area), structural diversity measured as PubChem fingerprints, and *Sa*FabI inhibition classes. Training set compounds were employed to train decision trees (DT), random forests (RF), multilayer perceptron (MLP), k-nearest neighbors (kNN), naïve Bayes (NB), and support vector machines (SVM) classification models, while test set compounds were employed in external validation.

Previously mentioned physicochemical properties, as well as twelve sets of fingerprints, were calculated with PaDEL-descriptor (Yap, 2011), namely Fingerprinter, Extended Fingerprinter, EState, Graph Only, MACCS, PubChem, Substructure, Substructure Count, Kleklota Roth, Kleklota Roth Count, Atom Pair 2D, and Atom Pair 2D Count. All fingerprints sets were used to generate MLT based models in combination with a variation of intrinsic parameters of each technique. A predefined parameter screening of each employed MLT was performed based on previous works reporting MLT applications (Nanda et al., 2018; Ghunaim & Dichter, 2016; Can et al., 2013; Wahono et al., 2014; Oikawa, 2015). DT models were constructed by varying the minimum number of records per node from 2 to 100. The parameters of RF models were screened heuristically by varying number of levels (from 10 to 50 in steps of 10 levels) and a number of models (from 10,000 to 50,000 in 10k steps). MLP parameters also were screened heuristically by varying a number of layers (from 1 to 5 in steps of 1 layer) and a number of hidden neurons per layer (from 20 to 100 in steps of 20 neurons). kNN models were generated by varying the number of "k" nearest neighbors from 1 to 27 in odd numbers. kNN models with neighbors weighted by distance were also generated using same k parameter variation. NB probability parameter was screened from 0.1 to 5 in 0.1 steps. And finally, SVM models were trained using three different kernels: radial basis function (RBF), hyper tangent (HT), and polynomial (Pol). For each kernel, a set of parameters was screened: for SVM-RBF, sigma varied from 0.5 to 300; for SVM-HT, kappa and delta were varied from 1 to; and 50 for SVM-Pol power, bias and gamma were varied from 1 to 5. Afterwards, overlapping penalty (C parameter) was also varied from 1 to 1500 for all three SVM kernel models. HCA step of training and test set selection, model generation and validation tests were performed by using KNIME 3.4.2 platform (Berthold et al., 2009).

Figure 1. Examples of active and inactive compounds from each series

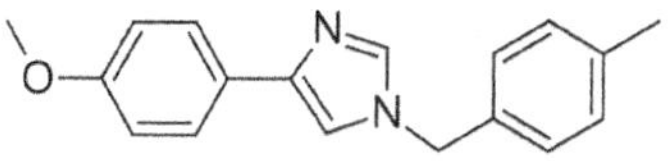

$IC_{50} = 360$ nM

(Heerding et al., 2001)

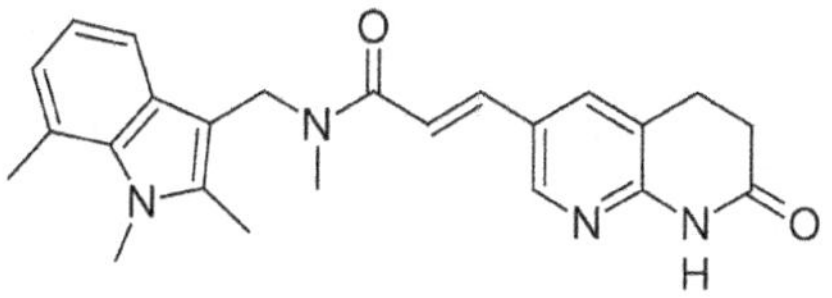

$IC_{50} = 20$ nM

(Seefeld et al., 2003)

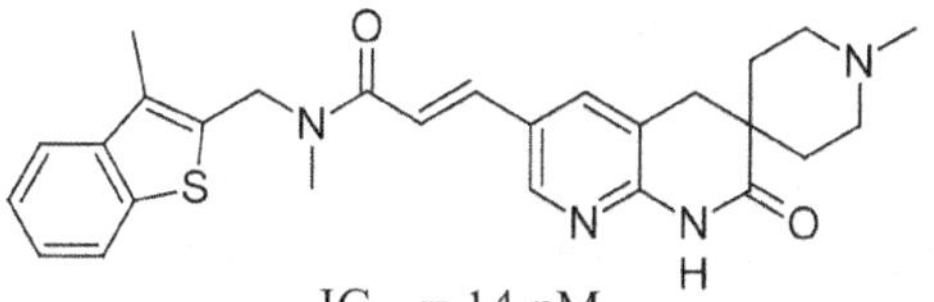

$IC_{50} = 14$ nM

(Sampson et al., 2009)

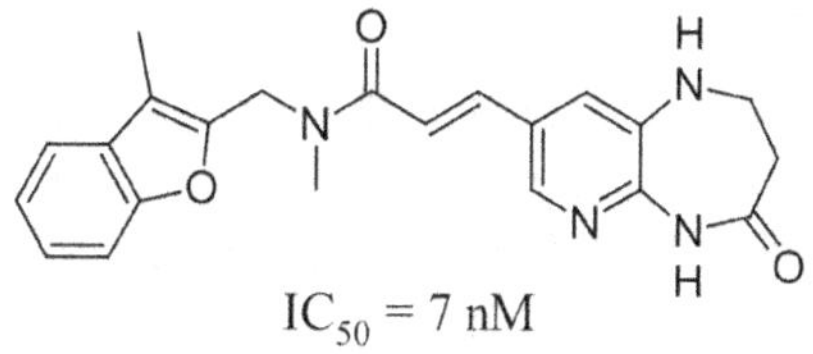

$IC_{50} = 7$ nM

(Ramnauth et al., 2009)

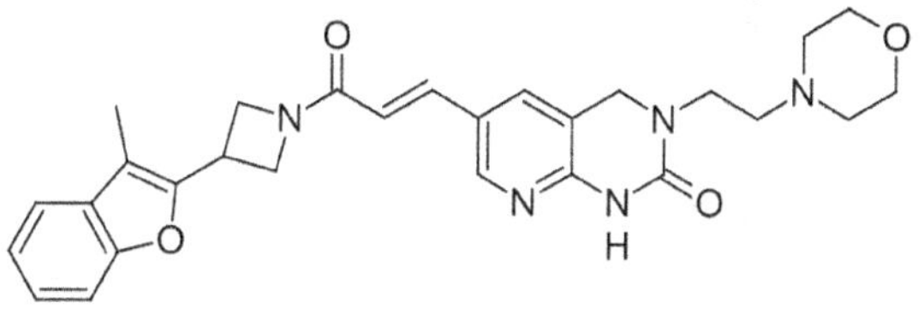

$IC_{50} = 58$ nM

(Takhi et al., 2014)

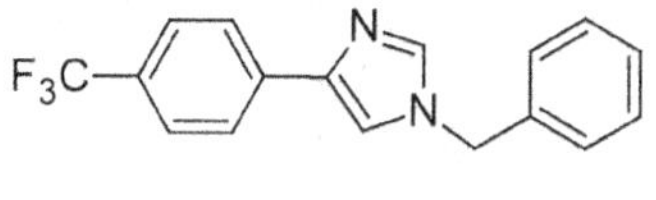

$IC_{50} > 100$ μM

(Heerding et al., 2001)

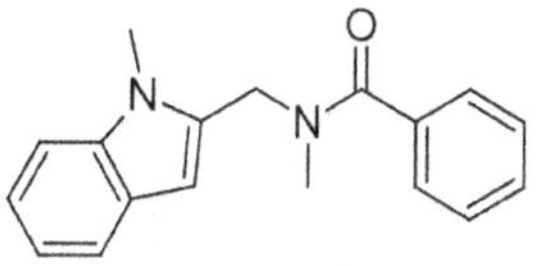

$IC_{50} > 100$ μM

(Miller et al., 2002)

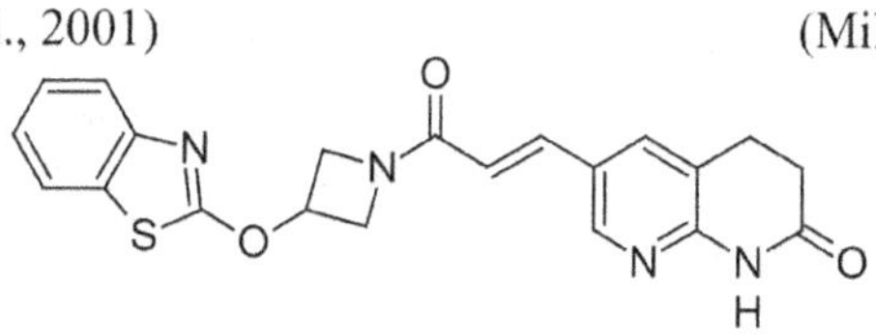

$IC_{50} =$ not determined

(16% inhibition at 1 μM)   (Takhi et al., 2014)

2.3. Validations and Model Selection

All generated models were validated by Mathews Correlation Coefficient (MCC, Equation 1), F1-Score (Equation 2), area under the curve (AUC) of a receiver operating characteristic curve (ROC) and true positive rate (TPR). The four selected validation parameters were obtained for test set compounds (external validation metrics) and in a 5-fold cross-validation (CV) (internal validation metrics) (Roy et al., 2015). For 5-fold CV, five replicates of validation leaving 20% of the training set for internal validation were performed.

$$MCC = \frac{TPxTN - FPxFN}{\sqrt{\left(TP + FP\right)\left(TP + FN\right)\left(TN + FP\right)(TN + FN)}} \tag{1}$$

$$F1Score = \frac{2TP}{2TP - FP - FN} \tag{2}$$

where TP: true positives; TN: true negatives; FP: false positives; and FN: false negatives.

Models were ranked according to MCC calculated with the test set (named extMCC), followed by extF1-Score, extAUC and extTPR. The metrics calculated with 5-fold CV were employed to verify the consistency of models. In other words, when the most predictive model (highest extMCC value) has a low cvMCC, a consistent model was also selected by selecting the highest average metrics (cvMCC + extMCC / 2, called avgMCC) and with the lowest difference (ΔMCC). Models highest external and average MCC values were selected for leave-many-out (LMO) and leave-one-out (LOO) cross-validation.

3. RESULTS AND DISCUSSION

The simultaneous screening of the parameters for the method with fingerprints sets generated in total 4,362 different models. Furthermore, 132 models were generated by DT, 300 each by RF and MLP, 180 each by kNN and kNN weighted methods, 600 by NB, 315 by SVM-RBF, 1,728 by SVM-HT, and 627 by the SVM-Pol method. From all SVM kernels, hyper tangent was the only one which did not produce predictive models and its generated models were not employed in the overlapping penalty screening step.

The best model produced with each technique was selected by the highest MCC value for external validation (Table 1). In some cases, models with highest external predictability also presented very low MCC values calculated with 5-fold CV internal validation. As an example, model 1 generated with DT and Atom Pair fingerprint set presented MCC calculated with test set being equal to 0.837 and MCC calculated with 5-fold cross-validation being equal to 0.494. This result indicates a low consistency of model 1, and a probability of the good external predictability could be obtained by chance. Then, models were also selected by concordance analysis (average and difference values of MCC calculated by internal and external validations).

Table 1. The fingerprint set, parameters, cvMCC and extMCC values of selected models of fingerprint and parameter screening step for each employed MLT

No.	Technique	Fingerprint set	Parameters	cvMCC	extMCC
1	DT	Atom Pair	minimum N records = 50	0.494	0.837
2	DT*	Pubchem	minimum N records = 8	0.791	0.757
3	RF	Klekota Roth	max_levels = 20 / n_models = 50,000	0.753	0.757
4	RF*	Atom Pair Count	max_levels = 50 / n_models = 40,000	0.911	0.717
5	MLP	PubChem	hidden layers = 4 / neurons/layer = 20	0.735	0.789
6	MLP*	PubChem	hidden layers = 2 / neurons/layer = 100	0.751	0.789
7	kNN	Atom Pair	23 neighbors	0.576	0.837
8	kNN *	Atom Pair	3 neighbors	0.684	0.789
9	kNN$_{weighted}$	Atom Pair	27 neighbors	0.578	0.743
10	kNN$_{weighted}$ *	Substructure Count	19 neighbors	0.767	0.701
11	NB	Atom Pair	probability = 0.1	0.409	0.887
12	NB*	Substructure Count	probability = 0.3	0.732	0.743
13	SVM-RBF	Atom Pair Count	sigma = 10 / C_parameter = 10	0.837	0.789
14	SVM-Pol	PubChem	power = 1 / bias = 4 / gamma = 2 / C = 1	0.600	0.789
15	SVM-HT	n.d.	n.d.	n.d.	n.d.

*models selected using consistency analysis (avgMCC and ΔMCC values); n.d.: not determined.

From all 15 presented models in Table 1, the five most predictive models based on avg MCC and ΔMCC (highlighted in grey) were selected for further analysis. From the comparison of models 2, 4, 5, 6 and 13 selected on this first analysis (Figure 2), it is possible to note that all RF, SVM-RBF, DT and MLP selected models are equivalent by the presented metrics. In addition, model 13 generated with SVM-RBF and Atom Pair Count fingerprint set generated the most equilibrated model by comparing selected metrics calculated with 3 validation methods.

From MCC values, RF* model (4) outperformed other models at 5-fold CV and the analysis of F1-score, and AUC indicates that all 5 models are equivalent. In general terms, the comparison of metrics suggests that DT produced a comparable model to RF technique which is a more computational expensive method. Indeed, DT outperformed RF in external validations when comparing TPR and MCC values, but the analysis of ROC curve (Figure 3) indicates that model 2 generated with DT has lower ability to distinguish active from inactive compounds. In early and late stages of ROC curve construction calculated with LOO cross-validation, inactive molecules were classified with high probability than active ones. Model 5 generated with MLP also presented a point of ROC curve under the random classification in external validation. From external validation ROC curve, model 4 (RF*), model 6 (MLP*) and model 13 (SVM-RBF) outperform other two models.

A consensus model considering the average predictions of models 4, 6 and 13 also was generated but did not improve the results (Table 2), indicating then that a single MLT is more suitable to predict *Sa*FabI inhibition than combined with other methods.

Figure 2. Comparison between MCC (A), F1-Score (B), TPR (C) and AUC (D) values calculated with LOO-CV (light grey), 5-fold CV (dark grey) and external validation (black)

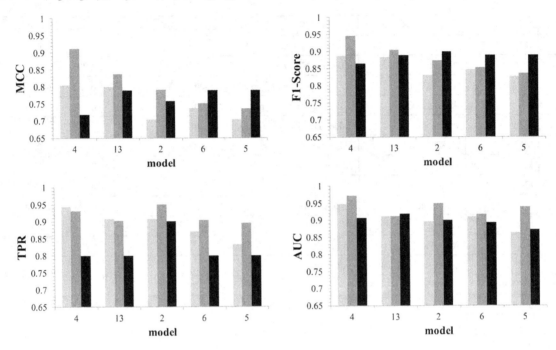

Figure 3. ROC curves of all five selected models generated with LOO-CV and external validation

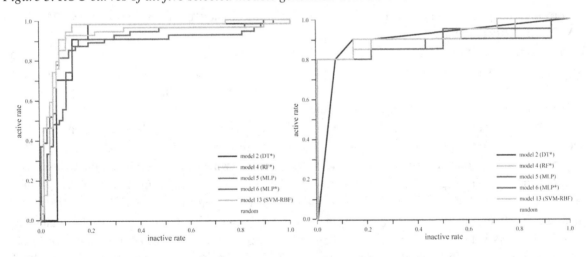

Table 2. Consensus model internal and external validation of calculated metrics

	TPR	MCC	F1-Score	AUC
LOO CV	0.944	0.819	0.895	0.939
5-fold CV	0.893	0.778	0.860	0.938
External Validation	0.800	0.789	0.889	0.918

Finally, confusion matrices were generated for RF*, MLP* and SVM-RBF using training and test set compounds (Table 3). Interestingly, all three selected models presented similar error rates for active compounds at test set (20, 25 and 20% for models 4, 6 and 13, respectively). RF* model presented 7.14% of inactive compounds wrongly predicted at test set compared to perfect predictions of MLP* and SVM-RBF. This finding indicates that all models could predict better inactive compounds than active ones. From internal validation confusion matrices, the SVM-RBF model presented a balanced error rates for inactive/active compounds predictions (10.25 and 9.25%, respectively), the MLP* model predicted inactives better than active compounds (8.97 and 18.51% of errors, respectively) and, in contrast with the test set, the RF* model predicted better active compounds (5.55% of error) than inactive ones (12.82%).

Table 3. Confusion matrices for internal and external validations for models 4, 6 and 13

Observed	Model 4 (RF*)		Model 6 (MLP*)		Model 13 (SVM-RBF)	
	Leave-One Out					
	Inactives	Actives	Inactives	Actives	Inactives	Actives
Inactives	68	10	71	7	70	8
Active	3	51	10	44	5	49
	External Validation					
	Inactives	Actives	Inactives	Actives	Inactives	Actives
Inactives	13	1	14	0	14	0
Active	4	16	5	15	4	16

After all validation steps, the RF model was employed for interpretation due to its more understandable algorithm in comparison with MLP and SVM (Gertrudes et al., 2012). Another important reason of the selection of the RF model is that it was generated with Atom Pair Count fingerprint which is considered a pharmacophore-based fingerprint (Awale & Reymond, 2014) allowing to discuss the influence of structural contribution to the model. The importance of fingerprint bins to RF model were measured by the rate between "the number of times a bin was employed to predict correctly the compound class in a tree root" and "the total number of times it was a candidate in a tree root". Fingerprint bins with a success rate higher than 70% were analyzed (Figure 4A). Then, nine features were selected to this step:

1. C-N atoms at topological distance 1 (D1_C_N);
2. C-C atoms at topological distance 2 (D2_C_C);
3. C-N atoms at topological distance 3 (D3_C_N);
4. N-O atoms at topological distance 6 (D6_N_O);
5. C-N atoms at topological distance 7 (D7_C_N);
6. C-C atoms at topological distance 8 (D8_C_C);
7. C-C atoms at topological distance 9 (D9_C_C);
8. C-C atoms at topological distance 10 (D10_C_C);
9. O-O atoms at topological distance 10 (D10_O_O).

Figure 4. Importance of each selected variable employed on RF model generation estimated by the ratio between a number of times employed feature at tree root and successfully predicted dataset classes (A). The average frequency of each feature for inactive and active compounds (B). Box plot of C_C and C_N distances for inactive and active compounds (C).

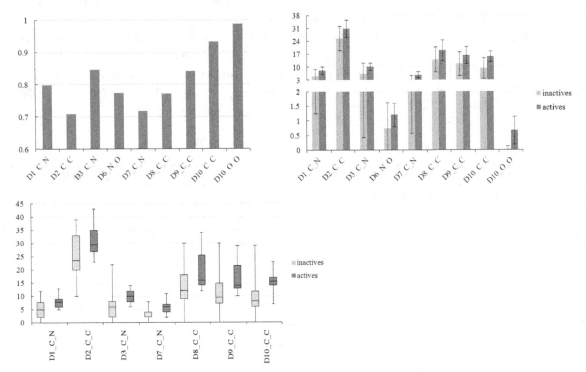

The most important features to distinguish *Sa*FabI inhibitors from non-inhibitors are D10_O_O and D10_C_C (Figure 4A). All the C-C atom pair counts, specifically at large topological distances such as 9 or 10, indicate that larger molecules could tend to be active. This finding agrees with the average values of features frequencies and a box plot of those features for inactive and active compounds (Figure 4B and 4C). In a previous QSAR reported study (Kronenberger et al., 2017), molecules with a molecular weight higher than 360 g/mol are considered actives corroborating current finding. Lu and collaborators (2012) reported that indole ring provides a hydrophobic contribution to FabI inhibitors and naphthyridinone ring has a positively steric contribution to biological activity, also indicating the importance of larger groups (large C_C topological distances). In addition, the indole ring interacts at Tyr-146 hydrophobic pocket which is reported as important to biological activity (Yang et al., 2017; Lu et al., 2012; Kronenberger et al., 2017). Likewise, mutations on Tyr-146 decreased significantly its activity (Mistry et al., 2016; Yao et al., 2013) indicating its importance to enzymatic function and to inhibitors binding.

Similarly, to the first analysis, C-N atom pair counts simply is related to the amount of N atoms in the compound structures, indicating that molecules with a larger number of N atoms trend to be actives. Indeed, aminopyridine derivatives (Figure 5A) were designed by Miller and collaborators (2002) aiming to form ionic interaction with NAD+ phosphate of *E. coli* FabI, but 3D structure obtained by X-ray crystallography revealed that proposed moiety formed hydrogen bonds with Ala-95. Therefore, the importance of C-N pair counts corroborates the literature where N atoms are involved in H-bonds with

Ala-95 region (Miller et al., 2002; Seefeld et al., 2003; Sampson et al., 2009; Ramnauth et al., 2009; Takhi et al., 2014; Lu et al., 2012; Kronenberger et al., 2017).

The D6_N_O feature describes the specific distance between N atom from the naphthyridinone ring (which interacts with Ala-95 residue) and carbonyl O atom from central amide (which interacts with NADPH and Tyr-156, cofactor and catalytic residue of *Sa*FabI active site, respectively) (Figure 5A). The D10_O_O also describes the specific distance between carbonyl O atom from the naphthyridinone ring and carbonyl O atom from central amide (Figure 5B). These two features are more present in active compounds and indicate the importance of these two structures (central amide and naphthyridinone ring) for the potency of FabI inhibition. Indeed, compounds with those scaffolds are the highest active compounds from all employed dataset (Figure 1). Both tyrosine residues (Tyr-146 and Tyr-156) comprise the catalytic triad of *Sa*FabI playing a crucial role in substrate reduction (Lu & Tonge, 2008). In 2016, Schiebel and collaborators (2015) stated that Tyr-157 of *Ec*FabI (here called Tyr-156 Tyr-146 due to *S. aureus* FabI different numbering) is responsible for substrate recognition and positioning of enoyl-ACP double bond for enzymatic reduction. Moreover, it was described that Ala-95 interacts with phosphopantetheine moiety of substrate additionally participating in its recognition (Schiebel et al., 2015). Recently, Daryaee and collaborators (Daryaee et al., 2016) reported the design of a triclosan derivative with increased potency and residence time at the binding pocket of *Sa*FabI by introducing a hydroxypyridinone ring to form H-bond with Ala-95.

Figure 5. Example of N-O and O-O pairs at topological distances 6 (A) and 10 (B), respectively, and its counts for inactive and active compounds (C and D)

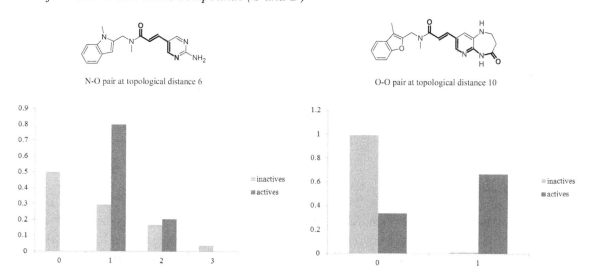

The Atom Pair 2D Count fingerprints do not explicitly indicate functional groups but describe specific distances between two atoms. Those distances could be translated into existing functional groups of dataset compounds, which successfully explain differences in biological activity. Therefore, SVM and RF models which were generated with Atom Pair 2D Count fingerprints as molecular descriptors could be employed as an important tool for the identification of new scaffolds able to forms known interactions of potent *Sa*FabI inhibitors.

For comparison, Wang and collaborators (2014) published a paper, which reported a virtual screening of new antibacterial agents against MRSA. The most predictive model was constructed employed naïve Bayes method and SciTegic extended-connectivity fingerprints LCFP and presented a MCC and AUC values for test set equal to 0.488 and 0.845, respectively. From 56 selected hits, 12 compounds presented activity against MRSA ranging from 4 mg/mL to >256 mg/mL (considered then inactives). The three most predictive models generated in current work presented MCC values equal to 0.717 (RF) and 0.789 (MLP and SVM) suggesting a great potential to virtual screening campaigns applications.

4. CONCLUSION

A dataset containing 166 *Sa*FabI inhibitors and non-inhibitors was employed to generate classification models with MLT and molecular fingerprints. From all employed techniques, RF, SVM and MLP outperformed and were selected for further validations. In addition, a consensus model was constructed but not produced a more predictive model indicating that a single MLT-based model could be preferred due to its simplicity than a consensus one. The RF model was selected for interpretation because the used set of fingerprints (Atom Pair count) is considered a pharmacophore-based fingerprinting method. The interpretation of RF model indicated that larger compounds, the high presence of N atoms and the presence of central amide group at a specific distance from naphthyridinone ring could discriminate active compounds from inactive ones in conformity with literature. Therefore, generated models could be considered an important and powerful tool for the design of new *Sa*FabI inhibitors as potential new antibacterial agents.

ACKNOWLEDGMENT

The author would like to thank CNPq (grant 456984/2014-3), FAPEMIG, CAPES and UFMG for the financial support and OpenEye Scientific Software for OMEGA and QUACPAC academic licenses. I would like to thank Dr Thales Kronenberger for valuable suggestions to the manuscript content.

REFERENCES

Allison, B. J., Allenby, M. C., Bryant, S. S., Min, J. E., Hieromnimon, M., & Joyner, P. M. (2017). Antibacterial activity of fractions from three Chumash medicinal plant extracts and in vitro inhibition of the enzyme enoyl reductase by the flavonoid jaceosidin. *Natural Product Research*, *31*(6), 707–712. doi:10.1080/14786419.2016.1217201 PMID:27482826

Awale, M., & Reymond, J. L. (2014). Atom pair 2D-fingerprints perceive 3D-molecular shape and pharmacophores for very fast virtual screening of ZINC and GDB-17. *Journal of Chemical Information and Modeling*, *54*(7), 1892–1907. doi:10.1021/ci500232g PMID:24988038

Baldock, C., Rafferty, J. B., Sedelnikova, S. E., Baker, P. J., Stuitje, A. R., Slabas, A. R., ... Rice, D. W. (1996). A mechanism of drug action revealed by structural studies of enoyl reductase. *Science*, *274*(5295), 2107–2110. doi:10.1126cience.274.5295.2107 PMID:8953047

Berthold, M. R., Cebron, N., Dill, F., Gabriel, T. R., Kötter, T., Meinl, T., ... Wiswedel, B. (2009). KNIME-the Konstanz information miner: version 2.0 and beyond. *ACM SIGKDD explorations Newsletter, 11*(1), 26-31. doi:10.1145/1656274.1656280

Braga, R. C., Alves, V. M., Silva, A. C., Nascimento, M. N., Silva, F. C., Liao, L. M., & Andrade, C. H. (2014). Virtual screening strategies in medicinal chemistry: The state of the art and current challenges. *Current Topics in Medicinal Chemistry, 14*(16), 1899–1912. doi:10.2174/1568026614666140929120749 PMID:25262801

Can, H., Jianchun, X., Ruide, Z., Juelong, L., Qiliang, Y., & Liqiang, X. (2013, May). A new model for software defect prediction using particle swarm optimization and support vector machine. In *Proceedings of the 2013 25th Chinese Control and Decision Conference (CCDC)* (pp. 4106-4110). IEEE. 10.1109/CCDC.2013.6561670

Centers for Disease Control and Prevention (CDC). (2016). Methicillinresistant Staphylococcus aureus (MRSA). Retrieved from http://www.cdc.gov/mrsa/

Chemaxon. Marvin Sketch 15.8.31 (2015). Retrieved from www.chemaxon.com/products/marvin/

Chirala, S. S., Huang, W. Y., Jayakumar, A., Sakai, K., & Wakil, S. J. (1997). Animal fatty acid synthase: Functional mapping and cloning and expression of the domain I constituent activities. *Proceedings of the National Academy of Sciences of the United States of America, 94*(11), 5588–5593. doi:10.1073/pnas.94.11.5588 PMID:9159116

Daryaee, F., Chang, A., Schiebel, J., Lu, Y., Zhang, Z., Kapilashrami, K., ... Tonge, P. J. (2016). Correlating drug–target kinetics and in vivo pharmacodynamics: Long residence time inhibitors of the FabI enoyl-ACP reductase. *Chemical Science (Cambridge), 7*(9), 5945–5954. doi:10.1039/C6SC01000H PMID:27547299

Davis, A., & Ward, S. E. (Eds.). (2014). *The handbook of medicinal chemistry: principles and practice.* Royal Society of Chemistry.

Gertrudes, J. C., Maltarollo, V. G., Silva, R. A., Oliveira, P. R., Honorio, K. M., & Da Silva, A. B. F. (2012). Machine learning techniques and drug design. *Current Medicinal Chemistry, 19*(25), 4289–4297. doi:10.2174/092986712802884259 PMID:22830342

Gerusz, V., Denis, A., Faivre, F., Bonvin, Y., Oxoby, M., Briet, S., ... Peltier, L. (2012). From triclosan toward the clinic: Discovery of nonbiocidal, potent FabI inhibitors for the treatment of resistant bacteria. *Journal of Medicinal Chemistry, 55*(22), 9914–9928. doi:10.1021/jm301113w PMID:23092194

Ghunaim, H., & Dichter, J. (2016). The Significance of Parameters' Optimization in Fair Benchmarking of Software Defects' Prediction Performances. *International Journal of Advanced Research in Computer Science, 7*(1), 1–7. doi:10.26483/ijarcs.v7i1.2610

Hafkin, B., Kaplan, N., & Murphy, B. (2015). Efficacy and safety of AFN-1252, the first staphylococcus-specific antibacterial agent, in the treatment of ABSSSI, including patients with significant co-morbidities. *Antimicrobial Agents and Chemotherapy*. doi:10.1128/AAC.01741-15

Hawkins, P. C., Skillman, A. G., Warren, G. L., Ellingson, B. A., & Stahl, M. T. (2010). Conformer generation with OMEGA: Algorithm and validation using high quality structures from the Protein Databank and Cambridge Structural Database. *Journal of Chemical Information and Modeling*, *50*(4), 572–584. doi:10.1021/ci100031x PMID:20235588

Hawkins, P. C., Skillman, A. G., Warren, G. L., Ellingson, B. A., & Stahl, M. T. (2016). OMEGA 2.5.1.4. OpenEye Scientific Software. Retrieved from www.eyesopen.com/

Heath, R. J., & Rock, C. O. (1995). Enoyl-acyl carrier protein reductase (fabI) plays a determinant role in completing cycles of fatty acid elongation in Escherichia coli. *The Journal of Biological Chemistry*, *270*(44), 26538–26542. doi:10.1074/jbc.270.44.26538 PMID:7592873

Heerding, D. A., Chan, G., DeWolf, W. E. Jr, Fosberry, A. P., Janson, C. A., Jaworski, D. D., ... Qiu, X. (2001). 1, 4-Disubstituted imidazoles are potential antibacterial agents functioning as inhibitors of enoyl acyl carrier protein reductase (FabI). *Bioorganic & Medicinal Chemistry Letters*, *11*(16), 2061–2065. doi:10.1016/S0960-894X(01)00404-8 PMID:11514139

Kim, Y. G., Seo, J. H., Kwak, J. H., & Shin, K. J. (2015). Discovery of a potent enoyl-acyl carrier protein reductase (FabI) inhibitor suitable for antistaphylococcal agent. *Bioorganic & Medicinal Chemistry Letters*, *25*(20), 4481–4486. doi:10.1016/j.bmcl.2015.08.077 PMID:26343826

Kitagawa, H., Kumura, K., Takahata, S., Iida, M., & Atsumi, K. (2007). 4-Pyridone derivatives as new inhibitors of bacterial enoyl-ACP reductase FabI. *Bioorganic & Medicinal Chemistry*, *15*(2), 1106–1116. doi:10.1016/j.bmc.2006.10.012 PMID:17095231

Klevens, R. M., Edwards, J. R., Tenover, F. C., McDonald, L. C., Horan, T., & Gaynes, R. (2006). Changes in the epidemiology of methicillin-resistant Staphylococcus aureus in intensive care units in US hospitals, 1992–2003. *Clinical Infectious Diseases*, *42*(3), 389–391. doi:10.1086/499367 PMID:16392087

Kronenberger, T., Asse, L. R. Jr, Wrenger, C., Trossini, G. H. G., Honorio, K. M., & Maltarollo, V. G. (2017). Studies of Staphylococcus aureus FabI inhibitors: Fragment-based approach based on holographic structure–activity relationship analyses. *Future Medicinal Chemistry*, *9*(2), 135–151. doi:10.4155/fmc-2016-0179

Kwon, J., Mistry, T., Ren, J., Johnson, M. E., & Mehboob, S. (2018). A novel series of enoyl reductase inhibitors targeting the ESKAPE pathogens, Staphylococcus aureus and Acinetobacter baumannii. *Bioorganic & Medicinal Chemistry*, *26*(1), 65–76. doi:10.1016/j.bmc.2017.11.018 PMID:29162308

Lima, A. N., Philot, E. A., Trossini, G. H. G., Scott, L. P. B., Maltarollo, V. G., & Honorio, K. M. (2016). Use of machine learning approaches for novel drug discovery. *Expert Opinion on Drug Discovery*, *11*(3), 225–239. doi:10.1517/17460441.2016.1146250 PMID:26814169

Ling, L. L., Xian, J., Ali, S., Geng, B., Fan, J., Mills, D. M., ... Xiang, Y. (2004). Identification and characterization of inhibitors of bacterial enoyl-acyl carrier protein reductase. *Antimicrobial Agents and Chemotherapy*, *48*(5), 1541–1547. doi:10.1128/AAC.48.5.1541-1547.2004 PMID:15105103

Lowy, F. D. (2003). Antimicrobial resistance: The example of Staphylococcus aureus. *The Journal of Clinical Investigation*, *111*(9), 1265–1273. doi:10.1172/JCI18535 PMID:12727914

Lu, H., & Tonge, P. J. (2008). Inhibitors of FabI, an enzyme drug target in the bacterial fatty acid biosynthesis pathway. *Accounts of Chemical Research*, *41*(1), 11–20. doi:10.1021/ar700156e PMID:18193820

Lu, X., Lv, M., Huang, K., Ding, K., & You, Q. (2012). Pharmacophore and molecular docking guided 3D-QSAR study of bacterial enoyl-ACP reductase (FabI) inhibitors. *International Journal of Molecular Sciences*, *13*(6), 6620–6638. doi:10.3390/ijms13066620 PMID:22837653

Maltarollo, V. G., Gertrudes, J. C., Oliveira, P. R., & Honorio, K. M. (2015). Applying machine learning techniques for ADME-Tox prediction: A review. *Expert Opinion on Drug Metabolism & Toxicology*, *11*(2), 259–271. doi:10.1517/17425255.2015.980814 PMID:25440524

McMurry, L. M., Oethinger, M., & Levy, S. B. (1998). Triclosan targets lipid synthesis. *Nature*, *394*(6693), 531–532. doi:10.1038/28970 PMID:9707111

Miller, W. H., Seefeld, M. A., Newlander, K. A., Uzinskas, I. N., Burgess, W. J., Heerding, D. A., ... Moore, T. D. (2002). Discovery of aminopyridine-based inhibitors of bacterial enoyl-ACP reductase (FabI). *Journal of Medicinal Chemistry*, *45*(15), 3246–3256. doi:10.1021/jm020050+ PMID:12109908

Mistry, T. L., Truong, L., Ghosh, A. K., Johnson, M. E., & Mehboob, S. (2016). Benzimidazole-based FabI inhibitors: A promising novel scaffold for anti-staphylococcal drug development. *ACS Infectious Diseases*, *3*(1), 54–61. doi:10.1021/acsinfecdis.6b00123 PMID:27756129

Nanda, M. A., Seminar, K. B., Nandika, D., & Maddu, A. (2018). A comparison study of kernel functions in the support vector machine and its application for termite detection. *Information*, *9*(1), 5. doi:10.3390/info9010005

Oikawa, R. T. (2015). Reconhecimento do Padrão Pluvial na cidade de Presidente Prudente-SP através de rede neural artificial [Master Thesis]. Universidade do Oeste Paulista. Retrieved from http://bdtd.unoeste.br:8080/tede/handle/tede/491

OpenEye Scientific Software. (2016). QUACPAC 1.6.3.1: Santa Fe, NM. Retrieved from www.eyesopen.com/

Passeri, G. I., Trisciuzzi, D., Alberga, D., Siragusa, L., Leonetti, F., Mangiatordi, G. F., & Nicolotti, O. (2018). Strategies of virtual screening in medicinal chemistry. *International Journal of Quantitative Structure-Property Relationships*, *3*(1), 134–160. doi:10.4018/IJQSPR.2018010108

Ramnauth, J., Surman, M. D., Sampson, P. B., Forrest, B., Wilson, J., Freeman, E., ... Awrey, D. E. (2009). 2, 3, 4, 5-Tetrahydro-1H-pyrido [2, 3-b and e][1, 4] diazepines as inhibitors of the bacterial enoyl ACP reductase, FabI. *Bioorganic & Medicinal Chemistry Letters*, *19*(18), 5359–5362. doi:10.1016/j.bmcl.2009.07.094 PMID:19682900

Roy, K., Kar, S., & Das, R. N. (2015). Statistical methods in QSAR/QSPR. In *A primer on QSAR/QSPR modeling* (pp. 37–59). Cham: Springer. doi:10.1007/978-3-319-17281-1_2

Sampson, P. B., Picard, C., Handerson, S., McGrath, T. E., Domagala, M., Leeson, A., ... Kaplan, N. (2009). Spiro-naphthyridinone piperidines as inhibitors of S. aureus and E. coli enoyl-ACP reductase (FabI). *Bioorganic & Medicinal Chemistry Letters*, *19*(18), 5355–5358. doi:10.1016/j.bmcl.2009.07.129 PMID:19682901

Schiebel, J., Chang, A., Merget, B., Bommineni, G. R., Yu, W., Spagnuolo, L. A., ... Sotriffer, C. A. (2015). An ordered water channel in Staphylococcus aureus FabI: Unraveling the mechanism of substrate recognition and reduction. *Biochemistry*, *54*(10), 1943–1955. doi:10.1021/bi5014358 PMID:25706582

Seefeld, M. A., Miller, W. H., Newlander, K. A., Burgess, W. J., DeWolf, W. E., Elkins, P. A., ... Manley, P. J. (2003). Indole naphthyridinones as inhibitors of bacterial enoyl-ACP reductases FabI and FabK. *Journal of Medicinal Chemistry*, *46*(9), 1627–1635. doi:10.1021/jm0204035 PMID:12699381

Seefeld, M. A., Miller, W. H., Newlander, K. A., Burgess, W. J., Payne, D. J., Rittenhouse, S. F., ... Janson, C. A. (2001). Inhibitors of bacterial enoyl acyl carrier protein reductase (FabI): 2, 9-disubstituted 1, 2, 3, 4-tetrahydropyrido [3, 4-b] indoles as potential antibacterial agents. *Bioorganic & Medicinal Chemistry Letters*, *11*(17), 2241–2244. doi:10.1016/S0960-894X(01)00405-X PMID:11527706

Shrivastava, S. R., Shrivastava, P. S., & Ramasamy, J. (2018). World health organization releases global priority list of antibiotic-resistant bacteria to guide research, discovery, and development of new antibiotics. *Journal of Medical Society*, *32*(1), 76. doi:10.4103/jms.jms_25_17

Soufan, O., Ba-alawi, W., Magana-Mora, A., Essack, M., & Bajic, V. B. (2018). DPubChem: A web tool for QSAR modeling and high-throughput virtual screening. *Scientific Reports*, *8*(1), 9110. doi:10.103841598-018-27495-x PMID:29904147

Takhi, M., Sreenivas, K., Reddy, C. K., Munikumar, M., Praveena, K., Sudheer, P., ... Reddy, Y. R. (2014). Discovery of azetidine based ene-amides as potent bacterial enoyl ACP reductase (FabI) inhibitors. *European Journal of Medicinal Chemistry*, *84*, 382–394. doi:10.1016/j.ejmech.2014.07.036 PMID:25036796

Wahono, R. S., Suryana, N., & Ahmad, S. (2014). Metaheuristic optimization based feature selection for software defect prediction. *Journal of Software*, *9*(5), 1324–1333. doi:10.4304/jsw.9.5.1324-1333

Wang, L., Le, X., Li, L., Ju, Y., Lin, Z., Gu, Q., & Xu, J. (2014). Discovering new agents active against methicillin-resistant Staphylococcus aureus with ligand-based approaches. *Journal of Chemical Information and Modeling*, *54*(11), 3186–3197. doi:10.1021/ci500253q PMID:25375651

Wenzel, R. P. (2004). The antibiotic pipeline—Challenges, costs, and values. *The New England Journal of Medicine*, *351*(6), 523–526. doi:10.1056/NEJMp048093 PMID:15295041

Yang, X., Lu, J., Ying, M., Mu, J., Li, P., & Liu, Y. (2017). Docking and molecular dynamics studies on triclosan derivatives binding to FabI. *Journal of Molecular Modeling*, *23*(1), 25. doi:10.100700894-016-3192-9 PMID:28064376

Yao, J., Maxwell, J. B., & Rock, C. O. (2013). Resistance to AFN-1252 arises from missense mutations in Staphylococcus aureus enoyl-acyl carrier protein reductase (FabI). *The Journal of Biological Chemistry*. doi:10.1074/jbc.M113.512905

Yao, J., Zhang, Q., Min, J., He, J., & Yu, Z. (2010). Novel enoyl-ACP reductase (FabI) potential inhibitors of Escherichia coli from Chinese medicine monomers. *Bioorganic & Medicinal Chemistry Letters*, *20*(1), 56–59. doi:10.1016/j.bmcl.2009.11.042 PMID:19959361

Yap, C. W. (2011). PaDEL-descriptor: An open source software to calculate molecular descriptors and fingerprints. *Journal of Computational Chemistry*, *32*(7), 1466–1474. doi:10.1002/jcc.21707 PMID:21425294

Zheng, C. J., Sohn, M. J., Lee, S., & Kim, W. G. (2013). Meleagrin, a new FabI inhibitor from Penicillium chryosogenum with at least one additional mode of action. *PLoS One*, *8*(11), e78922. doi:10.1371/journal.pone.0078922 PMID:24312171

This research was previously published in the International Journal of Quantitative Structure-Property Relationships (IJQSPR), 4(4); pages 1-14, copyright year 2019 by IGI Publishing (an imprint of IGI Global).

Chapter 18

Optimum Design of Carbon Fiber–Reinforced Polymer (CFRP) Beams for Shear Capacity via Machine Learning Methods:
Optimum Prediction Methods on Advance Ensemble Algorithms – Bagging Combinations

Melda Yucel

 https://orcid.org/0000-0002-2583-8630
Istanbul University-Cerrahpaşa, Turkey

Aylin Ece Kayabekir
Istanbul University-Cerrahpaşa, Turkey

Sinan Melih Nigdeli
Istanbul University-Cerrahpaşa, Turkey

Gebrail Bekdaş
Istanbul University-Cerrahpaşa, Turkey

ABSTRACT

In this chapter, an application for demonstrating the predictive success and error performance of ensemble methods combined via various machine learning and artificial intelligence algorithms and techniques was performed. For this reason, two single methods were selected, and combination models with a Bagging ensemble were constructed and operated with the goal of optimally designing concrete beams covering with carbon-fiber-reinforced polymers (CFRP) by ensuring the determination of the design variables. The first part was an optimization problem and method composing an advanced bio-inspired

DOI: 10.4018/978-1-6684-6291-1.ch018

metaheuristic called the Jaya algorithm. Machine learning prediction methods and their operation logics were detailed. Performance evaluations and error indicators were represented for the prediction models. In the last part, performed prediction applications and created models were introduced. Also, the obtained predictive success of the main model, as generated with optimization results, was utilized to determine the optimal predictions of the test models.

INTRODUCTION

Artificial Intelligence (AI) methods are effective in solving multidisciplinary engineering problems. Also, AI methods can be trained with optimization methodologies to provide the prediction of optimization results. In this chapter, the authors present a study showing the application of the predictive success and error performance of ensemble methods employing various machine learning and artificial intelligence algorithms. Two single methods were selected, and combination models with a Bagging ensemble were constructed. The optimal design is that of using concrete beams with a covering of carbon-fiber-reinforced polymers (CFRP) by ensuring the determination of design variables for the minimization of CFRP material in order to increase the shear capacity of the beam. For an RC beam using CFRP, the width, spacing, and application angle of the CFRP strip are the design variables. Their optimization has previously been done (Kayabekir, Sayin, Bekdas, & Nigdeli, 2017; Kayabekir, Sayin, Nigdeli, & Bekdas, 2017; Kayabekir, Sayin, Bekdas, & Nigdeli, 2018; Kayabekir, Bekdaş, Nigdeli, & Temür, 2018) by using several metaheuristic algorithms—namely, Flower Pollination Algorithm (FPA) (Yang, 2012), Teaching-Learning-Based Optimization (TLBO) (Rao, Savsani, & Vakharia, 2011), and Jaya Algorithm (JA) (Rao, 2016).

CARBON-FIBER-REINFORCED POLYMER (CFRP) BEAM MODEL

The Optimization Problem

The capacity of reinforced concrete elements may be insufficient due to reasons such as a change in the purpose of use of the structure (for examples, adding a new floor to the existing structure or retrofitting it for a capacity increase due to earthquake force mitigation; etc.). In such cases, various retrofit methods are utilized to increase the shear force, flexural moment, or axial force capacities. These methods generally necessitate the partial destruction of existing members; and the use of such structures may not always be possible in such case. Furthermore, since the total weight and rigidity of the structure are changed, a structural re-analysis is required. Another option is to use carbon-fiber-reinforced polymer (CFRP), having a linear deformation behavior with a large strain capacity, without changing the existing behavior of the structure. This method can be easily applied and provides for the use of the structure during its application.

In this chapter, optimal carbon-fiber-reinforced polymer design is presented with the goal of increasing the shear capacity of T-shaped RC beam members. This is done by considering the rules of regulation ACI 318 (Building Code Requirements for Structural Concrete); and by following various advanced machine learning applications that were carried out. It was likewise done by determining these designs rapidly and effectively in a short time—with the purpose of preventing the loss of effort, time, and cost while generating structural designs. In the optimization process, the Jaya Algorithm (JA)—a metaheuristic method—was utilized. Objective function was defined as being the minimization of the required CFRP area per meter. In other words, optimal design variables providing the minimum required CFRP area per meter and providing for structural safety are searched. The mentioned design variables are the spacing (s_f), width (w_f), and angle of CFRP strips (β). Structural model and design variables of the problem are shown in Figure 1.

Figure 1. Structural model and design variables of the problem
(Khalifa & Nanni, 2000)

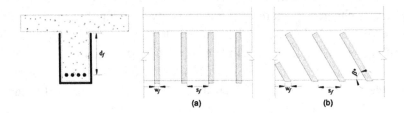

(a)   (b)

In the figure, d_f represents the depth of beam, where the wrapping of CFRP is applied. It can be calculated as

$$d_f = d - h_f \tag{1}$$

in which h_f represents the thickness of the slab, and d represents the effective depth of the beam.

In addition, objective function of the problem can be written as in Equation (2). Here, the total area covered with CFRP within the beam unit length (m), which is defined by A, is minimized.

$$A = \frac{w_f \left(\dfrac{2d_f}{\sin^2} + b_w \right)}{s_f} \, x1000 \tag{2}$$

Here, b_w represents the breadth of the beam.

Design constraints are determined according to the regulation of ACI 318. These constraints can be given as given in Eqs. (3-5);

$$g_1(x) : s_f \leq \frac{d}{4} \tag{3}$$

$$g_2(x) : 0.7R \frac{(2t_f w_f f_{fe})(\sin^2 + \cos^2) d_f}{s_f + w_f} > V_{add} \tag{4}$$

$$g_3\left(x\right):\frac{\left(2t_f w_f f_{fe}\right)\left(\sin^2+\cos^2\right)}{s_f+w_f}\leq\frac{2\sqrt{f'_c}b_w d}{3}-V_s \tag{5}$$

In these equations, V_{add}, R, t_f, f_{fe}, f'_c, and V_s indicate the required additional shear capacity, the reduction factor, the thickness of the CFRP, the effective tensile strength of the CFRP, and the compression strength of the concrete total shear force capacity of the rebar, respectively. In addition, the design constants and ranges of the design variables are summarized in Table 1.

Table 1. Design constants and variables

Components		Definition	Symbol	Unit	Value
Design constants		Breadth of the beam section	b_w	mm	200–500
		Height of the beam section	h	mm	300–800
		Effective depth of the beam	d	mm	0.9h
		Thickness of the CFRP	t_f	mm	0.165
		Reduction factor	R	mm	0.5
		Thickness of the slab	h_f	-	80–120
		Compression strength of the concrete	f'_c	MPa	20
		Effective tensile strength of the CFRP	f_{fe}	MPa	3790
		Additional shear force	V_{add}	kN	50–200
		Shear force capacity of the rebar	V_s	kN	50
Design variables		Width of the CFRP	w_f	mm	10–1000
		Spacing between CFRPs	s_f	mm	0–d/4
		Covering angle of the CFRP	β	°	0–90

Metaheuristic Method for Optimization: Jaya Algorithm

Jaya was originally a Sanskrit word, and its meaning (in English) is "victory." After testing the algorithm, Rao (2016) probably was the one who gave it this name because of its having achieved such successful results. The most important feature of this algorithm is that it does not require the user to enter any user-defined parameters. For that reason, it is easy to apply it to optimization problems. Similarly, as with other metaheuristics, the optimization process of Jaya can be explained in five steps. These steps are summarized in following section.

In the first step—that of optimization—the design constants, the ranges of the design variables, and population and termination criterion are determined. In this optimization problem, termination criterion is defined as being the maximum iteration number.

In the second step, the initial solution matrix—including candidate solution vectors (in other words, a set of candidate solutions)—is generated. These candidate solution vectors include randomly generated design variables. The initial solution matrix can be indicated symbolically as follows, in Equation (6).

$$CL = \begin{bmatrix} X_{1,1} & X_{1,2} & \cdots & X_{1,vn} \\ X_{2,1} & X_{2,2} & \cdots & X_{2,vn} \\ \cdot & \cdot & \cdots & \cdot \\ \cdot & \cdot & \cdots & \cdot \\ X_{pn-1,1} & X_{pn-1,2} & \cdots & X_{pn-1,vn} \\ X_{pn,1} & X_{pn,2} & \cdots & X_{pn,vn} \end{bmatrix} \tag{6}$$

Each column of the *CL* matrix represents a candidate solution set. The total number of these candidate solutions is a user-defined value, and it is called a vector number (*vn*). In the matrix, $X_{i,j}$ characterizes the value of the ith design variable in the jth solution vector. The values of the design variables are generated via Equation (7).

$$X_I = X_{I(\min)} + rand(X_{I(\max)} - X_{I(\min)}) \tag{7}$$

$X_{i(min)}$ and $X_{i(max)}$ indicate the ultimate limits of the design variables. Rand is a function producing a random number between 0 and 1.

In the third step, the objective function is calculated (Equation (2)) for each of candidate solution vectors. The calculated objective function values are stored in a vector for later comparison. Also, candidate solution vectors must provide design constraints in order to ensure structural safety. Therefore, for candidate solutions that do not provide design constraints, the objective function is punished with very large values.

These first three steps are similar for optimization processes of all metaheuristic algorithms. The differences start with the fourth step. In this step, a new solution matrix is generated, considering the rules of the algorithm. According to the rules of the Jaya algorithm, new values of design variables are generated by utilizing the best and worst solution vectors in the existing solution matrix.

The best and worst solution vectors are determined according to values of the objective function. In this optimization problem, since the design of the CFRP having a minimum area for 1 meter is searched for, the best solution represents a candidate solution vector providing a minimum value of the objective function. The worst solution represents a candidate solution vector giving a maximum value of the objective function. This situation can be expressed numerically via Equation (8).

$$X_{i,j}^{t+1} = X_{i,j}^t + rand\left(g^* - \left|X_{i,j}^t\right|\right) - rand\left(g^w - \left|X_{i,j}^t\right|\right) \tag{8}$$

Here, $X_{i,j}^{t+1}$, $X_{i,j}^t$ and t represent a new (or a next) candidate design variable, an existing (or an old) design variable, and an iteration number, respectively. On the other hand, g* indicates the values of ith design variables in the best candidate solution vector; and g^w indicates the values of ith design variables in the worst candidate solution vector.

New candidate solution vectors (including new design variables) which are generated are stored in a matrix. Candidate solutions that do not meet design constraints are penalized with large objective function values, as in Step Three. Then, comparisons are done between the existing solution matrix and the new solution matrix. This part of the comparison constitutes the last step of the optimization process. In this step, if the new candidate solution or solutions provides a better solution, the existing solution matrix is modified with a new candidate solution. Otherwise, no changes are made in the existing solution matrix.

The last two steps are repeated until the provision of termination criterion and the optimization process of JA can be summarized as follows, in Figure 2.

Figure 2. The optimization process of JA

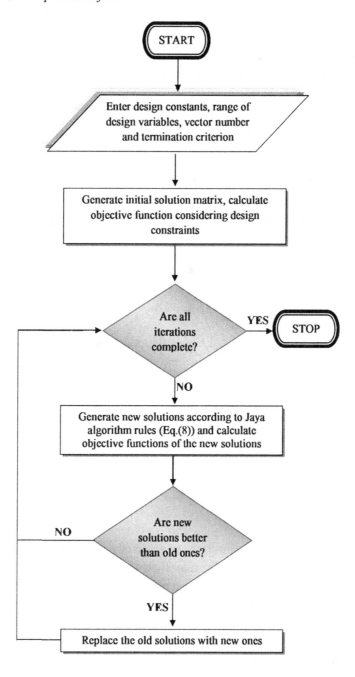

MACHINE LEARNING METHODS

Multilayer Perceptrons (MLP)

Artificial Neural Networks (ANNs) can be seen as being a machine learning method that ensures the mimesis of various behaviors unique to the human brain, in regard to different systems (Yucel, Bekdaş, Nigdeli & Sevgen, 2019). There are so many models and types of ANNs in the literature. One such ANN is that of multilayer perceptrons (MLPs), which have input, output, and one or more hidden layers.

These MLP neural networks can learn from samples. The input layer, hidden layers, and output layer includes input nodes, calculation nodes, and output node, respectively. The input and output nodes store the data samples and result predictions, respectively (Chou, Tsai, Pham & Lu, 2014). In these respects, MLPs have an ability to determine the effects of input parameters onto output parameters. This can result in the occurrence of a map of relation for input-output parameters (Maimon & Rokach, 2010). A multilayer perceptron structure is presented in Figure 3 for the prediction of two different FRP beam design outputs in this study.

Figure 3. Multilayer perceptron model generated for optimal design variables

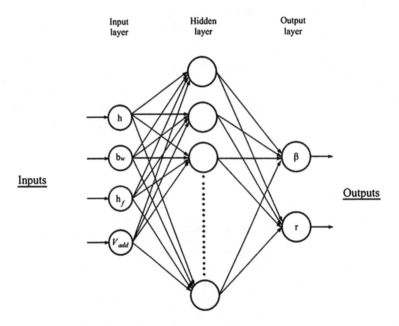

While realizing this process, a set of training stages is carried out with different algorithms with respect to the aim of determining the output result. The reason for this is the input data that can be nonlinear or unsuitable to operate by using a specific curve or an equation for predicting the output values directly. With this aim, MLP are trained by means of numerous input samples.

In this issue, an algorithm called back-propagation, which is one of the most frequently preferred algorithms nowadays, was proposed by G. E. Hinton, Rumelhart and R. O. Williams in 1986 in order to train neural networks (Raza & Khosravi, 2015).

This training process is realized after the spreading of input data, as a feed-forward mechanism. At this stage, firstly, there is an independent multiplication of each input with the connection weights belonging to nodes within the next layer; and a summation of these multiplications is obtained.

Moreover, this summation is carried out with the sum function (Σ), which benefits to determine the net input for any single node. Net input (net$_j$) is obtained as a combination of the weighted summation and the bias value (b) for any node j as follows, in Equation (9). Also, activation function (f) is beneficial for the calculation of output prediction by means of processing the net input (Equation (10)). Obtained prediction output and real output differences are named as being an error, and this value is used to update the connection weights via transference to the general network. These components and operations can be seen in Figure 3.

In addition to this, expressed in these equations and in Figure 4, i is input node, in other words, outputs existing in previous layer; j is current node that targets the determination of its net input; W_{ij} represents the connection weights between nodes i and j; X_i is the output value from the previous layer, and α is a constant value which ensures the function gradient (Topçu & Saridemir, 2008).

$$net_j = \sum_{i=1}^{n} W_{ij} X_i + b \tag{9}$$

$$f\left(net_j\right) = \frac{1}{1 + e^{-\alpha net_j}} \tag{10}$$

Figure 4. Calculation of the output for any node via activation of the sigmoid function
(Topçu & Saridemir, 2008)

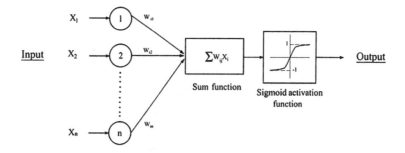

On the other hand, this activation function expressed in the above equation is a sigmoid/logistic function and is known as being a transfer function, too. Additionally, there are various types of functions such as a hyperbolic tangent, sine, cosine, linear, or identity function. However, the most-used one from among these is the sigmoid function, in virtue of advantages related to nonlinearity and good simulation with respect to the operation of human brain neurons intended for prediction applications (Maimon & Rokach, 2010).

Random Tree

The random tree method is a decision tree algorithm. In this respect, it is an algorithm applied to obtain an ultimate prediction result by splitting the tree according to defined labels of parameters via decisions made in the direction of the values of these labels. On the other hand, this algorithm is generally applied for generating random forest ensembles. Therefore, each of the random trees can be considered as being a member existing in forest. This decision tree algorithm is called Random Tree. It can be preferred/intended for the application of solving classification and regression problems. It was proposed by Leo Breiman and Adele Cutler (Kalmegh, 2015). During the constructing of the random decision tree model, root and internal labels must first be determined in order to branch the tree structure. However, there is no obligation to do that in an analysis of the problem data for the identification of attributes, which will be taking part in the interior nodes of the decision tree, because of the renewable and exchangeable structure of the tree (Jagannathan, Pillaipakkamnatt & Wright, 2009).

Bagging Learners

Bagging method is one of the independent ensemble learning techniques developed by Breiman, and its name occurred with respect to a combination of bootstrap and aggregation approaches (Cichosz, 2015; Skurichina & Duin, 2002). Ensemble models have an ability related to generalizing learning due to making mistakes less than that which base learners perform independently (Jagannathan et al., 2009).

This method applies an approach which is related to the fact that one basis prediction value is obtained by integrating the output results produced by different learner methods or classifiers, with the purpose of enhancing prediction accuracy (Rokach & Maimon, 2015). In this respect, this approach is carried out so that the major dataset is split into different subgroups by those data samples which are selected randomly. Hence, these can include the same data more than once. Also, these sub data samples can be trained via any method, which is named as the basic/main learning algorithm or classifier.

This random selection, which is realized for its determination of data belonging to K different subgroups, is performed by means of sampling with replacement (putting sampled data back into the dataset) of each data sample from the training set composed of n samples. As has been said before, some data can be selected many times. Therefore, some of these may not take part in the training set. On the other hand, each basic learner method in ensemble is trained with training sets/subgroups including n samples different from each other, and the results (predictions) are combined with voting of majority (Kılınç, Borandağ, Yücalar, Özçift & Bozyiğit, 2015). However, these prediction results of sub data groups can be combined by using the other rules, too (Skurichina & Duin, 2002). A chart about prediction process via the Bagging method is given as Figure 5.

PREDICTION AND ERROR EVALUATION INDICATORS

After performing output prediction, the evaluation of obtained values in comparison with real data is required. The aim of this operation is that validation of accuracy, reliability, and precision belonging to the generated prediction model is provided. By means of this, the possibility and measure of making mistakes by the prediction model can be observed, and the success and performance of the model can be sensed more clearly.

Figure 5. Prediction process via the bagging method

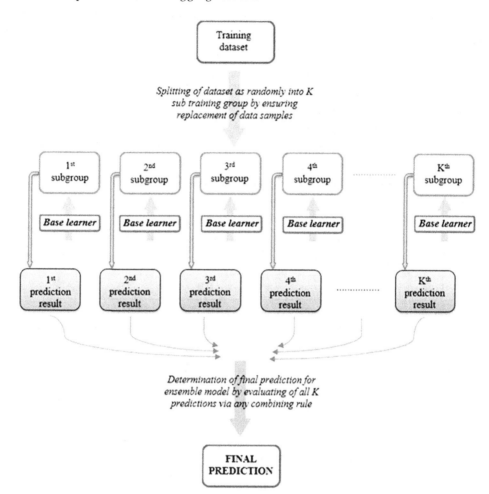

All of the presented evaluation criteria and error performance indicators, their formulations, and their components acting as these indicators are shown in Table 2.

Correlation Coefficient (R)

The *Correlation Coefficient (R)* metric is a measure of compatibility between real/actual and predicted values belonging to data samples. It shows how much these values are close or similar to each other. This coefficient value can take the form of values between -1 and 1. It can be said that if R is 0, then there is no similarity of values. In addition, if its value is 1 or close to 1, there is strong fitness between the actual and predicted results of the data.

Table 2. Error performance indicators and various details

Performance Indicator	Abbreviation	Formulation	Components
Correlation Coefficient	R	$$\dfrac{n\sum_{i=1}^{n}a_ip_i - \sum - \left(\sum_{i=1}^{n}a_i\right)\left(\sum_{i=1}^{n}p_i\right)}{\sqrt{n\left(\sum_{i=1}^{n}a_i^2\right)-\left(\sum_{i=1}^{n}a_i\right)^2}-\sqrt{n\left(\sum_{i=1}^{n}p_i^2\right)-\left(\sum_{i=1}^{n}p_i\right)^2}}$$	a_i: i[th] actual value p_i: i[th] predicted value m_a: mean of the actual data n: data number
Mean Absolute Error	MAE	$$\frac{1}{n}\sum_{i=1}^{n}\left|a_i - p_i\right|$$	
Mean Square Error	MSE	$$\frac{1}{n}\sum_{i=1}^{n}\left(p_i - a_i\right)^2$$	
Root Mean Square Error	RMSE	$$\sqrt{\frac{1}{n}\sum_{i=1}^{n}\left(p_i - a_i\right)^2}$$	
Relative Absolute Error	RAE	$$\frac{\sum_{i=1}^{n}\left|p_i - a_i\right|}{\sum_{i=1}^{n}\left|m_a - a_i\right|}$$	
Root Relative Square Error	RRSE	$$\sqrt{\frac{\sum_{i=1}^{n}\left(p_i - a_i\right)^2}{\sum_{i=1}^{n}\left(m_a - a_i\right)^2}}$$	

Mean Absolute Error (MAE)

Absolute error means the absolute value of the error occurring between the actual value and the predicted result of the data sample. For this reason, the *Mean Absolute Error (MAE)* metric is the mean value of these errors observed for all samples. In addition, the absolute function is beneficial when used for preventing the incorrect processing of negative error, which is generated in the case that the actual value is smaller than predicted.

It is possible that the MAE metric, which is an important indicator with respect to determining the best and most promotive solution in any case such as a regression problem, can be called an absolute loss (Cichosz, 2015).

Mean Square Error (MSE)

Square error expresses the squared error of difference. In other words, it shows error which is observed when actual values are compared with predicted values. Therefore, *Mean Square Error (MSE)* is an average value of the error squares of all samples. On the other hand, MSE error indicator benefits from enabling noticing and evaluating of errors more carefully, owing to the fact that the square function can perform an amplification of the observed error rate.

Also, increasing the success of prediction can be carried out by means of reducing the value of the MSE metric (Hill, Malone & Trocine, 2004).

Root Mean Square Error (RMSE)

The *Root Mean Square Error (RMSE)* metric is the root value of the MSE indicator. In other words, it shows the root of the mean of all occurred errors' squares, according to a specifically adjusted line. For this reason, this root value expresses ultimate error, and actually expresses the mean distance between actual and predicted results (Chou & Tsai, 2012).

Relative Absolute Error (RAE)

The *Relative Absolute Error (RAE)* metric, as seen in its formulation, is related to deviation from the mean value of actual data. Therefore, this metric is beneficial in that it helps users in noticing the mean deviation of the predicted results. Moreover, a case is suitable when relative absolute error value is smaller than 1, or when—in a good model—it even equals 0 (Cichosz, 2015). In addition, RAE metric generates the total absolute error value (Witten & Frank, 2005).

Root Relative Square Error (RRSE)

The *Relative Square Error (RSE)* metric, as in relative absolute error, is performed with normalization of errors. Therefore, RSE metric square errors of all samples are summed up and determined by dividing the squares of deviation from the mean of actual values belonging to that data. Also, the *Root Relative Square Error (RRSE)* metric is a root value of the RSE metric (Witten & Frank, 2005).

All of the evaluation criteria and error performance indicators, their formulations, and their components acting as these indicators are shown in Table 2.

PREDICTION APPLICATIONS VIA MACHINE LEARNING METHODS FOR OPTIMAL FRP BEAM DESIGNS

The Main Model

The optimization process was carried out with the aim of determining the design variables belonging to beams covered with carbon-fiber-reinforced polymers (CFRP). Values obtained for variables and design properties, which will be dealt with in prediction applications by machine learning algorithms, were used to generate a dataset.

As expressed in the optimization process, design constants composed of various numerical expressions and beam properties. These include h (height), b_w (breadth), h_f (the slab thickness of the beam), and V_{add} (additional shear force values). These were considered as being input parameters for the prediction model. In addition, design variables that engineers aim to optimize are β (CFRP covering angle), w_f (FRP width), and s_f (the amount of space between two consecutive CFRPs) values. However, a new parameter was generated by using w_f and s_f variables besides β, with the aim of its being used in a training dataset as one of the output parameters. This output is CFRP rate (r) and expresses CFRP width existing in length until the starting point of the next CFRP. The CFRP rate equation can be formulated as follows:

$$r = \frac{w_f}{w_f + s_f}$$ (11)

Also, machine learning algorithms and combinations of them were determined, together with the creating of dataset intended for prediction operations, owing to the performance of model training.

During predictions of optimal variables for CFRP beam designs, four different machine learning approaches as two single and two hybrid prediction models, generated from (and comprising) multi-layer perceptrons (MLPs), Random tree, and Bagging methods combined with MLP and Random Tree methods as separate base learner methods, were proposed. In this respect, the dataset—which includes four inputs (h, b_w, h_f and V_{add}) and two outputs (β and r)—was trained in the direction of these prediction models using Weka machine learning software (Witten et al., 2016).

For the main training model, the results of the optimal variables' predictions and indicators for error evaluations are shown in Tables 3 and 4 for β and CFRP rate, respectively.

Table 3. Error indicators and performance of prediction for β output

β (°)	Prediction Models			
	MLP	*Bagging+MLP*	*Random Tree*	*Bagging+Random Tree*
Correlation coefficient (R)	99.69%	99.77%	98.89%	99.38%
Mean absolute error (MAE)	0.0908	0.0776	0.1305	0.1069
Root mean squared error (RMSE)	0.1155	0.0998	0.2176	0.1684
Relative absolute error (RAE)	8.0829%	6.9034%	11.6068%	9.5150%
Root relative squared error (RRSE)	7.9472%	6.8622%	14.9707%	11.5845%
Total Number of Instances	231	231	231	231

Table 4. Error indicators and performance of prediction for CFRP rate (r) output

FRP Rate (r)	Prediction Models			
	MLP	*Bagging+MLP*	*Random Tree*	*Bagging+Random Tree*
Correlation coefficient (R)	99.70%	99.49%	99.36%	99.59%
Mean absolute error (MAE)	0.0121	0.0176	0.0123	0.0139
Root mean squared error (RMSE)	0.0175	0.0249	0.0258	0.0215
Relative absolute error (RAE)	6.4224%	9.3321%	6.5124%	7.3985%
Root relative squared error (RRSE)	7.6681%	10.9200%	11.3089%	9.4058%
Total Number of Instances	231	231	231	231

Table 5. Optimization results for designs in test model determined with the JA metaheuristic algorithm

h (mm)	b$_w$ (mm)	h$_f$ (mm)	V$_{add}$ (kN)	β (°)	w$_f$ (mm)	s$_f$ (mm)	CFRP Rate (r)
350	200	120	70000	65.016	35.170	61.271	0.365
530	420	85	55000	63.324	18.639	54.053	0.256
750	370	100	120000	63.593	83.198	59.184	0.584
680	500	95	110000	62.608	58.911	53.272	0.525
420	450	120	70000	62.753	61.816	110.000	0.360
300	300	100	100000	64.259	99.541	104.068	0.489
770	220	90	80000	64.974	58.013	93.878	0.382
400	510	85	90000	62.683	76.496	106.484	0.418
550	200	80	50000	64.839	31.058	102.775	0.232
800	300	100	120000	64.217	97.372	68.646	0.587

Test Models

After the training process, test models were handled for evaluation for the main model. These models are composed of 10 different design combination data, and optimal design parameters and variables for these combinations are expressed in Table 5.

The obtained results for optimal variable predictions, made by means of each machine learning training models, are shown in Tables 6–9 for β, together with the CFRP rate. Furthermore, in these tables, various performance error indicators—mean absolute (MAE), absolute percentage (MAPE), and square error (MSE)—are shown, with the purpose of comparing them according to JA used in optimization for analyzed prediction models.

CONCLUSION

For the main model, according to the results, it is seen that the *correlation coefficient (R)*—which expresses how well actual values are explained by predicted values—is observed as being extremely high in all models for both CFRP rate and β outputs. Moreover, the success of the ensemble models is (to a large extent) remarkable in terms of increasing predictive success for β via each hybridization of the bagging method. However, for the CFRP rate only, the ensemble model that operated by combining with Random Tree became successful in terms of moving in the right direction towards the achievement of this purpose.

According to the error evaluations for these four different prediction models, *mean absolute error (MAE)* values are extremely low for both outputs. However, MAE values decreased for β, and increased for the CFRP rate, from the point of view of the base learner methods (the MLP and Random Tree algorithms alone) in comparison to their combination with the Bagging algorithm. In addition, the *root mean square error (RMSE)* metric showed a similar behavior as MAE with respect to both design variables. Nevertheless, one difference was realized in CFRP rate prediction performance via the Bagging algorithm combined with Random Tree algorithm. This is a decreasing of the RMSE value for prediction in the CFRP rate model.

Table 6. β° and CFRP rate (r) predictions for the test model via the MLP algorithm

MLP Model					
	Error Values for JA			Error Values for JA	
β (°)	Absolute Error	Square Error	CFRP Rate (r)	Absolute Error	Square Error
63.657	1.359	1.847	0.604	0.239	0.057
63.644	0.320	0.102	0.240	0.016	0.000
64.902	1.309	1.714	0.377	0.207	0.043
63.930	1.322	1.747	0.372	0.153	0.023
61.858	0.895	0.801	0.456	0.096	0.009
61.944	2.315	5.358	0.910	0.421	0.177
65.969	0.995	0.991	0.220	0.162	0.026
61.508	1.175	1.382	0.545	0.127	0.016
65.498	0.659	0.435	0.212	0.020	0.000
65.531	1.314	1.726	0.353	0.234	0.055
	MAE	MSE		MAE	MSE
Mean	1.166	1.610		0.168	0.041
RMSE		1.269			0.202

Table 7. β° and CFRP rate (r) predictions for the test model via the Bagging algorithm in conjunction with the MLP algorithm

Bagging+MLP Model					
	Error Values for JA			Error Values for JA	
β (°)	Absolute Error	Square Error	CFRP Rate (r)	Absolute Error	Square Error
63.556	1.460	2.132	0.621	0.256	0.066
63.634	0.310	0.096	0.236	0.020	0.000
64.917	1.324	1.754	0.370	0.214	0.046
63.880	1.272	1.618	0.367	0.158	0.025
61.780	0.973	0.947	0.460	0.100	0.010
61.846	2.413	5.822	0.945	0.456	0.208
65.977	1.003	1.007	0.210	0.172	0.030
61.506	1.177	1.386	0.551	0.133	0.018
65.487	0.648	0.420	0.208	0.024	0.001
65.558	1.341	1.798	0.343	0.244	0.059
	MAE	MSE		MAE	MSE
Mean	1.192	1.698		0.178	0.046
RMSE		1.303			0.214

Table 8. β° and CFRP rate (r) predictions for the test model via the Random Tree algorithm

	Random Tree Model				
β (°)	**Error Values for JA**		**CFRP Rate (r)**	**Error Values for JA**	
	Absolute Error	**Square Error**		**Absolute Error**	**Square Error**
64.239	0.777	0.604	0.353	0.012	0.000
63.597	0.273	0.075	0.237	0.019	0.000
64.944	1.351	1.826	0.277	0.307	0.094
63.940	1.332	1.774	0.323	0.202	0.041
61.143	1.610	2.592	0.353	0.007	0.000
61.733	2.526	6.380	0.987	0.498	0.248
66.158	1.184	1.402	0.279	0.103	0.011
61.753	0.930	0.866	0.607	0.189	0.036
65.762	0.923	0.852	0.191	0.041	0.002
65.458	1.241	1.539	0.279	0.308	0.095
	MAE	MSE		MAE	MSE
Mean	1.215	1.791		0.169	0.053
RMSE		1.338			0.230

Table 9. β° and CFRP rate (r) predictions for the test model via the Bagging algorithm in conjunction with the Random Tree algorithm

	Bagging+Random Tree Model				
β (°)	**Error Values for JA**		**CFRP Rate (r)**	**Error Values for JA**	
	Absolute Error	**Square Error**		**Absolute Error**	**Square Error**
64.335	0.681	0.464	0.346	0.019	0.000
63.595	0.271	0.073	0.235	0.021	0.000
64.892	1.299	1.688	0.282	0.302	0.091
63.942	1.334	1.779	0.326	0.199	0.040
61.227	1.526	2.328	0.372	0.012	0.000
61.707	2.552	6.512	0.955	0.466	0.217
66.115	1.141	1.302	0.290	0.092	0.008
61.818	0.865	0.749	0.605	0.187	0.035
65.708	0.869	0.756	0.191	0.041	0.002
65.468	1.251	1.564	0.285	0.302	0.091
	MAE	MSE		MAE	MSE
Mean	1.179	1.722		0.164	0.049
RMSE		1.312			0.221

Following this, for the test model comprised of ten design samples, the prediction of optimal values for β and CFRP rate outputs were carried out by means of predictive success and low error of proposed machine learning methods, and their combinations created by using the bagging ensemble algorithm with respect to the main model. In this direction, two different error metrics comprised of MAE and mean square error (MSE) were calculated from the obtained results via Weka software, comparing this to the Jaya metaheuristic optimization algorithm.

For β output, MAE error is 1.166 and 1.192, respectively, in MLP and Bagging combined with MLP. Also, for CFRP rate, these values were 0.168 and 0.178, respectively in both models. In addition to this, MSE values showed increases from 1.610 to 1.698 for β, and 0.041 to 0.046 for CFRP rate, despite the main model not being successful only for the CFRP rate in terms of the MLP algorithm when comparing it to the Bagging algorithm according to correlation.

Both error metric values increased in comparison to real optimal design values for variables, too. Actually, these error values were pretty low, but if combinations for Bagging models are evaluated, the model/method that combined the Bagging and MLP algorithms can be considered as having failed in terms of its prediction of test model designs. Nevertheless, it can be seen that the increasing error rate for the β model is higher than that of the CFRP rate for the model that combined the Bagging and MLP algorithms. In addition, RMSE, which expresses ultimate (or what can be considered as being average) error for all models, is 1.269–1.303 for β, and 0.202–0.214 for the CFRP rate in MLP and Bagging with MLP hybridization, respectively. The obtained increase in this metric was lower in the CFRP rate, as was likewise the case for the other metrics.

On the other hand, another machine learning technique—and one used in combination with the Bagging algorithm—is the Random Tree algorithm.

By combining the Random Tree and Bagging algorithms relative to this method, this ensured that MAE values decreased for both β (1.215 to 1.179) and CFRP rate (0.169 to 0.164) outputs. Moreover, MSE errors were decreased similarly to MAE. MSE values changed from 1.791 to 1.722 for β, and from 0.053 to 0.049 for the CFRP rate. Thus, due to this model's low error rate, it can be said that the Bagging with Random Tree hybridization model is successful for the prediction of values. Also, errors could be reduced in a major part of design samples for the prediction of optimal results via this model. RMSE values were decreased, too.

As a result, it can be concluded that all four models are successful for the prediction of optimal values belonging to design variables by means of their good predictive performance and low error performance. As was especially the case for the CFRP rate, the error values obtained were very close to 0.

Differences were discovered between the two models and their combinations. The first combination, created via the Bagging algorithm in comparison with its base learner (MLP), was not successful with regard to outputs. The second one, though, performed better than the first one did, in terms of its achievement of its purpose of predicting β and the CFRP rate. However, if general evolution were to improve these four models even further, then MLP as a single algorithm, and Bagging with Random Tree as a combination of algorithms, would become considered as being even more suitable and efficient means of making output predictions.

REFERENCES

American Concrete Institute. (2005). *Building code requirements for structural concrete and commentary* (ACI 318M-05).

Chou, J. S., & Tsai, C. F. (2012). Concrete compressive strength analysis using a combined classification and regression technique. *Automation in Construction, 24*, 52–60. doi:10.1016/j.autcon.2012.02.001

Chou, J. S., Tsai, C. F., Pham, A. D., & Lu, Y. H. (2014). Machine learning in concrete strength simulations: Multi-nation data analytics. *Construction & Building Materials, 73*, 771–780. doi:10.1016/j.conbuildmat.2014.09.054

Cichosz, P. (2015). *Data mining algorithms: explained using R.* Chichester, UK: John Wiley & Sons. doi:10.1002/9781118950951

Hill, C. M., Malone, L. C., & Trocine, L. (2004). Data mining and traditional regression. In H. Bozdogan (Ed.), *Statistical data mining and knowledge discovery* (p. 242). Boca Raton, FL: CRC Press.

Jagannathan, G., Pillaipakkamnatt, K., & Wright, R. N. (2009). A practical differentially private random decision tree classifier. In *Proceedings of 2009 IEEE International Conference on Data Mining Workshops.* Miami, FL: IEEE. 10.1109/ICDMW.2009.93

Kalmegh, S. (2015). Analysis of weka data mining algorithm reptree, simple cart and randomtree for classification of Indian news. *International Journal of Innovative Science, Engineering & Technology, 2*(2), 438–446.

Kayabekir, A. E., Bekdaş, G., Nigdeli, S. M., & Temür, R. (2018). Investigation of cross-sectional dimension on optimum carbon-fiber-reinforced polymer design for shear capacity increase of reinforced concrete beams. In *Proceedings of 7th International Conference on Applied and Computational Mathematics (ICACM '18).* Rome, Italy: International Journal of Theoretical and Applied Mechanics.

Kayabekir, A. E., Sayin, B., Bekdas, G., & Nigdeli, S. M. (2017). Optimum carbon-fiber-reinforced polymer design for increasing shear capacity of RC beams. In *Proceedings of 3rd International Conference on Engineering and Natural Sciences (ICENS 2017).* Budapest, Hungary.

Kayabekir, A. E., Sayin, B., Bekdas, G., & Nigdeli, S. M. (2018) The factor of optimum angle of carbon-fiber-reinforced polymers. In *Proceedings of 4th International Conference on Engineering and Natural Sciences (ICENS 2018).* Kiev, Ukraine.

Kayabekir, A. E., Sayin, B., Nigdeli, S. M., & Bekdaş, G. (2017). Jaya algorithm based optimum carbon-fiber-reinforced polymer design for reinforced concrete beams. In *Proceedings of 15th International Conference of Numerical Analysis and Applied Mathematics.* Thessaloniki, Greece: AIP Conference Proceedings 1978.

Khalifa, A., & Nanni, A. (2000). Improving shear capacity of existing RC T-section beams using CFRP composites. *Cement and Concrete Composites, 22*(3), 165–174. doi:10.1016/S0958-9465(99)00051-7

Kılınç, D., Borandağ, E., Yücalar, F., Özçift, A., & Bozyiğit, F. (2015). Yazılım hata kestiriminde kolektif sınıflandırma modellerinin etkisi. In *Proceedings of IX. Ulusal Yazılım Mühendisliği Sempozyumu.* İzmir, Turkey: Yaşar Üniversitesi.

Maimon, O., & Rokach, L. (Eds.). (2010). *Data mining and knowledge discovery handbook* (Vol. 14). Springer Science & Business Media. doi:10.1007/978-0-387-09823-4

Rao, R. (2016). Jaya: A simple and new optimization algorithm for solving constrained and unconstrained optimization problems. *International Journal of Industrial Engineering Computations*, 7(1), 19–34.

Rao, R. V., Savsani, V. J., & Vakharia, D. P. (2011). Teaching–learning-based optimization: A novel method for constrained mechanical design optimization problems. *Computer Aided Design*, 43(3), 303–315. doi:10.1016/j.cad.2010.12.015

Raza, M. Q., & Khosravi, A. (2015). A review on artificial intelligence-based load demand forecasting techniques for smart grid and buildings. *Renewable & Sustainable Energy Reviews*, 50, 1352–1372. doi:10.1016/j.rser.2015.04.065

Rokach, L., & Maimon, O. (2015). *Data mining with decision trees: theory and applications* (2nd ed., Vol. 81). Singapore: World Scientific Publishing.

Skurichina, M., & Duin, R. P. (2002). Bagging, boosting and the random subspace method for linear classifiers. *Pattern Analysis & Applications*, 5(2), 121–135. doi:10.1007100440200011

Topçu, İ. B., & Sarıdemir, M. (2008). Prediction of mechanical properties of recycled aggregate concretes containing silica fume using artificial neural networks and fuzzy logic. *Computational Materials Science*, 42(1), 74–82. doi:10.1016/j.commatsci.2007.06.011

Witten, I. H., & Frank, E. (2005). *Data mining: Practical machine learning tools and techniques* (2nd ed.). San Francisco, CA: Morgan Kaufmann.

Witten, I. H., Frank, E., Hall, M. A., & Pal, C. J. (2016). *Data mining: Practical machine learning tools and techniques* (4th ed.). Cambridge, MA: Morgan Kaufmann.

Yang, X. S. (2012). Flower pollination algorithm for global optimization. In Jérôme Durand- Lose & Nataša Jonoska (Eds.), *International conference on unconventional computation and natural computation* (pp. 240-249). Berlin, Germany: Springer.

Yucel, M., Bekdaş, G., Nigdeli, S. M., & Sevgen, S. (2019). Estimation of optimum tuned mass damper parameters via machine learning. *Journal of Building Engineering*, 100847.

This research was previously published in Artificial Intelligence and Machine Learning Applications in Civil, Mechanical, and Industrial Engineering; pages 85-103, copyright year 2020 by Engineering Science Reference (an imprint of IGI Global).

Chapter 19
Knowledge Generation Using Sentiment Classification Involving Machine Learning on E-Commerce

Swarup Kr Ghosh

https://orcid.org/0000-0002-9312-4189

Brainware University, Kolkata, India

Sowvik Dey

Brainware University, Kolkata, India

Anupam Ghosh

Netaji Subhash Engineering College, Kolkata, India

ABSTRACT

Sentiment analysis manages the computational treatment of conclusion, notion, and content subjectivity. In this article, three sentiment classes such as positive, negative and neutral emotions have been demonstrated by appropriate features from raw unstructured data followed by data preprocessing steps. Applying best in class social analytics methodology to examine the sentiments embedded with purchaser remarks, encourages both producer and individual customers. Machine learning methods such as Naïve Bayes, maximum entropy classification, Deep Neural Networks were used upon the data, extracted from some websites such as Samsung and Apple for sentiment classification. In the online business arena, the application of sentiment classification explores a great opportunity. The subsidy of such an investigation is that associations can apply the proposed social examination framework to exploit the entire social information on the web and therefore improve their proper blueprint promoting strategies corresponding business.

DOI: 10.4018/978-1-6684-6291-1.ch019

1. INTRODUCTION

Nowadays, large amount of unstructured data are accessible online from different E-commerce site, social network site, some forum such as movie review forum, travel blog, hotel blog etc. Native online users are in trouble to access the actual information as per their requirement since size of data are becoming vast day by day and more unnecessary information occupy space rather than significant information. So users are getting confused to handle these. In this work, authors have focused on different e-commerce site for a different product to the benefit of both customer as well as producer on the basis of user's review on a particular product. Thus sentiment classification takes place on the user's review followed by text mining. Hence, automated systems could be developed that could effectively organize and classify this data, so that it could be leveraged by human users in a meaningful way. Sentiment analysis in reviews is the way towards investigating a product review on the web to decide the general sentiment or on the other hand feeling about a product. Reviews speak for the supposed client produced substance, and this is of developing consideration and a rich asset for promoting groups, sociologists and analysts and other people who may be worried about feelings, sees, open temperament and general or individual attitude.

As such, sophisticated sentiment classification techniques that can automatically classify, on the basis of any form of data, for e.g. the analyzed travel blogs, whether the overall reviews of a specific destination either positive or negative would certainly be useful to users. Sentiment classification is a class of recently developed web mining techniques that can perform analysis on sentiment or opinions (Liu et al., 2005). Generally speaking, sentiment classification aims at mining text of written reviews from customers for certain products or services, and classifying the reviews into positive or negative or neutral opinions. The classification method has been used in the computing fields of information retrieval and natural language processing (Godbole et al., 2007). Again, there are challenges associated with mining data from texts (Go et al., 2009). In this domain specific area, word semantics in a particular review could contradict with the inclusive semantic direction (good or bad) of that review. For instance, if we take an example of travel blogs, an ''unpredictable'' camera implies a negative meaning to that camera; whereas a tour with an ''unpredictable'' experience is positive to explorers. Sentiment classification aims to extract the text of written reviews of customers for certain products or services by classifying the reviews into positive or negative opinions according to the polarity of the review (Dave et al., 2003). With the results of sentiment classification, consumers would know the necessary information to determine which products to purchase and sellers would know the response from their customers and the performances of their competitors. With the wide adoption of computing technology, sentiment classification of reviews has become one of the foci of recent research endeavors. The method has been attempted in different domains such as movie reviews, product reviews, customer feedback reviews, and legal blogs. Other potential applications include extracting opinions or reviews from discussion forums such as blogs, and integrating automatic review mining with search engines to automatically provide useful statistical data of search results or to build sentiment analysis systems for specific products or services.

The present research can be divided into two sections. The first section consists of pre-processing steps from raw data which are directly collected merchant or e-commerce websites on some product such as Nokia x6067, Canon-1200D-Digital Camera Black, Apple iPod and Samsung Galaxy Tab S8.4 LTE. Since this work is based on unstructured data, so data pre-processing takes a decisive part and which consists of some phases. The TF-IDF method has been applied to assign polarities on sentential data by using dictionaries of unigram, bigram and trigram for sentiment classification. The second section of the work consists of machine learning algorithm such as Naïve Bays, Maximum entropy and Deep Neural Network for the classification of sentiment on a particular product and some discussion in this context.

The reminder of the paper is organized as follows: next section consists of related work in the literature. The methodology is covered in third section along with data processing steps and machine learning algorithms for sentiment classification. After that we represent the experimental evaluation of text mining and sentiment classification result of validation. Finally, we conclude the paper with some discussion and some areas for future development.

2. RELATED WORK

In recent time, a number of approaches have been developed on the classification of sentiment using several techniques. Engelson et al. (1998) described text categorization in natural language processing (Engelson et al., 1998). Adam et al. (1996) proposed text classification by using maximum entropy classifier (Adam et al., 1996). Text pre-processing on sentiment analysis was suggested by Haddi et al. (Haddi et al., 2013) at which SVM classifier used on feature vector. Thelwall et al. (2011) described sentiment analysis on twitter data by using time series analysis on the web based on hypothetical (Thelwall et al., 2011). They had experimented on the analysis of sentiment in the 30 largest spiking events in Twitter posts over a month of twitter post and achieved good accuracy level on positive sentiment than negative sentiment. The major drawback of the method that hypotheses was tested only one time period. A sentiment classification using feature relation networks on selected attribute had been reported by Abbasi et al. (Abbasi et al., 2011). Acharjya and Tripathy (2008) proposed a rough set based on fuzzy approximation space knowledge systems (Acharjya and Tripathy, 2008) which play outperforms on quantity of data but still suffer from qualitative data (Tripathy and Acharjya, 2010). Rough sets used on intuitionistic fuzzy approximation space and knowledge representation for decision system on the quantitative data (Acharjya and Tripathy 2009). Tan et al. (2011) proposed sentiment polarity classification using a linguistic approach on sentence (Tan et al., 2011). Lau et al. (2014) described a fuzzy-based product ontology for aspect-oriented sentiment analysis in social network analysis (Lau et al., 2014). A sentiment analysis in Facebook was proposed by Ortigosa et al. (2014) on the benefit of e-learning (Ortigosa et al., 2014). Das and Acharjya (2014) suggested a decision-making model based on rough set and soft set from which the authors had found the limitation of rough set in the decision system and introduced rough-soft set-based decision system (Das and Acharjya, 2014). A soft set based post-processing followed by rough set based pre-processing decision system was introduced by Das and Acharjya (2014) which provided a satisfactory result on both qualitative and quantitative data. A novel rough and real coded genetic algorithm-based prediction system proposed by Rathi and Acharjya (2017) which is a prediction framework of future instances of real time data (Rathi and Acharjya, 2017). Acharjya, and Anitha (2017) introduced a comparative study of statistical and rough computing models in predictive data analysis which could be a good predictor in several area (Acharjya, and Anitha, 2017). Recently, Rathi and Acharjya suggested another rule-based classification model by using the hybridization of rough set and genetic algorithm which classify vegetable production in Tiruvannamalai district in India (Rathi and Acharjya, 2018). There could be a new era in cultivation in India if it is applied properly in agriculture field.

The performance of the above methods discussed in literature decreases as the data size increases. Naive Bayes classifiers is based on Bayes' theorem that the features in a dataset are mutually independent. In practice, the independence assumption is often violated, but Naïve Bayes classifiers still tend to perform very well for small size of data. Raychaudhari et al., (2002) found that Maximum Entropy classifier performed better than Naïve Bayes and Nearest Neighbor classification. Unlike the Naïve Bayes machine learning, maximum entropy makes no independence assumptions regarding the prevalence of words. The Maximum Entropy modeling technique provides a likelihood distribution that's as getting ready for the uniform as potential provided that the distribution satisfies certain constraints. Maximizing entropy with feature expectation constraints turn out to be equivalent to maximizing likelihood in a log-linear model. In sake of comparison of Naïve Bays and Maximum Entropy classifiers, Maximum Entropy classifier is not well performed on outline noisy data. In this context authors have introduced deep neural network with 'softmax', which overcome the limitations of said methods.

3. METHODOLOGY

In the first step, authors have extracted user reviews from different E-commerce or merchant website in unstructured format. This step also involves data cleaning using some basic concept of text mining. The second step of this consists of the feature extraction using TF-IDF followed by Tokenization of the data with the help of dictionaries such as positive unigram, negative unigram, positive bigram, positive trigram, etc. In the third step, classification is done using popular machine learning algorithm such as Naïve Bayes, Maximum Entropy Classifier and Deep Neural Networks. Figure 1 shows the process by which sentiment classification is done for the acceptability of a particular product from the point of view of both producer and consumer.

Figure 1. Block diagram of sentiment analysis

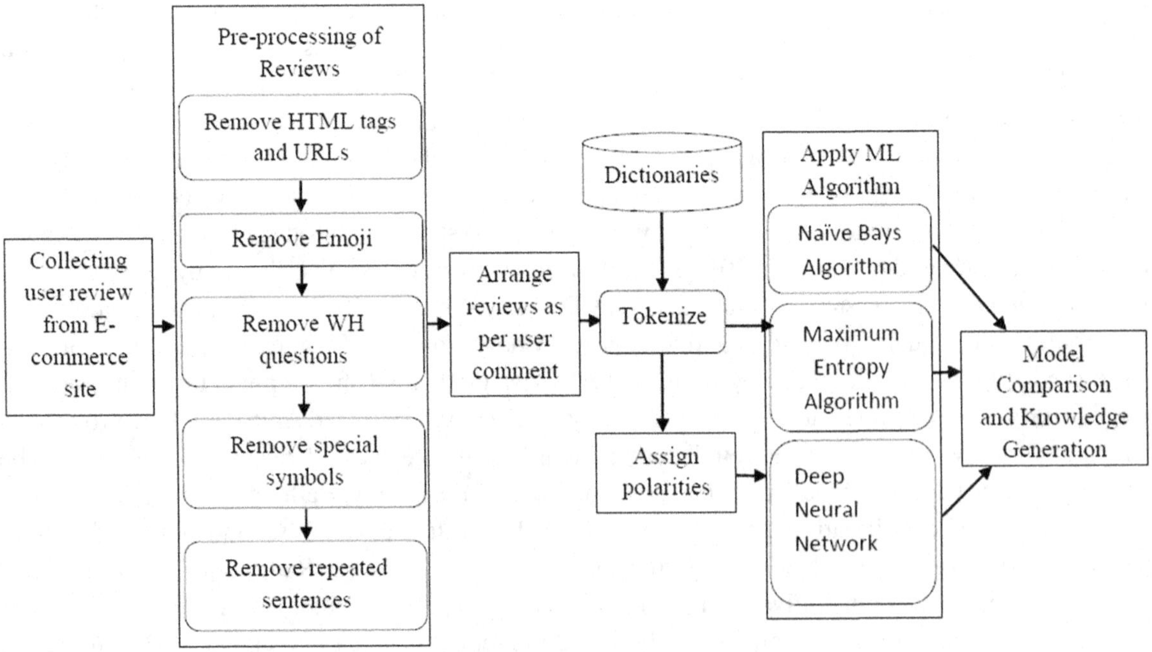

3.1. Data Collection Form E-Commerce or Merchant Website

The data collection is the most significant part of this work. The data have been collected from different websites such as E-commerce or some merchant website of a particular product. There are two types of reviews in merchant site or e-commerce site: first, the user review of a particular product that customer described about the product or some part of a product which all are in sentential form which are basically unstructured data. The second thing is rating of a particular product that is like score matrix which could be in table format that are structured data. In this paper, authors have focused on qualitative analysis and hence it is based on unstructured data. Data cleaning is the most significant part in this research.

3.2. Preprocessing of Data

Unstructured data are collected from different websites, that have different formats, different font and contain lots of unnecessary information such as URLs, HTML tags etc. Hence data preprocessing has a crucial role in this work. Raw data are preprocessed using text mining methods to remove HTML tags, URLs, emoji's, 'WH' questions, special symbols, repeated sentences etc. After that sentences have been reconstructed as per user which means they extracted all reviews and organize as per user wise. Cleaned data files are stored for further process.

```
Procedure Preprocessing_of_review:

Step1: Take User[i].feedback as argument.
Step2: Remove HTML tags by finding '<' and '>' symbols.
Step3: Remove URLs by getting "Http://" or "www" strings.
Step4: Remove Emoji by fetching ':' or ';' followed by another symbol like
')', '(' etc.
Step5: Remove 'WH' questions by scanning 'WH' words followed by question
mark.
Step6: Remove all Special symbols if any.
Step7: Remove repeated words or phrase.
Step8: Remaining terms are getting together to construct User[i].review
Step9: Return User[i].review.
```

3.3. Tokenization

It is obvious that each comment of every user contains unnecessary words or phrases which have not given any emotions. Dictionaries have been put in place to extract features from the sentences that are identifying the emotion words. Tokens include those extracted words from user feedback which have a few emotions. Three categories of dictionaries of both Positive emotions and negative emotions are utilized, viz. Unigram, bigram and trigram. Unigram: it is a single word which gives some emotion. A positive unigram dictionary contains a set of all words that gives a positive emotion, as an example good, like, easy, compact, better. A negative unigram dictionary consists of the set of all words that's give negative emotions as example bad, sad, expensive, complaint etc. Bigram: it defines a couple of words which give some emotion. Positive bigram dictionary encompasses set of all couple of words that's give positive emotions as example very good, heavy use, good wi-fi, running, etc. Negative bigram dictionary involves of set of all words that's give negative emotions as example bad, sad, expensive, complaint, etc. Trigram: it is three consecutive words which give some emotion. Positive trigram dictionaries contain a set of all trigrams that's give positive emotions as example most enjoyable thing, most beautiful baby, more frame rate, etc. Negative trigram dictionary includes set of all trigrams that's give negative emotions as example no proper comparison, auto restart problem, little bit slower etc. In this section, emotion words are extracted by using above dictionaries.

```
Procedure Tokenize_review

Step1: Take User[i]. review as input. //input
Step2: tokenize each words of User[i]. review as per Dictionaries and make
User[i].token
Step3: Return User[i].token
```

3.4. Feature Extraction Using TF-IDF

An existing method on statistical analysis or feature extraction TF-IDF (Term Frequency Inverse Document Frequency) is used to assign polarities to create feature vectors on the emotion words (Deng et al., 2014). The Term Frequency (TF) of a word defined by the probability of the occurrence of the word in a document in a particular document and it is formulated as:

TF(W, D) = (frequency of word W)/ (total frequency of all the feature words)

Inverse Document Frequency (IDF) is used to measure how important a word is from the documents. It can be defined as:

$IDF(D,f(D,W)) = \log_e((D)/f(D,W))$

where D=total number of documents, f(D, W) is function which finds number of documents among D which contains the word W.

To calculate TF-IDF, the number of occurrences of a word in the document called feature frequency, is needed (Haddi et al., 2013). The TF-IDF is formulized as follows:

TF-IDF(W, D) = TF(W)*IDF(D, f(D, W))

where N is the number of tokens, and DF is the number of tokens containing this feature. The TF-IDF and FF are called features matrices. W is the identified keywords in the user review and D is total number of users.

```
Procedure Assign_polarity:

Step1: Take User[i].token as input to this procedure.
Step2: Polarity value is calculated for every token using TF-IDF method.
Step3: Return all Polarity values.
```

3.5. Classification by Machine Learning Algorithm

The primary objective of this research is classified into three categories of emotions upon user reviews. Lots of classification algorithms have been applied by numerous researchers. The best fitted three classification algorithm based on machine learning has been discussed details in this section viz., Naïve Bayes, Maximum entropy classifier and deep neural network.

3.5.1. Classification by Naïve Bays

The Bayesian Classification signifies a crucial role in supervised learning for classification. This basically assumes an underlying probabilistic model and it agrees to imprisonment uncertainty about the model by determining probabilities of the outcomes (Geman et al., 1984). Bayesian classification be responsible for practical learning algorithms and preceding knowledge. Bayesian classification computes explicit probabilities for hypothesis and it is so robust for noise data. Naïve Bayes classifiers most significant in text classification and multiclass problems have higher success rate as compared to other algorithms on sentiment analysis. The limitation of Bayesian classifier is that decrease its performance on large data. The Bayes rule for the class $C_i \in C$ (set of classes) on the documents D is defined as:

$$P(C_i \mid D) = \frac{P(D \mid C_i)P(C_i)}{P(D)} \tag{1}$$

The maximum posteriori for classification by Bayes theorem is defined as the most likely class C_p is calculated as for all C_i in C:

$$C_p = \arg\max(P(D \mid C_i)P(C)) = \arg\max(P(x_1, x_2, ..., x_n) \mid C_i)P(C)) \tag{2}$$

by dropping denominator of Equation (1) and documents are divided into features x_1, x_2, …, x_n in feature set X.

The assumption is that the text features are independent and hence multinomial distribution have been applied for the final classification for the class C_i on features vector X as:

$$C_{NB} = \arg\max(P(C_i)\prod_{x \in X} P(x \mid C)) \tag{3}$$

Naïve table store the probabilities of feature vectors for a particular class and the algorithm is described as follows:

```
Procedure Naïve_Bays_Algorithm(User[1:N].polarity)
     forall User[i].polarity
          forall words W|W ∈ Naïve table
               User[i].polarity←User[i].polarity+ log
               cond_prob(User[i].polarity)
          End for
          If User[i].polarity > θ1 then
               User[i].message ← positive
          Else if User[i].polarity < θ2 then
               User[i].message ← negative
          Else
               User[i].message ← neutral
     End for
End procedure
```

3.5.2. Classification by Maximum Entropy

The Maximum Entropy classifier, a type of exponential models in a probabilistic classifier. Presence of conditional dependence among the features, makes maximum entropy distinguished from the Naïve Bays classifier. The Maximum Entropy classifier is based on the principle of maximum entropy. The application domain of maximum entropy classifier covers the solution to a large variety of text classification problems such as language detection, topic classification, sentiment analysis and more. Moreover, text classification domains have an inherent feature of conditional dependency, this makes the maximum Entropy classifiers is well suited in such a domain (Banea et al., 2011). The parametric form for a conditional maximum entropy is defined as:

$$P(C_i \mid D) = \frac{1}{Z(D)} \exp \sum_j \lambda_{j,i} f_{j,i}(D,C) \tag{4}$$

where $Z(D)$ is a normalize function, $f_{j,i}(C,D)$ is a feature or class function for the feature f_j and class C_i which has a feature weight parameter $\lambda_{j,i}$ indicates strong associated with $f_{j,i}(C,D)$ for large value of it. The optimization problem in maximum entropy classifier needs to be solved in order to estimate the parameters of the model, the maximum entropy classifier consumes more time than Naïve Bays classifier for training on a given dataset and the algorithm as follows:

```
Procedure Maximum_Entropy_Algorithm(User[1:N].polarity)
    forall User[i].polarity
        forall words W|W ∈ Naïve table
            User[i].polarity ← User[i].polarity+
                               User[i].polarity* log
                         cond_prob(User[i].polarity)
        End for
        If User[i].polarity > ϴ1 then
            User[i].message ← positive
        Else if User[i].polarity < ϴ2 then
            User[i].message ← negative
        Else
            User[i].message ← neutral
    End for
End procedure
```

3.5.3. Classification by Deep Neural Network

Neural system is a data handling prime example that capacities analogically to the organic sensory system. The fundamental component of this original is the novel structure of the data handling framework. The system structure is established by substantial number of exceptionally interconnected components (neurons) working in unanimity to order a particular issue. The encourage forward NN is a normally famous model in regulated learning science. It carries out arrangement of layered hubs and weighted association between each contiguous layer. Fundamentally it has three layers, first layer is the input layer, last layer is called the output layer and there is an arrangement of shrouded layer in the middle is called hidden layer. Feed-forward systems are often prepared utilizing a back spread learning plan as a result of the weight mistake revise rules. Back engendering learning work by making change in weight esteem beginning at the yield layer at that point being a step in reverse through the concealed layers in the system (Ghosh et al., 2018). In this work, there are more hidden layers with weight matrices are called deep neural network which can handle large data with more accuracy (Zhang and Chen, 2017). The working principle of deep neural network describes in Figure 2, at which tanh activation function has been used in each hidden layer and "softmax" function used in the output layer in the network for classification with three classes. The activation function tanh is used in each hidden layer and output will be generated after first hidden layers such as:

$$z^{[1]} = \left(W_1^T a^{[0]} + b^{[1]} \right) \text{ and } a^{[1]} = \tanh\left(z^{[1]} \right),$$

where $a^{[0]} = X$ is the input data stored in matrix, W_1 is the weight matrix at first hidden layer and b is bias. Thus above is calculated in each hidden layer taking whose input will be the output of previous layer. So in general formula at i[th] layer will be:

$$z^{[i]} = \left(W_i^T a^{[i-1]} + b^{[i]} \right) \text{ and } a^{[i]} = \tanh\left(z^{[i]} \right) \tag{5}$$

where $a^{[i-1]}$, $b^{[i]}$ and W_i denotes output of previous layer, bias unit and weight matrix in i^{th} layer. In this way values have been updated in each layer and finally softmax function has been applied in the output layer for final classification and it is defined by:

$$\sigma(z)j = \frac{e^{zj}}{\sum_{k=1}^{K} e^{zk}} \text{ for j} = 1, 2, \ldots, K \qquad (6)$$

where K is the number of classes.

Figure 2. Deep neural network architecture

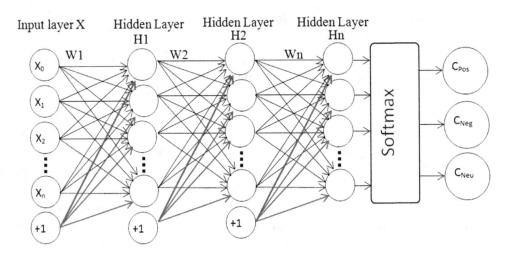

In this research, the hyper-parameter learning rate α has been varying 0.3 to 0.6 to achieve desired result.

3.5.4. Proposed Multi-Class Deep Neural Network for Sentiment Classification

In practice, different multi-level classification tasks are often solved by various neural network. Suppose, given an N training samples $\{(x_i, y_i)\}_{i=1}^{N}$ belongs to the K number of classes, where x_i represents sample data point and y_i denotes the relevant feature labels. Therefore, the basic concept of neural network is mapping between input vector x_i and output vector y_i by a predefined model F in entire training phase. The entire training process be completed under two learning phases, first is the forward propagation step and last is back-propagation step. Next the given train samples (x_i, y_i) is fed as input to neural network then the processed sample x_i is transferred from input layer to final layer with back-to-back steps. Hence, for an expected output O_i, the entire learning process of network is mathematically defined as follows (Liu and Wang, 2017):

$$O_i = F_L\left(F_{L-1}\left(W_{L-1}^T x_i + b_{L-1}\right)\right)o...o\left(F_1\left(W_1^T x_i + b_1\right)\right) \tag{7}$$

where L denotes the number of neuron layers and W_i is the weighted vector at ith layer in F_i. After complete those operations, the estimated weighted vectors W_i (for i= 1 to L) will be solved by a minimization of objective functions expressed as:

$$\arg\min \frac{1}{N}\sum_{i=1}^{N}\xi(y_i, o_i) \text{ for } W_1, W_2, ..., W_L \tag{8}$$

where $\xi(.)$ be a cross entropy or 'sumsqured' function. This minimization problem can be solved a gradient decent method such as probabilistic gradient decent method and back propagation process.

3.5.5. Loss Function and Dropout

In order to adjust the loss of trained model, we used the cross-entropy loss in each data that is defined as (Srivastava et al., 2014):

$$\phi(x) = -\frac{1}{N}\sum_{i=1}^{C}\left(\sum \log\left(\tilde{p}_i\left(x\right)\right)\right) \tag{9}$$

where $\tilde{p}_i(.)$ is the softmax class probability, which is defined in Equation (6).

The input to this loss function is real valued output predictions $x\varepsilon[-1,+1]$ from the last layer. In this work, we used the above loss formulation for all data sets in our experiments.

Due to the high dimensionality of dense layers with large size batches and limited available training samples, over-fitting is a serious problem in this method. In order to handle the issue, a recently introduced method named dropout is used (Srivastava et al., 2014). It is basically dropping some network basis on probability.

In experiment, authors have used ten to fifteen hidden layers in the network and select best possible outcome in training phase. The dropout ratio has set to 0.5 and it is fixed. In the end, all the nodes are equipped with 'soft-max' classifier to produce the corresponding labels.

4. RESULT AND DISCUSSION

The effectiveness of our algorithm along with comparisons is demonstrated on product's review data on a particular product discussed in this section. The result analysis is shown according to the phases of our proposed methodologies. Data clean take a crucial role on unstructured data and each of the steps has been shown here. Lastly result and comparisons of three standard classifications have been discussed.

4.1. Collection of Raw Data

Initial phase of our proposed method is tantamount to collect data from merchant websites or different E-commerce website such as Amazon and GSMArena on a particular product. In this work, four products have been applied to classify the sentiment viz. Nokia x6067, Canon-1200D-Digital Camera Black, Apple iPod and Samsung Galaxy Tab S8.4 LTE and user comments are directly collected from the merchant or different E-commerce website. The raw data which is stored in files contain lots of noise such as HTML tags, URL, emoji's, punctuations etc. The user's comments of each product contain more than ten thousand words which kept in four different files. Extraction of related words from bulk amount of unstructured data are achieved by using standard text mining method. In this paper, ETL (Extract Transform Load) has been used to obtain structured data. Various types of dissimilar words, emoji's, punctuations are present in raw data such as [+1], [8 MEG], want to start, in their reviews, about its, I'm in high school, and this, what I use it for which is shown in Figure 3.

Figure 3. Collection of raw data from merchant website

Line ID	Customer_ID	Brand	Product	Camera	Music Player	Target	Phone	Review
2	I Canon S 101	Canon	Camera	I	0	0		0 small[+1] I want to start off saying that this camera is small for a reason.
3	I Canon S 102	Canon	Camera	I	0	0		0 Some people, in their reviews, complain about its small size, and how it doesn't compare with larger cameras.
4	I Canon S 103	Canon	Camera	I	0	0		0 camera[+3],size[+2] I'm in high school, and this camera is perfect for what I use it for, carrying it around in my pocket so I can take pictures whenever I want to, of my friends and of funny things that happen. 7
5	I Canon S 104	Canon	Camera	I	0	0		0 memory[-2] The only thing I don't like is the small size (8 MEG) memory card that comes with it.
6	I Canon	Canon	Camera	I	0	0		0 room[-2] I have to move pictures off of it every day so I have room for more pictures the next, and I don't have enough money to buy the 256 MEG card that I've had my eye

4.2. Data Preprocessing

Data pre-processing is a fundamental step in this work since raw data have been directly collected from different websites which are in unstructured format. Raw data contain a lot of noise like symbols such as emoji, blank lines etc. Text tagging and annotation is a prevalent procedure established on natural language processing. This is the most significant component of a document processing and information retrieval system. Text tagging and annotation involves investigating free form text and identifying unnecessary terms such as proper nouns, numerical expressions etc. Text annotation is also brought up as a named entity distillation which deal a good degree of accuracy and are widely used in applications in text mining, information extraction and NLP. Sample output after removing noise is illustrated in Figure 4. After that, users comments are structured as per each user.

4.3. Tokenized by Using Dictionaries

Output of the noise free data has been classified as positive and negative emotion words. Each unigram contains approximately four thousand emotion words as well as each bigram dictionary contain approximately three thousand bigram words. Each comment per user has been tokenized with unigram or bigram or trigram emotion using both positive and negative dictionaries. The result of determining the positive and negative bigrams and trigrams has been shown in Figure 5 where bigrams such as 'professional battery', 'perfect pocket exposure', 'something', 'especially memory', 'picture quality digital', 'pictures' are detected as positive sentiments and they are indicated using green color and red indicates negative sentiment.

Figure 4. Noise free data as collected from merchant website

	Line ID	Customer Brand	Product	Camera	Music_Pla Target	Phone	Clean Data
1							
2	2	1 Canon S 101	Camera	1	0	0	0 I want to start off saying that this camera is small for a reason.
3	3	1 Canon S 102	Camera	1	0	0	0 Some people, in their reviews, complain about its small size, and how it doesn't compare with larger cameras.
4	4	1 Canon S 103	Camera	1	0	0	0 I'm in high school, and this camera is perfect for what I use it for, carrying it around in my pocket so I can take pictures whenev
5	5	1 Canon S 104	Camera	1	0	0	0 The only thing I don't like is the small size (8 MEG) memory card that comes with it.
6	6	1 Canon S 105	Camera	1	0	0	0 I have to move pictures off of it every day so I have room for more pictures the next, and I don't have enough money to buy th
7	7	1 Canon S 106	Camera	1	0	0	0 A larger memory card and extra battery are good things to buy.
8	8	1 Canon S 107	Camera	1	0	0	0 Other than that pictures taken in the dark are not as nice as I'd like them.
9	9	1 Canon S 108	Camera	1	0	0	0 I'd say that this camera is perfect.
10	11	2 Canon S 110	Camera	1	0	0	0 OK, not quite everything...but this camera is so compact that you will have it by your side when you need it.
11	13	3 Canon S 112	Camera	1	0	0	0 I bought this camera for the same reason many of you are considering it, or have already bought it--it's size.
12	14	3 Canon S 113	Camera	1	0	0	0 It is amazingly small, it's hard to believe all that has been packed into this camera.
13	15	3 Canon S 114	Camera	1	0	0	0 I take it with me everywhere, literally,
14	16	3 Canon S 115	Camera	1	0	0	0 It is so small that I am able to keep it in my pocket, and I don't have to fear that it will get ruined in my pocket because it is so

Figure 5. Determination and identification of both positive and negative sentiments

4.4. Concept Link Graph

Concept link graph defines how emotion words are connected or how to form a bigram or trigram emotions. It also identifies the most frequent words or a set of emotion words in which the features can be extracted. The detail explanation of concept link graph has been shown in Figure 6. The first sub image shows five words are connected with a central word 'love' which indicates that 'iPod', 'camera', 'feature', 'size', 'phone' form bigram emotion with the word 'love'. Among the five words, 'size' and 'iPod' are connected with the word 'love' with deep link which indicates that bigrams 'love size' and 'love iPod' have higher frequencies in the document. The '+' sign in the word indicates that those words also have more connected words which can form a bigrams or trigrams emotions.

Figure 6. Sample output of the visualization of detected keywords

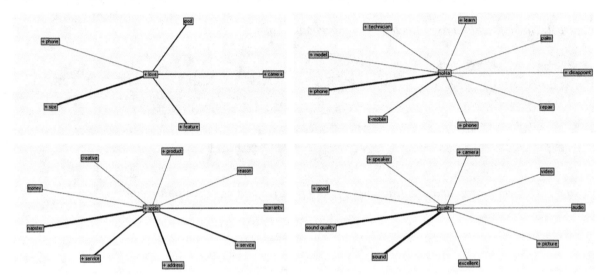

4.5. Feature Extraction by TF-IDF on a Particular Product

In this work, features are extracted from emotion words based on positive and negative viz. unigram, bigram and trigram by using statistical methods. The Term Frequency (TF) and Inverse Document Frequency (IDF) have been used to extract features from comments of each user at which positive polarities assign to the positive emotions words and negative polarities assign to the negative emotion words. The top ten most frequent words along with its polarities word per user review are presented in Figure 7.

Figure 7. Sample output of assignments of polarities to detected keywords

pictures	+3.996
digital	+2.983
quality	+2.722
picture	+1.998
especially	+1.993
something	+1.988
exposure	+1.880
pocket	+1.829
perfect	+1.764
Battery	+1.546
professional	+1.519

According to the proposed methodology, the keywords 'pictures', 'digital', 'perfect' for example are assigned the polarities +3.996, +2.983 and +1.764, respectively. Sample output of the polarities of feedback of users are shown in Figure 8.

Figure 8. Evaluation of polarities of reviews by the users of the merchant websites

I'm in high school, and this camera is perfect for what I use it for, carrying it around in my pocket so I can take pictures whenever I want to, of my friends and of funny things that happen.	7	↓	+0.4175
I have to move pictures off of it every day so I have room for more pictures the next, and I do n't have enough money to buy the 256 MEG card that I've had my eye on for a while.	9	↓	+0.4464
The picture quality surprised me. when I first saw this camera I saw how small it was an instantly assumed that the picture quality would not be good -- but I was wrong The picture quality of this camera is outstanding (taking its ' size and price into consideration).	10	↓	+0.5817
This camera uses a lithium battery. I find lithium battery to be highly inconvenient because what if you are on vacation, where the nearest place to buy batteries is just a gas station -- there is no way that you are going to find lithium battery there.	10	↓	-0.2874
This is n't uncommon in cameras, though, just as long as you bring your charger and spare batteries, you should be fine.	7	↓	-0.1752
These are all the flaws I found in the camera, it 's not my first choice in cameras, I have come across many other beginner cameras that I prefer over this camera, but the thing you have to keep in mind about this camera is the size.	10	↓	-0.3049

The final result of sentiment analysis for the statements are shown in Figure 8 at which polarities are calculated on a review as per user followed by TF-IDF.

4.6. Classification

Classification is a big challenge for unstructured data as well as increase the volume of the data. Three different classification algorithms have been applied on four separate products by keeping each product in training dataset to classify positive, negative and neutral emotions in this research. Three different classification algorithms that have been discussed in the proposed methodology are Naïve Bays classifier, Maximum Entropy classifier and deep neural network with 'softmax' classifier. Four different products that have been taken are Nokiax6067 mobile phone, Canon 1200D-DC camera, Apple iPod and Samsung Galaxy Tab. A snippet of output performed on Nokiax6067 mobile phone using three different algorithms are presented in Figure 9. As an illustration, Naïve Bays Classifier on the data set Nokiax6067 produces 67% positive emotion, 21% negative emotion and 17% neutral emotion. Similarly, Maximum Entropy Classifier classifies the entire user review on the product Nokiax6067 into 56% positive emotion, 20% negative emotion and 24% neutral emotion. Finally, the Deep Neural Network classifies the same data set to the product of Nokiax6067 into 61% positive emotion, 21% negative emotion and 18% neutral emotion. Other remaining products classifies by three emotions based on three different algorithms as shown in Figure 9.

Figure 9. Three different classifier algorithms applied on four datasets Nokiax6067, Canon 1200 D-DC, Apple iPod, Samsung Galaxy Tab

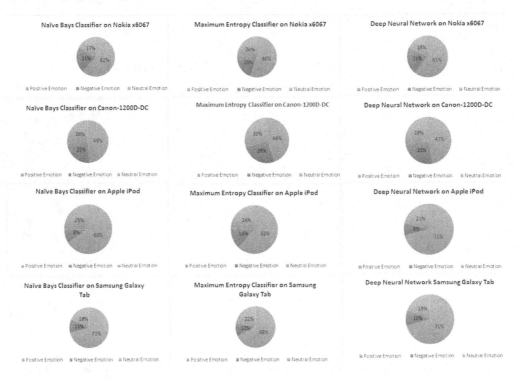

4.7. Validation

The Accuracy of a classifier on a given test set is the probability of test set that are correctly classified by the classifier and defined as:

$$accuracy = \frac{TP + TN}{TP + TN + FP + FN}$$

where TP = True Positive, TN = True Negative, FP = False Positive and FN = False Negative (Ghosh et al., 2018). In this paper, three classification algorithms have been applied to obtain the desired result. In order to get satisfactory classification, the entire data set has been classified into three parts while keeping particular product fixed. The three different classes are denoted as C_{pos}, C_{neg} and C_{neu} where C_{pos} is positive emotion class, C_{neg} is the negative emotion class and C_{neu} is the neutral emotion class. Figure 10 shows the comparative analysis of three classifier on four different products. As illustration, it can be seen that accuracy of the Naïve Bays classifier, Maximum Entropy classifier and deep neural network are 0.76, 0.73 and 0.81, respectively, while keeping the dataset of Nokiax6067. Hence, it can be observed from Figure 10 that the deep neural network produces the best result.

Figure 10. Comparative study on classification by three classifiers on the dataset of four products

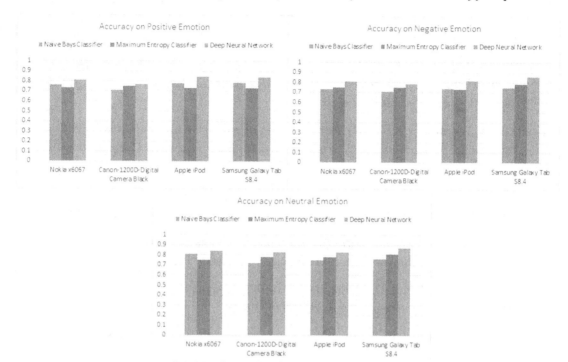

5. CONCLUSION

Electronic commerce or e-commerce is a term for any type of business, or commercial transaction that affects the transfer of information across the internet. Most of the machine learning algorithm work on structured data. As the amount of unstructured data are increasing day by day, this paper shows how the proposed methodology can be applied in the context of unstructured data. The proposed methodologies will help both the consumer as well as the producer. From the point of view of application, this proposed algorithm will enable native users to obtain information about a product from a merchant website. Hence, reduced time needs to find the acceptability of a particular product. On the contrary, producer can identify the acceptability of a particular product for the customer. Thus, the information obtained will be beneficial for consumers as well as manufacturers in making a better decision about the business and further lead to generation of knowledge about the perspective of a product in the same domain.

Furthermore, authors will focus on word embedding and word representation for feature extraction using Deep Recurrent Neural Network. It might be used for Bidirectional Recurrent Neural Network to classify emotions. Word generation and word to vector or GLOVE for word representation are promising better results.

REFERENCES

Abbasi, A., France, S., Zhang, Z., & Chen, H. (2011). Selecting attributes for sentiment classification using feature relation networks. *IEEE Transactions on* Knowledge and Data Engineering, *23*(3), 447–462.

Acharjya, D. P., & Anitha, A. (2017). A comparative study of statistical and rough computing models in predictive data analysis. *International Journal of Ambient Computing and Intelligence*, *8*(2), 32–51. doi:10.4018/IJACI.2017040103

Acharjya, D. P., & Tripathy, B. K. (2008). Rough sets on fuzzy approximation spaces and applications to distributed knowledge systems. *International Journal of Artificial Intelligence and Soft Computing*, *1*(1), 1–14. doi:10.1504/IJAISC.2008.021260

Acharjya, D. P., & Tripathy, B. K. (2009). Rough sets on intuitionistic fuzzy approximation spaces and knowledge representation. *International Journal of Artificial Intelligence and Computational Research*, *1*(1), 29–36.

Alvaro, O., José, M., Martín, J. M., & Carro, M. R. (2014). Sentiment analysis in Facebook and its application to e-learning. *Computers in Human Behavior*, *31*, 527–541. doi:10.1016/j.chb.2013.05.024

Banea, C., Mihalcea, R., & Wiebe, J. (2011) Multilingual sentiment and subjectivity analysis. In I. Zitouni & D. Bikel (Eds.), Multilingual Natural Language Processing. Prentice-Hall.

Berger, A. L., Stephen, A., Pietra, D., & Pietra, V. D. (1996). A maximum entropy approach to natural language processing. *Computational Linguistics*, *22*(1), 39–71.

Das, T. K., & Acharjya, D. P. (2014). A decision making model using soft set and rough set on fuzzy approximation spaces. *International Journal of Intelligent Systems Technologies and Applications*, *13*(3), 170–186. doi:10.1504/IJISTA.2014.065172

Dave, K., Lawrence, S., & Pennock, D. M. (2003). Mining the peanut gallery: opinion extraction and semantic classification of product reviews. In *12th international conference on World Wide Web* (pp. 519-528).

Deng, Z. H., Luo, K. H., & Yu, H. L. (2014). A study of supervised term weighting scheme for sentiment analysis. *Expert Systems with Applications*, *41*(7), 3506–3513. doi:10.1016/j.eswa.2013.10.056

Srivastava, N., Hinton, G., Krizhevsky, A., Sutskever, I., & Salakhutdinov, R. (2014). Dropout: A simple way to prevent neural networks from overfitting. *Journal of Machine Learning Research*, *15*(1), 1929–1958.

Geman, S., & Geman, D. (1984). Stochastic relaxation, Gibbs distributions, and the Bayesian relation of images. *IEEE Transactions on Pattern Analysis and Machine Intelligence*, *6*(6), 721–741. doi:10.1109/TPAMI.1984.4767596 PMID:22499653

Ghosh, S. K., Ghosh, A., & Chakrabarti, A. (2018). VEA: Vessel extraction algorithm by active contour model and a novel wavelet analyzer for diabetic retinopathy detection. *International Journal of Image and Graphics, World Scientific Publishing Company*, *18*(2), 1–20.

Go, A., Bhayani, R. and Huang, L. (2009). Twitter sentiment classification using distant supervision. *Stanford University. Stanford Digital Library Technologies Project.*

Godbole, N., Srinivasaiah, M., & Skiena, S. (2007). Large-Scale Sentiment Analysis for News and Blogs. In *International conference on web and social media.*

Haddi, E., Liu, X., & Shi, Y. (2013). The Role of Text Pre-processing in Sentiment Analysis. *Procedia Computer Science*, *17*, 26–32. doi:10.1016/j.procs.2013.05.005

Liu, B., Hu, M., & Cheng, J. (2005). Opinion observer: analyzing and comparing opinions on the Web. In *14ᵗʰ international conference on World Wide Web* (pp. 342-351).

Liu, W., Wang, Z., Liu, X., Zeng, N., Liu, Y., & Alsaadi, F. E. (2017). A survey of deep neural network architectures and their applications. *Neurocom*, *234*, 11–26. doi:10.1016/j.neucom.2016.12.038

Ortigosa, A., Martin, J. M., & Carro, R. M. (2014). Sentiment analysis in Facebook and its application to e-learning. *Computers in Human Behavior*, *31*, 527–541. doi:10.1016/j.chb.2013.05.024

Pang, B., Lee, L., & Vaithyanathan, S. (2002). Thumbs up? Sentiment classification using machine learning techniques. In *Empirical Methods in Natural Language Processing*. EMNLP.

Rathi, R., & Acharjya, D. P. (2018). A Rule Based Classification for Vegetable Production for Tiruvannamalai District using Rough Set and Genetic Algorithm. *International Journal of Fuzzy System Applications*, *7*(1), 74–100. doi:10.4018/IJFSA.2018010106

Rathi, R. and Acharjya, D. P. (2017). A Framework for Prediction using Rough Set and Real Coded Genetic Algorithm. *Arabian Journal for Science and Engineering*, *43*(8), 4215–4227.

Raychaudhuri, S., Chang, J. T., Sutphin, P. D., & Altman, R. B. (2002). Associating genes with Gene Ontology codes using a maximum entropy analysis of biomedical literature. *Genome Research*, *12*(1), 203–214. doi:10.1101/gr.199701 PMID:11779846

Raymond, Y. K. L., Chunping, L., & Stephen, S. Y. L. (2014). Social analytics: Learning fuzzy product ontologies for aspect-oriented sentiment analysis. *Decision Support Systems*, *65*, 80–94. doi:10.1016/j.dss.2014.05.005

Shlomo, A. E., Koppel, M., & Avner, G. (1998). Style-based text categorization: What newspaper am I reading? In *Proc. Of the AAAI Workshop on Text Categorization* (pp. 1–4).

Tan, L., Na, J., Theng, Y. and Chang, K. (2011). Sentence-level sentiment polarity classification using a linguistic approach. In *Digital Libraries: For Cultural Heritage, Knowledge Dissemination, and Future Creation* (pp. 77-87).

Thelwall, M., Buckley, K., & Paltoglou, G. (2011). Sentiment in twitter events. *Journal of the American Society for Information Science and Technology*, *62*(2), 406–418. doi:10.1002/asi.21462

Tripathy, B. K., & Acharjya, D. P. (2010). Knowledge mining using ordering rules and rough sets on fuzzy approximation spaces. *International Journal of Advances in Science and Technology*, *1*(3), 41–50.

Zhang, L., & Chen, C. (2017). Sentiment Classification with Convolutional Neural Networks: An Experimental Study on a Large-Scale Chinese Conversation Corpus. In *2016 12th International Conference on Computational Intelligence and Security (CIS)*.

This research was previously published in the International Journal of Business Analytics (IJBAN), 6(2); pages 74-90, copyright year 2019 by IGI Publishing (an imprint of IGI Global).

Chapter 20
An Exploratory Study on the Use of Machine Learning to Predict Student Academic Performance

Patrick Kenekayoro

https://orcid.org/0000-0003-0021-6584

Mathematics / Computer Science Department, Niger Delta University, Amassoma, Nigeria

ABSTRACT

Optimal student performance is integral for successful higher education institutions. The consensus is that big data analytics can be used to identify ways for achieving better student academic performance. This article used support vector machines to predict future student performance in computing and mathematics disciplines based on past scores in computing, mathematics and statistics subjects. Past subjects passed by students were ranked with state of art feature selection techniques in an attempt to identify any connection between good performance in a particular discipline and past subject knowledge. Up to 80% classification accuracy was achieved with support vector machines, demonstrating that this method can be developed to produce recommender or guidance systems for students, however the classification model will still benefit from more training examples. The results from this research reemphasizes the possibility and benefits of using machine learning techniques to improve teaching and learning in higher education institutions.

INTRODUCTION

Teaching is one of the main goals of Higher Education Institutions (HEIs), and part of the objectives of teaching is guiding students towards specialties that they may thrive in. If a student's strong areas can be determined from his/her previous performances, it takes us closer to automating the process of guiding students to specialties. Supervised learning techniques may also be used to identify those attributes (performance in certain subjects) that may influence success in a particular specialty. Accurately

DOI: 10.4018/978-1-6684-6291-1.ch020

identifying these attributes and adding significance to ensuring that those students who may want to advance to a particular specialty have a good grasp of its required (previously identified) subjects may increase the likelihood of students' success in their chosen specialties. This may also be reflected in the design curricula that adequately shows prerequisites or desired knowledge for respective specialties.

Traditional methods that have been used to investigate factors that affect student academic performance involve correlation and regression approaches (Figlio & Kenny, 2007; Myller, Suhonen, & Sutinen, 2002; Pritchard & Wilson, 2003), but data mining techniques may also be used for this purpose. Pahwa, Arora and Thakur (2011) succinctly defined data mining as "…efficient discovery of non-obvious information from a large collection of data…" Data mining is becoming an increasingly important tool for knowledge discovery, as there is an exponential increase in the amount of information available. Data mining deals with this information overload by finding patterns or relationships in data that would otherwise be unidentifiable, there by simplifying decision making for policy makers (Govindarajan & Chandrasekaran, 2012).

The use of data mining techniques such as supervised learning to explore educational data in order to improve student performance is an aspect of Educational Data Mining. This research uses a case study from a real higher education institution to determine if machine learning techniques can be used to predict student academic performance.

LITERATURE REVIEW

Educational Data Mining (EDM) has been defined as "…scientific inquiry focused on developments of methods for making discoveries with data from educational settings and using those methods to better understand students and the settings which they learn in…" (Baker, 2010). Understanding students through educational data mining can give new insights to ways that can improve student academic performance. Academic success is seen as a critical factor for individual success in contemporary society (Pritchard & Wilson, 2003). If students' academic performance can be previously predicted, it gives policy makers the opportunity to introduce policies that will improve student academic success rate, thereby increasing the likelihood of successful completion of a higher education degree. Also, creating predictive models that can be used for early identification of weak students who will be at risk is beneficial for reducing failure or dropout rates in higher education institutions (Raju & Schumacker, 2016).

Techniques for predicting student performance have been researched extensively. Historically, correlation and multiple regression are the traditional methods used to investigate the extent to which socioeconomic or psychological factors can positively or negatively affect a student's academic performance. For example, Figilo and Kenny (2007) have used correlation to investigate the relationship between teacher incentives and student performance. However, machine learning techniques can use these socioeconomic, psychological or other factors to also predict how well a student will perform in a particular subject, thus it is a useful technique that can be used in the design of systems that can provide real time guidance to students.

Although early studies have used regression to investigate factors influencing student performance (Myller et al., 2002; Pritchard & Wilson, 2003), there is still a dearth of research on how effective these models are for Educational Data Mining in higher education institutions (Raju & Schumacker, 2016). Linear regression may perform poorly and sometimes more elaborate classification models perform better than linear regression for student performance prediction (Myller et al., 2002), but in other times the average accuracy of more complex mathematical models like support vector machines or neural networks is not better than linear regression (Huang & Fang, 2013). A comparison of random forests, linear regression, decision trees and neural networks machine learning algorithms for academic analytics showed no difference in the misclassification rate (Raju & Schumacker, 2016), reaffirming the no free lunch theorem (Wolpert & Macready, 1997) that no method is guaranteed to always outperform others. However, machine learning techniques have an advantage over statistical methods like regression, correlation or discriminant analysis as machine learning techniques can identify more complex patterns and predictions with machine learning methods are more accurate when the data is not linearly separable.

Kotsiantis, Pierrakeas and Pintelas (2004) achieved the best results with Naïve Bayes algorithm in one of the earliest studies that used machine learning to predict student performance. Over the years, a number of other supervised learning algorithms, among which include decision trees, support vector machines, Bayesian networks (Thai-Nghe, Busche, & Schmidt-Thieme, 2009) and ensemble classifiers (Kotsiantis, Patriarcheas, & Xenos, 2010) have also been used with good results.

The features used to create a prediction model is a critical factor in determining the accuracy of the model. Márquez-Vera et al (2013) have divided these features into general survey and specific survey as shown in Table 1.

Table 1. Attribute types for predicting academic performance as described by Márquez-Vera et al. (2013)

Attribute Type	Description
General survey	Socioeconomic factors and past scores
Specific survey	Personal, social, family and institution facilities

Socioeconomic and psychological factors (non-cognitive attributes) play a big role in academic performance (Ransdell, 2001), which is why they are among the features used to predict student academic performance in a number of studies (Bekele & Menzel, 2005; Delen, 2010; Kotsiantis et al., 2004; Pritchard & Wilson, 2003). However, it sometimes may be difficult to gather data that contains these non-cognitive data. Data such as the quality of teaching could be gotten through quantitative surveys, but answers to questions such as "…rate the quality of teaching on a scale from 1 to 5…" will always be subjective, thus it can be difficult to repeat experiments.

Haung and Fang (2013) have predicted students' performance in an engineering course with acceptable results using only Grade Point Average (GPA) and past scores in statics, physics and calculus. The past subjects that were used as attributes were carefully selected, which means domain knowledge is needed to select appropriate subjects (features) that are to be used for prediction.

The use of feature ranking by importance reduces the need for specific domain knowledge for feature selection. All students' past scores can be the initial predictor variables, and then appropriate feature selection techniques used to select the most suitable combination of variables that will be used as features to create the classification model.

This study uses students past scores to predict the performance of students in five Computing or Mathematics subjects. The following research questions guided this study:

- How accurately can supervised learning correctly predict the performance of a student in a certain subject, based on his/her past performances in other subjects?
- Do highly ranked attributes (subjects) determined by machine learning feature selection methods have significant impact on student performance in selected fields?

METHODS

Past examination scores from a real university were collected to form the dataset that was used to answer the research questions posed in the previous sections.

To address the first research question, which is determining how accurately machine learning techniques can be used to predict student performance. Support Vector Machines (SVM) was used to create a classification model that maps past examination scores to future performance in a particular specialty. SVMs (Cortes & Vapnik, 1995) have been shown to perform better than Probabilistic Neural Networks (Modaresi & Araghinejad, 2014), K-Nearest Neighbors, C4.5 and Naïve Bayes supervised learning algorithms (Joachims, 1998). Also, the performance of support vector machines is not greatly reduced without feature selection (Joachims, 1998), making it suitable for the classification of high dimensional data. So, SVM was chosen as the machine learning algorithm for this study.

Two accuracy measures; simple accuracy (correctly predicted / total predicted) and F-Score were used to determine the accuracy of the classification models. F-Score is an accuracy measure that can show how well a model predicts individual classes.

To determine if certain past subjects have significant influence on a student's performance in another subject, features in the dataset were ranked, and then highly ranked features were manually examined to determine if there is any relationship between these highly ranked features (subjects) and the specialty that the classification model is to be created for.

Data

Data from a real university (Niger Delta University) was used in this study. This data contained the scores Computer Science students' obtained in their four year program.

Table 2. Structure of instances in examination performance predictor dataset

F_1	F_2	F_3	...	F_n	Class
5	4	2	...	45	G
10	3	2	...	0	P
...	...	...	...	...	...
23	24	12	...	34	G

Table 2 shows the structure of instances in an example dataset. $F_1...F_n$; $n=116$ are the scores for the subjects a student passed in his/her first 3 undergraduate years, while the class is the performance in a final year Computer Science or Mathematics subject. If a student did not take a particular course, the corresponding attribute value for that instance is zero. The 5 final year subjects (each as a standalone dataset) that are used in this study can be seen as students' chosen computing specialty. The final year subjects are shown in Table 3.

Students who scored less than 50 in the respective final year course in Table 3 are classified to have poor performance "P" in that course, while those who scored greater than 49 are classified to have good performance "G". Hence, this study is a two class supervised learning classification problem.

Table 3. Subject code for examination performance predictor datasets

Code	Subject
413	Expert Systems
421	Algorithms
422	System Simulation and Modeling
431	Numerical Methods II
436	Compiler Construction II

Preprocessing

Although there are five datasets, these datasets have identical features, with difference only in the class attribute. Class value can be good or poor, depending on the student's performance in that particular course.

There were 116 attributes, some of which are zero filled; where only few instances have values greater than zero. Dimension reduction is a way to improve generalization of machine learning algorithms. Low variance filter is one way to achieve dimension reduction as well as to remove zero filled attributes. This approach was used in this study, although principal component analysis and random forests are some widely used feature selection / dimension reduction techniques (Tang, Alelyani, & Liu, 2014).

Feature selection also filters out noise from data which is an important step in data mining, as has been shown in a number of data mining application domains such as Customer Relationship Management, where differentiating useful information from noise has been cited as one of the main challenges faced (Tolulope, Uwadia, & Ayo, 2013).

Classification

The dataset was divided into two disjoint parts; training set and test set. The test set contained a random 30% of the total instances in the dataset, while the training set contained the remaining 70%. SVM supervised learning algorithm was used to create classification models.

Support Vector Machines (SVM)

The SVM is similar to the perceptron (Rosenblatt, 1962) algorithm in that it aims to find a hyper plane that separates the instances of two classes in a dataset. However, the hyper plane separating the classes in the SVM is also the maximum distance between the two classes. Instances on the margins are called support vectors, while the hyper plane in the middle of the support vectors is the model that is used to predict the classes of future unseen examples.

Classes in a dataset may be linearly separable in a higher dimension in cases where they are not in its original dimension. Transforming this data to a higher dimension can be computationally and memory expensive. The SVM only needs to compute the dot product of pairwise examples in its algorithm, and there are functions that can compute the dot products of two vectors in a higher dimension without previously transforming the vectors to that dimension, thereby avoiding the computation and memory overhead of data transformation. Such functions are called kernel functions, the and process of using these kernel functions to compute the dot product of pairwise instances in a higher dimension instead of previously transforming instances is known as the kernel trick. Some kernel functions are the Radial Basis Function (RBF), polynomial and linear kernels.

The implementation of the SVM is readily available in the scikit-learn (Pedregosa et al., 2011) machine learning python package that is used in this study.

Training

The training set was used to determine the coefficients for the supervised learning classification models used in this study. Input parameters of supervised learning algorithms can be tuned to create more accurate classification models, because these parameters also determine the coefficients of classification models. Although there is no consensus as to how these parameters for supervised learning algorithms can be chosen, in some cases the default settings in machine learning software packages may be good enough. There are also algorithms that can be used to heuristically search the input parameter search space for optimal values (Bergstra, Bardenet, Bengio, & Kégl, 2011). The implementation of some of these algorithms such as random search (Bergstra & Bengio, 2012) and grid search are readily available in the scikit-learn python machine learning package. Although random search has been shown to be more efficient than the brute force grid search technique (Bergstra & Bengio, 2012), the parameter search space for the SVM is not wide, so grid search technique is adequate for this study.

Training Accuracy

Cross validation (Kohavi, 1995) is one of the accuracy measures widely used to determine the training accuracy of supervised learning models (Arlot & Celisse, 2010; Kenekayoro, Buckley, & Thelwall, 2014). In an n-fold cross validation, the training data is split into n equal disjoint sets. One set is used to test the accuracy of the classification model, while the union of the other n − 1 sets are used in training. This is repeated n times, with each of the n sets used to test the accuracy of the model exactly once. The final accuracy is the average accuracy for all n iterations.

Test Accuracy

30% of the dataset not used in training was used to determine the true accuracy of the supervised learning algorithms. Two accuracy measures; simple accuracy (1) and F-Score (3) are used to evaluate the accuracy of a supervised learning model.

The four parameters shown in Table 4 were used to compute the F-Score of supervised learning algorithms as shown in Equation (4):

$$\text{Simple Accuracy} = \frac{\text{Correctly predicted}}{\text{Total predicted}} \tag{1}$$

$$\text{Precision} = \frac{\text{TP}}{\text{TP} + \text{FP}} \tag{2}$$

$$\text{Recall} = \frac{\text{TP}}{\text{TP} + \text{FN}} \tag{3}$$

$$\text{F}_{\text{Score}} = \frac{2 * \text{Precision} * \text{Recall}}{\text{Precision} + \text{Recall}} \tag{4}$$

Table 4. Parameters used to compute F-Score for supervised learning algorithms for a two class classification problem

Parameter	Definition
True Positive (TP)	Number of instances in dataset correctly classified as true
True Negative (TN)	Number of instances in dataset correctly classified as false
False Positive (FP)	Number in instances in dataset incorrectly classified as true
False Negative (FN)	Number of instances in dataset incorrectly classified as true

When the test accuracy is worse than the training accuracy, the classification model is said to over fit the training set, if the training accuracy is not better than the test accuracy, generalization has been achieved. The machine learning assumption is that, the classification model will perform as well as it performs in the test set for future unseen cases.

Feature Importance

It is a consensus that feature selection through importance is necessary to improve generalization and for explaining/understanding data (Grömping, 2009). When it is necessary to rank features by importance, random forests, linear regression, relief and elastic net are among the state of art techniques used by researchers.

Important features in linear regression are determined by the coefficients of the linear model, while in random forests (Breiman, 2001), it is based on gini importance also referred to as the minimum decrease in impurity (Breiman, 2001; Sandri & Zuccolotto, 2008).

The impurity of a node in a tree is a measure that shows the extent of homogeneity (all instances belong to the same class) of that node, 0 being when the node is completely homogenous and 1 when the node is completely heterogeneous (each instance belongs to a different class). When a feature is used to split a node, the difference in impurities between the node and the resulting child nodes is computed. Features used to split nodes whose resulting child nodes are more homogenous have a higher decrease in impurity than those features whose node splits result in nodes that are heterogeneous, and are thus ranked as more important features. In random forests, the gini importance of a feature is the mean decrease in impurity for all nodes that have used that feature for splitting.

Random forests and linear regression may sometimes produce completely different feature rankings (Grömping, 2009), and they are both susceptible to missing some related features. The elastic net (Zou & Hastie, 2005) may be more suitable for data with correlated features when the purpose of feature selection is for understanding, as strongly correlated features are also included in the feature ranking list (Zou & Hastie, 2005).

The Relief algorithm (Robnik-Šikonja & Kononenko, 1997) is a method that uses nearest neighbors to determine feature importance, and it has been used to achieve good results (Kotsiantis & Pintelas, 2005). Compared to linear regression, the relief method may be more suitable for datasets that are not linearly separable.

Four feature selection techniques; linear regression, relief, random forests and elastic net were used to determine highly ranked features, and then these features were examined to identify any interesting patterns that may exist.

The 116 attributes (subjects from all disciplines) in each dataset were reduced to the 53 attributes that represented either a Mathematics, Statistics or Computer Science subject and then ranked with feature selection techniques (relief, linear regression, random forests and elastic net) to identify any existing relationships between attributes (past subjects) and classes (performance in future disciplines).

RESULTS

Table 6 shows the training and tests accuracy for 3 SVM kernels; RBF, Linear and Polynomial in the form of 0.98 (0.97), where 0.98 is the 5 fold cross validation accuracy and 0.97 is the accuracy of an unseen test set (not used in training) that was previously randomly selected and excluded from the dataset before training.

C, gamma and the degree of the polynomial kernel are the SVM parameters tuned in this study as shown in Table 5. Optimal parameters were identified by the grid search technique. *"Gamma defines how far the influence of a single training instance extends, with low values meaning high and high values meaning low"* (Pedregosa et al., 2011). C is the SVM parameter that controls the susceptibility of the SVM to outliners or noise. It is responsible for hard margins (Boser, Guyon, & Vapnik, 1992) and soft margins (Cortes & Vapnik, 1995). Higher C values (hard margins) means the model tries to correctly classify all instances in the training set, which could include outliners or noise and thus result in overfitting, while lower C values (soft margins) give room for misclassification of some instances in the training set that could be outliners. However, too low C could result in under fitting.

Table 5. Input parameters for support vector machines supervised learning algorithms

Kernel	C	Gamma	Class Weight	Degree
RBF	[1, 10, 100, 1000]	[0.01, 0,001, 0.0001]	[balanced, none]	NA
Linear	[1, 10, 100, 1000]	NA	[balanced, none]	NA
Poly	[1, 10, 100, 1000]	[0.01, 0,001, 0.0001]	[balanced, none]	[1, 2, 3]

Table 6. Cross validation and tests accuracy for the classification of student performance dataset with support vector machines RBF, linear and polynomial kernels

Dataset	RBF	CV(Test)	Linear	CV (Test)	Polynomial	CV (Test)
401	0.73 (0.80)	0.68 (0.59)	0.71 (0.64)
413	0.69 (0.70)	0.68 (0.62)	0.73 (0.71)
422	0.68 (0.64)	0.57 (0.75)	0.66 (0.62)
431	0.66 (0.67)	0.60 (0.62)	0.70 (0.67)
436	0.74 (0.74)	0.66 (0.71)	0.71 (0.64)

From the results shown in Table 6, the RBF kernel performed better than the linear and polynomial kernels. This is in line with Keerthi and Lin's (2003) suggestion that the RBF kernel will perform at least as well as the linear kernel if a complete model selection has been carried out. The RBF kernel is a good enough first choice to be used as the default kernel in the sckit-learn SVM package.

The polynomial kernel overfits the training set in all 5 datasets, so the learning model will benefit from more training examples to improve generalization. In two datasets, the test error is significantly less than the training error for the linear kernel which is counter intuitive to how supervised machine learning is supposed to work. This is likely because the test set had more hard cases than the training. Changing the random seed that is used to split the dataset into test and training influences the accuracy of the classification model, reaffirming that the learning model will benefit from more training examples.

Table 7 shows the how well individual classes (good and poor) were identified by the support vector machine supervised learning algorithm.

Table 7. Precision, recall and F-Score for predicting student's performance in computing disciplines with support vector machine (RBF Kernel)

Dataset	G	Precision(Recall)	P	Precision (Recall)	Average F-Score
401	0.77 (0.71)	0.61 (0.68)	0.70
413	0.77 (0.69)	0.61 (0.70)	0.70
422	0.78 (0.67)	0.44 (0.58)	0.65
431	0.82 (0.62)	0.51 (0.75)	0.67
436	0.80 (0.71)	0.69 (0.78)	0.74

Feature Ranking

Table 8 shows the top 10 features identified by relief, random forests, linear regression and elastic net. The symbol that represents each of the feature ranking methods appears in the cell of the corresponding attribute, if that attribute is in the top 10 features.

In line with the results previously shown by Grömping (2009), the top features for linear regression and random forests vary. Interestingly, relief and linear regression had similar top features, while random forest and elastic net had identical top features.

On a closer inspection of the datasets, the majority of values for some attributes, particularly in Mathematics and Statistics subjects were zero. These majority zero filled attributes were as a result of the elective subjects few students (sometimes only one) registered for. Perhaps the students who registered to take these courses needed extra credits. The relief and linear regression feature selection methods identified these majority zero filled attributes as top features. Even though these majority zero filled attributes may be useful for identifying an accurate linear classification model, it is not adequate for exploratory understanding of data, as it could be argued that not a lot can be learnt from zero filled attributes which will be filtered out by the low variance threshold feature selection technique. The random forest and elastic net seem more suitable for feature ranking for exploratory purposes for the dataset used in this research as they ignore the majority zero filled attributes.

The results shown in Table 8 did not suggest any obvious relationship between the performance in a particular subject and the future performance in another subject. Good students who on average performed well in all previous subjects were likely to perform just as well in the future subjects taken. However, not surprisingly the majority of Mathematics subjects appeared in the top features in the Numerical Analysis dataset, suggesting that a strong Mathematics background is necessary in order to achieve above average performance in Mathematics disciplines.

DISCUSSION AND CONCLUSION

The importance of developing ways to improve student performance cannot be overstated, which is why it has been the focus in a number of researches (Missildine, Fountain, & Summers, 2013; Yuretich, Khan, Leckie, & Clement, 2001). Using machine learning methods to predict student performance can help in identifying those students who may need special attention, or identifying if there are certain subjects whose performance greatly depends on the knowledge in another subject.

This study used support vector machines to predict the performance of students in computing subjects based on their past performance in other subjects. Up to 80% accuracy was obtained, which may also be improved with an increase in the training examples. Thus, the method described in this study is suitable for the design of recommender systems that can guide students into specialties that they may thrive in.

Results from the comparison of the radial basis function, polynomial and linear support vector machines kernel functions suggest that the radial basis function is a good first choice for the design support vector machines prediction models.

Tweaking the input parameters of supervised learning classification algorithms from the default settings in machine learning packages improves the accuracy of the resulting classification model. Although the random search has been shown to be effective in finding optimal input parameter combinations (Bergstra & Bengio, 2012), brute force methods such as the grid search technique that was used in this research is appropriate when the input parameter search space is not wide.

Subjects that determine the performance of students in certain disciplines were identified through feature ranking techniques. Elastic net and random forests seem to be appropriate feature selection techniques not only to improve generalization of classification models, but also for exploratory purposes in order to understand data. On close inspection of the identified top ranked features for the data used in this study, no single computing or Mathematics subject greatly influence the performance in another subject.

Table 8. Top 10 attributes or features in five datasets identified by relief ⊥, linear regression ■, random forests ✖ and elastic net ⊗ feature ranking techniques

Attribute	401	413	422	431	436
CMP201			✖	✖ ■ ⊗	✖ ⊗
CMP202	✖ ⊗		✖		
CMP203		⊗	⊗		
CMP301		■	✖ ⊗		
CMP303	✖ ⊗	✖ ⊗		✖ ⊗	
CMP305	■	✖		✖	
CMP307	✖	✖ ■ ⊗	✖ ■ ⊗		✖ ⊗
CMP308	✖ ■ ⊗			✖ ⊗	✖ ⊗
CMP309	✖ ⊗	✖ ⊗	✖ ⊗	✖ ⊗	
CMP311		✖ ⊗			⊗
CMP312		✖ ⊗			
CMP314			⊗		✖ ⊗
CMP322	✖		✖ ■ ⊗		
CMP336	✖ ⊗	✖ ⊗			
CMP338	✖ ⊗		✖	✖ ⊗	
MTH101			■		✖ ⊗
MTH104	⊗		■		✖ ⊗
MTH105	■	⊥ ■	⊥ ■	⊥ ■	⊥ ■
MTH106	⊥ ■	⊥ ■	⊥ ■	⊥	⊥ ■
MTH211		⊗	⊗		
MTH212					✖
MTH233				✖	
MTH235	✖ ⊗		■	✖	✖ ⊗
MTH236			■ ⊗	✖ ■ ⊗	
MTH258	⊗	✖ ⊗	✖ ⊗		
MTH302	⊗			✖ ■ ⊗	✖ ⊗
MTH313		⊥		⊥	
MTH316	■	⊥ ■	⊥ ■	⊥	⊥ ■
MTH319	⊥	⊥ ■	⊥ ■	⊥ ■	⊥ ■
MTH328	⊥ ■	⊥	⊥	■	⊥ ■
MTH344	⊥ ■	■	⊥	■	⊥ ■
MTH354	⊥ ■	⊥ ■	⊥ ■		⊥ ■
STA204	⊥			■	
STA261		✖ ⊗			
STA262		⊗			
STA336	✖ ⊗				
STA361	■	⊥ ■	⊥ ■	⊥	⊥ ■
STA362		✖ ⊗	⊗	⊥	
STA364	⊥ ■			■	■
STA365	⊥			⊥ ■	■
STA367	⊥ ■	⊥	⊥	■	⊥
STA374		⊥			⊥
STA375	⊗	⊗		⊥ ⊗	✖ ⊗

This research has described a method in which supervised learning can be used to enhance student learning in Higher Education Institutions, thus reemphasizing that machine learning can be applied to improve teaching and student performance in Higher Education Institutions as has previously been shown in other studies (Huang & Fang, 2013; Kotsiantis et al., 2004). This study also shows that using only past scores, without the subjective non-cognitive data can still produce good enough results for predicting student academic performance.

This research used data from for five computing subjects to demonstrate the possibility of applying machine learning techniques to the design of real time recommender systems for students. As only five computing subjects were considered in this study, further empirical analyses are necessary to understand how well the method used in this study can be used to accurately predict student performance across all disciplines.

REFERENCES

Arlot, S., & Celisse, A. (2010). A survey of cross-validation procedures for model selection. *Statistics Surveys*, *4*(0), 40–79. Retrieved from http://projecteuclid.org/euclid.ssu/1268143839 doi:10.1214/09-SS054

Baker, R. S. J. D. (2010). Data mining for education. International Encyclopedia of Education, 7(3), 112–118. doi:10.4018/978-1-59140-557-3

Bekele, R., & Menzel, W. (2005). A Bayesian Approach To Predict Performance Of A Student (BAPPS): A Case with Ethiopian Students. In *Artificial Intelligence and Applications* (pp. 189–194). Retrieved from http://www.actapress.com/Abstract.aspx?paperId=18917

Bergstra, J., Bardenet, R., Bengio, Y., & Kégl, B. (2011). Algorithms for hyper-parameter optimization. In *Advances in Neural Information Processing Systems* (pp. 2546–2554). Retrieved from http://papers. nips.cc/paper/4443-algorithms-for-hyper-parameter-optimization

Bergstra, J., & Bengio, Y. (2012). Random search for hyper-parameter optimization. *Journal of Machine Learning Research*. Retrieved from http://www.jmlr.org/papers/v13/bergstra12a.html

Boser, B., Guyon, I., & Vapnik, V. (1992). A training algorithm for optimal margin classifiers. In *Proceedings of the fifth annual workshop on Computational learning theory* (pp. 144–152). Retrieved from http://dl.acm.org/citation.cfm?id=130401

Breiman, L. (2001). Random forests. *Machine Learning*, *45*(1), 5–32. doi:10.1023/A:1010933404324

Cortes, C., & Vapnik, V. (1995). Support-Vector Networks. *Machine Learning*, *20*(273), 273–297. doi:10.1007/BF00994018

Delen, D. (2010). A comparative analysis of machine learning techniques for student retention management. *Decision Support Systems*, *49*(4), 498–506. doi:10.1016/j.dss.2010.06.003

Figlio, D. N., & Kenny, L. W. (2007). Individual Teacher Incentives and Student Performance *. *Journal of Public Economics*, *91*(5), 901–914. doi:10.1016/j.jpubeco.2006.10.001

Govindarajan, M., & Chandrasekaran, R. (2012). A Hybrid Multilayer Perceptron Neural Network for Direct Marketing. *International Journal of Knowledge-Based Organizations*, 2(3), 63–73. Retrieved from http://www.igi-global.com/article/content/68974 doi:10.4018/ijkbo.2012070104

Grömping, U. (2009). Variable Importance Assessment in Regression: Linear Regression versus Random Forest. *The American Statistician*, 63(4), 308–319. doi:10.1198/tast.2009.08199

Huang, S., & Fang, N. (2013). Predicting student academic performance in an engineering dynamics course: A comparison of four types of predictive mathematical models. *Computers & Education*, 61(1), 133–145. doi:10.1016/j.compedu.2012.08.015

Joachims, T. (1998). Text categorization with Support Vector Machines: Learning with many relevant features. In *European conference on machine learning* (pp. 137–142). 10.1007/BFb0026683

Keerthi, S. S., & Lin, C.-J. (2003). Asymptotic Behaviors of Support Vector Machines with Gaussian Kernel. *Neural Computation*, 15(7), 1667–1689. doi:10.1162/089976603321891855 PMID:12816571

Kenekayoro, P., Buckley, K., & Thelwall, M. (2014). Automatic classification of academic web page types. *Scientometrics*, 101(2). doi:10.100711192-014-1292-9

Kohavi, R. (1995). A Study of Cross-Validation and Bootstrap for Accuracy Estimation and Model Selection. *International Joint Conference on Artificial Intelligence*, 14(12), 1137–1143. doi:10.1067/mod.2000.109031

Kotsiantis, S. B., Patriarcheas, K., & Xenos, M. (2010). A combinational incremental ensemble of classifiers as a technique for predicting students' performance in distance education. *Knowledge-Based Systems*, 23(6), 529–535. doi:10.1016/j.knosys.2010.03.010

Kotsiantis, S. B., Pierrakeas, C., & Pintelas, P. (2004). Predicting students' performance in distance learning using machine learning techniques. *Applied Artificial Intelligence*, 18(5), 411–426. doi:10.1080/08839510490442058

Kotsiantis, S. B., & Pintelas, P. E. (2005). Predicting students' marks in Hellenic Open University. *Proceedings - 5th IEEE International Conference on Advanced Learning Technologies, ICALT 2005, 2005*, 664–668. doi:10.1109/ICALT.2005.223

Márquez-Vera, C., Cano, A., Romero, C., & Ventura, S. (2013). Predicting student failure at school using genetic programming and different data mining approaches with high dimensional and imbalanced data. *Applied Intelligence*, 38(3), 315–330. doi:10.100710489-012-0374-8

Missildine, K., Fountain, R., & Summers, L. (2013). Flipping the classroom to improve student performance and satisfaction. *Journal of Nursing*. Retrieved from http://www.healio.com/nursing/journals/jne/2013-10-52-10/%257Bfaa085a3-27be-4037-a63c-c87dc32391ba%257D/flipping-the-classroom-to-improve-student-performance-and-satisfaction?version=1

Modaresi, F., & Araghinejad, S. (2014). A Comparative Assessment of Support Vector Machines, Probabilistic Neural Networks, and K-Nearest Neighbor Algorithms for Water Quality Classification. *Water Resources Management*, 28(12), 4095–4111. doi:10.100711269-014-0730-z

Myller, N., Suhonen, J., & Sutinen, E. (2002). Using data mining for improving web-based course design. In *Proceedings - International Conference on Computers in Education, ICCE 2002* (pp. 959–963). 10.1109/CIE.2002.1186125

Pahwa, P., Arora, R., & Thakur, G. (2011). An efficient algorithm for data cleaning. *International Journal of Knowledge-Based Organizations*, *1*(4), 56–71. doi:10.4018/ijkbo.2011100104

Pedregosa, F., Varoquaux, G., Gramfort, A., Michel, V., Thirion, B., Grisel, O., ... Duchesnay, E. (2011). Scikit-learn: Machine Learning in Python. *Journal of Machine Learning Research*, *12*, 2825–2830.

Pritchard, M., & Wilson, G. (2003). Using emotional and social factors to predict student success. *Journal of College Student Development*, *44*(1), 18–28. Retrieved from https://muse.jhu.edu/article/40374/summary. doi:10.1353/csd.2003.0008

Raju, D., & Schumacker, R. (2016). Comparing Data Mining Models in Academic Analytics. *International Journal of Knowledge-Based Organizations*, *6*(2), 38–54. doi:10.4018/IJKBO.2016040103

Ransdell, S. (2001). Predicting college success: The importance of ability and non-cognitive variables. *International Journal of Educational Research*. Retrieved from http://www.sciencedirect.com/science/article/pii/S0883035501000325

Robnik-Šikonja, M., & Kononenko, I. (1997). An adaptation of Relief for attribute estimation in regression. In *Machine Learning: Proceedings of the Fourteenth International Conference (ICML'97)* (pp. 296–304). Retrieved from http://www.clopinet.com/isabelle/Projects/reading/robnik97-icml.pdf

Rosenblatt, F. (1962). *Principles of neurodynamics; perceptrons and the theory of brain mechanisms.* Washington: Spartan Books.

Sandri, M., & Zuccolotto, P. (2008). A Bias Correction Algorithm for the Gini Variable Importance Measure in Classification Trees. *Journal of Computational and Graphical Statistics*, *17*(3), 611–628. doi:10.1198/106186008X344522

Tang, J., Alelyani, S., & Liu, H. (2014). Feature selection for classification: A review. *Data Classification: Algorithms and Applications*, 37. Retrieved from http://eprints.kku.edu.sa/170/

Thai-Nghe, N., Busche, A., & Schmidt-Thieme, L. (2009). Improving academic performance prediction by dealing with class imbalance. In *ISDA 2009 - 9th International Conference on Intelligent Systems Design and Applications* (pp. 878–883). 10.1109/ISDA.2009.15

Tolulope, F. I., Uwadia, C., & Ayo, C. K. (2013). A Knowledge Mining Approach for Effective Customer Relationship Management. *International Journal of Knowledge-Based Organizations*, *3*(2), 76–86. doi:10.4018/ijkbo.2013040105

Wolpert, D. H., & Macready, W. G. (1997). No free lunch theorems for optimization. *IEEE Transactions on Evolutionary Computation*, *1*(1), 67–82. doi:10.1109/4235.585893

Yuretich, R. F., Khan, S. A., Leckie, R. M., & Clement, J. J. (2001). Active-learning methods to improve student performance and scientific interest in a large introductory oceanography course. *Journal of Geoscience Education*, *49*(2), 111–119. Retrieved from http://www.nagt-jge.org/doi/abs/10.5408/1089-9995-49.2.111 doi:10.5408/1089-9995-49.2.111

Zou, H., & Hastie, T. (2005). Regularization and variable selection via the elastic net. *Journal of the Royal Statistical Society. Series B, Statistical Methodology*, *67*(2), 301–320. doi:10.1111/j.1467-9868.2005.00503.x

This research was previously published in the International Journal of Knowledge-Based Organizations (IJKBO), 8(4); pages 67-79, copyright year 2018 by IGI Publishing (an imprint of IGI Global).

APPENDIX

Table 9. Names of features in datasets

CMP201 - Computer Programming I	MTH235 - Linear Algebra I
CMP202 - Computer Programming II	MTH236 - Linear Algebra II
CMP203 - Introduction to Computer Systems	MTH258 - Real Analysis I
CMP301 - Introduction to Digital Design and Micro Processor	MTH302 - Discrete Mathematics
CMP303 - Computer Architecture I	MTH313 - Elementary Differential Equations II
CMP305 - Data Structure and Algorithms	MTH316 - Introduction to Operational Research
CMP307 - Operating Systems I	MTH319 - Mathematical Modelling
CMP308 - Operating Systems II	MTH328 - Vector and Tensor Analysis
CMP309 - Database Design and Management	MTH344 - Dynamics of a Rigid Body
CMP311 - Automata Theory, Computability and Formal Language	MTH354 - Metric Space Topology
CMP312 - Systems Analysis and Design	STA204 - Statistics for Physical Sciences
CMP314 - Social and Ethical Issues in Computer Science	STA261 - Probability II
CMP322 - Numerical Methods I	STA262 - Inference II
CMP336 - Compiler Construction I	STA336 - Introduction to Operational Research
CMP338 - Computer Architecture II	STA361 - Probability III
MTH101 - Elementary Mathematics I	STA362 - Inference III
MTH104 - Elementary Mathematics III	STA364 - Lab for Inference III
MTH105 - Engineering Mathematics I	STA365 - Analysis of Variance
MTH106 - Engineering Mathematics II	STA367 - Sampling Theory and Survey
MTH211 - Mathematical Methods I	STA374 - Statistical Quality Control
MTH212 - Elementary Differential Equations I	STA375 - Operational Research I
MTH233 - Sets, Logic and Algebra	

Chapter 21
Machine Learning Based Taxonomy and Analysis of English Learners' Translation Errors

Ying Qin

Beijing Foreign Studies University, Beijing, China

ABSTRACT

This study extracts the comments from a large scale of Chinese EFL learners' translation corpus to study the taxonomy of translation errors. Two unsupervised machine learning approaches are used to obtain the computational evidences of translation error taxonomy. After manually revision, ten types of English to Chinese (E2C) and eight types Chinese to English (C2E) translation errors are finally confirmed. There probably exists three categories of top-level errors according to the hierarchical clustering results. In addition, three supervised learning methods are applied to automatically recognize the types of errors, among which the highest performance reaches F1 = 0.85 on E2C and F1 = 0.90 on C2E translation. Further comparison to the intuitive or theoretical studies on translation taxonomy shows some phenomenon accompanied by language skill improvement of Chinese learners. Analysis on translation problems based on machine learning provides the objective insight and understanding on the students' translations.

1. INTRODUCTION

Errors are unavoidable for EFL students during language learning. Error analysis plays an important role in language pedagogy by observing students' performances in real communication situations (Richards, 2015). And translation practice could reflect the primary ability of L2 learners as they process second language (Dodds, 1999, pp. 58-61). Compared to the errors in students' free essay writings, translation errors have some unique features because translation is an activity in a constrained language environment.

DOI: 10.4018/978-1-6684-6291-1.ch021

When transforming the source text into the target, students have to consider the semantic equivalence of the two texts as well as the expression in target language. Therefore, translation error could reveal the default of language application when L2 learners try to use the word and grammar to convert the original text into the target language. Additionally, Séguinot (1990) pointed out that translation error analysis could be used to deeply explore the procedure of translation besides being used to judge the quality of translation. Thus, translation error analysis is of great significance to L2 teaching and language study (Yakimovskaya, 2012).

However, the taxonomy of translation error lacks commonly agreed distinctions probably due to that the causes of errors are very complicated. Pym (1992) divided translation error into binary and non-binary error to study the division between translation teaching and language teaching. Binary error refers to the error with no ambiguity and usually could be corrected with the right one. For example, errors of spelling, inflection, word selection and syntax are typical binary errors. On the other hand, inaccurate or unfaithful translation is regarded as non-binary error. Another translation error taxonomy is whether the error is content-related or language-related (Secară, 2005). The former will lead to semantic difference between the source and the target text, such as mistranslation and omission. Language-related error is not as serious as the content-related, generally not leading to misunderstanding. For example, ignorance of case, misuse of possessive and improper collocation is usually viewed as minor errors. More categories of translation errors are summarized by Corder (1974) including addition, selection, omission and ordering according to different translation methods. Even more categories are proposed by American Translators Association (ATA) with as many as 24 kinds of common translation problems.

Some scholars put forward hierarchical categories of translation errors. According to Richards (1971), the top level of error type is a three-kind framework: a) interference errors, generated by L1 transfer; b) intralingual errors, resulted from incorrect (incomplete or over-generalized) application of language rules and c) developmental errors, caused by the construction of faulty hypotheses in L2. Each type of error can be further divided into several sub-types.

Chinese scholars have studied the translation problems made by different learners as well. Sun (2011) described four common Chinese to English (C2E) translation errors made by second-year English majors. Chen (2012) applied the corpus-based approach to study the top 10 C2E errors in the national university entrance exams. Both of them adopt single-layer error taxonomy. Nevertheless, the taxonomy of translation errors is subjective, varying with different researchers or purposes.

In recent years empirical approach in translation error analysis is attracting more and more attention (Campoy et al., 2010). The authors lately build a Chinese learners' translation corpus with comments of teachers on translation problems. Based on the learners' corpus, the authors attempt to apply machine learning methods including clustering and classification to explore the taxonomy of translation errors. The goal and contribution of this study is to generalize translation errors in Chinese EFL learners in a more objective way than the previous studies, which might provide a hint to language learning and translation teaching.

In the following paper the authors first give the introduction to the learners' translation corpus lately built, followed by the description of machine learning approaches including clustering and classification algorithms employed in this study. Section 4 is the experimental results and translation error instances and analyses based on the corpus. The authors also compare the results to the related studies on translation error taxonomy in this section. The last section contains the conclusion and future work.

2. LEARNERS' TRANSLATION CORPUS WITH NATURAL COMMENTS

The translation texts the authors collected are written translation assignments of English major post-graduate students. Besides the sources and students' translations, the authors collect the comments of the teachers. Due to the fact that translation errors may be attributed to numerous causes and located on numerous levels, the authors do not require the teachers to use pre-defined error types to markup the problems in the students' translation assignments. Instead, they can make comments on the translation problems in their own words. Most teachers prefer to use natural sentences to describe translation problems. Therefore, the comments can fully reflect the opinion of the commenter on the translation problems. The length of comments may vary from a single word to several paragraphs.

The corpus contains original texts of 23 topics, with 15 C2E and 8 E2C topics respectively. It is also a balanced corpus including six fields such as technology, politics, literature, and law. Table 1 shows the field distribution of translations in the corpus. Totally the corpus consists of 1091 students' translation texts over one million words. The number of commenters for C2E and E2C translations is 123 and 29 respectively. Most of them are teachers and some are their assistants, all with high translation competence. Therefore, the study of these comments may reflect the common viewpoints of professionals, not only individual opinion. Figure 1 illustrates a little portion of the corpus on C2E translation, in which the left part is the student's translation and the right is the teacher's annotations. The comments are translated into English since most comments are in Chinese in the corpus.

Table 1. Number of translation texts in different fields

Fields	Economy	Politics	Literature	Law	Technology	News
text number	382	334	201	70	110	46

Figure 1. Learners' translations corpus with comments

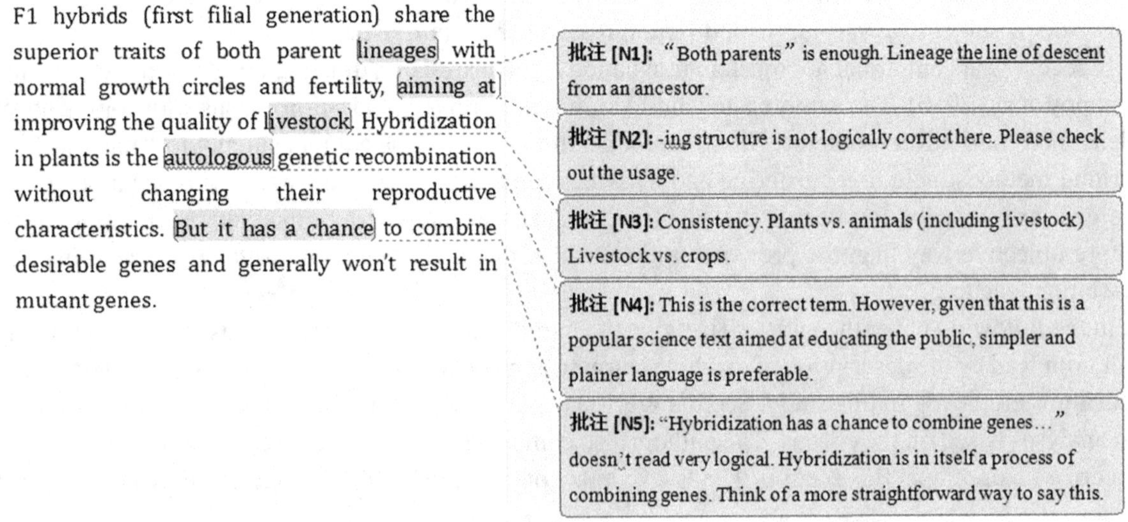

F1 hybrids (first filial generation) share the superior traits of both parent lineages with normal growth circles and fertility, aiming at improving the quality of livestock. Hybridization in plants is the autologous genetic recombination without changing their reproductive characteristics. But it has a chance to combine desirable genes and generally won't result in mutant genes.

批注 [N1]: "Both parents" is enough. Lineage the line of descent from an ancestor.

批注 [N2]: -ing structure is not logically correct here. Please check out the usage.

批注 [N3]: Consistency. Plants vs. animals (including livestock) Livestock vs. crops.

批注 [N4]: This is the correct term. However, given that this is a popular science text aimed at educating the public, simpler and plainer language is preferable.

批注 [N5]: "Hybridization has a chance to combine genes…" doesn't read very logical. Hybridization is in itself a process of combining genes. Think of a more straightforward way to say this.

The authors glean all the translation comments using VBA program to explore the taxonomy of translations problems. In the following, the authors will employ clustering and classification approaches to study the error types in the students' translations according to the comments.

3. MACHINE LEARNING METHODS

Machine learning is the method to automatically learn the pattern from the empirical data using computer. Generally it is divided into supervised learning, which learns from labeled data, and unsupervised learning, in which the data are not labeled by human, also called raw data. Clustering is a kind of unsupervised learning approach, that is, samples are grouped according to the similarity among them. And classification is a supervised task, in which the class of sample is assigned according to the model learned from manually labeled data.

3.1. Clustering

Two clustering methods, flat clustering and hierarchical clustering are widely used in data analysis. Flat clustering means all the classes are equally grouped. While in hierarchical clustering, some classes may be more general than others, so they are assigned to the top level. K-means and ISODATA are two classic flat clustering algorithms. Among the hierarchical clustering methods, the authors select agglomerative clustering which is easy to understand and implement.

3.1.1. K-Means Clustering

K-means is a ripe unsupervised machine learning algorithm with the advantage of simplicity and efficiency (MacQueen, 1967). Here is the principle of K-means.

For a given sample set of $\{x_1, x_2, \ldots, x_m\}$, each represented as a vector in the n-dimensional feature space $x_i = [x_1, x_2, \ldots, x_n]^T$, K-means aims to partition the samples into k clusters for each closing to its center with the minimum distance. The algorithm initially sets k centers of each cluster $\{m_1, m_2, \ldots, m_k\}$ and then iteratively proceeds between the following two steps until converging or the change is small enough to stop:

Step 1: Assign each sample to a cluster by the nearest distance, in Euclidean or cosine distance, that is,

$$\mathbf{x} \in \omega_i \ \ if \ \ d(\mathbf{x}, m_i) = \min(d(x, m_1), d(x, m_2), \ldots, d(x, m_k)) \tag{1}$$

Step 2: Calculate the mean of each cluster and then update the center with the new value.

In translation problem analysis, the authors convert the comment sentences into vectors. Thus, the distance between vectors indicates the relations or similarities between them, that is, the more similar meaning of the comment sentence is, the closer distance of vectors will be.

In K-means, the number of cluster k should be known as a priori, that is to say, the authors should specify the k value before running the algorithm. In the final, samples are grouped into the given number of clusters.

Obviously, K-means is suitable to group samples with the known number of class. From the statistical viewpoint, the clusters grouped by K-means can be interpreted as the Maximum Likelihood Estimates (MLE) of the sample partition assuming that each cluster comes from a spherical normal distribution with different means but identical variance (and zero covariance). In this study the authors assume the premise is satisfied.

3.1.2. ISODATA Clustering

ISODATA, abbreviated from Iterative Self-Organizing Data Analysis Technique Algorithm, is another well-known flat clustering algorithm (Ball & Hall, 1965). ISODATA is similar to K-means on distance computation. The distinct difference lies in that ISODATA allows for different number of clusters while K-means assumes that the number of clusters is fixed. Therefore, this algorithm includes the merging of clusters if their separation distance in the feature space is less than a user-specified value and the rules for splitting a single cluster into two clusters. Clusters are merged if either the number of members in a cluster is less than a certain threshold or if the centers of two clusters are too close, less than a certain threshold. Clusters are split into two different clusters if the standard deviation exceeds the predefined value and the number of members is twice the threshold for the minimum number of members. The desired number of clusters, minimum number of samples in each cluster (for discarding clusters), maximum variance (for splitting clusters) and minimum pairwise distance (for merging clusters) are known as the parameters of the algorithm. The setting of parameters is vital to the final clustering result.

The implementation of ISODATA is depicted as follows.

Step 1: Given a dataset of $\{x_1, x_2, \ldots, x_m\}$, each x be n-dimensional vector. Initialize the algorithm with a desired number of cluster $k=k_0$ and cluster centers $\{m_1, m_2, \ldots, m_k\}$.

Step 2: Assign each data x to the cluster $w_j(j=1\ldots k)$ with closest distance according to Equation 1.

Step 3: Discard clusters containing too few members and reassign its members to other clusters, $k=k-1$.

Step 4: For each cluster $w_j(j=1\ldots k)$, update the cluster center $\{m_1, m_2, \ldots, m_k\}$ according to Equation 2,

$$m_j = \frac{1}{n_j} \sum_{x \in w_j} x \tag{2}$$

and the covariance matrix as Equation 3 to obtain the variances $\sigma_1^2, \sigma_2^2, \ldots, \sigma_n^2$,

$$\sum_j = \frac{1}{n_j} \sum_{x \in w_j} (x - m_j)(x - m_j)^T \tag{3}$$

Step 5: If there are too few clusters, go to the step of splitting;

Else if there are too many clusters, go to the step of merging;

Step 6: Stop if the maximum number of iterations is reached. Otherwise go to Step 2.

Here the authors omit the details of splitting and merging for sake of simplicity and focus on the core principle of ISODATA.

The advantage of ISODATA over K-means lies in that the number of clusters k can be dynamically adjusted in the procedure. So ISODATA algorithm is more flexible than K-means. But all of the parameters listed above have effect on the result. The best setting is always empirical values after many trials. In the paper the authors use ISODATA to obtain the estimated number of translation error categories.

3.1.3. Agglomerative Clustering

According to the theoretical studies, some translation errors may be more abstract than others, for example, contented-related errors and language-related errors are more general than specific errors like word selection and wrong format. So the authors apply hierarchical clustering to observe whether there exist significant distinctions among error categories, the number of error type on top level and the relations among them.

Two strategies are usually adopted in hierarchical clustering, one is top-down splitting method and the other is bottom-up agglomeration. Agglomerative clustering belongs to the latter (Mullner, 2011). The basic idea of agglomerative clustering is merging. At the very beginning, the algorithm views each sample as one cluster, which is the deepest level. Then the merging procedure is iteratively carried on until reaching the specified number or single cluster. Finally, the samples are grouped into a tree-like structure or the hierarchical categories.

The authors implement a hierarchical clustering program to study the translation errors.

4. CLASSIFICATION

Classification is a supervised machine learning method. Classifier must be trained on labeled data before it is used to classify new or unlabeled data. To train the classifier of translation errors, the authors try three off-the-shelf methods including decision tree, logistic regression and SVM. The idea of classification in each method is quite different.

4.1. Decision Tree

Decision tree is used in the task of both classification and regression (Safavian & Landgrebe, 1991). The goal of decision tree is to build a model to predict the class the data belongs to by learning simple decision rules inferred from the data features. There are several famous implementations of decision tree such as ID3, C4.5, C5.0 (Hastie et al., 2009). Step by step, the algorithm finds the best feature to be used as the rule to divide the data. The common criteria of the best feature include information entropy and gain of information entropy, which are employed in ID3 and C4.5 respectively. Decision tree is widely used because it is able to interpret why the data is predicted to one class by tracing back the rules along the tree.

4.2. Logistic Regression

Logistic regression is also known as Maximum Entropy (Berger, 1996) or the log-linear classifier. It can combine different facts to make probability prediction of the class the data belong to. As a generative model, it makes no assumption of unknown facts, that is, the probability of prediction of each class is equal when there is no evidence to support the class prediction (Ratnaparkhi, 1998). The rules of classification are denoted as feature functions, which contextual information in the sentence is often considered. Usually the feature function $f(a,b)$ takes the simple form of indication.

$$f(a,b) = \begin{cases} 1 & if \quad b = b' \ and \ cp(a) = true \\ 0 & otherwise \end{cases}$$

where b is the contextual feature and $cp(a)$ is a prediction or assertion.

Feature selection is crucial to build a logistic regression classifier. Logistic regression is usually used in multiple classification tasks.

4.3. SVM

SVM (Support Vector Machine) is an effective non-linear classification algorithm in high dimensional spaces (Cortes & Vapnik, 1995). In SVM model, a sample is represented as a point in the high-dimensional space. The algorithm can divide the points by a clear gap, so the core idea of the algorithm is the support vector in classification. The so-called support vector is a hyperplane that can divide the data into two classes with the largest margin. Figure 2 depicts the concept of support vector in the partition of circle samples and triangle samples. Though the hyperplane H1-3 can correctly divide the two kinds of samples, H2 is the best one because it separates the two classes as wide as possible, namely the largest margin.

Figure 2. Support vector of SVM

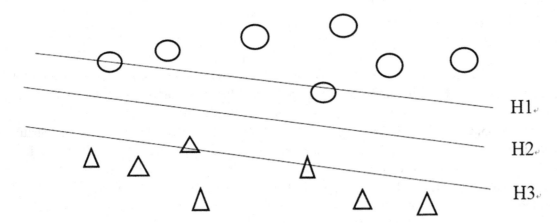

SVM maps non-linearly separated samples in finite-dimensional space into a higher dimensional space using a kernel function, which makes the samples linearly separated. Initially SVM is used in binary classification task. Here the authors take the binary classification task as an example to explain the principle. Given the training data set with n samples $((x_1, y_1), (x_2, y_2), ..., (x_n, y_n))$, where y_i is the label of class, either -1 or 1 in binary task, the maximum margin hyperplane is defined so that the distance between the hyperplane and the nearest point x_i from either group is maximized, that is, the vector satisfies, $w \cdot x - b = 0$ where w is a normalized vector to the hyperplane, and b represents the offset of the hyperplane from the origin along the normal vector.

SVM is proved to be a powerful algorithm in many tasks such as chunking (Kudo & Matsumoto, 2001) and POS tagging (Giménez & Marquez, 2004).

5. EXPERIMENTS AND COMPARATIVE STUDY

5.1. Design of the Experiment

The workflow of exploring translation error category based on the comments contains six stages including comment extraction, data cleaning, comment vectorization, clustering, classification and result analysis as depicted in Figure 3.

Figure 3. Workflow of experiment on translation error taxonomy

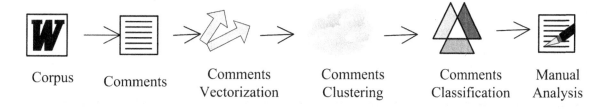

| Corpus | Comments | Comments Vectorization | Comments Clustering | Comments Classification | Manual Analysis |

The authors extract the teachers' comments in the corpus using a VBA script, one paragraph for one comment. Then it is followed by data cleaning such as removing the comments only containing single punctuation, hyperlink or other meaningless characters. Word-level processing including English word stemming and Chinese word segmentation is carried on subsequently. The authors then convert the comment sentences into vectors for clustering and classification. Totally there are 20744 comments in C2E translations and 6467 in E2C translations.

How to convert sentences into vectors? CBOW model, which is Continuous Bag-of-Words architecture proposed by Mikolov et al. (2013), is commonly used as neural networks inputs, by which the word semantic features are represented iteratively in lower dimension in form of word vector. In the experiment, the authors apply pre-trained Chinese word vectors with dimension size of 300 on the merged very large sale corpora including Baidu Encyclopedia, Wikipedia_zh, People's Daily News and so on (Li et al., 2018). The comment sentence vector is the averaged vector of all word vectors in the sentence. The dimension of word vector is determined by the generation algorithm. Word vector in low dimensional feature space could encode semantic relations among contextual words, resulting in dense hidden semantic representation (Mikolov et al., 2013). Limited by the computation capacity of a computer, the size of word vector is usually set as 300, 150 or 50. The lower dimension, the denser representation.

To analyze translation error types based on machine learning, the authors design the four-phase experiments: first, the authors use flat clustering ISODATA and K-means to obtain the natural translation error types, and manually check and refine the clustering results. In the next phase the authors train three classifiers using decision tree, logistic regression and SVM to automatically identify translation errors, and simultaneously inspect the boundary of error categories. Then hierarchical clustering is used to explore abstract relations among the error types.

5.2. Flat Clustering

Since it is not clear what the number of error categories is, the authors first use ISODATA to estimate the probable value. In ISODATA clustering, the authors try the initial number of clusters as 15, 13 and 10 respectively. Other parameters are listed as follows. The maximum number of pairs of clusters which can be merged is 5. The threshold value of minimum number of samples in each cluster is set 100 for discarding a cluster. When the standard deviation in each cluster is larger than 0.05, the cluster will be split and when the pairwise distance between clusters is less than 0.3, the clusters will be merged. The above parameters are kept consistent in clustering C2E and E2C translation comments. Table 2 shows the final number of clustering in different initial settings after dozens of iterations.

Table 2. ISODATA clustering results

Translation direction	Initial number of clustering	Final number of clustering
C2E	15	11
	13	10
	10	10
E2C	15	12
	13	10
	10	8

According to the table, the comments on C2E translations are naturally clustered as 10 types and the E2C translation error types range from 8-10 due to the different starting numbers. Based on the result of ISODATA clustering, the authors then specify the number of clusters in the following flat clustering. Though there is no fixed number of clusters, the result still tells us the estimated and objective number of translation error categories.

Further, the authors apply K-means to collect the clusters. After several trials in different k values, the authors obtain meaningful error classes when the value of k is set around eight. After closely checking the comments of each type, the authors affirm ten translation error types in E2C and eight in C2E translations. The name of each error type mainly comes from the keyword in the comments or simple induction. Figure 4 and 5 show the error types and their distributions in C2E and E2C corpus respectively.

Figure 4. C2E translation error types and distributions

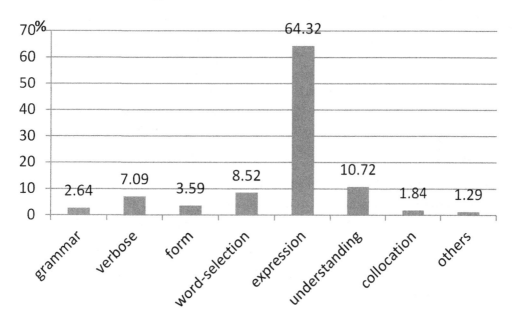

Figure 5. E2C translation error types and distributions

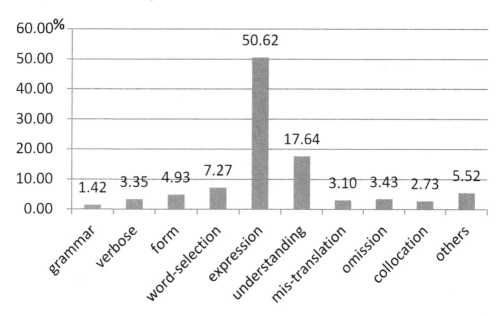

According to the above figures, the most frequent error type is expression both in E2C and C2E translations, accounting for more than half the amount. This type of errors is automatically clustered because the most frequent meaning in the comments is 'expression' or 'express'. In fact, expression problems can cover many translation errors. Therefore, it needs further study. The authors then divide the expression error into several subtypes through observing and analyzing. In E2C translations, 71.92%

expression problems are inaccurate translation, indicating that the source information is incompletely translated. The second most common expression problem is anaphora resolution and Chinese sentence structure, accounting for 11.24% and 11.42%. The other portion involves ambiguity and fluency of expression. With regard to C2E translation expression errors, the most frequently used word in comments is also inaccuracy, accounting for 63.93%, followed by improper sentence structure expression, for about 14.12%. The English expression problems also contain ambiguity and improper reference.

The translation error types clustered according to the comments give us an objective angle to analyze the translation mistakes made by the postgraduate students. Since the students have completed four years of adequate language and translation learning, there is a decreasing proportion of binary error. Most translation errors belong to non-binarism, which can be reflected in the teachers' comments. This can explain why the most frequent word in teachers' comments is 'expression' instead of a clear and specific error name. The phenomenon might serve as a hint of the hypothesis proposed by Pym (1992), that is, with the progress in language learning, the error type has the general tendency towards non-binarism.

Here the authors paste several typical errors and corresponding comments in the corpus to peer into translation error types. The underlined words or phrases in the sentence are problematic in the translation, marked by the teachers. The type that the error belongs to is assigned manually with reference to the automatic clustering.

C2E-e.g.1.

Source: 水月观音的披纱远看轻薄、欲隐欲现,细如蛛丝、薄如蝉翼,似乎能感觉到水月观音的微微呼吸。

Looking from afar, the scarf drapes over the bodhisattva's shoulders is lightweight, partly <u>hidden</u> and partly visible...

Comments: 藏哪了?欲隐欲现不能这么表达,hidden没有这个意思

(Where to hide? You cannot express the phrase like this, because 'hidden' does not mean it.)

Error type: expression-inaccuracy

Analysis: The student failed to find an accurate English word to translate the Chinese multi-word phrase.

C2E-e.g.2.

Source: 近看会发现这些都是极为细密的线条勾画成的网,上面呈现六棱形的花瓣,每一花瓣竟然都是由48根比发丝还细的金线组成

Yet upon a closer look, you may notice that the veil is veined with patterns of six-fold radial symmetry, each fold <u>laminated</u> with 48 golden lines thinner than hair.

Comment: 理解错laminate这个词了

(The understanding of 'laminate' is wrong.)

Error type: understanding

Analysis: The error may be attributed to lack of the knowledge of the English word.

C2E-e.g.3.

Source:诸如梵天肃穆,天王威武,金刚刚毅,天女妩媚,鬼子母慈祥,儿童天真,都真切生动

The dignified God of Creation (Brahma), the mighty Four *heavenly kings* (Caturm ahārājakayikas), the resolute Guardians (Kongōs), the beautiful Heavenly Maidens (Devakanyas), the loving mother Goddess (Hariti), the adorable children...

Comment: 如果只说heavenly kings,则体现不出天王"守护"之意,因此改为Guardian更妥当

(If you just say 'heavenly kings', it cannot reflect the meaning of 'guardian', so changing it to 'guardian' is better.)

Error type: word selection

Analysis: The error type belongs to under-translation with improper word selection.

C2E-e.g.4.

Source: 它已经转变成一种收集证据的方法。

It has mutated into a method of evidence collection.

Comment: 代词It,指代不明,此处将其指明比较好。

(The reference of pronoun is vague. It is better to make it explicit.)

Error type: expression-anaphora

Analysis: Translation explicitness of pronoun sometimes is needed to make it better understood.

E2C-e.g.5.

Source: *Encourage international cooperation actors to support disability-inclusive policies and programs and refrain from supporting any policy, program or practice that is inconsistent with the rights of persons with disabilities.*

鼓励国际合作伙伴对兼顾残疾的政策方案给予支持,禁止支持任何侵害残疾人权利的政策、方案或做法.

Comment: Inconsistent与侵害还是有差别的

('Inconsistent' is different from 'violation'.)

Error type: word selection

Analysis: The error is attributed to confusing the two synonyms.

E2C-e.g.6.

Source: *develop disability-related indicators to assess adequately the impact of all policies and programs on persons with disabilities.*

制定残疾相关指标以充分评估所有残疾人相关政策和方案的影响

Comment: 表达不够通顺

(Not fluent enough in expression.)

Error type: expression-fluency

Analysis: It is not an idiomatic Chinese sentence, probably affected by the source.

E2C-e.g.7.

Source: *The financial services sector, which must innovate to cut the costs of legacy systems and manage increasing regulation, is leading the way with block chain and taking advantage of the technology's security, immutability, transparency, and ability to cut out the middleman.*

作为率先使用区块链技术的行业,金融服务业利用了该技术的安全性、不可篡改行、透明行以及其剔除中间人的能力

Comment: "安全性"已经是名词了,后面再加"能力"则不合适。

(Since '安全性' is a noun, it is not suitable to add '能力' next to it.)

Error type: collocation

Analysis: Collocation is a kind of binary error.

E2C-e.g.8.

Source: *Urban density is about efficient resource use.*

<u>(控制)城市密度的关键在于有效地利用资源。</u>

Comment: 逻辑关系错误

(Logic relation is wrong.)

Error type: others

Analysis: The Chinese sentence has a different logic relation of the subject and object to English source.

5.3. Classification

Based on the clustering results, the authors manually check the error categories. Since some clusters include trifle phrases or ambiguous sentences, the authors remove them from the clusters and refine the training data. The authors also reassign the comments incorrectly clustered to the corresponding correct cluster. After tagging error type on translation comments, the authors train three classifiers based on decision tree, logistic regression and SVM. The authors extract the features in the comments using TF-IDF (Term Frequency and Inversed Document Frequency) (Blei et al., 2003). After the principal component analysis (Wold et al., 1987), 80-90% feature vectors are input to train the above classifiers. The ratio of training and test data is 4:1. The performances of three classifiers with F1 value are shown in Table 3.

Table 3. Performances of translation error classifiers

	Decision tree	Logistic regression	SVM
C2E	0.81	0.85	0.90
E2C	0.77	0.79	0.85

The best classification performance comes from SVM classifier as shown in Table 3. The lowest F1 value is from decision tree with 0.81 on C2E and 0.77 on E2C translation error classification. The high performance of classifiers reveals that the boundary of each error type is clear and easy to detect by the algorithms. It is interesting to notice that it is harder for all the classifiers to classify the E2C error comments than the C2E comments even though all the comments are in Chinese.

5.4. Hierarchical Clustering

The authors use Ward (a kind of distance algorithms) to calculate the minimum distance among clusters in the agglomerative clustering (Murtagh & Legendre, 2014). For clarity, the dendrogram (the tree-like clustering graph) is drawn on the top 20 clusters. Figure 6 and 7 are the dendrogram of C2E and E2C translation errors respectively. In the figures, the height of the horizon line reflects the distance of two merged clusters. The higher the line, the larger the distance between the two clusters.

It is easy to judge the number of errors on the top level according to the dendrogram. The authors think it is appropriate to divide the translation errors into three kinds on the top level because the distinction among them is rather significant. Under preliminary observation, the authors find that the top level error types are omission, mistranslation and others.

Figure 6. Hierarchical clustering dendrogram of C2E translation errors

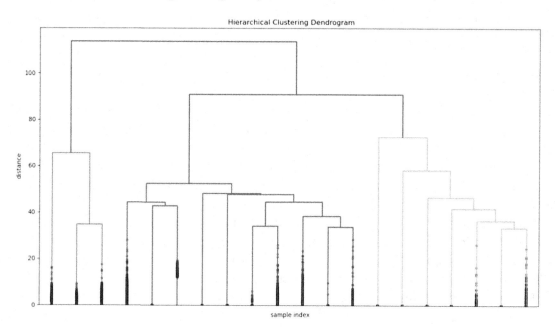

Figure 7. Hierarchical clustering dendrogram of E2C translation errors

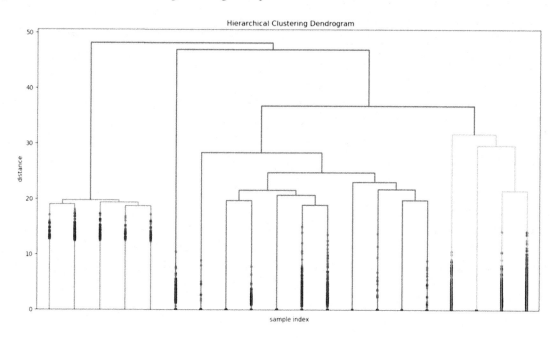

Though the number of categories is accidentally identical to the opinion of Richards (1971), the categories are not compatible with his findings. The authors owe the difference to the approach of semantic distance calculation which only utilizes the superficial information of comment sentences to measure the distance of comments. Compared to the abstract analyses on translation problems based on linguistics and cognition, the hierarchical clustering of translation errors is coarse and somewhat random. The result from hierarchical clustering seems to support the opinion that the top level of translation error category consists of three types.

5.5. Comparison to Related Studies

Many researchers proposed individual viewpoints on the taxonomy of translation errors. The authors coarsely compare the present work to the intuitive or theoretical error classification schema. According to the observation of students' translation assignments, Sun (2011) summed up four translation errors made by Chinese undergraduate students majoring in English. Based on the corpus of college entrance English exams in 2010, Chen (2012) obtained the most frequent translation errors and distributions. It is hard to compare the error types because the taxonomy is quite different.

The authors assume the progress of students' translation competence on different level. What is the change of translation error? After a careful analysis, the authors extract the error types overlapped with those in the study of Chen (2012). These C2E error types have similar names and contents but different distributions. Horizontal comparison of error distribution is improper because the categories are different. Therefore, the authors calculate the rate of error type change as shown in Table 4 and make longitudinal comparison among error types.

Table 4. Comparative study of translation error types

Type	Chen (2012)	This research	Change ratio
word selection	19.9%	7.27%	63.47%
grammar	23.8%	2.64%	88.91%
collocation	5%	2.73%	45.4%
mistranslation	13.3%	3.1%	76.69%
omission	9.4%	3.43%	63.51%
form	11%	4.93%	55.18%

The table shows that the translation error of grammar has the most significant decrease among all the errors. On the other hand, the rate of change on collocation error is less than others, with the lowest decreasing ratio. Years of language learning from high school to graduate school bring different declining rates of different translation errors. This is an interesting finding through comparative studies.

6. CONCLUSION

The authors build a large scale of Chinese students' C2E and E2C translation corpus with translation problem comments. In the paper the authors extract all the comment sentences and apply unsupervised and supervised machine learning approaches to study the taxonomy of translation errors. Flat clustering results reveal that there are 10 types of E2C and 8 types of C2E translation errors. The three classifiers based on decision tree, logistic regression and SVM trained on the manually revised error categories can identify translation problems automatically with a rather high performance. Hierarchical clustering results also give a hint to abstract analysis of translation problems. Translation error taxonomy using machine learning provides translation error analysis with objective insights and understanding.

ACKNOWLEDGMENT

This research was supported by the National Social Science Foundation of China [grant 17BYY047]

REFERENCES

Ball, G. H., & Hall, D. J. (1965). *ISODATA, a novel method of data analysis and pattern classification.* Stanford Research Inst Menlo Park CA.

Berger, A. L. (1996). A maximum entropy approach to natural language processing. *Computational Linguistics*, *22*(1), 39–71.

Blei, D. M., Ng, A. Y., & Jordan, M. I. (2003). Latent dirichlet allocation. *Journal of Machine Learning Research*, *3*(1), 993–1022.

Campoy, M. C., Cubillo, M. C. C., Belles-Fortuno, B., & Gea-Valor, M. L. (Eds.). (2010). *Corpus-based approaches to English language teaching.* A&C Black.

Chen, J. L. (2012). Corpus based interlanguage error analysis: Taking Chinese-English translation testing as an example. *China Examinations*, *9*, 25–31. (in Chinese)

Corder, S. P. (1974). Error analysis. In J. Alien & SP Corder (Ed.), The Edinburgh course in applied linguistics (pp. 122-131). Academic Press.

Cortes, C., & Vapnik, V. (1995). Support-vector networks. *Machine Learning*, *20*(3), 273–297. doi:10.1007/BF00994018

Dodds, J. M. (1999). Friends, false friends and foes or back to basics in L1 to L2.

Giménez, J., & Marquez, L. (2004). SVMTool: A general POS tagger generator based on support vector machines. In *Proceedings of the 4th International Conference on Language Resources and Evaluation.* Academic Press.

Hastie, T., Tibshirani, R., & Friedman, J. (2009). *The Elements of Statistical Learning New York*. NY: Springer. doi:10.1007/978-0-387-84858-7

Kudo, T., & Matsumoto, Y. (2001). Chunking with support vector machines. In *Proceedings of the second meeting of the North American Chapter of the Association for Computational Linguistics on Language technologies* (pp. 1-8). Association for Computational Linguistics.

Le, Q., & Mikolov, T. (2014). Distributed representations of sentences and documents. In *Proceedings of the International Conference on Machine Learning* (pp. 1188-1196). Academic Press.

Li, S., Zhao, Z., Hu, R., Li, W., Liu, T., & Du, X. (2018). Analogical reasoning on Chinese morphological and semantic relations.

MacQueen, J. (1967). Some methods for clustering and analysis of multivariate observations. In *Proceedings of 15th Berkeley Symposium on Math Statist Problem* (pp. 281-297). University of California Press.

Mikolov, T., Sutskever, I., Chen, K., Corrado, G., & Dean, J. (2013). Distributed representations of words and phrases and their compositionality. In *Proceedings of NIPS2013*. Academic Press.

Mullner, D. (2011). Modern hierarchical, agglomerative clustering algorithms.

Pym, A. (1992). Translation error analysis and the interface with language teaching. In C. Dollerup and A. Loddegard (Ed.), The Teaching of Translation. Amesterdam: John Benjamins.

Murtagh, F., & Legendre, P. (2014). Ward's hierarchical agglomerative clustering method: Which algorithms implement Ward's criterion? *Journal of Classification*, *31*(3), 274–295. doi:10.100700357-014-9161-z

Richards, J. (1971). *Error analysis and second language strategies. Language Sciences*. ERIC.

Safavian, S. R., & Landgrebe, D. (1991). A survey of decision tree classifier methodology. *IEEE Transactions on Systems, Man, and Cybernetics*, *21*(3), 660–674. doi:10.1109/21.97458

Secară, A. (2005). Translation evaluation: A state of the art survey. In *Proceedings of the eCoLoRe/ MeLLANGE Workshop*, Leeds (pp. 39-44). Academic Press.

Séguinot, C. (1990). Interpreting errors in translation. *Translators' Journal*, *35*(1), 68–73.

Ratnaparkhi, A. (1998). *Maximum entropy models for natural language ambiguity resolution* [PhD thesis]. University of Pennsylvania, Philadelphia, PA.

Richards, J. C. (2015). *Error analysis: Perspectives on second language acquisition*. Routledge. doi:10.4324/9781315836003

Sun, Y. J. (2011). An analysis of errors in C-E translation of second-year English majors. *Chinese Science & Technology Translators Journal*, *24*(3), 32–36. (in Chinese)

Wold, S., Esbensen, K., & Geladi, P. (1987). Principal component analysis. *Chemometrics and Intelligent Laboratory Systems*, *2*(1-3), 37–52. doi:10.1016/0169-7439(87)80084-9

Yakimovskaya, K. (2012). Applying corpus methodology to error analysis of students' translation into the L1: The context of audiovisual translation.

This research was previously published in the International Journal of Computer-Assisted Language Learning and Teaching (IJCALLT), 9(3); pages 68-83, copyright year 2019 by IGI Publishing (an imprint of IGI Global).

Chapter 22

Concerning the Integration of Machine Learning Content in Mechatronics Curricula

Jörg Frochte
Bochum University of Applied Sciences, Germany

Markus Lemmen
Bochum University of Applied Sciences, Germany

Marco Schmidt
Bochum University of Applied Sciences, Germany

ABSTRACT

Machine learning is becoming more and more important for mechatronic systems and will become an ordinary part of today's student life. Thus, it is obvious that machine learning should be part of today's student's curriculum. Unfortunately, machine learning seldomly is implemented into the curriculum in a substantial or linking manner, but rather offered as an elective course. This chapter provides an analysis of how machine learning can be integrated as a mandatory part of the curriculum of mechatronic degree courses. It is considered what the required minimal changes in fundamental courses should be and how traditional subjects like robotics, automation, and automotive engineering can profit most of this approach. As a case study, this chapter utilizes an existing German mechatronic degree course specialized on information technology, which covers most of the discussed aspects.

INTRODUCTION

Mechatronics is a multidisciplinary field that includes mechanical engineering, electronics, and computer engineering. Typical application areas are industrial automation, robotics, and automotive engineering. Especially for the latter two, control theory has become an important topic.

DOI: 10.4018/978-1-6684-6291-1.ch022

Within mechatronic systems, software and intelligent systems play a crucial role as they are the key drivers for innovation and added value of modern mechatronic systems. Nowadays, also machine learning is a new major factor in this field, and very often it interacts closely with control theory. Some techniques will be or are already integrated into modern mechatronic systems as standard components, like e.g. image and speech recognition. Usually, these components are simply licensed and integrated from suppliers. Nevertheless, in many cases the integration of machine learning requires a deep understanding of the technical behavior of a mechatronic system. Therefore, engineers should have a basic understanding of common machine learning approaches. This is especially true for the field of robotics, flexible manufacturing, vehicles and logistics.

This demand in mechatronic engineering practice has a strong impact on mechatronics and computer science engineering curricula at universities: While machine learning is increasingly important for the mechatronic systems, the mechatronic degree courses at universities often lack integration of this subject, and usually the different curricula are not ready to integrate this subject into fundamental courses of a degree curriculum. We will show, that with minor changes in the curriculum, seamless integration of machine learning contents is achievable. In that way, a university can enhance the attractiveness of a degree course without additional expenses.

In the following sections of this paper, we analyze the requirements for integrating machine learning into mechatronic degree courses based on an existing (example) degree course. In order to be able to choose a proper approach to integrate machine learning, it is essential to understand, which part of machine learning offers the strongest connections to the courses under discussion and therefore candidates are to be integrated into the courses. Next, the interaction to control theory and simulation will be highlighted; both topics have already (classically) a big influence on mechatronic degree courses. The subsequent section will show, which new requirements for degree courses have to be considered, and which already established approaches and topics can be utilized for this purpose by slight re-arrangements, e.g. in control theory.

AN OVERVIEW ON MACHINE LEARNING

Which aspects of machine learning are now the most important ones for mechatronics? One taxonomy for machine learning approach divides them into

- Supervised,
- Unsupervised
- And reinforcement methods.

Supervised methods can be broadly divided into two groups of tasks: regression and classification. Regression is about estimating or predicting a continuous quantity, like e.g. the probability of failure. Classification deals with assigning a given set of features into discrete categories, like e.g. categorizing objects into animal or furniture. Both techniques are important when it comes to mechatronics with a wide field of applications like Predictive Maintenance, see e.g. (Ahmad et al 2012), automated/autonomous driving (Vallon et al 2017) and Convolutional Neural Networks and Deep Learning are more and more used in medical systems see e.g. (Lee et al 2017) and healthcare, see e.g. (Esteva et al 2019). Beyond the technical application areas, it becomes more important in production planning, logistics and cost estimation (Börzel et al 2019) closely linked to curricula's and professional opportunities of engineers. One aspect is which methods one should teach to mechatronic engineers from the rich family of possible algorithms and techniques. To answer this question, it is important to mention the nature of the data. We have two major types of data: structured and unstructured data. Structured data is organized in a data frame, e.g. in rows (data records) and columns (features). In unstructured data, the information is in the data record, but there is no clear relation of the information and the individual data bits. Take for example the picture of a dog as a bitmap. It is clear that the picture shows a dog but the contribution of every pixel to this class is unclear. Both kinds of data suggest different tools. For unstructured data, the family of neuronal networks is most important. For classification of classes from pictures etc. convolutional neural networks are important and should be taught. For structured data, it is important for students to know approaches like CART because a learned tree addresses the problem of transparency in technical applications and leads easily to ensemble methods like random forest. A tool-kit could be set-up with the following methods:

- K-nearest neighbors (lazy learner, to illustrate the principle and often quite efficient)
- CART (Classification and Regression Trees)
- Random Forest
- Dense Neural Networks
- Convolutional Neural Networks (CNN)

Beyond this there is a class of tools like YOLO, see e.g. (Redmon, J. et al, 2016) widely used in robotics for real-time segmentation and classification. It is in general not possible in a mechatronic machine learning course to cover the detailed theory of this approaches, but they are related to CNN, therefore a less theoretical use in e.g. a practical session might still be possible.

Furthermore, there exists a different class of algorithms referred to as unsupervised learning. While supervised learning is based on datasets of labeled answers to learn from - e.g. sensor data, which is annotated either as a failure or as working correctly - unsupervised learning tasks identify patterns without labels. The main task here is clustering. Clustering refers to grouping things together in such a way, that members of a group are similar to each other. The last category is reinforcement learning. In order to be able to conduct reinforcement learning, it is essential to provide a signal suitable for rewarding and quantifying the amount of reward. Consequently, one does not in general know in advance, what the (final) solution will be. Thus, in general, the result is usually of less quality than in the supervised learning case. Reinforcement learning is very useful in cases, where the algorithm can be thought of as an agent interacting with its environment. In mechatronics that can be a robot, a vehicle or even a whole factory.

As one can see, every category of machine learning approaches can be used in mechatronic products like robots, vehicles, and factories. If one has to make a ranking, one might end up with reinforcement learning and supervised learning as most important categories, especially because modern approaches of reinforcement learning like Q-Learning require regression learning techniques like neural networks to represent the Q-Function (Wiering & Otterlo, 2012). Therefore, we will focus on the demands of reinforcement learning to illustrate connections and requirements, as an example.

MACHINE LEARNING AND MECHATRONICAL SYSTEMS

Machine learning enables predictions to be made based on data to elaborate knowledge and relationships out of experiences / data sets. For this purpose, it makes use of some mathematical fields, mainly regression, optimization, and statistics.

Application Areas

One area of application is Industry 4.0, also referred to as smart factory. In smart factory, production processes are connected and a lot of data can be collected in order to optimize the manufacturing process. In this context, machine learning supports e.g. process optimization by changing and adapting manufacturing settings or automatically improving quality assessment. In the application area of vehicle technology, machine learning can mainly be found as a tool to support autonomous driving and comfort functions or features. Furthermore, a lot of companies can make use of machine learning in maintenance and support services. By means of sensors the energy consumption of individual machines can be monitored, maintenance needs can be predicted, and maintenance cycles can be optimized. If a smart system is designed to continuously learn, it is very likely that it will improve performance based on more accurate and actual predictions.

Figure 1. Frequency range of control cycles, translated from (Hertzberg, J. et al. p. 262, 2012)

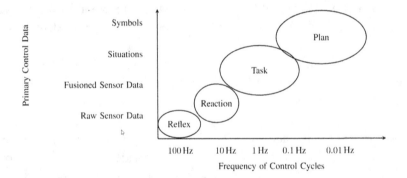

Links to Robotics and Control Engineering

Machine learning approaches for robotic applications have grown quite popular in the last decade. Recent success in the fields of robotics vision and AI robotics showed the benefits in many applications.

Prior to the increased popularity of machine learning in robotics, mainly control engineering approaches were used to ensure safe and autonomous operation of robotic systems.

Nowadays, robotic platforms are getting more and more complex, including a variety of different sensors, increasing computational power, and network capabilities.

The challenge to achieve intelligent behavior of the robot in an unknown and dynamic working environment leads to challenges combining recent machine learning approaches with traditional control engineering aspects in a neat manner.

At first glance, this seems quite difficult, as on the one hand control loops require real-time behavior of the system and on the other hand machine learning approaches are often computationally expensive. A common model for the design of a robot control system in a layered structure is given in (Hertzberg, Lingemann, & Nüchter, 2012) and is illustrated in figure 1.

The layers of the control structure in figure 1 can be seen as complexity levels to be handled from the robot, ranging from obstacle avoidance to path planning:

- **Reflex:** Describes the lowest level of control and uses raw sensor data to immediately react to changes in the environment. This layer is often directly implemented in hardware.
- **Reaction:** Implements reactions that rely on filtered or fused data. Software modules process the sensor data and build the basic behavior for robotics.
- **Task:** Controls the achievement of small tasks given to the robot. The task is only a small step to achieve a final goal.
- **Plan:** Creates a global plan to be executed from the robot. The global plan is divided into several tasks, which are executed from the layer below.

The execution frequency of the control cycles decreases with growing complexity. The lowest layer (reflex) directly uses the sensor data to react as fast as possible to changes in the environment, typically with a frequency of about 100 Hz. If an obstacle or hazardous area is detected, the system should stop its motion without any delays. It is highly required for security reasons that a real-time response of the system is possible, thus a direct implementation in hardware can be found in many systems. The frequency of the control layer above is already an order of magnitude larger. Reactions rely on fused sensor data, i.e. several sensors are used to derive more knowledge about the environment and to initiate behaviour of the robot. For example, the robot could avoid an obstacle by detecting an alternative path with a variety of navigation sensors. The two lower layers, reflex and reaction, are closely related to the hardware of the robot. In contrary, the upper layers are independent of the robot hardware, they are responsible for the planning process. In this context, planning is related to reaching a final goal or solving a given problem. The planning process on a global scale is performed from the highest layer (plan), which is only executed at minute intervals. The result of the global planning process is divided into several tasks, which are given to the task layer for execution. These upper layers are well suited to apply machine learning algorithms, as they are not time critical. The task and plan layers are commonly used for path planning and scheduling. This layered structure demonstrates, how the connection of control engineering and machine learning can be integrated into a modern robotic system.

Today, at first quite often simulated environments are being used. The reason is that for modern reinforcement approaches (e.g. (Otterlo, 2012)) using deep neuronal networks a lot of data is necessary for training purpose. This amount of data is typically hard to acquire just from real life tests.

Thus, pre-training based on simulation is quite commonly found.

A similar challenging application area is automotive engineering / vehicles. As established state-of-the-art vehicle technology, many control tasks have to be performed on a millisecond calculation time basis performing on cost-optimized ECUs, while the environment sensing, classification and path planning performs on a different scale, still.

In particular, in the context of fully automated driving, there are still many challenging aspects to provide suitable control structures and vehicle control architectures to cope with this challenge, though many OEMs and suppliers are working on these topics with very high effort and promising results.

Placing of Machine Learning Contents in a Generic Curriculum Framework

The analysis of the requirements necessitates mathematical fundamentals as well as programming skills to be taught prior to any machine learning module. As discussed, it makes sense to focus on reinforcement learning in mechatronics, since it is helpful to be able to rely on basics in physics, simulation, and control theory before the machine learning module pops up in the study curriculum. Control theory is not really mandatory but very useful, since many standard problems, like e.g. the inverted pendulum, are being used as examples in control theory courses.

These application examples from control theory courses can then be adopted in machine learning as well in order to illustrate to the students, how reinforcement learning approaches may achieve similar or equal results based on completely different approaches. A machine learning module can be sped up significantly if the students have already participated in such control engineering experiments and have prior knowledge in application examples.

Nevertheless, machine learning is by no means a separated degree course in mechatronics, and it makes the most sense if it is integrated into advanced courses of application areas like robotics, intelligent or automated driving or automation. Consequently, there should be still sufficient time following the machine learning course to integrate this approach into those fields of application.

Implications to Mechatronics Curricula and Deduction of a Generic Framework

In this section we will discuss the implication of successful integration of machine learning to the curricula of a mechatronic degree course plan; to the complete study plan as well as to individual existing modules. Even though today's European degree courses are based on the idea of modules, usually almost no module is separated from all other modules. Most courses base on fundamental courses and thus, rely on skills set up before.

Prerequisites and Requirements for Machine Learning Contents

Nowadays the availability of many easy-to-use machine and deep learning packages, such as scikit-learn (Pedregosa et al., 2011) (Python), Weka (Hall et al., 2009) (Java), Tensorflow (Abadi et al., 2015) (Python) etc. makes it easier for engineers to use state-of-the-art machine learning algorithms in and for their products. Especially the Keras-API was a big step forward for the usage by different professions than mathematicians and computer scientists (Chollet, 2015).

Nevertheless, machine learning is a field, that intersects statistics, optimization, computer science, and algorithmic aspects. Despite the immense possibilities of existing tools, at least a rough mathematical understanding of many of these techniques is necessary in order to obtain satisfactory or good results. Examples of this requirement are

- Selecting appropriate algorithms regarding aspects like e.g. the required accuracy, suitable training time, adequate model complexity, number of parameters and number of features.
- Choosing parameter settings and validation strategies.
- Identifying under- and over-fitting by understanding statistics, regression and function approximation.

Therefore, one can conclude, that the fundamentals for understanding machine learning are mainly programming skills and knowledge about algorithms and mathematics. Fortunately, a lot of the necessary concepts are already part of the mathematical education of e.g. mechanical engineers.

Let's have a look at the list of the main mathematical aspects needed for machine learning:

1. Ordinary one-dimensional basic calculus
2. Basic Linear Algebra, especially vector spaces, Projections, Eigenvalues & Eigenvectors, norms and metrics
3. Some parts of higher dimensional calculus, especially how to determine or estimate gradients and derivatives
4. Basics in optimization approaches like Gradient descent, Newton's Methods and similar methods
5. Curve fitting and basic regression like least squares methods
6. (Basic) Mathematical statistics

While the first five aspects are usually part of the mathematical education of engineers -- maybe optimization sometimes needs slightly more attention -- the last point is only rarely taught in engineering mathematics. Consequently, the question has to be answered, how deep and how much of these new aspects are needed?

The answer to this question cannot uniquely be given and depends on the choice, how machine learning is presented. If one chooses a more algorithmic approach in teaching of machine learning like in (Marsland, 2014) in contrast to a quite probabilistic perspective as in (Kevin, 2012), the topic of machine learning fits quite well to common fundamental engineering mathematics courses. The basics for an engineer can be handled in between three and five weeks during a semester. Therefore, 2 European Credit points (ECTS) are somehow a lower boundary for the additional statistics needed. Of course, more ECTS would allow for a broader basis, such as also up to 4 European credit points could be reasonable.

From fundamental computer science courses some other subjects including the following are required:

1. Procedural and Object-Oriented Programming
2. Practical skills in Python and/or Java
3. Basics in Algorithm analysis
4. From Physics, some newton mechanics and advanced topics like friction models are useful in order to understand some important effects within the simulated environments.
5. For a Simulation and Modelling course the concept of models in simulation is important as well as some basic practical skills in this topic.

The first two items are mainly covered in typical mechatronic degree courses as part of programming courses. The third topic, basics in algorithms, is not necessarily covered in a mechatronics curriculum. Nevertheless, it can be easily integrated into any computer science related lecture. From our perspective, reinforcement learning is one of the most relevant machine learning disciplines for mechatronics students, therefore items number four and five become mandatory. To understand the physics behind a system is especially important when reinforcement learning is applied to a real-world system.

Achieving this is more demanding within a six semester degree course, though these are quite common in traditional universities as bachelor degree curricula. Of course, it is much easier to realize it in a seven semester curriculum, which is often being chosen by most universities of applied sciences.

Figure 2. Generic Curricula Framework for 6 semester degree courses with application areas

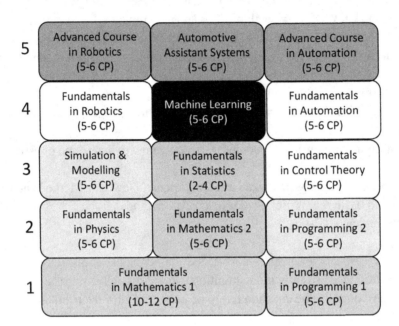

Figure 2 sketches some possible solutions to set up a curriculum for a six semester version of a bachelor study program. Dark grey filled elements highlight mandatory prerequisites for the machine learning module depicted in black. Light grey filled courses are highly desirable, while white filled courses are needed for the advanced machine learning courses filled in red.

Of course, the fundamentals of statistics need to be integrated into the general mathematics fundamentals. They are displayed separately because this is, in general, the only really new aspect next to machine learning itself required in the degree courses. On the one hand, it is very encouraging that this new topic fits in so well. Still, on the other hand, there are at least seven or eight credit points that need to be re-assigned in the existing bachelor courses. Beyond this, it only fits in easily, if the existing degree course comes up with sufficiently integrated credit points for mathematical fundamentals and focus on principals and ideas rather than training to solve more complicated integrals by hand or handle conic sections. Therefore, the integration of machine learning shifts the focus in mathematics from human computation to more general principals and more linear algebra and statistics.

In the whole degree course plan, it shifts the course plan more into the direction of computer science, because the total amount of credit points is limited and transferred from mechanics and/or electronics.

PERSPECTIVES AND BENEFITS OF LINKING MACHINE LEARNING, AUTOMOTIVE, ROBOTICS, AND AUTOMATION

In this section, we discuss, why in our option it is worth to integrate machine learning to keep mechatronic degree courses up-to-date and to satisfy the demands of the typical mechatronics application areas. Of course, the benefit strongly depends on the seamless integration of machine learning contents on module level and the cooperation of different lectures across module borders.

Table 1. Study Plan Bachelor Mechatronic & Information Technology (2019) from the Bochum University of Applied Sciences

Semester	Course / Module	Provides Prerequisites
1	• Analysis 1 • Linear Algebra • Fund. Programming 1	• One-dimensional basic calculus • Basic Linear Algebra • Curve fitting and basic regression • Procedural Programming • Basics in Algorithm analysis
2	• Analysis 2 • Physics 1 • Fund. Programming 1	• Higher dimensional calculus, Basics in optimization approaches • Basic Knowledge for e.g. simulated environments • Object-Oriented Programming
3	*No machine learning related contents in this semester*	
4	• System Analysis & Simulation • Fund. Control Theory	• Basics in Simulation and Modelling • Basics in Control Theory
5	• Machine Learning • Fund. Robotics • Fund. Automation	• (Basic) Mathematical statistics • Application areas
6	• Advanced Robotics • Advanced Automation	• Application areas

Examples of Machine Learning in Robotic Applications

Especially in the field of robotics, machine learning plays an important role. Thus, the students of mechatronic courses strongly benefit from integrated machine learning contents in their curriculum when working on robotics-related projects. It will be shown in the three following examples; how machine learning is used in robotics context to realize an application.

- Machine learning had a big influence on many computer vision approaches. Camera systems are standard equipment in any mobile robot platform, they are available as low-cost commercial of the shelf components. These camera systems in combination with machine learning are often used for the identification of objects in the robot environment or for obstacle detection in navigation tasks. Especially in the field of object detection are a number of libraries available, which can be easily adapted to detect objects in the robot's environment. It is important to have a basic understanding of the used key technologies to utilize the libraries appropriately in a robotic context. A well-known library to realize object detection in a robotic scenario is YOLO (Redmon et al., 2016). To use YOLO on a mobile robot, one has to take into account that many mobile platforms have only very limited computing resources. It is important to understand how neural networks work and what makes them computationally expensive when applied to a robotic application. An example picture from our Turtlebot is shown in figure 3 where YOLO is used on a Turtlebot platform for object detection. If students acquire skills in machine learning and neural networks, they are able to realize their own implementations in a timely manner.
- Another important application field of machine learning is the mobility of robots. The control of challenging robot kinematics, such as humanoid robots or mobile platforms with legged locomotion, is quite demanding. Control software development for unknown terrain or noisy environ-

ments is very sophisticated. Control engineering is in many mechatronic engineering courses already an integral part and is a necessary requirement for stabilizing the movement of a robot. But if the kinematics of a robot is very sophisticated and the environment is unknown and additionally very dynamic, reinforcement learning is an important tool to realize a stable and adaptive behavior of the robot. The idea of reinforcement learning is, to define a reward for the desired behavior (in this case a movement in the desired direction). While many movements of the legs to not lead to any movement of the robot, a combination of movements might lead to the goal of moving into the correct direction. A good example is the crawling robot (Tokic & Ammar, 2012), which is able to adapt its locomotion strategy according to the characteristics of the underground surface. Even further challenging is when the scenario involves multiple agents acting and learning (Weiss, 2013).

- A third example shows the importance of machine learning in the field of industrial manipulators. For many decades, industrial manipulators were mainly used for repetitive tasks with high accuracy requirements. In a pick and place scenario, where the manipulator moves a workpiece from a start location to an end location, the workpieces need to be placed with high accuracy in the work environment. Meanwhile, it is quite common to use vision systems to be able to dynamically grasp well-defined workpieces (see figure 4). Recent developments based on machine learning approaches do not even require the workpieces to be well defined or separated on a feeding system. The dex net project (Mahler et al., 2017) enables grasping of arbitrary objects with the help of a neural network approach.

Figure 3. Object detection with YOLO on a Turtlebot

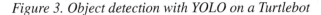

Figure 4. Grasping an object based on a visual system

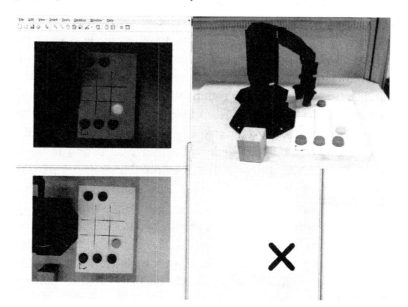

Examples of Machine Learning in the Field of Automotive Engineering

Similar developments to the ones just discussed within the fields of robotics can be observed in automotive engineering, too. Machine learning techniques have played crucial roles, in particular in the area of systems trying to investigate the environment of vehicles. Examples are camera systems for speed sign recognition, radar, lidar or ultrasonic sensors in addition to mono and stereo cameras. They are used to detect possible paths to follow for the car or to identify obstacles within or near to the planned paths as part of advanced driver assistance systems of manual-driven cars. Beyond this, they can be used as part of vehicle controllers for trajectory tracking of (partly) automated driving vehicles; see e.g. (Ersoy & Gies, 2017) as an introduction to these topics. The impact of machine learning techniques even become more important due to the very manifold development challenges, validation tasks for components, systems and full vehicles and also for the driving tasks of the individual vehicle to be engineered and during lifetime of each vehicle making use of modern driver assist systems or future (partly) automated driving.

Thus, summarized, machine learning will get increasingly important as the enabler for functions or features for vehicles to be engineered as part of components or systems, and machine learning is being investigated to support the tuning and validation processes of these functions or features, as well.

In order to give an example of how a university automotive application courses for machine learning could look like, will be discussed here. Already in classical (machine-learning-free) mechatronics engineering curricula we gained experience with some elective courses for problem-based-oriented model-based software development.

The task for the students of the course is to build up (step by step with the increasing complexity of tasks) some LEGO-EV3-based vehicle which should perform certain tasks.

During the course, the tasks get more and more complicated. At first, the students have to implement vehicle speed control and lateral control (following path marks) for arbitrary vehicle speed set points.

Then the next complex task is to implement an adaptive speed/distance control in order to prevent the own vehicle from crashing into a slower preceding vehicle. Next comes vehicle location and online map generation of the driven tracks. Then the task is to stop the vehicle at some pre-defined location of the map. The final task then is to re-use the sensors for adaptive speed/distance control for sideways detection of potential parking lots and implement automated reverse parallel parking to the left and then to the right including each time a return on the path markings (lane/street). These tasks have to be performed completely stand-alone on the EVO3-LEGO-Brick, which only has rather limited computation power and memory space. Last but not least the student's final task has been to re-do all these development steps for a new vehicle designed by the students themselves. The only restriction is, that it needs a driven rear axle (preferable with rear differential) and a steered front axle. Up to this point, the course does not need artificial intelligence or machine learning. This changes now, since the already developed tasks are extended by two very basic changes:

First, the reference vehicle set point (given from outside by the student) shall be overruled by traffic signs like "STOP" or speed limits. Second, the lateral vehicle controller based on the idea of controlling the desired measured reflected light intensity of a lane mark by the reference orientation calculated by a lane detection algorithm. Both additional tasks depend on cameras and additional computation power which the LEGO-Brick cannot perform by itself. For this purpose, a mobile phone has been fixed on the LEGO-vehicle, the camera-data is transferred to a computer in the lab performing the camera-based traffic sign recognition and the lane / track identification.

Figure 5 depicts the signal flow structure of the set-up. This setup and separation of tasks can be done since Matlab-EV3-Release 2018. Since then, a rather reliable UDP signal transmission is available for information fed from outside to the (comparable slow) real-time calculation being done on the LEGO-Brick EV3. Both tasks are being performed with AI tools, in particular, neuronal networks. The calculated information results in vehicle speed setpoint correction values for the vehicle speed controller and into steering angle set or yaw rate points for the lateral controller of the student's vehicle running on the LEGO-Brick.

Figure 5. Set-up for extending a LEGO-brick vehicle by AI camera-based traffic sign recognition and lane tracking (Simic & Heller, 2019)

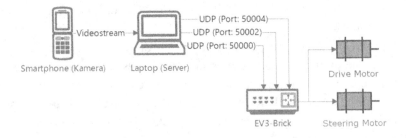

Figure 6 illustrates the tracking task, while figure 7 shows the situation for identifying a STOP-sign. For a bachelor course, the amount of content can be scaled by the amount of reduction of degrees in freedom for the student and increased predefined structures in terms of software running on the Brick and type and structure of networks and training methods and also for the used signals.

Figure 6. Tracking of the LEGO brick by identification of the lane markings (Simic & Heller, 2019)

Figure 7. Identification of a STOP-sign (Simic & Heller, 2019)

Case Study on the Bachelor Degree Course Mechatronic and Information Technology

The considerations mentioned above provide a theoretical approach to cover relevant machine learning contents into a curriculum. Now, it will be shown in a case study, how this has been achieved in an existing mechatronics degree program. The main issue with new content is, that existing study plans are quite often fully packed and there is no further degree of freedom to place new contents. In general, there are two approaches to this: On the one hand, the establishment of a suitable specialization subject or on the other hand, the development of a specialized degree program. The framework described in the section "placing of machine learning contents in a generic curriculum framework" places the machine learning lecture in the fourth semester of a six-semester course. In this way, a specialization subject in machine learning can be implemented. In the presented case study, we look at a seven-semester bachelor's degree program in mechatronics and information technology, which belongs to the genre of specialized degree programs. Table 1 shows an excerpt of the study plan, which only shows the contents related to the framework of the section "placing of machine learning contents in a generic curriculum framework".

The third semester contains lectures such as electrical engineering and mechanics. These are not contents of our framework; thus it is kept blank in Table 1. This is possible because it is a seven- and not six-semester degree course. The module System Analysis & Simulation mainly covers the required skills in modeling and simulation. The machine learning module will be followed by two specialization subjects. First of all, this shows that integration is possible in the sense of the framework. At the same time, however, there are also challenges that make a seamless integration difficult, which will be similarly found in other degree programs. The first challenge lies in teaching the subject of machine learning with regard to the available mathematical basics. Mathematics in the degree program is sufficiently represented with 18 ECTS credits and further expansion is not possible without going at the expense of other subjects. However, the mathematical courses are already filled with traditional engineering subjects and are under increasing pressure to deal with the heterogeneous admission requirements of the students. Therefore, statistical basics are only discussed in terms of the equilibrium calculation as they are necessary for the fitting of measurements. Corresponding contents are therefore first and foremost imparted in machine learning and partly in System Analysis & Simulation. This is accompanied by a reduction in the amount of the core substance, which has been minimized by an algorithmic orientation of machine learning.

The second challenge concerns the application areas. As it is often the case in modular degree programs, these are also used as compulsory or optional subjects in other degree programs. Therefore, the lecturers cannot assume that all participants have dealt with machine learning beforehand. This prevents integration as an integral part of the course, although the majority of participants are familiar with it. The chosen solution for this is the integration of modern teaching concepts which are especially suitable for advanced students. These events are partly enhanced by aspects of problem and project-based learning. This differentiation allows the integration of machine learning in selected projects and problems as well as a stronger practical activation of the advanced students. In general, problem-based learning has shown itself to be an excellent integration option, which offers interested students opportunities and at the same time takes the individual interests of the students into account. Focusing on the students as initiating partners leads to more active learning, better understanding and stronger anchoring of what has been learned. In addition, this learning approach promotes the acquisition of interdisciplinary skills -- important for mechatronics -- and soft skills, see e.g. (Wood, 2003) discussing this for medicine. The most common difficulties in implementation, which (Wood, 2003) also mentioned, are the need for more personnel and, in certain areas of expertise, for more equipment per student. Therefore, it is in general, a good approach to use this technique in higher semesters. Nevertheless, the open design of problem-oriented learning scenarios as well as in social aspects such as group dynamics are still aspects of research (Antonietti, 2001; Henry et al., 2012; Neville, 2009). The practical experience in the *Bachelor Mechatronic & Information Technology* of the Bochum University of Applied Sciences is that project and problem-based learning in the advanced courses can, as illustrated in the section before, in the context of machine learning in automotive, robotics and automation has the potential to provide experiences for students with this mathematical subject in an applied context. This includes problem solving in the application domain as well as applying methods learned in machine learning courses.

In our work, we focused mainly on machine learning contents to be integrated into the curriculum. It should be mentioned, that there is a strong demand to include in modern engineering curricula additional contents like personal and professional skills, like proposed in the CDIO approach (Crawley et al., 2011). These additional qualifications were not covered in this work, but a number of different courses (e.g. English classes, scientific writing courses) are available and are mandatory for all bachelor students in our engineering department. The feedback from the students regarding the new lecture contents was very positive. It was very motivating for them to apply latest approaches from the field of machine learning to different applications. In the lectures they were able to include their new skills in robotic projects and show impressively the application of machine learning in a mechatronic system. As many students study at our university in the scope of dual study program, they were even able to transfer their knowledge successfully in their companies, for example in a case study for CAD based cost estimations (Börzel 2019).

CONCLUSION

This work introduced a framework to integrate machine learning contents in a modern mechatronics curriculum. The relevance of machine learning disciplines for mechatronics applications has been discussed, and a framework with required course contents has been derived. The framework has been formulated in a modular way to enable seamless integration in any engineering degree program. The successful integration has been demonstrated with a case study at the University of Applied Sciences Bochum. Benefits and drawbacks of this solution have been presented and discussed. Beyond this and (Frochte, J. et. al) some examples for possible application areas and project-based learning in the context of robotics and autonomous driving where given and discussed.

REFERENCES

Abadi, M., Agarwal, A., Barham, P., Brevdo, E., Chen, Z., Citro, C., . . . Ghemawat, S. (2015). *Tensor-Flow: Large-scale machine learning on heterogeneous systems.* Software available from tensorflow. org: http://tensorflow. org

Ahmad, R., & Kamaruddin, S. (2012). An overview of time-based and condition-based maintenance in industrial application. *Computers & Industrial Engineering, 63*(1), 135–149. doi:10.1016/j.cie.2012.02.002

Antonietti, A. (2001). Problem based learning--A research perspective on learning interactions. *The British Journal of Educational Psychology, 71*, 344.

Börzel S., & Frochte, J. (2019). Case Study On Model-based Application of Machine Learning Using Small CAD Databases for Cost Estimation. *Proceedings of KDIR 2019.*

Castle, R. (in press). Shadowing a police officer: How to be unobtrusive while solving cases in spectacular fashion. *Professional Writers' Journal.*

Crawley, E. F., Malmqvist, J., Lucas, W. A., & Brodeur, D. R. (2011). *The CDIO Syllabus v2. 0: An Updated Statement of Goals for Engineering Education. In Proceedings of the 7 th Intl. CDIO conference.* Copenhagen: University of Demark.

Ersoy, M., & Gies, S. (Eds.). (2017). *Fahrwerkhandbuch: Grundlagen–Fahrdynamik–Fahrverhalten–Komponenten–Elektronische Systeme–Fahrerassistenz–Autonomes Fahren–Perspektiven.* Springer-Verlag. doi:10.1007/978-3-658-15468-4

Esteva, A., Robicquet, A., Ramsundar, B., Kuleshov, V., DePristo, M., Chou, K., ... Dean, J. (2019). A guide to deep learning in healthcare. *Nature Medicine, 25*(1), 24–29. doi:10.103841591-018-0316-z PMID:30617335

Frochte, J., Lemmen, M., & Schmidt, M. (2018). Seamless Integration of Machine Learning Contents in Mechatronics Curricula. In *2018 19th International Conference on Research and Education in Mechatronics (REM)* (pp. 75-80). IEEE. 10.1109/REM.2018.8421794

Hall, M., Frank, E., Holmes, G., Pfahringer, B., Reutemann, P., & Witten, I. H. (2009). The WEKA data mining software: an update. *ACM SIGKDD Explorations Newsletter, 11*(1), 10-18.

Henry, H. R., Tawfik, A. A., Jonassen, D. H., Winholtz, R. A., & Khanna, S. (2012). "I know this is supposed to be more like the real world, but...": Student perceptions of a PBL implementation in an undergraduate materials science course. *Interdisciplinary Journal of Problem-based Learning, 6*(1), 5. doi:10.7771/1541-5015.1312

Hertzberg, J., Lingemann, K., & Nüchter, A. (2012). *Mobile Roboter: Eine Einführung aus Sicht der Informatik*. Springer-Verlag. doi:10.1007/978-3-642-01726-1

Kevin, P. M. (2012). *Machine learning: a probabilistic perspective*. Academic Press.

Lee, J. G., Jun, S., Cho, Y. W., Lee, H., Kim, G. B., Seo, J. B., & Kim, N. (2017). Deep learning in medical imaging: General overview. *Korean Journal of Radiology, 18*(4), 570–584. doi:10.3348/kjr.2017.18.4.570 PMID:28670152

Mahler, J., Liang, J., Niyaz, S., Laskey, M., Doan, R., Liu, X., . . . Goldberg, K. (2017). *Dex-net 2.0: Deep learning to plan robust grasps with synthetic point clouds and analytic grasp metrics*. arXiv preprint arXiv:1703.09312

Marsland, S. (2014). *Machine learning: an algorithmic perspective*. Taylor & Francis Inc. doi:10.1201/b17476

Neville, A. J. (2009). Problem-based learning and medical education forty years on. *Medical Principles and Practice, 18*(1), 1–9. doi:10.1159/000163038 PMID:19060483

Pedregosa, F., Varoquaux, G., Gramfort, A., Michel, V., Thirion, B., Grisel, O., ... Vanderplas, J. (2011). Scikit-learn: Machine learning in Python. *Journal of Machine Learning Research, 12*(Oct), 2825–2830.

Redmon, J., Divvala, S., Girshick, R., & Farhadi, A. (2016). You only look once: Unified, real-time object detection. In *Proceedings of the IEEE conference on computer vision and pattern recognition* (pp. 779-788). IEEE. 10.1109/CVPR.2016.91

Simic, B., & Heller, A. (2019). *Autonomes Fahren: Spur- und Schilderkennung mit einem LEGO-Fahrzeug unter Matlab und Simulink. Bochum University of Applied Sciences, Höseler Platz 2, D-42579 Heiligenhaus*. Project Documentation.

Tokic, M., & Ammar, H. B. (2012). Teaching reinforcement learning using a physical robot. *Proceedings of the ICML Workshop on Teaching Machine Learning*.

Vallon, C., Ercan, Z., Carvalho, A., & Borrelli, F. (2017, June). A machine learning approach for personalized autonomous lane change initiation and control. In *2017 IEEE Intelligent Vehicles Symposium (IV)* (pp. 1590-1595). IEEE. 10.1109/IVS.2017.7995936

van Otterlo, M. (2012). *Reinforcement learning: State-of-the-Art*. Springer Berlin Heidelberg.

Weiss, G. (2013). *Multiagent Systems, ser.* EBSCO ebook academic collection.

Wiering, M., & Van Otterlo, M. (2012). *Reinforcement learning. Adaptation, learning, and optimization.* Academic Press.

Wood, D. F. (2003). Problem based learning. *BMJ (Clinical Research Ed.), 326*(7384), 328–330. doi:10.1136/bmj.326.7384.328 PMID:12574050

KEY TERMS AND DEFINITIONS

Machine Learning: A branch of artificial intelligence. Summarizes different approaches to "learn" from data.

Mechatronic Degree Courses: A complete mechatronics course at the university with a total length of 6 to 8 semesters. The student completes the course with a bachelor thesis.

Reinforcement Learning: Machine learning approaches often used in robotics. A reward is used to teach a system a desired behavior.

Supervised Learning: Machine learning approaches often used for regression and classification.

Unsupervised Learning: Machine learning approach used for clustering. Learns from unlabeled data (i.e., there is no supervision from a human who specifies the labels for the data).

This research was previously published in Revolutionizing Education in the Age of AI and Machine Learning; pages 75-96, copyright year 2020 by Information Science Reference (an imprint of IGI Global).

Chapter 23
A Process for Increasing the Samples of Coffee Rust Through Machine Learning Methods

Jhonn Pablo Rodríguez
University of Cauca, Popayán, Colombia

David Camilo Corrales
Telematic Engineering Group, University of Cauca, Popayán, Colombia and Department of Computer Science and Engineering, Carlos III University of Madrid, Madrid, Spain

Juan Carlos Corrales
Telematic Engineering Group, University of Cauca, Popayán, Colombia

ABSTRACT

This article describes how coffee rust has become a serious concern for many coffee farmers and manufacturers. The American Phytopathological Society discusses its importance saying this: "...the most economically important coffee disease in the world..." while "...in monetary value, coffee is the most important agricultural product in international trade..." The early detection has inspired researchers to apply supervised learning algorithms on predicting the disease appearance. However, the main issue of the related works is the small number of samples of the dependent variable: Incidence Percentage of Rust, since the datasets do not have a reliable representation of the disease, which will generate inaccurate predictions in the models. This article provides a process about coffee rust to select appropriate machine learning methods to increase rust samples.

1. INTRODUCTION

Coffee rust has become a serious concern for many coffee farmers and manufacturers. The American Phytopathological Society discusses its importance saying this: "the most economically important coffee disease in the world," while "in monetary value, coffee is the most important agricultural product

DOI: 10.4018/978-1-6684-6291-1.ch023

in international trade". Without a solution, the effects on the coffee industry may soon be reflected in price and availability (Arneson, 2000).

For several years, the disease was managed through the combination of various techniques such as quarantine, cultural management, fungicides and resistant crops. Due to the effectiveness of chemical control and the relatively limited damage caused by the disease, particularly at high altitudes, Meso-american coffee farmers and technical authorities considered it manageable. This view prevailed until the epidemic between 2008 and 2013 along Mesoamerica, from Colombia to Mexico, including Peru, Ecuador and some Caribbean countries (Avelino et al., 2015). Coffee farmers were desperate to obtain an answer to this terrible situation since the intensity was higher than anything previously observed, affecting a large number of countries including: Colombia, from 2008 to 2011, affecting an average of 31% of coffee production compared with the production in 2007; Central America and Mexico, in 2012–13, affecting an average of 16% of the production in 2013 compared with 2011-12 and an average of 10% in 2013-14 compared with 2012-13; and Peru and Ecuador in 2013 (Avelino et al., 2015). More specifically, in 2013, the Guatemalan government and the Guatemalan Nation Coffee agency declared a national state of emergency after a projection of nearly 15% crop loss in their region. The devastation has continued to spread due to higher temperatures in this region, which are making fungus growth at higher altitudes possible ("A Solution to the Coffee Rust Epidemic," 2015). Higher temperatures may be linked to climate change. And several/many experts are worried about the persistence of these conditions (high temperatures) will not change in the near future. In this regard, several reports and experts proposed solutions related with early detection of the disease and the eradication of infected plants.

The early detection has inspired researchers to apply supervised learning algorithms on predicting the disease appearance. The data collected about conditions and soil fertility properties, physical properties and management of a coffee crop, can be used to forecast the rust infection rate. In the same way, weather conditions such as the minimum and maximum levels of temperature, humidity and rainy days can help to estimate the behavior of the disease. Several Colombian and Brazilian researches in supervised learning attempt to detect the incidence percentage of rust (IPR) in coffee crops using Neural Networks, Decision Trees, Support Vector Machines, Bayesian Networks, K Nearest Neighbor, and Ensemble Methods (Cesare di Girolamo, 2013b; Cintra, Meira, Monard, Camargo, & Rodrigues, 2011; Corrales, Corrales, & Figueroa-Casas, 2015; Corrales, Figueroa, Ledezma, & Corrales, 2015; Thamada, Rodrigues, & Meira, 2015). However, the main drawback of the related works is the few data samples of the dependent variable: Incidence Percentage of Rust, since the datasets do not have a reliable representation of the disease, which will generate inaccurate classifiers (Corrales, Figueroa, et al., 2015).

This paper provides a process to increase coffee rust samples applying machine learning methods through a systematic review about coffee rust in order to select appropriate algorithms to increase rust samples. The paper is structured as follows: in the next section, we describe the coffee rust disease and supervised learning concepts. Section 3 exposes the supervised learning approaches applied to coffee rust detection and the main challenges due to low accuracy of rust detecting models; Section 4 shows a systematic review of the approaches to generate synthetic data. Section 5, proposes a process for building large dataset of coffee rust based on the Section 4. Finally, the section 6 presents the conclusions.

2. BACKGROUND

2.1. Coffee Rust

Coffee rust is caused by the fungus Hemileia vastatrix, among the cultivated species C. Arabica is the most severely attacked. The disease causes defoliation, sometimes this one can lead to death of branches and crop losses (Figure 1a). The first symptoms are small yellowish lesions that appear on the underside of the leaves, where the fungus has penetrated through the stomata (Figure 1b). These lesions grow, coalesce and produce uredospores with their distinctive orange color. Chlorotic spots can be observed on the upper surface of the leaves. During the last stage of the disease, lesions become necrotic (Avelino et al., 2015).

Figure 1. Coffee rust (Source (Lasso et al., 2017)). (a) Symptoms of strong defoliation in Libano, Tolima, Colombia; (b) Small yellowish lesions on the underside of a coffee leaf

(a)   (b)

The progression of coffee rust depends on four factors (Figure 2) that appear simultaneously (Rivillas Osorio, 2011):

- **The Host:** there are varieties of coffee plants susceptible and resistant to rust. Varieties such as Típica, Borbón and Caturra suffer severe rust attacks, while Colombia and Castillo varieties are highly resistant to rust.
- **Pathogenic Organism:** Hemileia vastatrix lifecycle begins with the germination of uredospores in 2-4 hours in optimal conditions. Within 24 – 48 hours, infection is completed. Once the infection is completed, the underside of the leaf is colonized and sporulation will occur through the stomata (Nutman, Roberts, & Clarke, 1963).
- **Weather Conditions:** Weather with constant precipitations, mainly in the afternoon and night with cloudy sky, high humidity in the plants and low temperatures are relevant factors for germination of rust. Spread of disease and its development is usually limited to the rainy season, while in dry periods the rust incidence is very low.

Figure 2. Factors for the progress of coffee rust. Source (Rivillas Osorio, 2011)

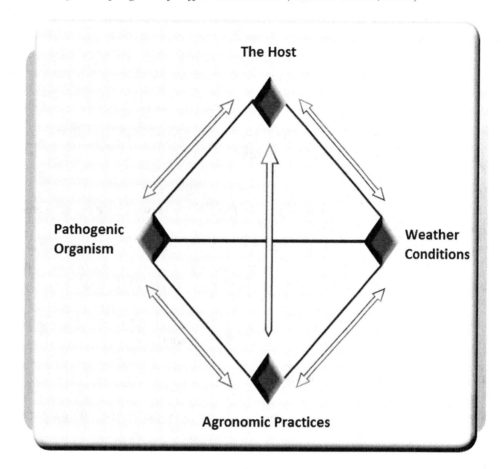

- **Agronomic Practices:** This practice refers to properties of crop sowing (plant spacing, percentage of shade, etc.), application of fungicides and fertilizations on coffee crops with the aim to avoid several rust attacks.

In Colombia the incidence of rust is measured through the methodology developed by Centro Nacional de Investigaciones de Café (Cenicafé) (Rivillas Osorio, 2011), which is explained as follows:

Incidence Percentage of Rust (IPR) is calculated for a plot with area lower or equal of one hectare. The methodology is composed by three steps:

1. The farmer must be standing in the middle of the first furrow, choose one coffee tree and pick out the branch with greater foliage for each level (high, medium, low); the leaves of the selected branches are counted as well as the infected ones for rust.
2. The farmer must repeat the step 1 for every tree in the plot until 60 trees are selected. It is worth mentioning that the same number of trees must be selected in every furrow (e.g. if the plot has 30 furrows, the farmer selects two coffee trees for each furrow).

3. Once the step 1 and 2 are finished, the Leaves of the selected Coffee Trees (LCT) are added as well as the Infected Leaves by Rust (ILR). Then, the Incidence Percentage of Rust (IPR) must be computed using the following formula:

$$IPR = \frac{ILR}{LCT} \; x100 \tag{1}$$

Furthermore, in Brazil, Procafé Foundation (A. Garcia, 2011) proposes a methodology that enables measuring the incidence of rust through the following steps:

1. The farmer selects a random region of 4 m2 from the plot.
2. From the region selected in the previous step, the farmer selects two coffee trees, located in different furrows, one in front of the other.
3. The trees are divided into three levels according to its height: high, medium, and low; and the branches are divided in quartiles by its size. One branch of the middle zone of the plant is chosen, then two leaves of that area are taken from the third or fourth part of the branch.

Finally, for each plot 25 regions are selected, from which 50 plants are chosen, therefore 100 leaves are collected. The samples are taken the first two days of each month.

2.2. Supervised Learning Techniques

Based on (Corrales, Corrales, et al., 2015), in this section the main supervised learning algorithms, from coffee rust domain are explained:

A supervised learning process is based on the iteration of a training process from a dataset named training data. The training data consist of a set of examples. Each example is represented by a pair (x_i, y_i), where x_i is an attributes vector and y_i is the desired output value (also called class) of the example. A SL algorithm analyzes the training data and produces an inferred function which is called classifier (if y_i is discrete) or regression function (if y_i is continuous) (A. Ng, 2003). In Table 1 an example of a dataset with three attributes is presented: Number of Days of Precipitation (NDP), average Daily Nighttime relative Humidity (DNH), average Daily Minimum Temperatures (DMT), which can take different values (discrete or continuous); and the desired output value (Corrales, Corrales, et al., 2015).

Table 1. Four sample for training dataset. Source (Corrales, Corrales, et al., 2015)

Attribute			Output Value
NDP	**DNH**	**DMT**	**IPR**
2	96.1	14	65.23%
3	93.8	16	62.54%
4	95.7	15	57.32%
1	98.2	14	61.12%

The goal of this family of algorithms, once the learning process is successfully completed, is to assign the value of the class that best represents the set of instances that belongs to a new case. It is important to note that the result of the learning process (or training) of the algorithm employed generates a classifier (hypothesis or model) for a set of specific training data. Thus, if there are n training data sets, an algorithm can generate n classifiers (Corrales, Corrales, et al., 2015).

The most commonly applied algorithms are Decision Trees (DT), Bayesian Networks (BN), Artificial Neural Networks (ANN), Support Vector Machines (SVM) and K Nearest Neighbor (KNN) (Corrales, Corrales, et al., 2015).

2.2.1. Decision Trees

Decision Trees are algorithms of classification that make an approximation discrete of values objective, in which the function learned is represented by a decision tree (Hierons, 1999). The DTs classifies an instance by sorting it through the tree to the appropriate leaf node, i.e. each leaf node represents a classification. Each node represents some attribute of the instance, and each branch corresponds to one of the possible values for this attribute.

Figure 3 shows a case study carried out in (Cintra et al., 2011) to detect the appearance of rust in coffee, making use of a decision tree and taking into account the attributes of relative humidity, average maximum temperature for the rust incubation period, and average temperature.

Figure 3. Rust detection using a decision tree. Source (Corrales, Corrales, et al., 2015)

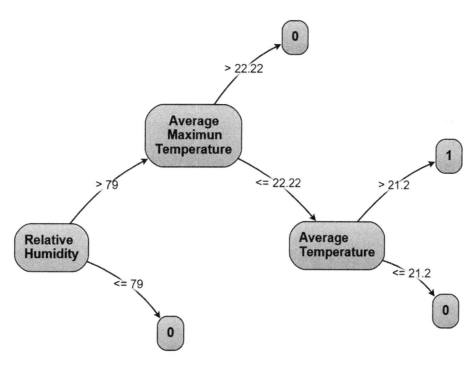

Each attribute is represented by an intermediate node depending on its value. It will take different paths to reach a leaf node. The leaf nodes of the tree correspond to a particular category of the dependent variable (class), in this case 0 (when there is no rust) and 1 (when rust is detected).

2.2.2. Bayesian Networks (BN)

Bayesian networks (BN) model a set of variables and the dependency relations between them, making use of Bayes theorem. The classifier BN requires all assumptions be explicitly built into models which are then used to derive 'optimal' decision/classification rules (Tsai & Chen, 2010). In Figure 4 is presented a Bayesian network for coffee rust detection, which consists of two variables - excess rainfall (ER) and rust - with an edge from the first to the second.

Figure 4. Coffee rust detection through Bayesian network (Source (Corrales, Corrales, et al., 2015))

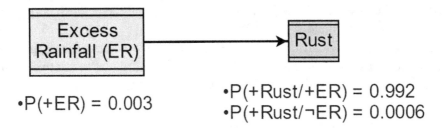

Thus, excess rainfall is a binary variable denoted by presence (+) and absence (-), and similarly with rust. For this example, the following values are calculated using Bayes Theorem (Corrales, Corrales, et al., 2015):

- P (+ER) = 0.003; indicates that the excess rainfall was present in 0.3%.
- P (+Rust/+ER) = 0.992; indicates the excess rainfall, increase to 99.2% probability of the occurrence of rust.
- P (+Rust/¬ER) = 0.0006; indicates that in the absence of excess rainfall there is a 0.06% probability of the occurrence of rust.

2.2.3. Artificial Neural Networks (ANN)

Artificial Neural Networks (ANNs) are a collection of nodes interconnected. The weights of these interconnections are tuned during learning so that the output of the network is as close as possible to the desired training targets for a set of training input examples. The most common type of neural networks consists of three layers of units: input layers, hidden layers, and output layers. It is called multilayer perceptron (MLP). A layer of "input" units is connected to a layer of "hidden" units, which is connected to a layer of "output" units (Tsai & Chen, 2010).

Figure 5 shows an ANN that calculates the rust infection rate (RIR) in coffee one month beforehand. This ANN is comprised of input, hidden and output layers. The input layer receives the number of consecutive days with relative humidity above 85% (DRH85), number of consecutive days with rain at night (DRN), and the percentage of shade in the lot (PSL). The hidden layer further solves problems when the data are not linearly separable, this way different hidden layers can be used depending on the organization of the data. Finally, the output layer calculates the rust incidence rate.

Figure 5. Rust infection rate using artificial neural networks Source (Corrales, Corrales, et al., 2015)

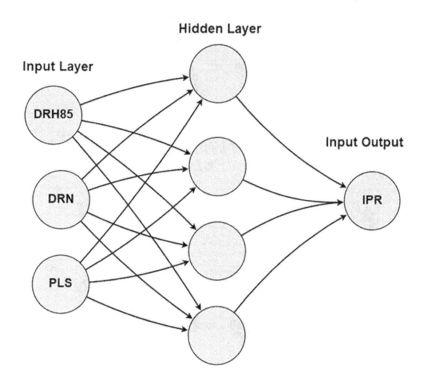

2.2.4. Support Vector Machines (SVM)

The Support Vector Machines (SVM) are learning machines using the method of support vector (SV), this is a general method for solving problems of classification and regression. It was proposed originally by Vladimir Vapnik (L & G, 2006).

Figure 6 presents a linearly separable binary SVM for the classification of leaves infected with rust. The possible hyperplanes separate healthy leaves and infected leaves. SVM is searching for the hyperplane that optimally separates the two leaf types.

2.2.5. K Nearest Neighbor (K-NN)

Nearest Neighbor is an classifier algorithm, classify a new input data, according to the k training data closest to those around them, where k is an integer defined by the user. As such, the class assigned to the new input data will be the most voted class among the k nearest neighbors from the training dataset. This algorithm was proposed by Fix and Hodges (Fix & Hodges, 1989).

Figure 6. Possible hyperplanes (left) and optimal hyperplane using SVM (right) (Source (Corrales, Corrales, et al., 2015))

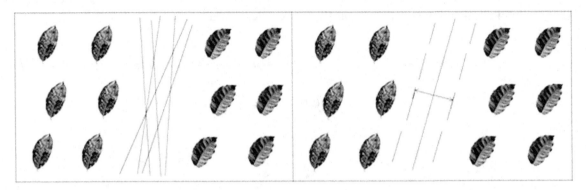

Figure 7. k =1 is classified as a healthy leaf (left), just as in the right image, where k = 4 is classified as healthy leaf (Source (Corrales, Corrales, et al., 2015))

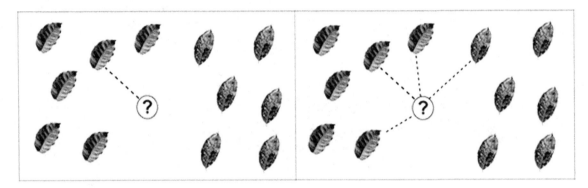

Based on example of classification of rust-infected leaves presented above, the K-NN algorithm classifies the new input data by the value of k. When k = 1 the new input data is classified as a healthy leaf (left side of Figure 7). Similarly, when k = 4, the k nearest neighbors are three healthy leaves and one infected leaf. The new input data is classified as a healthy leaf (right side of Figure 7) (Corrales, Corrales, et al., 2015).

3. SUPERVISED MACHINE LEARNING TECHNIQUES IN COFFEE RUST DETECTION

This systematic review took into account the inclusion criterion: Colombian and Brazilian research using supervised learning algorithms. And as an exclusion criterion: investigations not greater than 8 years. Systematic review was based on the following research question:

Are there researches that address the coffee rust by supervised learning?

18 papers were found (2008 - 2016) from 4 sources of information: IEEE Xplore (1 paper), Science-Direct (1 paper), Springer Link (6 paper) and Google Scholar (10 papers). We defined 2 search queries: "coffee rust prediction" and "coffee rust detection".

The papers found in the systematic review, contain approaches for coffee rust detection in Colombian and Brazilian crops, using supervised learning algorithms. These researches are detailed below:

3.1. Supervised Learning for Coffee Rust Detection in Colombian Crops

The dataset built in the Colombian researches was obtained for 18 plots from experimental farm Los Naranjos (21° 35'08 "N, 76 ° 32'53" W), of the Supracafé enterprise, located in Cajibío (Cauca) [26]. The samples were recollected among years 2011 – 2013, with 147 instances and 21 attributes: 6 of weather conditions, 5 soil fertility properties, 6 physic crop properties, 4 crop management; the class represents the Incidence Percentage of Rust (IPR). This dataset was used in several works presented in Table 2:

Table 2. Related works for coffee rust detection in Colombian crops

Work	Year	Algorithm
(Corrales et al., 2014)	2014	ANN, SVM, RT
(Corrales, Figueroa, et al., 2015)	2015	ANN, SVM, RT
(Corrales, Casas, Ledezma, & Corrales, n.d.)	2016	Two-level classifier ensembles using Back Propagation Neural Networks, Regression Tree M5 and Support Vector Regression
(Corrales & Peña, 2014)	2014	SVM
(Lasso, Thamada, Meira, & Corrales, 2015)	2015	DT

Briefly, Colombian researchers using SVM (4 papers), ANN (2 papers) and DT/RT (4 paper), but the most used are SVM and ANN, since this class of algorithms deliver results accurate to the end user, these are less prone to overfitting than other methods, tolerance to the noise, Accuracy in general, Tolerance to irrelevant attributes, easy to understand and speed in its learning and classification (Corrales, Corrales, et al., 2015).

3.2. Supervised Learning for Coffee Rust Detection in Brazilian Crops

Brazilian researchers built a dataset from physic crop properties and weather conditions. These data were collected in the experimental farm Procafé (South latitude 21°34'00" longitude West 45°24'22" and altitude 940 m) located in Varginha, Minas Gerais, during the years 1998 - 2011 (Meira, Rodrigues, & Moraes, 2008). The final dataset includes 182 instances. Table 3 are presented the works related with the Brazilian dataset:

Thus, the algorithms used in Brazil are DT, SVM, SVR, ANN, RF and BN, focusing in its priority to generate an easy interpretation model based on graphs like the DT and generate accurate results with SVM.

3.3. Discussion

The algorithms used in the last years are Support Vector Machines (SVM), Decision Trees (DT), Bayesian Networks (BN), Nearest Neighbor (KNN) and Artificial Neural Networks (ANN), but the algorithms

Table 3. Related works for coffee rust detection in Brazilian crops

Work	Year	Algorithm
(Meira et al., 2008)	2008	DT
(Pérez-Ariza, Nicholson & Flores, n.d.)	2012	BN
(di Girolamo, 2013a)	2013	ANN, DT, Random Forest (RF), SVM
(Thamada et al., 2015)	2015	Ensembles Methods with SVM, ANN, DT
(Meira, 2009)	2009	DT
(Cintra et al., 2011)	2011	DT
(Di Girolamo Neto, Rodrigues, & Meira, 2014)	2014	SVM, ANN, DT, RF
(Luaces, Rodrigues, Alves Meira, & Bahamonde, 2011)	2011	SVR
(Luaces, Rodrigues, Meira, Quevedo, & Bahamonde, 2010)	2010	SVR

SVM and ANN are the most used for the precision in the categorization of results, however the algorithms present deficiencies in their interpretation, since classifiers built by these algorithms do not generate a visual representation, in contrast to the DT and algorithms the BN, which allow the user to observe the classifier through a representation based on graphs (Corrales, Corrales, et al., 2015). On the other hand, algorithms such as: KNN and BN are good by their speed of learning (training phase) (Bhavsar & Ganatra, n.d.; Kotsiantis, 2007; Segrera Francia & Moreno García, 2006).

In accordance with the system review, Brazil and Colombia are the countries that address the coffee rust detection through supervised learning. However, the researchers found are limited due lack of data in measures of Infection Percentage of Rust, due to the high costs and time invested for the collection of data rust infection. As a result, datasets cannot represent faithfully the total population, generating low accuracy in the results obtained by classifiers (Corrales, Figueroa, et al., 2015). Section 4 describes approaches for resolving this kind of problem, through the generation of synthetic data.

4. SYNTHETIC DATA GENERATION

The few number of samples do not let to the models to represent important characteristics of the population, therefore the models constructed are affected in its precision (Corrales, Figueroa, et al., 2015). For this systematic review, the inclusion criterion was taken into account: research to increase the number of samples in a dataset. And as an exclusion criterion: proposed researches that do not have a benchmark analysis with traditional algorithms. Systematic review was based on the following research question:

Which are synthetic data approaches most used for lack of data?

We found 26 papers (2000-2015), considering 5 search queries: "Synthetic Data Generation", "Imbalanced Dataset", "Over-Sampling", "Virtual Sample Generation" and "Interpolation Algorithm", it was found from 4 sources of information: IEEE Xplore (10 papers), ScienceDirect (5 papers), Springer Link (7 papers) and Google Scholar (4 papers).

From the systematic review conducted previously, were found 4 approaches to addressing the lack of data and their respective algorithms for synthetic data generation as shown in Table 4:

Table 4. Approaches and synthetic data algorithms

Approach	Algorithms	Description	Works
OverSampling	MDO, SMOTE, ADASYN, RWO SAMPLING, BORDERLINE SMOTE2 MSMOTE, BORDERLINE SMOTE1, BORDERLINE SMOTE, C-SMOTE, SMOTE-I, DSMOTE	Creates new synthetic instances for the minority class.	(Abdi & Hashemi, 2016; Chawla, 2005; Galar, Fernández, Barrenechea, Bustince, & Herrera, 2012; Han, Wang, & Mao, 2005; G. He, Han, & Wang, 2005; Haibo He & Garcia, 2009; H. He & Ma, 2013; Kerdprasop & Kerdprasop, 2011; Mahmoudi, Moradi, Akhlaghian, & Moradi, 2014; Pengfei, Chunkai, & Zhenyu, 2014; Thanathamathee & Lursinsap, 2013; Wong, Leung, & Ling, 2013; Zhang & Li, 2014)
Interpolation	Stair, S-Spline, Bicubic, Lanczos, Nearest Neighbor, Fractals, Linear.	Determinates the values of a function at positions lying between its samples.	(Bentbib, El Guide, Jbilou, & Reichel, n.d.; Hung & Siu, 2015; Malpica, 2005; Rui & Qiong, 2012; Shi, Yao, Li, & Cao, 2008)
Classifiers	AdaBoost, RAMOBoost, AdaBoost.M2, AdaBoost.M1, DataBoost.IM, SMOTEBoost, DataBoost, SMOTE Bagging, OverBagging	Classification or regression model that aims to predict the value of output variable from certain independent input variables.	(Abdi & Hashemi, 2016; Chawla, Lazarevic, Hall, & Bowyer, 2003; Galar et al., 2012; Guo & Viktor, 2004a; Sun, Kamel, & Wang, 2006; Thanathamathee & Lursinsap, 2013; Viktor & Guo, 2004)
Copy of Data	Bagging, Regression Trees, Random Forest, Stattistical Distributions	Creates a copy from original data with a different representation that not reveal private information.	(Albuquerque, Lowe, & Magnor, 2011; Anderson, Kennedy, Ngo, Luckow, & Apon, 2014; Drechsler & Reiter, 2011)

To construct the guideline for increasing coffee rust samples, we used the approaches: oversampling, interpolation, and classifiers. Copy of data is not used because for this kind of problem is necessary use the original representation of data.

5. A PROCESS FOR BUILDING LARGE COFFEE RUST SAMPLES

In this section, we propose a process to increase coffee rust samples. Figure 8 presents the process for generate discrete or numeric rust samples.

When the coffee rust samples are discrete, the imbalance ratio must be evaluated. Commonly the Imbalance Ratio (IR) is used to measure the distribution of the classes:

$$IR = \frac{C^+}{C^-} \tag{2}$$

where C+ represents the size of the majority class and C- the size of the minority class (Verbiest, Ramentol, Cornelis, & Herrera, 2012). *Oversampling* techniques are used if IR > 1; otherwise *Classification* techniques are applied. The techniques for increase the discrete coffee rust samples are presented below.

Figure 8. Process for increase coffee rust samples

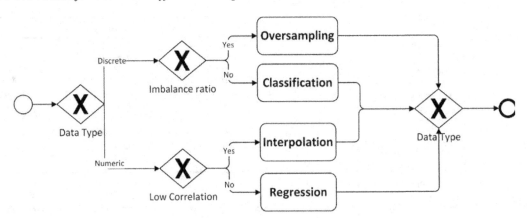

5.1. Oversampling

Oversampling is used to increase examples from minority classes with aim have equitable distribution of the classes (H. He & Ma, 2013). The algorithm most used are called SMOTE: Synthetic Minority Over-sampling Technique (Chawla, 2005); RUS Boost (Seiffert, Khoshgoftaar, Hulse, & Napolitano, 2010), Balance Cascade (S. Albayrak, 2013) and Easy Ensemble (S. Albayrak, 2013) also are considered Oversampling algorithms. Other algorithms used are MDO (Abdi & Hashemi, 2016), SMOTE (Kerdprasop & Kerdprasop, 2011; Pengfei et al., 2014; Wong et al., 2013), ADASYN (Haibo He & Garcia, 2009; Thanathamathee & Lursinsap, 2013), RWO SAMPLING (Zhang & Li, 2014), BORDERLINE SMOTE2 (Han et al., 2005), MSMOTE (Galar et al., 2012), BORDERLINE SMOTE1 (Han et al., 2005), BORDERLINE SMOTE (Han et al., 2005), C-SMOTE (G. He et al., 2005), SMOTE-I (Nitesh V., Kevin W., Lawrence O., & W., 2002), DSMOTE (Mahmoudi et al., 2014). The Figure 9 shows an example of the oversampling approach for coffee rust apparition (CRA).

The minority class is represented when exists the coffee rust (CRA = YES), while the majority class when the coffee rust does not exist (CRA = NO). Thus, the oversampling approach will generate samples in the minority class until to approximate the number of samples of the majority class.

5.2. Classification

Classification algorithms are efficient methods to increase discrete samples where each new value is obtained from related cases in the whole set of records (Figure 10). Besides the capability to increase the coffee rust samples with plausible values that are as close as possible to the true value, classification algorithms should preserve the original data structure and avoid to distort the distribution of the original samples. The algorithms based in neighbours are the most used (Beretta & Santaniello, 2016). The algorithm most used are AdaBoost (Abdi & Hashemi, 2016; Galar et al., 2012; Sun et al., 2006; Thanathamathee & Lursinsap, 2013), RAMOBoost (Thanathamathee & Lursinsap, 2013), AdaBoost. M2 (Galar et al., 2012), AdaBoost.M1 (Galar et al., 2012), DataBoost.IM (Guo & Viktor, 2004b), SMOTEBoost (Chawla et al., 2003; Galar et al., 2012; Thanathamathee & Lursinsap, 2013), DataBoost (Guo & Viktor, 2004a), SMOTE Bagging (Galar et al., 2012), OverBagging (Galar et al., 2012). Figure 10 presents an example of classification of occurrence of coffee rust.

Figure 9. Oversampling

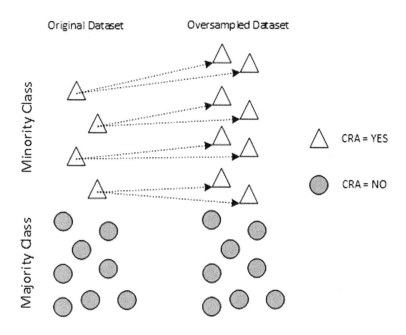

Figure 10. Classification

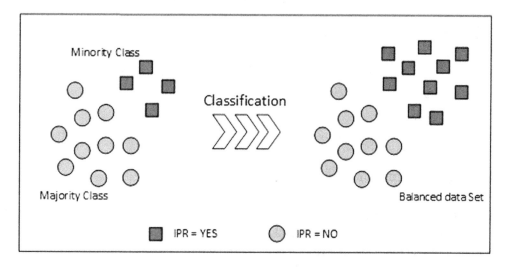

The minority class is represented when exists the incidence percentage of rust (IPR = YES), while the majority class when the coffee rust does not exist (IPR = NO). Thus, the oversampling approach will generate samples in the minority class until to approximate the number of samples of the majority class.

5.3. Interpolation

Interpolation is the process of determining the values of a function at positions lying between its samples. It achieves this process by fitting a continuous function through the numeric input samples. The interpolation can be addressed of two ways: univariate and multivariate (Mohanty, Reza, Kumar, & Kumar, 2016). Figure 11 shows an example of interpolation of Incidence Percentage of Rust (IPR). The original measurements are represented by the 5 white dots. The remaining black dots are synthetic measurements created by an interpolation algorithm.

Figure 11. Interpolation IPR

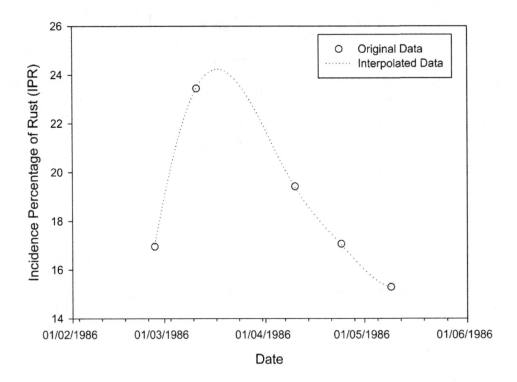

5.3.1. Univariate Interpolation

The univariate interpolation is defined for values of a function f(x) = y, where only take part two variables (x,y), in which x is the series with full data and y is the incompleteness variable in the serie. Inside univariate interpolation, there are algorithms that interpolate the y values, of which three obtain good results: lineal interpolation, K-nearest neighborhood (KNN), and cubic spline interpolation (Hamed, Shafie, Mustaffa, & Idris, 2015; Keogh, Chu, Hart, & Pazzani, 2001; Li, Wan, Liang, & Gao, 2014; Phillips, 2003).

5.3.2. Multivariate interpolation

The univariate interpolation fitted of two-dimensional data points, while the multivariate interpolation make the points fit finding the surface that provides an exact fit to a series of multidimensional data points, considering a series of N distinct dimensional data points (x1, y1), (x2, y2),... (xN, yN), where

$Xi = \left(X_i^1, X_i^2, \ldots X_i^d \right)$ is a vector for each i = 1,2,….N. By this interpolation we find a function f: $R^d \rightarrow R$ such that: f(x1) = y1, f(x2) = y2, … f(xN) = yN (Schaback, 1995). The algorithms most used are Inverse Distance Weighting (IDW) and Kriging (Peralvo, 2002).

5.4. Regression

Similarly, to Classification algorithms, the coffee rust is treated as dependent variable and a regression is performed to increase coffee rust samples. Regression analysis is a machine learning approach that aims predict the value of continuous output variables (coffee rust samples) from certain independent input variables (e.g. temperature, humidity, etc.), via automatic estimation of their latent relationship from data (Yang, Liu, Tsoka, & Papageorgiou, 2017). Figure 12 presents an example of regression of Incidence Percentage of Rust (IPR).

Figure 12. Regression models

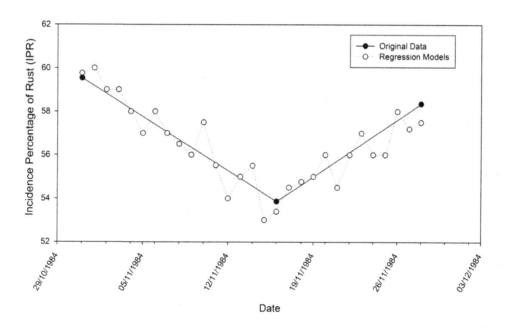

In the Figure 12 shows an example of the regression models applied to data generation in the IPR. From a set of training data, regression models learn and generate new data to increase the volume of IPR information. Linear regression, logistic regression (2004), regression trees (Breiman, Friedman, Stone, & Olshen, 1984), support vector regression (Vapnik, Golowich, & Smola, 1997) and multi-layer perceptron (Haykin, 1998) are typical choices for regression models.

6. CONCLUSION

In this paper, a process for increasing the coffee rust samples was made. The first step to create the process was to make a systematic review about coffee rust in order to select appropriate algorithms to increase rust samples.

When the process for increasing the coffee rust samples is used, we consider important follow the next observations (Corrales, Gutierrez, Rodriguez, Ledezma, & Corrales, 2017):

- **Distance Between Meteorological Station and Coffee Trees:** If a weather station is away from a coffee plot, the weather measurements are inaccurate, because coffee plot can have micro-climate influenced by: coffee plot orography and properties of crop sowing such as: plant spacing, shade on coffee trees, etc. Unfortunately, the weather stations are very expensive to have one per coffee plot.
- **Information About Application of Fungicides on Coffee Plots:** If fungicides are applied on coffee plots before germination of rust, the weather conditions cannot be relevant factors to increase the rust incidence. We consider necessary this information to build a correct regression model based on meteorological variables.
- **Consider a Margin of Error in IPR Measurements:** The insufficient data due to the expensive collection process that requires large expenditures of money and time. The farmers must select 3 branches for each 60 coffee trees (minimum) per plot (Rivillas Osorio, 2011). Usually one plot have 10000, 5000, or 2500 coffee trees (Arcila, Farfan, Moreno, Salazar, & Hincapie, 2007), given that the maximum number of IPR measures that we can obtain for one plot are: 0.6%, 1.2%, or 2.4% respectively. Besides a coffee farm has over one coffee plot.
- Due to the coffee rust is an element of an agronomic pathosystem, it is necessary to study how the factors about crop administration (fungicides, production levels, and so on), the meteorological factors (humidity, temperature and so on) and the fungus development interact with each other, and how this interaction contribute to increase the coffee rust disease.

ACKNOWLEDGMENT

We thank to the Telematics Engineering Group (GIT) of the University of Cauca for the technical support. In addition, we are grateful to Colciencias (Colombia) for PhD scholarship granted to MsC.David Camilo Corrales. This work has been also supported by Innovacción-Cauca (SGR-Colombia) under project "Alternativas Innovadoras de Agricultura Inteligente para sistemas productivos agrícolas del departamento del Cauca soportado en entornos de IoT - Convocatoria 04C-2018 Banco de Proyectos Conjuntos UEES - Sostenibilidad".This paper is an extended revised version of "A Guideline for Building Large Coffee Rust Samples Applying Machine Learning Methods" presented at the International Conference of ICT for Adapting Agriculture to Climate Change (AACC'17), November 22-24, 2017, Popayán, Colombia. AACC'17, Advances in Intelligent Systems and Computing Proceedings pp.97-110.

REFERENCES

Abdi, L., & Hashemi, S. (2016). To Combat Multi-Class Imbalanced Problems by Means of Over-Sampling Techniques. *IEEE Transactions on Knowledge and Data Engineering, 28*(1), 238–251. doi:10.1109/TKDE.2015.2458858

Albayrak, S. A. S. (2013). Alleviating the Class Imbalance problem in Data Mining. Retrieved from http://worldcomp-proceedings.com/proc/p2013/DMI8016.pdf

Albuquerque, G., Lowe, T., & Magnor, M. (2011). Synthetic Generation of High-Dimensional Datasets. *IEEE Transactions on Visualization and Computer Graphics, 17*(12), 2317–2324. doi:10.1109/TVCG.2011.237 PMID:22034352

Anderson, J. W., Kennedy, K. E., Ngo, L. B., Luckow, A., & Apon, A. W. (2014). Synthetic data generation for the internet of things. In *Proceedings of the 2014 IEEE International Conference on Big Data* (pp. 171–176). 10.1109/BigData.2014.7004228

Arcila, J., Farfan, F., Moreno, A., Salazar, L., & Hincapie, E. (2007). *Sistemas de produccion de cafe en colombia*. Cenicafe.

Arneson, P. A. (2000). *Coffee rust*. The Plant Health Instructor. doi:10.1094/PHI-I-2000-0718-02

Avelino, J., Cristancho, M., Georgiou, S., Imbach, P., Aguilar, L., Bornemann, G., ... Morales, C. (2015). The coffee rust crises in Colombia and Central America (2008–2013): Impacts, plausible causes and proposed solutions. *Food Security, 7*(2), 303–321. doi:10.100712571-015-0446-9

Bentbib, A. H., El Guide, M., Jbilou, K., & Reichel, L. (n.d.). A global Lanczos method for image restoration. *Journal of Computational and Applied Mathematics*. doi:10.1016/j.cam.2015.12.034

Beretta, L., & Santaniello, A. (2016). Nearest neighbor imputation algorithms: A critical evaluation. *BMC Medical Informatics and Decision Making, 16*(Suppl. 3), 74. doi:10.118612911-016-0318-z PMID:27454392

Bhavsar, H., & Ganatra, A. (n.d.). A Comparative Study of Training Algorithms for Supervised Machine Learning.

Breiman, L., Friedman, J., Stone, C. J., & Olshen, R. A. (1984). *Classification and Regression Trees*. Taylor & Francis.

Carlos, A. A., & Meira, L. H. A. R. (2009). Warning models for coffee rust control in growing areas with large fruit load. *Pesquisa Agropecuária Brasileira, 44*(3), 233–242.

Cesare di Girolamo, L. H. R. (2013a). Desenvolvimento e seleção de modelos de alerta para a ferrugem do cafeeiro em anos de alta carga pendente de frutos.

Cesare di Girolamo, L. H. R. (2013b). Potencial de técnicas de mineração de dados para modelos de alerta da ferrugem do cafeeiro.

Chawla, N. V. (2005). Data Mining for Imbalanced Datasets: An Overview. In O. Maimon & L. Rokach (Eds.), *Data Mining and Knowledge Discovery Handbook* (pp. 853–867). Springer. Retrieved from http://link.springer.com.bd.univalle.edu.co/chapter/10.1007/0-387-25465-X_40 doi:10.1007/0-387-25465-X_40

Chawla, N. V., Lazarevic, A., Hall, L. O., & Bowyer, K. W. (2003). SMOTEBoost: Improving Prediction of the Minority Class in Boosting. In N. Lavrač, D. Gamberger, L. Todorovski, & H. Blockeel (Eds.), *Knowledge Discovery in Databases: PKDD 2003* (pp. 107–119). Springer Berlin Heidelberg; Retrieved from http://link.springer.com.bd.univalle.edu.co/chapter/10.1007/978-3-540-39804-2_12 doi:10.1007/978-3-540-39804-2_12

Cintra, M. E., Meira, C. A. A., Monard, M. C., Camargo, H. A., & Rodrigues, L. H. A. (2011). The use of fuzzy decision trees for coffee rust warning in Brazilian crops. In *Proceedings of the 2011 11th International Conference on Intelligent Systems Design and Applications (ISDA)* (pp. 1347–1352). 10.1109/ISDA.2011.6121847

Corrales, D. C., Casas, A. F., Ledezma, A., & Corrales, J. C. (n.d.). Two-Level Classifier Ensembles for Coffee Rust Estimation in Colombian Crops. *International Journal of Agricultural and Environmental Information Systems*, 7, 41–59.

Corrales, D. C., Corrales, J. C., & Figueroa-Casas, A. (2015). Towards Detecting Crop Diseases and Pest by Supervised Learning. *Ingeniería Y Universidad*, *19*(1), 207–228. doi:10.11144/Javeriana.iyu19-1.tdcd

Corrales, D. C., Figueroa, A., Ledezma, A., & Corrales, J. C. (2015). An Empirical Multi-classifier for Coffee Rust Detection in Colombian Crops. In O. Gervasi, B. Murgante, S. Misra, M. L. Gavrilova, A. M. A. C. Rocha, C. Torre, … B. O. Apduhan (Eds.), *Computational Science and Its Applications -- ICCSA 2015* (pp. 60–74). Springer International Publishing. Retrieved from http://link.springer.com/chapter/10.1007/978-3-319-21404-7_5

Corrales, D. C., Gutierrez, G., Rodriguez, J. P., Ledezma, A., & Corrales, J. C. (2017). Lack of Data: Is It Enough Estimating the Coffee Rust with Meteorological Time Series? In *Computational Science and Its Applications – ICCSA 2017* (pp. 3–16). Cham: Springer; doi:10.1007/978-3-319-62395-5_1

Corrales, D. C., Ledezma, A., Q, A. J. P., Hoyos, J., Figueroa, A., & Corrales, J. C. (2014). A new dataset for coffee rust detection in Colombian crops base on classifiers. *Sistemas Y Telemática*, *12*(29), 9–23. doi:10.18046/syt.v12i29.1802

Corrales, D. C., & Peña, A. J. (2014). Early warning system for coffee rust disease based on error correcting output codes: A proposal. *Revista Ingenierías Universidad de Medellín*, *13*(25), 59–64.

Di Girolamo Neto, C., Rodrigues, L. H. A., & Meira, C. A. A. (2014, July 22). Modelos de predição da ferrugem do cafeeiro (Hemileia vastatrix Berkeley & Broome) por técnicas de mineração de dados. Artigo em periódico indexado (ALICE). Retrieved February 3, 2016, from http://www.alice.cnptia.embrapa.br/handle/doc/991078

Drechsler, J., & Reiter, J. P. (2011). An empirical evaluation of easily implemented, nonparametric methods for generating synthetic datasets. *Computational Statistics & Data Analysis*, *55*(12), 3232–3243. doi:10.1016/j.csda.2011.06.006

Fix, E., & Hodges, J. L. (1989). Discriminatory Analysis. Nonparametric Discrimination: Consistency Properties. *International Statistical Review / Revue Internationale de Statistique, 57*(3), 238–247. doi:10.2307/1403797

Galar, M., Fernández, A., Barrenechea, E., Bustince, H., & Herrera, F. (2012). A Review on Ensembles for the Class Imbalance Problem: Bagging-, Boosting-, and Hybrid-Based Approaches. *IEEE Transactions on Systems, Man and Cybernetics. Part C, Applications and Reviews, 42*(4), 463–484. doi:10.1109/TSMCC.2011.2161285

A. Garcia, A. L. (2011). Resumo metodológico de avaliação das variáveis fenológicas e fitossânitárias do sistema de avisos fitossânitários do mapa/ procafé.

Guo, H., & Viktor, H. L. (2004a). Boosting with Data Generation: Improving the Classification of Hard to Learn Examples. In B. Orchard, C. Yang, & M. Ali (Eds.), *Innovations in Applied Artificial Intelligence* (pp. 1082–1091). Springer Berlin Heidelberg. Retrieved from http://link.springer.com.bd.univalle.edu.co/chapter/10.1007/978-3-540-24677-0_111 doi:10.1007/978-3-540-24677-0_111

Guo, H., & Viktor, H. L. (2004b). Learning from Imbalanced Data Sets with Boosting and Data Generation: The DataBoost-IM Approach. *SIGKDD Explorations, 6*(1), 30–39. doi:10.1145/1007730.1007736

Hamed, Y., Shafie, A., Mustaffa, Z. B., & Idris, N. R. B. (2015). An application of K-Nearest Neighbor interpolation on calibrating corrosion measurements collected by two non-destructive techniques. In *Proceedings of the 2015 IEEE 3rd International Conference on Smart Instrumentation, Measurement and Applications (ICSIMA)*. doi:10.1109/ICSIMA.2015.7559030

Han, H., Wang, W.-Y., & Mao, B.-H. (2005). Borderline-SMOTE: A New Over-Sampling Method in Imbalanced Data Sets Learning. In D.-S. Huang, X.-P. Zhang, & G.-B. Huang (Eds.), *Advances in Intelligent Computing* (pp. 878–887). Springer Berlin Heidelberg. Retrieved from http://link.springer.com.bd.univalle.edu.co/chapter/10.1007/11538059_91 doi:10.1007/11538059_91

Haykin, S. (1998). *Neural Networks: A Comprehensive Foundation* (2nd ed.) Neural Networks: A Comprehensive Foundation. Retrieved from https://www.researchgate.net/publication/233784957_Neural_Networks_A_Comprehensive_Foundation_2nd_Edition_Neural_Networks_A_Comprehensive_Foundation

He, G., Han, H., & Wang, W. (2005). An Over-sampling Expert System for Learing from Imbalanced Data Sets. In *International Conference on Neural Networks and Brain, 2005. ICNN B '05* (Vol. 1, pp. 537–541). doi:10.1109/ICNNB.2005.1614671

He, H., & Garcia, E. A. (2009). Learning from Imbalanced Data. *IEEE Transactions on Knowledge and Data Engineering, 21*(9), 1263–1284. doi:10.1109/TKDE.2008.239

He, H., & Ma, Y. (2013). Foundations of Imbalanced Learning. In *Imbalanced Learning: Foundations, Algorithms, and Applications* (p. 216). Wiley-IEEE Press. Retrieved from http://ieeexplore.ieee.org/xpl/articleDetails.jsp?arnumber=6542481

Hierons, R. (1999). Machine learning. Tom M. Mitchell. Published by McGraw-Hill, Maidenhead, U.K., International Student Edition, 1997. ISBN: 0-07-115467-1, 414 pages. Price: U.K. £22.99, soft cover. *Software Testing, Verification & Reliability, 9*(3), 191–193. doi:10.1002/(SICI)1099-1689(199909)9:3<191::AID-STVR184>3.0.CO;2-E

Hung, K.-W., & Siu, W.-C. (2015). Learning-based image interpolation via robust k-NN searching for coherent AR parameters estimation. *Journal of Visual Communication and Image Representation, 31,* 305–311. doi:10.1016/j.jvcir.2015.07.006

Hunterlab. (2015, January 12). A Solution to the Coffee Rust Epidemic: How Spectrophotometry May Provide the Answers. Retrieved February 13, 2017, from https://www.hunterlab.com/blog/color-food-industry/searching-solution-coffee-rust-epidemic-spectrophotometry-may-provide-answers/

Keogh, E., Chu, S., Hart, D., & Pazzani, M. (2001). An online algorithm for segmenting time series. In *Proceedings 2001 IEEE International Conference on Data Mining* (pp. 289–296). 10.1109/ICDM.2001.989531

Kerdprasop, N., & Kerdprasop, K. (2011). Predicting Rare Classes of Primary Tumors with Over-Sampling Techniques. In T. Kim, H. Adeli, A. Cuzzocrea, T. Arslan, Y. Zhang, J. Ma, … X. Canción (Eds.), *Database Theory and Application, Bio-Science and Bio-Technology* (pp. 151–160). Springer Berlin Heidelberg. Retrieved from http://link.springer.com.bd.univalle.edu.co/chapter/10.1007/978-3-642-27157-1_17

Kotsiantis, S. (2007). *Supervised Machine Learning: A Review of Classification Techniques.* Ljubljana: Informatica.

L, J. E. H., & G, S. S. (2006). Implementación de una maquina de vectores soporte empleando FPGA. *Scientia Et Technica, 2*(31). Retrieved from http://revistas.utp.edu.co/index.php/revistaciencia/article/view/6383

Lasso, E., Thamada, T. T., Meira, C. A. A., & Corrales, J. C. (2015). Graph Patterns as Representation of Rules Extracted from Decision Trees for Coffee Rust Detection. In E. Garoufallou, R. J. Hartley, & P. Gaitanou (Eds.), *Metadata and Semantics Research* (pp. 405–414). Springer International Publishing; Retrieved from http://link.springer.com/chapter/10.1007/978-3-319-24129-6_35 doi:10.1007/978-3-319-24129-6_35

Lasso, E., Valencia, O., Corrales, D. C., López, I. D., Figueroa, A., & Corrales, J. C. (2017). A Cloud-Based Platform for Decision Making Support in Colombian Agriculture: A Study Case in Coffee Rust. In *Advances in Information and Communication Technologies for Adapting Agriculture to Climate Change* (pp. 182–196). Cham: Springer; doi:10.1007/978-3-319-70187-5_14

Li, H., Wan, X., Liang, Y., & Gao, S. (2014). Dynamic Time Warping Based on Cubic Spline Interpolation for Time Series Data Mining. In *Proceedings of the 2014 IEEE International Conference on Data Mining Workshop* (pp. 19–26). 10.1109/ICDMW.2014.21

Luaces, O., Rodrigues, L. H. A., Alves Meira, C. A., & Bahamonde, A. (2011). Using nondeterministic learners to alert on coffee rust disease. *Expert Systems with Applications, 38*(11), 14276–14283. doi:10.1016/j.eswa.2011.05.003

Luaces, O., Rodrigues, L. H. A., Meira, C. A. A., Quevedo, J. R., & Bahamonde, A. (2010). Viability of an Alarm Predictor for Coffee Rust Disease Using Interval Regression. In N. García-Pedrajas, F. Herrera, C. Fyfe, J. M. Benítez, & M. Ali (Eds.), *Trends in Applied Intelligent Systems* (pp. 337–346). Springer Berlin Heidelberg. Retrieved from http://link.springer.com/chapter/10.1007/978-3-642-13025-0_36 doi:10.1007/978-3-642-13025-0_36

Mahmoudi, S., Moradi, P., Akhlaghian, F., & Moradi, R. (2014). *Diversity and separable metrics in over-sampling technique for imbalanced data classification. In Proceedings of the 2014 4th International eConference on Computer and Knowledge Engineering* (pp. 152–158). doi:10.1109/ICCKE.2014.6993409

Malpica, J. A. (2005). Splines Interpolation in High Resolution Satellite Imagery. In G. Bebis, R. Boyle, D. Koracin, & B. Parvin (Eds.), *Advances in Visual Computing* (pp. 562–570). Springer Berlin Heidelberg. Retrieved from http://link.springer.com.bd.univalle.edu.co/chapter/10.1007/11595755_68 doi:10.1007/11595755_68

Matteo Magnani. (2004). Techniques for Dealing with Missing Data in Knowledge Discovery Tasks.

Meira, C. A. A., Rodrigues, L. H. A., & Moraes, S. A. (2008). Análise da epidemia da ferrugem do cafeeiro com árvore de decisão. *Tropical Plant Pathology*, *33*(2), 114–124. doi:10.1590/S1982-56762008000200005

Mohanty, P. K., Reza, M., Kumar, P., & Kumar, P. (2016). Implementation of Cubic Spline Interpolation on Parallel Skeleton Using Pipeline Model on CPU-GPU Cluster. In *Proceedings of the 2016 IEEE 6th International Conference on Advanced Computing (IACC)* (pp. 747–751). 10.1109/IACC.2016.143

Ng, A. (2003). CS 229 Machine Learning Course Materials. In S. Learning (Ed.), *University of Stanford*.

Nitesh, V. C., Kevin W., B., Lawrence O., H., & W., P. K. (2002). SMOTE: Synthetic Minority Over-sampling Technique. Retrieved from https://www.cs.cmu.edu/afs/cs/project/jair/pub/volume16/chawla02a-html/chawla2002.html

Nutman, F. J., Roberts, F. M., & Clarke, R. T. (1963). Studies on the biology of Hemileia vastatrix Berk. & Br. *Transactions of the British Mycological Society*, *46*(1), 27–44. doi:10.1016/S0007-1536(63)80005-4

Pengfei, J., Chunkai, Z., & Zhenyu, H. (2014). A new sampling approach for classification of imbalanced data sets with high density. In *Proceedings of the 2014 International Conference on Big Data and Smart Computing (BIGCOMP)* (pp. 217–222). 10.1109/BIGCOMP.2014.6741439

Peralvo, M. (2002). Influence of DEM interpolation methods in Drainage Analysis. Retrieved February 20, 2017, from https://www.researchgate.net/publication/237116945_Influence_of_DEM_interpolation_methods_in_Drainage_Analysis

Pérez-Ariza, C. B., Nicholson, A. E., & Flores, M. J. (n.d.). Prediction of Coffee Rust Disease Using Bayesian Networks. In M.G.-O. Andrés Cano, & T.D. Nielsen (Ed.), *The Sixth European Workshop on Probabilistic Graphical Models* (Vols. 1).

Phillips, G. M. (2003). Univariate Interpolation. In *Interpolation and Approximation by Polynomials*. Springer New York. Retrieved from http://link.springer.com/chapter/10.1007/0-387-21682-0_1

Rivillas Osorio, C. A. (2011). La roya del cafeto en Colombia, impacto, manejo y costos de control. Cenicafé: Chinchiná - Caldas - Colombia.

Rui, L., & Qiong, L. (2012). Image sharpening algorithm based on a variety of interpolation methods. In Proceedings of the *2012 International Conference on Image Analysis and Signal Processing (IASP)*. doi:10.1109/IASP.2012.6425043

Schaback, R. (1995). Multivariate Interpolation and Approximation by Translates of a Basis Function. Retrieved February 20, 2017, from http://www.codecogs.com/library/maths/approximation/interpolation/multivariate.php

Segrera Francia, S., & Moreno García, M. N. (2006, March). Multiclasificadores: métodos y arquitecturas [Informe técnico]. Retrieved December 29, 2015, from http://gredos.usal.es/jspui/handle/10366/21727

Seiffert, C., Khoshgoftaar, T. M., Hulse, J. V., & Napolitano, A. (2010). RUSBoost: A Hybrid Approach to Alleviating Class Imbalance. *IEEE Transactions on Systems, Man, and Cybernetics. Part A, Systems and Humans, 40*(1), 185–197. doi:10.1109/TSMCA.2009.2029559

Shi, Z., Yao, S., Li, B., & Cao, Q. (2008). A Novel Image Interpolation Technique Based on Fractal Theory. In *Proceedings of the International Conference on Computer Science and Information Technology ICCSIT '08* (pp. 472–475). 10.1109/ICCSIT.2008.185

Sun, Y., Kamel, M. S., & Wang, Y. (2006). Boosting for Learning Multiple Classes with Imbalanced Class Distribution. In *Proceedings of the Sixth International Conference on Data Mining ICDM '06* (pp. 592–602). 10.1109/ICDM.2006.29

Thamada, T. T., Rodrigues, L. H. A., & Meira, C. A. A. (2015). Predição da taxa de progresso da ferrugem do cafeeiro por meio de ensembles. Retrieved from http://www.sbicafe.ufv.br:80/handle/123456789/4134

Thanathamathee, P., & Lursinsap, C. (2013). Handling imbalanced data sets with synthetic boundary data generation using bootstrap re-sampling and AdaBoost techniques. *Pattern Recognition Letters, 34*(12), 1339–1347. doi:10.1016/j.patrec.2013.04.019

Tsai, C.-F., & Chen, M.-L. (2010). Credit rating by hybrid machine learning techniques. *Applied Soft Computing, 10*(2), 374–380. doi:10.1016/j.asoc.2009.08.003

Vapnik, V., Golowich, S. E., & Smola, A. J. (1997). Support Vector Method for Function Approximation, Regression Estimation and Signal Processing. In M. C. Mozer, M. I. Jordan, & T. Petsche (Eds.), Advances in Neural Information Processing Systems (Vol. 9, pp. 281–287). MIT Press. Retrieved from http://papers.nips.cc/paper/1187-support-vector-method-for-function-approximation-regression-estimation-and-signal-processing.pdf

Verbiest, N., Ramentol, E., Cornelis, C., & Herrera, F. (2012). Improving SMOTE with Fuzzy Rough Prototype Selection to Detect Noise in Imbalanced Classification Data. In *Advances in Artificial Intelligence – IBERAMIA 2012* (pp. 169–178). Berlin, Heidelberg: Springer. doi:10.1007/978-3-642-34654-5_18

Viktor, H. L., & Guo, H. (2004). Multiple Classifier Prediction Improvements against Imbalanced Datasets through Added Synthetic Examples. In A. Fred, T. M. Caelli, R. P. W. Duin, A. C. Campilho, & D. de Ridder (Eds.), *Structural, Syntactic, and Statistical Pattern Recognition* (pp. 974–982). Springer Berlin Heidelberg. Retrieved from http://link.springer.com.bd.univalle.edu.co/chapter/10.1007/978-3-540-27868-9_107 doi:10.1007/978-3-540-27868-9_107

Wong, G. Y., Leung, F. H. F., & Ling, S.-H. (2013). A novel evolutionary preprocessing method based on over-sampling and under-sampling for imbalanced datasets. In *IECON 2013 - 39th Annual Conference of the IEEE Industrial Electronics Society* (pp. 2354–2359). 10.1109/IECON.2013.6699499

Yang, L., Liu, S., Tsoka, S., & Papageorgiou, L. G. (2017). A regression tree approach using mathematical programming. *Expert Systems with Applications*, *78*, 347–357. doi:10.1016/j.eswa.2017.02.013

Zhang, H., & Li, M. (2014). RWO-Sampling: A random walk over-sampling approach to imbalanced data classification. *Information Fusion*, *20*, 99–116. doi:10.1016/j.inffus.2013.12.003

This research was previously published in the International Journal of Agricultural and Environmental Information Systems (IJAEIS), 9(2); pages 32-52, copyright year 2018 by IGI Publishing (an imprint of IGI Global).

Section 3
Tools and Technologies

Chapter 24
Artificial Intelligence and Machine Learning Algorithms

Amit Kumar Tyagi

(iD) https://orcid.org/0000-0003-2657-8700

School of Computing Science and Engineering, Vellore Institute of Technology, Chennai, India

Poonam Chahal

(iD) https://orcid.org/0000-0002-2684-4354

MRIIRS, Faridabad, India

ABSTRACT

With the recent development in technologies and integration of millions of internet of things devices, a lot of data is being generated every day (known as Big Data). This is required to improve the growth of several organizations or in applications like e-healthcare, etc. Also, we are entering into an era of smart world, where robotics is going to take place in most of the applications (to solve the world's problems). Implementing robotics in applications like medical, automobile, etc. is an aim/goal of computer vision. Computer vision (CV) is fulfilled by several components like artificial intelligence (AI), machine learning (ML), and deep learning (DL). Here, machine learning and deep learning techniques/algorithms are used to analyze Big Data. Today's various organizations like Google, Facebook, etc. are using ML techniques to search particular data or recommend any post. Hence, the requirement of a computer vision is fulfilled through these three terms: AI, ML, and DL.

INTRODUCTION ABOUT ARTIFICIAL INTELLIGENCE& MACHINE LEARNING

Computer Vision is a subdivision of computer science which is integrated with the usual mining, analysis and consideration of constructive information. In simple words, computer vision means "How machines can/ a machine sees/ solves problems without a human-being". In the past decade, this area is too popular and has still attracted several research communities to develop machines better than human being (in terms of work-efficiency, thinking-level or solving problems). For example, Sophia is a recent and enhanced robot which is being developed by the Hong Kong based company Hanson Robotics. It is the first robot

DOI: 10.4018/978-1-6684-6291-1.ch024

to come to get the Saudi Arabia citizenship in 2016. So, it can be said that the computer vision domain is the becoming the upcoming field of research that can solve various problems related to virtualization. The computer vision has been expanding and emerging with the new and advanced technologies or concepts (like Blockchain, Internet of Everything, etc.) and applications that utilize different computer vision techniques. Among all existing technologies (in recent years), over a hundred applications/ many organizations have moved to the practice and execution of Artificial Intelligence techniques.

Machine Learning techniques required in their business/ to give boost to the aim of computer vision. Hence, to fulfil the vision of smart worlds/ requirements, artificial intelligence, and machine learning allows tools/ applications to become more accurate (in terms of values) in predicting results (without being explicitly programmed). For artificial intelligence algorithms, several inferences, rules and logic that were used in the systems which were created using traditional techniques of Artificial Intelligence are not meeting the today's requirement of the changing world. In divergence, systems that focus on the analysis and detection the patterns that are existing in dataset for classification, clustering, regression, are becoming the overriding system of AI. In addition to the existing mechanisms, the domain of AI can be further taken into the form of three main groups like Artificial Slight intellect, Artificial Overall Intelligence, and Artificial Super Intelligence. On the other way round there are numerous categories of existing techniques of Machine Learning (ML) algorithms used in fulfilling the objective of computer vision like supervised (regression, decision tree, random forest, classification) and unsupervised (Clustering, Association Analysis, Hidden Markov Model (HMM), etc.) and semi-supervised. In simple words, computer vision is the science and technology of machines that a machine sees (without a human-being). Computer vision is an exploration extent that comprises numerous methods to approach several graphic problems. In recent years, over a hundred applications/ many organizations have been replaced by Artificial Intelligence, Deep Learning and other Machine Learning techniques to give boost to the aim of computer vision. Hence, to fulfil the vision of smart worlds/ requirements, artificial intelligence, and machine learning allows tools/ applications to become more accurate (in terms of values) in predicting results (without being explicitly programmed).

BACKGROUND

Artificial Intelligence (AI)

It is a division of Computer Science which tracks technology, i.e., generating the computers or machineries that behave as intelligent and rational as human beings. In general, the definition of Artificial Intelligence includes the designing and creation of systems that can understand the human intelligence and behave accordingly in an environment provided. It will include the learning, planning etc. to behave the system rationally. AI not only creates the intelligent systems or expert systems but it also expand to the biologically observable. In addition to this the father of AI named as John McCarthy, "The science and engineering of creating intellectual machines, specifically intellectual system programs".

In other words, Artificial Intelligence (AI) is a means of constructing a computer, a robot controlled by computer, or software that contemplates intelligently, similar to a human/individual. Artificial Intelligence accomplish its aims by deeply studying the structure and thinking process of an individual brain to find out the ways of learning, planning, decision capability, and taking action in a particular situation. In the previous years, Artificial Intelligence has increased acceptance due to growing people's curiosity in numerous novel research domains like big data, Blockchain technology etc., because of the enhancement in the speed of generation of data, its huge size and its various varieties. The use of AI also helps in businesses by making the use of the techniques of business intelligence embedded with the AI techniques. In an organization, the tools, methodologies used to enhance their business processes in real world when combined with the AI tools, give better results.

In the domain of computer science, where programming perspective is very strong and allied, AI deals with the searching, planning, learning, computational linguistic, etc. It also includes the representation of knowledge in the knowledge base or production system y considering the characteristics of the problem to be solved and all the possible issues related to the same. In general, the knowledge base constructed for the intelligent system should be systematic and it should have a control strategy and motion. By motion, it means that whenever a rule is selected to be applied while solving a problem it should cause the current state to be enhanced in the state space search. The control strategy should be designed like that the same rule is not be selected again and again, the rule selection should be based on the learning mechanism which is to be embedded in the system that can access the knowledge base.

The knowledge base is basically the collection of facts and rules. The facts act as the terminating statements for a problem which can be solved by applying various rules. So, to solve a particular problem we should be able to define the problem, its input, its output, the set of rules/facts, its cost of computation to find the efficiency of the system. There are various applications of AI like computer vision, creation of expert system, computational linguistic, Natural Language Processing (NLP), Machine Learning (ML), etc. Hence, an Artificial Intelligence (AI) method that exploits knowledge, which is used to characterize:

- The knowledge apprehensions generalizations that segment properties, are grouped together, rather than being acceptable distinct representation.
- It can be tacit by people who must make available it. For numerous programs, most of the data comes inevitably from interpretations.
- In numerous AI domains, how the people comprehend the similar people must source the knowledge to a program.
- It can be simply adapted to precise faults and reproduce changes in actual circumstances.
- It can be extensively used even if it is inadequate or imprecise.
- It can be used to aid stunned its own issues or problems by serving to slender the variety of options.

Data Mining

In general terms, Data Mining is a process to finding several new patterns in huge collection of data sets using numerous techniques like classification, clustering (Tyagi &Tyagi, 2014), regression, etc. to predict future trends (see figure 1). In old days (from 1990 to 2010), data mining techniques was used quite a lot. But, when the revolution in smart technology enters, a lot of data is being collected at server side (for all organisations). In other words, data mining was used in past decades to discover hidden pattern/ information/ unknown facts from a data. These hidden patterns play an essential role in increasing profit for organisation. On the other hand, a lot of data has been produced by several (integration of internet connected devices together) Internet of Things (via machine to machine/ device to device communication). But available traditional data mining tools were not sufficient to handle this data or finding hidden patterns. So, a new term "Machine Learning" was created by Arthur Samuel (Anderson, 1987) and the definition of Machine Learning as "ML is a field of study that gives computers the capability to learn without being explicitly programmed". Today's era the domain of Machine learning is being used in several applications like e-healthcare, retail, defence, etc., to make some useful decision (prediction). For that, it works on indicative based learning, instance based learning, neural network (i.e., based supervised, unsupervised and semi-supervised learning) (refer figure 3).

Figure 1. An overview of tasks and main algorithms in data mining

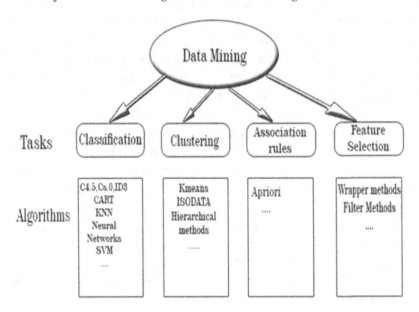

In recent days (or in the past decade), data mining technique have been used in analysing of data. Generally, Data mining can be directed or undirected data mining. The data mining techniques based on directed approach extracts the data from the past records to detect the existing patterns that gives a particular framework for the outcome of the problem which includes clustering, regression, prediction, classification etc. Whereas, the undirected data mining extracts the data through the similar records for detecting the patterns that are hidden using the association rules, clustering etc.

Generally, Data Mining never aspect for precise goal, but it continuously emphases on extracting novel or hidden knowledge considering semantics. Data mining is achieved on following kinds of databases, i.e., Relational databases, Advanced Data bases, Data warehouses, and material repositories, Object-oriented concepts and object-relational databases,, Heterogeneous with legacy databases, Transactional and Spatial databases (considering space), Multimedia with streaming database, Text mining, Text based data storage, and Web information mining (Tyagi, 2019). So, Data Mining techniques can be summarized as:

- **Classification:** This technique classifies the data based on different classes. It is mainly used to invent the class tag for new samples of data.
- **Clustering:** Clustering analysis technique to identify data similarities by projecting the data on n-dimensional space.
- **Regression:** Regression analysis finds the relationship between variables by identifies the possibility of a definite variable, given the existence of additional variables.

- **Rules based on Association:** This technique creates the connotation between diverse items in the system of rules. It determines a concealed pattern in the data set.
- **Outlier recognition:** This technique is used to uncover the unexpected pattern or unexpected behavior from the dataset. It is used in several areas/domain, such as invasion detection, deception or fault uncovering, etc. Alternative name for outlier recognition is outlier investigation or outlier mining.
- **Sequential based Patterns:** It works on transactional data bases and assistances to determine the like patterns or drifts occur in transaction data sets for firm passé of time.

In conclusion, Data Mining is all round amplification the precedent and envisaging the prospect based on analysis. It aids in mining of treasured information from huge volume of data. It is the method of mining knowledge from data. Data mining (Guleria & Sood, 2019; Bathela, 2018) (term introduced by Gregory Piatetsky-Shapiro, in KDD-1989 workshop, as "knowledge discovery in databases" first workshop of same topic) includes Business Considerate, Data Considerate, Data Grounding, Exhibiting, Progression, and Distribution. Some of significant Data mining techniques are: Categorization, Classification, Clustering, Regression, Association rules, Outlier analysis, and Sequential patterns (as shown is figure 1). For implementation, the protuberant data mining tools used are Weka, R Tool and Oracle server based Data mining. Data mining technique benefits organisations/ companies to get knowledge-based information to progress their revenue (with reference to their products). The bid of data mining techniques has been implemented in numerous businesses such as insurance, education, communication, manufacturing, banking, retail, ecommerce, service providers and many more.

Machine Learning

Machine learning algorithms are frequently characterized as supervised or unsupervised. Supervised algorithms require a data analyst or scientist with machine learning techniques aids to run both effort and anticipated outcome. Further, to furnish the response about the correctness of estimates while training the algorithm. Data Scientists works on extracting the features that will help in prediction. The feature extraction then leads to the training of data set so that the system designed can learn to give the desired output. This needs deep learning which is based on unsupervised learning techniques that come under the umbrella of neural network. The unsupervised learning techniques are used in many applications like image recognition, natural language generation, computational linguistic etc.

Figure 2. Process of machine learning

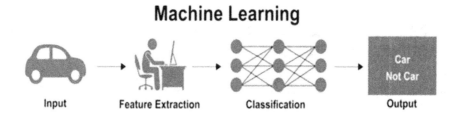

Hence, figure 2 discusses the method of machine learning, i.e., in Machine Learning (ML) is done using past data (including human intervention), for example, IBM Watson, Google search algorithm, email spam filer, etc. Whereas, figure 3 explains machine learning algorithms in terms of inductive based learning, instance based learning, genetic algorithms, neural networks and Bayesian approaches.

Figure 3. Classification of main machine learning algorithms

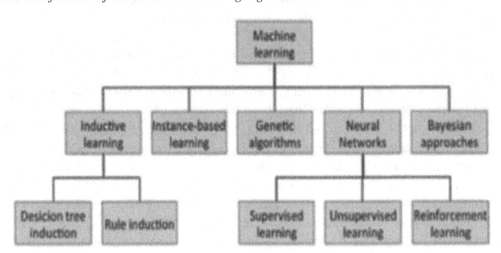

Hence in general, Machine learning is a subdivision of artificial intelligence, where as deep learning is a subdivision of machine leaning (Tyagi, 2019). Whereas data mining are tools or techniques used in old days to refine or process data, but fails to refine or process large amount of data (and different format of data), so we sued machine learning. Today various organizations like Google, Facebook etc., are using Machine Learning techniques to search particular data or recommend any post/ finding friends or finding respective picture of a user. Hence, the requirement of a computer vision is fulfilled by these three terms, i.e., by AI, ML, and DL. Now due to the recent development in technologies and integration of millions of internet of thing's devices, a lot of data is being generated everyday (known as Big Data). This is required to analysis for improving growth of several organizations or in applications like e-healthcare. Here, data mining or machine learning techniques/ algorithms used to analysis this Big Data for producing a decision for future (or for prediction purpose). Hence, this section discusses about artificial intelligence, data mining and machine learning as introduction in brief. Now next section of this chapter will discuss several raised problems in artificial intelligence and machine learning.

PROBLEMS WITH ARTIFICIAL INTELLIGENCE (AI) AND MACHINE LEARNING (ML)

There are numerous branches occur of Artificial Intelligence (AI), which are: Logical AI, Pattern detection, Common intellect Knowledge and interpretation, Ontology, Heuristics, Genetic Programming, etc. The mentioned branches are only some to be named here and AI does not restrict to only these but extends to many more. Moreover this, even all branches are not discovered yet, even though AI, ML and DL have several problems in it. Now some problem in AI (area-wise), ML is being discussed here as:

Problems That Occur in Artificial Intelligence

Intelligence does not infer perfect considerate; every intellectual being has inadequate perception, retention and computation. AI looks to comprehend the computations essential from intellectual behaviour and to yield computer systems that revelation intellect. Characteristics of intelligence studied by AI comprise perception, communicational using human dialects, reasoning, planning, learning and retention. The following queries are to be well-thought-out before we move advancing:

- Fundamental norms about intelligence?
- Techniques used for problem solving using AI?
- How to model Level of human intelligence?
- When and How to realize that an intelligent program has been built?

To solve the above mentioned problems/issues AI can be amended a lot using machine learning and other methods in near future.

Problems of Machine Learning

Deep learning techniques are in infancy stage. They require large amount of data-sets (properly structured and arranged) to provide precise answers to existing questions. An Organization occupied on a realistic machine learning appliance requires to devote time, assets, and take extensive threats. Artificial Neural Network (ANN) requires millions of parameter, whereas a training set (in ANN) uses millions of records (i.e., used as input for processing). While an association is accomplished of retention the training dataset sample and providing answers with 100 percent correctness, but this accurateness may become useless when we collect/ receive new data. This process is called over-fitting (or overtraining) and one popular limitation of deep learning techniques.

1. **Problem based on Black Box:** The initial phase of machine learning fitted to moderately modest, superficial methods. For example, a tree algorithm based on decision acts firmly according to the convention its superior skilled it: "if something is oval and green, there is a probability P it is a cucumber". These forms were not very good at recognizing a cucumber in a image, but at slightest everybody knew how they effort. Deep Learning algorithms are diverse. They construct a hierarchical demonstration of data layers which them to construct their own perceptive. After analyzing this huge amount of data-sets, neural networks can discover how to identify cucumbers with good precision. But here the difficulty is that machine learning engineers/data scientists do not recognize "how they received these results"? In summary this problem is called a black box problem.

Artificial Intelligence controller appreciated the input (the data that the algorithm works) and the output (the resolution it makes). While the engineers are able to appreciate "how a single prediction was made"? Here, it is a lack of lack of transparency, interpretability. Generally, it is very complicated to appreciate "how the whole model works"? As discussed in, one of popular limitations of deep learning (a subset of AI and ML) is: we do not know that how a neural network reaches at a particular solution. It is impossible to look inside of it to see how it works (called black box problem). It is a major barrier in the growth of other AI applications like provides efficient formulas for medicine (in medical-care), or automatic assessment of credit rating. Now thing, what if an algorithm's analysis comes incorrect? How will a car producer explain the performance of the autopilot when a deadly calamity occurs? How will a bank reply a customer's grievance? By many researchers (which has done previously), we find that artificial intelligence causes fright and other unconstructive passion in people (or human-being). Most of the People are anxious of an object seeing and behaving "almost like a human" (i.e., this phenomenon is known as "uncanny valley").

2. **Talent Deficit:** A data scientist can understand machine learning good but he/ she can not have sufficient knowledge of software engineering. Knowing every areas/ subject knowledge is a big problem now days. There are few (at the near end of 2017, there were approximate 300,000 researchers, educationist, academicians, practitioners, industrialist working with AI globally, according to). Apart that, who are skilled one require serious artificial intelligence research. For top companies like Google, Amazon, etc., machine learning engineers and data scientists are pinnacle precedence choices. In area of machine learning, there are lot of incentives and good salaries given to talented people who know how to work with machine learning. Several organisations are doing brain drain with the help of organising job fair, etc.

3. **Data is Paid:** To train a machine learning prototype, we require massive data. However, it is not a difficulty anymore, since everybody can work to accumulate and process petabytes of information. While storage space may be inexpensive, it needs time to gather a enough quantity of data. But, retailing ready-sets of data is costly. There are also issues of a diverse nature. Preparing data after pre-processing for training of any algorithm is a complex task (takes a lot of time). Using algorithms like classification, clustering, regression, etc., we prepare meaningful data. Also, we require to accumulate data compilation methods and reliable formatting. Then, we have to decrease data with characteristic sampling, record sampling, or aggregating sampling. We require to divide the data and scaling of the same needs to be done. It is a composite task that requires highly knowledgeable engineers and time. So even if we have unlimited disk storage available, the process is too costly. On another side, if attempt to use individual data, people will begin facing extra challenges like leaking of their information/ knowledge (or defending their isolation), trust, protection, etc. Individual data and big data actions have also become more complicated, dangerous and expensive with the foreword of novel regulations defending individual data, like the well-known European General Data Protection Regulation (Mrakovic & Vojnomic, 2019), HIPAA (Marcos & Garcia, 2019; Benett & Verceler, 2018).

4. **Based on Technology:** The Alphabet Inc. (former Google) bids TensorFlow, whereas Microsoft liaises with Facebook emerging Open Neural Network Exchange (ONNX). The systems constructed by them are overloaded with data generated in each business across the world. Although the environments created are novel like the very primary version of TensorFlow available in 2015 February, PyTorch, which is a remarkable library released in 2016. In today's era of technology the solutions required for problem solving needs too much of efforts and contemplation to build a product and make it ready for release to the outside world. This requires time to achieve the promising and efficient results. In general, the development of the code for any machine language algorithm is

also complex and needs intelligence so that the machine can perform the desired task. In addition to this the learning is also complex and it requires the coding in the form of layers which helps the machine to get trained to perform the task as required. Further, the working on AI project is a high hazard, high recompense innovativeness. We require to be persistent, plan prudently, reverence the challenges of advanced technology, and find people who really comprehend machine learning and are not demanding to vend and vacant ability.

Now days using machine learning-based strategies in computer vision is an extremely critical issue (due to rising of several critical challenges in ML). For example, object acknowledgment and image grouping, colossal advancement has been made in applying deep learning systems. Then again, there are a few discussions with regards to the explanations behind the high achievement of the profound learning-based techniques, and about the restrictions of these strategies. Hence, this section discusses several problems raised in AI and ML in the previous decade. Now next section will deal with some real world's examples with respect to AI and ML in detail.

Artificial Intelligence and Machine Learning: Real World's Examples

Artificial Intelligence is a method of constructing a computer, a robot controlled by the computer, or software contemplates intelligently, similar to a human who can contemplate intelligently. As deliberated in preceding sections, area or field of Artificial Intelligence is firm to define, since it is used in many other domains now days. For example, Google (search engine which searches results as per user query), Wikipedia (used for getting outcomes in brief), etc. Artificial Intelligence (AI) is firm to define, because intelligence is firm to define in the primary place. Artificial Intelligence is not natural- living, it is a constructed machine made by human which is running on code. AI systems can make decisions that take into account numerous factors, such as how an individual brain functions (in dissimilar scenarios). In modest terms, "robot" is not a synonym for Artificial Intelligence. Artificial Intelligence is a reference to the software that establishes intelligence, however robots deduce a physical component, a shell which conveys out the decisions made by the AI engine overdue it. Not all AI desires a robot to carry out its functions, i.e., an AI desires to envisage an incident/decision earlier occurring, but not all robots desire accurate AI to power its functionality.

As we nurture and together this technology evolves, the definition of AI also gets variations. In fact, John McCarthy, who invented the term "Artificial Intelligence" in 1956 (Albert et. al., 2018), focussed that "as soon as it works, no one demands it AI anymore". Today's many of the rules- and logic-based systems that were earlier considered Artificial Intelligence are no extended classified as AI. In contrary, systems that analyse and detect patterns in data (using machine learning) are becoming a fragment of Artificial Intelligence. Hence, the level of AI can be fragmented down into three key categories.

1. **Artificial Narrow Intelligence:** Narrow AI (or weak AI) is the only method of Artificial Intelligence that humankind has attained so far. This is virtuous at performing a solitary task, such as playing chess or Go, making procurement suggestions, sales forecasts and weather predictions. Computer vision and computational linguistic are in the present stage narrow AI. Speech and image detection are narrow AI, even if their developments seem enthralling. Even Google's transformation engine, Self-driving car skill, etc., is a system of narrow AI. In over-all, narrow AI works within a very inadequate framework, and cannot take on errands beyond its field. Narrow AI (or weak AI)

does not mean incompetence. On additional side, it is so decent at routine jobs, both physical and cognitive. It is narrow AI which is intimidating to substitute (or rather displace) numerous human jobs. And it is slight AI that can explore required patterns and associations from data that would take years for people to find. But, it is still not individual-level AI (i.e., contented/ part of Artificial General Intelligence).

2. **Artificial General Intelligence:** General AI (individual-level AI or robust AI) is the kind of Artificial Intelligence that can comprehend and reason its environment as an individual would. General AI has constantly been subtle. In the previous decades, we are using it in escalate the miracles, i.e., behind the individual brain or to know concealed patterns in individual brain. This is very hard to define (or achieve) each and every action of human being (how we perceive input the things form the environment, disguise between numerous unrelated opinions and memories) by general AI. Also, the competence of general AI is firm to define. Humans might not be able to process and work on data as fast as computers, but they can contemplate abstractly and design, resolve problems at a wide-ranging level without going into the specifics. They can revolutionize, come up with opinions and thoughts that have no superiority. Several inventions like ships, telescopes, telephone, concepts such as gaming, graphics, e-mail, social media, and virtual reality, has been done by humans which cannot be done by computers. It is very firm to make a computer which can invent things that are not available which is possible only by human's by making the use of brain only.

3. **Artificial Super Intelligence:** According to a scholar from University of Oxford, AI expert Nick Bostrom, when AI develops much smarter than the best human brains in essentially each field, including technical creativity, general knowledge and social aids, we have attained Artificial Super Intelligence (ASI). ASI is even indistinct (vague) than AGI at this point. By some accounts, the remoteness between AGI and ASI is very short. It shall occur in few months, weeks, or maybe the blink of an eye and will continue at the speed of light. What happens then, no one (i.e., human-being) knows for sure. Some scientists such as Stephen Hawking see the development of full artificial intelligence as the potential end of humanity. Even in previous decades, several movies have made to show such reality/ on such incidents. On other side, Google's Demis Hassabis (founder of DeepMind, 2010), believe the shrewder AI gets, the improved humans will develop at saving the environment, curing illnesses, discover the universe, and at thoughtful themselves (Powel & Hodson, 2017).

Some other applications of Artificial intelligence are Expert System, Planning, learning, Machine Learning, probability based learning, computational linguistic, Theorem Proving, virtual reality, Symbolic Mathematics, animation, Game Playing, semantic similarity, Natural Language Processing, uncertainty dealing, Robotics, etc. Apart that, some applications of machine learning are weather forecasting, health-care, sentiment analysis, fraud detection, and e-commerce, etc.

TYPES OF ARTIFICIAL INTELLIGENCE AND MACHINE LEARNING ALGORITHMS

There are a lot of benefits of AI in in today's life for a human life. AI has reduced work load and increase productivity and serving better for good for humanity. In summary, AI is using several algorithms to serve or perform human's work. On the another side, some benefits of machine learning are powerful processing, better decision making and predication, quicker processing, accurate results/ decisions, affordable data management, inexpensive services to users and analysing complex (large) big data. Hence, such services or benefits are provided by using several learning algorithms like supervise, unsupervised and re-enforcement techniques. Each learning technique will be discussed in this section in detail (Horowitz, 2018).

Artificial Intelligence Algorithms

Artificial Intelligences being used in an extensive range of applications today, for example, Google Search, Facebook's News Feed. Google Search practices AI to find or to give reply to individual query by searching among huge amount of data (on web i.e. WWW). Also, the News Feed practices machine learning to engrave every member's feed. For example, if any person stops reading or scrolling or liking a post posted by any friend, then using machine learning technique the News feed will show more activities related to that friend as compared to activities that were shown earlier. Any software used for any kind of machine learning needs the statistical and predictive analysis for detecting the hidden patterns in the dataset of the user and then further uses these patterns in feeding the news. AI and ML are also emerging as an array of applications in enterprise domain like customer relation management (CRM), supplier chain management (SCM), human resource management (HRM, business intelligence (BI) etc. CRM basically uses the machine learning models to read the emails for responding the sales team on time regarding the delivery of any product or service. BI uses the models of machine learning to identify the significant points in their business processes and decisions which can impact the profit of an organization. HRM uses the models of machine learning to detect the characteristics of their employees, their training, development program so that they work to the best of their knowledge. Machine learning algorithms/techniques also play an important role in automation like it creates the self- identifying and driving car to reduce man work/efforts. Neural Networks which include machine learning with deep learning helps in determining the optimal and rational solution/action for steering a car round the road to avoid any kind of accidents. This technology is called virtual assistant which is also gained by machine learning. Smart assistants combine numerous deep learning models to construe natural speech, fetch in appropriate context, i.e., similar to a user's personal plan or formerly defined predilections and take an accomplishment, like booking an aircraft or pulling up driving directions. Hence, AI practices all machine learning and deep learning technique to do any kind of processing. In AI some algorithms are A*, AO*, production, heuristic search, etc., but these algorithms are used to detect an optimal/rational solution. Apart that, AI uses all knowledge algorithms like supervised and unsupervised listed in figure 4. Also, it practices the significant deep learning techniques like Convolutional Neural Networks (CNNs), Back-propagation, Recurrent Neural Networks (RNNs), and Reinforcement Learning (RL).

Machine Learning Algorithms

As discussed there are many applications/ uses of machine learning techniques, hence there exists variety of machine learning algorithms. They vary from the fairly simple (less time complexity) to the highly complex (high time complexity). The class of machine learning algorithm includes categorizing an association, i.e., among two variables and using that association to make predictions about imminent data points. Some of the most commonly used techniques are:

Figure 4. Structure of machine learning techniques and algorithms

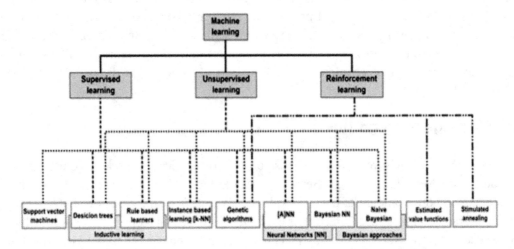

- **Decision trees:** The decision tree is a hierarchical representation of a problem solving technique. It uses observations about firm actions and finds an optimal path for receiving an outcome that is desired.
- **K-means clustering:** This is type of clustering which forms the clusters depending on the value of k provided by the user. The cluster specifies a group of data points that are similar in characteristics.
- **Neural networks:** It includes machine leaning with deep learning methods that utilizes huge amounts of training data to detect association among various variables. This association helps in learning of the process which manages the incoming data in near future. The types of Neural Networks are Artificial Neural Network (ANN), Convolution Neural Network (CNN), Recursive Neural Network (RNN), Deep Neural Network (DNN) and Deep Belief Network (DBN).
- **Reinforcement Learning:** This area of deep learning includes methods which iterate over various steps in a process to get the desired results. Steps that yield desirable outcomes are content and steps that yield undesired outcomes are reprimanded until the algorithm is able to learn the given optimal process. In unassuming terms, learning is finished on its own or effort on feedback or content based learning.

In next section each machine learning algorithms (Burio et al. 2019) is been discussed in details (with respect to supervised learning and unsupervised learning).

SUPERVISED LEARNING

Decision Trees

A tree or hierarchical representation based on decision is a sustenance tool that aids the use of a tree-like hierarchical structure or form of decisions and their feasible cost, with chance-event effect, foundation costs, and utility role. From the analysis point of big business view, a decision tree is the least number of yes/no questions that one has to request, to measure the probability of creation an accurate decision.

As a technique, it allows us to move in the direction of the difficulty in an ordered and methodical way to attain at a logical conclusion (Galley & Raje, 2012).

Naive Bayes Classification

Naive Bayes classifiers are an intimate of straightforward probabilistic classifiers build on pertaining Bayes' theorem with vigorous (naive) eccentricity supposition among the characteristics. The characteristic representation is the equation, i.e.,with P(A|B) which is known as posterior probability, P(B|A) which is called as likelihood, P(A) which is called as class prior probability, and P(B) which is called as predictor prior probability. Nearly of real world examples of Naive Bayes Classification are:

* Finding of an email marked as spam.
* Classifying the articles of news article based on technology, politics, or sports.
* To do sentiment analysis of a text which finds its polarity?
* Software based on face/image recognition.

Ordinary Least Squares Regression

When we have consequence with statistics, we need linear regression for prediction. Here, least square is a technique for accomplishment linear regression. Linear regression is the mission of appropriating a straight line through a given set of points. There are manifold probable conducts to do this, so here "ordinary least squares" plan used, i.e., we can illustrate a line, and then for every of the data points, calculate the vertical remoteness among the point and the line, and append these up; the built-in line would be the solitary where this addition of distances is as minute as achievable (see figure 5).

Figure 5. Ordinary least squares regression

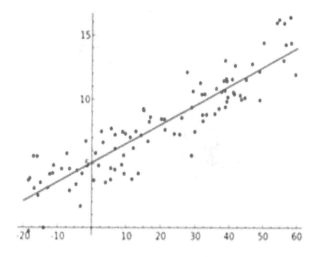

Logistic Regression

It is type of regression based on logistics (or logit regression) is a influential numerical way of modelling a binomial effect more than one explanatory variables. It is the method in which relationship among the categorical variable which is dependent and more than one independent variables by approximating probabilities using mathematical function based on logistic, which is the collective logistic distribution (see figure 6). It is used to approximate the values which are discrete in nature (Binary values like 0/1, yes/no, true/false) based on known set of autonomous variable (s). In simple words, it estimates the probability of result of an event by correcting data to a logic function. Note that it estimates the probability, its outcome values always lays in range of 0 and 1 (as expected) (Turner, 2019).

There are many real world applications of regressions such as:

- Scoring of credit
- accomplishment rates measurement of crusades used for marketing
- Recognising the revenues of a firm service or product
- Forecasting of weather

For example, if a puzzle needs to be solved and then there exist two possibilities wither the puzzle is solved or remains unsolvable. Now envisage that we are being specified with diverse range of puzzles/quizzes in an effort to understand which subjects we are decent at. The result to this study would be like a trigonometry based problem of tenth grade and so we are likely to solve it to the extent of 70%. Whereas the question from history related to grade five then the possibility of solving reduces to 30% (Avati et. al., 2018).

Figure 6. Regression with logistic concept

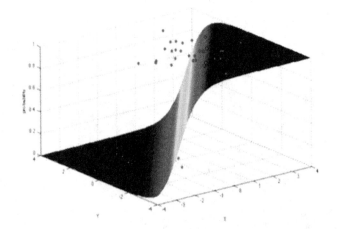

Support Vector Machines (SVM)

It is a dual classification algorithm. For example, for set of two kinds of points in a agreed N dimensional space, SVM constructs (N-1) dimensional hyper-plane to different the known N points into two groups. Suppose we have some points of two different types that can be separated linearly. By using SVM a straight line can be constructed which divides the two types of points as shown in figure 7.

Figure 7. Support vector machine (linear classification)

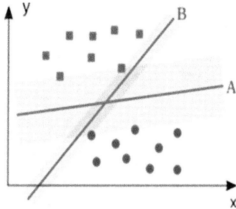

In the past decade, various complex problems have been solved efficiently with less time and space complexity using SVMs. The classification method used in SVM is highly remarkable and attained from the domain of data mining. In the algorithm of SVM the data items are plotted in N dimensional space where, N is the count of features that have been extracted from the data points. The SVM classification is shown in Figure 8.

Figure 8. Support vector machine showing classification

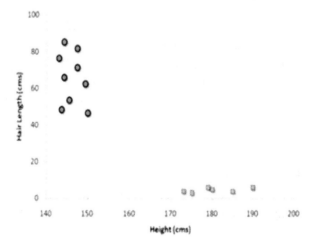

In Figure 8 the data points are clustered and now the line is to be created that actually separates the data points so that the classification of two groups is done. The line constructed is the major division between the two types of data types to show two groups.

Figure 9. Support vector machine showing two groups

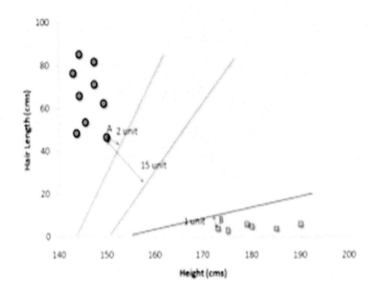

In figure 9, the black line is constructed which separates the data into two contrarily classified groups. This black line is the classifier created by SVM. Whereas, the red lines on either side of the black line is the one on which the user tests the classification done by SVM.

kNN (k- Nearest Neighbors)

It can be used for the problems based on classification and regression. K-nearest neighbors is a modest algorithm that stores all accessible cases and classifies novel cases by a common voting of its neighbors k. The case being allocated to the class is most communal amongst its nearest neighbors k measured by a function based on distance. These distance functions can be Euclidean, Manhattan, Minkowski and Hamming distance. First three functions are continuous function and fourth one (Hamming) is based on categorical variables. If K = 1, then the case is simply allocated to the class of its nearest neighbor. It is important to note that choosing the value of K is also a challenging task while implementing the kNN modeling. Also, kNN is extensively used in industry problems based on classification.

k-Means

It is a unsupervised algorithm to resolve clustering based problem, i.e., it is using simple process to classify a assumed data-set through a firm number of clusters (assume k-clusters). It is to be noted that data points privileged a cluster may be homogeneous or heterogeneous (for peer groups).Figure 11 shows approximately shapes like ink blots. Using these shape and feast, the different clusters/ categorization can be determined which are present in a given data-set.

Figure 10. k- nearest neighbors (KNN)

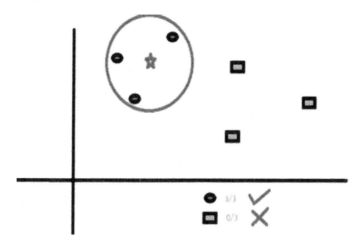

Figure 11. An example of k-means showing constructed clusters

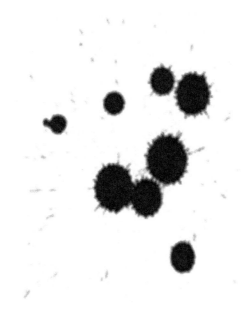

Process Used by k-Means to Construct the Cluster

1. k-means input value of k which is number of points for each cluster also called as centroids.
2. Each data point constructs a cluster with the minimum distance from centroids, i.e., k clusters.

3.   Each cluster centroid is determined based on existing members of the cluster. Here we have novel centroids.

4.   After finding new centroids, step 2 and 3 are repeated. Again, the closest distance for each data point from new centroids is calculated using any distance formula and the data points get associated with new k-clusters. This process is repeated until merging occurs i.e. centroids remains fixed or does not change.

Figure 12. Process of setting value of k used in k-means algorithm

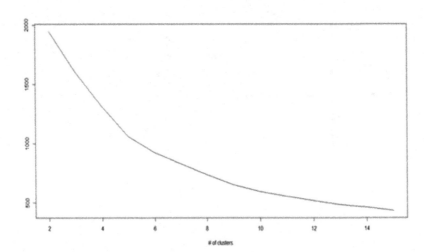

Random Forest

Random Forest (RF) is based on assembly of decision trees thus called as "Forest". To classify a novel object based on characteristics, each tree gives arrangement, i.e., the tree "votes" for individual class. The forest selects the classification having the maximum votes covering all the trees available in the forest. In RF, each and every tree is constructed as follows:

1.   If the numeral of cases in the training set is N, then sample of N cases is taken at random but with replacement. This sample will be the training set for growing the tree.

2.   If there are M input variables, a number m<<M is specified such that at each node, m variables are selected at random out of the M and the best split on these m is used to split the node. The value of m is held constant during the forest growing.

3.   Each tree is grown to the largest extent possible. There is no pruning.

Ensemble Approaches

Ensemble approaches are learning algorithms that creates a classifier based on the set of data points and then categorize novel data points by considering a prejudiced vote of their forecasts. The innovative ensemble technique is based on averaging Bayesian, but more current established algorithms comprise error-correcting output coding.

Figure 13. Ensemble learning algorithms (ELA)

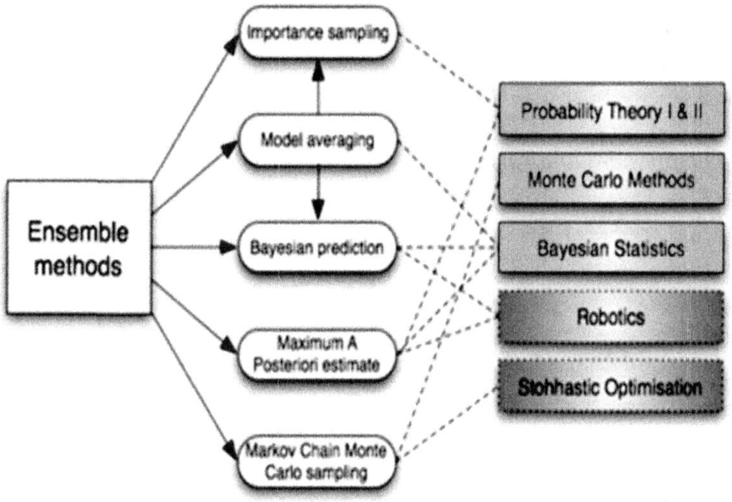

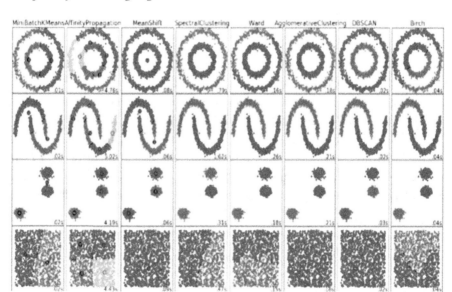

UNSUPERVISED LEARNING

Clustering is the undertaking of collecting a set of substances in a way that substances in the similar group (also called as cluster) are alike to each other as compared to those in previous groups. Every algorithm used for clustering algorithm is diverse as shown in figure 14.

Figure 14. Examples of clustering algorithms

Few algorithms used for Clustering are: Connectivity-based, Centroid-based, Density and Probabilistic based, Dimensionality Reduction based, neural networks based, Deep Learning based.

Principal Component Analysis (PCA)

It is a statistical process that utilizes an orthogonal alteration to change a set of annotations of probably associated variables into a dataset of standards of linearly non-associated variables are known as principal components as shown in figure 15.

Figure 15. Principal component analysis (PCA)

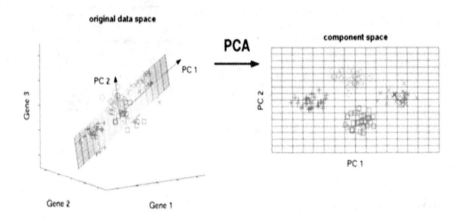

Few of the appliances of PCA comprise compression of image/ videos, abridge data for relaxed learning, imagining etc. For all the applications the knowledge related to a domain is actually significant while selecting that the execution is to go frontward with PCA or still carried out with other available techniques. It is also found that PCA is not appropriate in cases where datasets are noisy i.e. the data points have elevated variance.

Singular Value Decomposition (SVD)

It is a representation of actual matrix that is complex in nature, for example, m * n representing multiplication of two matrices m and n and the result is stored in matrix M, then the decomposition exist as $M = U\Sigma V$. In which U and V are the matrices are unitary and Σ is the matrix which represents diagonal.

Generally, PCA is a modest appliance of SVD. In the field of computer vision, to identify and filter a face, PCA and SVD are used in order to signify faces as a linear mixture of "Eigen-faces", then dimensionality decrease is done, and then counterpart faces to individualities via modest techniques. This technique provides a modest way to identify any image as compared to other existing traditional or modern methods.

Figure 16. Singular value decomposition (SVD)

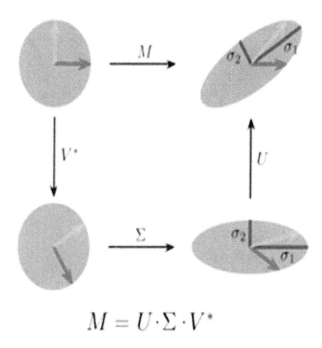

$$M = U \cdot \Sigma \cdot V^*$$

Independent Component Analysis (ICA)

ICA is a numerical method for skimpy concealed factors that lie behind groups of random variables, dimensions, or signals. It defines a generative prototype for the experiential multivariate data, i.e., for a huge database of samples. In this prototype, the data variables are presumed to be linear combinations of approximately unidentified latent variables as shown in figure 17. The latent variables used are presumed to be non-Gaussian and communally independent (also known as independent elements of the experiential data).

Generally, ICA is also connected to PCA (like SVD). But, ICA is additionally influential method which is accomplished of detecting the underlying factors of emerged from various sources when the traditional methods does not provide the desired outcome. Today's ICA is used in numerous domains showing its appliances like digital formed images, document based, economic calculation sign and dimensions of psychometrics, etc.

HOW ARTIFICIAL INTELLIGENCE AND MACHINE LEARNING WILL INFLUENCE BUSINESS/ IT INFRASTRUCTURE IN FUTURE

Till now, we have been uses of AI and ML algorithms in various applications like medical-diagnosis, weather forecasting, etc. Using machine intelligence, cities, transportation, manufacturing, etc., are getting more productive (also smarter). Artificial Intelligence is also using its intelligence (in form of its subsets like machine learning and deep learning) in several uses cases like future of insurance, and

Figure 17. Independent component analysis (ICA)

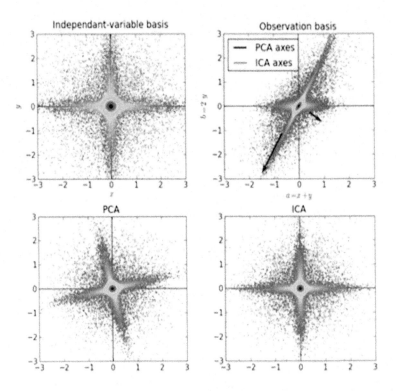

future on market (e.g., social media market, e-commerce, integrating chat-bots, automation in industry (operation, accounting, payroll/ HR automation, etc.), business). Such industries/ areas are getting a huge growth with integration/ use of AI. The organisation/ company can use machine learning to up-sell the right product, to the right customer, at the right time. In simple words, machine learning is about understanding data and statistics, and Artificial Intelligence has to fulfil this demand using its intelligence (e.g., manufacturing of 1 million of BMW cars in one year using automation systems). As discussed in (Tyagi, 2019), Internet of Things (IoTs) and machine learning are going to change future, these are technologies which will be used together for produces prediction, i.e., IoTs will generate a lot of data (i.e., Big Data, and machine learning or artificial intelligence will make prediction for future (after applying efficient analysis methods/ tools).

Also in future, AI-assisted robots will be there to perform tasks or serve human being. In areas like medical-care, robots can help patient to move, live more as younger, etc. In general, Artificial intelligence is a type of automation where machines can "outwit people on every dimension". But, AI can make a major impact in the enterprise as discussed before also, i.e., particularly with any mission with adequate data that has a "set of inputs that map to a set of outputs". On another side, machine learning algorithms have been available since many decades (but got more attention in 20's century), they have also attained new popularity as Artificial Intelligence (AI). Hence, some future enhancements using machine intelligence (AI and ML together) will be like deeper personalization, self-driving cars, automatic translation, smarter investment opportunities, better medical diagnosis, number plate detection, instance segmentation, etc.

Today's in medical care system, we require patients at little risk for difficulties to outpatient conduct, preserving hospital beds and the consideration of medical staff. For that, scientists are recommending to use several algorithms to doctors. The neural network is giving far better results than any of the other methods. But, note that without the extra care of a patient, hospital's patient records may changes, i.e., outcomes could have been received different (called "explainability" problem). In summary, we do not want to create systems that aids us with medical dealings, transportation possibilities and profitable opportunities to detect out after the statistic that these systems do not actually work, i.e., they give/ make errors when they needed most (in cases of human lives and happiness). Hence, a lot of research is required (also on-going) by research community to fix that problem. Table 1 provides some undeveloped research concern in machine earning with big data.

Table 1. Undeveloped research issues in ML on big data

Elements	Parameters	Issues
Big Data	Volume	• cleaning and condensing big data • Huge scale dispersed characteristic extraction • Workflow organization and job development
	Velocity	• factual time online wisdom for streaming data
	Variety	• Multi-view knowledge for diverse multimedia data • Multimedia neural semantic annotations
	Veracity	• Assessing data reliability • information with changeable or denying data
	Value	• comprehensible ML for resolution support • Multi-user supportive decision maintain based on big data testing
User	Labeling	• multitude sourced vigorous learning for real large scale data Annotation
	Assessment	• widespread assessment method for ML (e.g., usability-based method)
	Privacy	• confidentiality protecting dispersed ML
	User Interface	• envisaging big data • intellectual user interfaces for interactive ML • Declarative ML
Domain	Information	• integrating general field knowledge (e.g., ontology, first-order logic (FOL), business rules) in ML
System	Infrastructure	• Novel infrastructure that seamlessly afford decision sustain based on factual time investigation of huge amount of assorted and unpredictable data. • wide-ranging big data middleware

In current following are the areas where subset of AI like ML and Deep Learning is being applied. Some of these areas are included here:

- **Computer Vision:** AI is used for dissimilar applications as vehicle plate identification on which number is written and also in facial recognition.
- **Information Retrieval:** ML and DL learning techniques are used in applications like searching by search engines, text matching and search by finding similarity, and image filtering.
- **Marketing:** ML learning technique is used in automated email marketing and target identification.

- **Diagnosis in medical domain:** ML and DL learning techniques are used in this area, i.e., in applications like cancer recognition and anomaly recognition, etc.
- **Computational Linguistic:** To identify handwritten languages by machine (using its intelligence), we refer machine learning and deep learning techniques.
- **Others:** ML and for applications like opinion mining, sentiment analysis, online Advertising, etc.

In summary, Artificial intelligence, is intelligence done by machines to learn "how a human being things and react"? In simple words, it creates some intelligent machines which work and react like humans. Hence, AI is used in several applications like Speech recognition, Text matching, semantic similarity, Learning, computational linguistic, robotics, Planning, and Problem solving, etc. Now in next section, this chapter will be concluded with some essential remarks.

CONCLUSION

This chapter discusses about Artificial Intelligence and its sub-related areas, algorithms and their uses in various applications like Natural image processing, Speech recognition, Learning, Planning, and Problem solving, etc. In this chapter, we find that AI is a technique which enables machines to mimic human behavior, for example, IBM Deep Blue chess, and Electronic game character. Whereas, Machine Learning (ML) is a technique which uses statistical methods, enabling machines to learn from their past data (including human intervention), for example, IBM Watson, Google search algorithm, email spam filer, etc. On another side, deep learning (also a sub-set of AI) is a subset of ML composing algorithms that allow a model to train itself (without human intervention) and perform tasks for example, Alpha Go, Natural Speech Recognition, etc. Hence, the aim of this chapter is to study algorithms/techniques used in artificial intelligence and machine learning. It also focuses on the application areas like virtual reality, image processing, robotics, automation, weather forecasting, etc. In modest terms, this chapter also explains the goals of a computer vision. This chapter aims to showcase the latest advances and trends in computer vision/ AI and machine learning algorithms for various applications. This chapter shows that methods involved in AI usages in machine learning techniques, which are analogous to data mining and predictive modelling, as both the techniques require searching and mining through data to look for hidden patterns and regulating program actions accordingly. Hence, machine learning techniques include cases like fraud discovery, spam sieving, network security threat recognition, predictive conservation and constructing news feeds, etc.

Apart above discussion, we also found that un-scalability and centralization, non-dynamic and uniform data structure are the biggest limitation in existing analysis algorithms (supported by ML, and DL learning techniques). Using this big data (collected from Internet of things/ machine communication), data mining, machine learning techniques are able to identify hidden trends and associations. Several benefits of AI are: providing cost reduction, quicker, better verdict making, new goods and services, product recommendation, and fraud discovery. AI uses data mining, machine learning techniques to make machine intelligent which used metrics to measure performance of respective machine (or used algorithms). Data mining algorithms are measures using accuracy, reliability, and usefulness. Some other evaluation metrics for data mining tasks are: cross-validation, holdout technique, arbitrary sub-sampling, k-fold cross authentication, leave one out technique, bootstrap, confusion matrix, Receiver Operating Curves (ROC). Also, there are several metrics for association rule mining like Support, Confidence, Lift,

Succinctness and Conviction. Some metrics like confusion matrix, Receiver Operating Curves (ROC), precision call etc., are also used in machine learning techniques.

REFRENCES

Albert, J. R. G., Orbeta, A. C. Jr, Paqueo, V. B., Serafica, R. B., Dadios, E. P., Culaba, A. B., & Bairan, J. C. A. C. (2018). *Harnessing government's role for the Fourth Industrial Revolution*. Academic Press.

Anderson, C. W. (1987, January). Strategy learning with multilayer connectionist representations. In *Proceedings of the Fourth International Workshop on Machine Learning* (pp. 103-114). Morgan Kaufmann. doi:10.1016/B978-0-934613-41-5.50014-3

Avati, A., Jung, K., Harman, S., Downing, L., Ng, A., & Shah, N. H. (2018). Improving palliative care with deep learning. [PubMed]. *BMC Medical Informatics and Decision Making*, *18*(4), 122. doi:10.118612911-018-0677-8

Bathaee, Y. (2018). The artificial intelligence black box and the failure of intent and causation. *Harvard Journal of Law & Technology*, *31*(2), 889.

Bennett, K. G., & Vercler, C. J. (2018). When Is Posting about Patients on Social Media Unethical "Medutainment"? [PubMed]. *AMA Journal of Ethics*, *20*(4), 328–335. doi:10.1001/journalofethics.2018.20.4.ecas1-1804

Buriro, A., Crispo, B., & Conti, M. (2019). AnswerAuth: A bimodal behavioral biometric-based user authentication scheme for smartphones. *Journal of Information Security and Applications*, *44*, 89–103.

Gallege, L. S., & Raje, R. R. (2017, April). Parallel methods for evidence and trust based selection and recommendation of software apps from online marketplaces. In *Proceedings of the 12th Annual Conference on Cyber and Information Security Research* (p. 4). ACM. doi:10.1145/3064814.3064819

Guleria, P., & Sood, M. (2014). Data Mining in Education: A review on the knowledge discovery perspective. *International Journal of Data Mining & Knowledge Management Process*, *4*(5), 47–60. doi:10.5121/ijdkp.2014.4504

Horowitz, M. C. (2018). *Artificial Intelligence, International Competition, and the Balance of Power*. Texas National Security Review.

Kumar, A., Tyagi, A. K., & Tyagi, S. K. (2014). Data Mining: Various Issues and Challenges for Future A Short discussion on Data Mining issues for future work. *International Journal of Emerging Technology and Advanced Engineering*, *4*(1), 1–8.

Marcos-Pablos, S., & García-Peñalvo, F. J. (2019). Technological Ecosystems in Care and Assistance: A Systematic Literature Review. [PubMed]. *Sensors (Basel)*, *19*(3), 708. doi:10.339019030708

Mraković, I., & Vojinović, R. (2019). Maritime Cyber Security Analysis–How to Reduce Threats? *Transactions on Maritime Science*, *8*(1), 132–139.

Powles, J., & Hodson, H. (2017). Google DeepMind and healthcare in an age of algorithms. [PubMed]. *Health and technology*, 7(4), 351–367. doi:10.100712553-017-0179-1

Sergeev, A., & Del Balso, M. (2018). *Horovod: fast and easy distributed deep learning in TensorFlow.* arXiv preprint arXiv:1802.05799

Turner, J. (2019). Controlling the Creators. In *Robot Rules* (pp. 263–318). Cham: Palgrave Macmillan; doi:10.1007/978-3-319-96235-1_7

Tyagi, A. K. (2019). Building a Smart and Sustainable Environment using Internet of Things. In *Proceedings of International Conference on Sustainable Computing in Science, Technology and Management (SUSCOM)*. Amity University Rajasthan, Jaipur - India. Available at SSRN: https://ssrn.com/abstract=3356500 or http://dx.doi.org/ doi:10.2139/ssrn.3356500

Tyagi & Rekha. (2019). Machine Learning with Big Data. In *Proceedings of International Conference on Sustainable Computing in Science, Technology and Management (SUSCOM)*. Amity University Rajasthan. Available at SSRN: https://ssrn.com/abstract=3356269 or http://dx.doi.org/ doi:10.2139/ssrn.3356269

Wei, W. A. N. G. (2018). *Prediction of protein-ligand binding affinity via deep learning*. Academic Press.

KEY TERMS AND DEFINITIONS

Artificial Intelligence: Artificial intelligence (AI) deals with the creating of machines with the mind. The creation of machines that can work better than human.

Computer Vision: AI is used for dissimilar applications as vehicle plate identification on which number is written and also in facial recognition.

Data Mining: In general terms, data mining is a process of finding several new patterns in a huge collection of data sets using numerous techniques like classification, clustering, regression, etc. to predict future trends.

Information Retrieval: ML and DL learning techniques are used in applications like searching by search engines, text matching and search by finding similarity, and image filtering.

Machine Learning: Machine learning (ML) is the branch of computer science that comes under the umbrella of Artificial Intelligence. ML deals with the learning of machines to perform various tasks that can be done better than human beings.

Neural Networks: It includes machine learning with deep learning methods that utilizes huge amounts of training data to detect association among various variables.

Reinforcement Learning: This area of deep learning includes methods which iterates over various steps in a process to get the desired results. Steps that yield desirable outcomes are content and steps that yield undesired outcomes are reprimanded until the algorithm is able to learn the given optimal process. In unassuming terms, learning is finished on its own or effort on feedback or content-based learning.

Chapter 25
Machine Learning, Data Mining for IoT–Based Systems

Ramgopal Kashyap
https://orcid.org/0000-0002-5352-1286
Amity University, Raipur, India

ABSTRACT

This chapter will addresses challenges with the internet of things (IoT) and machine learning (ML), how a bit of the trouble of machine learning executions are recorded here and should be recalled while arranging the game plan, and the decision of right figuring. Existing examination in ML and IoT was centered around discovering how garbage in will convey garbage out, which is extraordinarily suitable for the extent of the enlightening list for machine learning. The quality, aggregate, availability, and decision of data are essential to the accomplishment of a machine learning game plan. Therefore, the point of this section is to give an outline of how the framework can utilize advancements alongside machine learning and difficulties get a kick out of the chance to understand the security challenges IoT can be bolstered. There are a few extensively unmistakable counts open for ML use. In spite of the way that counts can work in any nonexclusive conditions, there are specific standards available about which figuring would work best under which conditions.

INTRODUCTION

The Internet of Things (IoT) perspective is making through the general social event of perceiving and getting humbler scale and nano-contraptions dove in standard conditions and interconnected in low-control, lossy frameworks. The aggregate and consistency of certain contraptions construct all around requested and after that the rate of unforgiving data open for managing and examination exponentially grows-up. More than ever, conceivable strategies are required to treat data streams with the last goal to give a great illustration of recuperated information (Puthal, 2018). The significant information name was built up to mean the innovative work of data mining systems, what's more, affiliation structures to direct "volume, speed, grouping, and veracity" issues rising correctly when immense proportions of information make a joke of what's more, ought to control. Like this, Machine Learning (ML) is under-

DOI: 10.4018/978-1-6684-6291-1.ch025

stood to build unpalatable data and settle on needs to be arranged to decision help and computerization ("Special issue of Big Data Research Journal on "Giant Data and Neural Networks," 2018). Advance in ML estimations and change keeps running with advances of certain advances and Web-scale data affiliation structures, with the objective that specific focal spotlights have been passed on from the data examination reason behind the watching by some unimportant inadequacies are 'before clear concerning the creating multifaceted nature and heterogeneity of specific figuring difficulties. Mainly, the nonattendance of imperative, machine real depiction of yields from setting up ML structures is a perceptible cutoff for a possible abuse in entirely autonomic application conditions.

This fragment exhibits a general structure showing redesign standard ML examination on IoT data streams; relate semantic frameworks to information recuperated from the physical world, rather than inconsequential portrayal names. The key idea is to treat a typical ML plan issue like a levelheadedness drove resource introduction. Steps join producing a reason based depiction of quantifiable data dispersals and playing out fine-grained event attestation, misusing non-standard reasoning relationship for matchmaking (Rathore, Paul, Ahmad and Jeon, 2017). Each remark recommends a power giving the conceptualization and vocabulary to the particular taking in a territory, an influenced matchmaking on metadata set away in seeing and getting contraptions dove in an exceptional situation, lacking settled databases. Affirmation assignments float among devices which give unessential computational cutoff points. Stream thinking systems give the expecting to manage the flood of semantically remarked on invigorates gathered from low-level data, remembering the ultimate objective to interface with versatile setting attentive practices. Alongside this vision, creative examination frameworks related with data cleared by simple off-the-rack sensor contraptions can give solid results in event confirmation without requiring far-reaching computational resources. The methodology was tried and affirmed in a proper examination for road and headway opposing a certified educational gathering amassed for tests. Results were isolated from eminent ML figurings reviewing an authoritative objective to contemplate execution. The test campaign and early starter's groundwork assess both probability and plausibility of the differing strategies.

MOTIVATION

The standard motivation for this zone moves from the affirmation of honest to goodness cutoff focuses in the IoT, regardless of confirmation decreasing and accessibility interconnection invigorates physical structures, liberal data corpora show up without having amazingly the probability of destroying them from start to finish locally. Generally got data mining techniques to have two central detriments: i) they on a fundamental level do just about a social event errand and ii) their precision is widened whenever related on large data adds up to so making unfeasible an on-line examination (Yildirim, Birant and Alpyildiz, 2017). These sections foresee perceived the probability of seeing reasoning things: the IoT is deciphered likewise as recognized by the earth while is inconceivably secured the likelihood of settling on decisions and taking exercises locally after the perceiving forms. It should be seen as that in IoT conditions; information is collected through cut back scale contraptions identified with general things or sent in given situations and interconnected remotely. In a general sense, by the righteousness of their little measure, such demand has scarcest overseeing limits, a dash of securing and low-throughput correspondence restrict — they for the most part pass on repulsive data whose volume impacts fundamentally to be set to up by cutting-edge remote applications. A sharp comprehension of recuperated information diminishes estimations and possibly settles on decisions on what perceived, paying little identity to whether at a primitive stage. Standard machine learning frameworks have been, as it were, used for that; regardless, their huge deficiency is without a telling and first depiction of revealed events (Noel, 2016). IoT criticalness could update by explaining bona fide ask for, the data they gather and the conditions they make a plunge with brief, made what's more, semantically rich portrayals. The mix of the IoT and Semantic Web accomplishing the ensured Semantic Web of Things (SWoT). This perspective hopes to interface with novel classes of quick applications and affiliations grounded on Knowledge Representation (KR), misusing semantic-based revamp enlistments to interpret specific information starting from a specific event correspondingly, setting introduction. By right hand a shaped and machine-certifiable delineation in standard Semantic Web vernaculars, every social event yield could expect a non-obscure gigantic-ness (Jara et al., 2014). Also, clarification limits gave by the supporting semantic matchmaking grant to legitimize occurs, so expanding trust in structure response. If certain little scale devices are fit for capable onboard overseeing on the furtively recouped data, they can portray themselves and the setting where they are planned toward external contraptions what's more, applications. Would upgrade interoperability, flexibility, drawing in certain data based systems with high degrees of automaticity not yet allowed by ordinary IoT establishments and methodology. Machine learning, web on things and great information are reliant on one another while completing an exceptional development as found in figure 1.

Web of Things encourage joining between the physical world and computer correspondence systems, and applications, for example, foundation administration and ecological observing make protection and security procedures essential for future IoT frameworks. IoT frameworks need to ensure information protection and address security issues, for example, mocking assaults, interruptions, forswearing of administration assaults, circulated disavowal of administration assaults, sticking, listening in, and malware. For example, wearable gadgets that gather and send the client wellbeing information to the associated cell phone need to evade protection data spillage.

Figure 1. Machine learning interoperability

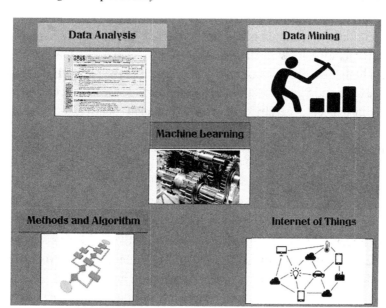

Machine Learning and IoT

It's for the most part restrictive for IoT gadgets with limited calculation, memory, radio transfer speed, and battery asset to execute computational-escalated and inactivity delicate security assignments, particularly under overwhelming information streams (Urquhart and Rodden, 2016). In any case, most existing security arrangements produce vast calculation and correspondence stack for IoT gadgets, for example, shoddy sensors with light-weight security insurances are usually more powerless against assaults than computer frameworks.

Forecast of Information Patterns

In this article, we explore the IoT confirmation, get to control, secure offloading, and malware identifications:

- Authentication enables IoT gadgets to recognize the source hubs and address the personality based assaults, for example, parodying and Sybil assaults.
- Access control counteracts unapproved clients to get to the IoT assets.
- Secure offloading methods empower IoT gadgets to utilize the calculation and capacity assets of the servers and edge gadgets for the computational-serious and inertness delicate errands.
- Malware recognition shields IoT gadgets from security spillage, control exhaustion, and system execution corruption against malware, for example, infections, worms, and Trojans with the improvement of ML and brilliant assaults, IoT gadgets need to pick the safeguard approach and decide the critical parameters in the security conventions for the tradeoff in the heterogeneous and dynamic systems. This undertaking is trying as an IoT gadget with confined assets more often than not experiences issues precisely assessing the current system and assault state in time.

Bunching of Information

The verification execution of the plan in is delicate to the test limit in the speculation test, which relies upon both the radio proliferation show and the mocking model. Such data is inaccessible for most open-air sensors, prompting a high false alert rate or miss location rate in the parodying identification. Machine learning systems (Kashyap and Piersson, 2018) including managed learning, unsupervised learning, and fortification learning have been generally connected to enhance security, for example, verification; get to control, against sticking offloading and malware location figure 2 shows how uncommon machine learning estimations give various results for that correct theory is required.

Supervised Learning System

Support vector machine (SVM), K-nearest neighbor (K-NN), neural network, deep neural network (DNN) can be utilized to mark the system activity, or application hints of IoT gadgets to construct the grouping or then again relapse demonstrate. For instance, IoT gadgets can utilize SVM to organize interruption and ridiculing assaults apply K-NN in the system interruption and malware recognitions, and use the neural system to recognize organize interruption and DoS assaults. IoT gadgets can connect devices in the interruption location, and irregular timberland classifier can be utilized to identify malware. IoT gadgets with adequate calculation and memory assets can use DNN to identify caricaturing assaults.

Figure 2. Machine learning methods case astute result comparison

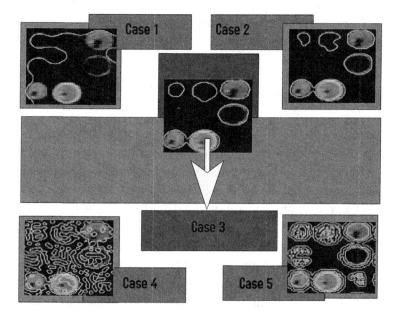

Unsupervised Learning System

Unsupervised learning does not require marked information in the supervised learning and explores the likeness between the unlabeled information to bunch them into various gatherings. For model, IoT gadgets can utilize multivariate connection investigation to recognize DoS assaults furthermore, apply IGMM in the PHY-layer validation with security assurance.

Reinforcement Learning System

Q-learning empowers an IoT gadget to pick the security conventions and additionally the key parameters against various assaults using experimentation. For instance, Q-learning as a model reinforcement learning method has been utilized to enhance the execution of the validation, hostile to sticking offloading, and malware identifications.

Learning-Based Access Control

It is trying to configuration get to control for IoT frameworks in heterogeneous systems with numerous sorts of hubs and multi-source information. ML strategies, for example, SVM, K-NN, and neural system have been utilized for interruption discovery. For example, the DoS assault identification as proposed in utilizes multivariate connection examination to extricate the geometrical relationships between system activity highlights. This plan builds the discovery exactness by 3.05% to 95.2% contrasted and the triangle region based closest neighbors approach with knowledge (Kashyap and Gautam, 2017). IoT gadgets, for example, sensors open air, as a rule, have a strict asset and calculation imperatives yielding difficulties for peculiarity interruption discovery strategies more often than not have corrupted identification execution in IoT framework. ML systems enable the form to lightweight get to control conventions to spare vitality and expand the lifetime of IoT frameworks. For instance, the anomaly recognition plot as created in applies K-NN to address the issue of unsupervised exception location in WSNs and offers adaptability to characterize anomalies with diminished vitality utilization. This plan can spare the most extreme vitality by 61.4% contrasted and the Centralized plan with comparable normal vitality utilization.

System Administration Advancements for IoT

It is extremely an expansive space, and there are many contending answers for the transference of information. Contrasts between arrangements originate from various guidelines and correspondence conventions connected in the segments which much of the time are not steady with each other. It can make troubles when choosing the parts for the IoT speculation's organizing because it is questionable which advancements will end up overwhelming renditions for the IoT segments. It would imply that picking the wrong innovation could turn out to be testing or exorbitant to supplant (Chen and Liu, 2016). Networking innovations, as a rule, can be partitioned into wired and remote advancements with regards to IoT, the remote advances are all the more fascinating because of the adaptability permitted by not associating things with wires into the web. Another grouping factor for the remote advancements is the inclusion region which can be separated into short range and long-extend advances. Short-run advances incorporate innovations with inclusion regions littler than an ordinary house whereas long-extend advances cover significantly more large regions. In some IoT cases, the short-extend advances can be more appropriate because of their better vitality productivity and lower costs (Wang, McMahan and Gallagher, 2015). This list contrast between short-extend advancements and long-ago innovations being the more drawn out inclusion region, generally bring down arrangement costs, an abnormal state of security and less demanding administration for long-ago advances. Short-go remote innovations incorporate both remote particular region organizing advancements and remote neighborhood advances. This innovation associate gadgets together inside little separations while WLAN advancements interface PCs together from a bigger territory, more often than not around the measure of a substantial building this require a switch to interface into the web. Short-extend remote advancements incorporate a wide range of innovations, for example, Bluetooth, ZigBee, Z-wave, Insteon, BACnet, Modbus, ANT, and Wi-Fi separate these advancements into four noteworthy application zones: client checking, home computerization, building mechanization and autos. Some short-run remote innovations can connect in different regions, for example, Wifi and Zigbee while different advances are more application territory particular, for example, BACnet and Modbus which utilized in building mechanization. Contrasts between advancements made from to the way that they work in various layers on the short-run remote innovation stack. Short-run remote innovation stack layer comprises from the physical layer, interface layer, arrange layer, transport layer and application layer. Specialized contrasts likewise originate from various working extents, frequencies and convention between operability (Hussain and Cambria, 2018). Long-extend remote correspondence in the IoT setting incorporates cell innovations and remote wide territory organizing advances. Cell innovation implies many interconnected transmitters each in charge of a specific zone or cell. Cell advancements are typically arranged in the ages beginning from the original of innovations (1G) to the present fourth era of advances (4G). The cutting-edge forward is the fifth era which is intended to sent from the year 2019 advances. The fifth era (5G) of cell innovations is extremely applicable to the IoT because it empowers significantly more effective correspondence. The 5G advancements give noteworthy upgrades in some gadgets associated, information rate, inclusion, and nature of administration estimates contrasted with the past fourth era innovations. The fifth era of cell advancements likewise give better security, portability, nature of administration bolster and worldwide reach than current innovations. Key wellspring of upgrades for 5G innovations is the utilization of higher frequencies called millimeter waves. Another factor for 5G enhancements is beamforming capacities and full duplex abilities, which mean centering transmission all the more insightfully and having the capacity to send two-way correspondences utilizing similar frequencies all the more effective (Tofan, 2014). Wide zone organizing innovations incorporate for instance Coronis, NWawe, and On-Ramp remote. Key highlights are wide inclusion region, proficient vitality utilization and utilization of low transmission capacity. Wide territory organize advances, and cell advances are good innovations where WAN advances are more suited for shorter range machine-to-machine, additionally called M2M correspondence, and current cell advances all the more longer-run correspondence with past referred to benefits contrasted with WAN advances.

Computing Paradigm for Machine Learning

The registering worldview for the IoT venture is an essential viewpoint in the IoT speculation, particularly when the extent of the created information approaches big data levels (Yao, 2014) contend that information administration is one of the greatest difficulties for IoT speculations because of the large measures of information that IoT venture can create. Distinctive processing ideal models incorporate for instance centralized server registering, pc figuring, distributed computing, and edge figuring, applications of machine learning shown in figure 3.

Figure 3. Machine learning applications

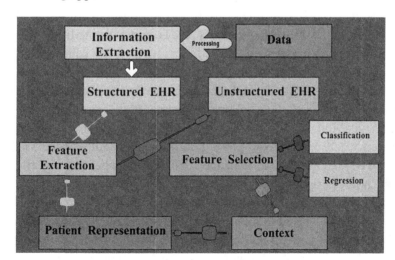

IoT speculations, the most intriguing figuring ideal models have distributed computing and edge processing. Distributed computing is a registering worldview where progressively versatile assets given over the web, and a significant part of the information handled elsewhere than where it made. Advantages of distributed computing incorporate versatility, valuing and high accessibility (Kashyap and Pierson, 2018). Distributed computing enables clients to get too tall measures of assets, for example, preparing power, stockpiling, servers and applications on-request and pay by the utilized sum without the need to put resources into the IT foundation. Difficulties for distributed computing dependent on incorporate security, protection and a certain level of un-customizability of the cloud stages. One testing angle is further trouble in changing distributed computing suppliers due to the area of the information.

Cloud Figuring

It can order in three areas, private, open and a half and a half private distributed computing are given solely to one customer who permits more prominent control on security, information control, and more customization capacities. Outsider suppliers or clients themselves can give private mists. Open distributed computing is a processing administration given by an outsider where different customers, for the most part, share the equipment, which means servers, stockpiling frameworks and systems. Mixture registering is a blend of private cloud and open cloud. Principle contrast between these kinds of distributed computing is security. Private mists can open mists which as a rule can be in broad daylight utilize and can't be overseen just based by specific customer's needs (Kashyap and Tiwari, 2018). Cloud registering is partition in three administration levels: Software as a Service (SaaS), Platform as a Service (PaaS) and Infrastructure as a Service (IaaS). SaaS benefit demonstrates it gives clients access to applications without the need to work the IT foundation by any stretch of the imagination. It implies SaaS benefit show clients can buy an entrance to the application using a permit or a membership. SaaS benefit demonstrates clients the entire IT stack, which means application, middleware, database, working framework, virtualization, and IT framework foundation, as an administration. There are two classes of SaaS arrangements: level and vertical. Level SaaS arrangement gives application to particular capacity crosswise over various enterprises whereas vertical SaaS arrangement comprises from items customized to specific ventures. PaaS benefit show offers clients finish IT stack where they can run distinctive applications, yet the apps themselves excluded in the administration display. In this way, clients gain admittance to the middleware, database, working framework, virtualization and IT framework foundation which is required to have a domain where to run applications. IaaS benefit display gives clients the IT framework foundation and virtualization and the IaaS client set up the working frameworks and the critical applications themselves. (Dzbor, Stutt, Motta and Collins, 2007). Edge figuring, or mist registering as it can likewise b a figuring worldview where an enormous piece of information handling occurs close to the cause of the information at the edge of the system. Machine learning challenges like security, specific troubles, and interoperability shown in figure 4. For the event, for applications that don't give zone benefits the exchanging of zone information may have all the earmarks of being horrifying. In any case, an exchange may be tolerable tolerating uncovered in a confirmation approach.

Edge registering worldview comprises from putting a unit with preparing, putting away and dissecting abilities into the system. For instance, switches or switches with these capacities can be utilized as a haze hub. Haze hub, likewise called an IoT entryway gadget, imparts between different hubs in the system by utilizing some remote systems administration innovations introduced beforehand. The IoT door hub is likewise associated with the web so it can send and get information from the cloud stage. Edge figuring can be appropriate for instance in mechanical IoT situations where moving substantial measure of information into the cloud for preparing and over into the blue pencils and actuators probably won't be proficient due time or different requirements. Edge registering would then be able to be appropriate concerning constant investigation arrangements since it permits quicker response times. Activities would be dependent on given standards in the system itself, and just certain information would be sent into the cloud stage for more profound examination. (Cisco, 2015) Benefits for edge figuring show up when the IoT setting requires quick reactions for information importance there is a low idleness prerequisite for correspondence. Edge registering is valuable in a circumstance where the system is expansive topographically, and there are a unique number of units associated with the system. Utilization of edge processing can likewise give some additional protection and security into the IoT venture since every one of the information doesn't need to be sent into the cloud stage and back. This likewise diminishes the required bandwidth and transmission costs if the information can be handled and acted inside the system. Edge figuring isn't selective of distributed computing, and there are fascinating conceivable outcomes in a mix of edge processing worldview into the as of now a mainstream pattern of grasping the distributed computing potential outcomes (Kim, 2018).

Figure 4. Challenges with machine learning

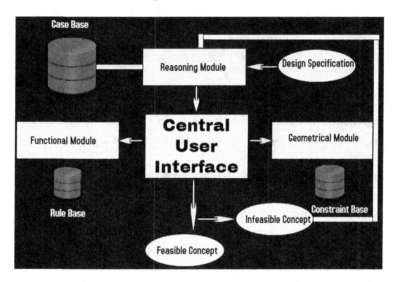

FOUNDATION

This domain quickly reviews contemplations on machine learning and description logics, recollecting a final goal to make the segment free and effortlessly sensible and it takes a gander at original related work.

Intelligence Layer in the IoT

Venture comprises from the information examination and central leadership after the information from the blue pencils in the detecting layer has been gathered and handled through the system layer. The normal popular expression Big Data is particularly connected to the IoT idea because of the large measures of information IoT blue pencils can create. An IoT venture can deliver large measures of information which can be considered as Big Data. One standard definition for Big Data is data with huge volume, assortment, and speed or essentially the three V's of information (Neath and Cavanaugh, 2011) as shown in figure 5.

Figure 5. Big data processing model

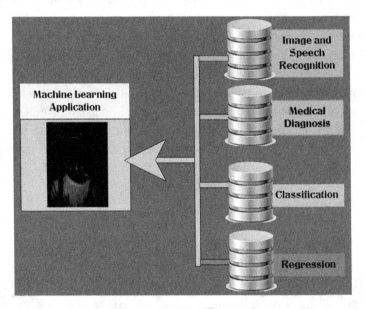

The Big Data component in numerous IoT venture implies that the insight layer is the most important perspective in the IoT speculation. Enter components in the insight layer are:

Analytic Solutions and Decision Support Systems

Artificial Intelligence Figure 5 portrays the insight layer of the IoT venture understanding what the gotten data means and capacity to settle on choices dependent on these discoveries are significant in the IoT setting without these capacities, the equipment and systems administration arrangements can't create noteworthy esteem. IoT speculation is an approach to gather a lot of information from different sources and to utilize expository answers to transform that information into experiences which at that point could be transformed into benefits (Kashyap, 2018). Refining the control level information is finished by utilizing examination arrangements which are usually called business knowledge or business investigation arrangements. Another important piece of the IoT venture is choosing how to deal with the information and how to settle on educated choices dependent on this information. Basic leadership in the IoT setting may require a type of choice emotionally supportive networks because of large measures of data created. On the off chance that the measure of data ascends over the human decision makers abilities even with applying choice emotionally supportive networks human-made reasoning arrangements may be required to remove all the possible incentive from the IoT speculation.

Decision Making

Examination implies breaking down information with the utilization of different strategies, systems, advancements, practices, and applications to have a clear comprehension of the circumstance. The objective of the expository arrangement is to transform data into bits of knowledge and permit activity dependent on those bits of knowledge. This is the motivation behind why logical arrangements are very basic viewpoint in the IoT speculation. Investigation consolidates perspectives from various fields, for example, data frameworks, software engineering, insights, and business. Regular terms utilized with regards to examination are business insight (BI) and business administration (BA). (Borisova, 2014) few perspectives to think about while breaking down investigation arrangements are information distribution center, information taking care of which are otherwise called extraction, change, stacking forms, database questioning, online expository handling and announcing and the distinctive instruments which to use in these procedures (Tiwari S., Gupta R.K., & Kashyap R., 2019).. The investigation can be partitioned into classes of clear examination, prescient investigation, and prescriptive investigation. Spellbinding investigation gives by and large lucidity to circumstances by giving general level answers from chronicled information. The graphics examination comprises from general rundowns of information properties and measurements, design disclosure, and division (Little, 2010).Prescient examination gives probabilistic responses to what may occur later on dependent on the chronicled information. These should be possible by some relapse examination or by characterization. The prescient examination is otherwise called determining or extrapolating from past information. Prescriptive examination incorporates both unmistakable and prescient investigation and produces distinctive choices to act dependent on the circumstance. Prescriptive examination computes various distinctive movements dependent on future activity by utilizing apparatuses from a few controls. Graphic examination answers what occurred previously though prescient investigation gives forecasts what may occur later on. The prescriptive examination takes both past kinds of an investigation into thought and gives significant responses to decision-making circumstances (Toivonen and Gross, 2015) the investigation arrangement in the IoT speculation is in charge of refining the vast crude information that originates from the blue pencils and different sources into significant data. (Zhang, Xiang, and Wang, 2010) notice multiprotocol capacities, de-centralization, enhanced security and data mining as a future element to be incorporated into the investigation arrangements. Multiprotocol capacities mean supporting diverse sorts of conventions and models both in accepting information and sending it. This element is exceptionally essential given the different principles and conventions in the IoT area. De-centralisation implies that sensors and information they created isn't attached to a single stage however that different kind of frameworks can collaborate and participate. Enhanced security is imperative for all levels in the IoT venture; however, investigation arrangements are likely the most basic part in the security for the entire IoT arrangement. Enhanced data mining capacities are required to examine past and current data all the more effectively with large measures of information produced by the IoT gadgets and from different sources (Punyavachira, 2013). The measure of information produced by the IoT arrangement may be big to the point that conventional investigation arrangements probably won't be satisfactory and particular big data arrangements must be incorporated into the knowledge layer of the IoT venture. Enormous data arrangements vary from common examination arrangements by their capacity to deal with bigger measures of more mind-boggling information by using for instance hugely parallel handling databases, information mining networks, disseminated databases, distributed computing, and versatile stockpiling frameworks. Difficulties with big data arrangements are security, integrational issues between customary social databases and NoSQL database frameworks, a prerequisite of more proficient answers for accelerate handling calculations and enhancement of information stockpiling.

Decision Support System (DSS)

It is an intelligent computer-based framework intended to enhance central leadership in complex circumstances where there is excessively information for people to process. A decision support system can likewise be connected to settle on the central leadership more goals and deliberate. The reason for diagnostic arrangements is to give better comprehension of the information which at that point makes the best open doors for central leadership. frameworks have been made which are usually eluded as choice emotionally supportive networks. Choice emotionally supportive networks can be utilized from various perspectives, for example, to settle on decisions between different alternatives, building distinctive choices for the procedure and even to recognize chances to make basic leadership circumstances (Huby, Cockram and Fleming, 2013). Decision models can be spoken to with three parts right off the bat, the inclination of goals besides the potential alternatives accessible. Thirdly, the measure of vulnerability in the model in regards to the impact of factors into the choice and the results. The general structure for a choice emotionally supportive network is three-separated application comprising from the database, backend-arrangement, and frontend-arrangement (Islam, 2018). The database stores all the required information, the backend essentially runs the required tasks, and the frontend composes the association between the client and the choice emotionally supportive network. DSS is a general term for any computer application intended to upgrade the client's capacity to decide. There are five general classes of DSS: interchanges driven DSS, information-driven DSS, report driven DSS, learning driven DSS, and model-driven DSS.

Artificial Intelligence (AI)

It is a subsection of software engineering which is centered on creating personal computers (PCs) capacities to coordinate people concerning knowledge. As of late, there has been a ton of enthusiasm for AI, and uniquely towards machine learning and all the conceivable application zones, AI could be utilized. Human-made intelligence connected in the IoT speculation is extremely intriguing because of the possibly large measures of information created by the IoT controls. This measure of enormous information can undoubtedly be excessively to include people in central leadership if the required activities must be made close continuously. The produced information can be so colossal and complex that people probably won't have the capacity to distinguish every single significant component in the information. In this manner, applying AI appears a legitimate component to consider in an IoT venture. IoT speculation can likewise be thought as a venture to embed blue pencils into a present framework to make changes to apply AI capacities. Human-made consciousness is where the point is to enhance PCs capacities in spaces where people have been altogether superior to machines, for example, learning, and imagination, arranging, thinking and central leadership (Sun and Betti, 2015). The point in human-made brainpower is to comprehend knowledge and after that make insightful PCs. Human-made intelligence comprises from a wide range of zones connected to human insight, for example, normal dialect handling, information portrayal, thinking, computer vision, mechanical technology, and machine learning. The field of AI joins a few trains, for example, software engineering, arithmetic, logic, brain science, etymology, financial matters, and science (Misra, Krishna, and Abraham, 2010). There are numerous subfields of

AI, for example, apply autonomy, discourse preparing, arranging, master frameworks, which are firmly connected to choice emotionally supportive networks, artificial neural systems, transformative calculation, and machine learning. In the IoT setting the most interesting subfield of AI could be machine learning. Machine learning is a subset of AI which examines how to influence PCs to perform errands without expressly letting them know and making PCs make enhancements for their own by utilizing different calculations (Abdolkarimi, Abaei, and Mosavi, 2017) arranges machine learning calculations in five fundamental gatherings: imagery, connectionism, transformative, Bayesian and analogism. Every single one of these gatherings applies diverse sorts of calculations as their fundamental technique in machine learning. In imagery the calculation connected is different reasoning, in connectionism, it is back propagation, in developmental it is genetic programming, in Bayesian calculation Bayesian surmising is utilized as the fundamental strategy and in analogism, it bolsters vector machine. Different sorts of these calculations are utilized in zones, for example, administered learning, unsupervised learning, neural systems and strengthened learning. These calculations perform distinctively on various kinds of errands they are relegated (Hasan and Mishra, 2012). IoT venture where there are a huge number of blue pencils and actuators introduced into an organization's frameworks give a fascinating chance to apply human-made brainpower and particularly machine learning. Human-made brainpower could be utilized progressively central leadership in a circumstance where it would be inconceivable by human administrators to settle on choice as productively as machines (Coufal, 2016). Uncovering the IoT improved framework to machine learning gives chances to distinguish potential approaches to utilize the framework gainfully which probably won't be effectively found by people. Applying machine learning effectively into the IoT venture could therefore capable of finding fascinating discoveries which could conceivably then be connected either to expand deals or abatement operational expenses.

Information Mining

We abuse semantic web advancements for a few reasons right off the bat, semantics empowers an explicit depiction of the importance of sensor information in an organized way, with the goal that machines could comprehend it. Besides, it encourages interoperability for information joining since unrelated IoT information is changed over as indicated by a similar vocabulary (Hasan and Mishra, 2012). Thirdly, semantic thinking motors can be effectively utilized to find abnormal state deliberations from sensor information. Fourthly, setting mindfulness could be actualized utilizing semantic thinking. At long last, in principle, semantics facilitates the learning sharing and reuse of space learning skill which ought to evade the reexamination of the wheel. Each time a new area particular vocabulary is characterized.

Big Information Mine Information

The IoT information is a sort of informational collection, which incorporates that regular arrangement of preparing information, administration information, so this information is the principal focus of enormous information handling. Huge information starts with information securing at each step, which makes a first the web of things information interface, and guaranteeing the precision of the different circles. Huge information gets information on unit client hubs. However, the number of hubs develop exponentially, creating a lot of the web of things information, and requires more rational calculations for improvement (Kashyap, and Tiwari, 2017). The Internet of Things possesses information learning abilities that enable enormous information innovation to get the data from the immense Internet, and advance data limit, securing rate, and detecting strategies. The web of things learning strategies incorporate that situation learning, scale learning, informal learning and complex data adapting, so the web of things will take in the calculation stretched out to the setting, additionally progress information handling proficiency (Kashyap, R., 2019a). What's more, enormous information can play its claim focal points, which understand the synchronous improvement of informal learning and information investigation by dissecting techniques, for example, stream information, change point identification, and time arrangement forecast (Little, 2010). Customary information investigation has been not used to plan suitable learning capacities, while enormous information can be handled through a summed up model to the dispersed informational collection in the web of things, which can accomplish programmed information mining of complex systems, for example, picture order, dialect, right and content examination. Right now, the Lambda design empowers bunch information investigation of enormous information, which accomplishes the auspiciousness and assorted variety of the web of things information preparing, so the Lambda design is broadly utilized in Hadoop and Spark.

THE UTILIZATION OF ENORMOUS INFORMATION ON THE WEB OF THINGS

Enormous data delves profoundly into organized, semi-organized and unstructured data in an Internet of things information, and successfully organizes its inward information and recovers data significantly. The measure of information handled by huge information is billions, and the records framed by it achieve several billion (Schumaker, 2013). At present, enormous information is fundamentally connected to arrange deals, client visits, web-based life, portable information and such, which not just spare Internet of things information handling costs, yet also, enhance information gathering and advancement capacities.

Healthcare Industry

Enormous information predicts the patient's hospitalization; release what's more, treatment time by breaking down the therapeutic information and then the patient's connected records, to enhance the treatment impact. At that point, the healing center dependent on the mediation of huge information to diminish the patient's costly doctor's facility costs. A few doctor's facilities are growing new data items, fundamentally to gather quiet inpatient data and give alluring proposals and advantages to patients (Waoo, Kashyap & Jaiswal, 2010). As indicated by Internet insights, clinic treatment costs increment half every year, multiplying like clockwork, while the development of enormous information can decrease the aggregate expense of 60% predicts that as of the finish of 2020, individuals depend more on enormous information to keep clinic treatment costs down to 42% of the present circumstance. At present, Baidu has two noteworthy sorts of information accumulation frameworks, basically for client look portrayal of interest information, crawler information, and open web information (Ott and Houdek, 2014).What's more, enormous information employments an assortment of information preparing strategies to ace the healing facility's patient information and treatment information to frame an information investigation chain dependent on client connections to all the more likely anticipate the patient's treatment conduct, movement of the illness, furthermore, the future danger of sickness.

Financial Administrations Industry

Huge information enables budgetary administrations associations to mine information in profundity, and which make adjust money related information in general by tweaking client information. Among them, Apache arrange is the primary advancement of defense parcel exchanged system in the US Department, which is the start of the world wide web, and transmission control convention/web convention that is the most essential web convention, so the huge information Furthermore, a web of things additionally for the IP convention and TCP convention dependent on data correspondence. The use of enormous information in the money related field should start with the digitization of simple flags, and seal the information parcels of clients with the end goal to guarantee the security of money related information, with the goal that their business extension is more extensive, and the administration level is higher (Brookman, Rouge, Alva and Yeung, 2017).

Resource Investigation

Enormous information can improve the investigation of assets, which utilize constant creation information to enhance the operational proficiency of asset improvement undertakings, and make more great utilization of existing assets. Enormous information influences early recognizable proof of profitability advancements, which find different wellsprings of information that incorporate gas logging, quakes, tests, and gamma beams, and to set up a logical model of asset improvement (Tango, Minin, Tesauri and Montanari, 2010). At the equivalent time, enormous information breaks down the peculiarities in the penetrating procedure by the chronicled information of asset advancement with the end goal to enhance penetrating strategies, enhances resource usage and prescient support, and diminishes downtime. Moreover, enormous information takes into account a thorough building examination to better than anyone might have expected, which comprehend Earth's assets through successful information investigation. The effect of enormous information on the web of things is essentially reflected in the midstream also, downstream businesses of asset advancement, so as the examination and checking of continuous sensor information, the examination of unrefined petroleum lab parts results in the decrease of important time, which can diminish related expenses furthermore, the enhancement of forecast exactness (Zhang, 2016).

Retail and Coordination

Huge information utilizes radio frequency identification (RFID) innovation to track the pattern of coordination items conveniently, for example, labels, which can give retailers more exact and effective coordination data. In the meantime, huge information can enhance the exactness of stock administration data, and lessen the occurrence of robbery. Moreover, huge information can help coordination undertakings to acquire focused chances to streamline their coordination activities, which incorporate conveyance is estimating, course improvement and gauging of turnaround time. During the time spent coordination's administration, the organization can get more data, benefit level data, production network hazard data, sensor figure data, coordination and transmission data, and geographic data with enormous information innovation (Sądel and Śnieżyński, 2017). Enormous information can help the Internet of Things early distinguishing proof, physical measurements, faculty planning, active investigation, with the end goal to accomplish the extension of the Internet of things itself.

Profound Learning for the Web of Things

The multiplication of internetworked handy and implanted gadgets prompts dreams of the IoT, offering to ascend to a sensor-rich reality where physical things in our normal the condition is progressively enhanced with registering, detecting, and correspondence capacities. Such abilities guarantee to upset the collaborations between people and physical articles. Undoubtedly, critical research endeavors have been spent toward building more intelligent and more easy to use applications on portable and installed gadgets and sensors (Tango, Minin, Tesauri and Montanari, 2010). In the meantime, late advances in profound learning have enormously changed the manner, in which that is registering gadgets process human-driven substance, for example, pictures, video, and discourse, what's more, sound. Applying profound neural systems to IoT gadgets could in this manner realize an age of utilizations equipped for performing complex detecting and acknowledgment errands to help another domain of communications between people and their physical environment (Kashyap, R.,2019b). This article talks about four key examine inquiries toward the acknowledgment of such novel associations between people and (profound) learning-empowered physical things, specifically: What profound neural system structures can viably process and wire real info information for different IoT applications? How to lessen the asset utilization of profound learning models with the end goal that they can be proficiently conveyed on did asset oblige IoT gadgets? How to figure certainty estimations in the accuracy of profound learning forecasts for IoT applications? At long last, step by step instructions to limit the requirement for marked information in learning?

To expand on the above difficulties, first, see that IoT applications regularly rely upon joint effort among different sensors, which requires planning novel neural system structures for multisensory information combination. These structures ought to be ready to demonstrate complex connections among various tangible contributions over time and adequately encode highlights of real data sources that are appropriate to wanted acknowledgment and different errands. We survey a general profound learning structure, for this reason, called deep sense that gives a brought together yet the adjustable answer for the adapting needs of different IoT applications (Mawdsley, Tyson, Peressotti, Jong and Yaffe, 2009). It exhibits that specific mixes of profound neural system topologies are especially appropriate for gaining from sensor information. Second, IoT gadgets are typically low-end frameworks with restricted computational, vitality, and memory assets (Shukla R., Gupta R.K., & Kashyap R., 2019). One key obstacle in sending profound neural systems on IoT gadgets in this manner lies in the high asset request for prepared profound neural system models. While existing neural system pressure calculations can successfully decrease the number of model parameters, not these models prompt grid portrayals that can be productively executed on item IoT gadgets (Ghotekar, 2016). Ongoing work portrays an especially compelling profound learning pressure calculation, considered Deep IoT that can straightforwardly pack the structures of normally utilized profound neural systems. The compacted model can be conveyed on ware gadgets. An expansive extent of execution time, vitality and memory can be lessened with little impact on the last forecast precision. Third, unwavering quality affirmations are vital in digital physical and IoT applications. The requirement for advertising such confirmations call for all around aligned estimation of vulnerability related with learning results (Zhang, 2016). We present straightforward strategies for producing well-calibrated vulnerability gauges for the forecasts figured in profound neural systems, called RDeepSense. It accomplishes precisely and very much aligned estimations by changing the goal capacity to reflect expectation rightness steadfastly. At last, naming information for learning reasons for existing is tedious. One must show detecting gadgets to perceive articles and ideas without the advantage of (many) precedents, where ground truth esteems for such protests, what's more, ideas are given. Unsupervised what's more, semi-supervised arrangements are expected to fathom the test of learning with constrained marked and for the most part unlabeled examples while moving toward the execution of gaining from completely marked information (Chen, Liu, and Yang, 2016). We expand on these center issues, what's more, their rising answers for help establish a framework for building IoT frameworks advanced with successful, effective, what's more, solid profound realizing models.

Deep Learning Models for Sensor Data

A key research test toward the acknowledgment of learning-empowered IoT frameworks lies in the plan of profound neural system structures that can viably assess yields of intrigue from boisterous time-arrangement multisensory measurements. In spite of the expansive assortment of installed and portable registering assignments in IoT settings, one can, for the most part, arrange them into two regular sub-types: estimation undertakings and characterization assignments, contingent upon whether the expected results are persistent or straight out, individually. The inquiry thusly moves toward becoming regardless of whether general neural system engineering exists that can viably take in the structure of models required for estimation and grouping undertakings from sensor information. Such a general profound learning neural arrange engineering would, on a fundamental level, conquered disservices of the present approaches that depend on systematic model improvements or the utilization of hand-created built highlights (Houeland and Aamodt, 2017). Generally, for estimation-arranged issues, for example, following and confinement, sensor inputs are prepared based on the physical models of the marvels included. Sensors create estimations of physical amounts such as increasing speed and rakish speed. From these estimations, other physical amounts are inferred, (for example, dislodging through twofold coordination of increasing speed after some time). In any case, estimations of product sensors are loud. The commotion in estimations is nonlinear and may be associated after some time, which makes it hard to display. It is along these lines testing to separate flag from the clamor, prompting estimation mistakes and predisposition (Li, Jiang, Zhang, Pang and Huang, 2014). For characterization arranged issues, for example, action and setting acknowledgment, a common methodology is to figure proper highlights inferred from crude sensor information. These high-quality highlights are then nourished into a classifier for preparing. Structuring great hand-made highlights can be tedious; it requires broad investigations to sum up well to different settings, for example, unique sensor commotion designs and different client practices. A general profound learning system can successfully address both of the previously mentioned difficulties by consequently adjusting the scholarly a neural system to complex corresponded clamor designs while, in the meantime, uniting on the extraction of maximally hearty flag includes that are most suited for the job that needs to be done. An ongoing structure called deep sense shows a case for achievability of such a general arrangement. Deep sense incorporates convolution neural systems (CNN) and recurrent neural systems (RNNs). Tangible information sources are adjusted and isolated into time interims for handling time-arrangement information. For every interim, deep sense first applies an individual CNN to every sensor, encoding applicable nearby highlights inside the sensor's information stream. At that point, a (worldwide) CNN is connected on the separate yields to display collaborations among numerous sensors for successful sensor combination. Next, an RNN is connected to remove practical examples. Finally, either a relative change or a softmax yield is utilized, contingent upon regardless of whether we need to demonstrate an estimation or a characterization assignment (Schwab and Ray, 2017). This engineering takes care of the general issue of learning multisensory combination errands for reasons for estimation or then again grouping from time-arrangement information. For estimation-situated issues, deep sense takes in the solid framework what's more, clamor models to yield yields from boisterous sensor information straightforwardly. The neural system goes about as an inexact exchange work. For classification-oriented issues, the neural system goes about as a programmed highlight extractor encoding nearby, worldwide, and transient data. The focal thought of the model-based way to deal with oversee machine learning is to make a custom show uniquely fitted particularly to each new application. Once in a while, the model together with a detailed assembling calculation may stand out from a common machine learning system, while a huge piece of the time it won't. Normally, show based machine learning will be executed utilizing a model particular vernacular in which the model can be depicted utilizing decreased code, from which the thing finishing that model can be made hence (Dehestani et al., 2011) as showed up in figure 6 how exhibit base and case base model are expecting fundamental part in machine learning.

Figure 6. Model-based machine learning

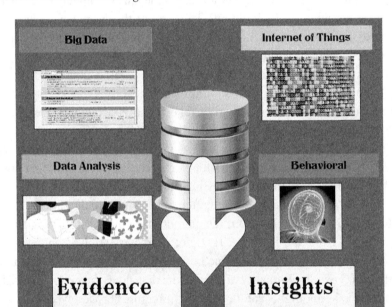

DISCUSSION

Basic learning is essential for overseeing unmistakably settled issues in computer vision and trademark vernacular managing, yet it normally does everything considered by using epic central processing unit and graphical processing unit resources. Standard vital learning methodologies aren't genuine to looking out for the challenges of the Internet of Things applications, regardless, since they can't have any effect a close level of computational resources. While using translated figuring and structure weight there will be a condition of reliable episodes. Push diminishing in structure or spotlight point size may pass on prohibited drops inexactness and accuracy. Immense learning is the best response for different examination and perceiving affirmation issues. Correctly when used with an eye to sparing system, memory, and power resources, important learning can pass on data to IoT contraptions. These structures join a critical number of passed on contraptions reliably making a high volume of data. Changing sorts of contraptions make particular sorts of data, prompting heterogeneous enlightening accumulations, yet the data typically joins timestamps and zone information. Finally, IoT applications must be proposed to drive forward hubbub in the data as a result of transmission and anchoring goofs. Fake care is expecting a growing part in IoT applications and affiliations. Financing interests in IoT new affiliations that are using AI are up tenaciously. Affiliations have acquired different affiliations working at the relationship of AI and IoT over the latest two years. Additionally, crucial merchants of IoT deal with making PC programs are beginning at now offering cemented AI limits, for instance, machine learning-based examination. Artificial intelligence is expecting an including a part in IoT in light of its ability to quickly wring bits of picking up from data. Machine taking in, an AI movement, brings the ability to frequently see plans and perceive oddities in the data that shocking sensors and devices impact information, for instance, temperature, to weight, suppleness, air quality, vibration, and sound. The compelling blend of AI and IoT movement is helping affiliations avoid unconstrained downtime, increase working advantage, interface new things and affiliations, and enhance hazard affiliation. Big data sums and in this manner, people may require help from choice emotionally supportive networks and even computerized reasoning, so these perspectives are additionally important components to consider in the IoT speculation. The second research question was what the most important business measurements for the IoT venture are? Based on the writing three measurements were distinguished: IoT biological system, the plan of action decided for the venture and the application region of the speculation. IoT biological community is the network of the considerable number of organizations, authorities, and people collaborating in the IoT condition. Examination of the IoT biological community is essential for the IoT venture because the environment is a vital factor in the improvement of different innovations, models and conventions. Not understanding the IoT biological system can make difficulties if the picked IoT advancements, guidelines, and conventions. Plan of action is the applied model of the organization's business portraying how an organization makes, conveys and catches esteem. For the IoT venture, this is exceptionally essential since one noteworthy test in IoT speculations is the way to adapt the information got. The IoT innovations can anyway permit changes in the organization's plans of action which can be the best wellspring of the benefit of the IoT venture. Application territory of the venture is an important measurement of the IoT speculation because distinctive zones have enormously extraordinary necessities. Atzori et al. (2010) separate the application zones into four primary sections of transport and coordination, therapeutic services, brilliant condition, and individual and social area. Prerequisites for IoT interests in these application regions can vary for instance with venture needs, support costs, vitality utilization, information administration necessities and client association (Gubbi et al., 2013). The third research question was, does IoT speculation require further developed productivity investigation strategies because of the idea of these mechanical components and business measurements?

Conventional gainfulness investigation techniques, for example, clear, present esteem strategy, recompense strategy and inside rate of return strategy are usually connected strategies however probably won't be most appropriate for the IoT ventures because of the high vulnerability identified with the IoT speculations. Genuine choice valuation strategies anyway are more suited to incorporate the vulnerability of venture into the productivity examination. The examination of the gainfulness investigation techniques with a whole situation where add up to cost of proprietorship investigation was performed on two modern machines where one of the machines had IoT-capacities, and the other one didn't. In the light, the speculation case figured, and benefit investigation was performed utilizing the common gainfulness examination strategies and a genuine alternative valuation strategy for fluffy result technique. The aftereffects of the correlation of the benefit examination demonstrated that incorporating the vulnerability level in the gainfulness investigation is important for the IoT speculations. Counting the good choices found for the situation expanded the net present estimation of the speculation 5 percent, however, the accurate estimation of the true alternative valuation is showing the vulnerability related in the appraisals. This vulnerability can be utilized all the more effective in the venture procedure because of an incredible wellspring of the IoT speculations' qualities produced in the most dubious esteem sources which are difficult to gauge with conventional gainfulness investigation techniques. Consequences of the case show that accurate choice valuation is a conventional technique for breaking down IoT ventures since it can help recognize the most significant parts of various speculations which normally are the most unverifiable segments of the speculations. In this manner, including the good choice valuation in the benefits investigation of IoT speculations is a decent decision which can enable organizations to recognize the most potential esteem creating ventures which can here and there incorporate a lot of vulnerability. Consequences of the proposition show that organizations ought to think about IoT as a potential wellspring of an upper hand. IoT ventures can give organizations numerous choices either to robotize their present activity or even develop new items, administrations, and methods for working. Organizations ought to likewise incorporate good choice valuation strategies in their capital planning while breaking down IoT ventures.

CONCLUSION

The motivation behind the investigation was to break down the productivity examination of a general IoT speculation. Breaking down the productivity of an IoT speculation previously required investigating the components of the IoT venture. IoT speculation's investigation comprises for the most part from two sections: what data is basic from a business perspective and in what capacity should this data be given by the IoT innovation. Based on the past writing three mechanical layers and three business measurements were distinguished. In the wake of distinguishing the significant components of the IoT venture, various benefit techniques were broken down to think about how the IoT speculations productivity would be assessed ideally. Investigation of the unique gainfulness strategies finished with a genuine case with an IoT-competent mechanical machine. Principle look into the issue of the investigation was the assurance of profit for speculations for the IoT venture and based on that three research questions were framed. To start with, what are the principal mechanical components of an IoT speculation? Second, what are the most critical business measurements for the IoT venture? Third, does an IoT venture require further developed benefit examination strategies because of the idea of these innovative components and business measurements? The first and second research questions considered in the second section of the proposal, and the third research question examined in the third and fourth parts of the postulation. The first research question was what the fundamental innovative components of an IoT venture are? Based on the writing the three mechanical components of general IoT venture were recognized as detecting layer, organizing layer and insight layer. Detecting layer is where assembling all the data created by the information sources and following up on the information is finished. Detecting layer comprises from different edits and actuators. Key advances are radio recurrence recognizable proof innovation, close field correspondences innovation, and remote sensor systems. Systems administration layer is where the information is exchanged from the detecting layer into insight layer for investigation and central leadership with various systems administration advancements. There are many systems administration advances in the IoT worldview, for example, Wi-Fi, Bluetooth and the fifth era of cell advances. Another key part of the IoT speculation is the registering worldview. Distributed computing and edge registering offer intriguing conceivable outcomes for IoT interests in regions, for example, scaling capacities and speed while more conventional centralized computer processing gives more advantages in regions, for example, security. Knowledge layer comprises from the components identified with the investigation and central leadership, and it tends to be viewed as the most critical piece of the IoT venture. Enter advances in the insight layer incorporate examination answers for the IoT information, choice emotionally supportive networks for following up on that information and potentially some AI-answers for assuming control over a few sections of the basic leadership process when the measure of information achieves levels past human capacities. IoT ventures can be considered as a strategy to extricate information from different information sources, understanding the importance of that information and settling on choices and activities based on that information. The sum and speed of the potential IoT information can achieve effectively. Generally, organizations may underestimate the most intricate and potentially the most significant speculations because of the conventional productivity examination techniques' powerlessness to incorporate all the important parts of the IoT interests in the gainfulness investigation. Based from the aftereffects of the theory it very well may be presumed that in the IoT speculation's benefit investigation the good alternative valuation strategies ought to be connected because conventional gainfulness examination techniques are not ideally suited to break down all the important parts of IoT ventures without anyone else. From the aftereffects of the proposition it very well may be presumed that one angle which may diminish the market interest for IoT speculations may be the underestimating of the IoT ventures because of the failure to examine the benefit of IoT speculations accurately. This might be caused from to the high utilization of conventional productivity examination techniques which can exclude all the pertinent parts of the IoT interest in the benefits investigation. There are numerous confinements of the proposition. IoT is an exceptionally wide worldview so breaking down all the pertinent territories is very testing and was impractical in the extent of this proposition. Likewise, past writing of the IoT is intensely centered on building and software engineering spaces which cause difficulties in understanding the true capability of the IoT for the laymen of those fields. Another constraint of the proposition is the avoidance of security and protection parts of the IoT which are significant components of the IoT venture yet require further investigation than was conceivable in theory. There are many fascinating exploration territories in regards to productivity investigation of IoT speculations. Intriguing further research theme would be an examination of various genuine choice valuation strategies to one another in productivity investigation of IoT speculations. Another point would be administrative adaptability for instance in scaling the IoT speculations or the parts of reversibility in the IoT ventures. The likelihood to oversee IoT speculations and the chances to incorporate genuine alternatives in them would be a fascinating region of research, the adaptability of changing mechanical arrangements in the IoT speculation.

REFERENCES

Abdolkarimi, E., Abaei, G., & Mosavi, M. (2017). A wavelet-extreme learning machine for low-cost INS/GPS navigation system in high-speed applications. *GPS Solutions*, *22*(1), 15. doi:10.100710291-017-0682-x

Borisova, N. (2014). An Approach for Ontology-Based Information Extraction. *Information Technology and Control, 12*(1). doi:10.1515/itc-2015-0007

Brookman, J., Rouge, P., Alva, A., & Yeung, C. (2017). Cross-Device Tracking: Measurement and Disclosures. *Proceedings On Privacy Enhancing Technologies, 2017*(2). doi:10.1515/popets-2017-0020

Chen, W., Liu, T., & Yang, X. (2016). Reinforcement learning behaviors in sponsored search. *Applied Stochastic Models in Business and Industry, 32*(3), 358–367. doi:10.1002/asmb.2157

Chen, Z., & Liu, B. (2016). Lifelong Machine Learning. *Synthesis Lectures On Artificial Intelligence And Machine Learning, 10*(3), 1–145. doi:10.2200/S00737ED1V01Y201610AIM033

Coufal, D. (2016). On the convergence of kernel density estimates in particle filtering. *Kybernetika*, 735–756. doi:10.14736/kyb-2016-5-0735

Dehestani, D., Eftekhari, F., Guo, Y., Ling, S., Su, S., & Nguyen, H. (2011). Online Support Vector Machine Application for Model-Based Fault Detection and Isolation of HVAC System. *International Journal Of Machine Learning And Computing*, 66-72. doi:10.7763/ijmlc.2011.v1.10

Dzbor, M., Stutt, A., Motta, E., & Collins, T. (2007). Representations for semantic learning webs: Semantic Web technology in learning support. *Journal of Computer Assisted Learning, 23*(1), 69–82. doi:10.1111/j.1365-2729.2007.00202.x

Ghotekar, N. (2016). Analysis and Data Mining of Call Detail Records using Big Data Technology. *IJARCCE, 5*(12), 280–283. doi:10.17148/IJARCCE.2016.51264

Hasan, M., & Mishra, P. (2012). Robust Gesture Recognition Using Gaussian Distribution for Features Fitting. *International Journal Of Machine Learning And Computing*, 266-273. doi:10.7763/ijmlc.2012.v2.128

Houeland, T., & Aamodt, A. (2017). A learning system based on lazy metareasoning. *Progress In Artificial Intelligence, 7*(2), 129–146. doi:10.100713748-017-0138-0

Huby, G., Cockram, J., & Fleming, M. (2013). Through-life Data Exploitation to Reduce Downtime and Costs. *Procedia CIRP, 11*, 50–55. doi:10.1016/j.procir.2013.07.070

Hussain, A., & Cambria, E. (2018). Semi-supervised learning for big social data analysis. *Neurocomputing, 275*, 1662–1673. doi:10.1016/j.neucom.2017.10.010

Internet of Things & Creation of the Fifth V of Big Data. (2017). *International Journal Of Science And Research, 6*(1), 1363–1366. doi:10.21275/art20164394

Islam, N. (2018). *Business Intelligence and Analytics for Operational Efficiency.* SSRN Electronic Journal. doi:10.2139srn.3163429

Jara, A., Olivieri, A., Bocchi, Y., Jung, M., Kastner, W., & Skarmeta, A. (2014). Semantic Web of Things: An analysis of the application semantics for the IoT moving towards the IoT convergence. *International Journal of Web and Grid Services, 10*(2/3), 244. doi:10.1504/IJWGS.2014.060260

Kashyap, R. (2018). Object boundary detection through robust active contour-based method with global information. *International Journal Of Image Mining, 3*(1), 22. doi:10.1504/IJIM.2018.093008

Kashyap, R. (2019a). Security, Reliability, and Performance Assessment for Healthcare Biometrics. In D. Kisku, P. Gupta, & J. Sing (Eds.), Design and Implementation of Healthcare Biometric Systems (pp. 29-54). Hershey, PA: IGI Global. doi:10.4018/978-1-5225-7525-2.ch002

Kashyap, R. (2019b). Geospatial Big Data, Analytics and IoT: Challenges, Applications and Potential. In H. Das, R. Barik, H. Dubey & D. Sinha Roy (Eds.), Cloud Computing for Geospatial Big Data Analytics (pp. 191-213). Springer International Publishing.

Kashyap, R., & Gautam, P. (2017). 'Fast Medical Image Segmentation Using Energy-Based Method,' Biometrics. *Concepts, Methodologies, Tools, and Applications, 3*(1), 1017–1042. doi:10.4018/978-1-5225-0983-7.ch040

Kashyap, R., & Piersson, A. D. (2018). Impact of Big Data on Security. In G. Shrivastava, P. Kumar, B. Gupta, S. Bala, & N. Dey (Eds.), *Handbook of Research on Network Forensics and Analysis Techniques* (pp. 283–299). Hershey, PA: IGI Global. doi:10.4018/978-1-5225-4100-4.ch015

Kashyap, R., & Piersson, A. D. (2018). Big Data Challenges and Solutions in the Medical Industries. In V. Tiwari, R. Thakur, B. Tiwari, & S. Gupta (Eds.), *Handbook of Research on Pattern Engineering System Development for Big Data Analytics* (pp. 1–24). Hershey, PA: IGI Global. doi:10.4018/978-1-5225-3870-7.ch001

Kashyap, R., & Tiwari, V. (2017). Energy-based active contour method for image segmentation. *International Journal of Electronic Healthcare, 9*(2–3), 210–225. doi:10.1504/IJEH.2017.083165

Kashyap, R., & Tiwari, V. (2018). Active contours using global models for medical image segmentation. *International Journal of Computational Systems Engineering, 4*(2/3), 195. doi:10.1504/IJCSYSE.2018.091404

Kim, L. (2018). DeepX: Deep Learning Accelerator for Restricted Boltzmann Machine Artificial Neural Networks. *IEEE Transactions on Neural Networks and Learning Systems, 29*(5), 1441–1453. doi:10.1109/TNNLS.2017.2665555 PMID:28287986

Li, G., Jiang, S., Zhang, W., Pang, J., & Huang, Q. (2014). Online web video topic detection and tracking with semi-supervised learning. *Multimedia Systems, 22*(1), 115–125. doi:10.100700530-014-0402-0

Little, B. (2010). Concerns with Learning-Management Systems and Virtual Learning Environments. *Elearn, 2010*(7), 2. doi:10.1145/1833513.1837142

Mawdsley, G., Tyson, A., Peressotti, C., Jong, R., & Yaffe, M. (2009). Accurate estimation of compressed breast thickness in mammography. *Medical Physics, 36*(2), 577–586. doi:10.1118/1.3065068 PMID:19291997

Misra, S., Krishna, P., & Abraham, K. (2010). A stochastic learning automata-based solution for intrusion detection in vehicular ad hoc networks. *Security and Communication Networks, 4*(6), 666–677. doi:10.1002ec.200

Neath, A., & Cavanaugh, J. (2011). The Bayesian information criterion: Background, derivation, and applications. *Wiley Interdisciplinary Reviews: Computational Statistics, 4*(2), 199–203. doi:10.1002/wics.199

Noel, K. (2016). *Application of Machine Learning to Systematic Allocation Strategies*. SSRN Electronic Journal. doi:10.2139srn.2837664

Ott, D., & Houdek, F. (2014). Automatic Requirement Classification: Tackling Inconsistencies Between Requirements and Regulations. *International Journal of Semantic Computing*, *08*(01), 47–65. doi:10.1142/S1793351X14500020

Punyavachira, T. (2013). *Forecasting Stock Indices Movement Using Hybrid Model: A Comparison of Traditional and Machine Learning Approaches*. SSRN Electronic Journal. doi:10.2139srn.2416494

Puthal, D. (2018). Lattice-modeled Information Flow Control of Big Sensing Data Streams for Smart Health Application. *IEEE Internet of Things Journal*. doi:10.1109/jiot.2018.2805896

Rathore, M., Paul, A., Ahmad, A., & Jeon, G. (2017). IoT-Based Big Data. *International Journal on Semantic Web and Information Systems*, *13*(1), 28–47. doi:10.4018/IJSWIS.2017010103

Schumaker, R. (2013). Machine learning the harness track: Crowdsourcing and varying race history. *Decision Support Systems*, *54*(3), 1370–1379. doi:10.1016/j.dss.2012.12.013

Schwab, D., & Ray, S. (2017). Offline reinforcement learning with task hierarchies. *Machine Learning*, *106*(9-10), 1569–1598. doi:10.100710994-017-5650-8

Shukla, R., Gupta, R. K., & Kashyap, R. (2019). A multiphase pre-copy strategy for the virtual machine migration in cloud. In S. Satapathy, V. Bhateja, & S. Das (Eds.), *Smart Innovation, Systems and Technologies* (Vol. 104). Singapore: Springer. doi:10.1007/978-981-13-1921-1_43

Sun, H., & Betti, R. (2015). A Hybrid Optimization Algorithm with Bayesian Inference for Probabilistic Model Updating. *Computer-Aided Civil and Infrastructure Engineering*, *30*(8), 602–619. doi:10.1111/mice.12142

Tango, F., Minin, L., Tesauri, F., & Montanari, R. (2010). Field tests and machine learning approaches for refining algorithms and correlations of driver's model parameters. *Applied Ergonomics*, *41*(2), 211–224. doi:10.1016/j.apergo.2009.01.010 PMID:19286165

Tiwari, S., Gupta, R. K., & Kashyap, R. (2019). To enhance web response time using agglomerative clustering technique for web navigation recommendation. In H. Behera, J. Nayak, B. Naik, & A. Abraham (Eds.), *Computational Intelligence in Data Mining. Advances in Intelligent Systems and Computing* (Vol. 711). Singapore: Springer. doi:10.1007/978-981-10-8055-5_59

Tofan, C. (2014). Optimization Techniques of Decision Making - Decision Tree. *Advances In Social Sciences Research Journal*, *1*(5), 142–148. doi:10.14738/assrj.15.437

Toivonen, H., & Gross, O. (2015). Data mining and machine learning in computational creativity. *Wiley Interdisciplinary Reviews. Data Mining and Knowledge Discovery*, *5*(6), 265–275. doi:10.1002/widm.1170

Urquhart, L., & Rodden, T. (2016). *A Legal Turn in Human-Computer Interaction?* Towards Regulation by Design for the Internet of Things. SSRN Electronic Journal. doi:10.2139srn.2746467

Wang, D., McMahan, C., & Gallagher, C. (2015). A general regression framework for group testing data, which incorporates pool dilution effects. *Statistics in Medicine*, *34*(27), 3606–3621. doi:10.1002im.6578 PMID:26173957

Waoo, N., Kashyap, R., & Jaiswal, A. (2010). DNA nano array analysis using hierarchical quality threshold clustering. In *Proceedings of 2010 2nd IEEE International Conference on Information Management and Engineering* (pp. 81-85). IEEE. 10.1109/ICIME.2010.5477579

Waoo, N., Kashyap, R., & Jaiswal, A. (2010). DNA nanoarray analysis using hierarchical quality threshold clustering. In *2010 2nd IEEE International Conference on Information Management and Engineering*. IEEE.

Yao, M. (2014). Research on Learning Evidence Improvement for kNN Based Classification Algorithm. *International Journal Of Database Theory And Application*, *7*(1), 103–110. doi:10.14257/ijdta.2014.7.1.10

Yildirim, P., Birant, D., & Alpyildiz, T. (2017). Data mining and machine learning in the textile industry. *Wiley Interdisciplinary Reviews. Data Mining and Knowledge Discovery*, *8*(1), e1228. doi:10.1002/widm.1228

Zhang, B., Xiang, Y., & Wang, J. (2010). Information Filtering Algorithm Based on Semantic Understanding. *Dianzi Yu Xinxi Xuebao*, *32*(10), 2324–2330. doi:10.3724/SP.J.1146.2009.01393

Zhang, N. (2016). Semi-supervised extreme learning machine with wavelet kernel. *International Journal of Collaborative Intelligence*, *1*(4), 298. doi:10.1504/IJCI.2016.10004854

KEY TERMS AND DEFINITIONS

Artificial Intelligence: Computerized thinking is understanding appeared by machines, as opposed to the trademark learning appeared by individuals and changed animals. In programming designing, AI asks about is described as the examination of "sharp masters": any device that sees its condition and goes for broke exercises that intensify its danger of successfully achieving its objectives. Casually, the articulation "artificial intellectual competence" is associated when a machine mimics "emotional" limits that individuals interface with other human identities, for instance, "learning" and "basic reasoning."

Artificial Neural Network: An artificial neural network (ANN) is information taking care of perspective that is animated by the way tangible natural frameworks, for instance, the cerebrum, process information. The key segment of this perspective is the novel structure of the information taking care of the system. It is made out of a broad number of incredibly interconnected getting ready segments (neurons) filling in as one to deal with specific issues. ANNs, like people, learn by case. An ANN is intended for a specific application, for instance, plan affirmation or data gathering, through a learning strategy. Learning in regular structures incorporates changes as per the synaptic affiliations that exist between the neurons.

Chapter 26
Object Detection in Fog Computing Using Machine Learning Algorithms

Peyakunta Bhargavi
Sri Padmavati Mahila Visvavidyalayam, India

Singaraju Jyothi
Sri Padmavati Mahila Visvavidyalayam, India

ABSTRACT

The moment we live in today demands the convergence of the cloud computing, fog computing, machine learning, and IoT to explore new technological solutions. Fog computing is an emerging architecture intended for alleviating the network burdens at the cloud and the core network by moving resource-intensive functionalities such as computation, communication, storage, and analytics closer to the end users. Machine learning is a subfield of computer science and is a type of artificial intelligence (AI) that provides machines with the ability to learn without explicit programming. IoT has the ability to make decisions and take actions autonomously based on algorithmic sensing to acquire sensor data. These embedded capabilities will range across the entire spectrum of algorithmic approaches that is associated with machine learning. Here the authors explore how machine learning methods have been used to deploy the object detection, text detection in an image, and incorporated for better fulfillment of requirements in fog computing.

INTRODUCTION

Fog computing conjointly called fogging could be a distributed computing infrastructure during which some application services are handling at the network edge in a elegant device. Fog computing is a paradigm which monitors the data and helps in detecting an unauthorized access. According to Cisco, the spacious geological involve the Fog computing, and it is well suitable for real time analytics and big data. Fog computing involve an intense geographical allocation of network and provide a trait of site access.

DOI: 10.4018/978-1-6684-6291-1.ch026

With this any unauthorized activity within the cloud network will be detected. To get the advantage of this method a user ought to get registered with the fog. Once the user is prepared to filling up the sign up form he can get the message or email that he's able to take the services from fog computing. A learn by IDC estimates that by 2020, 10 percent of the world's information will be formed by edge devices. This will additional drive the necessity for a lot of economical fog computing solutions that give low latency and holistic intelligence at the same time.

Machine learning could be a branch of artificial intelligence that aims at enabling machines to perform their jobs skillfully by exploitation intelligent software system. Machine Learning is a natural outgrowth of the intersection of Computer Science and Statistics. The statistical learning methods constitute the backbone of intelligent software that is used to develop machine intelligence. Because machine learning algorithms need information to find out, the discipline must have connection with the discipline of database. Similarly, there are familiar terms such as Knowledge Discovery from Data (KDD), data mining, and pattern recognition. Machine learning algorithms are helpful in bridging this gap of understanding. The goal of learning is to construct a model that takes the input and produces the specified result. The models are often thought-about as an approximation of the method we would like machines to mimic. In such a scenario, it's doable that we have a tendency to acquire errors for a few input, however most of the time, the model provides correct answers. Hence, a new calculation of performance (moreover recital of metrics of speed and memory usage) of a machine learning algorithm will be the correctness of result.

FOG COMPUTING

Fog computing is that the thought of a network stuff that stretches from the outer edges of wherever information is made to wherever it'll eventually be hold on, whether or not that is in the cloud or in a customer's data center.

Fog is another layer of a distributed network location and is closely related to cloud computing and also the internet of things (IoT). Public infrastructure as a service (IaaS) cloud vendors will be thought of as a high-level, global endpoint for data; the edge of the network is where data from IoT devices is created.

Fog computing is that the plan of a distributed network that connects these two environments. "Fog provides the primitive link for what information must be pushed to the cloud, and what can be analyzed locally, at the edge," explains Mung Chiang, dean of Purdue University's College of Engineering and one in all the nation's prime researchers on fog and edge computing.

Fog computing will be perceived each in hefty cloud systems and big data structures, making reference to the growing difficulties in accessing information objectively. This leads to an absence of quality of the obtained content. The things of fog computing on cloud computing and big data system might vary. However, a common aspect is a limitation in accurate content distribution, an issue that has been tackled with the creation of metrics that attempt to improve accuracy.

To extend cloud computing and bring high performance computing capability to the edge of an enterprise's network, fog computing was introduced by Cisco (Bonomi et al., 2017). Fog computing, also known as edge computing or fogging, is a computing model that provides high performance computing resources, data storage, and networking services between edge devices (e.g., wireless router and wide area network access device) and cloud computing data centers (Bonomi et al., 2014; Aazam & Huh, 2014; Yi, Li & Li, 2017). In cloud computing, the massive amounts of data have to be transmitted to data centers on the cloud, yielding significant performance overhead. As opposed to cloud computing, computationally intensive workloads such as training large datasets and visualizing data analytics are conducted in fog computing at locations where large volumes of data are collected and stored instead of centralized cloud storage. One of the key benefits of fog com-putting is that it enables users to avoid transferring numerous data between edge devices and cloud computing data centers by moving computing nodes closer to local physical objects or devices and executing applications directly on big data. Because fog computing is in close proximity to the source of raw data, fog computing is able to considerably reduce latency.

Figure 1. Architechture of fog computing
(Source from google)

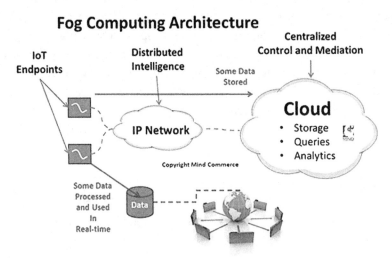

Benefits of Fog Computing

Fundamentally, the event of fog computing frameworks provides organizations, additional decisions for process data where it's most acceptable to act thus. For some applications, information might process as quickly as potential – as an example, during a producing use case wherever connected machines got to be ready to respond to an incident as soon as possible.

Extending the cloud never to the items that generate and act on data profit the business within the following ways:

- **Bigger Business Agility**: With the proper tools, developers will quickly develop fog applications and deploy them wherever required. Machine manufacturers can offer MaaS to their customers. Fog applications program the machine to control within the means every client desires.
- **Higher Security**: Defined your fog nodes exploitation a similar policy, controls, and procedures you utilize in alternative elements of your IT environment. Use the same physical security and cyber security solutions.

- **Deeper Insights, With Privacy Control**: Analyze sensitive information domestically rather than causation it to the cloud for analysis. Your IT team will monitor and manage the devices that collect, analyze, and store information.
- **Lower Operating Expense**: Conserve network bandwidth process designed information domestically rather than causation it to the cloud for analysis

Fog computing will produce low-latency network connections between devices and analytics endpoints. This architecture in turn reduces the amount of bandwidth needed compared to if that data had to be sent all the way back to a data centre or cloud for processing. It can even be employed in situations wherever there's no bandwidth association to send information, therefore it should be processed getting ready to wherever it's created. As one more profit, users can place security features in a fog network, from segmented network traffic to virtual firewalls to protect it.

Working of Fog Computing

The devices wherever the info is generated and even collected don't have the type of computation power or the storage resources so as to perform all types of advanced analytical calculations nor machine learning tasks. As a result, fogging comes to participate since it plant on the edge and is capable to bring the cloud nearer in logic. Cloud servers have all of the necessary ability to do this stuff and they are normally excessively far away to actually aid in a appropriate approach. Because fogging works to attach the endpoints nearer, it's capable of bring regarding enormous results. In a fog setting, all of the processing generally takes place within a specific smart device or particular gateway. As a consequence, all of the data needs of what is being sent to the cloud are effectively reduced.

Fog Computing and Internet of Things

Because cloud computing is not viable for IoT devices, it is necessary to utilize fog computing instead. This as a result provides superior overall distribution capabilities and addresses the requirements of IoT much better in the finish. It is accomplished of managing the size of information that these kind of devices end up generate which make it the idyllic style of compute to hold them. Because fogging can successfully lessen the quantity of bandwidth that is necessary and since it has the potential to lessen the required back and forth contact with the cloud and the variety of sensors, it is going to assist string the whole thing jointly lacking falling the overall presentation of the process or devices.

Applications of Fog Computing

Fog computing is that the adorning stages of being extended in formal deployments, however there are a mixture of use cases that are known as potential ideal scenario for fog computing.

- **Connected Car:** Autonomous vehicle is that the new trend going down on the road. Software that is used to add automatic steering, enabling literal "hands free" operations of the vehicle. Starting out with testing and release self-parking operations that do not need oblige a person behind the wheel. Fog computing are going to be the most effective choice for all internet connected vehicles why as a result of fog computing provides real time interaction. Cars, access purpose and traffic lights are able to move with one another and then it makes safe for all. At some purpose in time, the connected car will start saving lives by reducing automobile accidents.

- **Smart Cities and Smart Grids:** Like associated cars, utility systems are gradually more using real-time information to extra powerfully run systems. Sometimes this information is in remote areas, so processing close to where it's created is essential. Other times the information must be aggregate from an outsized variety of sensors. Fog computing architectures may well be devised to resolve each of those problems.

- **Real-Time Analytics:** A bunch of use cases incorporate period analytics. From construct systems that want to be clever to retort to events as they occur, to financial institution that utilize real-time information to notify trading decision or check for con. Fog computing deployments can help facilitate the transfer of data between where its created and a variety of places where it needs to go.

- **Self Maintaining Train:** Another request of fog computing is self maintaining trains. A train ball-bearing watching detector can sense the changes within the temperature level and any disorder can mechanically alert the train operator and create maintenance in keeping with. Thus we can avoid major disasters.

- **Wireless Sensor and Actuator Networks (WSAN):** The actual Wireless Sensor Nodes (WSNs), were designed to extend battery life by operating at predominantly low power. Actuators serves as Fog devices which control the measurement process itself, the consistency and the oscillatory behaviours by creating a closed-loop system. For example, in the lifesaving air vent sensors on vent monitor air environment flowing in and out of mine and mechanically change air-flow if situation suit risky to miners. Most of those WSNs entail less bandwidth, less energy, very low processing power, functioning as a sink in a unidirectional manner.

- **Smart Building Control:** In localised sensible building manage wireless sensors are installed to assess temperature, humidity, or levels of diverse gaseous components in the building atmosphere. Thus, information can be exchanged among all sensors in the floor and the reading can be combined to form reliable measurements. Using distributed high cognitive process, the fog devices react to information. The system gears up to figure along to lower the temperature, input contemporary air and output wetness from the air or increase wetness. Sensors reply to the movements by shift on or off the lights. Observance of the outlook the fog computing is applied for elegant buildings which might maintain basic wants of preserving external and internal energy.

- **IoT and Cyber-Physical Systems (CPSs):** Fog computing has a major role in IoT and CPSs. IoT is a network that can interconnect ordinary physical objects with identified address using internet and telecommunication. The characteristic of CPSs is the combination of system's computational and physical elements. The association of CPSs and IoT will transform the world with computer-based control and communication systems, engineered systems and physical reality. The object is to integrate the concept and precision of software and networking with the vibrant and uncertain environment. With the growing cyber physical systems, we will be able to develop intelligent medical devices, smart buildings, agricultural and robotic systems.

- **Software Defined Networks (SDN):** SDN is an emergent computing and networking notion. SDN notion jointly with fog computing will choose the key topic in vehicular networks unequal connectivity, collision and high package loss rate.SDN chains vehicle to-vehicle with vehicle-to transportation communications and main control. It splits manage and communication layer, manage is finished by central server and server decides the communication path for nodes.

MACHINE LEARNING ALGORITHMS

The term 'machine learning' is often, incorrectly, interchanged with Artificial Intelligence, but machine learning is actually a subfield/type of AI. Machine learning is also often referred to as predictive analytics, or predictive modelling. At its most basic, machine learning uses programmed algorithms that receive and analyse input data to predict output values within an acceptable range. As new knowledge is fed to those algorithms, they learn and optimise their operations to enhance performance, developing 'intelligence' over time. There are four types of machine learning algorithms: supervised, semi-supervised, unsupervised and reinforcement.

Supervised Learning

In supervised learning, the machine is tutored by example. The operator provides the machine learning algorithm with a far-famed dataset that features desired inputs and outputs, and also the formula should realize a way to see a way to arrive at those inputs and outputs. While the operator knows the correct answers to the problem, the algorithm identifies patterns in data, learns from observations and makes predictions. The formula makes predictions and is corrected by the operator – and this method continues till the formula achieves a high level of accuracy/performance. Under the umbrella of supervised learning fall: Classification, Regression and Forecasting.

1. **Classification**: In classification tasks, the machine learning program must draw a conclusion from observed values and determine towhat category new observations belong. For example, once filtering emails as 'spam' or 'not spam', the program must look at existing observational data and filter the emails accordingly.
2. **Regression**: In regression tasks, the machine learning program must estimate – and understand – the relationships among variables. Regression analysis focuses on one variable and a series of alternative dynamical variables – creating it notably helpful for prediction and forecasting.
3. **Forecasting**: Forecasting is the process of making predictions about the future based on the past and present data, and is commonly used to analyze trends.

Semi-Supervised Learning

Semi-supervised learning is analogous to supervised learning, but instead uses both labelled and unlabelled data. Labelled information is basically info that has purposeful tags so the formula will perceive the info, whilst unlabelled data lacks that information. By using this combination, machine learning algorithms can learn to label unlabelled data.

Unsupervised Learning

Here, the machine learning algorithm studies information to spot patterns. There is no answer key or human operator to supply instruction. Instead, the machine determines the correlations and relationships by analysing available data. In an unsupervised learning method, the machine learning algorithm is left to interpret large data sets and address that data accordingly. The formula tries to organise that information in how to explain its structure. This might mean grouping the data into clusters or arranging it in a way that looks more organised. As it assesses more data, its ability to make decisions on that data gradually improves and becomes more refined. Under the umbrella of unsupervised learning, fall:

1. **Clustering**: Clustering involves grouping sets of similar data (based on defined criteria). It's useful for segmenting data into several groups and performing analysis on each data set to find patterns.
2. **Dimension Reduction**: Dimension reduction reduces the number of variables being considered to find the exact information required.

Reinforcement Learning

Reinforcement learning focuses on regimented learning processes, where a machine learning algorithm is provided with a set of actions, parameters and end values. By process the system, the machine learning algorithm then tries to explore different options and possibilities, monitoring and evaluating each result to determine which one is optimal. Reinforcement learning teaches the machine trial and error. It learns from past experiences and begins to adapt its approach in response to things to realize the most effective attainable result.

Use of Machine Learning Algorithms

Choosing the right machine learning algorithm depends on several factors, including, but not limited to: data size, quality and diversity, as well as what answers businesses want to derive from that data. Additional concerns embrace accuracy, training time, parameters, data points and much more. Therefore, choosing the right algorithm is both a combination of business need, specification, experimentation and time available. Even the foremost full-fledged information scientists cannot tell you which ones algorithm program can perform the most effective before experimenting with others. We have, however, compiled a machine learning algorithm 'cheat sheet' which can assist you notice the foremost acceptable one for your specific challenges.

Common Popular Machine Learning Algorithms

Naive Bayes Classifier Algorithm (Supervised Learning: Classification)

The Naïve Bayes classifier is predicated on Bayes theorem and classifies each worth as sovereign of the other value. It permits us to forecast a class/category, base on a set of quality, using likelihood. Despite its ease, the classifiers does unexpectedly well and is often used owing to the fact it outperforms more sophisticated classification methods.

K Means Clustering Algorithm (Unsupervised Learning: Clustering)

The K Means Clustering algorithmic program could be a form of unsupervised learning, which is employed to reason unlabeled information, i.e. data without defined categories or groups. The algorithmic program works by finding teams at intervals the information, with the amount of teams drawn by the variable K. It then works iteratively to assign each data point to one of K groups based on the features provided.

Support Vector Machine Algorithm (Supervised Learning: Classification)

Support Vector Machine algorithms are unit of supervised learning models that analyze information used for classification and regression analysis. They primarily filter information into classes, which is achieved by providing a set of training examples, each set marked as belonging to one or the other of the two categories. The algorithm then works to build a model that assigns new values to one category or the other.

Linear Regression (Supervised Learning/Regression)

Linear regression is that the most elementary form of regression. Simple linear regression allows us to understand the relationships between two continuous variables.

Logistic Regression (Supervised Learning: Classification)

Logistic regression focuses on estimating the likelihood of an occasion occurring supported the previous information provided. It is accustomed cowl a binary dependent variable quantity, which is where only two values, 0 and 1, represent outcomes.

Artificial Neural Networks (Reinforcement Learning)

An artificial neural network (ANN) contains 'units' organized during a series of layers, each of which connects to layers on either side. ANNs are motivated by biological systems, such as the brain, and how they process information. ANNs are essentially a large number of inter connected processing elements, working in unison to solve specific problems.

ANNs also study by instance and through practice, and they are really helpful for modeling non-linear relations in high-dimensional information or where the association amongst the effort variables is tricky to recognize.

Decision Trees (Supervised Learning: Classification/Regression)

A decision tree is a flow-chart-like tree structure that uses a branching method to illustrate every possible outcome of a decision. Each node at intervals the tree represents a check on a particular variable – and every branch is that the outcome of that check.

Random Forests (Supervised Learning: Classification/Regression)

Random forests or 'random decision forests' is correlate ensemble learn technique, combining several algorithms to produce better result for classification, regression and other responsibilities. Each individual classifier is frail, but when mutual with others, can produce excellent results. The algorithmic program starts with a 'decision tree' (a tree-like graph or model of decisions) associated an input is entered at the highest. It then travels down the tree, with data being segmented into smaller and smaller sets, based on specific variables.

Nearest Neighbours (Supervised Learning)

The K-Nearest-Neighbour algorithm estimates however seemingly an information purpose is to be a member of one group or another. It essentially looks at the data points around a single data point to determine what group it is actually in. For example, if one aim is on a grid and therefore the formula is making an attempt to work out what group that information point is in (Group A or Group B, for example) it might look into the information points close to it to visualize what cluster the bulk of the points are in.

Clearly, there are a bunch of belongings to deem when it comes to choose the accurate machine learning algorithms for your business analytics. Conversely, you don't require to be a data scientist or skilled statistician to utilize these models for your trade. At SAS, our products and solutions utilize a comprehensive selection of machine learning algorithms, helping you to develop a process that can continuously deliver value from your data.

Machine Learning Algorithm in Fog Computing

In present days each human is allied to network using their pocket-sized mobile devices every time. The internet is interconnected with elastic communication network facilitate quality of human. The demand for human resources to understand the knowledge due to every present use of the networked static and mobile cameras has made many efforts in past decades. Normally the system depends on human operations to influence the process of capture video or image. Now a days there are many approaches for human operation to maintain the full concentration on the video for a longer time but it also not scalable as the number of cameras as sensors grows significantly. Mostly the human is aimed at the object detection and the task of irregular activity detection is taken by many types of machine learning algorithms (Sifre, 2014). The algorithm mechanically process to collect video frames in a cloud to detect, track and report any strange situation. The system is classified in three levels:

Level 1: Each object is identified through low-level feature extraction from video data or image
Level 2: The activities of each object are detected/renowned, quick alarm raise; and
Level 3: Doubtful activities profile build and past statistical analysis and also fine tuning during online training the decision-making algorithm.

In the above operation level 1 and level 2 by the edge devices in this detection and tracking tasks are done the results are outsourced to the fog layer for data analyzing and decision making and in the level 3 function is placed in fog computing level or even away on the cloud center allowed on edge processing power (Chen et al., 2016; Ribeiro, Lazzaretti & Lopes, 2017). In level 1 is mainly focus on the human object detection is essential as missing any objects in the frame will lead to undetected behavior. However human body can have different looks in different ambient lighting which has the harder for the kinds of models to achieve high detection accuracy.

In fog computing based object detection we load partial computation tasks from cloud to fog nodes. The operation includes different object detection in an image (ex: persons, cars, traffic signals etc), image preprocessing, feature extraction and clustering generation are deployed on fog nodes. The completed operations on fog are transferring only the identified objects to the cloud rather than original image.

The object detection consists of three main parts are as follows client, fog and cloud.

- **Client:** Client is liable for collecting images from the different spying camera and requesting the object service from fog nodes.
- **Fog Node:** Fog Nodes are situated at the edge of the network. This network edge device has the dedicated fog server. In practical client devices are directly access to the internet which can be used as fog node. Fog node is responsible for object detection, text detection and color clustering. The fog nodes are responsible for requests the resolution service to cloud. Finally, the object detector is transmitted to cloud for identity resolution.
- **Cloud:** Cloud is interred related with Fog Nodes, resolution server, information server. These are scheduled for resources and allocating computing tasks. It provides a standard object detection resolution service interfaces and fog nodes are accessed as connectivity in various IOT applications.

Edge Detection Method

There are different types of edge detection techniques. Each method detects the edges of an image. The Robert cross method performs simple and quick for computing. The input image may be grayscale and output will be the same. The next way is prewitt algorithm which is used to approximation the magnitude and orientation of an edge. The estimate needs to calculate different magnitudes in x and y directions the prewitt edge detection is simpler than sobel method (Cortes & Vapnik, 1995). This is a directional operator on the basis of odd size template. The algorithm consists the edge of the image is located at the place in which the brightness changes significantly, the neighborhood of the pixel gray value of pixels exceeds a set entry depending on the explicit steps for the edge. In this Laplacian of Gaussian smoothes and computes the Laplacian, this yields a double edge image. Locate edges then consists of verdict the zero crossings amid the double edges.

The edge detection of image has done to analyze the boundaries of object to work with the discontinuities in brightness as shown in below Figure 2.

Figure 2. (a) Normal image (b) Rainy traffic image (c) Traffic image (d) airport image (e) – (h) Images obtained after edge detection for input images (a)-(d)
(Sources from Google, STL Today, n.d.)

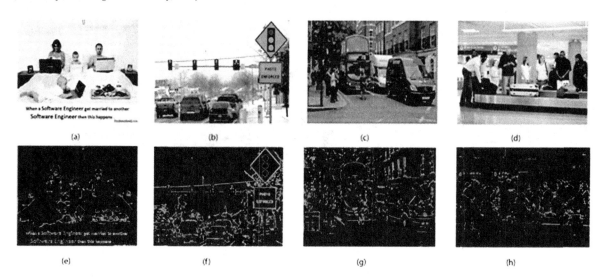

SVM and CNN Method

The SVM is a supervised learning method for binary classification (Kingma & Ba, 2014) it objective is to find the optimal hyper plane f (w, x) = w. x+ b which is to separate the given class in to two data sets with features x $\in$ R^m. SVM reads the parameters w by solving an optimization problem in Equation 1

$$\min \frac{1}{p} W^T W + C \sum_{I=1}^{P} MAX \left(0,1 - y_i' \left(W^T X_i + b \right) \right) \tag{1}$$

Where W^T W is l1 norm, C means penalty parameter, y' is a main label, $W^T X_i + b$ is a predictor function. This can be interring connected to the CNN for the object identification in the image or video.

CNN is widely applied for the object classification and is challenging task for the CNN to fit in the network edge devices due to restrict constraints on resources. The time consuming and computing can be outsourced to the cloud and the network layer. The edge devices cannot afford the storage space for parameters and weight values of filters of the neural networks. In implementation CNN architecture depth wise separable convolution is used to reduce the computational cost of CNN without making much sacrificing the accuracy of the whole network which is specialized for human detection to reduce the unnecessary huge filter numbers in each layer this makes network implementation in edge (Chen et al., 2017).

The object detection is done with the image using SVM and CNN methods where object of each thing in the image is identified and mentioned with the type of the object as shown in Figure 3.

Figure 3. (a) Normal image (b) Rainy traffic image (c) Traffic image (d) Airport image (e) – (h) Images obtained after object detection for input images (a)-(d)
(Sources from Google)

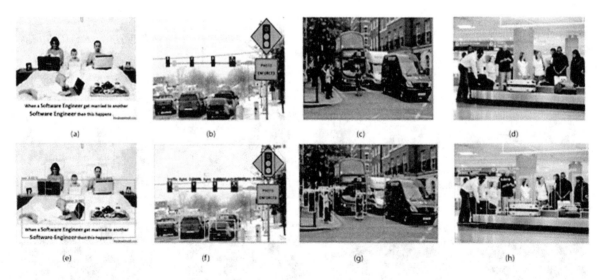

K-Means Algorithm

K-means clustering is a one of the unsupervised learning which is used for exploratory data analysis of labeled data the process of grouping a set of physical objects into classes of same objects is called clustering (Muthukrishnan & Radha, 2011; Rasmussen & Williams, 2006). A clustering is a collection of data objects that are same in the cluster and dissimilar to the objects in other clusters. It is useful method for the discovery of data distribution and pattern that under the k-means. The method is simple and very easy to classify a given data set through a certain number of clusters which assumes the k-mean clusters. The idea is to derive k centers for each cluster the centers should be in sly way because different location causes different output. Next step is each point belonging to a given data set and associate to its nearer center. When there is no point then the step1 is completed and grouping is done. By these k centroids a loop is generated by this we may notice the K-centers change their locations step by step until no more changes takes place.

The cluster number specifies the maximum numbers of colours are used in the image as shown in the Figure 4.

Figure 4. (a) Normal image (b) Rainy traffic image (c) Traffic image (d) Airport image (e) – (h) Images obtained after clustering for input images (a)-(d)
(Sources from Google)

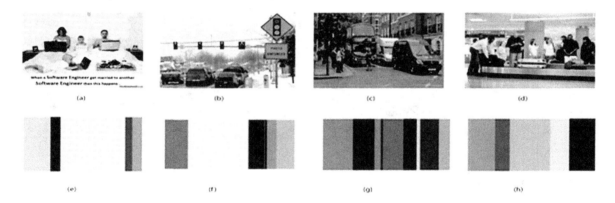

Neural Network

A Neural Network usually involves a large number of process operation in parallel and arranged in tier. In this human visual system is one to effortlessly recognize a numbers or text in the image. The difficulty of visual pattern recognition becomes apparent to write or detect the text in an image. Neural network approach the program in a different way. These can be stated with Gaussian process and random forest regression.

- **Gaussian Processes (GP):** the outputs probabilistically by use of Gaussian distribution for approximating a set of functions (processes) in a high-dimensional space (Segal, 2004). The main argument for using GP is the fundamental assumption that the mapping of independent to dependent variables cannot be sufficiently captured by a single Gaussian process. GP also uses lazy learning, which delays generalization about training data until after a query has been made.

- **Random Forest Regression:** Random forests are a popular ensemble model belongs to the decision-tree class of ML algorithms. Random Forest Regression (RFR) works by fitting a number of decision trees, to various subsamples of the dataset that are then averaged to improve accuracy and reduce over-fitting in a popular process known as bagging.

The text can be recognized in any image using neural network along with Gaussian process and random forest regression, but it is difficult to identify the noisy (blur) text as shown in Figure 5.

Figure 5. (a) Normal image (b) Rainy traffic image (c) Traffic image (d) Airport image (e) – (h) Images obtained after text detection for input images (a)-(d)
(Sources from Google)

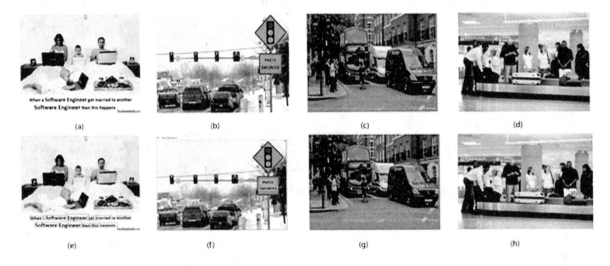

CONCLUSION

This paper analyzed the machine learning algorithms in fog computing to detect objects, text in an image using different methods. Firstly, studied what is fog computing and how it vary with the cloud computing. Secondly, described about the different algorithms in machine learning algorithms and application of the machine learning algorithms. Finally, described how fog computing uses or take the images or videos for object detection. By using the images, founded edge detection with Gaussian model. And detected the objects using the methods SVM and CNN, founded the clustering in an image using K-means clustering algorithm, and also observed how to identify text in an image using neural network along with Gaussian and random forest regression. We can also detect face, identifying the person, and can analyze the live video and image through the machine learning algorithms.

REFERENCES

Aazam, M., & Huh, E.-N. (2014). Fog computing and smart gateway based communication for cloud of things. *Proc. Future Internet of Things and Cloud (Fi Cloud).International Conference on*, 464–70.

Bonomi, F., Milito, R., Natarajan, P., & Zhu, J. (2014). *Fog computing: A platform for internet of things and analytics, Big Data and Internet of Things: A Roadmap for Smart Environments*. Springer.

Bonomi, F., Milito, R., Zhu, J., & Addepalli, S. (2017). Fog computing and its role in the internet of things. *Proc. Proceedings of the first edition of the MCCworkshop on Mobile cloud computing*.

Chen, N., Chen, Y., Blasch, E., Ling, H., You, Y., & Ye, X. (2017). Enabling smart urban surveillance at the edge. *2017 IEEE International Conference on Smart Cloud (Smart Cloud)*, 109–119. 10.1109/SmartCloud.2017.24

Chen, N., Chen, Y., Song, S., Huang, C.-T., & Ye, X. (2016). Smart urban surveillance using fog computing. *Edge Computing (SEC), IEEE/ACM Symposium on*, 95–96.

Christopher, M. (1995). *Bishop, Neural networks for pattern recognition*. Oxford University Press.

Cortes, C., & Vapnik, V. (1995). Support-vector Networks. *Machine Learning*, *20*(3), 273–297. doi:10.1007/BF00994018

Kingma, D., & Ba, J. (2014). *Adam: A method for stochastic optimization*. Ar Xiv preprint ar Xiv: 1412.6980

Muthukrishnan & Radha. (2011). Edge Detection Techniques for Image Segmentation. *International Journal of Computer Science & Information Technology*, *3*(6).

Rasmussen, C. E., & Williams, C. K. (2006). Gaussian processes for machine learning. MIT Press.

Ribeiro, M., Lazzaretti, A. E., & Lopes, H. S. (2017). A study of deep convolutional auto-encoders for anomaly detection in videos. *Pattern Recognition Letters*.

Segal, M. R. (2004). *Machine learning benchmarks and random forest regression*. Center for Bioinformatics & Molecular Biostatistics.

Sifre, L. (2014). *Rigid-motion scattering for image classification* (Ph.D. dissertation). PSU.

Waheetha & Fernandez. (2016). Fog Computing And Its Applications. *International Journal of Advanced Research in Basic Engineering Sciences and Technology*, *2*(19), 56-62. Retrieved from https://www.networkworld.com/article/3243111/what-is-fog-computing-connecting-the-cloud-to-things.html

Yi, S., Li, C., & Li, Q. (2017). A survey of fog computing: concepts, applications and issues. *Proc. Proceedings of the 2015 Workshop on Mobile Big Data*, 37–42.

This research was previously published in Architecture and Security Issues in Fog Computing Applications; pages 90-107, copyright year 2020 by Engineering Science Reference (an imprint of IGI Global).

Index

L

M

N

T

U

V

W

Z

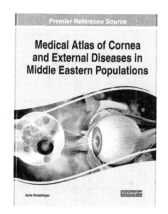

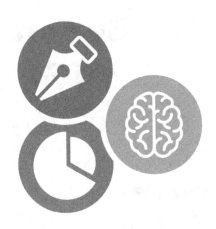

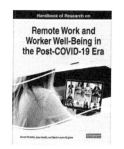
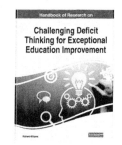

Printed in the United States
by Baker & Taylor Publisher Services